Accounting Principles:
A Canadian Viewpoint

Accounting Principles

R.M. Skinner, FCA
Partner
Clarkson, Gordon & Co.

Foreword

The term 'generally accepted accounting principles' has had a long history. In recent years, however, those who are interested in fair financial reporting – corporate executives, shareholders, financial analysts, the financial press and members of accounting and business faculties in the universities, as well as professional accountants – have voiced increasing concern about the lack of precision in the term. Just what do we mean by 'generally accepted' principles? Is the term to be interpreted broadly or narrowly? How do we make sure that generally accepted principles are meeting the needs of all parties concerned with fair financial reporting?

With questions such as these in mind, the Accounting and Auditing Research Committee some years ago initiated the present Study. It is regarded as one of the most important projects ever undertaken by the Committee. Two basic issues are explored – the current state of accounting principles and the directions in which developments should be taking place. In initiating the project, the Research Committee deliberately kept the terms of reference fairly broad, and Mr. Skinner was asked to do the following:

(1) To review financial accounting (as distinct from internal management accounting) in Canada as it may be interpreted from available financial reports, both for profit seeking and for non-profit institutions.

(2) To identify accounting principles and practices that may be said to have received some general acceptance.

(3) To codify such principles and practices in a rational articulated manner, so as to reveal insofar as is possible the theory or assumptions underlying such principles and practices.

(4) To compare and contrast Canadian principles and practices with those found in other countries, particularly the United States of America and Great Britain.

(5) To consider areas where Canadian accounting practices appear to be in conflict and areas where practices found are in apparent conflict with authoritative accounting literature, including official recommendations of professional accounting institutes or their committees.

(6) To recommend areas where existing Canadian financial reporting should be improved and areas where the accounting profession should undertake further study with a view to modification of existing accounting principles so as to make them more accurate or of more widespread usefulness.

Consistent with these terms of reference "Accounting Principles – A Canadian Viewpoint" is somewhat broader and more future-oriented than has been attempted in Canadian research studies to date. It is more than an inventory of generally accepted accounting principles; Mr. Skinner's consideration of accounting principles involves not only where we are today but also where we should be going.

The Study expresses the views of the author and should not be interpreted as representing an official position either of the Accounting & Auditing Research Committee or of the Institute. Although it is not to be expected that everyone will agree with every conclusion expressed in a Study of this length, the Committee's objectives in commissioning the Study have clearly been fulfilled – it paints a recognizable picture of the history and present state of the theory underlying present accounting principles and suggests the sorts of questions we should be considering in our efforts to improve financial reporting.

The Accounting and Auditing Research Committee was most fortunate in having Mr. R. M. Skinner, FCA, Clarkson, Gordon & Co., Toronto accept responsibility for the project and authorship of the Study. Mr. Skinner, a former member and Chairman of the Accounting and Auditing Research Committee and National Director for Accounting Standards for Clarkson, Gordon & Co., was eminently qualified to undertake this important work. "Accounting Principles – A Canadian Viewpoint" bears evidence of his tremendous commitment of time and effort over an extended period of years.

G. MULCAHY, FCA,
Director of Research

March 1972

Preface

This work has been in preparation over a period of several years. During that time great changes have taken place in accounting. When I began I was impressed by the number of problems in accounting that had been identified in the 1930's, or earlier, but remained unresolved thirty years or more later. As I write this, I am impressed by how much has been accomplished in the last six or seven years. The widespread criticisms of accounting principles in the financial press and our own professional literature give a very misleading impression of the real achievements of our profession in recent years. Yet the criticisms do not lack for substance. While much has been accomplished, much more remains to be done. This work attests to that.

The Study also focuses on a second issue – namely, how accounting principles should be arrived at. The Study was commissioned as a survey of 'generally accepted accounting principles'. One of its major conclusions is that 'general acceptance' is not a sound basis for the formulation of accounting principles. This conclusion merely substantiates a development that is taking place in practice. In the last ten years, we have been witnessing the transfer of responsibility for the formulation of accounting principles to the technical committees of the professional institutes of accountants – to the CICA Accounting and Auditing Research Committee, the AICPA Accounting Principles Board, and the Accounting Standards Steering Committee of the several accounting institutes in Great Britain and Ireland.

This development is in the right direction but it raises a host of questions. When we think of it, no other profession has attempted to do what we are attempting. When an economist talks about principles of economics, you cannot know what he means with any degree of precision unless you read his text book. No association of economists attempts to define a set of principles of economics that all economists would adhere to in their advice. Why then do accountants attempt to define common principles? We do it in the interests of users of financial statements who are not in a position to question how the statements are made up. There must be rules of the game to ensure that the user understands what the person providing the report had to say. But the task we have undertaken is not an easy one.

As a profession we need to think about the implications of our quasi-legislative responsibility for the formulation of accounting principles. What kind of person should be appointed to a quasi-legislative body? How should he be selected? Should non-accountants play a part? What research support should be supplied? What provision should be made for the interpretation of rules in particular cases?

Should there be an appeal procedure? Should accounting principles be set out in broad terms, or should they be fairly detailed? If they are set out in broad terms, how do we prevent the well-known tendency to erosion of principles as particular situations are interpreted as not being subject to a given rule, each situation being more debatable than the last, but by so small a degree that it is hard to differentiate between them? If the principles are formulated in fairly detailed form, can we avoid rather arbitrary and unrealistic rules of application and the sort of loophole searching that goes on in tax legislation?

We had better start out with the realization that in the real world we are not going to get perfect answers to problems in defining principle. Accounting, like politics, is the art of the possible. Accountants might well adopt Reinhold Niebuhr's prayer –

> "O God, give us
> serenity to accept what cannot be changed,
> courage to change what should be changed, and
> wisdom to distinguish the one from the other."

Rather less of the first characteristic and more of the second and third would seem the most desirable mix.

My thanks are due to members of the CICA Research Committee of 1970/71 for helpful criticism of this Study in the draft stage. Many others, too numerous to mention, also responded valiantly to my request for help; I would be remiss, however, if I did not acknowledge the very comprehensive commentaries furnished by W. B. Bolton, CA, Professor R. H. Crandall, CA and J. R. M. Wilson, FCA. Discussions with R. M. Parkinson, FCA, who is currently engaged on a comprehensive study of problems in accounting for foreign currency translation, greatly assisted in the writing of Chapter 19. I am also grateful for three perspectives from non-accountants – to C. T. P. Galloway, FSA and G. R. Wallace, FSA for comments on Chapters 12 and 25, and to W. O. C. Miller, QC for a general overview. Much as I would like to attribute errors of omission or commission in this Study to the aforementioned criticisms and comments, honesty (and the force of custom) compel me to admit them as my own. Over the years this work was in process, first Sylvia Ego, then Laila Hill, and in the later stages Mickey Hubbert, bore up stoically and efficiently under the burden of transcribing the weight of words.

Logan Lake,
Thanksgiving, 1971   R. M. Skinner

Contents

PART II – CHANGE AND DEVELOPMENT

Summary statement of generally accepted accounting principles for business enterprises

The following summary statement of accounting principles which are generally accepted in Canada as of 1971 is based on the discussion found in Chapters 5 to 22. This statement does not include principles of accounting for financial institutions or non-profit organizations. The accounting methods of such entities are considered too diverse to be included in a generalized summary. Following this statement is a summary of basic assumptions or concepts (which are discussed in Chapter 3) considered to underlie present generally accepted accounting principles.

Transaction Recognition and Measurement

A. Principles governing the initial recognition given to transactions in the accounts of an entity

Financial transactions

1. Transactions involving the issue or retirement of debt or equity capital should be recorded in the accounts as of the date a legal commitment is established. Interest expense on debt obligations is accrued in accordance with the passage of time. Dividends payable are recorded when declared.

Investment transactions

2. Transactions involving the purchase or sale of investments should likewise be recorded at the contract date. Interest income on investments not in default is accrued at the stated rate of interest in accordance with the passage of time. Dividends receivable should be recorded when a legal right to them arises.

3. Acquisition of capital assets for use rather than resale is normally recorded at the earlier of the date of delivery or the date of transfer of title to the asset.

Operating transactions

4. Business or operating transactions should be recorded at the earlier of:
   (a) the date of performance by the purchaser (i.e. payment according to the contract),
   (b) the date of performance (or partial performance in the case of services) by the vendor.

   Exception – A few expenses which relate directly to particular time periods are accrued with the passage of time, even in advance of receipt of the service to be rendered or of any obligation to pay.

B. Principles governing measurement of transaction amounts

1. Transaction amounts are measured by reference to values involved in the transaction at the date it is recognized in the accounts.
   (a) Transactions involving payment on normal short-term credit or cash terms are measured at the contract amount. Cash discounts, where allowed, should be deducted in the measurement.
   (b) Transactions involving significant delay in payment after performance contain a financing element. Such transactions should be measured at a discounted amount. The appropriate amount of discount may be estimated by reference to the alternative price of the asset in a cash transaction, the market value current for similar debt obligations or, if neither of these yardsticks is available, by applying an imputed interest factor to the face amount of the debt.[*]
   (c) Barter transactions should be measured by the fair value of the asset given up, or the asset acquired, whichever is the more reliably ascertainable. Shares issued for property or services should be measured by the same rule. Where the values in such share issues are inherently difficult to measure reliably, additional disclosure should be made in the description in the balance sheet of the asset acquired.
   (d) Gifts received by an entity, and dividends and donations in kind, should be measured at the fair value of the assets received or distributed.[*]

2. The total amount assigned to a 'basket purchase' transaction should be allocated according to the fair value of the identifiable tangible and intangible assets acquired. Where the total transaction amount exceeds the aggregate of such asset values the remainder should be assigned to 'goodwill'. Where the total transaction amount (including provision for any costs or losses expected to be associated with the transaction) is less than the aggregate of asset values the difference should be deducted from the amount of those assets whose value appears less certain, or deducted pro rata from the amount assigned to all non-cash assets.

3. Where more than one type of security is sold in units for one price, the consideration received should be assigned to each type of security sold on a reasonable basis – usually in proportion to the value of each separately.[*]

---

[*] This principle is not invariably followed in practice.

Accounting for Operations

A. Principles governing recognition of revenue as earned

1. Revenue from business activity should be regarded by a vendor as earned as soon as:
   (a) significant uncertainty about the amount that will be realized from the sale of the product or service is removed;
   (b) significant uncertainty about the costs that will be incurred in producing the goods or rendering the service is removed; and
   (c) a reasonable basis exists for relating the revenues deemed earned with the work accomplished in the course of production or rendering the service.

   In the majority of situations these criteria are not considered to be fulfilled until the shipment of goods or completion of services. It is therefore desirable that any departure from a basis of regarding revenue as earned at point of shipment or sale be disclosed in the financial statements.

   Such departures will normally be associated with one or more of the following conditions:
   (a) Advance revenue recognition
       (i) revenue may be associated with services rendered on a fairly predictable basis, but actual billing is made irregularly;
       (ii) the work carried on consists of a few large projects, and the earning of profits will not be well portrayed unless revenue is accrued as the work is done;
       (iii) the market for the product is so highly organized that reliable prices for it are always obtainable, and selling is not an important activity of the producer.
   (b) Delayed revenue recognition
       (iv) there is great uncertainty about ultimate realization of the transaction amount.

B. Principles governing allocation of costs among accounting periods and to income, retained earnings or capital accounts

The matching principle

1. Costs recorded in the accounts should be matched with revenues for the purpose of determining income of individual accounting periods in a manner which best reflects the 'cause and effect' relationship existing between costs and revenues. To formulate particular rules to implement the matching principle, costs incurred are customarily divided into several categories – viz. costs of acquiring and producing goods for resale, costs of capital assets, other costs of goods or services that may be expected to assist in earning future revenue and costs of goods or services from which no benefit is derived beyond the period in which the costs are incurred.

Measurement of inventory cost and cost of goods sold

2. Inventory costs comprise all costs that can reasonably be attributed to the purchase and manufacture of goods.

(a) Costs reasonably attributable to inventory include at least the cost of materials entering into the production of inventory, the cost of labour directly expended in the fabrication or processing of inventory, and overhead costs that may be seen to vary in amount more or less proportionately to the volume of production.

(b) Inventory costs may also include an allocation of overhead costs that do not vary with the volume of production. Such allocation for a period should not exceed the proportion which the number of units in inventory bear to an assumed normal or standard number of production units for the period.

3. The portion of inventory costs that are matched with earned revenues may be arrived at by specifically identifying unit costs of goods sold, or by making some assumption as to flow of costs such as FIFO, average cost, etc. The method of matching selected depends on the circumstances of the business.

4. If costs remaining in inventory at the end of an accounting period are unlikely to be recoverable without loss, or reflect inefficiencies or mistakes in the accounting period, an appropriate portion of such costs should be written off against the income of the period, by means of a reduction to 'market'. One method of writing-down to market in common practice is to compare the cost of each item in inventory
   – with replacement cost (buying market) for raw materials
   – with net realizable value (selling market) for finished goods, and
   – with replacement cost or realizable value less costs to complete and sell (whichever is determined more conveniently) for work-in-process.
   Other definitions of market, however, may be appropriate in given circumstances, and it may equally be appropriate to compare the aggregate market for inventory as a whole, or major categories of it, with aggregate cost, rather than item by item. The objective should be to reflect most fairly the results of the trading activities in the accounting period.

   (a) When the nature of the business is to trade or speculate in commodities, goods on hand at the end of the accounting period should not be valued at more than net realizable value less a discount to cover any probable abnormal delay in realization.

   (b) Where a business speculates in raw materials to the extent that it may on occasion buy more than normal quantities in anticipation of price rises, any decline in replacement market should be reflected at least to the extent of the above normal stocks.

   (c) Where a business deals in fashion goods, a valuation of any sizeable amounts of inventory at the end of the period should be sufficiently below net realizable value to allow for normal gross margins. Otherwise the current period may reflect higher margins than can be sustained in the following period when goods in inventory are sold off.

   (d) Where a business deals in seasonal non-fashion goods, any inventories left over at the end of the season should be valued at not more than net realizable value less a discount to cover the carry-over period until next season. If sizeable amounts are carried over, it may also be desirable to allow for a normal gross margin below realizable value to cover overheads during the period of disposal in the following period.

(e) Discontinued lines of merchandise should also be valued at not more than net realizable value less a discount to recognize probable delays in realization.

5. Where a business has purchase commitments with respect to inventory, these also should be considered in connection with the valuation at 'market' as though the goods for which the business is committed were actually in inventory at the end of the accounting period.

Measurement of cost of tangible capital assets and depreciation

6. The recorded cost of a tangible capital asset should include all costs necessary to put the asset in a position to render service. In the case of self-constructed assets, these would include costs of material and labour, overheads attributable to the construction, and actual out-of-pocket charges to finance construction costs during the construction period.

7. The cost of wasting tangible capital assets must be apportioned and charged off in determining the income of accounting periods benefiting from their use.
   (a) If, however, some other valuation (e.g. an appraisal value) has been substituted for cost in the accounts, the new carrying value should form the basis of the depreciation charge.

8. The period over which an asset or group of assets is depreciated should correspond with estimated economic life. The pattern of depreciation charges within that period should be systematic (which may be achieved by the use of one of the formulas such as diminishing balance or straight-line) and rational.
   (a) Round amount judgments of the amount of depreciation applicable to the entire plant of a sizeable business, made on a year to year basis, do not qualify as a systematic calculation of depreciation.
   (b) The present system of calculating capital cost allowances for income tax purposes is not designed to provide allowances related to the economic lives of the assets of individual businesses and therefore only by coincidence represents a satisfactory measure of depreciation. In particular, the fact that capital cost allowances are available on assets not yet in service, the existence of highly accelerated rates for incentive purposes and the occasional deferment of normal rates to act as economic depressants frequently make the amount of capital cost allowance unsuitable as a depreciation provision.

9. Since depreciation rates for a business can only represent estimates, they are subject to revision from time to time in the light of experience and current information.

Treatment of costs of intangible capital assets, prepaid expenses, deferred charges, period costs and costs of raising capital

10. The accounting for costs of intangible capital assets may depend on whether the useful life of such assets is limited or not.
    (a) If the economic life of a specific intangible right or thing is limited, its cost should be amortized against income over the period benefited.

(b) If a limit to the economic life of a general intangible asset is not foreseeable, its cost need not be amortized. However, amortization over an arbitrary period is permissible in recognition of the fact that no asset (except land) may be expected to last forever. Alternatively, such assets may be written off against accumulated retained earnings in one lump sum.

11. Costs that are not attributable to the acquisition of tangible or intangible capital assets or of inventory will normally be written off against the income of the period in which they are incurred, but such write-off may be deferred if:
    (a) costs are attributable to services yet to be received, or otherwise clearly relate to future time periods (in which case the costs represent 'prepaid expenses');
    (b) costs of services already rendered may reasonably be expected to produce benefits in future periods (in which case the costs will be treated as 'deferred charges').
    Prepaid expenses and deferred charges should be assigned to the periods considered to benefit from the expenditure.

12. Costs of raising capital should be accounted for according to the nature of the capital acquired.
    (a) Costs of raising fixed term debt capital should be written off over the term of the debt issue in proportion to the amounts outstanding from time to time, along with the interest expense on the debt.
    (b) Costs of raising share capital may be carried as an intangible asset indefinitely, but alternatively may be written off against contributed surplus or retained earnings.

Treatment of costs under a pension plan or deferred compensation arrangement

13. Where an employer has adopted a pension plan or entered into deferred compensation arrangements, the cost of such obligation should be recognized over the working life of the employees covered.

14. When the current cost of future benefits must be estimated (usually by actuarial calculations):
    (a) the underlying assumptions as to future interest, mortality, terminations, etc., should be realistic,
    (b) the actuarial method used to estimate cost should be applied consistently, and
    (c) adjustments consequent upon revisions in estimates from time to time should be included in pension costs of the current year or spread over a reasonable number of years (such as the period elapsing until the next revaluation) as seems appropriate in the circumstances.

15. Past service costs or prior service costs arising from introduction of a plan or improvement in its benefits should not be charged against earnings of prior years. The cost should be charged against income over a reasonable period of future years which need not coincide with the period over which such cost is funded.

Accounting for income taxes

16. For accounting purposes, corporate income tax is treated as a cost to be taken into account in the determination of net income for the year.

17. A proper presentation of the income tax cost related to reported income before tax requires:
   (a) when items of gain or loss are treated as extraordinary items or are credited or debited direct to a surplus account the tax or tax reduction attributable to such items should be segregated from the amount of tax that otherwise would be shown, and should be grouped with the item of gain or loss in the financial statements;
   (b) when revenues reported as earned in the accounts are not taxed currently but will be brought into account as an element of taxable income in future years, provision should be made for the future tax on such revenues;
   (c) when costs are claimed for tax purposes before being written off in the accounts, the resulting tax reduction should be deferred, to be brought back into income account at the future date when the cost is brought into account in the determination of reported income;
   (d) when costs are written off for accounting purposes in a current year, but these expenses will not be accepted as taxable deductions till future years (e.g. as in the case of warranty provisions), the benefit of the expected future tax reduction should be accrued, thereby reducing the amount of tax cost charged against the current year's income;
   (e) when revenues are taxed which have been treated as unearned for accounting purposes, the associated tax cost should be deferred to be charged against income in future periods when the revenue is regarded as earned.

18. For balance sheet purposes the credits or debits resulting from the allocation procedures applied to the income tax charge in the income statement should be regarded as deferments, the purpose of which is merely to allocate tax effects related to revenues, costs and gains or losses to the income account of the same year as that in which the related items are reported. Deferred tax credits or debits should not be regarded in the same light as ordinary amounts payable or receivable.

19. Recoveries resulting from tax losses carried back or carried forward should be treated as follows:
   (a) a recovery resulting from a loss carry-back should be taken in as a credit in the year of loss;
   (b) a recovery resulting from a loss carry-forward should also be considered applicable to the year of loss. However, since the actual recovery is contingent upon taxable profits being earned within the loss carry-forward period no credit should be taken in the year of loss unless some special circumstances exist that make such recovery virtually certain. When, and if, a recovery is realized in the carry-forward period the resulting credit should be treated as an extraordinary credit in the income statement of the year of recovery;

(c) when deferred tax credits exist at the same time as a loss carry-forward, it usually will be appropriate, depending on circumstances, to draw down into income account deferred tax credits associated with timing differences, up to the amount of the potential future tax reduction from the loss carry-forward.

Treatment of extraordinary items

20. Extraordinary items (less any income tax applicable) should be separately disclosed as the last item before 'net income' in the income statement. Extraordinary items are defined as material gains and losses connected with transactions that are significantly different from those resulting from the normal or typical activities of the entity. As a result, such gains or losses would not normally have great weight in an evaluation of the business. They do not include gains or losses which would normally be regarded as a risk incidental to the business carried on, even though such gains or losses might be abnormal in amount or occur only infrequently.

Treatment of capital transactions

21. Gains, losses or adjustments resulting from capital transactions* should in no case be credited or charged to income account.

22. A 'contributed surplus' account resulting from a capital transaction may be used to absorb charges that are the opposite to those that gave rise to the contributed surplus.

23. A charge that would otherwise have to be made against income may not be written off directly against a contributed surplus. If operations result in an accumulated deficit, such deficit should be shown as a deduction from capital and contributed surplus, and may only be written off against contributed surplus as a result of formal reorganization or quasi-reorganization proceedings. After any such write-off the accumulated earnings (or deficit) position should, for a reasonable period of years (say, five), indicate the date from which it has accumulated.

Treatment of prior period adjustments

24. Prior period adjustments are of two types:
    (a) adjustments to give retroactive effect to changed accounting methods, and
    (b) adjustments that represent corrections to previously reported figures.

---

* Capital transactions may be defined as including:
  (a) transactions involving contributions of capital by, or accruing to the benefit of, the equity interest (including preferred and common shareholders in the case of a corporation),
  (b) transactions involving withdrawal or reduction of such capital,
  (c) restatement of the capital interest as a result of:
    – reorganizations (in this case, adjustments to debt interests as well as share interests may be involved),
    – quasi-reorganizations, and
    – write-up of fixed assets on appraisal.

25. Corrections of previous estimates are inevitable given the uncertainty under-
    lying all economic activity. To avoid continual revision, corrections should
    only be treated as prior period adjustments when:
    (a) the transaction(s) whose record is being corrected clearly took place
        entirely in a prior period or periods, and
    (b) the determination of the outcome of the transaction was the result of
        action by forces or parties external to the entity, and not by its manage-
        ment alone, and either
        (i) the event or transaction was unusual to the entity (e.g. a lawsuit), or
        (ii) the transaction was of a kind that normally could be recorded with-
             out need for material correction (e.g. liability for income tax).

C. Principles governing the measurement of assets, liabilities and equities, and classification of equities

Assets

1. Accounts receivable arising from transactions with outside parties should be
   carried at their face value after allowance for discount to cover extended credit
   terms and for costs and losses associated with bad debts.

2. Accrued revenue should be recorded at a figure based on the contracted total
   revenue and proportionate to the recipient's entitlement based on his performance, the passage of time, or other factor governing the amount that may
   reasonably be regarded as earned.

3. Inventory should be valued at acquisition at the sum of all costs that can reasonably be attributed to it. Costs of goods remaining in inventory at any particular
   date are determined by the cost flow assumption adopted by the enterprise.
   Costs in inventory at the end of a period should be reduced to 'market' on a
   basis appropriate to the business. When inventory is written down to market,
   which is below cost, at the end of one period, the written-down value will be
   maintained until the inventory is sold (or further written down).

4. Fixed assets:
   (a) Land should be valued at cost except when the value of the land is depend-
       ent on some other factor that is consumed in the course of the business,
       in which case the land cost or an appropriate portion should be amortized
       as its value is exhausted.
   (b) Buildings and equipment, etc. should be valued initially at acquisition
       cost, which includes installation costs. The accumulated allowance for
       depreciation should be shown as a separate deduction from cost in the
       balance sheet and the net amount only shown as an asset.
   (c) An alternative acceptable basis of accounting for fixed assets is appraised
       value (allowing for any loss of value attributable to lack of tax-deduct-
       ibility) less an allowance for accumulated depreciation appropriate to
       the said appraised value.

5. Prepaid expenses should be carried at the unexpired portion of their cost
   determined on the basis of lapse of time or other basis appropriate to the nature
   of the prepayment.

6. Deferred tax debits attributable to accumulated timing differences between taxable and accounting income should be carried at the actual increase in tax paid with respect to (a) revenues taxed before their recognition in the accounts as earned, or (b) expenses incurred, not deductible for tax purposes until future years. Deferred tax debits relating to loss carry-forwards (where realization of such is virtually certain) should be carried at the amount of the estimated future tax recovery.

7. Other deferred charges should be carried at cost, less amounts written off to reflect the proportion of benefits already received to total expected benefit.

8. Intangible assets (where not written off against retained earnings upon acquisition):
   (a) if of indefinite life, are carried at cost, or are systematically amortized over an arbitrary term of years;
   (b) if of limited life, are carried at cost, less amortization related to the estimated expired useful life.

Liabilities

9. Accounts payable arising from transactions with outside parties should be shown at face value (after deducting any cash discounts allowed), less a discount for payment deferred beyond the normal credit terms at a discount rate established at the time the transaction was recorded.

10. Accrued costs or charges should be recorded at a figure based on contracted cost, proportionate to the creditor's entitlement based on his performance, the passage of time, or other factor governing the cost that should reasonably be recognized in the accounts.

11. Provisions for future costs or losses arising out of activities prior to the balance sheet date should be based on estimates of their amount.

12. Dividends payable should be shown at the amount declared.

13. Income tax payable should be shown at the estimated amount assessable.

14. Deferred revenue should be that proportion of revenue proceeds received which is not yet earned, determined on the basis of the degree of performance by the vendor.

15. Deferred tax credits attributable to accumulated timing differences between taxable and accounting income should be recorded at the amount of actual reduction in tax achieved (a) by postponement of taxation of revenues recognized in the accounts as earned or (b) by claiming for tax purposes costs not yet charged against income for accounting purposes.

16. Debt should be shown at the discounted present value of the amount contracted to be repaid in future, the discount rate being that established when the contract was entered into. By custom, however, debt having a nominal or face amount may be carried at that figure, and the difference between that figure and the original transaction amount be carried as a deferred charge or credit to be amortized over the period to maturity of the debt.

Equity

17. Capital contributed is carried at the amount established by the transactions through which the capital was issued. Such capital is usually subdivided between:
    (a) stated value (par value, or value assigned in the case of no par value stock), and
    (b) contributed surplus (amounts received in excess of stated capital).

18. Where share capital is redeemed for less than its stated value, the difference remains part of the equity but is transferred to contributed surplus.

19. Where share capital is redeemed for more than its stated value the difference is charged to contributed surplus to the extent that there were previous amounts paid in or gains on redemptions on the same issue, and against retained earnings if such contributed surplus is not available.

20. Any credit to equity resulting from a write-up of assets on appraisal over their former carrying value may be carried as a separate section of contributed capital indefinitely. Alternatively, to the extent that depreciation has been written on the appraisal increment, or some part of the write-up has entered into the determination of gain or loss on disposal of appraised assets, a transfer may be made from the appraisal surplus account to the retained earnings account.

21. Retained earnings represent a residual amount consisting of the accumulated sum of annual earnings since the inception of the enterprise, less dividends declared, and minus any adjustments resulting from capital transactions which could not be charged against contributed surplus.

Reorganizations or quasi-reorganizations

22. Any of the foregoing values are subject to readjustment through formal proceedings to a basis which appears to be fair and realistic. In the rare cases where this occurs, the retained earnings account for a period thereafter should be dated to indicate the 'fresh start' given to the accounting for the enterprise at the date of the reorganization.

Accounting for Investments

1. Investments held by trading companies may be classified as:
   (a) investments in subsidiaries or in other members of an affiliated group of companies,
   (b) other investments held for continuing business advantage, which usually may be described as 'investments in associated companies', and
   (c) other investments.
   Current assets include only such of the third group as are both readily marketable and not intended to be held for an extended period of time.

A. Accounting for investments other than in affiliated or associated companies

1. The primary basis of valuation of investments is cost. Provision should be made for the diminution in value:

(a) where the market value of the investments carried as current assets is materially below cost at the balance sheet date,

(b) in other cases where the decline in value of the investment appears to be enduring.

In exceptional cases where the current value of investments held has appreciated so much that the cost figure is meaningless, investments may be reappraised at the higher value, the write-up being credited to an appraisal increment account.

2. The basis of valuation of investments should be disclosed. In addition:

(a) the market value of investments carried as current assets should be disclosed,

(b) the market value of significant holdings of marketable securities which are carried as non-current assets should also be disclosed,

(c) where the current value of other investments is significantly different from carrying value, some indication of current value is desirable.

3. Where a part only of the holding of a particular security is sold, the average carrying value of the entire holding should normally be used for determining the figure to be written off against sales proceeds.

4. Receipt of a stock dividend does not constitute income to the recipient.

B. Accounting for investments in affiliated and associated companies

1. Where a holding company owns directly or indirectly over 50% of the voting shares of a subsidiary, consolidated financial statements are ordinarily necessary to a fair presentation of the financial position of the holding company. Exceptions to this general rule are:

(a) where control is expected to be temporary or where control has been lost, e.g. because the subsidiary is in receivership or because a foreign government is creating substantial interference with its operations or its right to remit dividends;

(b) where there is an extremely sizeable minority interest;

(c) where inclusion of a subsidiary would have an extremely distorting effect on the consolidated financial statements – e.g. where the parent company controls a financial institution.

2. The aim of consolidated financial statements is to present the financial position and results of operations as though the group of companies were one company. Therefore, all interlocking accounts between companies in the group must be eliminated. Also, since one company cannot make a profit dealing with itself, provision must be made for elimination of profits made by one company on sale to another in the group where the assets sold are still included as assets in the consolidated balance sheet, so that the assets will be restated on a cost basis in accordance with normal accounting practice. Income tax paid by individual companies with respect to such profits eliminated should be deferred.

3. The consolidation policy followed by the holding company should be disclosed. If any subsidiaries are not consolidated the reasons for such exclusion and the amount of their profits for the year and since date of acquisition, to the extent that they have not been reflected in the holding company's accounts, should be disclosed. If unremitted subsidiary company profits included in the consolida-

tion would be subject to tax on remittance this fact should be disclosed, preferably with an estimate of the amount of tax that would have been paid had all the year's earnings been remitted.

4. Investments in unconsolidated subsidiaries should normally be accounted for on the equity basis rather than the cost basis, except where control has been lost or is likely to be temporary.

5. Investments in associated companies (where ownership is 50% or less) are usually accounted for at cost. In 50% owned companies, companies which are effectively controlled with less than 50% ownership, or joint ventures, the equity basis is an acceptable alternative. (Where the joint venture is of the cost-sharing type, rather than being a profit-oriented venture, 'line-by-line' consolidation may also be appropriate.)

6. On either the cost or equity basis of investment accounting, if there appears to be a more than temporary decline in the value of the investment below the figure at which it is carried in the accounts, a write-down should be made.

C. Accounting for business combinations

1. Business combinations should be classified either as purchases, where one party is clearly acquiring control of the other business or businesses, or poolings of interests where, as a result of share exchanges carried out by the residual equity interests, there is a genuine mutual exchange of proportionate interests with the result that the operations and control of the former independent entities are pooled.

   (a) Poolings of interests

   In the minority of cases that are poolings of interests the assets and liabilities of the combining entities (after adjustment to place them on a uniform accounting basis) should be added together to form the basis of the combined entity's accounts. The various equity accounts should likewise be added together, except to the extent that surplus has to be capitalized to meet the requirements of corporate law. In historical statements of earnings the figures for the combining entities should likewise be added together.

   (b) Purchases

   (i) The consideration given to effect a purchase should be valued at fair market value at the approximate date the agreement is struck. In the case of quoted share issues fair value may be taken as indicated by the market price of the stock for a reasonable period before the acquisition, but allowance should be made for limitations on marketability of the stock issued, or the pressure on market price and costs of issue that would be entailed in a direct issue of the stock to the public.

   (ii) The total consideration arrived at should be allocated to assets purchased according to their fair value. Any excess of consideration over the fair value of all the identifiable tangible and intangible assets should be carried as goodwill. Where shares of a subsidiary company are purchased, rather than assets directly, the allocation of the purchase consideration for purposes of consolidation should follow the same general principle. In this case the liabilities assumed will also have to be valued and allowance made in the valuation for any difference between the values assigned to assets and liabilities and their status for tax purposes. If the total consideration is less than the fair value of all assets conservatively valued, the difference should be treated as a provision for future identifiable costs arising from the combination or as a deferred credit, suitably described, whichever is the more appropriate. A deferred credit should be amortized against income subsequently over a period which appears reasonable according to the circumstances.

Translation of Accounts in Foreign Currencies

Translation of accounts of foreign subsidiaries or branches

1. The usual procedure for balance sheet accounts is to translate current assets and liabilities at year-end exchange rates and long-term assets, liabilities and paid-in capital at the exchange rates prevailing when the assets were obtained, liabilities incurred, or capital contributed. Retained earnings are translated at the rate required to balance the balance sheet when it is expressed in the parent company's currency.

   Exceptions
   (a) Frequently inventory is translated at historic exchange rates rather than year-end rates especially if the inventory was imported by the foreign subsidiary.
   (b) Long-term monetary assets and liabilities are often translated at year-end rates rather than historic rates.
   (c) After a major revaluation of the foreign currency it may be considered desirable to abandon the historic rates for translation of long-term assets and liabilities in favour of the year-end rate, possibly in conjunction with a revaluation of the assets in terms of the foreign currency.
   The first two of these exceptions are more frequently encountered in connection with the translation of accounts in currencies subject to a long-term declining trend in value.

2. Income statement amounts for the most part are translated at rates designed to fairly represent the actual exchange rates prevailing during the period. This may be achieved by the use of averages, or rates changed every month or quarter, or a combination of these methods. However, income statement amounts associated with balance sheet items which are translated at historic rates (e.g. depreciation associated with fixed assets, cost of sales associated with inventory carried at historic rates, etc.) should be translated having regard to the rates used in the translation of the asset account.

3. Gains appearing in translation should be deferred until realization except to the extent they counteract losses previously written off. Losses on translation should be charged against previously deferred gains and any balance not so covered should be written off.

Exceptions

(a) After a major currency revaluation it may be considered appropriate to treat gains or losses on debt incurred just before the revaluation as an adjustment of the cost of assets acquired out of the proceeds of the debt.

(b) If a change in exchange rate may reasonably be expected not to be reversed in future (as in the case of a steadily declining currency), either gains or losses may be reflected in income account as they occur.

4. The use of standard translation rates which are changed only infrequently is acceptable when the currency to be translated is stable in relation to the parent company currency.

5. The accounts of foreign subsidiaries or branches should not be consolidated if the parent company's control is jeopardized by government action or unsettled conditions in the foreign country so that the ability of the parent company to receive the income earned from operations of the subsidiary or branch is in doubt.

Translation of foreign currency assets and liabilities arising from transactions not involving branches or subsidiaries

6. Current monetary assets and liabilities should be translated at year-end rates and any gain or loss recognized in income.

Exceptions

(a) A gain on translation at the new rate of an asset or liability other than cash may be deferred until date of settlement in cash.

(b) After a major revaluation it may be appropriate to treat *gains or losses* on liabilities incurred just before the revaluation as an adjustment of the cost of *inventory* acquired with the proceeds, if the realizable selling price of the inventory is expected to reflect the change in the cost of importing it. Similarly, it may be appropriate to treat such a *gain* as an adjustment of the cost of a *fixed asset* acquired, but ordinarily a *loss* should not be capitalized owing to the difficulty of establishing that the increase in carrying value will be recoverable.

7. Non-current monetary assets and liabilities may be treated in any of three ways:

(a) Translation may continue at the historic rate until the asset or liability becomes current.

(b) Translation may be at the new rate and
  (i) gains deferred until the item becomes current or is settled, and
  (ii) losses recognized in income or deferred until the item becomes current.

(c) If the change in exchange rate is expected not to be reversed, translation may be made at the new rate and both gains and losses reflected immediately in income.

The Fair Disclosure Principle

1. Disclosure in financial statements should be sufficient to make them not misleading to a typical investor. Assets, liabilities, revenues and expenses should be

accurately described. Non-recurring factors affecting information reported should be separately disclosed. The following matters particularly should be the subject of disclosure:

(a) details of accounting policies and methods, particularly where judgment is required in the application of an accounting method, the method is peculiar to the reporting entity, or alternative accounting methods could be used;

(b) additional information to aid in investment analysis or to indicate the rights of various parties having claims upon the reporting entity;

(c) changes from the preceding year in accounting principles or methods of applying them and the effect of such changes;

(d) assets and liabilities, costs and revenues arising out of transactions with parties such as controlling interests, or directors or officers, that have a special relationship to the reporting entity;

(e) contingent assets, liabilities and commitments;

(f) financial or other non-operating transactions after the balance sheet date which have a material effect on the financial position shown by the year-end statement.

Principles of Analysis

A. Calculation of earnings per share

1. Earnings per share data should be disclosed in the financial statements so that it becomes part of the audited information.

2. Basic earnings per share should be calculated for common stock and each other class of stock which has participation in earnings such that it is similar to common. Such calculations should be on the 'two class' method.

3. Fully diluted earnings per share figures should be calculated to show the effect of the existence of other securities that may, under certain conditions, become common stock.

4. The calculation of earnings per share on the fully diluted basis should follow certain rules:

(a) When convertible securities exist, the calculation should be on the 'if converted' basis. That is, dividends or after-tax interest on the convertible securities should be added back to earnings and the resulting total divided by the weighted average number of common shares outstanding during the period, as it would be if the securities had been converted at the beginning of the period (or at the date of issue of the convertible securities if they were issued after the beginning of the period).

(b) When warrants or options exist, cash proceeds on their exercise should be deemed used in the business, and imputed earnings at an appropriate rate (after tax) should be added to actual earnings. The earnings so adjusted should then be divided by the weighted average number of common shares, including the shares issuable upon the exercise of the rights, assuming such rights were issued at the beginning of the period (or at the date the rights were granted if that is later than the beginning of the period).

(c) Where shares are issuable in future subject to certain conditions, the calculation of earnings per share should assume earnings and a number of shares outstanding which will be consistent with the terms and conditions applicable to the contingent issue of shares in future.

(d) Where the calculation with respect to a given security under the above rules would increase the figure of fully diluted earnings per share, such security should not be taken into account in the calculation.

B. Classification of current assets, current liabilities and working capital

1. Working capital is defined as the difference between current assets and current liabilities.

2. The operating cycle is the average time intervening between the acquisition of materials or services for inventory and the final cash realization from inventory sold.

3. Current assets are those assets realizable within one year from the balance sheet date or, in the case of operating assets, within the operating cycle of the business if that is longer than one year.

(a) Certain operating assets, such as prepayments, although not held for sale and therefore not realizable in the customary sense, are includable as current assets to the extent that their existence reduces the need for cash within the next year (or operating cycle if longer than one year).

(b) Cash not available for current spending or cash intended to be spent on the acquisition of non-current assets or liquidation of non-current liabilities should be excluded from current assets.*

(c) Other non-operating assets (e.g. investments) are excluded from current assets if they are not intended to be realized within one year, even though they may be readily realizable.*

4. Current liabilities are those liabilities which will require the use of current assets to liquidate them:

(a) within the longer of one year or, if the liabilities arise from operations, the operating cycle,

(b) within one year in the case of other liabilities.

   (i) Current maturities of long-term debt are includable as current liabilities.

   (ii) Debt which is expected to be refunded on a long-term basis, however, need not be classified as a current liability.

5. Deferred tax debits or credits should be classified as current if they relate to assets or liabilities classified as current, and otherwise as non-current. If both deferred tax debits and credits occur within a category they are usually netted.

---

* This principle is not invariably followed in practice.

Summary of Underlying Accounting Concepts

A. Characteristics of the accounting environment.

    1. Accounting is related to identifiable entities.

    2. Such entities may normally be assumed to have continuing existence.

    3. The existence of an exchange economy supports a system of accounting in monetary terms.

B. The objectives of financial accounting.

    1. The primary objective is usefulness.

    2. General purpose statements must fairly balance the information needs of all interested parties.

C. Standards of useful reporting.

    1. Financial reporting should be on a regular, periodic basis (the period being not longer than once a year) and the reports should be timely, i.e. be issued soon after the close of the period reported on.

    2. In reporting economic events, accounting should look to the substance of the transaction rather than legal form.

    3. An accounting entity should maintain consistency in accounting methods used from year to year. When the occasional change becomes necessary to improve the reporting, the fact of the change and its effect should be clearly disclosed.

    4. Information reported should be as reliable as possible, consistent with fair reporting of economic substance.

    5. Where accounting estimates are subject to major uncertainty, the estimate should be conservative – i.e. it should tend to understate, if anything, the expected revenue or gain, and overstate expected cost or loss.

    6. Meticulous accuracy in accounting for, and reporting, immaterial amounts is not required.

1   Introduction

Accountants have used the phrase 'generally accepted accounting principles' for some thirty-five years. In spite of this long history of usage, it would be difficult to reach general agreement today as to what, specifically, is meant by the words 'accounting principles'. Nor does any precise definition of the phrase 'generally accepted' exist.

Nevertheless, accounts are kept and financial reports are prepared in accordance with accounting and reporting methods well recognized as being appropriate. In fact, so well recognized are they that innovations may well be the subject of comment, critical or otherwise, in the financial press and elsewhere.

It may therefore be asked why the Accounting and Auditing Research Committee of the Canadian Institute of Chartered Accountants (hereafter CICA Research Committee) should have commissioned this Study. At least three reasons can be discerned:

1. As a result of widespread usage, the phrase 'generally accepted accounting principles' has acquired a significance beyond the confines of the accounting profession. It has, in fact, entered into the public domain. It is customarily included in auditors' reports on annual financial statements. (Indeed its use is now mandatory in audit reports on corporations incorporated under the laws of Canada and of several of its provinces.) The words are found in trust deeds and in other contractual arrangements between parties. The accounting profession, therefore, has a responsibility to make the meaning of the phrase reasonably clear.

2. A swelling tide of criticism has been voiced in recent years about the variety of accounting treatments possible in given situations, the effect of this variety on corporate financial reporting, and the consequent difficulty that readers of financial statements have in making decisions based (in part) on such statements.

3. Accounting principles are not static. They change and develop to meet changed conditions. To cite only two examples – the growth of pension plans and the practice of financing by long-term leases in the last two decades have caused accounting problems which are not yet solved in a manner universally recog-

nized as satisfactory. Changes in accounting principles also mirror changes in social attitudes. Forty years ago the provision of reserves out of income, at the discretion of management, was commonplace in financial statements. Today the practice is rare, if not non-existent. The accounting profession through its professional societies has, over the years, accepted increasing responsibility for the formulation of accounting principles and the direction of change in them. If this is to be done rationally the profession must at all times be conscious of its existing body of principles, so that new rules complement, rather than conflict with, existing rules.

It is an assumption of this Study and its terms of reference that accounting principles are, or should be, consistent one with another. This is implicit in the third and fifth terms of reference:

> " – to codify such principles and practices in a rational articulated manner, so as to reveal insofar as is possible the theory or assumptions underlying such principles and practices.
> – to consider areas where Canadian accounting practices appear to be in conflict, and areas where practices found are in apparent conflict with authoritative accounting literature, including official recommendations of professional accounting institutes or their committees."

This view has to be reconciled with the fact that accounting principles have evolved over a century and a half, and under the influence of economic, legal and social institutions that have varied from time to time and place to place. Some considerable inconsistencies as between principles would seem therefore to be inevitable. On the other hand, there are also elements that would lead one to expect some degree of common practice in accounting:

1. Accounting is a means of communication of relevant information to interested parties. The needs of such parties for information influence the form in which it is presented. Historically, the development of accounting has been geared to provide information to the owner-manager, the short-term creditor, the long-term creditor and the equity investor. While the needs of all these for information are not identical, they are sufficiently similar to have imposed some sort of pattern on accounting.*

2. In order to communicate effectively, accounting must classify and condense its material. If, then, there is any pattern to the raw material of accounts, it is likely to be reflected in the accounting reports. To the extent that a pattern exists in business, there should be a pattern in accounting for business.

3. Business activity, no matter how diverse its product, can be described as consisting of relatively few functions – buying, manufacturing, transporting,

---

* More recently, the information produced by accounting has been used to serve other purposes – for example, the calculation of income subject to taxation, the regulation of public utilities, and the production of national income figures and other statistical measures. For some of these special purposes some deviation from a strict adherence to generally accepted accounting principles may be required. Special exceptions may be made, say to facilitate the administration of income tax, or to implement a particular theory in utility rate regulation that is in conflict with accounting principles. In the main, however, they rely upon a logical uniform accounting process to provide the tools of control and administration.

storing, selling, research and design, product development, exploration, and financing the whole activity. It is reasonable to expect this repetitive activity to be accounted for by methods that will find general acceptance.

4. Similarly, in accounting for non-profit organizations, those interested in the accounting – the contributors and occasionally governments – are interested in relatively simple information – where the money came from and how it was spent.

Accordingly there are grounds for the belief that accounting principles are likely to show some unity in pattern. One of the purposes of this Study is to delineate this pattern for the better information of practitioners, students of accounting and the public at large.

This Study is in two parts. The objective of Part I, entitled "The Present State of the Art", is to satisfy the Study's terms of reference:

> " – to identify accounting principles and practices that may be said to have received some general acceptance.
> – to codify such principles and practices in a rational articulated manner so as to reveal insofar as is possible the theory or assumptions underlying such principles and practices."

The meaning of the term 'generally accepted accounting principles' is first explored, followed by a review of certain fundamental observations and assumptions (themselves called principles by some authors) that influence accounting principles. The Part continues with a brief statement of the historical development of accounting principles and the influences that have moulded them. This leads into the detailed exposition of accounting principles generally accepted today.

In Part I the attempt is to deal with principles as they are and explain how they came to be that way. If certain principles are inconsistent, or if practice condones the use of two or more accounting treatments that are logically incompatible, these facts will necessarily be brought out. However, the primary objective in Part I is to catalogue principles as they exist, and not to evaluate them critically.

Part II, entitled "Change and Development", takes up the challenge of the terms of reference,

> " – to recommend areas where existing Canadian financial reporting should be improved and areas where the accounting profession should undertake further study with a view to modification of existing accounting principles so as to make them more accurate or of more widespread usefulness."

In this Part the findings will be less objective, more a matter of opinion. There are three topics considered: (1) the foundations required for a logical development of accounting principles; (2) the machinery necessary to facilitate changes in accounting principles when required; and (3) a critical analysis of current accounting principles and practices.

These two Parts contain the substance of this Study. There are also two Appendices. Appendix A contains discussions in greater depth of a number of accounting issues mentioned in Part I. These detailed discussions have been removed to this Appendix in order to avoid extensive interruption of the natural progression of ideas in Part I, but are referenced to the related Chapter in the main work. Appendix B contains excerpts from the statements on accounting principles published by the professional associations of accountants in three countries, Canada, the United States and England. These excerpts are also arranged in the order of development of this Study and referenced to related Chapters in it.

Part I

The present state
of the art

2   Definitions

Accounting rules are developed to ensure that the users of accounting data get reliable information in the form best suited to their wants. An enquiry into the uses for which accounting data is required, therefore, casts light upon the nature of accounting principles.

The first use of accounting is merely to keep track of assets and liabilities. In this function it supplements the fallible human memory. The need for accounting in this purely recording aspect is directly proportional to the scale of wealth involved – the greater the wealth, the greater the need for accurate records. The rules for processing data however are not *accounting* principles as that term is used in this Study. Rather they are principles of bookkeeping or of bookkeeping systems. Accounting principles are concerned with the measurement, classification and interpretation of data, not with its compilation.

A second use of accounting data is to assist the management of an enterprise to make business decisions. Management however is in the fortunate position of being able to specify what information it wants, and how it should be presented. While such information obviously should be realistic and reflect the economic situation fairly, so long as management understands the basis upon which it is prepared it is not essential that it be, for example, highly objective, or conservatively estimated, or consistent with information presented previously for other purposes. In other words management accounting is largely free of the constraints applicable to external reporting and need not be concerned with a rigorously defined body of accounting principles.

The third use of accounting is to report to outside interested parties how the management of an enterprise or institution has fulfilled its responsibility. This is accomplished traditionally through the medium of the annual report and in particular the annual financial statements. We call the process that culminates in the production of financial statements 'financial accounting'. Financial accounting has in view the communication of information by those who manage an enterprise to those who have a legitimate interest in it, but do not have access to its internal information systems.

The role of financial accounting as a means of communication is central to the existence of accounting principles. If communication through financial statements is to be successful there must be an understanding among the parties concerned as to the nature and character of the accounting. Principles of accounting therefore (as the term is used here) refer to those standard rules for accounting action that are necessary to make for fair and effective communication through the medium of financial statements.

Meaning of the term 'generally accepted'

The term 'generally accepted' is difficult to define in a precise manner. Its meaning can perhaps best be conveyed by describing the conditions under which an accounting method will be recognized as generally accepted. To qualify, an accounting method must meet at least one, and usually more, of the following conditions:
- The method will be in actual use in a significant number of cases where the circumstances are suitable.
- The method would have support in the pronouncements of the professional accounting societies, or other authoritative bodies such as the Securities and Exchange Commission in the United States.
- The method would have support in the writing of a number of respected accounting teachers and thinkers.

To state these conditions however is not to solve the problems connected with the meaning of the term 'generally accepted':

1. Just as one swallow does not make a summer, an isolated example of usage does not establish a method as generally accepted. There should be some evidence that the method is usually or frequently applied in the particular conditions for which it is designed.

2. On the other hand, a method need not be frequently encountered to qualify as generally accepted. The special conditions which it is designed to meet may be rare. An example of this is the sinking fund depreciation method which is well documented in accounting literature but is used in practice only when asset lives are long, demand for the assets' product is well established and likely to persist over their assumed life, and operating costs of service are unlikely to increase materially as the assets age. These conditions are rare in a competitive business environment.

3. It is not always easy to discover what specific accounting methods are being followed by a business. Corporate annual reports do not furnish details of their accounting policies except in isolated cases, and then usually only when the accounting treatment used is a special case.

4. Generally accepted accounting methods differ from country to country and the differences are not always explainable by differences in the legal or economic backgrounds. This difficulty is particularly acute for Canadian accountants who are influenced both by English and American precedents. To cite only two examples – the valuation of fixed assets at appraised values is frowned on in the United States, but is commonplace in the United Kingdom, and certainly permissible, though less frequent, in Canada. Inventory valuation by the 'direct costing' method is likewise frowned on in the United States (although there is evidence that it is used to some extent) but would be considered perfectly justified in the United Kingdom.

5. Specific accounting methods are not mutually exclusive. That is to say, there is not just one method usable in a particular set of circumstances. Examples of this diversity abound. FIFO or LIFO may be used in inventory cost accounting. Depreciation patterns may follow the straight-line or the diminishing balance methods. Product development costs may be capitalized and amortized or written off immediately, and so on.

Accounting principles and accounting methods

In the first section of this Chapter accounting principles were defined as "standard rules for accounting action that are necessary to make for fair and effective communication through the medium of financial statements". In the second section it was noted that there is considerable diversity in accounting methods. The question naturally arises – how is the distinction drawn between rules of general application and methods that are found in many alternative forms?

Consider for example, the following directions to be followed in accounting:

1. Match costs incurred with revenues recognized in order to arrive at accounting income.

2. Follow depreciation accounting in order to match costs of plant and equipment with revenues.

3. Use the straight-line depreciation method.

Each of these statements gives guidance in the making of entries in the accounts. The guidance given however differs in its degree of generalization and each succeeding instruction rests upon the preceding. In describing accounting rules therefore, one has to recognize different levels of generalization. It is almost like an inverted pyramid with a succession of practical rules resting upon the foundation of a few generalized principles.

A further point may be noted, however – that the more specific the instruction, the more likely it is that there is an alternative rule resting upon the same general principle. In the illustration above for example, there are in practice several alternatives to the instruction – "use the straight-line depreciation method" – for example, the diminishing balance depreciation method, the sum-of-the-years' digits method, the unit-of-production method, and so on. Thus, there are generalized accounting principles that admit no alternatives (e.g. Numbers 1 and 2 in the illustration) and specific accounting methods that are found in several alternative forms.

Herein lies a partial answer to a question that frequently puzzles accountants – "how can improvements in financial reporting be made if published financial statements must always follow current generally accepted accounting principles?" New accounting *methods* may be adopted so long as they are not inconsistent with a governing principle. The decision whether a proposed method is or is not acceptable, of course, may still be a difficult one. For example, if the revenue recognition principle is stated as "revenue is to be recognized at point of sale" it may be difficult to choose some other time for revenue recognition unless it is argued that a sale occurs in substance at some time other than the date of legal transfer of title. If however the principles is stated as "revenue is to be recognized as soon as the effort required to earn it is largely completed and the amount of revenue that will be received is known with reasonable certainty" it will be easier to select accounting methods that achieve the desired goal.

Alternative definitions of 'accounting principle'

From the foregoing discussion it might be concluded that generally accepted accounting principles consist only of a very few, very broad, guidelines. A number of writers in accounting adopt this type of definition, possibly influenced by a natural reluctance to attach the word 'principle' to the miscellany of alternative methods and procedures that make up the practice of accounting. Such a definition, however, is not satisfactory for a study such as this, since the difficult problems in today's accounting do not arise at the level of broad principle. Almost everyone agrees, for example, that costs and revenues should be matched and reported in the income statement of the period to which they relate. The difficult problems arise in the application of such a broad principle – for example in deciding what is the appropriate income tax expense to attribute to income for a year when taxable income is reduced below accounting income because the tax act permits or prescribes a different timing for recognition of revenues or costs than the timing adopted for accounting purposes. 'Accounting principles' would be a relatively meaningless phrase if it were restricted to generalizations so broad that they afford little practical guidance in dealing with the important issues that arise in accounting.

On the other hand, some authorities have adopted all-encompassing definitions of accounting principles. In 1957, when introducing a recommendation that the auditor's report contain a reference to generally accepted accounting principles, the CICA Research Committee said:

> "Basic concepts of sound accounting have evolved over the years, and have been developed and recognized generally by accountants. Within the framework of basic concepts of sound accounting, certain rules, conventions, or practices have gained general acceptance as appropriate methods of applying these concepts in particular circumstances. The basic concepts of sound accounting and the acceptable methods of applying them are referred to as 'generally accepted accounting principles'."[1]

Statement No. 4 of the Accounting Principles Board of the American Institute of Certified Public Accountants (hereafter AICPA Accounting Principles Board) states:

> "Generally accepted accounting principles therefore is a technical term in financial accounting. Generally accepted accounting principles encompass the conventions, rules, and procedures necessary to define accepted accounting practice at a particular time. The standard of 'generally accepted accounting principles' includes not only broad guidelines of general application, but also detailed practices and procedures."[2]

In addition most accounting writers identify a number of observations about the environment of accounting and the uses of accounting information that are pertinent to the development of principles. Paul Grady referred to these as basic concepts to which accepted accounting principles are oriented or "which underlie or permeate accepted accounting principles".[3] To some accountants these concepts, too, are part of the body of accounting principles.

To avoid confusion it is proposed to adopt the following definitions in Part I of this Study. These are believed to be consistent with the general line of development of current accounting theory (even though the terminology used by individual writers varies):

1. Accounting concepts are those observations about the economic and social environment and the uses to which accounting information is put, which are pertinent to the development of accounting principles. (Accounting concepts will be discussed in Chapter 3.)

2. Accounting principles are rules which give guidance to the measurement, classification and interpretation of economic information and communication of the results through the medium of financial statements. These rules are characterized as 'principles' by the fact that no alternative rule is generally recognized as permissible for the operation to which the principle relates. Most accounting principles are relatively broad guidelines which may be implemented by two or more alternative procedures. However, this fact reflects the way that accounting theory has historically developed and is not necessitated by this definition. Under this definition an accounting principle may be a quite specific guide for action in a particular situation, provided that no alternative procedures are recognized as permissible in the same situation.

3. Accounting procedures, practices or methods are acceptable ways of implementing governing accounting principles which even in similar situations may differ from one accounting entity to another at the sole discretion of the management of the entity. Over a period of time a particular accounting method may come to be recognized as the only appropriate way to deal with a particular situation. It then will have become a principle. The activities of the professional societies of accountants in recent years have accelerated the process by which accounting procedures make the transition to the status of accounting principles.

Accounting principles for non-profit institutions and specialized enterprises

When we survey the whole field of accounting however, it is clear that it is very difficult to find any accounting principle that is applied without exception throughout the whole range of economic activity, non-profit making as well as profit making. To cite but one example, depreciation accounting is the invariable rule for business enterprises but is the exception, rather than the rule, in the accounting of non-profit organizations such as charities, municipalities, churches, and universities.

To solve this dilemma it is necessary to distinguish between systems of accounting principles, each system having its own set of rules designed to meet its own particular needs for information. One can recognize for example one system for business enterprises generally, another for hospitals, another for charities, and so on. Ideally then, in using the phrase generally accepted accounting principles we would add a few words explaining what system of principles we are talking about – e.g. generally accepted accounting principles for municipalities, for hospitals, for business enterprises, etc. In practice, the distinction is not ordinarily spelled out, but rather is understood merely from the description or title of the organization for which the accounting is being performed.

The question then arises what basis exists for distinction between various sets of accounting principles. The answer to this may lie in reference back to the basic purpose of accounting – the communication of pertinent information to parties interested in an enterprise. This suggests that accounting rules can be distinguished or classified according to the parties to whom the communication is addressed and the type of information they require. Three broad categories may be suggested:

– Accounting for business enterprises – where the communication is primarily addressed to the investor and creditor.

– Accounting for financial institutions – where the interests of the depositor or policyholder, or society generally, are deemed to outweigh the interests of the investors, and accounting principles are strongly influenced by government regulation in the interests of these other parties.

– Accounting for institutions that are not profit seeking – where the communication is primarily addressed to the providers of funds – whether such be the donors of charitable gifts, taxpayers, government officials controlling disbursements to hospitals, universities, and so on.

There is room for argument that sets of accounting principles should be much more finely differentiated. Certainly the accounting principles of a life insurance company exhibit substantial differences from those of a chartered bank – merely because of the different nature of the two institutions. Nevertheless, for the purpose of this Study in which the main emphasis will be on accounting principles for ordinary business enterprises the classification is convenient.

The emphasis on accounting for business enterprises in this Study follows both from the fact that this is the area of widest interest, and the fact that accounting principles are most highly developed in this field. Traditionally, relatively little attention has been paid to the accounting of financial institutions and non-profit enterprises and as a result there is relatively little to be said about generally accepted accounting principles in these fields. To illustrate the point we quote from the introduction to Bulletin 43 issued by the AICPA Committee on Accounting Procedures:

> "The committee has not directed its attention to accounting problems or procedures of religious, charitable, scientific, educational, and similar non-profit institutions, municipalities, professional firms, and the like. Accordingly, except where there is a specific statement of a different intent by the committee, its opinions and recommendations are directed primarily to business enterprises organized for profit."[4]

Similarly, the Preface to the Recommendations issued by the CICA Research Committee contains these words:

> "Recommendations are intended to apply to all types of profit oriented enterprises, unless a particular recommendation makes a specific exemption or extension. However, pending further study, the recommendations do not necessarily apply to the special problems of banks, trust companies and insurance companies."[5]

In this Study, discussion of the accounting principles of financial institutions will be found in Chapter 25 and of non-profit organizations in Chapter 26. The remainder of the Study will deal with generally accepted accounting principles for business enterprises.

References

1. The Committee on Accounting and Auditing Research, *Bulletin No. 17, The Auditor's Report* (Toronto: Accounting and Auditing Practices: Canadian Institute of Chartered Accountants, 1959), par. 6.
2. The Accounting Principles Board, *Statement No. 4 – Basic Concepts and Accounting Principles Underlying Financial Statements of Business Enterprises* (New York: American Institute of Certified Public Accountants, Inc., 1971), par. 138.
3. Paul Grady, *Inventory of Generally Accepted Accounting Principles for Business Enterprises* (New York: American Institute of Certified Public Accountants, Inc., 1965), p. 23.
4. Committee on Accounting Procedure, *Bulletin No. 43 – Restatement and Revision of Accounting Research Bulletins* (New York: American Institute of Certified Public Accountants, 1953), p. 8.
5. The Accounting and Auditing Research Committee, *Research Recommendations* (Toronto: Canadian Institute of Chartered Accountants, 1969), p. 7.

3   Basic accounting concepts

OFR & Qualtatative CRiteriA

Chapter 2 has suggested that there are certain concepts which underlie accounting principles but which may be distinguished from them in that the concepts do not, in themselves, furnish direct guidance for measuring, analyzing or interpreting economic data. These concepts include certain observations about the economic environment, and assumptions about the uses of accounts and the objectives of accounting which, taken together, shape the development of accounting principles. Collectively they might be called the preconditions of modern accounting.

Accounting writers are in broad agreement in identifying the accounting concepts set out below.

Observations about the economic environment

The first environmental observation pertinent to accounting is that in a highly developed, industrialized society economic activity is carried on through the medium of identifiable *entities*. We recognize these entities as being distinct from their owners. In the case of corporations this distinction is institutionalized by the law, but recognition of a separate entity is not primarily dependent on any action of law. We have no difficulty in recognizing Smith's Drug Store as a separate entity from Mr. Smith even though the business is unincorporated. Indeed Mr. Smith may die, and yet the entity may carry on under the same name and in the same location, the business having been sold to new owners. Entities with real economic substance thus exist apart from the people who own them, and the focus in accounting and financial reporting is on the economic entity.

Secondly, in a mature economy most forms of business and other enterprises are carried on by '*going concerns*' – i.e. entities that have a continuing existence, and are not just established to carry out one venture.

Thirdly, in a mature economy most goods and services are produced for sale to other entities, or to ultimate consumers, not for use by the owners of the producing entity. This requires highly developed market facilities and the use of money as a medium of exchange. As a result market prices are available to assist in measuring (valuing) economic data, and *accounts recording assets owned and their increase can be maintained primarily in monetary terms*.

The objectives of accounting

It is commonly said that accounting is a pragmatic art – its primary objective is usefulness. The goal of usefulness raises questions as to who are the users, and what they want to know. As mentioned earlier, the principal users of financial reports are owners, creditors and investors, but many other parties also have an interest in accounting information. It is presumed that all these users are interested in statements of financial condition and changes in financial condition over the reporting period resulting from income earned and other causes. Because of the complex nature of economic activity, financial condition and changes in it are not adequately portrayed for the typical entity by mere statements showing cash received and disbursed. The objective of usefulness therefore requires the use of accrual accounting for most entities (i.e. accounting based on recording the effect of transactions on financial condition and income when the transactions take place, not merely when they are settled in cash).

The fact that so many different parties have an interest in the results of financial reporting means that financial statements are used for many purposes. It is unfortunately true that the statements may not serve all such purposes equally well. For example, the creditor might feel that extremely conservative accounting methods would be most useful for his special interests, whereas a shareholder wishing to dispose of his shares would prefer methods designed to portray the real economic situation more closely, even if this meant writing up assets above cost to reflect enhanced current market values. Ideally it might be felt that special purpose statements should be prepared on different accounting bases for each special class of users, but this is almost entirely impractical. The general purpose statements must be prepared to meet the needs of all parties as far as possible (presumably taking into account the legitimacy of the interest in the entity of each type of interested party – e.g. a government department merely seeking statistical information is less entitled to consideration than the shareholder group). Some accounting writers therefore lay great stress on *fairness* in the presentation of general purpose financial statements. This test extends the concept of usefulness, since it is conceivable that a distorted presentation would be more useful to some parties (using the word 'useful' in a narrow, selfish sense) than would an unbiased presentation.

Standards of usefulness

Certain standards of financial reporting are considered to contribute to the usefulness of accounting information. In the first place, the reports should be made *periodically* at frequent intervals. A comprehensive report at annual intervals is mandatory and condensed reporting of key figures on an interim basis is becoming standard. To be most useful the reports should be *timely*.

Accounting methods adopted should endeavour to convey the *substance of the economic events portrayed, rather than mere form*. While legal rights and obligations are important, it is also important that they not be permitted to obscure the economic effect of transactions entered into. (It is not unknown that the legal form of a transaction is determined largely with this purpose in mind.) *Consistency* in accounting methods from year to year is also necessary to avoid confusing the reader and to enable proper evaluation of trends. While changes to improved accounting methods are necessary from time to time they should be held to a minimum and be clearly disclosed.

The usefulness of financial statements will obviously depend on the *reliability* of the measurements (valuations) in them, as well as the appropriateness of the accounting methods followed. This standard must be modified, however, by the realization that absolute reliability is unattainable, given the uncertainty inherent in many accounting estimates. Moreover, even if absolute reliability were attainable, it would undoubtedly be at the expense of fairness in reporting. Older accounting literature tended to state the standard of reliability in the words "accounting should be based on objective evidence". From the requirement for objectivity two sub-concepts (or principles) were deduced, namely (1) the realization concept – revenue should not be regarded as earned until it is 'realized', and (2) the cost concept – assets should be carried in the accounts on the basis of cost (or lower) until another transaction provides objective evidence of increase in value. Under the definitions of this Study, at this point, the line is crossed between accounting concepts and accounting principles. Hence discussion of the latter two propositions is deferred. A further derivation from the objectivity concept and cost concept may have been the assumption that the unit of currency has a constant purchasing power. To assume otherwise would mean adjusting the accounts on the basis of indices or other evidence that would be considerably less factual than that furnished by actual transactions.

Many measurements in accounting depend on estimates of the future – the amount that will be collected on accounts receivable, the realizable value of inventory, the future economic life of fixed assets, the amount of costs that will be incurred on product warranties and so on. While experience provides guidance for these estimates, there are many occasions when it is quite limited. For example, future warranty costs on a product involving new technology or design may be quite uncertain. Similarly the outcome of lawsuits is frequently unpredictable. In circumstances of uncertainty, it is accepted that estimates should be weighted on the *conservative* side, although there is virtually no authoritative evidence as to the degree of conservatism. In earlier accounting literature and practice conservatism was a virtue esteemed more highly than it is today. At one time there was little objection to rapid asset write-offs, or the creation of excessive provisions for liabilities (and sometimes secret reserves) even though it was known income and shareholders' equity was thereby understated. Today the conflict between practices and the standard of fair presentation is recognized and conservative accounting estimates and methods are more properly reserved for situations where the inherent uncertainty justifies them.

A final concept significant to the usefulness of financial reporting is that of *materiality*. Stated simply this concept suggests that it is not worthwhile bothering with meticulous accounting for, or reporting of, small amounts. In the first place, such meticulous accounting makes work and is therefore expensive. In the second place, small amounts separately identified in the financial statements usually have no significance to the decision-making processes of the reader. In the third place, small amounts may so clutter the financial statements that the pertinent information therein is obscured.

Limitations on the usefulness of accounting information

Some writers include among 'accounting concepts' cautionary observations about the limitations of financial reporting. For example they emphasize that because of the necessary role of judgment in making accounting estimates figures reported are necessarily approximate and tentative. Also the value of the results is subject to the limitation that accounting cannot measure many intangible factors, such as the skill and life expectancy of management. Also comparability of accounting information between entities is limited because of the freedom of the management of two entities under the present state of the accounting art to choose alternative accounting practices in similar situations.

While all these statements are true and it is important that users of financial statements be aware of such limitations, it seems rather odd to classify such statements among "basic concepts which underlie accounting principles".

In summary, the following accounting concepts may be identified:

A. Characteristics of the accounting environment.

　1. Accounting is related to identifiable entities.

　2. Such entities may normally be assumed to have continuing existence. *Going Concern.*

　3. The existence of an exchange economy supports a system of accounting in monetary terms.

B. The objectives of financial accounting.

　1. The primary objective is usefulness.

　2. General purpose statements must fairly balance the information needs of all interested parties.

C. Standards of useful reporting.

　1. Financial reporting should be on a regular, periodic basis (the period being not longer than once a year) and the reports should be timely, i.e. be issued soon after the close of the period reported on.

　2. In reporting economic events, accounting should look to the substance of the transaction rather than legal form.

　3. An accounting entity should maintain consistency in accounting methods used from year to year. When the occasional change becomes necessary to improve the reporting, the fact of the change and its effect should be clearly disclosed. *$ 500.*

　4. Information reported should be as reliable as possible, consistent with fair reporting of economic substance.

　5. Where accounting estimates are subject to major uncertainty, the estimate should be conservative – i.e. it should tend to understate, if anything, the expected revenue or gain, and overstate expected cost or loss. *But Relate to CFR.*

　6. Meticulous accuracy in accounting for, and reporting, immaterial amounts is not required. *Materiality.* *ie Revenue measurement*

Some of these concepts are discussed in greater depth in the supplementary material in Appendix A.

4   The historical development of accounting principles

Wherever there is wealth some form of accounting records will also be found. Accounts therefore are associated with the most ancient civilizations. Accounting principles however (that is rules of general application for recording and reporting information about wealth) do not predate the 19th Century. The following conditions had to exist before such rules were either needed or possible:

1. A recognized medium of exchange and a developed market for goods so that values could be provided for incorporation in the accounts – Manorial accounts in feudal times were likely to be listings of goods themselves rather than the monetary value of such goods. This would prevent such records from giving the overall view that is the essence of communication through financial statements.

2. Business carried on on a continuing basis – In a continuing business periodic reports become necessary. When business is carried on in the form of separate ventures, owners can wait for the liquidation of each venture to learn of its success or failure.

3. Large-scale enterprise – In large complex businesses it is more difficult for anyone not intimately acquainted with the business to assess its progress without financial reports, and the valuations embodied in such reports are more difficult to come by. Hence, the need for recognized accounting rules is greater.

4. Separation of ownership and management – Rules for accounting are not essential when the manager is responsible only to himself. It is only when an outsider must understand what management has done that rules become essential.

5. The existence of an undefined group of owners – The problems of separation of ownership and management are reinforced when ownership is divided up among many people and the rights of ownership are freely transferable, as is the case with public companies listed on the stock exchange. Financial statements and periodic reports then become the only practicable means of communication of reliable information about the progress of the business.

The first of these conditions was probably satisfied by the 14th or 15th Century, and at this time we find the first treatises on accounting method, and the development of the double entry bookkeeping system associated with the name of Pacioli. The new accounting texts however were largely expositions of bookkeeping method rather than guides to accounting principles. There was no positive influence imposing accounting unity and each businessman could choose his method to suit himself.[1] Typically, in this period business was carried on by individuals, fixed capital investment was small and inventory was usually not far from the saleable state. The simplest way to assess the progress of a business, therefore, was simply to carry out an informal valuation of its assets and liabilities whenever required.

The remaining conditions listed above were not fulfilled until the 19th Century. Essentially it was the industrial revolution that brought them about. The following important developments may be noted:
– The expansion of credit for business purposes
– The introduction of the principle of limited liability in connection with joint stock companies
– The growth of enterprise on a large scale, such as railways and new factories built to take advantage of the early mechanical inventions.

Credit initially was short-term in nature, and the creditors followed the banker's tradition of looking to the 'pounce' value of the debtor's assets as security. The principal business assets at the time were receivables and inventory (the latter being much closer to realizable form than is the case today). Hence was developed one of the oldest principles of accounting – that assets of a current nature should never be valued at more than realizable value.

The 19th Century also saw the development of the joint stock company. The first general companies act permitting incorporation by registration was passed in England in 1844. Provisions permitting limited liability were introduced in 1855. For these new companies it became necessary to account in such a way as to show the amount available for dividends, i.e. the amount that could be paid without representing an illegal reduction of capital. The focus on dividends meant that the profit calculation should result in a figure of *distributable* profits and this tended to introduce a realization test into the accounting measurement of profit. (Subsequently, as a result of a number of legal cases decided towards the end of the century, the legal restriction on payment of dividends proved to be much less stringent than had been originally thought. By this time however, the accounting principle of realization was firmly established.) The realization rule, of course, meant that no credit could be taken for appreciation of value in assets prior to sale.

The advent of large-scale enterprise may be said to have created the need for accounting principles. Among the earliest forms of large-scale enterprise in England were the railroads and public utilities. For these, the so-called 'double account' form of balance sheet was developed. Essentially this represented a division of the balance sheet into two sections. In a capital section were shown the fixed assets at their original cost, and the capital subscribed to finance the purchase of these assets. It was recognized that market value was a phrase with no meaning with respect to individual assets of such large undertakings, and the original carrying value therefore remained unchanged. In the other section of the balance sheet were shown the working assets comprising 'circulating capital' which would be subject to regular revaluation. A surplus of such working assets then formed a convenient measure of the amount available for dividend distribution. Frequently no depreciation of fixed assets was charged, in view of the prospective long life of the assets and on the assumption that maintenance absorbed currently would be enough to keep the fixed plant in working order indefinitely.

In contrast to the rules for accounting for current assets, therefore, early practice in accounting for fixed assets was often not conservative, and as a result a number of companies got into difficulty when the time came that the plant needed renewal. By the end of the 19th Century, the necessity for depreciation provisions in the normal business began to be recognized. Depreciation was thought of, however, more as a means of holding back from distributable profits a fund to replace capital assets, than as a charge required in the proper measurement of income.

Essentially, at this time the outside shareholder was looked on as having a long-term interest in the business, even though he was not in a position to manage it. The directors were his representatives for this purpose, and his rights were limited to a right to receive dividends after all other claims on the business were satisfied and the financial needs of the firm were prudently provided for. Under this view, the main test of sound accounting would be to present a statement of financial position that was not overvalued, and a figure for income that represented an amount unquestionably available for dividends. Since the shareholder was thought of as holding a long-term interest in the business, there was no strong objection to directors holding back secret reserves from reported distributable profits against the proverbial 'rainy day' provided that, in so doing, they were acting in good faith.

Such a system of financial reporting was probably understandable given the background of small-scale individual enterprise from which it sprang, but it was not well suited to the requirements of the 20th Century. To begin with, the concept of the shareholder as a person having a long-term continuing interest in the enterprise became unrealistic. It did not fit with the development of an organized market for company shares on the basis of freely transferable instruments. Secondly, that market could not function efficiently and well without a steady flow of accurate up-to-date information. The annual release of limited information, carefully doctored by the use of reserves, simply did not meet the needs of the capital market.

Thirdly, the system was open to abuse and the temptation to abuse it was not always successfully resisted, especially when the sale of securities was being promoted. A particular weakness was the lack of sufficiently strong rules governing the valuation of fixed assets. Public utilities, particularly, took advantage of this lack to write up their fixed assets to vastly inflated heights and issue stock on the strength of such valuations. The use of secret reserves also was a weakness. There may be arguments in favour of understating profits by creation of secret reserves in good times. It is harder to justify the release of secret reserves to inflate profits in poor years, particularly if securities are being sold on the strength of such reported profits.

The 1929 crash and the beginning of the great depression ushered in a period of intensive rethinking of accounting philosophy. The ensuing decades of the 1930's and 1940's were marked by:

– The beginning of large-scale, organized efforts by the accounting profession to clarify and enunciate accounting principles. In the United States five accounting rules or principles were recommended to the New York Stock Exchange by the Committee on Cooperation with Stock Exchanges of the American Institute of

Accountants in 1932. These, with one further rule, were adopted by the membership at large in 1934. Continuing development was promoted by the establishment of committees on accounting procedure and on terminology which, beginning in 1938, issued a series of Accounting Research Bulletins and Terminology Bulletins to make recommendations on new and demanding problems. In England, the Council of the Institute of Chartered Accountants in England and Wales commenced publication of a series of Recommendations on Accounting Principles in 1942. In Canada the CICA Research Committee commenced publication of Bulletins on Accounting and Auditing Practices in 1946.

– More active governmental regulation of financial reporting. In the United States the Securities Act of 1933 and the Securities Exchange Act of 1934 granted the Securities and Exchange Commission broad authority over financial reporting in prospectuses and annual reports required to be filed under the acts, including authority to prescribe accounting methods. In Canada the Dominion Companies Act of 1934 prescribed relatively advanced standards for the time for financial reports furnished by companies to their shareholders.

– A proliferation of accounting literature attempting to provide comprehensive statements of accounting theory to provide a setting and indicate a conceptual basis for accepted accounting principles. Particularly noteworthy were the publications of the American Accounting Association (largely consisting of accountants on university faculties) beginning with "A Tentative Statement of Accounting Principles Underlying Corporate Financial Statements" published in 1936, and revised and supplemented from time to time. Three other notable works of this period may be mentioned – by Sanders, Hatfield & Moore[2], by Stephen Gilman[3], and by Paton & Littleton[4].

As a result of these developments, by the end of the 1930's the older approach to financial reporting was largely overturned, and the foundations of present day accounting theory were firmly established.

The essence of the change was a shift from the older valuation approach to accounting to an approach emphasizing analysis, classification and allocation of the effects of actual transactions engaged in by the entity. The earlier approach had evolved naturally from the nature of enterprise in earlier periods. To an individual or to a small businessman, the economic question that really interests him is "how much am I worth today?". The question of how much he earned in a particular period is of secondary importance. However, if he has reliable statements of wealth at two different points of time he can by simple subtraction (after allowing for withdrawals or injections of capital in the period) readily determine his income. In a simple economy therefore, the natural approach to accounting is the valuation approach. In cases of doubt a few simple maxims like "don't count your chickens before they are hatched" or "anticipate no profits but provide for all losses" are sufficient guides to the sort of problems encountered.

In a complex economy however, the picture changes. In the first place, valuation becomes more difficult. When the assets include complicated productive assets, or inventory at all stages of production, independent market data to aid the valuation process are lacking to a considerable degree. In the second place, the separation of ownership and management means that valuation is more open to management manipulation. In the third place, the interest of individual shareholders of a large enterprise in the current values of its assets is smaller since, in the normal course, the business is not going to be liquidated and its assets distributed. What the shareholder is interested in is what the income of the business is, what share of that income he will receive by way of dividends and how that income will be reflected in the valuation of his shares in the market place.

For these sorts of reasons the emphasis of accounting in the 1930's began to switch away from valuation, and towards rules to ensure:

– No recognition of income or gain before confirmation by actual transactions.
– A fair matching of costs and revenues to determine earned income properly.
– No arbitrary reductions of income by the use of reserves, or bonusing of income by the release of reserves previously accumulated or by direct write-off of costs against reserves or capital surpluses.*

On this basis the realization test for the recognition of income was confirmed. Revenues received but not earned became deferred credits in the balance sheet and were treated as liabilities. Rules were developed for the matching of costs against earned revenues. Because of the emphasis on proper allocation of costs of earning income, the figures assigned to productive assets in the balance sheet were conceived of not so much as a listing of values, but rather a listing of costs incurred but not yet used up in the revenue earning process. Depreciation on a systematic pattern was recognized as a necessary charge in determining income; the older idea that depreciation was a provision for asset replacement or an allowance to reduce assets to current value was abandoned. Appraisals of fixed assets were not actually prohibited but in practice, after the experience of the 1920's and 1930's, few appraisals were given recognition in the accounts (until quite recently when interest has been revived as a result of present inflationary conditions).

As a result the focus of accounting theory shifted from the balance sheet to the income statement, from asset and liability valuation procedures to revenue and cost allocation procedures. Perhaps, more broadly, it may be said that accounting switched its aim to a more limited, if more attainable, objective. From the pursuit of a 'true and fair view' of financial condition (to use the historic English expression) its aim changed to that of a fair and reasonable presentation of the results of objectively verifiable transactions.

1970's Interest Rise Rt An end to the current Value Concept. Now S.16235 - Only. (handwritten)

---

* Changes of course did not come overnight, and it was not uncommon to find reserves affecting income determination throughout the 1940's. As late as 1953 the CICA Research Committee noted in Bulletin No. 9 "During World War II the Excess Profits Tax Act permitted the deduction of certain inventory reserves. Many companies created these reserves by charges against income since they resulted in large tax reductions and in these circumstances the creation of the inventory reserves from earned surplus would have distorted the income account. *Subsequently the necessity for a clearer delineation between amounts required for a proper determination of income and discretionary reserves has become more apparent*; also, new accounting practices have been developed to overcome, through allocation of income taxes, the distortion caused when large charges to earned surplus result in substantial savings in the current year's taxes." (Emphasis supplied.)

References

1. See B. S. Yamey, "Some Topics in the History of Financial Accounting in England, 1500–1900" in *Studies in Accounting Theory*, W. T. Baxter and Sidney Davidson eds. (Homewood, Ill.: Richard D. Irwin Inc., 1962).
2. T. H. Sanders, H. R. Hatfield and U. Moore, A *Statement of Accounting Principles* (New York: American Institute of Accountants, 1938).
3. Stephen Gilman, *Accounting Concepts of Profit* (New York: The Ronald Press Company, 1939).
4. W. A. Paton and A. C. Littleton, *An Introduction to Corporate Accounting Standards* (Columbus, Ohio: American Accounting Association, 1940).

5 Initial recognition of transactions in the accounts

Under the new accounting theory that developed through the 1930's and 1940's accounting principles and procedures were primarily directed to determining when various transactions should be selected for recognition in the accounts, what amounts were involved in each transaction and how such amounts should be classified and then allocated to time periods to make up a picture of financial position (assets, liabilities and equities) and income (revenues and expenses). The first two of these problems – the timing of transaction recognition and the measurement of transaction amounts will be dealt with in this Chapter and the next.

A brief classification of transactions will be useful in consideration of these questions. An entity may engage in the following types of transactions:

1. Financial transactions – These are transactions in which an entity receives funds by way of issue of debt obligations or equity capital or by way of other contributions of capital, or conversely repays or redeems debt or capital previously issued. Also included in this category are payments of interest or dividends on such debt or capital.

2. Investment transactions – These are transactions in which an entity acquires securities or other forms of investments to be held for production of income and also the transactions reflecting the receipt of investment income. For the present purposes we will also classify as investment transactions the purchase of capital assets required for carrying on a business.

3. Business or operating transactions – These are transactions in which an entity engages for the purpose of carrying on its normal business or other activity, including the acquisition of goods and services, the employment of labour and the making of sales or rendering of service to others.

This classification has been developed for the purpose of the discussion that follows and does not have any particular authority behind it. Moreover, the above definitions are not mutually exclusive since one transaction may fall into more than one category. For example, a purchase of a piece of equipment on the instalment plan would represent a combination of an investment transaction and a financial transaction.

Recognition of transactions

For the most part, financial transactions involving the issue or retirement of debt or equity capital are recorded at the date the legal contract is effective. Usually when debt is issued there is little lapse of time between the signing of the contract and the transfer of funds to the debtor. If there were such a delay however, the fairest presentation of the financial position would be to show both the obligation for the debt and the funds which will be derived from it in the balance sheet (assuming receipt of such funds is reasonably assured). Similarly when shares are subscribed for and allotted, the normal practice is to record the share issue immediately, at least to the extent calls have been made on the shares. Amounts yet to be received on unpaid subscriptions, however, are shown as deductions from shareholders' equity rather than as part of the assets of the entity. The interest payable on debt is accrued on a time basis related to the amount of debt outstanding from time to time, since interest is specifically a payment for the use of money for a stated period. Dividends on stock, on the other hand, are recorded as a liability only when declared, i.e. at the date the shareholders obtain a legal right to payment.

Transactions for the purchase and sale of investments similarly are usually recorded on the legal contract date. (Investment dealers, however, may record investment trades at the value date, rather than the contract date. To them trades in securities are operating transactions rather than investment transactions and different considerations thus apply.) Interest receivable on a debt security not in default technically should be accrued over the time period during which the right to interest accrues, while dividend income may be recorded as of the record date for entitlement to payment. (As a matter of convenience however, many entities record interest and dividend income only when cash is received, particularly when the amounts involved are not very material.)

The purchase of capital assets for a business is sometimes recorded in the same manner as a similar operating transaction (i.e. upon delivery of the goods). For larger acquisitions however, earlier recognition may occur when title to the asset is obtained. In Canada, selection of the date of transfer of title for recognition of the transaction is reinforced by the fact that a purchaser becomes entitled to claim capital cost allowance on the asset for income tax purposes at that date.

Practice in recognition of business or operating transactions does not adhere so closely to the legal status of the transaction as in the case of financial and investment transactions. At one time, when the emphasis in accounting was directed more to the presentation of a balance sheet reflecting legal rights and legal obligations, the transfer of legal title was an important criterion determining when a transaction for purchase or sale of goods should be recorded. Thus it was common for a business to record an asset and liability for inventory in transit to it from suppliers. With the passage of time this practice has largely disappeared, to be replaced by some practical test of performance under the contract – such as shipment by the vendor, or receipt of shipment by the purchaser.

In general, a business transaction reflects a relationship established between a vendor and a purchaser of goods or services. The elements of that relationship are (1) a contract between the two parties, (2) performance of the service or fabrication and/or delivery of the property (performance by the vendor), and

(3) payment according to the contractual terms (performance by the purchaser). Recognition of transactions in the accounts must hinge upon one of these three elements.

Sometimes the three elements in the relationship occur simultaneously, as in the case of the ordinary retail cash sale. Below the retail level, however, the order (contract) usually precedes the other two, and in the case of goods made to order, the time interval may be considerable. Again, in certain industries, it is common to find contracts for the supply of goods or service covering long periods of time, e.g. twenty to thirty year contracts between gas pipeline and distribution companies.

In a very real sense the order position affects the financial position of a business. For example, a contractor may have a certain productive capacity, given his equipment, financial resources and especially his complement of skilled workers and supervisors. A thin order book position means probable losses through idle capacity. A full order book is usually more desirable although much may depend on the prices at which the work is taken.

The correct interpretation of the order position is thus not a simple matter and it may be for this reason that the order position is not incorporated within the formal system of accounts, although it may very properly be the subject of comment in any narrative report on company financial statements. At any rate, for accounting purposes the usual practice is that contractual relationships between parties do not affect the accounts, so long as neither party has rendered performance under the contract that has not been paid for.

Performance seems to be a logical criterion for transaction recognition in an accounting system that depends primarily on the allocation of completed transactions to time periods. Rarely would it be necessary, for example, to write off an asset not yet received. On the other hand, if the accounting system were based on a process of valuation of assets and liabilities there would be less justification for the failure to record unperformed contracts in the accounts. In point of fact, in those few cases where valuations are recorded, commitments should be taken into account if possible. For example, where inventory is written down to market under the 'lower of cost and market' rule, commitments for purchases should be evaluated on the same basis as inventory actually on hand, and provision made for losses on commitments where appropriate.

With these few exceptions initial recognition of a business transaction in the accounts depends on performance by one or the other of the parties. Performance by the purchaser is the easier to analyze. Typically it consists merely of payment on the due date according to the terms of the contract. In most cases payment does not fall due until after the performance of the vendor, but occasionally this is not so. The following are some examples of payments made prior to the vendor's performance:

— Subscriptions to magazines and newspapers
— Advance payment for telephone service or water service (if not on a metered basis)
— Insurance premiums
— Advances on long-term construction contracts.

In all such cases the receipt of cash by the vendor forces the recording of an entry in the accounts. Since the vendor has not performed his part of the contract, however, the credit must necessarily be made to an unearned revenue account. Such account cannot enter into the determination of income, and is therefore to be treated as a liability. The ultimate transfer of this credit from unearned revenue account to earned revenue depends on performance by the vendor and the rules adopted to reflect such performance (which are discussed in Chapter 7). *[handwritten: go to ch 7]*

On the other hand, from the purchaser's point of view a payment in advance of performance by the vendor creates an asset – the right to future service or delivery of goods – which, depending on the nature of the right required, will be treated as a prepaid expense, inventory, or charge to capital work-in-progress.

Performance by the vendor may take the form of rendering services or delivery of goods. In the case of services rendered, ideally revenue should be recorded as earned gradually as performance proceeds if it can be reliably measured; in the case of delivery of goods, revenue is usually not recorded as earned until shipment of the goods. If the vendor has been paid in advance the act of performance will trigger an entry transferring revenue from the unearned (liability) category to the earned (income) category. If, on the other hand, the vendor's performance precedes performance by the purchaser, such performance will be the occasion of the initial record of revenue in the accounts. *[handwritten: A/R – Rev. Asset]*

From the standpoint of the purchaser, if he is buying services he normally should record the cost and liability in step with performance – i.e. as the work progresses. If he is buying goods the normal test of performance will be delivery of goods (whether or not that date coincides with transfer of title, as we have already seen). A few exceptional types of costs however are considered to relate to time periods and are accrued in the accounts according to the passage of time rather than in accordance with a performance test. Such accrual may take place even before an obligation to pay arises, e.g. the accrual of municipal taxes in the early months of the municipality's fiscal year before the tax rate is struck. The purpose of this is to make sure that the cost that ultimately will be incurred is matched with income of the period to which the cost relates. An extreme example of a cost related to time periods is the audit fee, which is accrued as a cost of a particular accounting period, even though the auditors may have actually performed little or no work until after the end of the fiscal period.

Principles Governing Transaction Recognition

The foregoing principles governing the recognition of transactions in the accounts may be summarized as follows:

Financial transactions

1. Transactions involving the issue or retirement of debt or equity capital should be recorded in the accounts as of the date a legal commitment is established. Interest expense on debt obligations is accrued in accordance with the passage of time. Dividends payable are recorded when declared.

Investment transactions

2. Transactions involving the purchase or sale of investments should likewise be recorded at the contract date. Interest income on investments not in default is

accrued at the stated rate of interest in accordance with the passage of time. Dividends receivable should be recorded when a legal right to them arises.

3. Acquisition of capital assets for use rather than resale is normally recorded at the earlier of the date of delivery or the date of transfer of title to the asset.

Operating transactions

4. Business or operating transactions should be recorded at the earlier of:
   - (a) the date of performance by the purchaser (i.e. payment according to the contract),
   - (b) the date of performance (or partial performance in the case of services) by the vendor.

Exception – A few expenses which relate directly to particular time periods are accrued with the passage of time, even in advance of receipt of the service to be rendered or of any obligation to pay.

6   Transaction measurement

One of the primary objectives of an accounting theory based on matching of completed transactions and their allocation as revenues and expenses to time periods is to get away from the problems associated with valuation of assets and liabilities. Perhaps nineteen times out of twenty this objective is successfully achieved. When the transactions are for cash or are consummated on normal short-term credit terms, and the contract is between parties dealing at arm's length, it may be presumed that the contract amount represents fair value for the transaction (or at the very least it reflects the relative bargaining skill of the parties which should properly be reflected through their income accounts). In a significant number of transactions however, these conditions do not hold good and accordingly such transactions involve measurement problems. In addition, certain transactions involve the purchase of more than one asset or the giving up of more than one form of consideration so that problems of distribution of the transaction amount arise. These special measurement and distribution problems involve:

1. Transactions on delayed payment terms.
2. Barter transactions.
3. Acquisition of goods or services in exchange for shares issued.
4. Gifts.
5. Dividends and donations in kind.
6. Transactions involving the acquisition of several assets at one time (the 'basket purchase').
7. Transactions involving the sale of several forms of securities.

In addition, certain complex types of transactions raise questions not only as to the measurement of amounts involved in the transaction but also questions as to the time when initial recognition should be given to the transaction in the accounts and the manner in which revenues and expenses involved should be allocated to time periods. Such transactions include certain lease arrangements, pension plan and deferred compensation arrangements, stock options, and all kinds of non-arm's-length transactions. The problems in dealing with these complex transactions are so interrelated that discussion on them is reserved until Chapter 12, after com-

pletion of the discussion of measurement and allocation of simpler forms of transactions.

Transactions on delayed payment terms

It has been suggested that the contract price in an arm's-length contract represents
a fair measure of the transaction amount when the terms of payment are cash or
normal short-term credit. In strict logic, since a dollar receivable tomorrow is not
worth as much as a dollar receivable today there should be a discount factor
applied to the contract amount whenever payment is delayed, in order to measure
the transaction fairly at the date it is recorded. However, the extra bookkeeping
work required to do so would rarely be worthwhile when the credit given is
short-term, and in practice normal trade transactions are usually recorded at the
principal amount of the payment to be received. Frequently, however, the contract
provides a discount for cash payment within a certain period. In such cases:

1. The better accounting treatment by the vendor would be to record the sales
   transaction at the contract amount less discount, and treat any discounts not
   taken by customers as miscellaneous financial income. The more frequent
   accounting practice, however, is to record the sale transaction at the gross
   amount, and charge off the amount of any discount taken by customers, either
   as a financial expense or as a reduction of sales revenue.

2. The better accounting treatment by the purchaser would be to record the purchase transaction at the contract amount less discount and charge any discounts
   missed as a miscellaneous financial expense. This is the practice followed in a
   majority of cases, the alternative being to record the purchase at the gross
   amount and credit a miscellaneous income account for discounts taken at time
   of payment.

In transactions where payment is not called for within a short period of time
after performance it is clear that fair measurement of the amount of the transaction requires that the payments provided for under the contract be discounted,
unless a reasonable rate of interest is provided for in the contract.

For example, in certain lines of business it is quite common to buy equipment
and other types of capital assets upon the instalment plan. That is, instead of
buying a piece of machinery for, say, $10,000 cash, arrangements may be made for
a schedule of payments extending over three years totalling, say, some $12,000.

The economics of this situation are clear. The cost of such an asset is not $10,000
if the purchaser happens to acquire it for cash and $12,000 if he acquires it on the
instalment plan. The difference between the two figures is clearly the concession the
purchaser makes in order to avoid paying right away, i.e. it is from his point of view
an interest charge.

In order to give effect to this in the accounting, the purchaser should record the
asset and liability at the $10,000 figure. He should then calculate the rate of interest
implicit in the schedule of payments (which can be done by trial and error if need
be), and as each instalment is paid it should be divided into an interest element and
principal element, with the latter only being applied to reduce the liability.

Alternately, some accountants would prefer to show the full face amount of the
liability assumed, and this can be achieved by recording the transaction:

Dr.	Cost of asset	$10,000	
Dr.	Deferred finance charges	2,000	
	Cr. Liability payable in instalments		$12,000

If the deferred finance charges are amortized on the basis of the principal amount outstanding from time to time on the loan, the result will be the same as the method previously described insofar as the determination of income is concerned.

In the foregoing example the implicit rate of interest in the contract can be objectively determined by comparison of the contract price with an alternative known cash price. In other transactions involving delayed payment, an alternative cash price or even a reasonable estimate of market value of the asset sold may not be readily available. In such cases, it will be necessary to assume a reasonable implicit interest rate in order to measure the current transaction value. What is a reasonable interest rate will necessarily be a matter of judgment and may vary quite widely from one contract to another, depending upon the circumstances of the transaction and the security offered by the purchaser. However, application of a judgment rate of interest, even though arbitrary, will almost always provide a better measure of the transaction value than would ignoring the discount factor altogether.

When transaction contract prices are discounted a further complication will be introduced if the transaction is not treated the same way for income tax purposes as it is for accounting purposes. When this occurs the costs incurred by the purchaser or the revenues received by the vendor as a result of the transaction will be reflected in accounting income partly as imputed interest over the period of the transaction. There will then be differences in timing between the accounting income in the periods affected and the taxable income, because the interest charge or credit will not be recognized as such for tax purposes. In such cases two conclusions presumably follow:

1. The interest rate assumed to apply to the transaction should be a net-of-tax rate, since it is not recognized for tax purposes.

2. Tax allocation accounting (see Chapter 13) should be followed to compensate for the difference in timing of recognition of costs and revenues for accounting and tax purposes.

From the standpoint of the vendor particularly there are further theoretical complications in delayed payment transactions. Presumably, in entering into such a transaction, as opposed to a cash transaction, the vendor will not only want to receive recompense for waiting for payment, but also he will take into account any other consequences of the transaction on his cash position. Thus, for example, if the sale proceeds are taxed earlier than the date of their realization in cash, the vendor will need to build into his gross sale price not only an interest return for waiting for payment, but also something to offset the interest cost on cash required for the tax prepayment on the transaction. As a result, in this situation a simple comparison of the ultimate contract sale price with an alternative cash sale price could indicate a higher rate of interest than the real interest return earned by the vendor when all aspects of the transaction are taken into consideration. In theory then, the real interest return applied to the actual cash effects of the transaction should be used in accounting for it. In practice, the bookkeeping involved in accounting for a large number of such transactions on such a basis could become extremely onerous.

Thus, while the concept of discounting delayed payment transactions is obviously economically sound, it has complications in practice. Since most business transactions do not involve abnormal payment delays there may be a tendency in practice to ignore the discount factor implicit in the occasional transaction involving delayed payments. The error in this has recently been recognized in APB Opinion No. 21, entitled "Interest on Receivables and Payables".

Barter transactions

A barter transaction is one in which the purchaser acquires something in exchange for giving up an asset or performing a service, rather than in exchange for cash. In such cases there is a question on what basis to measure the cost of the asset or service acquired. Where the purchaser parts with an asset in the exchange, he may have a figure in his accounts for the asset given up. It is not correct however to assign this book value to the thing acquired if the accounts are to disclose the real result of the transaction. For example, suppose a company owned 1,000 shares in a readily marketable stock and this investment were carried on the books at $10,000 or $10 a share, while the shares were trading freely on the market at $20 a share. If these shares were exchanged for some other asset in a bona fide transaction, it is clear that the purchaser would have given up a value of $20,000 in the transaction and this is the cost that should attach to the thing acquired. If accounted for on this basis, the accounts would also show a gain realized on disposal of the investment.

In practice however, the valuation of assets or services entering into a barter transaction is frequently not as simple as in this illustration. The general rule is that the transaction should be recorded as a figure representing the market value of the thing acquired, or the market value of the thing given up, whichever can be measured the more reliably. In the absence of reliable indicators of value the management of the business must be asked to place a value on the transaction which, to be rational, must be a figure at which management would have been willing both to sell the asset given up, and buy the asset acquired in two independent transactions.

It is often logical to depart from what might appear to be market values on the surface. For example, a television station might well sell unused advertising time to a newspaper in return for advertisements displayed in the paper. Neither party might be willing to buy advertising from the other independently at the normal rate, but they may think it worthwhile to incur the little additional extra cost in running an advertisement for the other in return for what they get. In such a case a valuation of the transaction at a figure as low as the marginal cost of running the advertisement for the other party would reflect the economics of the situation.

Aquisition of goods or services in exchange for shares issued

When goods or services are acquired in consideration for the issue of shares, the rule of cost measurement on the basis of value of things acquired or value of things given up, whichever is the more readily ascertainable, likewise holds good. In the case of public companies there exists a readily available indicator of value of the shares issued in the form of quoted market prices. Some caution however must be exercised in the use of this indicator. Market values of an individual stock typically vary over a period of a year by as much as one-third of the high price for the year. It does not seem reasonable that the valuation which it is possible to put on a transaction should vary by as much as one-third in a period of a few months. In addition, it has to be remembered that the value quoted in the market is not necessarily the value which could be obtained on distribution of a sizeable block of shares. Moreover, a company would incur certain costs in distributing shares which would reduce its net return. For these reasons a valuation of shares issued in a barter transaction should probably be made on the basis of recent average market prices, rather than spot prices at the date of the transaction, less an allowance to reflect such factors as the costs which the company would incur if it had raised cash by a share issue.

If the shares issued are par value shares, the problem may become somewhat confused. Since for the most part company law prohibits the issuance of par value shares at a discount, an effective floor is put under the valuation of the transaction. The issuance of par value shares, however, does not establish that the transaction should not be valued at more than the par value, recognizing in effect a premium received on the issuance of shares. This fact is sometimes overlooked by company directors, and some share issues in consideration of asset acquisitions have, in fact, been valued at par value.[*]

In Ontario, mining companies (unlike other companies) may issue par value shares at a discount. Frequently these companies, while in the exploration stage, issue blocks of shares for unproven mining claims. Because of their nature it is practically impossible to obtain any independent indication of the value of such claims. At one time it was common to value these transactions at the par value of the stock issued. Now however, the customary approach, which seems much more satisfactory, is to value the claims and the stock issued at the same price at which shares are being issued concurrently out of the company treasury for cash, or a somewhat lower but still related figure if the shares issued for claims are subject to escrow.

As a matter of general practice, it is important for the directors to consider seriously the appropriate valuation when shares are issued and to assign this valuation at the time of share allotment, whether such shares be without par value or with par value.[**] Where the asset acquired through the means of a share issue

---

[*] In 1962, the auditors of City of London Real Property Limited became enmeshed in a controversy with the directors of the company upon the question of valuation of shares issued to acquire an interest in another real estate holding company. The directors proposed to state the value of shares issued at par value although recognizing that the share interest the company was acquiring had a much higher real value. The auditors conceded that the directors' proposals were sanctioned by practice in the United Kingdom, but nevertheless felt that this basis of accounting for the transaction would prevent a proper presentation of the financial statements. The directors ultimately accepted the auditors' suggestions.

[**] In the United States, the S.E.C. permits companies in the development stage to file financial statements in which no value is assigned to shares issued for intangible assets acquired when no independent evidence of value of the assets, or shares, exists. Subsequently, when such values become more clearly established a value may be retroactively assigned to the transaction. No similar provision exists in Canada, and most of the corporations acts require that a valuation be placed on shares at the date of issue.

is difficult to value, it is further desirable that the asset description in the balance sheet should be amplified to disclose the basis upon which cost is arrived at. This recommendation is contained in paragraph 3080.02 of the CICA Research Recommendations – "Where an intangible asset has been acquired other than through payment of cash or its equivalent, the basis of valuation should be fully described as, for example, 'at cost, being the value assigned to shares issued therefor'."

Gifts

Only rarely does an operating business receive an asset by way of gift. When it happens however, the question arises as to how the asset should be accounted for. If the accounts are to record the transactions of the business as they happen, it is necessary that the asset acquired be assigned a carrying value corresponding with its economic value. Accordingly the best estimate of value for the asset should be made and recorded in the accounts with a corresponding credit to contributed surplus.

Dividends and donations in kind

When readily marketable assets are distributed as a dividend or donation in kind, the substance of the transaction is best reflected by stating it at the fair market value of the assets distributed, rather than the carrying value of such assets on the books. Practice on this however appears to be mixed.

The preferable rule is subject to the exception that if a business were to pay a dividend or make a donation of its own product, evidence would frequently be lacking that it could dispose of all such product at current selling prices. In the absence of such evidence it would seem acceptable to record the dividend or donation at the inventory carrying value of the product.

Transactions involving the acquisition of several assets at once

Frequently a business will acquire the assets and undertaking of another business for a lump sum. It then becomes necessary to split up the cost of this 'basket purchase' into its components on the books of the purchaser – so much for inventory, so much for fixed assets, so much for goodwill, etc. The apportionment made has important consequences, since the subsequent accounting is determined by it. The more cost that is assigned to inventory, the more that will have to be absorbed as cost of sales in the near term. If cost is assigned to fixed assets it will be absorbed more slowly as depreciation or, if assigned to land or goodwill, it may never become a charge in determining future income.

Only the management of the purchasing business is in a position to estimate the several items of value acquired in a basket purchase and to say just what was paid for. Frequently however, the dominant motive of the purchaser is to acquire earning power and he has given little or no thought to just how much he has paid for the individual assets acquired in the transaction. The accountant therefore must get him to consider the matter and make such an analysis while his memory is fresh, as soon after the transaction is completed as is possible.

One thing is certain. In an arm's-length transaction, the values on the books of the vendor are irrelevant to the purchaser. Even if the total purchase price should, by coincidence, correspond with the total book value of the assets on the books of the vendor, there is no reason to assume correspondence with individual assets. The purchaser may want some assets badly and be willing to pay a high price for them, and take others merely because they are included in the overall deal.

The customary approach to this problem is to first value the accounts receivable, prepaids and tangible assets and subtract the total of these values from the total consideration, to arrive at a difference applicable to intangibles (if the difference is positive). There is usually little problem in valuing the accounts receivable and prepaids, and frequently the amounts at which they are carried in the books of the vendor will be satisfactory. Likewise the valuation of inventory on the books of the vendor may be satisfactory if his inventory costing methods are similar to those of the purchaser. The valuation of fixed assets presents more of a problem and it may be necessary to call in expert appraisers to arrive at a value and assign it to individual assets. Should the appraised values of fixed assets, together with the values attached to the current assets (as above), exceed the total purchase price, the excess would usually be subtracted from the fixed asset values on the grounds that these are inherently more difficult to value; but the available evidence might suggest a different treatment, such as reducing all asset values proportionately. If on the other hand, there remains a balance of cost attributable to intangible assets, it will frequently be classified as goodwill. However, if other intangibles have also been acquired, such as patent rights, these also should be valued, and only the remainder attributed to goodwill.

Sometimes the total consideration for a parcel of goods may include some that are desired and some that are not. In such cases there is justification for not apportioning the total purchase price until enough time has elapsed that the assets not desired can be disposed of. The purchase price less proceeds of disposal can then be allocated. Too long a period cannot be allowed to elapse however, since, until the purchase price is finally allocated, any calculation of cost of goods sold and depreciation can be tentative only.

A variation of the basket purchase problem occurs when one company acquires a majority of the shares of another company. In this situation, in order to produce consolidated financial statements it is necessary to assign the net purchase price of the shares to the assets and liabilities acquired. In addition to the general problems of any basket purchase discussed above, the following special problems are encountered:

1. Differences between tax and fair values of assets of the company acquired – The assets of the company acquired may have a fair market value either above or below the amounts at which they are carried for tax purposes by the company acquired. Thus, when such assets are written off for tax purposes, the deduction may be less or greater than it would be based on fair market value. As a result, to the purchaser, the assets will be worth something less or more than normal fair market value because of this tax effect, and they must be valued accordingly for the purpose of consolidated accounts.

2. Unrecorded assets – When a purchaser buys the assets of another undertaking all the assets acquired will be enumerated in greater or lesser detail in the

purchase agreement. He need be concerned, therefore, only with apportioning his total purchase price among the assets covered by the agreement. Where a purchaser acquires shares however, he must allocate his purchase price not only among the assets appearing in the accounts of the company taken over, but also must consider the possibility that unrecorded assets exist, e.g. inventories of supplies and small tools, intangibles such as blueprints, designs, patterns, etc., development work-in-progress and so on.

3. Unrecorded liabilities – A purchaser must also be alert to the possibility of unrecorded liabilities at the date of takeover, such as provisions for warranties, accruals for vacation pay, etc., unfunded past service obligations and other liabilities not set up.

4. Liability valuation – The current value of a liability may be different from that shown on the books of the company taken over. For example, interest-bearing debt issued by the latter at an earlier date may be more or less onerous to a purchaser because of changes in the general level of interest rates between the date the debt was issued and the date of purchase. The purchaser should reflect the debt at a figure which will yield an interest and amortization cost equivalent to the current cost of borrowing (allowing of course for the fact that amortization of discount or premium resulting from such a revaluation of outstanding debt will not be recognized for tax purposes).

These problems are dealt with in greater detail in Appendix A in the Supplement to Chapter 18 on Business Combinations.

Transactions involving the sale of several forms of securities

A somewhat similar allocation problem occurs in transactions where several forms of securities are sold as units or for one price. These transactions are sufficiently unusual that accounting theory does not seem to have developed a very consistent approach to them.

One common form of such transaction is the sale of debt securities together with detachable warrants giving the purchaser the right to buy common stock on stated terms. In Opinion No. 14 issued in March 1969, the AICPA Accounting Principles Board concluded that proceeds received from such sales should be allocated in proportion to a fair valuation of the warrants and of the debt separately. The Board recommended that the value attributed to these warrants should be accounted for as paid-in capital. The remainder of the proceeds, attributable to the debt, should be accounted for as such. In the normal case this would result in the debt being recorded at a discount from par value, which would need to be amortized against income over the life of the debt.

In the same Opinion the Board decided that proceeds from the sale of convertible debt should not be allocated between the convertibility privilege and the straight debt obligation. This decision ran counter to a recommendation previously made in Opinion No. 10 issued in December 1966. The Board's reason for reversing its previous recommendation was that the convertibility privilege was inseparable from the debt instrument and therefore should not be accounted for separately. A lesser influence in the decision was that, because of the lack of separability, it was impossible to obtain reliable evidence of the value of the convertibility privilege. The failure to require a separate accounting for the value of the convertibility privilege, however, meant that the discount attached to the debt feature of the issue as such was reduced and consequently the combined interest and amortization charged against income was reduced. The result is that a debt obligation which is inferior in security in all other characteristics (except for the convertibility privilege) to other debt of the same company, or to debt of other companies, may appear to cost less than the other debt – an anomaly which in the words of dissenting members of the Board "belies economic reality".

No comparable Canadian pronouncements on this subject have been made. General practice however appears to be to make no separate accounting for the convertibility feature of securities issued (consistent with APB Opinion No. 14) and not to allocate any portion of the issue price to share purchase warrants issued in conjunction with debt (contrary to APB Opinion No. 14).

A similar problem arises when securities are sold in units consisting of, say, debentures with a certain face value plus a given number of common shares. This type of issue is fairly frequent in companies without a proven earnings record which are developing a new undertaking. Sometimes the units are not immediately separable into their component parts. Here, in spite of the lack of separability it is necessary to assign a value to the shares immediately in order to show the amount of legal capital in the accounts. The consequences of undervaluation of the shares again would be that the discount applicable to the debt, and consequently its annual cost, would be understated. The problem of assigning value to the shares may be easier if trading in the shares develops on the basis of delivery when they become separable. Nevertheless, in some cases at least, it appears that straight par value has been assigned to the shares, or a relatively nominal value to shares without par value, which appears to be low in relation to the price developed for the shares in subsequent trading. Thus effectively the real contributed equity capital is understated.

Principles Governing Transaction Measurement

The foregoing discussion can be summarized as follows:

1. Transaction amounts are measured by reference to values involved in the transaction at the date it is recognized in the accounts.
   (a) Transactions involving payment on normal short-term credit or cash terms are measured at the contract amount. Cash discounts, where allowed, should be deducted in the measurement.
   (b) Transactions involving significant delay in payment after performance contain a financing element. Such transactions should be measured at a discounted amount. The appropriate amount of discount may be estimated by reference to the alternative price of the asset in a cash transaction, the market value current for similar debt obligations or, if neither of these yardsticks is available, by applying an imputed interest factor to the face amount of the debt.[*]

---

[*] This principle is not invariably followed in practice.

(c) Barter transactions should be measured by the fair value of the asset given up, or the asset acquired, whichever is the more reliably ascertainable. Shares issued for property or services should be measured by the same rule. Where the values in such share issues are inherently difficult to measure reliably, additional disclosure should be made in the description in the balance sheet of the asset acquired.

(d) Gifts received by an entity, and dividends and donations in kind, should be measured at the fair value of the assets received or distributed.[*]

2. The total amount assigned to a 'basket purchase' transaction should be allocated according to the fair value of the identifiable tangible and intangible assets acquired. Where the total transaction amount exceeds the aggregate of such asset values the remainder should be assigned to 'goodwill'. Where the total transaction amount (including provision for any costs or losses expected to be associated with the transaction) is less than the aggregate of asset values the difference should be deducted from the amount of those assets whose value appears less certain, or deducted pro rata from the amount assigned to all non-cash assets.

3. Where more than one type of security is sold in units for one price, the consideration received should be assigned to each type of security sold on a reasonable basis – usually in proportion to the value of each separately.[*]

---

[*] This principle is not invariably followed in practice.

7 Allocation of revenue to accounting periods

In Accounting Terminology Bulletin No. 2, the term 'revenue' is defined as follows:

> "*Revenue* results from the sale of goods and the rendering of services and is measured by the charge made to consumers, clients, or tenants for goods and services furnished to them. It also includes gains from the sale or exchange of assets (other than stock in trade), interest and dividends earned on investments, and other increases in the owners' equity except those arising from capital contributions and capital adjustments."[1]

This definition is broadly conceived to encompass all proceeds from business and investment activity that would be reported in the income statement. Some authorities prefer a narrower definition of revenue, as being the proceeds from the business activity being carried on excluding investment income and proceeds on occasional disposals of capital assets, etc. For the purposes of discussion of accounting principles this narrower definition is convenient, and will be adopted here. In other words, the definition of revenue as it is used in this Study is comprised in the first sentence of the quotation above. Accounting for investment income, or gain or loss on assets not produced or acquired for resale, will not be dealt with under this heading.

The term 'revenue' should be distinguished from the term 'income'. Revenue is the gross amount of consideration received or receivable by a vendor of goods or services from his business operations. Net income (or loss) of an entity for a year is the net balance arrived at by deducting all costs allocated to that year from all revenues of the year and including as well other gains or losses and investment income. Thus, in essence, income is a net concept, revenue is gross.

Revenue arises from dealings with parties outside the entity.* As we have seen, a revenue transaction receives initial recognition in the accounts of a vendor at the earlier of the date of payment by the purchaser, or the date of performance

---

* Thus it is to be distinguished from 'holding gains or losses' – i.e. increases or decreases in the value of assets or liabilities held by an entity not attributable to transactions with other parties. Some authorities (e.g. APB Statement No. 4) classify holding gains and losses which are given recognition in the accounts as 'revenues' as well. For the purpose of the present discussion however, the narrower definition is preferred.

by the vendor. If payment precedes performance the revenue is unearned, and the credit will be deferred in the accounts to a subsequent accounting period or periods when the vendor performs his part of the transaction. If performance precedes payment revenue will be recorded as earned depending on two factors: (1) extent of performance, and (2) assurance of collectibility of payment.

The principle governing the timing of recognition of earned revenue is conventionally called the 'realization' principle. As the name implies, realization was once considered to be completed only when performance had taken place and a liquid asset was received (cash, or a right to cash). That is to say revenue was considered earned at the time of delivery of goods or completion of service and receipt of a right to payment enforceable in a short period of time. But these criteria are not now followed in all circumstances and the term 'realization', when used to stand for the time when revenue is recognized as earned, has lost its clarity and is apt to be misleading.[2]

In general, revenue may be regarded as earned on one of three bases:

1. The accrual basis
2. The 'critical event' basis
3. The completed venture basis.

The accrual approach to recording revenue as earned

Modern business for the most part is carried on continuously and involves diverse activities – purchasing, manufacturing, storage, selling, delivery, etc. Many accountants have pointed out, and most would agree, that profit, the incentive and ultimate reward, is attributable to the whole of the activity carried on in an accounting period and not just to one particular point of time.[3] One might think therefore that revenue should be accrued as work progresses so that a profit or loss would be computed with respect to work done as it is done.

There are practical reasons, however, why revenue accrual as business activity proceeds is not common:

1. In most businesses much of the activity takes place before a sale transaction is concluded. Therefore, the amount of revenue that will be applicable to work done is unknown, and even approximation of what will be received on sale may be difficult.

2. Even where the sale contract is signed before work commences, the revenue to be received will apply to all the activities to be performed. How much revenue is attributable to completed activities can only be estimated arbitrarily.

3. Even when an arbitrary basis for attribution of revenue to activities is adopted – say on the assumption that each dollar of labour cost earns a proportionate part of total revenue – the amount of costs yet to be incurred on work-in-progress may be quite uncertain, so that the amount of revenue to be accrued is likewise uncertain.

Thus measurement uncertainties are a powerful deterrent to revenue accrual in most situations. Moreover, since business is carried on more or less continuously, it often makes little difference, insofar as reported income is concerned, whether revenue is recorded as earned on an accrual basis or only at point of sale.

There are two situations in particular, however, in which failure to accrue revenue can result in serious distortions of resulting reported income – namely in the case of the individual or firm rendering professional or similar services, and in the case of construction or heavy engineering contractors.

The accounting of doctors, lawyers, architects, accountants and similar professionals has tended historically to use a cash test for revenue recognition. In part this may be because these professions were originally carried on largely by individuals and, to an individual, income is not usually felt to be income until it is in cash form and therefore spendable. When practice is carried on by a firm however, questions of financial position and measurement become more important for the purpose of the annual division of profits, and more particularly for measurement of the interest of individual partners in the firm's assets when a partner enters or withdraws from the firm. For these reasons a firm may move first to a position of recognizing revenue when it is billed, and finally of measuring revenue as it accrues. The latter procedure conceptually represents the most satisfactory basis of measuring income earned (unless billings are issued promptly and regularly), and results in a far better portrayal of financial position, since otherwise the value of unbilled work is completely ignored. Also, frequently the difficulty of measuring revenue on an accrual basis is less for a professional firm than for other business, given adequate records of work done, since the revenue charged is likely either to be calculable on a fairly well-established scale or to bear a reasonably close relationship to time spent. On the other hand, the accrual basis does require more record-keeping, which may be regarded as an onerous burden in such a firm. This, together with the force of tradition and the use of cash-basis accounting for taxation purposes, probably explains why the accrual basis is not followed more often by such firms.

The other situation in which revenue recognition on the accrual basis is particularly desirable is that of the long-term contractor. In this type of business the longer the term of the contract the less chance there is that the results of completed contracts will portray the results of the business activity actually taking place in the accounting period. For this reason revenue may be recognized on the 'percentage-of-completion' basis wherever it is considered that progress towards completion and costs to complete can be estimated with a reasonable degree of accuracy.

Adoption of this accounting method entails certain decisions:

1. It is necessary to decide what activities justify recording revenue as earned. For example, a particular contract may call for design, materials purchase, construction, testing and so on. If a separate price is negotiated for each function then revenue accrual would be indicated as the function is performed.* Otherwise, a decision has to be made as to what is being paid for. For example, a contractor would usually be entitled to little reward for the simple act of buying

---

* As a matter of bookkeeping mechanics, often it is the profit element that is accrued, not the gross revenue. That is to say, rather than set up an asset 'accrued revenue receivable' and crediting 'earned revenue' account the contractor will merely add the accrued profit element to his 'contract work-in-progress' account, and credit 'profit earned on contracts in progress'. The latter figure is often only analyzed into its two components 'revenues' and 'costs' when a contract is closed out.

materials. Therefore very little, or no, profit would be accrued as this function is performed.

2. It is necessary to arrive at some practical basis for implementing this decision as to how to allocate profit to functions:

   (a) It may be possible to divide the contract up into distinguishable segments and assign a portion of the total contract price to each segment. Such information is often readily obtainable from the estimates made in preparation for bidding on the contract. Then as each segment is completed, its costs would be written off against the predetermined revenue for that segment and profit determined. The chief problem here is to make sure that all costs applicable to each completed segment are known and written off when its revenue is taken up.

   (b) Alternatively the allocation may be made literally on a 'percentage-of-completion' basis. This basis requires an estimate of total costs to be incurred on the contract, including those yet to come. On the basis of these total costs subtracted from the total contract price an estimate of profit on the total contract is arrived at, which should be prorated as between the work already done and the work yet to be completed. This division will usually be based on the ratio of costs already incurred to estimated costs to complete. Material costs (usually) and any other costs not considered reasonable indicators of performance under the contract will be excluded from the calculation. Thus it may be based on direct labour costs only, or direct labour plus direct overheads where overhead rates vary from one division to another, and so on. In view of the uncertainty inherent in estimates of future costs, there often is a policy that no profit will be recognized on a contract until it has reached a given percentage of completion.

Most long-term contracts call for progress payments or advances as the contract proceeds. Unless progress billings are rendered on a basis that accurately reflects performance, however, the billing should not be taken as the basis for recording revenue earned. Contracts are sometimes negotiated on an 'unbalanced' basis, whereby progress payments exceed a reasonable measure of the value of work done in the early stages of the contract.

Reliable accounting for long-term contracts is extremely difficult to achieve. Costs are difficult to forecast. On-site conditions frequently make them difficult to control. Changes in the work to be done under the contract are often made after construction is commenced, and sometimes the addition to the contract price for such changes is subject to considerable negotiation. It takes a first-class information system and constant vigilance to cope with these conditions. Not every contractor's accounting system is adequate to do the job and, in any event, every so often a disastrous error occurs which is difficult to avert even under the best of cost estimating and control systems. In view of the inherent uncertainties some contractors recognize profits only when contracts are completed, in spite of the conceptual superiority of the percentage-of-completion method. Some also account for smaller contracts on the completed contract method and try to reduce distortions by using the other method for larger contracts. Since surprises are almost always unpleasant it is the common practice to make full provision for all known or estimated losses on uncompleted contracts as soon as they can reasonably be estimated.

Earned revenue recording upon occurrence of a critical event

The principal alternative to the accrual approach to recognizing earned revenue is one in which the recognition is triggered by an event which is regarded as crucial to the earning process. Usually that event is the completion of a sale, but in special circumstances other events may be taken as critical events – namely:
– completion of production
– receipt of payment
– termination of warranty or guarantee.

Sale completion

There are a number of reasons why the time of completion of sale is usually the most suitable time to record earned revenue:

1. The amount of revenue to be received is not known with certainty until a sales order is placed and accepted.

2. Delivery of goods sold normally marks the completion of all the major activities connected with the business transaction, and hence costs can be known at this point with fair certainty.

3. Sale implies realization, in the sense of acquisition of a claim upon another person.

These points are discussed more fully below.

The first point merely recognizes that the test of the market is supreme in business activity. A businessman may think he has a valuable and attractive product. He cannot know until he sells it that he is right. Sale removes a major uncertainty. It does not however remove all uncertainties. The customer may or may not take a cash discount for prompt payment, if such is offered. He may take five days or five hundred days to pay, thereby causing lost interest to the vendor. He may return the goods for credit, or demand and receive an allowance for damaged or poor quality goods. He may keep the goods and not pay for them, or heavy costs may be incurred to achieve collection.

It is customary to make some allowance for these possibilities in the valuation of accounts receivable. Logically, the allowance should cover all the possibilities described. In practice however, the allowance is usually calculated largely by reference to estimates of amounts that will prove uncollectible,[4] and occasionally also to estimates of cash discounts that will be granted. Frequently however, the allowance is rounded off on the generous side which may be considered to make some provision for the other contingencies mentioned. The failure to make a precise calculation and allowance for all these contingencies is not normally sufficiently serious to distort the figure for earnings reported in the financial statements.

The second point reflects the fact that most business effort must have been completed before a sale to a customer can be completed. Some activity, however, remains. Certain effort is involved in recording and collecting accounts receivable. In addition, the vendor may give a product guarantee that will require some future effort. The amount cannot be known at the time of sale but estimates can be made. In practice, no provision is usually made for future costs of collection unless they can be said to be covered in the allowance against accounts receivable. An allowance for warranty costs is also sometimes ignored on the grounds that the costs tend to be constant from year to year, so that income will be fairly stated even if no allowance appears in the balance sheet. It would appear better practice, however, to make provisions for warranties as the product guaranteed is sold, and this practice is widely accepted.

The question arises whether the warranty provision represents a deferment of a portion of the revenue on sale or a provision for future costs arising out of the sale. The logical answer would seem to be that it is deferred revenue. In some cases appliance manufacturers give dealers a choice of buying with a service contract thrown in, or buying without warranty and doing their own service. Here the difference between a service-included price and a bare-bones price for the appliance is clearly an item of revenue which should logically be deferred and recognized only as the warranty period progresses. In practice however, it is probably more common to find the provision of an allowance for warranties treated as a cost. Again it is unlikely that the difference in treatment would materially distort reported earnings.

The third reason for recognition of revenue at point of sale, namely that it coincides with realization, suggests that profits should be in a separable form before revenue is recognized as earned. This seems to be a less powerful argument, under modern conditions, for recording earned revenue only at point of sale. If revenue can be demonstrated with certainty, it gives rise to an asset that can be pledged as security (e.g. banks frequently take an assignment of payments under contract as security on contractors' loans). Thus revenue need not be in an immediately distributable form.

Completion of production *Recognize Revenue @ this time.*

It is possible to conceive of circumstances in which the major business activity would have been completed and revenue known with comparative certainty at some time prior to the point of sale of the product. In some cases revenue may be determined under a firm long-term sales contract. In other cases a stable market exists for a standard commodity so that there is no real question whether the product will be sold, or at what price, and no substantial effort is required to sell it. In these circumstances inventories of the commodity may be valued at estimated net realizable value, and revenue is therefore established by the act of inventory valuation rather than by the act of recording a sale.[*] Any variance of the ultimate selling price from the inventory valuation then will represent an adjustment of revenue previously recorded. *By a Gain / Loss - Regular Business.*

The ideal example of such a product is gold. In this case the product can be exactly defined in terms of standards of purity, weight, etc. The market price is well known (until recently, precisely known) and it cannot be influenced by individual producers. It is not surprising then to find gold producers valuing their production at selling price less a provision for costs associated with transportation to market.

Some producers of other minerals follow a similar practice in valuing production. Here the uncertainty as to value of production is a little greater, because market

---

[*] Thus, in this case, the description of current accounting theory as being a process of allocation to time periods of the results of actual transactions with outside parties proves to be inadequate. We have to stretch the theory to take into account transactions which have not yet been entered into, but which are predictable on a reliable basis.

conditions are less stable and there may be a necessary lapse of time between production and sale. There are two practical reasons for accepting this degree of uncertainty:

1. Where more than one kind of mineral is produced from the same ore body the cost of ore production is joint and no rational basis exists for assigning that cost to any of the minerals once they have been separated from the native ore.

2. In most businesses an increase in productive effort will usually produce more product and an increase in cost per unit is often reflected in rises in selling prices per unit. In mining the correlation between costs and revenues is not nearly so close and therefore the practice of valuing inventory at cost of production produces less significant figures.

The problem of joint costs is also encountered in the meat-packing industry and as a result the traditional method of inventory valuation is at market price. Agricultural producers would also have costing problems and for them a direct valuation of inventory would often be logical.[5] (However, where crops are marketed under a system of delivery quotas involving occasional extended carry-overs, income determination, other than 'cash income', would be hazardous on any basis of accounting.) In practice of course farming has traditionally been carried on by individuals not accountable to others, and its accounting practices are not highly developed.

Critical events after sale date

The reverse situation, where revenue is not regarded as earned until some point after the goods are parted with, is rare. The act of shipment of goods usually means that major business activity is complete and after that point activity will be confined to installation and warranty service over a period. There are cases where on-site installation is sufficiently important to be regarded as part of production, and to delay the point of revenue recognition. Normally however, warranty service would not be sufficiently important to cause postponement of revenue recognition.

Moreover, the vendor is unlikely to part with goods irrevocably without having a fair degree of certainty that payment will be received. He may do so, of course, if he retains some right to repossession of the asset. In the latter situation it may depend on circumstances whether revenue should be recognized at the point of sale of the goods or not until a later date. It would seem, however, that the probability that contracts will not be fulfilled would have to be very great before the uncertainty would be such that it should be dealt with through postponement of recording earned revenue rather than by an allowance for profits that might be lost on sales that do not ultimately get completed. The sale of real estate on speculative terms (which may in substance be no more than the granting of an option) represents an example found in practice. Similarly the sale of goods on extended credit with the purchaser having rights to return the goods with little or no penalty may be little more than a consignment.

The situation is sometimes confused in the case of goods sold on an instalment plan. Here the proceeds to be received represent compensation for two activities – the production or handling of goods and the financing of the purchaser. Obviously, the revenue relating to the financing part of the transaction should be

[handwritten: ⁓ Gross Profit]

postponed to be taken in over the period of the financing. The question arises, should the revenue on production also be deferred until the financing function has been completed and the debt liquidated? The problem may be clarified by consideration of the common situation where a vendor will sell either on cash or on terms. If he sells for cash, he undoubtedly recognizes revenue. If he sells on an instalment plan, one would expect that he would recognize the same revenue that would accrue on a cash sale. On instalment sales he will normally protect himself against loss on repossession and costs of collection by a down payment, and a schedule of instalment payments that keeps ahead of the probable decline in real value of the goods. In such circumstances there are strong arguments that the cash sale price should be recognized as revenue at the time the goods are sold, and the balance of the total instalment price should be taken in over the life of the instalment contract. In practice however, cases will be found where the whole profit on an instalment sale is deferred, and recognized on a basis that would be appropriate to that used for the profit on financing. Frequently, in such cases it will be found that instalment selling is not the major part of the vendor's business and the practice does not cause significant distortion in the earnings he reports.

Cut-off *[handwritten: (must match Rev. Recognition method chosen)? GAAP & other Constraints]*

The use of a critical event as marking the point when revenue can be taken as earned makes an accurate record of such events, and a clean cut-off of those occurring before and after the end of each accounting period extremely important. The critical event therefore must be of such a nature that it is perfectly obvious when it has occurred.

If for example, the critical event is completion of sale, there must for recording purposes be some consistent way of defining when a sale has taken place. Because of past tradition it is fairly commonly believed that the theoretically correct time is when title to the goods is legally transferred. But the time when transfer of title takes place may vary considerably depending on the sales terms quoted, and sometimes the nature of the goods. Title may pass upon delivery to the customer at the factory door, or upon delivery considerably later, or even within the factory if goods to the specifications ordered are set aside. The result of adopting legal transfer of title as a test, therefore, is to introduce an unnecessary haphazard element into the determination of income, and one which is difficult to determine consistently and accurately in practice. The better answer is to record a sale at a time corresponding with a physical event so that the record will be made at a consistent level of achievement. The time commonly selected is at the point of shipment from the factory or warehouse door, which provides a convenient checkpoint for consistent recording.

Revenue earned upon completion of a venture

There are cases when an enterprise is undertaken, costs are incurred, revenues come in, but whether the final result will be a profit or loss is shrouded in uncertainty until near the end of the venture. To take a simple example – a man may contract with a farmer for a quantity of Christmas trees, which he trucks to the city and offers for sale on a rented lot. By December 23 he may have sold half his trees, but he would regard as foolish a question as to how much profit he had made on the trees sold. In his mind he will have made no profit until he is sure he will recover all the costs embarked upon the enterprise.

In circumstances such as these, the businessman reverts to one of the earliest forms of accounting – 'venture' accounting or 'voyage' accounting, wherein all costs and revenues of the venture are entered in one account and carried forward as a net figure in the balance sheet (subject to write-downs if losses appear probable) which is not closed out until the issue is finally determined. This form of accounting was used first to record the trading voyages of Italian merchants in the 15th Century, and persists today in the accounting of tramp freighter companies. The 'completed contract' method of accounting for contractors may be regarded as a variant of it. In general the basis would have application where the business carried on naturally falls into a small number of large projects, and where the project is highly speculative either as to final total cost or revenue, so that early experience is no assurance of the final result.

Principles of Revenue Accounting

The foregoing discussion of revenue accounting principles may be summed up in the following statement.

Revenue from business activity should be regarded by a vendor as earned as soon as:

(a) significant uncertainty about the amount that will be realized from the sale of the product or service is removed;

(b) significant uncertainty about the costs that will be incurred in producing the goods or rendering the service is removed; and

(c) a reasonable basis exists for relating the revenues deemed earned with the work accomplished in the course of production or rendering the service.

In the majority of situations these criteria are not considered to be fulfilled until the shipment of goods or completion of services. It is therefore desirable that any departure from a basis of regarding revenue as earned at point of shipment or sale be disclosed in the financial statements.

Such departures will normally be associated with one or more of the following conditions:

(a) Advance revenue recognition

(i) revenue may be associated with services rendered on a fairly predictable basis, but actual billing is made irregularly;

(ii) the work carried on consists of a few large projects, and the earnings of profits will not be well portrayed unless revenue is accrued as the work is done;

(iii) the market for the product is so highly organized that reliable prices for it are always obtainable, and selling is not an important activity of the producer.

(b) Delayed revenue recognition

(iv) there is great uncertainty about ultimate realization of the transaction amount.

References

1. Committee on Terminology, *Bulletin No. 2 – Proceeds, Revenue, Income, Profit, and Earnings* (New York: American Institute of Accountants, 1955), p. 2. This definition of revenue has now been superseded by APB Statement No. 4 which defines 'revenue' as:
   "*Revenue* – gross increases in assets or gross decreases in liabilities recognized and measured in conformity with generally accepted accounting principles that result from those types of profit-directed activities of an enterprise that can change owners' equity." (par. 134)
   The older definition seems more descriptive for general purposes.
2. Cf. discussion in H. E. Arnett, "Recognition as a Function of Measurement in the Realization Concept", *The Accounting Review* (October 1963), pp. 733–741.
3. See, for example, discussion in R. T. Sprouse and M. Moonitz, *A Tentative Set of Broad Accounting Principles for Business Enterprises* (New York: American Institute of Certified Public Accountants, Inc., 1962) beginning at page 10.
4. See discussion in *CICA Research Recommendations*, paragraphs 3020.04–.14.
5. *Recommendation on Accounting Principles No. 22* of The Institute of Chartered Accountants in England and Wales reports that inventories of tea and rubber plantations are valued at net prices actually realized after the balance sheet date (par. 20).

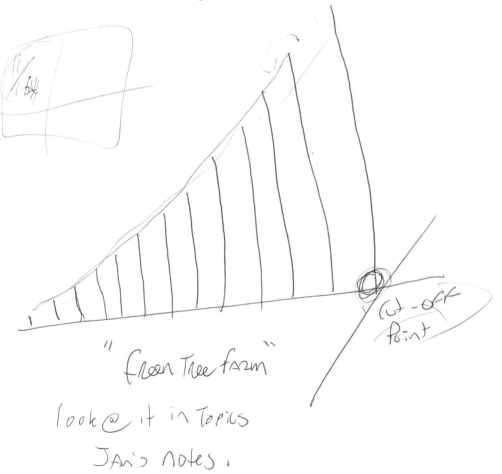

8 Cost allocation: the matching principle

AICPA Accounting Terminology Bulletin No. 4 defines the term 'cost' as follows:

> "*Cost* is the amount, measured in money, of cash expended or other property transferred, capital stock issued, services performed, or a liability incurred, in consideration of goods or services received or to be received. Costs can be classified as unexpired or expired. Unexpired costs (assets) are those which are applicable to the production of future revenues.... Expired costs are those which are not applicable to the production of future revenues, and for that reason are treated as deductions from current revenues or are charged against retained earnings...."*

That is to say, 'cost' is the amount of consideration given, or contracted to be given, for goods or services received or to be received. Cost is measured by the money paid or the current monetary equivalent of the obligation incurred or property given up. Costs are 'matched' with revenue earned in the process of income determination for an accounting period, and until they are so matched represent unexpired costs or, in the accounting sense of the term, 'assets'.

The basis to be adopted for matching costs with revenues is often far from obvious. The cost of a particular identifiable item of inventory naturally must be written off when the item is sold. But what is to be done with costs that can neither be directly related to identifiable units of inventory, nor otherwise closely identified with revenues of any particular accounting period? In most enterprises the majority of costs are of this character. Hence some reasonable ways must be found to allocate such costs to accounting periods, or else the transaction allocation approach to accounting won't work.

The objective of cost allocation rules must obviously be to reflect the 'cause and effect' relationship between costs and revenues. The starting point, then, is consideration of costs according to their nature and the benefits directly obtained from their outlay. Thus purchase of goods for resale provides an asset in tangible

---

* This definition uses the word 'cost' in the sense of acquisition price, or 'historical cost' which is the sense in which it is used in present generally accepted accounting principles. As APB Statement No. 4 points out, terms such as replacement cost, opportunity cost or economic cost have different meanings.

form directly available for production of revenue. Transportation of goods to a warehouse or distribution point gives them location utility which may justify attaching the transportation cost to the inventory carrying value of the goods. Employment of factory labour on an hourly basis provides a pool of service, the cost of which should usually attach to inventory worked on (but part of which may not pertain to inventories because of inefficiencies in labour use). Acquisition of a piece of equipment provides capacity to produce, and the cost thus may ultimately attach to inventory or may merely result in idle capacity losses.

Then follows consideration of how the various cost classifications contribute to revenues or otherwise relate to accounting periods. Goods sold from inventory of course directly contribute to revenues, but there may be problems in deciding how much inventory cost relates to goods sold if units of inventory and costs attaching to them are not separately distinguishable one from another. The capacity to serve of a piece of capital equipment may be exhausted by usage or by the mere passage of time, and this must be reflected in the way its cost is allocated either to inventory, and hence ultimately against revenues, or to accounting periods.

Succeeding Chapters deal with the ways in which costs are classified in major categories and the problems encountered in associating each category of cost either with revenues when they are recognized as earned, or directly with accounting periods. The major cost categories referred to are:

1. Costs of acquiring or producing goods for sale. Some of these costs are laid out to acquire tangible assets – e.g. raw materials. Some are laid out for intangibles such as labour or services. If, however, a reasonably close relationship can be shown between the cost and the ultimate product, these costs will be considered to attach to the goods. Inventory accounting conventions are concerned with the determination of the types of costs that attach to goods, and the subsequent matching of such inventory costs against revenues.

2. Costs of permanent capital assets – such as land or certain types of investments. Since these are not consumed in the course of carrying on business, there is no problem of matching them with revenues. The only occasions upon which they enter into the determination of income occur when they are sold, or revalued.

3. Costs of wasting capital assets. A capital asset is, by definition, one which will contribute service over more than one accounting period. Costs of wasting capital assets, then, must be spread on some logical basis over their useful lives. For tangible capital assets such as machinery, the process of allocation is known as depreciation accounting. For natural resource assets such as oil in place, the process of allocation is known as depletion accounting. For intangible assets, e.g. patents, the process of allocation is known as amortization.

4. Costs that will produce future benefits, but cannot immediately be classified in one of the other categories, including:
   (a) Costs of supply inventories – factory supplies when used may become part of product inventory costs; office supplies when used will become a charge against the period of use; inventories of spare parts when used may be added to the cost of capital assets or may be charged as part of repairs and maintenance cost of the period when used.
   (b) Prepaid expenses – i.e. amounts paid in advance of performance by the supplier of service, e.g. rent paid in advance or the unexpired portion of an

insurance premium. These costs, when expired, may be treated as **period costs** or may enter into the determination of the cost of inventory produced in that period.

(c) Deferred costs – i.e. costs (mostly intangible) of specific projects which are expected to have a beneficial effect on future revenues even though no saleable or productive assets resulted from the expenditure. These costs occasionally enter into inventory accounting when amortized – e.g. deferred engineering and design costs – but more often are written off directly as the deferment period expires.

5. All other costs. These are treated as costs to be absorbed in the fiscal period in which they are incurred, or 'period costs', because they cannot be fitted under any of the other cost categories with reasonable precision. Costs of administration of a business are a typical example. Some part of administration cost undoubtedly contributes to the production of goods, and theoretically could be treated as inventory costs. Another part, possibly a very important part, of top management administration costs will represent costs of planning which should benefit the future, and theoretically could be treated as deferred costs. The practical difficulties of making a reliable apportionment of such costs, however, are so great that they are almost universally treated as being applicable to the period in which they are incurred.

The Cost Allocation Principle

The overriding principle of cost allocation, then, can be summarized as follows:

Costs recorded in the accounts should be matched with revenues for the purpose of determining income of individual accounting periods in a manner which best reflects the 'cause and effect' relationship existing between costs and revenues. To formulate particular rules to implement the matching principle, costs incurred are customarily divided into several categories – viz. costs of acquiring and producing goods for resale, costs of capital assets, other costs of goods or services that may be expected to assist in earning future revenue and costs of goods or services from which no benefit is derived beyond the period in which the costs are incurred.

Initial : Direct Can Be Allocated to Different Related
Revenue Periods .

Direct Cost Are Period Cost Except for the amount
Allocated to Initial's Direct .

9   Inventory and cost of sales

Problems in inventory accounting fall into three main categories:

1. Determination of costs that are properly assignable to inventory, particularly costs associated with inventories of in-process and finished goods.

2. Selection of a basis for separation of accumulated inventory costs as between those attributable to goods sold and those assignable to goods still on hand – i.e. determination of cost of goods sold.

3. Determination of 'market' value for the purpose of application of the inventory valuation rule 'cost or market, whichever is lower'.

Inventory Cost Determination

In principle all costs associated with the acquisition of inventory, and with its manufacture, should be treated initially as costs of the goods in inventory. The problem in each case is to define just what costs should be considered to be associated with inventory acquisition and production. Every experienced accountant knows that considerable variety exists in methods used for costing inventory – especially inventory that has passed through some or all of the production stages. Some of these variations reflect the differing circumstances of the businesses in question. For example, very few businesses assign any portion of their administration costs to inventory, even though some administrative effort is necessarily associated with the purchasing of materials and production. For accounting purposes the connection between administrative effort and inventory acquisition is usually considered too remote. However, a contractor working on a 'cost plus percentage' or 'cost plus fixed fee' contract may well find that a better matching of costs with revenue is obtained if administrative costs, for which he will receive reimbursement, are inventoried.

Commonly however, variations in methods of assigning cost to inventory reflect merely a broader or narrower concept of production costs, or occasionally reflect purely accounting convenience. (The more indirect the relationship between a cost and the production process the more work will be involved in making allocations to inventory, and the more arbitrary the basis of allocation is likely to become). Examples of variations commonly found in practice are – the salary of a factory superintendent and his office expenses might be considered as administrative costs in one business or inventoried as factory overhead in another. Employee fringe benefits and costs (workmen's compensation, unemployment insurance, medical insurance, vacation pay) may be treated as administrative costs or may be allocated as production costs following the allocation of labour. Product development and engineering costs in some cases are written off in the period incurred, while in others they are amortized on some basis. If amortized the basis may be units produced, in which case the amortization per unit would probably be carried as an inventory cost, or the basis might be units sold, in which case the amortization would not figure in inventory costs.

Technical problems may also lead to variations in treatment. Sometimes two or more distinct products emerge from a common source of material. Examples are various cuts of meat, hides for tanning and other products derived from a single animal, oil and gas derived from one well, a variety of refined products derived from crude oil, and several metals derived from one ore body. In these cases a figure of cost after common production and processing costs that is uniquely assignable to one particular product cannot be arrived at. Arbitrary costing rules have to be followed. There are two recognized approaches to this. Under one approach (by-product costing) one or more of the outputs are regarded as the main products and the remainder as by-products. No cost as such is assigned to the latter, but rather, any revenues arising from their sale (or expected to be realized) are treated as reductions in the cost assignable to the main product(s). Under a different approach (the joint-costing approach) an arbitrary method for allocating joint costs to the several outputs is devised. For example total cost may be divided up in proportion to the sales value of the several forms of outputs, or the sales value after deducting any further processing and selling costs. Or cost may be divided in proportion to certain physical characteristics such as weight, B.T.U. content, or other factors. A variety of allocation bases may be available in a particular situation. But all are, in essence, arbitrary.

Thus extensive variations in inventory costing methods occur. The following generalizations, however, can be made:

1. It would be generally accepted that the cost of materials in inventory and direct labour effort expended (prime cost) should be the minimum costs assignable to inventory.

2. On the North American continent, it is generally conceded that inventory costs should also include at least such factory overhead costs as vary with volume of production. For example, the CICA Research Recommendations state (paragraph 3030.02) "In the case of inventories of work in process and finished goods, cost will include the laid-down cost of material plus the cost of direct labour applied to the product and ordinarily the applicable share of overhead expense properly chargeable to production. Where the storage of goods for a significant period of time is an integral part of the manufacturing process, cost may also include the applicable share of warehousing expense and, in a few cases, carrying charges." AICPA Accounting Research Bulletin No. 43 states "As applied to

inventories, cost means in principle the sum of the applicable expenditures and charges directly or indirectly incurred in bringing an article to its existing condition and location." This statement is discussed at greater length in the Bulletin and in the course of the discussion this sentence appears, "It should also be recognized that the exclusion of all overheads from inventory costs does not constitute an accepted accounting procedure." Although it is not entirely clear from the text of the Bulletin and particularly the sentence just quoted, it has been authoritatively stated that the Committee did not intend to sanction the 'direct costing' method of application of overhead to inventories (see discussion below) in this statement. Practice in Great Britain appears to be more permissive as is evidenced by Recommendation No. 22 of the English Institute.

3. The greatest area of debate in inventory costing revolves around the question of the treatment of fixed overhead costs. Accounting literature has been filled in the last twenty years with arguments for and against inventory valuation on a basis of 'direct', 'marginal' or 'variable' costs rather than on a basis of costs including a factor representative of fixed overhead (absorption costing). Some comments on this controversy follow.

Direct costing and absorption costing

Costs contributing to the production of goods may be classified in two categories – i.e. costs of creating capacity to produce, e.g. annual costs of capital equipment, rent of factories, municipal taxes on factories, etc., and costs that are directly caused by actual production, e.g. direct labour, and usage of materials and consumable supplies. Broadly speaking, the magnitude of the former costs are fixed by initial management decisions on the scale of production and do not change in character unless management decides to change its capacity. The latter costs, however, are caused by the act of production and tend to vary with volume.

The distinction between the two types of costs (i.e. those that are fixed and those that vary with volume) is not clear-cut but rather is one of practical convenience. In the long run and over the whole range of possible production volumes, all costs are variable. If management wishes to expand production beyond a certain point it must sooner or later expand capacity. Even in the short run, some costs are neither completely fixed nor completely variable – they are semi-variable. That is to say, they change with changes in the volume of production but not by a proportionate amount. In spite of the difficulty of making a precise separation of costs as between fixed and variable, such an analysis has great practical value as management information. It helps management understand how costs will behave over given ranges of production, and consequently helps it in its pricing decisions and general business strategy.

Proponents of 'direct costing' argue that only costs that can be directly related to production should be included in inventory. Essentially their thesis is that profit is only realized through sales and therefore accounting rules should be designed so that income reported in financial statements will also fluctuate in step with sales and only with sales. They point out that if an amount in respect of fixed overhead is added to inventory, the more inventory produced the greater the amount of fixed costs included in inventory and the less that remains to be charged to income for the year. In other words, under absorption costing profits reported are influenced not only by the level of sales but also by the level of production. It is possible therefore to improve the level of reported profits under this method merely by increasing production regardless of the expectations for sale of the increased stock in the succeeding accounting period. A simple illustration is frequently given showing how profits reported can vary widely in two accounting periods of identical sales, if production is high in one and low in the other.*

Advocates of absorption costing concede that under their method reported profits are influenced by production rates as well as sales. They would argue however that this is perfectly proper. Profit is the result of all activity, not just sales. Other things being equal, if two enterprises in the same line of business have identical sales volumes but Company A is bursting with activity in the factory at the fiscal year-end while Company B is just limping along, Company A is likely to be better off. This is on the assumption that the management of both companies have correctly planned their production programme to reflect anticipated sales in the next period. There ought to be a presumption to this effect, since investment in inventory costs money (interest, etc.) to carry, and therefore a management is foolish to carry any more inventory than is necessary, taking into account current demand estimates, the requirements to have a balanced stock of finished goods, required production time and necessary material procurement time.

In other words, at every level of expected sales volume a business has in theory an optimum inventory size. So long as management has kept its commitment in inventory approximately equal to the optimum level in relation to reasonable current sales expectations, it is perfectly proper to carry fixed costs in inventory costs. To illustrate the point, consider a company that creates facilities to produce a new product line. It takes two months' lead time to produce an accumulated stock so that sales orders can be filled in expected amounts. Production begins November 1; volume shipments do not begin until January. At December 31 is it not proper to carry forward all costs of manufacturing stock (except for costs of capacity as yet unused)? If revenue recognition is to be deferred until crystallized by sale, should not all costs attributable to revenue earning activities likewise be deferred?

In theory therefore, the inclusion of fixed manufacturing costs in inventory (at rates appropriate to planned operational levels) is justified *provided* the inventory is not larger than that required, together with production possible in the future, to meet future sales demand. The size of this inventory limit may require a rather nice calculation. Consider for example this simplified illustration (which ignores

---

* A further criticism sometimes leveled against absorption costing is that fixed manufacturing costs per unit of production will be low when activity levels are high and the fixed costs are spread over a large number of units of production and, conversely, will be high when production activity is low. This criticism can be disposed of summarily. It is, of course, nonsensical that unit costs for inventory purposes should vary inversely with the level of production. To avoid this it is necessary to relate fixed costs to an estimate of normal or planned production volumes and calculate unit fixed costs for inventory purposes using the number of units in normal planned production as a base. If, then, production is lower than planned, not all fixed costs can be assigned to or absorbed by actual production and the difference should be written off as a loss due to idle plant or low activity levels.

such factors as balancing the effect of interest on money tied up in inventory against extra costs of operating above optimum levels through overtime, etc.):

Optimum plant operating level	10,000 units per month
Expected sales – Month 1	5,000 units
Month 2	5,000 units
Month 3	5,000 units
Month 4	20,000 units
Month 5	30,000 units
Month 6	20,000 units
Months 7 to 12	5,000 units each month

The justified inventory level at the beginning of period 1 would be 25,000 units. This would be arrived at by calculating total sales to the end of the 6th period (at which time sales demand falls to a point where it can be taken care of by current production) – 85,000 units, less production possible at optimum levels in these six periods – 60,000 units. (This illustration, although unusual, is by no means impossible. Demand for many, if not most, consumer goods is highly seasonal. Consider ice skates, for example.)

In practice this important limitation on the propriety of carrying fixed overhead charges in inventory is not widely recognized. The author is not aware of a single company using absorption costing that makes a conscious calculation of justifiable inventory levels, and values excess inventory at variable costs only. As a practical method of inventory valuation, therefore, there is something to be said for the direct costing basis which can be applied automatically to the whole inventory. There is the further point that even if absorption costing were followed subject to a limitation on inclusion of fixed costs, calculation of the appropriate limitation would necessarily involve estimates of future sales, which may or may not be . realized. This difficulty could be avoided if inclusion of fixed overheads were restricted always to very minimum basic quantities which would be revised only when plant facilities and planned scale of operations changed. If this basis were followed, the amount of fixed overheads in inventory would be relatively constant and variations in profits reported as between absorption costing and direct costing would be insignificant. The chief difference would be in the balance sheet valuation of inventory which would be higher under absorption costing. In the long run also, in the typical business there would probably be a tendency for profits reported under absorption costing to be slightly higher as the value of fixed charges in inventory grew with increasing automation (which substitutes fixed for variable costs), increasing scale of operation, and rising prices of the components of fixed cost.

To summarize – absorption costing is theoretically more nearly correct. However, the failure to recognize a limit on the amount of fixed overheads that should be included in inventory constitutes a defect in the common application of absorption costing that becomes serious when a business gets into an overstocked position (as happens not infrequently). It may be noted that when goods are produced to order (i.e. are presold), this difficulty does not exist. Also when sales and revenue recognition are sporadic in incidence (as in the case in a job order type of industry), it becomes more important to defer all costs properly attributable to production until the point of revenue recognition. Absorption costing is therefore most necessary for the inventories of a business making goods to order under large contracts with consequent irregular recognition of revenue.*

When goods are produced for stock, so that there is a risk of overstocking, the arguments for direct costing grow stronger. However, the problems connected with the determination of an overstocked position can be avoided if a conservative estimate is made of the minimum work-in-process and finished goods inventory position and fixed overheads are included for these quantities only. This compromise procedure would go some distance to meet most of the criticism directed against absorption costing as it is commonly practised.

Practice

While, as indicated earlier, there may be some variation in the precise definition of material costs and direct labour (e.g. whether fringe benefits are included in labour costs or not), most Canadian business would treat these two costs as elements of inventory on a reasonably comparable basis. There may still be some industries that do not make any addition for factory overhead in their valuation of work-in-process and finished goods, and a few more who might include it in finished goods but not work-in-process, usually for reasons of convenience. A large majority however make some allowance for overhead in inventory.

As has been indicated above, there may be argument whether in a particular case manufacturing overhead should include fixed costs or should recognize only variable costs. In many cases it is not possible to tell where a company's management stands on this question. It is not uncommon to find a company including overhead in inventory at a fixed rate, say 125% of direct labour costs, and keeping this rate unchanged for years on end. Such a determination is obviously not very scientific and it is often doubtful that management has given specific consideration to the question of what manufacturing overheads are supposed to be covered by the fixed percentage. While very rough and ready, this method is not seriously wrong in a business with relatively stable operations. Over an extended period however, it is obviously likely to accumulate errors.

Methods for Determination of Cost of Goods Sold

As goods are sold, the costs previously accumulated in inventory applicable to them must be removed from the inventory account and charged to the cost of sales account. This presents theoretical problems in some circumstances and the common costing assumptions are discussed below.

Identification methods

Wherever the goods dealt in by a business are individual in nature, the specific identification method of assigning costs is likely to be used. For example, the

---

* Under these same conditions, it may be decided to accrue revenue on a percentage-of-completion basis, in which case the problem of costing of inventory in process disappears.

dealer in fine art or in precious gems will know what each item in his inventory cost him and can match that cost with the sales proceeds he ultimately realizes. This method of accounting will give him the best guide to his success as a dealer since he can pinpoint his successes and failures. He would not be nearly as well served by an accounting method that accumulated costs in terms of averages, say, per type of picture or per square foot of canvas, for the purpose of calculating costs of pictures sold.

Similarly, a business that makes specialized goods to order will want to match the costs of individual orders against sale proceeds to pinpoint poor performance – whether through bad estimating, poor labour efficiency or poor materials, etc. Almost invariably such a business will have a costing system that accumulates costs by jobs so that specific identification of each job cost is possible.

Where goods sold are highly perishable, the management will have to take care to make sure that there is an orderly movement of goods and older lots do not accumulate. In such cases there might be specific identification of goods sold through costing by lots. Alternatively, if this requires more record keeping than is warranted, a first-in first-out (FIFO) assumption may be used for costing goods sold. In these circumstances, FIFO would come very close to being equivalent to specific identification.

The problem of homogeneous goods

The foregoing methods of costing goods sold are applicable where the goods in inventory must be kept track of individually, either because of their intrinsically individual character or because they deteriorate rapidly with age. Such goods however are in the minority in business inventories.

The majority of goods in inventories are homogeneous in character – that is to say, one unit in inventory can be exchanged for another of the same type without problems. For example, one billet of copper or a pig of iron can be freely exchanged for another of the same weight and shape. One pencil produced by a pencil factory can be exchanged for another. One nut can be exchanged for another of the same specification. In these circumstances, there is no operating reason why inventory costs should be accounted for by units. Instead, it will be convenient and less work to account for inventory costs by type of product, grade of product and size and content specifications.

Even where there are small differences in the character of goods in inventory, the costs may in practice be treated as interchangeable. In the case of tea for example, there are small differences in character between tea of the same type from different gardens, and also between tea from the same garden picked at different times in the growing season. However, some of these differences are so small and their price significance so little that they can legitimately be ignored in the inventory cost records. Further, some goods may be perishable over a long period of time but the deterioration is so slow that there is no practical difficulty in disposing of the older stock in the normal course, so that no special accounting is required. The problem then, where costs are accumulated by type of inventory rather than by specific units, is to find a basis for assigning costs to the units sold. A number of different concepts receive some recognition in practice, and these are discussed below.

Physical flow of goods

The problem is sometimes viewed as one of ascertaining a basis for assigning costs to goods sold that corresponds reasonably well with the physical flow of goods. Essentially this represents an attempt to maintain an identification of inventory costs with the physical goods for which the costs were incurred, regardless of the fact that physically identical goods may have been acquired at different costs.

Using this concept, one would have to look at the methods of handling the physical goods to ascertain the most appropriate basis of costing. If goods were stored in piles and goods sold or used were withdrawn from the top of the pile, the appropriate formula might be last-in, first-out (LIFO). If inventory were stored in hoppers, loaded at the top and extracted from the bottom, the opposite formula, first-in, first-out (FIFO), would be appropriate. For goods stored in the normal fashion in storerooms, the most appropriate formula would probably be FIFO or average cost (i.e. a formula whereby cost of inventory acquisitions are averaged in with costs of goods on hand, and goods issued or sold are costed out at the latest average).

It will be apparent that, in practice, mechanical formulas such as these will rarely correspond exactly with the physical flow – they can only be an approximation. Moreover, the concept may be criticized from the standpoint of usefulness of results. Theoretically, two plants carrying on the same business but with different plant layouts might, under this concept, adopt different inventory methods. It is difficult to argue that identification of inventory costs with the flow of physical goods necessarily results in the best measurement of income.

Average cost of identical goods

The average cost method gives better recognition to the interchangeable nature of homogeneous goods. The reasoning underlying this method is as follows – in total, a certain amount of costs have been incurred to acquire a certain number of units of inventory. Since all units are identical it is reasonable to strike an average cost per unit and cost all goods sold at the average for purposes of matching costs with revenues. When more such goods are acquired, their cost will be added to amounts pertaining to inventory still on hand of the same type, and a new average struck.

This basis of dealing with the costs of homogeneous goods seems more satisfying intellectually than the attempt to tie inventory methods to the physical flow of goods. However, the need to recompute averages on a regular basis involves more effort, unless the inventory accounting is computerized. Probably for this reason it is not encountered nearly as frequently as FIFO and, in practice, its results are usually not substantially different from those that would be achieved under the FIFO method.

Logical flow of costs – LIFO

In some cases, it is argued that a more meaningful statement of income results if the costs charged as cost of goods sold can in some way reflect management's decisions in establishing selling prices for such goods. This concept first came to prominence in connection with the early arguments for LIFO in the 1930's and early 1940's. Briefly these arguments were as follows. Many businesses take a basic raw material and process it into a more advanced form for their customers. Sometimes in such cases the management has a particular concept of that company's business role. They regard it as being in business primarily as a processor or fabricator and not as a speculator in materials. Accordingly they establish their price structure on the basis that prices for finished products reflect a standard processing charge to recompense the business for its effort, plus an amount equivalent to the current replacement cost of the principal material(s) in the product. In these circumstances it is argued that the cost that should be charged as cost of goods sold should be a cost equivalent to that included in the price structure. Normally, the latest cost incurred would best reflect the material cost postulated in the price structure, and therefore a LIFO inventory assumption is most appropriate in these circumstances.

It was always recognized, however, that many businesses do not operate in such a way as to make a LIFO assumption logical for them. Therefore, in early literature on the subject certain tests were set out to determine whether the use of LIFO would be appropriate in a particular case.

– The sale price of the finished product should closely reflect the current replacement cost of the material content (this established the logical justification for charging the latest material costs against revenues).
– Purchases of materials should be matched with sales of finished products. (If the latest purchase price is to be a proper approximation of the material cost component included in current selling prices, this condition must be fulfilled. If, for example, purchases did not keep up with sales, inventory costs charged off under the LIFO method would be forced back to earlier periods, and there would no longer be a good match between LIFO costs and revenues.)
– Speculation in materials is avoided. (This is essential to the basic argument that income results only from the processing charge and not from profits on materials. The avoidance of speculation would, of course, automatically follow if purchases and sale quantities are matched.)
– The business has a slow turnover and must maintain a large inventory. (This condition merely suggests the situation in which correct inventory accounting is most important – whether a LIFO assumption is appropriate or otherwise.) *

It will be apparent that the LIFO cost assumption will not always give a cost for raw material exactly equivalent to the material cost component in the selling price (some authors have suggested that 'NIFO', next-in, first-out, would give a closer match) – but the approximation is usually fair enough. There may be times however when the business is unable to keep its purchases up to its sales (say because of war conditions, a strike at a supplier, etc.) and the LIFO assumption results in matching costs incurred at much earlier dates against current revenues. Such 'involuntary liquidation' may well result in a very poor portrayal of operating

---

* These conditions justifying the use of LIFO were accepted by the Exchequer Court of Canada in the tax case, *Anaconda American Brass Limited versus MNR, 52 DTC 1111*, and were sustained by the Supreme Court of Canada, but the decision was upset on appeal to the Judicial Committee of the Privy Council, *MNR versus Anaconda American Brass Limited, 54 DTC 1179*.

income and in such circumstances special consideration would have to be given to the disclosure in the financial statements.

The early use of LIFO, in accordance with the tests mentioned above, was confined to a relatively few industries – metal processors, leather tanners, oil refineries, etc. These industries were characterized by their dependence on one or a few basic raw materials which were frequently subject to wide price fluctuations on world markets. In Canada the use of LIFO has remained confined to a very few industries of this character.

In the U.S.A. however, the concept of the conditions in which LIFO is considered appropriate has steadily broadened (partly under the influence of a more favourable tax climate than in Canada). Once it was conceded that the inventory costing method need not be tied to the physical flow of goods, the question as to what was the most logical way to associate inventory costs with goods sold was thrown wide open. It is clear that when selling prices are tied very closely to current costs by a more or less automatic process of pricing, LIFO is appropriate. What if such connection does not exist? What assumption of flow of costs is best for a typical business that merely tries to buy or manufacture as cheaply as it can, and sell as advantageously as it can? Some would argue that the general price structure is more likely to be influenced by the current cost levels than by previous levels, and a LIFO assumption is therefore more realistic for reflection of current operating performance. Under the impetus of this kind of thinking, the use of LIFO has spread into many lines of business.*

Flow of costs – base stock

A few instances are also found in practice of the use of the base stock method of inventory valuation. This method dates back to the early years of the 20th Century. It has considerable similarity to LIFO in its effect on the financial statements, although it was developed by a different line of reasoning.

Essentially the base stock method is founded on the proposition that a going business concern must have on hand at all times a minimum stock in inventory in order to operate efficiently. From an economic point of view therefore, the investment in this basic stock is as much fixed as is investment in plant, and it follows that this part of the inventory investment should be excluded entirely from the normal inventory flow of costs. To accomplish this, basic stock quantities are defined and accounted for at constant prices from year to year, so that fluctuations in the current price of these inventory quantities have no effect on the income reported. Inventory held, over and above the basic stock quantities, is accounted for using one or other of the common costing methods.

Some difficulties are encountered in the practical application of base stock. In the first place, the definition of basic quantities must be arbitrary. The valuation placed on the basic stock is also sometimes arbitrary. It may represent price levels prevailing at the time the base stock method is adopted, or a figure may be selected

---

* Because this Study is concerned primarily with accounting principles that are common in Canada, a full summarization of arguments for and against the extended use of LIFO has not been attempted. Such arguments do exist however and can be readily found by reference to U.S. accounting literature.

that is lower than the lowest price that inventory materials are ever expected to reach. For this reason the method is sometimes criticized as not being a valuation method based on cost. As a practical matter also, the base stock method is only likely to prove workable for primary processors of staple commodities such as base metals, sugar, etc. Other enterprises are likely to find that the character of their business changes so much with technological progress and shifts in demand, that no definition of basic stock can be made to remain valid for extended periods.

Cost layers

There may be variations in the practical application of any of the inventory cost flow assumptions to meet bookkeeping convenience. One such variation frequently encountered is the averaging of costs within periods (or layers) in place of a rigid application of the cost assumption to the daily movement of goods.

For example, suppose a business used the FIFO assumption and typically had one and one-half months' inventory on hand. On a strict application of FIFO, each sale would be costed out at the actual cost of the acquisition that occurred approximately one and one-half months earlier, from which the sale is deemed to be made. However, if monthly layers were used the cost of all acquisitions for each month would be averaged. December sales would be costed out at the average cost per unit of October acquisitions until such were exhausted, and thereafter at the average cost of November acquisitions. January sales would be costed out at the average cost of November acquisitions until such were exhausted, and so on.

The use of cost layers can be fitted in with any costing assumption. The periods or layers chosen may be one week, one month, or even as long as a year in some LIFO applications.

Summary

In summary, it may be said that there are a variety of inventory costing assumptions, designed to fit a variety of circumstances.

Where the goods dealt in by the business are highly individual in character, so that each item handled is priced individually, there is no question that the records must keep track of costs by individual items.

Where goods are highly perishable a method of specific identification with inventory units or lots may also be used. Since, however, perishable goods are likely to have low unit value specific identification costing may be more expensive than is warranted, in which case a FIFO assumption would seem most appropriate.

When goods dealt in are interchangeable in character and not perishable, a greater variety of costing assumptions is found. Many businesses use a FIFO costing assumption, not so much because of its intrinsic merits but because some orderly method must be used to match costs with revenues and FIFO seems as good as any. An average cost assumption would seem, logically, to recognize the interchangeable nature of goods a little better than FIFO.

The LIFO and base stock methods, proceeding from different premises, both seek to find a more logical relationship between revenues recognized and costs allocated to cost of sales than is implicit in FIFO. The early LIFO applications stressed the relationship that existed in certain businesses, as a result of business policy, between current material costs and selling prices. It was argued, because of this, that income was most fairly presented by matching latest incurred costs against revenues. Later LIFO applications in the United States rested on an extension of this argument. Even though it was conceded that in most businesses prices are determined by general market conditions and not merely by building on costs, it was felt that the operations of a business are best reflected by matching costs being incurred currently with current revenues.

LIFO and base stock are accepted accounting methods in Canada even though they are used relatively infrequently. There are accountants, however, who disapprove of these methods. They are critical of the fact that the LIFO method only approximately attains its objective of matching current costs against current revenues, and they are critical of the difficulties the method encounters in situations such as 'involuntary liquidation'. Over and above these technical criticisms, they point out that the effect of both LIFO and base stock is to leave a large part of the inventory at a fixed value. They suggest that a change in the going value of inventory represents a real gain or loss to the business (apart from such changes as merely reflect changes in the general price level) and should be reflected in the accounts.

Supporters of the LIFO and base stock methods would deny that these price changes represent real gains to the business, or at least gains that should be reflected in the accounts. They point out that so long as an entity continues in business it is locked into an inventory position. It cannot liquidate its inventory and realize its inventory gains. They point out further that a rise in the price of certain inventories of materials can be harmful to the business to the extent that it encourages the use of substitute materials (e.g. aluminum for copper, sugar substitutes for sugar). In these circumstances the inventory gains, if gains they are, are at least of a different quality from other operating profits.

These differing points of view cannot be easily reconciled since they rest mainly on personal opinions which may differ as to what information is most useful in the financial statements. Unfortunately, the FIFO and LIFO methods of inventory valuation can give markedly different results when inventory cost levels are changing rapidly. The continued existence of both methods represents one of the unfortunate inconsistencies in accounting theory. In Canada this lack of uniformity has not been so serious since the use of LIFO and base stock has been very largely restricted to the few businesses which met the early traditional LIFO tests. In the U.S.A. the discrepancy in accounting methods is more serious.

The retail method of inventory valuation

Mention should be made of a method of inventory valuation which is marked more by its distinctive technique than by any difference in theoretical concept. The retail method is a way of arriving at the approximate total cost (or lower of cost and market value) of an inventory made up of many hundreds or thousands of inventory items without having records of the individual cost of any of the items that make up the inventory. The method is used mainly in the accounting of retail stores.

The method depends on keeping track of the total selling price assigned to goods bought for inventory and the total mark-up of such selling price over cost (or obtaining a valid statistical sample of such figures). Whenever the approximate cost of inventory on hand is required it can then be ascertained by totalling the retail price of all goods on hand and subtracting the average mark-up percentage derived from the records.

The validity of the cost figure so arrived at depends upon the average mark-up on goods in inventory corresponding to the average mark-up on all purchases for the period from which the mark-up percentage is calculated. Thus the method is most reliable when the mark-up on different goods does not vary widely. Where this is not the case it may be possible to improve the accuracy by arriving at different mark-up percentages for goods carried in different departments or categories.

The method has great flexibility. Where goods have been marked down after the initial selling price is established, application of the initial mark-up percentage to retail prices after mark-downs results in a valuation equivalent to 'lower of cost and market', on an item by item basis, which normally would be desired in preference to an actual cost figure. If it should be felt that goods in inventory at the end of the busy season are likely to be marked down further, a special percentage can be developed to allow for this, as well. In essence, a situation requiring costing or other valuation of large numbers of items each of small value relative to the total inventory value lends itself very well to methods based on statistical approximations.

Determination of Inventory 'Market' Value

The practice of valuing inventory at 'the lower of cost and market' had its origin in the 19th Century when accounting principles consisted mainly of rules for balance sheet valuation. The practice reflected the interest of the banker or other short-term credit grantor in realizable values of assets that formed the security against his loan. The rule has been carried on into the period when income determination principles have become predominant, under the rationalization that costs that are not recoverable should be treated as losses of current accounting periods rather than costs to be matched against revenues of future periods.

Variations occur in the precise definition of 'market'. Methods of application of the rule also may vary – i.e. each individual item in stock may be examined and its carrying value written down if market is below cost or alternatively, the total cost and market values of broad categories of goods, or even of the inventory as a whole, may be compared for purposes of the test. These variations largely reflect differences in the underlying view as to the purpose of the rule of 'lower of cost and market'. On extended discussion of these matters may be found elsewhere[1] so the commentary here will be brief.

The broad objective of the inventory valuation rule is to charge against income of the current reporting period the amount of future losses that may be attributable to events that have taken place in the current period. Interpreting this objective in specific circumstances suggests the following comments:

(a) In a fashion business, much of the success of the business lies in its ability to produce or buy goods that will catch the fancy of the consumer so as to be saleable at a satisfactory margin over cost (a satisfactory margin being defined as one that will cover selling and administration costs and yield an adequate return on capital). If goods are left in inventory at the end of the season that will not yield such a margin, this will largely be a reflection of irretrievable mistakes in procurement and poor sales effort, and it will be logical to reflect the effect of such mistakes by writing inventory down to estimated realizable value less the margin sought for on acquisition.*

(b) In a business dealing in staple non-perishable goods, buying mistakes are less important. Because the goods are staples, presumably they will be saleable sooner or later, and mistakes in procurement reflect themselves mainly in an overstocked inventory position. Also the business is less likely to have one single standard margin objective that is applicable to each line of goods in inventory. Some lines may have high margins and some low, yet it will be necessary to carry the low margin goods to round out the lines available to customers. If a less than satisfactory margin is being earned overall, this will be reflected in the income statement through the matching of costs of goods sold with revenues, and a further write-down of inventory would seem merely to shift profit from the current to future accounting periods. Three provisos to this general statement might be made, however:

(i) If certain lines, or the inventory as a whole, have been permitted to get into an overstocked position, costs of carrying unnecessary inventory will be incurred in the future, and it would be logical to make some provision for these future costs by way of an allowance against a cost valuation of slow moving or overstocked lines.

(ii) If replacement cost has dropped below the cost of goods in inventory, to the extent that the inventory is over normal quantities an opportunity has been lost to procure the goods at lower cost, and it may be considered logical to recognize this loss by writing excess inventory quantities down to replacement cost (and especially so if lower replacement costs are likely to be reflected in lower ultimate selling prices).

(iii) If there are any goods in inventory belonging to discontinued lines, such obsolete items should unquestionably be written down to estimated net realizable value less a discount factor to allow for the period of time that may elapse before realization.

It should be noted here that such refinements of reasoning are not usually found in ordinary business practice. One is likely to find the average business looking at its inventory item by item and, where applicable, writing down finished goods to net realizable value or realizable value less

---

* This margin by definition will cover normal selling and other costs so that the 'market' valuation will be at estimated selling price less the gross margin. If, however, special selling costs are associated with the goods in question, these should be allowed for as a reduction of the estimated selling price. For example some retailers, when they want to move goods, will pay special commissions (called 'spiffs') to salesmen on sales of the slow moving goods.

a 'normal' gross margin, its raw materials to replacement cost, and its work-in-process to one of these three interpretations of market, whichever is most conveniently arrived at.[2]

(c) In a business that is speculating in commodities – i.e. one that gets in and out of the market for commodities, or operates more or less by way of a series of separate individual ventures (e.g. it may buy a particular lot of goods and dispose of it and not repurchase similar goods for some time) – inventory valuations should not be above net realizable value (less a discount factor if realization is likely to be protracted). If the business deals in a well organized commodity market (such as the grain market) the results of operations may be most fairly presented by always valuing the inventory at market, thereby reflecting fully the results of trading to the reporting date, whether such be favourable or unfavourable.

(d) In a contracting or special order business costs accumulated to date on work-in-process should obviously not be valued at more than realizable value. The question arises, however, whether losses should also be provided for with respect to costs yet to be incurred to complete contracts which are in process at the year-end date, and if so, in what amount. In practice it is customary to make provision for future losses on contracts in progress. Sometimes the amount of such loss would be measured by comparison of future estimated costs on the contract with the net amount recoverable. Since, however, such contracts will occupy some or all of the capacity of the plant for a period of time, it may be argued that the comparison should be between the estimated costs to come on the contract and contract revenue less a margin to cover selling and administration costs, and profit during the period that the plant is occupied.

(e) The case of the contracting business may be considered a special case of the general rule that inventory valuation should take into account any purchase and sale commitments in existence at the year-end, and provide for losses on such where required.

From the foregoing it may be observed that the appropriate interpretation of 'market' may vary considerably depending on the circumstances of the business. Accordingly it is difficult to phrase an all-inclusive rule other than in terms of the objective of providing for losses attributable to actions or events in the current accounting period.

In practice, inventory write-downs to market have not been a large problem in the last thirty years (apart from the occasional business that has accumulated obsolete inventory) owing to the fairly high level of prosperity that has prevailed throughout the period, and the slow gradual increase in the general price level that has helped keep actual inventory costs below replacement costs.

Principles for Determination of Inventory Costs Applicable to Earned Revenues

The foregoing discussion may be summarized in the following principles:

1. Inventory costs comprise all costs that can reasonably be attributed to the purchase and manufacture of goods.

(a) Costs reasonably attributable to inventory include at least the cost of materials entering into the production of inventory, the cost of labour directly expended in the fabrication or processing of inventory, and overhead costs that may be seen to vary in amount more or less proportionately to the volume of production.

(b) Inventory costs may also include an allocation of overhead costs that do not vary with the volume of production. Such allocation for a period should not exceed the proportion which the number of units in inventory bear to an assumed normal or standard number of production units for the period.

2. The portion of inventory costs that are matched with earned revenues may be arrived at by specifically identifying unit costs of goods sold, or by making some assumption as to flow of costs such as FIFO, average cost, etc. The method of matching selected depends on the circumstances of the business.

3. If costs remaining in inventory at the end of an accounting period are unlikely to be recoverable without loss, or reflect inefficiencies or mistakes in the accounting period, an appropriate portion of such costs should be written off against the income of the period, by means of a reduction to 'market'. One method of writing-down to market in common practice is to compare the cost of each item in inventory
   – with replacement cost (buying market) for raw materials
   – with net realizable value (selling market) for finished goods, and
   – with replacement cost or realizable value less costs to complete and sell (whichever is determined more conveniently) for work-in-process.

Other definitions of market, however, may be appropriate in given circumstances, and it may equally be appropriate to compare the aggregate market for inventory as a whole, or major categories of it, with aggregate cost, rather than item by item. The objective should be to reflect most fairly the results of the trading activities in the accounting period.

(a) When the nature of the business is to trade or speculate in commodities, goods on hand at the end of the accounting period should not be valued at more than net realizable value less a discount to cover any probable abnormal delay in realization.

(b) Where a business speculates in raw materials to the extent that it may on occasion buy more than normal quantities in anticipation of price rises, any decline in replacement market should be reflected at least to the extent of the above normal stocks.

(c) Where a business deals in fashion goods, a valuation of any sizeable amounts of inventory at the end of the period should be sufficiently below net realizable value to allow for normal gross margins. Otherwise the current period may reflect higher margins than can be sustained in the following period when goods in inventory are sold off.

(d) Where a business deals in seasonal non-fashion goods, any inventories left over at the end of the season should be valued at not more than net realizable value less a discount to cover the carry-over period until next season. If sizeable amounts are carried over, it may also be desirable to allow for a normal gross margin below realizable value to cover overheads during the period of disposal in the following period.

(e) Discontinued lines of merchandise should also be valued at not more than net realizable value less a discount to recognize probable delays in realization.

4. Where a business has purchase commitments with respect to inventory, these also should be considered in connection with the valuation at 'market' as though the goods for which the business is committed were actually in inventory at the end of the accounting period.

References

1. See Gertrude Mulcahy, *Use and Meaning of "Market" in Inventory Valuation* (Toronto: The Canadian Institute of Chartered Accountants, 1963).
2. *Ibid.*, Appendix II.

10   Fixed assets and depreciation

In an oft-quoted phrase Hatfield observed "All machinery is on an irresistible march to the junk heap, and its progress, while it may be delayed, cannot be prevented by repairs."[1] The same may be said of virtually any productive asset, save land. The asset that is fresh and new today will, five, ten or fifty years hence become useless and be discarded or sold for what it will bring. This being so, it is clear that the cost of each such capital asset (less whatever salvage value may be realized upon its disposal) is a proper charge against the revenues of the periods in which it has been in use.

The process of allocating capital cost to accounting periods which benefit from the use of capital assets is known as depreciation accounting. AICPA Accounting Terminology Bulletin No. 1 defines depreciation accounting as follows:

> "*Depreciation accounting* is a system of accounting which aims to distribute the cost or other basic value of tangible capital assets, less salvage (if any), over the estimated useful life of the unit (which may be a group of assets) in a systematic and rational manner. It is a process of allocation, not of valuation. *Depreciation for the year* is the portion of the total charge under such a system that is allocated to the year. Although the allocation may properly take into account occurrences during the year, it is not intended to be a measurement of the effect of all such occurrences."

To implement depreciation accounting, it is necessary first to determine the cost or other basic carrying value of wasting tangible capital assets, and second to decide on a logical basis for matching this carrying value year by year with the benefits from the use of the asset.

Determining the Depreciation Base

The identification of the cost of an individual fixed asset is not usually very difficult. In the great majority of cases a business buys its productive plant and machinery from outside suppliers and the cost is readily identifiable from their invoices. It is accepted that the full capital cost of an asset to a business includes all material charges necessarily required to put the asset in question in a position to render service. Thus installation costs, for example, special foundations for a machine, wiring costs, etc. must be identified and capitalized.

There are however a number of practical problems to be dealt with in establishing the depreciation base, in the following areas:

1. Setting practical criteria for amounts to be capitalized

2. Accounting for plant retired or abandoned

3. Distinguishing between repair and maintenance work and costs to be capitalized

4. Determining the cost of self-constructed assets

5. Ensuring that the depreciation base corresponds with the carrying value of fixed assets in the accounts.

Criteria for capitalization

In theory any tangible asset acquired for use and not for resale, and having a usefulness extending beyond one yearly accounting period, is a capital asset. In practice most businesses are likely to modify this definition in recognition of the fact that accounting for fixed assets makes work, and the information obtained by keeping track of very small units is not worth the cost involved. Such modification usually takes the form of a policy decision not to capitalize additions beneath a stated dollar amount. In addition the policy may dictate that short-lived capital assets (say under three years) be written off immediately unless their cost is very substantial. The limits adopted will vary from business to business, since amounts that would be significant to a business of one size may be quite immaterial to another. The policy for any one business should similarly be adjusted from time to time, as the business grows.

Accounting for plant retired or abandoned

When capital assets are disposed of entries should be made to write off their cost, or other carrying value, in order that only plant in service be shown as an asset and in order to maintain a correct base for depreciation. To accomplish this there are two practical requirements: there must be some system whereby the accounting department is notified of disposals or retirements of units of plant; and it must be possible to ascertain from the records the carrying value of individual items of plant. In a business of any size the latter requirement effectively means that the business should maintain a detailed record of units of property owned.

Unfortunately, in many businesses fixed asset records are neglected or non-existent and controls to see that all disposals are reported are lacking. If this situation exists it is essential at least to have some safeguard against overdepreciation as a result of basing the depreciation calculation on plant that does not exist. The importance of the problem depends on the method of depreciation followed. For example, if depreciation is calculated on the straight-line method, plant additions must at least be classified by year of addition so that the depreciation provision may be cut off when a particular year's additions become fully depreciated. If however, the diminishing balance basis is used the potential problem is much less serious since the annual provision under this system diminishes towards zero as the age of the plant depreciated increases.

A few businesses that follow the straight-line method of depreciation solve the problem caused by failures in reliable reporting of plant retired by writing off all plant that has become fully depreciated against accumulated depreciation, whether it has been retired or not. The practice would seem to be less than fully satisfactory, however, since it follows that the accounts will no longer show the cost of plant actually in service.

Another common question concerns plant that is taken out of service but not actually sold or scrapped. The normal rule is that plant that is only temporarily idle, or is held on a standby basis, would not be removed from the accounts. Plant that is likely to be out of service for a protracted period, however, should be segregated from plant in service in the accounts and on the financial statements. If, as will frequently be the case, such plant is of doubtful value it should be written off completely as though it had been scrapped.

A few businesses, principally public utilities to whom plant accounting is particularly important, develop lists of 'retirement units' for their particular plant to aid in accounting for fixed assets. A retirement unit is defined as the minimum plant unit which, upon retirement, will be the subject of entries to remove its cost from the accounts. The preparation of a list of retirement units requires the use of informed judgment. Retirement units would generally be defined so that the unit represented something readily separable from the plant, and something that is useful in its own right. Any item of plant which is not on the list of retirement units would be a subsidiary part of a retirement unit and is denoted a 'minor item'. If an item of plant constituting a retirement unit is retired it will be written out of the accounts. If a minor item is retired it will not be written out of the accounts until the retirement unit of which it is a part is written off.

Distinguishing between repair and maintenance costs and costs to be capitalized

A frequent problem in fixed asset accounting arises when work of a repair nature has the incidental effect of improving the service given by the asset or extending its useful life beyond that originally estimated. Alternatively some capital project, say an addition to the building, may involve some repair work on existing capital assets. In such cases some division of the cost between repair cost and an amount to be capitalized should be made. Such allocation will often require estimates by some expert such as an engineer or architect.

Major maintenance work also presents a problem in fixed asset accounting. It often happens that a large portion of an asset needs renewal before its full life is exhausted. In a building, for example, the roof, the plumbing, the electrical wiring or the heating equipment may require renewal half way through the life of the building. Various treatments are possible. For example, the cost of those parts of the building with shorter lives might be accumulated in a separate account and depreciated accordingly. In such a case the expenditures required for renewal would be capitalized and the initial costs written out of the accounts. The practical problem with this approach is that the cost of all the parts which may need renewal before the end of the life of the asset to which they are attached is not always determinable. For example, the cost of a roof as opposed to the remainder of the building would not normally appear separately.

An alternative approach would be to use a depreciation rate on the building reflecting a weighted average of the lives of its components. For example, a rate based on a 40-year life might represent an expectation of a 50-year life for the building shell and 20 years for its wiring, heating and plumbing fixtures and roof. If this is done the renewal costs of shorter-lived components could be charged against the accumulated depreciation when incurred.

A further alternative would be to make a regular provision for major repairs so that the costs when incurred could be charged off against the provision. This practice is rather uncommon, probably because it is difficult to estimate major repairs with any degree of accuracy and the provision would therefore be some-what arbitrary. This basis of accounting, however, is found in the shipping industry where provisions are made for the annual and quadrennial survey costs of ships required by law. Here the legal requirement to have surveys at stated intervals introduces an element of certainty into the situation. Similar provisions are found in the steel industry to meet the regularly recurring costs of relining blast furnaces.

Finally, in some cases major repair costs may be charged off as they are incurred. The objection to this is that it distorts the earnings of the year in which the major repair is made. If the business is sufficiently large, however, this objection may not be serious.

Determining the cost of self-constructed assets

Occasionally a business will construct a capital asset for itself rather than acquire it from outside suppliers. How the asset should be costed or valued for the purposes of the accounts then becomes a problem. Had the business acquired the asset from an outside supplier in the normal course, presumably it would have paid a price that would cover all the supplier's costs and yielded him a profit. Should a corresponding figure be recorded in the accounts of the business that builds its own asset?

The direct answer to this question is 'no'. A self-constructed asset is not valued at the figure that would have been required to acquire it from an alternative supplier. Apart from any other reasons a reliable figure for such an alternative price would often be difficult to obtain, and in any event there is no assurance that the entity would have been willing to pay an outside supplier's price. The valuation of a self-constructed asset is confined to costs incurred by the entity itself; but the definition of such costs may substantially affect the total figure to be capitalized.

For purposes of discussion costs related to construction may be classified as direct costs, construction overheads and financing costs. There is no question but that costs to be capitalized for a self-constructed asset include direct costs, such as material, labour and outside services. More of a question is raised about con-struction overheads, such as supervision costs, engineering and design, and factory overheads (where applicable). Some writers take the view that overheads should not be capitalized to the extent that such costs would have been incurred anyway in the absence of the construction work. A somewhat similar view is that overheads should only be capitalized where self-construction has meant that current pro-duction has had to be curtailed. Other writers argue that the use of available capacity in a productive fashion rather than letting it go to waste justifies capitalization of the overhead cost, subject to a limitation on cost capitalized to the price for which the asset could have been obtained from other sources.

In the writer's opinion the best answer may depend on the circumstances. For example a machine tool company making a tool for its own use should be able to feel confident that a cost, including overheads developed by its normal costing procedures, is not more than a fair measure of the worth of the self-constructed asset. On the other hand, where the asset constructed is different from the normal form of output of the enterprise, capitalization of identifiable incremental costs of construction only would seem to be the course of prudence.

Financing costs (interest and amortization of debt discount or expenses of borrowing during the period of construction) related to self-constructed assets are also a problem. The older view, expressed by some writers, was that construction costs and financing costs are two different things and the latter should not be capitalized as part of an asset's costs. Otherwise the cost of two identical self-constructed assets would appear to be different if one were financed by borrowed funds and the other by equity funds. The further possibility that an imputed cost might be ascribed to equity funds and capitalized as part of the costs of self-constructed assets, was rejected on the grounds that this would be tantamount to an enterprise recording a profit on dealings with itself.

On the other hand, failure to capitalize costs attributable to funds borrowed to finance construction during the construction period means either that such costs need to be deferred (which has a result little different from that of capitalization) or else they fall as a charge against income of the period of construction. The distortion of income which the latter course causes has meant that practice has accepted the capitalization of interest costs where large amounts are involved, usually as part of the asset cost rather than as a separate deferred charge.

The fact that interest during construction is capitalized only with respect to borrowings made specifically to finance construction remains an anomaly except in the case of public utilities. Most public utilities for the last 25 years have been more or less continuously expanding their plant, and to a considerable extent this work is accomplished by their own employees. In these circumstances a careful accounting for plant costs is important, and this is reinforced in the case of the investor-owned utilities by the fact that the accounting adopted will probably be reflected in the rate base used in the regulation of its rates for service. As a result it is customary practice among utilities to capitalize overheads during construction calculated on ordinary cost allocation bases. It is also customary to capitalize what is called 'interest during construction'. In some cases, the amount of 'interest' capitalized is restricted to a rate equivalent to that actually incurred on long-term debt. In other cases a higher rate is used reflecting the estimated average cost of funds derived from all sources (whether debt or equity) to the company. In other words, in the case of some utilities an exception is made to the general rule that only actually incurred interest cost can be taken into account.

The credit arising from the entry capitalizing interest during construction as part of plant cost seems to be invariably carried to the income account for the period under review. Where the rate of interest capitalized reflects only actually experienced interest costs, this achieves the same result as that which would follow from an allocation of some part of actual interest cost to capital. Where, however, the rate of 'interest' capitalized is higher than any actually experienced rate the company is, in effect, taking up a profit on self-construction in its income account. This result could be avoided if the portion of interest capitalized attributable to equity funds were regarded as a return foregone by the owners and therefore, in effect, a further contribution of capital by them which could be accounted for as 'contributed surplus' but this approach is not followed in practice.°

Ensuring that the depreciation base corresponds with the carrying value of assets in the accounts

Once the carrying value of capital assets in the accounts is determined such carrying value must be written off against revenues over the useful life of the asset. Methods by which this is accomplished will be described in the next section.

It is fundamental that the depreciation calculations must be made by applying the appropriate rate to the balance as shown in the accounts. Yet this simple point is occasionally overlooked in certain situations, for example:

(a) Sometimes the carrying value of fixed assets is written up in the accounts to reflect an appraisal, or for some other reason. Yet management may decide, consciously or perhaps without thinking, that the depreciation provision should continue to be calculated on the old basis. The failure to carry the revaluation of assets through to its logical conclusion is now, however, recognized as improper. Paragraph 3060.06 of the CICA Research Recommendations states "If an appraisal of fixed assets has been recorded, subsequent charges against income for depreciation should be based on the new values."

(b) Occasionally a business receives a contribution from a government or other source to help finance the cost of a capital asset. At this point, it has a choice in accounting for the grant.[2] If it is believed that the grant merely offsets the uneconomic cost of the asset (and there would be a strong presumption that this is so if the cost is subsidized) the amount of the grant should be offset in the accounts against the asset cost (with appropriate disclosure) and only the net amount, being the effective cost to the accounting entity, should be depreciated. On the other hand, if it is believed that the grant is a pure windfall it should be credited to contributed surplus, being in the nature of a gift. On this basis depreciation should be provided against the full cost of the asset since the accounts have treated it as being worth its full cost.

Instances have occurred, however, where businesses have treated grants as being contributed surplus, and yet have based the depreciation provision on the cost of the asset less the amount of the grant. The logical inconsistency in treatment is apparent.

(c) When one company acquires the shares of another the amount paid rarely corresponds with the net carrying value of the assets and liabilities

---

° In its initial years TransCanada PipeLines Limited did credit interest during construction to Capital Surplus account, and charged actual interest and amortization incurred against that account. This policy was changed in 1958, however, "in conformity with the practice followed by other gas transmission companies".

in the books of the company acquired. For example, one company may pay $10 million for all the shares of another company which shows a net asset value of $7 million. When consolidating the accounts of the two companies for the purpose of presenting the financial statements of the parent company after acquisition, the difference of $3 million must be dealt with in some way. If it is felt that some or all of it can be attributed to specific assets of the subsidiary that are worth more than they were arrived at in the books of the subsidiary, the amount will be so distributed in the consolidation of accounts. For example, perhaps $2 million of the difference might be added to the carrying value of depreciable fixed assets.

If this is done, it should be apparent that for purposes of consolidated financial statements thereafter, the $2 million must be depreciated over the remaining useful life of the fixed assets owned by the subsidiary at the date of acquisition. Otherwise, the accounting would be contradictory in attributing $2 million to fixed assets, and yet not following through with appropriate depreciation provisions.

The Application of Depreciation Accounting

As was indicated at the beginning of this Chapter, depreciation accounting seeks to allocate the cost less salvage value of capital assets in an orderly and reasonable fashion over their economic lives. There are two problems associated with this. The first problem is that of estimating in advance the economic life of any particular capital asset. The second problem is that of finding a sensible basis on which to apportion the total amount to be written off as between the several accounting periods within that economic life. In addition, a number of issues arise in the practical application of depreciation accounting methods.

Estimating economic life

The problem of forecasting economic life may be illuminated by a consideration of the causes that will bring that life to an end. In the first place, the cause may be physical deterioration. This may be merely the result of exposure to the elements, or may be more the result of the wear and tear on the asset caused by its daily use. The former type of physical deterioration is probably more applicable to buildings and structures and is more predictable, being mainly a function of time. The latter type of deterioration tends to be more important for machinery and equipment and is less predictable, being largely a function of production volumes. When considering the physical limit to asset lives, one has to take into account the standard of maintenance. A high standard of preventive maintenance may prolong asset lives and in certain circumstances reduce the appropriate depreciation rate.

In the second place, the economic life of a capital asset may be ended or greatly diminished by obsolescence. Obsolescence, likewise, may arise from more than one cause. There may be advances in technique which make a particular machine obsolete even though its original physical capacity is completely unimpaired. There may be a growth in the market that makes larger equipment, with lower unit costs, feasible. Or there may be shifts in the demand for the product of a machine so that its services are no longer required, or not required on the scale that once they were.

Obsolescence may be partial or complete. Consumer demand may lessen for a machine's product, but there may still be enough demand to make it worthwhile to continue producing on a reduced scale. Similarly, technological advances may make it certain that a business would not buy an identical machine to the one it has if it were considering a replacement. Yet the savings possible through buying a new machine to replace the existing one may not be sufficient to justify the additional expenditure of funds required to effect replacement. In either case the machine will be partially but not wholly obsolete.

The importance of obsolescence as a factor in depreciation is evidently much greater today than it was thirty years ago. Both the pace of invention and the speed of change in consumer demand have increased tremendously in the past few decades. The result is that estimates of required depreciation write-offs must have a higher degree of uncertainty today than they have ever had. This fact is not appreciated by many people who still think that the establishment of depreciation rates and methods falls solely within the province of the engineer because of his familiarity with physical asset lives. An engineering background is still most useful in arriving at depreciation estimates but the judgment of the statistician, the economist and the experienced businessman are also of value.

Estimates of economic life are usually made in terms of the number of years for which the asset in question may be expected to render service. If obsolescence is likely to be the limiting factor in that life, a time estimate would seem to be most appropriate. The estimate however might also be expressed in terms of units of production if it is felt that the ultimate cause of the asset's retirement is likely to be wear and tear rather than obsolescence.

Depreciation patterns

Once the economic life of an asset is estimated, there remains the problem of allocating the cost less salvage value over that life. Various more or less arbitrary methods exist to accomplish this. These may be summarized as follows:

- (a) decreasing charge methods
    - – diminishing balance method
    - – sum-of-the-years' digits method
- (b) level annual charge (straight-line) method
- (c) unit-of-production method
- (d) increasing charge (interest) methods
    - – annuity method
    - – sinking fund method

As these methods are all described in standard accounting reference works, they will not be defined in detail here. It is sufficient to say that the most popular methods in this country are the diminishing balance method (under the influence of income tax considerations) and the straight-line method. Increasing charge methods in contrast are very rarely used.

A depreciation pattern is supposed to be 'systematic and rational'. It is undeniable that each of these methods is systematic, since given the basic choice of rate each can be applied without further exercise of judgment. The question arises, however, whether each is equally rational. In practice any one of several patterns may be initially selected by a business, almost at will. Depending on the selection, the depreciation provision with respect to any single asset in a given year may vary widely. Also, even when applied to a reasonably typical aggregation of assets, there may be substantial differences in the amount of the depreciation provision under different methods, depending on the average age of the assets. It does not seem reasonable to suggest that methods yielding different results can be equally rational. It would be more logical to think that one method would be preferable in one set of circumstances and another in a different set. The criteria by which a selection between available methods can be made have not been clearly delineated in accounting literature, nor is it certain it is possible to do so. Some lines of inquiry, however, are suggested in Appendix A.

Practical problems in the calculation of depreciation

Depreciation in the year of acquisition

When an asset is acquired the question arises as to what date should be used for beginning the calculation of the depreciation provision. Theoretically, of course, the date used should be that when the asset in question comes into regular service after the completion of any trial runs. This date is not always easy to determine since a piece of equipment may require a fairly extended working-in period and thus may take some time to achieve top efficiency. In practice, many businesses have a rule of thumb by which they take full depreciation in the year in which an asset is first put into service and none in which it is disposed of, or half in the year when it is acquired, half in the year of disposal. These are however only rules of convenience which can be justified on the grounds that the appropriate amount of the depreciation provision must, of necessity, be approximate. If a very large acquisition is made relative to the size of the business, a more precise calculation of the depreciation applicable to the portion of the year in which the asset is serviceable should be, and usually is, made to avoid distortion.

Assets which do not attain full serviceability for some time also raise a question about the appropriate amount of depreciation applicable to them in their early years. This problem occurs infrequently with routine acquisitions of capital assets, but is more common with the installation of large new units of productive capacity. For example, in electricity generating plants it is common to find the structures for a new plant built to house six or eight generating units, but only two, three or four units are installed initially. Similarly, any large industrial unit, say a new oil refinery or pulp and paper plant, is likely to be built with capacity somewhat in excess of the immediately foreseeable demand. If it is accepted that the depreciation provision should be related to anticipated service values of the asset or plant, it would seem that a lower initial rate of depreciation would be justified in these cases, balanced by a somewhat higher rate in the full service years. The period of lower depreciation, however, should be clearly defined at the outset to avoid the danger that depreciation provisions might be regularly understated if the plant production did not come up to its expected levels. While this type of depreciation provision allowing for lesser economic value of the plant in the early years of its life seems justified, it is not common in practice.

Individual item provisions and group provisions

It is conceivable, under depreciation accounting principles, that the actual mechanical calculation of the depreciation provision for a business for an accounting period might take the form of a separate calculation with respect to each individual fixed asset. That is to say, each asset would have its own individual rate of depreciation and the accumulated depreciation would be related to individual asset accumulations. Until the recent advent of computer processing methods however, such a method of calculation has been, for the most part, impractical and it has been customary to classify fixed assets in fairly broad groupings and apply one representative depreciation rate to each group. In a few cases one composite rate for all fixed assets of a business is used. To ensure that the composite rate of depreciation is appropriate however, it is necessary to make regular studies of the balance of assets owned as between short-lived and long-lived assets, and the effort involved in such studies might just as well be expended in calculating and recording depreciation on the group basis.

Where depreciation is calculated and recorded by groups, the method may be thought of merely as a short-cut substitute for a separate calculation for each asset, or instead it may be viewed as an application of an average rate which will reflect the average experience of the group as a whole, but which will not necessarily be right with respect to any individual asset in the group. The difference in viewpoint is reflected in the accounting for plant retired:

(a) Under the 'individual reserve' concept, when an individual item of plant is retired the depreciation accumulated with respect to it will be calculated, and both the asset carrying value and that amount of depreciation will be removed from the accounts. If the proceeds on disposal of the asset exceed or are less than the asset carrying value less accumulated depreciation, the difference will be recorded as an item of profit or loss for the period.

(b) Under the 'group reserve' concept, when an individual item of plant is retired its carrying value is merely removed from the asset account and this amount, less any recovery from disposal proceeds, is charged against the accumulated depreciation of the group. Thus, no profit or loss is recognized on sale, since it is assumed that profits on disposal of some assets in the group will be offset by losses on others. This underlying assumption, however, should be reviewed in the case of large disposals to see how well it corresponds with the facts. If, for example, there were only two buildings in a group and one is disposed of, it may be obvious that some profit or loss should be recorded on the disposal of the one building if the accumulated depreciation left for the remaining building is to be a reasonable figure.

Either of these concepts may be associated with any given depreciation pattern.

Round amount depreciation provisions

As was pointed out in Chapter 4, some sixty years ago the depreciation provision was thought of as a more or less discretionary appropriation of income for the purpose of building up a fund for the replacement of fixed assets, and there was no requirement that any particular amount be appropriated in any given year. In such circumstances, a round amount charge for depreciation determined by the directors was customary. The practice of providing depreciation in round amounts persisted on a gradually decreasing scale well into the 20th Century. Probably in many cases the thinking underlying the appropriation changed from the old idea of depreciation to the modern concept of depreciation as an allocation of property cost over its useful life without a corresponding change in the form of provision. A round amount approximate provision covering the entire plant is unsatisfactory, however, in that it lacks the substantiation afforded by a quantitative analysis of individual assets or asset groups. In other words, while judgment is inherent in the process of establishing depreciation rates, judgment cannot be exercised in a vacuum. There must be a background of factual information to guide judgment and the better the presentation of facts the better will be the judgment. Consequently it can be stated that sweeping round amount judgments on the depreciation provision applicable to the entire plant of a business of any size would not be acceptable and would not meet the requirement that the depreciation provision be 'systematic and rational'.*

Revisions in depreciation rates

The necessary uncertainty in any depreciation accounting plan suggests that as experience unfolds some adjustments in rates may appear desirable. The question then arises whether the amount of depreciation previously accumulated is too large or too small, and if so what should be done about it. Two courses of action are open. The difference may be picked up over the remainder of the useful lives of assets in existence. This is the general approach when service life reviews are conducted at regular intervals and depreciation rates changed accordingly. In other words, it is considered that depreciation is necessarily an estimate. Accounting based upon best current estimates need not be revised retroactively on the basis of later information that is itself only an estimate. All that is required is a periodic revision of rate to keep the accumulated amount of depreciation moving towards the amount it should be on the basis of the latest and best informed judgment.

The alternative is to adjust the amount of accumulated depreciation immediately.** This would be more appropriate where the adjustment is the result of a substantial change in depreciation assumptions.

Only a minority of businesses, however, make any such adjustment since relatively few businesses conduct the necessary studies to ascertain how their actual experience compares with the assumptions implicit in their depreciation policy. In a business where capital acquisitions and disposals are going on regularly, this lack is less serious than it might seem at first glance. If there is a continual turnover of assets the depreciation provision tends to be self-correcting inasmuch as

---

* A depreciation provision arrived at in the normal fashion, and then rounded to indicate the approximate nature of depreciation estimates, would of course be acceptable. It is not the round amount result, but rather the method of arriving at the result, which is subject to criticism.

** Not very many years ago such an adjustment would have been debited or credited to retained earnings (earned surplus) account. Current CICA Research Recommendations however call for such adjustments to be treated as items of ordinary income, presumably with special disclosure if material. (See paragraphs 3480.12 and 3600.03.) APB Opinion No. 20 does not countenance an immediate cumulative adjustment in any event. Changed estimates may be reflected prospectively only.

overdepreciation on assets newly acquired may be offset by underdepreciation on assets held for some time. Alternatively, if depreciation rates are too low, under-depreciation on newly acquired assets may be offset by losses taken on disposal of older assets or overdepreciation on such assets still in service. This conclusion will not be fully valid in any particular case, of course, because errors on new and old assets will not be exactly compensatory if the company is either growing or declining, or if asset acquisitions come in fits and starts instead of steadily (as is usually the case). It may be concluded, however, that there should be clear evidence before changes are made in a depreciation policy. Obviously also, more care is required when assets are long-lived than when they are short-lived.

Depreciation and capital cost allowances

The provision of a reasonable amount for depreciation is obviously a very difficult problem requiring a good deal of study and judgment. In practice, the problem does not receive the attention it deserves. The treatment of capital assets and capital cost allowances for tax purposes unfortunately has great weight, especially in smaller companies. Before 1949, allowances in lieu of depreciation under the Canadian scheme of taxation usually followed the straight-line method, with rates of 2½% on brick and concrete buildings, 5% on frame buildings, 10% on machinery, equipment and office furniture, and so on. There was no deduction for estimated salvage value and the rates on the whole were reasonably generous, especially in comparison with those prevailing in the United States. After 1948 the tax system changed over to the diminishing balance method. In view of the increasing importance of the obsolescence factor in the lives of capital assets this changeover had a considerable amount to recommend it. The rates of depreciation allowed were usually set at twice the old straight-line rates so that the new tax allowances were increased where assets were less than 50% depreciated and decreased where assets were more than 50% depreciated.

In general the normal rates allowed for tax purposes, although on the generous side, have seemed to be reasonable in view of the uncertainty and room for judgment inherent in the whole subject of depreciation. It therefore was convenient for taxpayers to adopt these rates for accounting purposes as well as for tax purposes, and this has been widespread practice for many years. Many business-men as a result have come to associate tax allowances with the depreciation that should be written in the accounts. This association however has no basis in accounting principles, and in some cases accountants have had to emphasize this fact. For example, under the straight-line depreciation basis in force before 1949 it used to be the practice of the Department of National Revenue to require the taxpayer to record depreciation at half rates in loss years. Accounting principles however hold that the depreciation provision is not affected by the profitability or otherwise of a business and the practice of accruing only half depreciation for accounting purposes was discouraged. Later on, in 1951 when capital cost allowances for tax purposes were temporarily deferred on new asset acquisitions in order to damp down inflationary pressures, Bulletin No. 8 of the CICA Research Committee was issued pointing out that an accounting provision for depreciation was required regardless of whether allowances for tax purposes were granted. Again, when the diminishing balance system was introduced for tax allowances but the allowance initially was limited to the amount of depreciation written in the accounts, the accounting profession made representations to the effect that tax allowances should not be permitted to influence a proper depreciation provision for accounting purposes.

More recently there seems to be an increasing tendency towards the use of the income tax statutes as a means of providing economic incentives or disincentives, and extremely generous capital cost allowances have been granted under restricted circumstances. These allowances cannot by any stretch of the imagination be considered to represent a reasonable allocation of the capital cost related to the economic life of the assets concerned, and it is clear that they are not acceptable for accounting purposes. There is some danger that the previous history of equivalence between allowances for tax purposes and the amounts reasonably taken in the accounts as depreciation could lead businessmen to overlook the divergence which frequently exists today and is likely to recur regularly in the future.

Principles of Depreciation Accounting

The foregoing discussion may be summarized in the following principles:

1. The recorded cost of a tangible capital asset should include all costs necessary to put the asset in a position to render service. In the case of self-constructed assets, these would include costs of material and labour, overheads attributable to the construction, and actual out-of-pocket charges to finance construction costs during the construction period.

2. The cost of wasting tangible capital assets must be apportioned and charged off in determining the income of accounting periods benefiting from their use.
   (a) If, however, some other valuation (e.g. an appraisal value) has been substituted for cost in the accounts, the new carrying value should form the basis of the depreciation charge.

3. The period over which an asset or group of assets is depreciated should correspond with estimated economic life. The pattern of depreciation charges within that period should be systematic (which may be achieved by the use of one of the formulas such as diminishing balance or straight-line) and rational.
   (a) Round amount judgments of the amount of depreciation applicable to the entire plant of a sizeable business, made on a year to year basis, do not qualify as a systematic calculation of depreciation.
   (b) The present system of calculating capital cost allowances for income tax purposes is not designed to provide allowances related to the economic lives of the assets of individual businesses and therefore only by coincidence represents a satisfactory measure of depreciation. In particular, the fact that capital cost allowances are available on assets not yet in service, the existence of highly accelerated rates for incentive purposes and the occasional deferment of normal rates to act as economic depressants frequently make the amount of capital cost allowance unsuitable as a depreciation provision.

4. Since depreciation rates for a business can only represent estimates, they are subject to revision from time to time in the light of experience and current information.

References

1. H. R. Hatfield, *Accounting, Its Principles and Problems* (New York: D. Appleton – Century Company Inc., 1927), p. 121.
2. See discussion in *CICA Research Recommendations*, Section 3065.

11 Intangible capital assets, prepaid expenses, deferred charges and period costs

We have seen that the costs of tangible capital assets are matched against revenue through depreciation accounting, and costs of goods for sale are matched through inventory accounting methods. The usage of parts and supplies is also accounted for by inventory accounting methods, but the charge for supplies consumed may be accounted for in several different ways. The cost of a repair part for a capital asset may itself be capitalized when put into service and thereafter be subject to depreciation accounting. The cost of factory supplies used may be treated as a factory overhead cost and thus may be incorporated into the cost of goods manufactured, to be ultimately written off through the entry recording costs of goods sold. The cost of office supplies used will usually be written off directly against revenues of the current period.

There remain for consideration a large number of costs that cannot be identified with tangible objects. Despite this fact, these costs do represent assets at the date acquired – if it were not so, the business would not buy them. A week of a secretary's time is as much an asset as a typewriter, a research scientist's skill as much an asset as a truckload of steel. These assets, then, must also be written off on a rational basis against revenue.

Many of these costs are exceedingly transitory assets. The value of a secretary's time, for example, is unlikely to be felt in revenues for long after the period in which the work is done. The most convenient and sensible practice, therefore, is often to write off these costs immediately, thus in effect matching them against the revenues of the period in which the cost is incurred. Costs so treated are known as 'period' costs.*

* In this connection, something depends upon the period under consideration. A cost that may reasonably be treated as a period cost for purposes of annual accounts may need to be treated more carefully for purposes of monthly reporting. For example, it is customary to treat advertising costs as period costs for purposes of annual financial reporting (except occasionally with costs of special campaigns just prior to the year-end). For internal monthly reporting however, many companies find it more satisfactory to write off advertising costs according to a predetermined budget, rather than distort reported monthly income by the somewhat erratic fluctuations in the level of actual costs from month to month.

Other intangible costs clearly have, or it is hoped they will have, a more lasting value. These may be classified as:

1. Costs of purchased intangible capital assets

2. Prepaid expenses

3. Other costs bringing with them future benefits (deferred charges).

With respect to the many types of costs that fall into these three categories, the following questions arise:
– Is the future benefit sufficiently assured to warrant treating the cost as an asset in the balance sheet?
– If so, should the cost be written off gradually against revenues (amortized) and on what basis?
– Alternatively, if there is no particularly rational basis for amortization should the asset be written off at one stroke against accumulated retained earnings from prior years?

Purchased Intangible Capital Assets

These may be classified as follows:

1. Intangibles representing legal rights – e.g. rights to a leasehold, franchises, patents, copyrights, trademarks and trade names, licence and royalty agreements.

2. Intangibles representing superior earning power – these are frequently embraced by the omnibus term 'goodwill', but there may be many factors contributing to superior earning power such as monopoly position, secret product processes or formulae, etc.

3. Intangibles representing 'going concern' value – customarily this represents the amount which a purchaser would pay to avoid incurring certain costs or losses attendant on breaking into a business. For example, a business that has built up a chain of retail stores might find another chain willing to pay something for a takeover rather than have to expand its own business. Or a magazine on the verge of failing may yet find another publisher in a related field willing to pay for its circulation lists. It is somewhat similar to 'goodwill' in character but is not necessarily represented by superior earning power, at least not to the vendor.

Such a classification is illustrative merely, and it is impossible to draw too precise dividing lines. For example, it may be difficult to distinguish to what degree superior earning power is the result of patent rights, trade names, or other factors.

For accounting purposes it is useful to distinguish between intangibles with a limited life, and those for whose life no limit can be seen at the time of acquisition. In the former category fall all intangible costs whose life is limited by law or contract, e.g. patents and licence agreements. In the latter category may fall costs of perpetual franchises, trademarks or goodwill.

Intangibles with a limited life must be amortized or written off against revenues over a reasonable period of years. In this they are exactly like fixed assets which must be depreciated on a reasonable basis. Where the life of the intangible is limited by law or contract, it may be reasonable to spread the cost evenly over its legal life. But this is not always so – the economic benefits from the asset may expire before its legal life. Just as a machine may need to be written off over a shorter period than its physical life because of the obsolescence factor, so a patent, say, may need to be written off over a shorter period than its legal term. The exercise of judgment in amortization policy is thus as inescapable as it is in depreciation policy.

Intangibles that have no readily apparent limit to their useful life present in practice a more difficult problem. At first glance it would seem that these assets should not be amortized, since no logical period for writing off the asset is apparent. On the other hand, common sense tells us that, with the single exception of land, the business asset with indefinite economic life is very rare, if not non-existent. Goodwill in the form of superior earnings power is under constant attack by the forces of competition. The value of secret processes, patents and trademarks is constantly eroded by advances in invention and technology. For these reasons it is fairly common to amortize the cost of purchased intangibles against income, even when no terminus to their existence appears on the horizon. Of necessity the period chosen for such amortization is arbitrary.

Goodwill

The treatment of purchased goodwill is a particularly difficult case of this general problem. Here the underlying reason for the difficulty is that while purchased goodwill figures in the accounts, goodwill developed through the business' own exertions does not.

Goodwill accrues insensibly to a business over time, as a result of many factors – effective marketing, effective location and product planning, efficient production – in short, good management, and sometimes luck. Goodwill can be dissipated as well as built up. For accounting purposes, however, the existence of goodwill is ignored except when it is purchased. The reason for this is simple – there is no known way by which periodic increases or decreases in the value of business goodwill can be measured with any degree of reliability.*

When consideration is given to the accounting for the cost of purchased goodwill, then, the following dilemma arises:
– It is reasonable to expect that the goodwill relating to the business at the time of purchase will eventually disappear. The products of the business purchased will decline in importance, or competition may strengthen, and so on. Therefore, the particular goodwill purchased might well be written off.
– On the other hand, the new owners of the purchased business will be continuing the efforts to maintain a successful business. As previously existing goodwill is eroded, new goodwill may be accruing so that, over all, the net value of the goodwill of the total business is no less than before.

---

* The reader of financial statements will do well to remember that because of this inability to account for goodwill creation and dissipation accurately, accounting methods tend to understate the 'economic' income attributable to proprietors of businesses enjoying healthy growth, and to overstate that of those going into a decline.

In this situation, strong arguments may be made in support of more than one accounting treatment:

1. There are those who argue that the cost of purchased goodwill should be amortized against income, even though new goodwill may be in the process of creation by the current efforts of management of the business. They feel that accounting principles call for the writing-off against income on some basis of all costs of assets purchased that do not have unlimited life. The manner of write-off, they believe, should be determined by the expectations of the purchaser when the acquisition is made. In other words, if the amount paid for goodwill was based on, say, five years' expectation of super profits, the write-off should be over this period. The fact that efforts are being made currently to maintain and build up goodwill is not pertinent, they feel, since normal accounting methods give no recognition to goodwill created by the internal efforts of the business. They point out that this accounting method will show consistent results as between a business that purchases goodwill and one that builds its own goodwill. The earnings of the former will bear the charge for amortization of purchased goodwill. The earnings of the latter will bear the costs of building goodwill. Also, after the amortization period each will be comparable in that goodwill will show on the balance sheet of neither.

2. Others believe that it does not make sense to amortize goodwill when the overall value of goodwill owned by the business is maintained. To do so, they think, involves an inconsistency in accounting for goodwill that has the effect of artificially depressing reported profits. That is to say, they feel that purchased goodwill should not be amortized unless internally created goodwill is capitalized – a procedure which is generally recognized as impractical. As a practical matter, they feel that the amortization of purchased goodwill would make the income statement of the acquiring company non-comparable with other companies that have not purchased goodwill, and would thus detract from its usefulness. For these reasons, they would advocate carrying the cost of goodwill as an asset in the balance sheet without amortization. If, however, it should subsequently appear that the goodwill of the business has in fact disappeared, it may be written off as a special charge against income or retained earnings.

   This latter suggestion has been criticized on the grounds that it is never possible to tell just when, or over what period, goodwill has lost its value. Generally, however, it is obvious that goodwill must have lost its value when earnings are persistently low, a time when management is most reluctant to countenance write-offs. A practical paradox therefore results – a business which can afford to write off goodwill should not do so; a business which cannot afford to write it off, should.

3. A third group would generally support the initial arguments in the preceding paragraph. They would go further, however, and write off the cost of purchased goodwill as a special charge, immediately upon acquisition. They suggest that it is inconsistent to carry purchased goodwill in the balance sheet without also carrying a value for internally generated goodwill, and that the figure for purchased goodwill alone may be misleading to the reader, since it may be much lower than the total goodwill of the business.

The anomalous result of these procedures, however, is that as a result of the purchase of goodwill, a transaction presumably expected to be profitable, the financial position reported in the balance sheet may appear to have suffered considerable deterioration.

All three of these differing views would find support in Canadian practice. The immediate write-off of purchased goodwill is not acceptable in the U.S.A. and since October 31, 1970 purchased goodwill is required to be amortized to comply with APB Opinion No. 17.

Prepaid Expenses

Prepaid expenses and deferred charges both represent costs incurred or laid out from which benefit is expected to be derived after the current accounting period. As the name implies however, prepaid expenses represent costs laid out ahead of the period to which they relate, or that in which the service purchased will be received. For example, for prepaid rent the business has the right to future occupation of the premises rented, for prepaid insurance the business has the right to future protection. In contrast, in the case of deferred charges the business will not receive any additional future service. The cost is deferred solely on the basis that the service previously received is expected to have a continuing beneficial effect on future revenues. For example, an advertising campaign might be planned, executed, and over before a fiscal year-end. If, however, the campaign were expected to have a beneficial effect on the following year's revenues, some part of its costs might be deferred.

Prepaid expenses are not ordinarily a problem for accounting. The fact that service is to be received in the future, or that the cost can be related to a future time period, is normally sufficient to warrant carrying the cost as an asset. The future write-off period is usually determined by the period covered by the prepayment.

When the period arrives to which a prepaid cost relates, the cost may be treated then as a 'period cost' or may enter into the determination of cost of inventory produced in that period.

Deferred Charges

Almost every cost has some value extending beyond the moment in which it is incurred. No hard and fast dividing line, therefore, can be drawn between costs that are treated as period costs as soon as they are incurred and those that may be treated as deferred charges. The dividing line is established by practical judgment involving examination of the nature of the cost, the reliability of the estimate of its potential contribution to future revenues, the materiality of the cost, and so on. Costs that qualify for treatment as deferred, however, will usually be readily identifiable in the cost system, frequently being costs of a specific project collected on an individual work order. The case for deferment of, say, more or less arbitrary percentages of an ordinary administrative cost or distribution cost, would rarely be convincing.

No list of deferred charges can possibly be comprehensive, but the following includes some of the more common types:
– Research and new product development costs
– Design and engineering for new models of existing products
– Past service pension costs
– Exploration and development expenses in oil and gas or mining companies
– Major renovation or plant rearrangement costs
– Start-up costs and initial losses
– Bond issue expense and discount
– Stock issue expense
– Organization expense.

Research and new product development costs

Some companies may conduct a 'pure' research program, but most research is likely to have as an objective the development of new products or improvement of existing products.

If research effort is directed towards the development of new products, deferment of costs to the future is clearly justifiable so long as the results appear hopeful. A continuing surveillance must be maintained however, and if a program appears ineffectual its cost should be written off. When a product gets to the commercial production stage, amortization of any research and development costs carried forward in relation to it must commence, on a basis commensurate with the product's prospects.

Many companies write off research and development costs as incurred, on the basis that these are recurring costs necessary to maintain the company's position. If the costs are incurred fairly evenly over the years, and if the company is a large one, this policy does not distort the income of any particular year, and has the advantage that it avoids the necessity of making inherently difficult decisions as to the potential future value of specific research programs. Smaller companies and newcomers, however, may be unable, or may not wish, to follow this policy since the fluctuations in research and development expenses in their cases may well be more substantial in relation to their reported net income.

Design and engineering costs

If a design and engineering department is maintained at a more or less constant level, its cost will probably be absorbed as part of manufacturing overhead and not be treated on a deferred charge basis. If, however, costs of new models fluctuate greatly from year to year, it may be convenient to classify such costs by product model and defer them until the model comes into production. Thereafter, amortization would be in step with the model's estimated future production or sales – normally over a relatively short period.

Past service pension costs

Frequently, as a result of labour negotiations or a review of its employee compensation policies, a business will adopt an employee retirement plan by which it will undertake to provide pensions on a stated formula to retiring employees who meet certain conditions of eligibility. In such cases provision is made for employees to receive certain benefits in respect of years worked after inception of the plan, and commonly also benefits are provided in respect of years of service before inception of the plan. Similarly, 'prior service' benefits may arise when a retirement plan is improved. A valuation of past service or prior service benefits arising upon inception or improvement of a plan may be made by actuarial methods and frequently the business will pay some or all of the amount over to a separate pension fund.

Detailed consideration of problems in accounting for past service costs is reserved for Chapter 12.

Exploration and development expenses – mining, oil and gas companies

Exploration expenses, to companies formed to exploit natural resources, are not unlike research expenses to an industrial concern. In both cases they represent the costs of organized and systematic efforts to bring into being a future source of income. In both cases there is no assurance that the efforts will be crowned with success; certainly the relationship between costs expended and results achieved is much less direct than with normal expenditures.

Detailed discussion of accounting for exploration and development expenses is included in Chapter 24 on the extractive industries.

Major renovation or plant modernization costs

Any business that has been in operation for some time, particularly a manufacturing business, is likely to find it necessary or desirable from time to time to undertake a program of major maintenance and repair to its capital assets, or to undertake heavy expenditures to modernize its plant, say by redesigning and streamlining its production line. Such occasional bursts of expenditures are likely to distort the picture of the recurring income-earning capacity of the business, if they are written off as a period cost in the year when the money is laid out.

As noted earlier in Chapter 10, to the extent that the expenditure represents major repairs some provision for it may have been made in previous years by anticipatory charges against income of those years. This practice, however, is not very common in North America and if such provision has not been made the problem of how to match these costs against revenues arises in an acute form.

One answer to this problem is to write off such costs immediately as period costs, but to give special disclosure of them. Alternatively, it is not uncommon to find these costs treated as deferred charges. If this is done an amortization period must be selected. The decision must be arbitrary to some degree, but it can be guided by the relationship between the amount of costs deferred, and what might be considered a normal long-term charge for repair and maintenance work. The normal desire would be to keep the amortization period as short as possible. This would be especially true if there were any suspicion that part of the repair costs deferred merely represented a catching-up of preventive maintenance work not performed in previous years.

Start-up costs and initial losses

Any business which is in the process of getting established is likely to incur some costs, other than costs of intangible assets, before it gets into business. Likewise, it may be in operation for some time before a profitable level of operations is attained. Similar start-up costs and initial operating losses will be encountered by an established business that embarks on a new venture.

Costs of this nature are absorbed currently in the vast majority of situations. Disclosure of the existence of start-up costs may be made outside the financial statements in the directors' report or by other means. There have, however, been exceptions to the normal practice of absorbing such costs immediately. Some finance companies have deferred costs in connection with new offices opened. An oil company has deferred costs and initial losses in connection with a new refinery. A tobacco company carried forward initial losses in an establishment account.

The theory behind such deferments cannot be called unsound. If management knows before commencing a project that it is going to incur start-up costs and initial losses, and yet the project shows overall profitability, such costs and losses are clearly part of the investment required to arrive at the eventual position of profitability. There is, however, a very practical problem in determining how much of such costs and losses may properly be deferred. If, for example, costs turn out to be higher than first anticipated, or losses continue longer, it is obvious that the excess should be written off and some doubt may be cast upon the validity of deferring even the originally anticipated amount. It may be difficult, however, to be sure that costs or losses are worse than originally anticipated, since frequently projects are modified after they are first embarked upon, and anticipations adjusted accordingly.

If these costs are deferred, the same question arises as with purchased goodwill and purchased going concern value – should the cost be amortized, written off, or carried indefinitely? – and exactly the same considerations apply as in these other situations.

Bond discount and issue expenses[1]

When a company borrows by way of bond or debenture, or similar instrument, it undertakes an obligation to pay a given amount at maturity and interest on the face amount at a stated rate before maturity. Normally the amount received by the company will differ from the face amount of the obligation, the difference reflecting the fact that the effective rate of interest demanded by the market is more, or less, than the stated rate attaching to the issue. If the effective yield rate required is higher than the stated rate, the bonds will sell at a discount from the face amount; if lower, at a premium over the face amount. The former situation is more common in practice.

In recording the debt obligation it is customary to set up the liability at the face amount and to record the difference between this and the cash actually received as a deferred charge (or as a deferred credit, if a premium). Many accounting theorists have argued that bond discount is not a true deferred charge, in that it does not represent a cost laid out, and have suggested instead that the debt should be recorded initially at the net amount received, which presumably represents the fair valuation of the obligation at that date. Traditional practice, however, ignores this argument.[2]

In most bond issues there are related costs, such as costs of a prospectus (including legal, auditing and printing costs), costs of engraving certificates, possibly underwriters' commission, and so on. These are costs incurred to obtain the use of funds borrowed over the period of the loan and thus are true deferred charges. It would be normal to match bond discount and issue expenses against revenue over the period in some fashion.

Older practice frequently was to write off bond discount and expenses directly against income or retained earnings. It is clear in logic, however, that these costs relate to the whole period of the loan, and therefore amortization against income over the period is the preferable practice. The method of amortization should recognize the term to maturity of the loan, and the amount of bonds outstanding from time to time (since many issues will be of a serial or sinking fund nature whereby a substantial principal amount of the loan is retired before maturity). The most accurate method of amortization is based on a calculation of the effective interest cost to the company of borrowing the net amount of cash received for the loan period, and writing off the deferred bond discount and expenses in such a way that the coupon interest, together with the amortization, will always equal the effective rate of interest applied to the net amount of loan from time to time outstanding. Approximations to this result may be calculated which avoid the complexities of a completely accurate calculation. A straight-line basis of amortization over the term to maturity of the issue will not normally be significantly in error if the full principal amount of the loan is outstanding to maturity, but will be quite wrong if material amounts of the issue are redeemed under sinking fund provisions before maturity.

Stock issue expense

Costs are frequently incurred in connection with share issues just as in the case with bond issues. The problem of accounting for them, however, is more difficult, because share issues ordinarily do not have a fixed maturity or redemption date.

The possible accounting treatments are:

1. To carry the cost of share issues as an intangible asset indefinitely

2. To write off the cost when incurred:
    (a) against contributed surplus,
    (b) against retained earnings,
    (c) against income

3. To carry the cost as a deferred charge and amortize it over an arbitrary period of years.

To begin with, it may be argued that it is presumably advantageous to carry on business in the corporate form, or it would not have been incorporated. This being so, share issue costs which are a necessary cost of raising capital represent the price of obtaining an economic benefit. Since the capital is permanent in nature, it is appropriate to carry the costs connected with its issue as an asset, indefinitely. (One may note in connection with this argument that the attribution of permanence to share capital is not necessarily justified in the case of redeemable preference shares, particularly if there are repurchase obligations in the share conditions.)

To some extent the strength of the argument for carrying share issue costs indefinitely depends on one's concept of the accounting entity (see Appendix A). If the entity is thought of as the equity interest in the corporation, the carrying of share issue costs as an intangible asset is logical. If the entity is thought of as the business itself, apart from its owners, then it would be logical for it to account only for the net proceeds entrusted to it. That is, in the case of no par value shares only the amount received less the costs of issue would be credited to capital; in the case of par value shares the costs of issue would be written off against any premium received on the issue (contributed surplus) if such existed.

The practical difficulty with this proposal is that most corporations acts require the balance sheet of a company to show the amount of issued capital, and 'issued capital' is defined as par value in the case of shares having a par value, and the consideration for which the shares were issued in the case of shares without par value.[3] Thus, except where share issue expenses can be written off against contributed surplus, to meet this suggested accounting treatment and also comply with the law it would be necessary to show in the balance sheet the amount of the legally defined 'issued capital' and subtract therefrom the share issue expense. This rather complicated presentation is unlikely to appeal to many. The alternative chosen in many cases, then, is to write off share issue expenses against retained earnings and this would seem to be relatively unobjectionable.

Still another alternative occasionally found is to write off share issue expenses against income. Some public utility companies have been known to do this on the grounds that their demands for capital for expansion are such that costs of this nature are regular recurring outlays. In this special case, if such outlays are accepted as part of the costs allowed by the regulatory authority as 'cost of service' in rate determination, it may be arguable that the costs are properly matched against revenues in the determination of income. In the ordinary case however, there would seem to be little logic to a deduction in the determination of *income* attributable to equity interest, of costs incidental to raising *capital* from such interests.

Finally there is the practice of amortizing share issue costs over a period of years. In the case of costs attributable to redeemable preferred share issues that may be expected to be redeemed sooner or later, there is probably some logic to amortization, especially if there is a mandatory purchase fund attached to the shares. Here again, however, it would be logical to write off the cost against retained earnings account where it would be associated with the dividends on the preferred shares so as to represent the total cost of raising capital in this form. Apart from redeemable preference shares however, it is difficult to see any logic in the amortization of share issue costs. Where done, it is probably more from a desire not to make too heavy a charge against retained earnings at one time, than from any other motive.

Organization costs

Organization costs are somewhat similar to share issue costs in that they represent costs not of doing business, but of setting up in business. Similar arguments apply, therefore, whether to carry them indefinitely as an intangible asset, write them off immediately, or amortize them. Most businesses usually want to write these costs off sooner or later. Probably this instinct, and indeed the prejudice in favour of writing off all intangibles, is a carry-over from the days when the issuance of stock for organization services, or other intangibles of doubtful worth, represented a convenient and not uncommon method of 'watering' the stock of a company.

Principles of Accounting for 'Other' Costs

The foregoing discussion may be summarized in the following principles:

1. The accounting for costs of intangible capital assets may depend on whether the useful life of such assets is limited or not.
    (a) If the economic life of a specific intangible right or thing is limited, its cost should be amortized against income over the period benefited.
    (b) If a limit to the economic life of a general intangible asset is not foreseeable, its cost need not be amortized. However, amortization over an arbitrary period is permissible in recognition of the fact that no asset (except land) may be expected to last forever. Alternatively, such assets may be written off against accumulated retained earnings in one lump sum.

2. Costs that are not attributable to the acquisition of tangible or intangible capital assets or of inventory will normally be written off against the income of the period in which they are incurred, but such write-off may be deferred if:
    (a) costs are attributable to services yet to be received, or otherwise clearly relate to future time periods (in which case the costs represent 'prepaid expenses');
    (b) costs of services already rendered may reasonably be expected to produce benefits in future periods (in which case the costs will be treated as 'deferred charges').
    Prepaid expenses and deferred charges should be assigned to the periods considered to benefit from the expenditure.

3. Costs of raising capital should be accounted for according to the nature of the capital acquired.
    (a) Costs of raising fixed term debt capital should be written off over the term of the debt issue in proportion to the amounts outstanding from time to time, along with interest expense on the debt.
    (b) Costs of raising share capital may be carried as an intangible asset indefinitely, but alternatively may be written off against contributed surplus or retained earnings.

References

1. A full discussion of the treatment of bond discount and issue expenses and share issue costs may be found in H. S. Moffett, *Accounting for Costs of Financing* (Toronto: The Canadian Institute of Chartered Accountants, 1964).
2. However, *APB Opinion No. 21* issued in August 1971 recommends that the discount or premium be shown as a direct deduction from or addition to the face amount of the debt.

3. For example, pertinent sections of *The Business Corporations Act, 1970* (Ontario) read as follows:

"32.—(1) Where all the shares of a corporation are with par value, its issued capital shall be expressed in Canadian or other currency, or partly in one currency and partly in another, and is an amount equal to the total of the products of the number of issued shares of each class multiplied by the par value thereof less such decreases in the issued capital as from time to time have been effected by the corporation in accordance with this Act.

(2) Where the shares of a corporation are without par value or where part of its shares are with par value and part are without par value, its issued capital shall be expressed in Canadian or other currency, or partly in one currency and partly in another, and is an amount equal to the total of the products of the number of issued shares of each class with par value multiplied by the par value thereof, together with the amount of the consideration for which the shares without par value from time to time outstanding were issued and together with such amounts as from time to time by by-law of the corporation may be transferred thereto and less such decreases in the issued capital as from time to time have been effected by the corporation in accordance with this Act."

12 Complex transactions: problems of recognition, measurement and allocation

Previous Chapters have dealt with the principles governing the allocation of revenues and costs associated with ordinary transactions to accounting periods. There are, however, a number of types of transactions that for one reason or another do not fit very easily under normal transaction recognition and measurement rules. The special nature of these transactions raises fundamental questions as to the point or points of time at which they should receive recognition in the accounts, how they are to be measured, and how their results are to be reflected in income. These questions are so interrelated that it is necessary to discuss such complex transactions in all their aspects in one place. This Chapter, accordingly, deals with accounting problems associated with the following special types of transactions or events:

1. Lease transactions

2. Pension plans

3. Deferred compensation arrangements

4. Stock options

5. Non-arm's-length transactions.

Lease transactions

Leasing of assets has become increasingly common in business in the past twenty-five years. Earlier it was pointed out that accounting recognition of a business transaction does not take place until performance by one of the parties. In a contract for sale of tangible assets 'performance' is usually taken as delivery, and the transaction is recorded at that time. In a contract for services performance may be gradual and the transaction then is recorded either on an accrual basis as the services are rendered, or when billed. The question is whether a lease contract is more like a contract for delivery of tangible property or a contract for services, and if the former at what date it is performed.

Accounting by lessees

The traditional accounting practice has been to treat lease contracts as though they were contracts for services – no more. It is to be remembered, however, that this practice grew up in a period when:

1. Most property leases were 'commercial' leases. That is to say they were for relatively short periods, the property rented was of a general purpose character (e.g. space in an office building) and the lessor was largely in the business of providing services (cleaning and maintenance, elevator service, etc.) as well as making space available.

2. Accounting was more heavily legally oriented (in the English tradition) and the fact that title to the space leased did not pass was decisive.

The traditional practice began to be questioned after World War II when it became apparent that in many cases leasing was being used as an alternative to ownership and, although the legal form was different, frequently a lease was little more than a means of financing acquisition of an asset, very similar to an instalment purchase of property.

In Bulletin No. 38 issued in 1949, the AICPA Committee on Accounting Procedure recommended that where a lease arrangement was in substance an instalment purchase of property, the lessee should value the lease and set up an asset and related obligation in the accounts.

In 1962, AICPA Accounting Research Study No. 4 on "Reporting of Leases in Financial Statements" was issued. The author, J. H. Myers, advocated capitalization of that portion of all leases involving the acquisition of 'property rights' as distinct from services. Myers took the view that any capital asset purchased by a business is acquired to be used. A lease represents an alternative way for a business to acquire property use rights. If then the use of a capital asset is acquired through a lease contract such property rights should, to make the accounting consistent, be valued and shown as an asset in the balance sheet even when the lease does not, in substance, convey ownership. Thus there is no significant difference in substance between long-term leases and short-term leases except that the property rights involved in the latter are less material (and frequently the current services supplied by the landlord in the short-term lease account for a higher proportion of the rental payment than under the long-term lease). On the other side of the coin, Myers argued that the obligation to make rental payments under a lease was very similar in economic substance to the obligation to pay interest and principal under a debt obligation, and this likewise would suggest inclusion of the discounted value of the lease obligation in the balance sheet.

APB Opinion No. 5 issued in September 1964 rejected Myers' arguments for recognition of the property rights element in all leases, and reaffirmed the earlier recommendation of Bulletin 38 that only leases which were in substance purchases of assets should be capitalized. Opinion No. 5 also stated that except in rare cases material gains or losses resulting from a sale of property which was then leased back to the previous owner, together with the related tax effect, should not be recognized immediately in the accounts but should be amortized over the life of the lease as an adjustment of rental cost.

Thus the first question in accounting for lease transactions is whether a lessee, when he signs a lease contract, should capitalize the asset value and related lease obligation in the balance sheet. The official U.S. position (in APB Opinion No. 5) is that in the ordinary situation a lease should be capitalized only when it is in substance a purchase of property.* There is no official Canadian statement on the subject of lease accounting and in practice capitalization of leases is extremely rare.

Under the U.S. approach a second question is by what criteria shall it be decided that a lease represents in substance a purchase. APB Opinion No. 5 stated that a lease should be regarded as a purchase if the lease was essentially non-cancellable and the terms of the lease created a 'material equity' in the property. The following conditions would usually create a material equity:

1. Where the initial term of the lease is materially less than the useful life of the property, and the lessee has the option to renew the lease for the remaining useful life of the property at substantially less than the fair rental value, or

2. The lessee has the right, during or at the expiration of the lease, to acquire the property at a price which at the inception of the lease appears to be substantially less than the probable fair value of the property at the time or times of permitted acquisition by the lessee.

The Board also named the following circumstances as suggesting conditions in which a lease probably would be in substance a purchase:

(a) The property is acquired by the lessor to meet the special needs of the lessee and would probably be usable only for that purpose and only by the lessee;

(b) The term of the lease corresponds substantially to the estimated useful life of the property, and the lessee is obligated to pay costs such as taxes, insurance and maintenance which are usually considered incidental to ownership;

(c) The lessee has guaranteed the obligations of the lessor with respect to the property leased;

(d) The lessee has treated the lease as a purchase for tax purposes.

It is doubtful that the 'material equity' test is a good one for distinguishing leases which are in substance purchases of property, and in any event it appears that it has been possible to structure new leases so that few have been required to be capitalized under the provisions of APB Opinion No. 5.

---

* An exception to this rule occurs when the lessor and lessee are related, the primary purpose of property ownership by the lessor is to lease the property to the lessee, and (1) the lease payments are pledged to secure the debts of the lessor or (2) the lessee is able directly or indirectly to control or significantly influence the activities of the lessor with respect to the lease (APB Opinion No. 5, paragraph 12). APB Opinion No. 10 also states that the accounts of all subsidiary companies whose primary business activity is leasing property or facilities to the parent company or another affiliated company should be consolidated. Thus, the consolidated statements will show the property asset and any related debt obligation, which has much the same effect as if the lease had been capitalized in the unconsolidated statements of the lessee. There has been no statement however that deals with the situation where companies use technically unrelated entities as financing intermediaries in acquiring capital assets and in effect guarantee the debt of such other entity through their lease or other contractual relationships. (See further comment at page 320.)

In view of the lack of capitalization in practice, problems in implementation of lease capitalization procedures have not received widespread attention. Such problems would include:

1. Determining what portion of the rentals should be attributed to services rendered by the lessor, such as maintenance, repairs, payment of taxes, etc., and what portion is purely for the use of the property (which should form the basis of the amount capitalized).

2. Ascertaining at what figure the asset and liability should be capitalized. As in the case of measurement of delayed payment transactions, this could be approached either by valuation of the asset or by applying an appropriate discount rate to the assumed obligation.

3. Deciding on what basis the capitalized lease asset should be amortized against income. Since the interest on the lease obligation would decline over the term of the lease, the depreciation on the asset would have to follow an increasing-charge pattern to produce the same level charge against income as would the normal rental charge under a lease. Increasing-charge depreciation patterns for capital assets are rare, and serious consideration would be required before it was decided that they were appropriate in a particular case. If it was decided that they were not appropriate, of course, this fact would be evidence of the desirability of lease capitalization in order to obtain the appropriate basis for charging the cost of rented property against income.

In particular cases, these problems could only be resolved through fairly arbitrary judgment decisions.

Accounting by lessors

APB Opinion No. 7, issued in May 1966, examined the accounting problems of leases from the standpoint of the lessor. The opinion suggested that leases could be classified into two basic types:

1. A lease which passed most of the risks and rewards of ownership to the lessee. Such a lease would cover most of the life of the property leased or would have purchase or renewal options which the lessee would be likely to exercise; the residual value of the property, if any, at the probable termination of the lease would be low; the lessor would have little or no responsibility for services to the asset leased; and the lessee would have a reasonably secure credit standing. Under these conditions the rentals would usually be designed to assure recovery of the lessor's investment in his property and yield a reasonable interest return thereon. Consequently, the lease could be accounted for by the 'financing' method whereby rentals received would be divided into a portion representing interest on the investment and a portion representing return of capital. When rentals are level the interest portion of successive rental payments would decline and the principal recovery portion would rise as the balance of unrecovered investment declined, just as would be the case in accounting for a mortgage or limited term annuity receivable.

2. Other leases under which the usual risks and rewards of ownership were retained. These leases would usually be for a shorter term than the economic life of the asset, might involve responsibility for maintaining the property or render-

ing related services, and sometimes might be tied in with other business operations of the lessor. In such cases, the 'operating method' of accounting would be followed under which rentals would be treated as earned revenue as they accrued (except in rare cases where the rentals departed from the straight-line basis without relation to the economic usefulness of the property leased) while costs of operation and depreciation would be absorbed according to conventional accounting methods for such costs.

Opinion No. 7 went on to say in essence that where a manufacturer (or a middle-man under certain conditions) entered into a lease of a product on terms which would qualify the lease for the use of the financing method under the above criteria, the manufacturer could regard the lease transaction as being tantamount to a sale, and report a manufacturing profit at that time. The figure to be used in recording the notional sale transaction would be the lower of the amount which would have been realized in a regular sale or the value of future rentals discounted at market rates.

It has been suggested that Opinion No. 7 presented more reasonable criteria for determining whether a lease was in substance a purchase of an asset than did the 'material equity' test in APB Opinion No. 5, and consequently a lease which qualified for use of the financing method of accounting by the lessor should be capitalized in the accounts of the lessee. On the other hand, some difficulties have been encountered in interpretation of the criteria in practice, particularly with respect to the question whether certain manufacturers are entitled to record a manufacturing profit upon leasing their equipment.

No Canadian statement has been issued on the subject of accounting for lessors. In some cases at least U.S. precedents have been followed, but it may be that some companies that should use the financing method under the guidelines of APB Opinion No. 7 continue to use the operating method.

Pension cost accounting

Forty or fifty years ago many employers did not pay pensions to retired employees. Moreover, most of those that did pay pensions did so ex gratia, making individual decisions with respect to amounts to be paid to individual employees and making no promises that amounts would be continued throughout the employee's retirement regardless of the employer's business fortunes. Only a minority of employers had pension *policies* whereby amounts determined by stated formulae were payable to all employees (or all employees in defined categories) and even in such cases the pension policy was virtually always stated to represent an intention only, and not a firm legally binding commitment. Given this view of pension payments as voluntary in nature, it was natural that accounting recognition of pension transactions was limited to recording pension cost only as cash was paid out.

As the social environment changed however, the concept of pension obligations changed. Concern for income after retirement became part of the general concern for social security that developed just before and during World War II. After the war, more and more employers adopted pension plans and the existence of adequate pension benefits became a factor in attracting and retaining good employees. Thus, gradually, pension benefits became part of the compensation package and in the case of organized workers became one of the subjects of bargaining between employers and unions. Sometimes as a result of this bargaining, and sometimes as a result of the desire to increase the assurance that benefits would be available under the pension plan when needed, employers began to set aside sums to pay for promised future benefits in trust funds or by buying insured annuities. Thus, even though accounting for pension transactions continued to reflect only related cash receipts and payments, this type of advance funding tended to move cost recognition closer to the time when compensable service was rendered by employees.

The discrepancy between the results of accounting for pension costs on a pay-as-you-go basis and accounting for recognition of costs associated with advance funding hastened reconsideration of the nature of pension costs. Further impetus to reconsideration was given by cases where employers varied their contributions to pension funds from year to year in order to affect cost and income reporting. A consensus gradually developed to the effect that pension contributions were not a voluntary outlay but rather a regular cost of doing business. Notwithstanding any legal right of the employer to discontinue the plan and limit his liability, as a practical matter an employer who wished to continue in business could not withdraw benefits once they were granted. It followed that pension costs were part of the costs of earning annual income whether or not cash was paid over to the pension plan in the year and irrespective of the amount of such payment. This then raised the question how the cost was to be measured and led to the realization that a pension plan arrangement constitutes a particularly complex form of delayed payment transaction.*

The first authoritative statement on pension cost accounting was Accounting Research Bulletin No. 36 issued by the AICPA Committee on Accounting Procedure in November 1948. This was followed by Accounting Research Bulletin No. 47 in September 1956, Accounting Research Study No. 8 in 1965 and Accounting Principles Board Opinion No. 8 in November 1966. The CICA Research Committee published a Research Study on the subject in October 1963 which was followed by authoritative recommendations in Bulletin No. 21 issued in August 1965 (now Section 3460 of the CICA Research Recommendations). In general, the U.S. studies were more exhaustive and more detailed in their recommendations. These studies and statements had to deal with the following problems of pension transaction accounting:

1. What method should be used to estimate future pension costs?

2. How should such costs be allocated to years of service of the employee group?

3. Since any measurement method must be based on estimates that require revision from time to time, how should such revisions be handled?

4. When a pension plan is introduced or benefits are improved:

   (a) What immediate recognition should be given in the accounts to the 'past

---

* The following discussion does not relate to pension plans of the type where a defined contribution is made to the plan by the employer (and perhaps the employees also) each year, and the pension benefits depend entirely on the amounts which such contributions will accumulate to by the time pensions become payable. The cost under such plans is a known amount and does not give rise to accounting problems.

service' obligation incurred with respect to benefits under a new plan or the 'prior service' obligation incurred with respect to improved benefits?

(b) To what period or periods should the cost of such benefits be assigned?

(c) On what pattern should such costs be absorbed when amortized over a period of years?

Estimation of costs of providing future pension benefits

Only in rare cases can the cost of providing future pensions be known with certainty. If the future benefit payable in respect of each year of service is completely defined, if the employer buys a deferred annuity to yield that benefit in the year it is earned, and if title to the annuity vests absolutely in the employee immediately, then the pension cost for each year attributable to each employee can be known with certainty. But all these features are found only infrequently in pension plans. The following factors contribute to uncertainty in measuring the amount of pension costs:

(a) The benefit payable under the plan may be defined in terms of factors which are not known with certainty at the time the employee renders his service. For example, the pension entitlement for each year worked might be stated to be 2% of the average earnings of the employee in his last five years before retirement. The ultimate obligation will then be affected by the way in which earnings levels change between the year of service and the employee's final five years of employment.

(b) The plan may not provide a value to the estate of an employee who dies which is equivalent to the commuted value of the annuity he would have received had he lived to retirement. Accordingly, the number of deaths of employees before retirement may affect the amounts paid under the pension plan obligation.

(c) Pension entitlements may not vest in the employee until after a further period of service. Costs will therefore be affected by the number of employee terminations before full vesting has occurred.

(d) Pension benefits ultimately will be provided partly by the contributions of the employer and employee and partly by earnings of the pension fund. Thus, an estimate of future return on investment is necessary to know the amount of contributions required and the real cost of providing the pension benefits. Even in the case where an employer does not fund his contributions the true pension cost should be valued on a discounted basis since the benefits will not be paid until the future. This requires the assumption of a reasonable rate of interest to discount the liability. (In the former case however, the interest assumed should be the best estimate of the earnings rate of the pension fund. In the latter case, it is arguable that the interest factor assumed should represent the cost of capital to the employer since he is in effect holding back on funding his pension obligation to save raising capital in other ways – but there is no authoritative guidance on this subject.)

The existence of these uncertainties means that estimates must be made which are recognized as being actuarial in character for the most part. Paragraph 3460.08 of the CICA Research Recommendations says "While an actuary is required to make the calculations, the accountant should satisfy himself that such calculations are made by the actuary on a basis that will provide for the accrual of pension costs over the working lives of the employees to whom the pensions will be payable, that the basis selected is applied consistently, and that the assumptions on which the computations are based are realistic." It is doubtful that the latter part of this recommendation is of much practical effect. For example, pension cost calculations are frequently made today using an interest factor in the range of 3½% to 5% which is a rate substantially below that at which insurance companies will guarantee annuities for periods of fifteen years or so and therefore presumably well below that which should be earned by a well managed fund. Unless large sums are already locked into the pension fund earning a low rate of interest, or unless the understatement of interest cost is intended to compensate for possible under-estimation of the effects of inflation on pension benefits (see further comment below), the use of such a low rate of interest has the effect of overstating pension costs until actual interest earnings of the fund begin to be reflected in adjustments to pension costs.

Allocation of estimated costs to accounting periods

A considerable number of actuarial methods exist for allocating pension plan costs to particular periods. It should be appreciated that these methods were originally developed by the actuarial profession for the purpose of providing alternative patterns for payment of contributions required to fund a pension plan. Factors that would influence the choice of a funding method include:
- the degree of assurance required that funds will be available to honor the pension obligations to all employees,
- the degree of risk that the employer might not be able to make good on his pension undertakings (because of the volatile nature of the industry, etc.),
- the ability of the employer to set aside funds in advance,
- the desirability of keeping the pension funding requirements fairly constant in relation to payroll costs.

Such factors as these do not directly reflect the accounting objective of providing a means of measuring that portion of the cost of providing pension benefits that properly relates to the service of one employee, or a group of employees, for a year.

How such an objective should be implemented is not easily answered. Presumably in every case there is a cause and effect relationship between an employee's service and his pension, but it will depend on the pension formula how direct that relationship is. For example, suppose a company had a policy that all employees who were employed for at least twenty years would obtain a vested right to receive a pension of $100 a month at age sixty-five. For any given employee who started work, it would be impossible to know whether he would stay for twenty years and thus qualify for a pension and whether, if he did stay, for what period he would continue to work. Presumably any accrual of pension costs in such a case would have to be based on the expectation (1) as to what percentage of employees at each level would fulfill the twenty-year service requirement, and (2) how many further years each might expect to be employed. While this example would be an unusual formula, even the more common pension benefit formulae raise similar questions. For example, consider a plan that provides a pension benefit

of 2% of earnings for each year worked, subject to a maximum thirty years' service:
- Under such a plan an employee who works for 35 years would receive the same pension as an employee who starts 5 years later and works only 30 years at the same rate of pay. Should no cost be accrued for five years of the first employee's service (which years?) or is an average rate of accrual applicable? It would seem that an average would need to be struck, and since it cannot be known at the start of an individual employee's service how long he will work, the average should be based on expectations for the employee group as a whole.
- A promise to provide a benefit equal to 2% of each successive year's earnings will cost more with respect to an individual employee with every passing year, since the cost of purchasing a deferred annuity at a fixed age rises steadily as a person ages. If we are already thinking in terms of an average experience for the group however, can we think also in terms of an average cost (say cost per year, or per dollar of wages) to provide an employee's pension over his working career? In other words, can we relate the total pension benefit to career earnings by assuming a constant percentage of pension cost to payroll dollar for a given employee, year by year, rather than an increasing cost as he gets older?
- It is widely believed that interest rates at current levels (say 8 or 9%) reflect a 4 or 5% allowance to recompense borrowers for the effect of inflation on the purchasing power of the funds loaned, leaving only 3–5% as the true interest return. If this is accepted, is it appropriate to cost pension obligations assuming only a 3–5% return on pension contributions on the assumption that any excess returns on such contributions will be required to meet improvements in pension obligations made necessary by the inflation? If so pension cost figures, in effect, will be building in an allowance for future improvements in the benefits.*

Such questions as these, as they relate to accounting for pension costs, do not seem to have been thoroughly discussed and resolved.

In part, the answer to such questions may depend on the view taken of the nature and purpose of a pension plan. One view regards a pension plan fairly narrowly as an arrangement to provide specific benefits to specific employees who are members of the plan. The cost, therefore, must be closely related to service performed by those employees. At the other extreme a pension plan may be viewed as a means of satisfying the needs for security of the employee group as a whole and encouraging its efficiency. On this view, the provision made for pension cost should ensure that funds will be available to meet pension obligations as they occur, but need not relate closely to what would be the actual cost of buying annuities for specific employees. In particular, it is sometimes argued that past or prior service obligations need not be provided for, so long as interest on such unfunded obligations is paid to prevent the obligation from growing. This is on the basis that so long as the employer continues in business, contributions to fund the current costs accruing, plus interest on the past service cost, are likely to be sufficient to meet all benefits required to be paid.

---

* Frequently where benefits under a plan are based on 'final earnings' a reduction in the interest assumption to eliminate the effect of inflation is used to eliminate the necessity to estimate the increase in final earnings from the same cause. On the other hand, if a plan is of the 'career average earnings' type a reduction in the interest assumption because of inflation would mean that the actuary was assuming that benefits would be improved in future and providing for it currently.

In practice, different forms of actuarial calculations produce different results for a number of reasons:

1. One very important difference concerns the way in which benefits and costs are related. One actuarial cost method (the 'accrued benefit cost' method or 'unit credit' method) is based on measuring the cost to fund the future benefits actually earned by the employees for services rendered in each year. Thus, with respect to an individual employee the cost figure derived increases each year.[*] Other actuarial cost methods look not just to the benefits earned in the particular year but rather to the projected total pension benefits for the employee or the employee group, and relate that total amount to the total years of service, or total earnings involved, over the working lifetime of the employees, thereby developing an average level premium contribution required over the working period. The concept is rather similar to the level premium which is calculated for a whole life insurance policy as contrasted with the increasing premium (commencing at a lower figure and ending higher) which would be charged for the same amount of insurance under a yearly renewable term plan. Such actuarial methods based on projected benefits include the 'individual level premium' method, the 'entry age normal' method, the 'aggregate' method and the 'attained age normal' method. (This list is not exhaustive; other methods or variations of methods exist.)

2. The treatment and calculation of past service or prior service cost also depends on the actuarial cost method selected and possibly, also, the method of funding.
   (a) Under some methods as usually applied (the individual level premium method, and the aggregate method) no separate calculation of the amount of past service or prior service is made, and the cost of such is automatically included in the method's determination of annual cost.
   (b) Where past service is calculated separately, the 'entry age normal' method differs from other methods in its basis of calculation of the amount of past service or prior service cost. Under most methods past service cost is calculated as the present value of future benefits credited to employees on account of service prior to the introduction or improvement of the plan. Under the entry age normal method, past service is calculated as the amount which would have been in the pension fund, had the new plan always been in effect and contributions been made on the entry age normal basis from the date of first employment or participation in the plan of the participants. Since the entry age normal method provides for level rates of contribution over an employee's working life, rather than contributions required to buy accrued benefits (which are lower in the early years of an employee's career and higher in the later years), this calculation results in a higher estimate of past service cost than do the other methods.
   (c) The method of funding also may affect the calculation of past service cost.

---

[*] For an employee group as a whole, the cost per dollar of payroll could remain constant if terminations of older employees compensated for increasing age of continuing employees and other cost inducing factors remained stable. In a growing group, however, the cost often tends to rise year by year because employee terminations are in the younger age group, while the remaining older employees become increasingly expensive each year.

If the plan is not insured, the past service cost will ordinarily be calculated allowing for the probability of some employee withdrawals before pension rights have vested. On the other hand if the plan is insured the insurer must calculate past service costs to cover all employees because employee terminations are (partially) under the control of the employer and thus are an uninsurable contingency. Any past service payments not required because of terminations are recovered by the employer after the event and are not reflected in his cost until that time.

3. Different methods vary in their treatment of surpluses or deficits calculated when the funds are valued (actuarial gains or losses). In some cases a revised contribution rate automatically spreads such gains over future years. In other cases the gains or losses may be reflected immediately as an adjustment of pension cost for the next succeeding year. In still other cases they may be rolled in to unfunded past service cost to be handled in the same way it is handled.

One might expect that when different methods of calculation produce different cost figures (especially in the simple case of calculations of past service cost) some extended consideration would have been given to the question of which method best meets the accounting objective of providing a rational matching of costs and benefits under the various types of plans that may be encountered.* The problem is, of course, a difficult one since the benefits from a pension plan are so intangible, and this may account for the failure to resolve the issue. It is now conceded that neither pay-as-you-go nor terminal funding (purchase of an annuity and recognition of cost at the date an employee retires) is an acceptable basis for pension cost recognition since neither recognizes any cost during the period when the employee is rendering service. Presumably, at the other extreme, recognition of the whole cost of providing a pension at the date an employee is hired would be equally unacceptable. But within these limits any systematic method that relates pension cost to an employee's (or group of employees') service period is accepted for accounting purposes.

Revisions of estimates (actuarial gains or losses)

After a period of time it will naturally be found that the actual experience under a pension plan will be different from the estimates on which previous pension costs were calculated. The earnings of pension fund assets will be different from those estimated, mortality and termination rates will differ from estimates, and so on. As a result, a valuation of the plan's obligations and assets will reveal surpluses or deficits. Where the plan is funded by deposits with trustees or by deposit administration arrangements with an insurance company such 'actuarial gains or losses' represent adjustments to be picked up in pension costs. (Where the pension benefits have been funded through insurance policies similar causes will be re-

---

* The problem is very like that of finding the 'best' depreciation pattern for various types of fixed assets – and like that problem it has not been authoritatively answered. Hicks in AICPA Accounting Research Study No. 8 expressed a preference for the 'entry age normal' method, on the pragmatic grounds that a method tending to produce level annual amounts of pension cost is desirable because of the long-range nature of pension commitments and the extent of the uncertainties involved in estimating pension costs.

flected in dividends received or surrender payments on individual policies, or experience rating refunds and termination credits on group policies.) In addition, from time to time it may be found desirable to change some of the actuarial assumptions for the future, which likewise will affect the apparent surplus or deficit shown upon revaluation of the plan. The question then arises as to how such gains or losses should be reflected in pension costs.

The Canadian recommendations are that adjustments brought about by an actuarial revaluation should be included in pension costs of the current period or allocated to operations over the period expected to elapse before the next revaluation. (At the time this recommendation was made revaluations were usually made at three to five-year intervals.) APB Opinion No. 8 contains more extensive discussion. The Opinion recommended that actuarial gains or losses should be recognized immediately if they arise from single occurrences not directly related to the operation of the pension plan and not in the ordinary course of the business. For example, if there were a plant closing the gain or loss in the pension plan attributable to resulting employee terminations should be treated as an adjustment of the net gain or loss from that occurrence. In other cases the Opinion recommended that actuarial gains or losses should be (1) spread over future years, (2) averaged by some method or (3) credited against past service so that they are reflected over its remaining amortization period, or through a reduction of future interest on such past service liability if it is not being amortized. In some cases (as indicated earlier) such spreading is automatically accomplished by the actuarial cost method followed. In still other cases the spreading would be accomplished by special adjustment to the normal pension cost as otherwise calculated. In the latter cases the Board recommended a period of from ten to twenty years for spreading.

Thus, there is some difference between the U.S. and Canadian recommendations on this point. The matter is complex and it does not seem that one simple rule is appropriate to all situations. The writer's views are:

1. He would agree with the U.S. position in favour of immediate recognition of the effect on pension cost of the unusual event not in the ordinary course of business. (Presumably such result would be classified as an 'extraordinary item', or be otherwise disclosed, in the income statement.)

2. The treatment of gains or losses resulting from differences between estimates and actual results might appropriately differ depending on their cause. For example:
   (a) If the gain or loss arose because of a difference between earned interest and interest assumed it would be reasonable to spread that gain or loss over a similar period to that in which it arose. That is to say, if the period between revaluations was three years the gain or loss would be amortized over three years.
   (b) On the other hand, if the gain or loss were attributable to such a factor as unusual mortality or terminations the adjustment might appropriately be spread over several years even though the period between revaluations was short. This is because one might expect to get wider deviations from estimates in a factor such as mortality over a shorter period than over a longer period. Thus if annual valuations are made and gains or losses are reflected immediately, the annual cost would fluctuate widely, whereas

if valuations were made, say, only at five year intervals, the differences between actual and expected mortality could be expected to largely cancel out over the period and little adjustment would be necessary from this cause.

3. Finally, the adjustment resulting from a change in the basic actuarial assumptions is of a different character altogether. It would seem much more reasonable to spread such an adjustment over a relatively lengthy arbitrary period – such as the ten to twenty year period recommended in APB Opinion No. 8.

As valuations are made currently there would be a practical problem in implementation of these suggestions because usually no separate calculation is made of the separate causes of actuarial gains or losses. With some additional work however, it should be possible for an actuary to estimate approximately the allocation of a net surplus or deficit to the various factors giving rise to it.

It may be noted that the amount of actuarial gains or losses at a valuation date is itself an estimate. One of the actuarial assumptions upon which cost estimates are based is that of an 'interest' return. In practice, if a pension fund is invested in assets that do not bear a fixed rate of interest (such as common stock), or if the fund is an active trader rather than following a 'buy and hold' investment policy, part of its return on investment will consist of gains or losses on its holdings. At any given valuation date there will be unrealized gains or losses on securities held, as well as realized gains or losses. The question is, how should the unrealized gains or losses be dealt with? On the one hand it may be argued that the investments could have been realized at the valuation date and therefore any unrealized gain or loss is properly counted as part of the investment return over the period since the last valuation date. On the other hand, it has to be recognized that the market for stocks (and to some degree for other forms of investment) fluctuates widely and it is not practical for a pension fund to operate so as to take advantage of the swings of the market, selling at the high point and reinvesting at the low. Hence it is to some degree unrealistic to measure return on investment by taking in unrealized gains or losses at any one point of time. Moreover, to do so would impart a volatility into figures for actuarial gains and losses, and consequently into the pension cost estimates that would be unrealistic in view of the long-run nature of pension obligations.

On the other hand, it would be equally unrealistic to ignore unrealized gains or losses completely, since over the long run some gain or loss on such forms of investment are the normal expectation. Consequently actuaries have developed various methods of giving partial recognition to unrealized appreciation or depreciation of investment holdings – including giving recognition to such gains or losses on a moving average basis, writing up investments on the basis of an assumption as to long-term yield that will be realized, and so on. Again no consensus has developed (nor may it be possible) as to the one best method.

Treatment of past service or prior service costs

When a pension plan is first introduced or benefits are improved, very frequently the employees are credited with some or all of their years of service before introduction or change of the plan as qualifying for the new benefits. The employer's assumption of an obligation for benefits related to past service or prior service raises three questions:

1. What immediate recognition should be given in the accounts to the past service obligation taken on?

2. To what accounting periods should such cost be charged?

3. On what basis or pattern should the costs be allocated to the appropriate periods?

As to the first of these questions, both the U.S. and Canadian recommendations take the position that recognition of the past service obligation in the accounts is only required as the cost becomes chargeable against income. Presumably the reasoning behind this conclusion is that although the past service obligation is a commitment that will result in payments in the future, it is not a legal liability and the commitment does not require recognition until the employees, in effect, earn their right to it as indicated by the time when the cost is recognized. The Canadian recommendation also makes an exception to this general rule by requiring that past service benefits that have vested in employees (i.e. to which they have received a right not contingent upon further service with the employer) but which have not been charged to operations, should receive recognition as a liability in the accounts offset by a deferred charge. Presumably it was thought that any obligation that is irrevocable should be recorded.*

At one time it was common for businesses to charge the amount of past service liabilities direct to the retained earnings account on the grounds that payments attributable to past service must represent adjustments of prior years' income. Today the accepted theory is that even though the past service obligation is calculated by reference to service rendered in previous years, the purpose of undertaking the obligation is to gain advantages for the employer in current and future years and any charge must accordingly be made to income of those years.

The Canadian recommendations say only that past service or prior service costs should be charged to operations "over a reasonable period of years". Under the pension legislation of some of the provinces, past service and prior service obligations are now required to be funded over a period not longer than 15 years, or 25 years from the date the legislation was introduced if that is longer. Although in theory the funding period should not govern the period over which the cost is written off for accounting purposes, in practice accounting does tend to follow the cash payment pattern.

The U.S. recommendations are somewhat different from the Canadian. APB Opinion No. 8 states that past service and prior service costs should not be amortized at a rate faster than 10% per annum. On the other hand, it is permissible to

---

* The merits of this treatment of vested benefits are extremely doubtful. The probable total obligation for past service payments is indicated by the total calculation of past service cost. If the business continues as a going concern it is the latter amount (modified by actuarial gains or losses) that will become payable. If it does not, in most cases the employees would not be able to recover even the vested obligation, because most pension plans are written so that the company's liability is limited to amounts funded. Thus, it is hard to see what value there is to information as to the amount of unfunded vested obligation.

make no amortization at all (merely providing for interest on the obligation to keep it from compounding) subject to a requirement that a provision for vested benefits must be made each year to the extent of the lesser of:

1. The amount required to reduce by 5% in the year the figure for the excess of the amount of vested benefits over:
   (a) the amount in the pension fund
       plus
   (b) the amount of any accruals for pension obligations in the balance sheet
       less
   (c) the amount of any prepayments or deferred charges with respect to pension obligations in the balance sheet.

2. The additional pension cost that would be required to amortize the past service obligation over a forty-year period.

Quite apart from the obvious artificiality of the U.S. guidelines a substantial question can be raised as to the practice in both countries. As indicated, amortization of past service obligation takes place over periods ranging from fifteen to forty years. Unless one accepts the theory that adoption or improvement of a pension plan produces an enduring benefit (which the writer does not) can such long amortization periods be justified? In some cases, for example, pension benefits may be the subject of union negotiations on a more or less regular basis. It may be questioned whether the benefits of improvements in plans so negotiated are felt for a period as long as fifteen to forty years but little evidence is available on this subject.

The common pattern by which the past service cost is amortized is also open to question. Usually the amount charged as past service cost is the level amount required to fund the liability over the period selected. Thus, at a 5% interest factor, the amount required to amortize a past service cost of $100,000 over 20 years would be $7,642 annually. But if the employer funded the $100,000 by an immediate payment, the level charge to amortize the $100,000 over twenty years would be only $5,000. Why the difference? It is obvious that in fact some of the so-called past service pension cost represents interest on the unfunded obligation, not a pension cost at all. Thus, the normal practice misclassifies part of the past service payment as an operating cost when it should be shown as a financial charge. (This fact would be more readily apparent if the past service obligation were actually recorded as a liability in the balance sheet.)

Moreover, since the annual amount paid is a constant amount, while the unfunded principal diminishes, it is clear that the interest portion of the payment is higher in the early years and declines constantly as the amortization period goes on. Consequently, the actual amortization of past service contained in the annual $7,642 charge against income must be lower in the earlier years and steadily increasing thereafter.* Can it be argued that the past service cost should be amortized in an increasing charge pattern? Surely, if anything, the benefit to an employer from a new or improved pension plan is greater in the years just after it is introduced and tails off subsequently. Or if we relate the past service cost directly to the

---

* In some cases, termination credits or actuarial gains or losses may have the effect of reducing the amounts charged against later years.

employees who are benefited by being credited with past service, and amortize it in proportion to the remaining years of service of such employees, again we would find a decreasing charge pattern.

Thus, it can be concluded that there are still many open questions in pension cost accounting, even though practice is much improved over what it was twenty-five years ago.

Deferred compensation arrangements

The CICA Research Recommendations state that "any formal arrangement for the deferred compensation of executives after retirement must be considered to be a pension plan" (paragraph 3460.02). While this statement is obviously correct in principle there are some practical differences between deferred compensation arrangements and pension plans which merit brief comment.

1. Deferred compensation arrangements frequently provide for executives to render consulting or other continuing services after retirement. Normally such services would not be extensive but, if they were, some part of the deferred compensation would be applicable to such services and need not be provided for during the active working period of the executive.

2. An individual employer would normally have deferred compensation arrangements with only a few executives and the terms of such arrangements might well vary from one individual to another. Consequently, there is not a large enough group to make valid actuarial assumptions about probable mortality or terminations affecting the deferred compensation liability. The accrual for such costs, therefore, must be made on some reasonable basis separately for each individual employee – perhaps on the basis of the premium that would be payable for an annuity that would yield the stated amount of post-retirement income to the executive.

3. If the employer does not in fact buy an annuity to fund the deferred compensation arrangement he would have to accrue interest in addition to the basic amount provided annually.

4. So long as the deferred compensation involves a life contingency, presumably a cost accrued but not funded will usually prove to be more or less than is required depending on the actual date of death of the executive and any dependents covered. The resulting gain or loss is similar in origin to actuarial gains or losses under a pension plan, but in principle should not be averaged and spread over future years since in the absence of a large group covered by the arrangements it cannot be assumed that gains on one individual will be offset by losses on another. In practice, there might be justification for deferring recognition of, or spreading, a gain if other executives look like they might outlive the provision made for the obligation to them.

Stock options

An interesting theoretical question in cost determination arises when companies grant options to executives or others to buy stock in the company at stated prices for a limited period of years. Usually such optioned shares are issuable out of the company treasury. The company could, however, buy some of its own shares on the market to hold against the possible exercise of the option (if not prohibited under the applicable corporations act) and the accounting problems would be the same. The questions that arise are – is there a cost associated with stock option arrangements; if so, how should it be measured and how should it be charged off against income?

In Canada these problems have been almost universally ignored. The customary practice is not to make an entry in the accounts when an option is granted. If subsequently the option is exercised cash received will be recorded on exactly the same basis as cash received on any other issue of shares. Disclosure, however, is usually made of details of commitments under share options granted but not exercised, in accordance with CICA Recommendations (par. 3240.03), as follows: "Number of shares reserved to meet rights outstanding under conversion or share option privileges, the prices at which such rights are exercisable and the dates of expiry."

In the United States stock option plans seem to be more widespread than in Canada and on average somewhat more complicated, and more consideration has been given to associated accounting problems. There, stock option arrangements have been recognized as clearly a form of compensation. The primary accounting problems have been how to measure the amount of compensation or its cost to the corporation, when to recognize the option obligation in the accounts, and finally over what period to write off the compensation expense.

In Accounting Research Bulletin No. 37 issued in 1948 it was recommended that the value of the option given and hence the measure of the total compensation cost should be considered to be the excess of the market value of the shares over the option exercise price at the date that the employee acquired irrevocable property rights in the option (even though there might be a further waiting period before it could be exercised). Subsequently, in 1953 the recognition and measurement date was moved ahead to the date of the grant of option. At this time and until quite recently it was usually advantageous under tax rules to set the exercise price very little below the market value of the stock at the date of grant. Consequently, the 1953 decision yielded the anomalous result that effectively very little compensation expense was recognized in connection with option arrangements designed primarily as compensation schemes.

In the last two or three years, the apparent anomalies have become more acute. Changes in U.S. tax legislation have made qualified stock option plans less attractive and as a result a wide variety of plans have been entered into. Under some of these an employee or employer may have a choice as to whether to take down stock or receive cash payments measured by the increase in the value of the stock over the option period. In such cases, the fact that there appears to be a higher cost if the cash alternative is taken than if the stock alternative is taken casts doubt on the whole basis of accounting for stock options. It appears that reconsideration of the whole area of stock option accounting will be necessary to resolve such questions as these.

Non-arm's-length transactions

A final problem in an accounting theory oriented to the recognition, measurement and allocation of transactions, is what to do about non-arm's-length transactions.

(The term 'non-arm's-length' is used here loosely to refer to any transactions which are not arrived at by a process of bargaining between completely independent parties.) As has been noted already, the abandonment of the valuation approach to accounting was brought about largely by the practical difficulties associated with obtaining objectively verifiable values; and the resort to the transaction allocation approach was largely justified by the assumption that completed transactions would automatically represent fair value because of the process of bargaining between parties.

But this assumption is just not true for a very large number of transactions that have to be recorded. Consider for example the following situations:

1. In an unincorporated business the owner charges only a nominal salary for his full-time services.

2. In a one-man corporation the owner takes his earnings from the business in a combination of forms, through salary, dividends and other distributions, with the purpose of minimizing the combined tax bill of the company and himself, and not to reflect a reasonable salary cost for his services.

3. Managers or directors engage in transactions with the company which may be difficult to evaluate.

4. Transactions between companies in an affiliated group may depart from a normal business basis:

   (a) Product transfer prices may not be fairly established to reflect the underlying economics.

   (b) Administrative, advertising and research services may be furnished by the parent company without adequate recompense or alternatively excessive charges may be made.

   (c) A related company may finance receivables on favourable terms for a parent company.

   (d) A parent company may guarantee debt thus permitting favourable interest costs to a subsidiary.

   (e) The parent company may lease property to a subsidiary on favourable terms.

In such situations as these, can it be said that income of the entities affected is fairly presented? Or is their financial position fairly presented if the amounts at which their assets are carried have been affected by such arranged transactions? For the parent company of a group of companies, the solution to this problem is frequently to present its financial statements in consolidated form, which makes provision for elimination of the effects of transactions between companies in the group. In effect, the accounting entity for reporting purposes is taken as the group and not the individual company. This does not, however, solve the problem of the individual subsidiary company which must also present accounts to fulfill the requirements of company law. Such accounts have validity for certain purposes – e.g. they serve as a basis for computation of income tax, but they do not necessarily show income or financial position fairly.

Accounting literature has not dealt extensively with the problems of fair presentation of the operations of an accounting entity that is materially affected by transactions not at arm's length. Insofar as it has, however, the emphasis appears to be on special disclosure in the statements of the matters affected by non-arm's-length relationships. For example, the CICA Research Recommendations call for special disclosure of:

- significant holdings of securities issued by affiliated companies included in temporary investments,
- long-term investments in subsidiaries and in other affiliates,
- amounts due from subsidiary companies and from other affiliates, and amounts owing to them,
- the amount of any loans made by a company or its subsidiary during the year, other than in the ordinary course of business, to the directors or officers,
- full description of the basis of valuation of intangible assets acquired other than through payment of cash,
- income from investments in non-consolidated subsidiary and affiliated companies,
- the amount of any increase or decrease in the parent company's equity in non-consolidated subsidiary companies, since acquisition and for the year under review,
- the aggregate of shares and of any other securities of the parent company held by non-consolidated subsidiaries.

The Committee has also been concerned with the limitations of financial statements of unincorporated business. Among its recommendations are:
- that the financial statements indicate clearly the name under which the business is conducted;
- that it be made evident that the business is unincorporated and that the statements do not include all the assets, liabilities, revenues and expenses of the owners;
- that any salaries, interest or similar items accruing to owners be clearly indicated showing such items separately either in the body of the income statement or in a note. If no such charges are made in the accounts, this fact should be disclosed.

Such recommendations are useful but it may nevertheless be questioned whether they are sufficiently comprehensive. The existence of non-arm's-length transactions affecting an accounting entity is always a significant fact in the appraisal of its financial statements. The significance of the existence of such transactions, however, is not easy to convey since it is usually impossible to judge what would have been the position if the non-arm's-length relationship had not existed. It is not just that the prices at which some transactions were consummated might have been different – perhaps the transactions would not have taken place at all.

While it is thus not easy to prescribe precisely what steps should be taken to deal with the problem it would seem that financial statements prepared for public distribution should contain:

1. A description of the basis of major business transactions with affiliates and other persons with whom the entity does not deal at arm's length.

2. Disclosure of the amounts of revenues and costs arising from transactions with affiliates or such other persons during the year.

On the other hand, where financial statements are not intended for general public distribution, it would seem sufficient to indicate that the statements are affected (to a greater or lesser degree) by transactions carried on with parties in a position to influence the results.

Principles of Accounting for Pension and Deferred Compensation Costs

In the absence of authoritative statements and development of practice in Canada in the fields of lease, stock options and non-arm's-length transactions it cannot be said that there are special principles applicable in these areas other than rules governing disclosure (which are summarized in Chapter 20).

The following principles, however, are applicable to accounting for pension or deferred compensation costs:

1. Where an employer has adopted a pension plan or entered into deferred compensation arrangements, the cost of such obligation should be recognized over the working life of the employees covered.

2. When the current cost of future benefits must be estimated (usually by actuarial calculations):
   (a) the underlying assumptions as to future interest, mortality, terminations, etc., should be realistic,
   (b) the actuarial method used to estimate cost should be applied consistently, and
   (c) adjustments consequent upon revisions in estimates from time to time should be included in pension costs of the current year or spread over a reasonable number of years (such as the period elapsing until the next revaluation) as seems appropriate in the circumstances.

3. Past service costs or prior service costs arising from introduction of a plan or improvement in its benefits should not be charged against earnings of prior years. The cost should be charged against income over a reasonable period of future years which need not coincide with the period over which such cost is funded.

13 Income taxes and income tax allocation

Taxation is a prominent feature of all countries with advanced technologies. In part this reflects the very great need that highly developed economies have for 'social capital' (schools, roads, bridges, airports, etc.). In part also, it reflects the welfare measures common to such communities.

The expansion in the role of government spending is comparatively recent. In 1926, for example, taxes taken by all levels of government in Canada amounted to only 13.9% of the gross national product. In 1970, it had reached 31.4%.[1]

Taxation may take several forms, and different countries place differing emphases on various types of tax. In Canada, the major forms of taxation are indicated by the following table showing tax revenues derived in 1968/69 by all levels of government[2]:

	(Millions)
Personal income tax	$6,099
Corporation income tax	2,873
General and other sales taxes	3,752
Real and personal property taxes	2,531
Customs and excise duties and taxes	1,646

These taxes may enter into the accounts of business and other enterprises in various ways:

- Personal income tax does not affect the accounts, except to the extent that businesses have to act as agents for government in withholding and remitting.
- Similarly, retail sales taxes do not affect the accounts except to the extent that business acts as a collector.
- The manufacturers' sales tax is generally treated in a similar manner to the retail sales tax, although in certain cases there may be a question whether it represents merely an add-on to selling price, or a cost of doing business.
- Real property and business taxes represent costs to an enterprise which will be accounted for through its normal cost allocation procedures, just like other costs such as light, heat and power.
- Customs duties form part of the cost of goods acquired and are accounted for accordingly.

Accounting problems associated with the foregoing are minor. The same cannot be said of the corporation income tax, and the remainder of this Chapter will be devoted to problems connected with it. The history of the treatment of corporate income taxes in the accounts is, incidentally, a good example of the way in which accounting principles develop to meet changing circumstances.

The nature of corporation income tax

To begin with, some disagreement exists as to the nature of corporate income tax. The majority view is that income tax is a cost necessarily associated with the earning of income. An accounting objective is to show the net income attributable to the equity ownership in the corporation and, to do this, applicable income taxes must first be accounted for and deducted.

There are some, however, who hold that income tax more properly represents a distribution of corporation income after it is earned, rather than a cost of earning income. They point out qualities that differentiate income tax from other costs. For example, the corporation receives directly no tangible goods or services as a result of the payment of tax. The cost may or may not be incurred, depending on whether profits are earned; indeed, there may be a negative cost in unprofitable years as a result of loss carry-backs or carry-forwards. The essential difference perhaps may be summed up by saying that most costs are incurred for the purpose of earning revenue, but income tax is incurred because revenue has been earned. In other words, the 'cause and effect' relationship between costs and revenues is reversed in the case of income tax.

It will be observed that whether income tax is defined as a cost or as a distribution of income rests upon the concept of the accounting entity. (See discussion in Appendix A.) If the entity is conceived of as the corporation itself, then income taxes represent a distribution, albeit a forced distribution, of its income. On the other hand, if the accounting entity assumed is the proprietary interest in the corporation, income taxes are a kind of cost – i.e. something that must be provided for before net income for the shareholders can be determined.

It has been argued that if income tax is not a cost, cost allocation procedures are inappropriate and the controversy over income tax allocation is unnecessary. By this reasoning the income tax distribution in a year is simply the amount required in accordance with the law for that year. This conclusion, however, does not stand up under examination.

If one were following through the accounting using the 'separate enterprise' concept of the entity in a logical manner, one would be almost certain to find that the financial statements included in some form information about the distribution of the corporation income. For example, the statements might take the form:

Statement of income	
Revenues earned	$10,000,000
Costs of operation, including materials, wages, services, supplies and salaries	9,000,000
Net income from operations	$ 1,000,000

Statement of distribution of income

Interest on debt capital	$ 120,000
Income taxes	440,000
Preference share dividends	70,000
Residual share of income for common shareholders	370,000
	$ 1,000,000

In this illustration, it would be necessary to consider whether the income taxes reported in the distribution statement were applicable to the net income reported in the income statement. If the income tax were not fairly stated in relation to the reported income the residual income for common shareholders would be mis-stated as well, since income tax ranks prior to the equity interest as a claim upon income.

In practice, as has been stated earlier, accounting principles generally are based on the proprietary view of the accounting entity. It may be concluded, however, that whatever the view of the accounting entity the problem of income tax alloca-tion remains in some form.

History of the development of income tax allocation procedures

The proper treatment of income taxes was not a problem that concerned account-ants greatly prior to 1940. For this, two causes may be discerned. In the first place, by today's standards income tax rates were relatively modest. In the second place, the differences between accounting income and taxable income were probably less important then than they are today. As a result, the normal procedure was to provide in the accounts merely the amount of the income tax liability expected to be assessed in respect of the year.

With the onset of the Second World War income tax rates rose steeply, and a meaningful presentation of income taxes became more important. In December, 1944, the AICPA Committee on Accounting Procedure issued Bulletin No. 23 dealing with two kinds of income tax allocation:

1. Allocation of income tax between surplus and income accounts when material taxable items were credited or debited to surplus account rather than being shown in the income account (intra-period allocation).
2. Allocation of the charge or credit for income tax expense where material items were recognized for tax purposes in years different from those in which they were recognized in the determination of accounting income (inter-period allo-cation). The scope of Bulletin No. 23 was specifically restricted however to cases where differences between the tax return and the income statement did not recur regularly over a long period of time.

Bulletin No. 23 pointed out that if all items affecting taxable income were also reflected in the income statement, each item of gain would be accompanied by the related tax cost and only the net gain would appear in the reported net income after tax. Conversely, each taxable loss would carry through as a net loss in the reported income. If, however, an item of taxable gain or loss were excluded from the determination of reported income, but the reported tax for the year remained unchanged at the figure of actual tax payable, the reported income after tax would be reduced or increased by the tax effect. In other words, the effect of a taxable gain would be to reduce reported income, and of a taxable loss would be to increase reported income.

To cure this problem in cases where gains or losses were credited or debited to surplus account rather than the income statement, the Committee recommended that the related tax cost or reduction should also be debited or credited to surplus, with appropriate disclosure. This simple solution of intra-period allocation of income tax was obviously sensible and has been generally adopted over the years.

The Bulletin was less clear-cut in connection with items of revenue or expense that were taxed in a period different from that in which they entered into the determination of accounting income. Generally it suggested what has come to be known as 'net-of-tax' accounting. For example, if a cost deferred to future periods were claimable currently for tax purposes, an amount equal to the tax reduction from this claim would be charged against the income account and credited against the cost carried forward as an asset. In subsequent years, then, only the net amount of the deferred cost had to be absorbed in determining accounting income. The Bulletin, however, did not insist on net-of-tax accounting. It stated:

> "Where the treatments recommended above are considered to be not practicable, the amount of taxes estimated to be actually payable for the year may be shown in the income statement, provided that the pertinent facts, including the amount of the increase or decrease attributable to other accounts, are clearly disclosed either in a footnote or in the body of the income statement."

The Bulletin also stated:

> "Neither allocation nor disclosure is necessary, however, in the case of differences between the tax return and the income statement where there is a presumption that they will recur regularly over a comparatively long period of time."

These exceptions tended to create difficulties in practice. In what circumstances, for example, should the recommended treatment be considered to be "not practicable"? What is a "comparatively long period of time" and how reliable is the accountant's ability to forecast that differences between the tax return and the income statement will recur regularly over such a period?

The problem of depreciation and tax allowances for depreciation

The problem of long-run differences between taxable and accounting income became urgent about the same time in Canada and the United States, and in connection with the same subject – namely differences between depreciation allowed for tax purposes and depreciation charged in the determination of accounting income.

The U.S. Internal Revenue Act of 1954 granted permission for the use of declining balance and similarly accelerated depreciation patterns for Federal income tax purposes, as well as the previously recognized straight-line method. The effect of this change was to allow higher depreciation write-offs against taxable income in the early years of an asset's life than had previously been the case. In some cases companies changed their depreciation accounting patterns to conform to the accelerated methods now available for tax purposes. In others, no change was made in the books but advantage of the accelerated depreciation was taken in filing the tax return and, as a result, the tax payable for the fiscal year was based on taxable income different, at least to this extent, from reported accounting income.

The Canadian Income Tax Act had prescribed the use of diminishing balance methods to control the amount of 'capital cost allowances' in 1949 – five years before the change in the American Code. The problem of differences between accounting and taxable income, however, did not arise immediately because of a regulation that an amount equal to depreciation claimed for income tax purposes must also have been written on the books. This regulation was withdrawn effective in 1954, so that the problem of differences between accounting depreciation and tax allowances for depreciation arose at about the same time in Canada as in the United States. The problem was much more acute in Canada because (1) the new form of allowances was applicable to all assets, not just to assets acquired after the date of change, as in the United States, and (2) tax allowances were available on assets from the date title was acquired, not just when assets were first put into service, as in the U.S.A.; thus potential differences between capital cost allowances and depreciation were much larger in Canada.

The acceleration of depreciation allowable for tax purposes in most cases had the immediate effect of reducing taxes payable below their previous level. Since the total amount claimable for tax purposes was not increased, however, it was to be presumed that the tax reductions obtained in the earlier years of any asset's life would be offset by lower tax allowances in the later years. If, notwithstanding, the tax provision in the accounts were based on taxes actually payable for the year, the whole tax reduction obtained from the accelerated depreciation charge would 'flow through' as an increase in the net income after tax, and no allowance would be made in recognition of the heavier taxes that would result in later years.

Faced with this situation, in September 1954 the CICA Research Committee issued its Bulletin No. 10 on Depreciation, Capital Cost Allowances and Income Taxes. The Committee concluded that income taxes in Canada were of such a character that in appropriate circumstances they might properly be allocated between accounting periods. In the case at hand, they felt that the principle of matching costs and revenues would logically suggest that the reduction in income taxes arising from claiming additional capital cost allowances (i.e. amounts in excess of the depreciation recorded in the accounts) should be treated as applicable to those future years in which the corresponding depreciation provisions would be recorded in the accounts, rather than flowing through to income of the year in which the taxes were reduced. They therefore recommended that the reduction in income taxes resulting from excess capital cost allowance claims should not be brought into income of the year but rather should be carried in the balance sheet as a deferred credit, to be brought back into the income computation in some future year when tax depreciation was less than capital cost allowances. In view of the possibility of divergent opinions and the lack of development in practice however, the Committee did not go so far as to state that the 'taxes payable' method, with suitable disclosure, was unacceptable.

In October 1954, the AICPA Committee on Accounting Procedure issued Bulletin No. 44 dealing with the same general subject. In its opinion, the Committee distinguished between tax postponements which were expected to be short-lived, and postponements that might last for a relatively long time. It felt that ordinarily deferred taxes need be provided only with respect to the short-lived postponement. Subsequently, however, in July of 1958 the Committee issued a revised version of Bulletin No. 44 in which it reversed this position. The Committee stated that since the issuance of the original Bulletin studies of published reports and other source material had indicated that, where material amounts were involved, recognition of deferred income taxes in the general accounts was needed to obtain an equitable matching of costs and revenues and avoid income distortion. Alternatively, if the accumulated difference between taxable income and accounting income seemed likely to persist for a long period, additional depreciation might be written to recognize the loss of future deductibility. (In effect, this was the net-of-tax accounting method.)

While a majority of companies in both countries accepted these authoritative recommendations, a sizeable minority did not. As time passed, this disparity in practice on a relatively clear-cut issue became less and less tolerable, since income reported could differ widely depending on the method selected, and the existence of the discrepancy (which was emphasized by the disclosure usually given to the effect of the choice) cast doubt on the whole structure of accounting principles. Accordingly the CICA Research Committee in September 1967, and the AICPA Accounting Principles Board in December 1967, issued new statements dealing in a comprehensive fashion with the accounting problems caused by differences in timing between the recognition of revenues and costs for taxation purposes and for financial reporting purposes.* The Institute of Chartered Accountants in England and Wales also updated its recommendations in July 1968. As a result of the issuance of these statements, variations in methods of accounting for income taxes were largely eliminated. (Exceptions were the oil industry in Canada, which in large measure did not accept the recommended treatment, and certain specialized industry situations in the United States which were not covered by APB Opinion No. 11.)

The statements clarified the following matters:

1. The distinction between 'permanent' differences between taxable and accounting income, and 'timing' differences;

2. The concept of comprehensive tax allocation;

3. The appropriate treatment to be given in the balance sheet to debits or credits arising from differences between tax expense as charged against income for the year, and the amount of tax actually payable with respect to that year's taxable income;

4. The treatment of credits arising from tax loss carry-backs and carry-forwards.

---

* A somewhat related problem, namely how to account for government incentives given in the form of tax reductions, tax holidays or credits against tax, was not dealt with in these bulletins. The treatment of the 'incentive tax credit' was a matter of considerable controversy in the United States (see APB Opinion Nos. 2 and 4) which was not resolved. Similar problems exist, or have existed, in Canada (e.g. the 'tax holidays' granted new industry in depressed areas as alternatives to outright cash grants, and the recent provisions for 115% capital cost allowances by the Federal government and 5% tax credits on purchase of capital assets by the Ontario government) but have not aroused much discussion. Normal practice is to reflect in income any tax reduction not related to timing differences, as it occurs.

Differences between taxable income and accounting income

The statements pointed out that there were two types of differences between income reported for accounting purposes for a year and taxable income for a year. On the one hand certain gains, losses, revenues or expenses may be included in accounting income, but may not be subject to tax or allowable for tax. For example (as of 1971 before the 'tax reform' amendments), dividends received from taxable Canadian corporations are not taxable to another corporation, amortization of goodwill is not an allowable deduction and capital gains and losses are not taxed or deductible. On the other hand, other differences between accounting income and taxable income merely represent differences in the timing of recognition of costs and revenues under the two systems. That is to say, an item of revenue (say proceeds on an instalment sale) may be regarded as earned in one period for accounting purposes, but be subject to tax in another period. Similarly a cost (say cost of future warranty service) may be expensed in one period for accounting purposes but be allowed for tax in another period.

Differences between taxable income and accounting income of the former type are known as 'permanent' differences. That is to say, the transaction as recorded in one period has no tax effect in that or any other period. Consequently it is agreed that the figure for income tax charged against income in the period or any other period should be unaffected by the transaction. It may be, however, that the distortion of the normal relationship between income before tax shown in the accounts and the amount of tax expense is such that attention should be called in the financial statements to the existence of the permanent differences.

The other type of difference between taxable and accounting income is known as a 'timing' difference. The bulletins concluded that to avoid distortion in figures for reported net income, the tax effects of timing differences should be reflected in the income account of the period in which the associated revenues, expenses, gains or losses were recognized for accounting purposes, regardless of the period in which actual taxes payable were increased or reduced by such items. The reasoning underlying this 'tax allocation' approach is set out below.

The concept of comprehensive tax allocation

The fundamental objective of income accounting is to show the consequences of income-earning activities and other events giving rise to gain or loss that are attributable to the period.

Because we live in a world of uncertainty all we can hope to show is the probable effect. We cannot be sure we are right. But this has long been accepted in accounting. Accounting statements depart from certainty the moment they go beyond a simple statement of cash received and spent. If we show inventory as an asset or a machine as an asset, we are saying that probably we can recover at least their carrying value from future sales or use.

Within this context if we show revenue as part of this year's income, say on instalment sales, but this revenue may be deferred for tax purposes, it is probable that it will be taxed next year or the year after. Therefore we should provide in this year's expenses for the probable future effect of the revenue recognized as earned this year. Similarly if we provide this year for the probable cost of making good our warranty on goods sold this year, and such costs are not allowed for tax purposes until actually paid out, it is also probable that we will receive a tax benefit in the future year in the form of a deduction when the warranty costs do occur. Accordingly we are entitled to take credit for this probable future benefit in the current year, because it results from events of the current year – namely the sale of the goods.

In the case of fixed assets there are frequently differences in any given year between the amount that may be claimed for tax purposes as capital cost allowances, and the amount written off in the accounts as depreciation. Capital cost allowance of course is not exactly the same as accounting depreciation, since it is not aimed primarily at the apportionment of fixed asset costs over their useful life. The write-off period prescribed for tax purposes may be shorter or, in a few cases, longer than the useful life. Nevertheless, for this purpose capital cost allowance can be equated with depreciation because it is based on the *cost* of the fixed asset and permits write-off of the whole amount,* less salvage, over a period of years. This being so any excess of capital cost allowance over depreciation in the early years of an asset's life will be reversed in later years, and vice versa. On the other hand, if the business is not continued there will be 'terminal losses' or 'terminal profits' subject to tax.

There are three arguments commonly made against the position here described. The first is that we cannot know the tax rates that will prevail in the future or even that there will be an income tax along the lines presently computed. The answer to this is that while this is true, there is a much higher degree of probability that there will be a broadly similar tax at about the same rate (at least) than that there will not be.

A second argument is that we cannot know there will be taxable profits, even if the system remains unchanged. Once again, an answer is that if we have a currently profitable going concern there is more likelihood that it will have taxable profits in the future than that it will not. There is a further unanswerable argument where depreciation being written on fixed assets is less than the amount of capital cost allowance currently claimed for taxes. If in these circumstances taxable profits in the future cannot be expected, then the depreciation being written in the accounts should be increased, and should not be less than the amounts claimed for tax purposes. Depreciation is the spreading of asset cost over estimated economic life. If depreciation written today is less than capital cost allowance there *must* be an assumption that there will be enough income to absorb depreciation in future when it exceeds capital cost allowance.

The third argument, and that which is most commonly urged against tax allocation accounting, is that in a going concern the effect of differences in timing between tax and accounting recognition of costs and revenues cancels out. If there is an instalment sale this year that will not be taxed until next year, then next year there will be another instalment sale that will not be taxed until the following year. If we reduce taxes this year by claiming more capital cost allowance on a fixed

---

* Purists may object to this statement since the diminishing balance system never accomplishes a 100% write-off if there is no salvage. The balance not allowed, however, becomes very small with the passage of time and tends towards zero, so that the statement is, for practical purposes, true.

asset than the depreciation we write, with corresponding reduction in available capital cost allowance claims in future years, then in future years we will buy more fixed assets and be able to claim excess capital cost allowance on them. This 'roll-over argument' might be persuasive on purely practical grounds (why go to unnecessary work in your accounting?) if business were completely repetitive – but the fact is that it is not. At any given time a business may be in a decline or relatively stable or growing. So the tax effects of timing differences do *not* cancel out in most individual businesses and income reporting will be distorted by accounting as though they did. The fundamental error in the 'roll-over' proposition is that assumed future transactions are allowed to influence the accounting for current and past transactions. This cannot help but be unsound. Accounting must confine itself to recording the results of activities that have taken place. In so doing, admittedly it has to consider the probable future effects of current and past activities, but this is far different from reflecting currently the effects of forecast future activities.

Finally, consider two identical companies with identical incomes before tax in their fiscal years ended December 31, 19X1. Assume, however, that Company A acquired a large new machine on December 31, whereas Company B acquired the identical machine at an identical cost on January 1, 19X2. It is ridiculous to suggest that the final profits of Company A for 19X1 are substantially higher than those of Company B simply because it became entitled to claim capital cost allowance on its new machine in 19X1, particularly when it has thereby reduced its entitlement to capital cost allowance in future years below that of Company B. Yet this is what occurs if the effect of tax/accounting timing differences is not, in some way, recognized in income determination.

The effect on the balance sheet of tax allocation procedures

It was noted earlier that some of the early recommendations for dealing with tax/accounting timing differences approved the net-of-tax method, whereby the tax effect of timing differences was to be recognized in the valuation of the asset or liability. Thus if accelerated depreciation were taken for tax purposes, the normal accounting depreciation would be increased by an amount equal to the tax reduction resulting from the excess of accelerated tax depreciation over accounting depreciation. The rationale for this was that the value of the asset was reduced by using up its tax-deductible status. Conversely, if provision were made for warranty cost which was not deductible for tax until incurred, the amount of the provision could be reduced by the expected future tax reduction, on the grounds that the weight of the future liability was best calculated after allowance for future tax benefits.

On the net-of-tax method therefore, the charge shown in the income statements for taxes was the amount of tax actually payable for the year, and the effect of timing differences was reflected solely by adjustments of the valuation of the assets and liabilities involved and the related expense and revenue amounts. This method of reflecting tax effects, however, was rejected by both the Canadian and U.S. recommendations in 1967.

Instead, it was recommended that the provision for income tax expenses in the income statement should be based on the accounting income before tax (after due allowance for permanent differences), so that the tax effects of timing differences were automatically recognized in the period when the basic revenues and expenses were recognized. This recommendation meant that there would normally be a difference between the amount of tax expense recorded in the income account of a year and the actual tax liability. Where the tax charge against income exceeded taxes currently payable a deferred credit would be thrown up to be dealt with in the balance sheet; where the opposite situation prevailed a deferred debit remained.

The nature of these deferred debits and credits, and particularly the latter, aroused some discussion. Some accountants felt that the credit balance should be regarded as an accrual of taxes payable in the future. In other words they felt it was closely akin to a liability. Consequently the amount of the liability needed to be adjusted from time to time as future tax rates appeared likely to change. Others regarded the deferred credits and debits as merely the automatic result of the matching principle for income determination, representing cost reductions or costs applicable to future years, but not representing receivables or payables in the normal sense of those words. (This was the initial concept in the Canadian Bulletin No. 10.) In the event, both the U.S. and Canadian statements espoused the deferral theory, rather than the accrual theory. The English statement, on the contrary, opted for the latter. Perhaps consistent with this view the English statement recommended that a debit balance resulting from timing differences should be written off rather than deferred unless its recovery against profits of the next accounting period were reasonably certain. Further discussion of this theoretical issue is included in Appendix A.

Tax recoveries resulting from losses carried back and tax reductions resulting from losses carried forward

Tax recoveries resulting from losses carried back or forward from other years present a special aspect of tax allocation.

No problem exists with respect to recoveries from loss carry-backs. In this case the recovery becomes receivable in the year of loss, and credit for the recovery is recognized as a factor in arriving at net income (loss) for that year. More of a question arises with respect to losses carried forward. Should the recovery be assigned to the year of loss, or to the future year when the recovery is realized?

The attitude of the authorities on this has been somewhat ambivalent. The feeling seems to be that the credit for a tax reduction caused by a loss carry-forward really belongs to the year of loss, but that because of uncertainty the expected tax benefit should not be recorded as an asset until the year when the benefit is realized by earning profits. Thus at one time the Canadian recommendation (in Bulletin No. 12 issued in 1956) was that the reductions from loss carry-forwards should be given no recognition until realized but, at that time, the credit preferably should be treated as a prior period adjustment, not a factor affecting income of the year of realization. The American position at the same time was that "*as a practical matter* ... the resulting tax reduction should be reflected in the year to which such losses or unused credits are carried". The amount of reduction, however, was to be disclosed and "where it is believed that misleading inferences would be drawn from such inclusion [in income], the tax reduction should be credited to surplus". (emphasis supplied) (Accounting Research Bulletin No. 43, Chapter 10B.)

Since the 1967 statements the Canadian and U.S. positions have been in agreement to the effect that:

1. Potential tax benefits of loss carry-forwards should not be recognized in the year of loss unless, at the time, realization appears "virtually certain" or "assured beyond any reasonable doubt".

2. If the benefit is not recognized in the year of loss, it should not be recognized in any subsequent year until it is realized.*

3. When the credit is reflected in the year of realization, it should be treated as an 'extraordinary item' in the statement of income, and should not be netted with the normal tax provision in arriving at profits for the year.

4. The existence of material amounts of unrealized loss carry-forwards should be disclosed in the financial statements.

The English position, although not spelled out in as great detail, agrees generally with the North American statements.

There may be some interaction between tax allocation accounting for timing differences, and accounting for loss carry-forward credits. Suppose, for example, that a contractor has deferred tax credits in the balance sheet with respect to revenue represented by untaxed holdbacks receivable, and at the same time suffers an operating loss which cannot be carried back. In future years when the holdback proceeds enter into taxable income, if the result is positive taxable income the tax will be reduced by the loss carry-forward. On the other hand, if no taxable income is earned in that year, the deferred tax credits with respect to the holdback will prove not to have been required. In these circumstances it is usually considered that the deferred tax credits may be restored to income account in the year of loss, which has the same effect on income as though the benefit of the tax loss carry-forward had been set up as an asset.**

Conversely, the existence of tax loss carry-forwards may indicate a situation in which the recoverability of tax benefits represented by deferred tax debits (re timing differences) appears more doubtful than at the time the deferred debits

---

* If the probability of realization is a factor in recognition of loss carry-forward tax benefits (as is implied by the 'virtual certainty' test), there may be some inconsistency in the refusal to recognize a credit in a year subsequent to that of the year of loss when the realization becomes virtually certain. Contrast, for example, the Accounting Principles Board recommendation for the use of the instalment method or cost recovery method of profit recognition on delayed payment receivables where collectibility is uncertain. "When such circumstances exist, *and as long as they exist*, either the instalment method or the cost recovery method of accounting may be used." (APB Opinion No. 10, footnote 8, emphasis supplied.)

** In relatively unlikely circumstances this draw-down of the deferred tax credit might prove to be unwarranted. However, the flexibility of the Canadian capital cost allowance system and administration of income tax usually permits remedial action to be taken to offset this contingency. The U.S. tax system is not as flexible and consequently the ability to draw down deferred tax credits when losses are incurred is more restricted.

were recorded. Occasionally, but infrequently, it may become necessary to write off such deferred tax debits and this possibility should be borne in mind in the accounting.

Principles of Accounting for Income Taxes

The foregoing discussion may be summarized as follows:

1. For accounting purposes, corporate income tax is treated as a cost to be taken into account in the determination of net income for the year.

2. A proper presentation of the income tax cost related to reported income before tax requires:
   (a) when items of gain or loss are treated as extraordinary items or credited or debited direct to a surplus account the tax or tax reduction attributable to such items should be segregated from the amount of tax that otherwise would be shown, and should be grouped with the item of gain or loss in the financial statements;
   (b) when revenues reported as earned in the accounts are not taxed currently but will be brought into account as an element of taxable income in future years, provision should be made for the future tax on such revenues;
   (c) when costs are claimed for tax purposes before being written off in the accounts, the resulting tax reduction should be deferred, to be brought back into income account at the future date when the cost is brought into account in the determination of reported income;
   (d) when costs are written off for accounting purposes in a current year, but these expenses will not be accepted as taxable deductions till future years (e.g. as in the case of warranty provisions), the benefit of the expected future tax reduction should be accrued, thereby reducing the amount of tax cost charged against the current year's income;
   (e) when revenues are taxed which have been treated as unearned for accounting purposes, the associated tax cost should be deferred to be charged against income in future periods when the revenue is regarded as earned.

3. For balance sheet purposes the credits or debits resulting from the allocation procedures applied to the income tax charge in the income statement should be regarded as deferments, the purpose of which is merely to allocate tax effects related to revenues, costs and gains or losses to the income account of the same year as that in which the related items are reported. Deferred tax credits or debits should not be regarded in the same light as ordinary amounts payable or receivable.

4. Recoveries resulting from tax losses carried back or carried forward should be treated as follows:
   (a) a recovery resulting from a loss carry-back should be taken in as a credit in the year of loss;
   (b) a recovery resulting from a loss carry-forward should also be considered applicable to the year of loss. However, since the actual recovery is contingent upon taxable profits being earned within the loss carry-forward

period no credit should be taken in the year of loss unless some special circumstances exist that make such recovery virtually certain. When, and if, a recovery is realized in the carry-forward period the resulting credit should be treated as an extraordinary credit in the income statement of the year of recovery;

(c) when deferred tax credits exist at the same time as a loss carry-forward, it usually will be appropriate, depending on circumstances, to draw down into income account deferred tax credits associated with timing differences, up to the amount of the potential future tax reduction from the loss carry-forward.

References

1. *The National Finances 1971-72* (Toronto: Canadian Tax Foundation, 1972), Table 1-5.
2. *Ibid.*, Table 1-13.

14 Special items: capital transactions, prior period adjustments and extraordinary gains and losses

The preceding Chapters have dealt with the accounting treatment of revenues and costs that arise from ordinary day-to-day operations of a business. From time to time in any business however, transactions will take place that are not everyday normal transactions. In addition, adjustments or corrections may have to be made to transactions previously recorded. These occurrences may result in gains or losses to be reflected in the accounts, and the treatment of these unusual items does not fit neatly into the rules for handling ordinary revenues and costs.

The following description embraces most types of special items:

1. Gains or losses on dealings in the capital stock of the company – e.g. premiums paid on redemption of preferred shares.

2. Gains or losses on transactions relating to debt capital – e.g. differences between the face amount of bonds redeemed plus or minus related unamortized premium or discount, and the actual reacquisition cost of such bonds.

3. Gains or losses on sale, disposal or abandonment of assets not originally acquired for resale – e.g. fixed assets or investments.

4. Adjustments of values recorded in prior periods:
   (a) to correct errors,
   (b) to reflect adjustments to previous estimates in the light of new knowledge,
   (c) as a result of a quasi-reorganization,
   (d) to give effect to changes in accounting methods.

5. Business gains or losses of sporadic incidence and of a non-routine nature – e.g. provisions for losses on discontinuance of a business or a department of a business including separation payments to employees, costs of start-up, moving, plant rearrangement, etc., gains or losses on discontinuance of a pension trust, costs and damages under lawsuits, write-offs of intangible assets, and special provisions such as for unexpected renegotiation refunds, for accumulated but previously unrecognized inventory obsolescence, and so on.

6. Gains or losses from causes external to the business – e.g. gains or losses from devaluation or appreciation of assets or liabilities in foreign currency, losses from fires, earthquakes, floods, wars, riots or revolutions.

Are capital gains and losses part of income?

The first question to be asked is how these items are regarded by accountants – are they part of the earned income of the business and, if not, how should this affect their treatment? It will be noted that the first three categories above, and a number of items in the other categories represent capital gains or losses under a legalistic definition of the term. Fifty years ago accountants would be inclined to follow such a definition, and to credit capital gains to a 'capital surplus' account,* thus maintaining at least some verbal equivalence. Capital losses would be charged against capital surplus if such existed and, if not, against retained earnings.

Accounting opinion in this area, however, gradually changed. It was recognized that gains or losses on disposal of capital assets, as well as inventory assets, are an almost inevitable concomitant of being in business. In addition, it is frequently difficult to separate the true capital gain from gains on trading. The general view of accountants today, then, is that all elements of profit and loss should be reflected in the accumulated net income of the business, with two exceptions:

1. Gains or losses resulting from so-called capital transactions. These are transactions involving contributions of capital by, or accruing to the benefit of, the equity interest and transactions involving withdrawal or reduction of such capital. They also include adjustments of the type mentioned in point 2 below. It follows from the proprietary view of the accounting entity that a gain or loss from capital transactions between the entity and its equity interests is not part of the income of the entity. Such gains, therefore, should be credited to contributed surplus rather than income or retained earnings account. Losses on this type of transaction may be charged against contributed surplus to the extent that they are less than amounts previously credited on the same type of transaction. If they exceed this figure, the excess must represent a use of retained earnings and should be charged against that account.

2. Adjustments on reorganization or quasi-reorganization. When a company gets into difficulty it may go through a reorganization sanctioned by the courts, whereby holders of debt capital and the various classes of shareholders give up some of their rights and claims upon the company, and the assets of the company are written down to values that are more realistic under current operating conditions. A quasi-reorganization is similar except that the adjustments required need not be sanctioned by the courts, but rather are made as a result of formal proposals consented to by the shareholders. In either case the write-down of asset values must first be applied against any balance in retained earnings account (if any) but thereafter these write-downs, along with any other balance in deficit account, may be charged off against contributed surplus created by the reduction in claims of creditors and shareholders. A reorganization or quasi-reorganization is regarded as a 'fresh start' for the business and thus the carry-forward of any retained earnings position is inappropriate. In subsequent financial statements for some time the retained earnings account

---

* We do not refer here to that statutory monstrosity, the 'capital surplus' required to be set up under Section 61 of the Companies Act (Canada) when preferred shares "not redeemable out of capital" are redeemed.

is dated to show that it reflects earnings history only since the time of the reorganization.

For all practical purposes therefore, the accountant's view of business income is all-inclusive. Income consists of all gains or losses accruing to the enterprise from whatever source or cause, with the two exceptions mentioned.* Gains or losses on capital transactions are excluded from business income because they are not associated with the enterprise activities as such. Reorganization adjustments are excluded from income because they represent merely the connecting link between old and new in an enterprise receiving a fresh start. They are not part of the income of the new enterprise, obviously, nor are they part of the income of the old since they would not have been recorded as such in the absence of a reorganization transition to the new form.

The relationship of extraordinary gains or losses to the annual income figure

A new dimension is added to the question of the composition of net income, however, when we try to define net income for a particular year. For example, is a gain or loss on disposal of an investment really part of the income of the year of sale, or was it income of that period of years over which the gain or loss built up? To put it another way, is the recognition of income at point of sale a fair and useful procedure in the case of gains and losses on the sale of assets not acquired for resale, as it (normally) is in the case of trading assets? To take another example, is a gain or loss suffered on revaluation of a foreign currency attributable to the moment when the revaluation takes place (if indeed that point of time can be identified – changes in the 'official' rate of exchange may well have been foreshadowed by the free rate or black market rate over a period of months or years), or is it attributable to the whole period in which foreign operations have been carried on, in full knowledge of the risk of changes in the exchange rate? In other words, can there be some elements of income which, even though they are recognized as income *in* a period, are not part of the income *for* the period?

Until recently this was one of the more important unresolved questions in accounting theory. One school of thought argued for an *all-inclusive* concept of income for a year. Another held to the view that the figure reported for net income of a given year would be more useful if it excluded gains or losses not related to the ordinary ongoing operations of the business, and thus reflected the *current operating performance* of the business. The arguments of these two schools may be summarized as follows:

Current operating performance
1. One of the chief values of the income statement is the indication it gives of the earning power of the business. Earning power derives from normal recurring operations. Emphasis on the figure of income from normal operations is justi-

---

* Dividend distributions are also excluded, of course, because they are distributions of income (and sometimes of capital), not losses that enter into the determination of income.

fied, and is useful in making analyses of trends and comparisons between companies.

2. If adjustments that represent corrections of prior years' estimates are permitted to fall into income reported for the current year, a double distortion will result. The error in the earlier year will have under or overstated its income. The correction in the current year will affect its income in the opposite direction. Any reading of the trend from year to year, then, may be quite mistaken.

All-inclusive concept

1. Logically, the accumulated net income of a business must represent the sum of the net incomes of the business for the years in which it has been in operation.

2. Many statement users are unaware that they must look beyond the income statement for pertinent information about the achievements of the business. They may be misled, as a result, if substantial gains, losses or adjustments are made through retained earnings account.

3. Whether an item is normal or extraordinary is often a matter of opinion. Inconsistencies are therefore bound to result from attempts to separate them.

4. Any study of the subject has revealed that losses treated as 'extraordinary' exceed extraordinary gains. Over the years therefore, the exclusion of these items from income tends to overstate the long-run earning power of the enterprise.

Criteria for determining what gains and losses are extraordinary; practical problems

The application of either theory bristles with practical difficulties of definition and classification. These are particularly acute for the 'current operating performance' concept, but they are not avoided under the 'all-inclusive' concept since, even on the latter basis of reporting, the amount and existence of extraordinary items must be identified and separately disclosed.

The problem, essentially, is to establish criteria for the identification of gains and losses that are to be given special treatment for reporting purposes – either by carrying them directly to retained earnings account under the 'current operating performance' theory, or by segregating them within the income account as being 'extraordinary' under the 'all-inclusive' theory. Traditionally three criteria have been recognized:

1. Special treatment is indicated for gains or losses that are 'non-operating'. The point here is that to the reader of financial statements income that is largely fortuitous has a different significance than income that is attributable to the planned efforts of management;

2. Special treatment is also indicated for items that are 'non-recurring'. Here again, obviously, a 'one-shot' gain or loss has different significance to a reader of financial statements than has income from business operations that are carried on a regular basis;

3. Finally, special treatment is indicated for gains and losses that are essentially

attributable to transactions and events that occurred prior to the current period. Readers of financial statements give more weight to the latest income figures than to earlier figures in appraising a business. They are also influenced by the trend in income from year to year. Any adjustments recognized in the latest income period that really result from business carried on in earlier years, therefore, should be carefully disclosed.

The size of an item also has had a considerable influence in determining whether it should be treated as a 'special item' or form part of ordinary reported income. As has been mentioned earlier, materiality of an item, event or transaction is often an important consideration in determining how it will be treated in the accounts or reported in the financial statements. It may be questioned, however, whether it would not be better to draw distinctions only on the basis of the nature of the item in question. In many situations, a material item is taken to mean an item of a size of upwards of 5% or 10% of net income. The accepted range of percentages makes it difficult to decide in any particular case whether or not an item is material, and even if a firm dividing line is decided on, one can easily get into irrational situations where an 8% item is included in the determination of net ordinary income for the year and a 12% item is excluded. Moreover, the inclusion in net income one year of an extraordinary *credit* equal to 9% of the net income, coupled with the inclusion of an extraordinary *debit* of the same size next year, would give a most misleading picture of trends in ordinary income in the two years.

The kinds of practical problems that arise in applying the above three criteria are indicated by the following discussion of individual gains or losses:

(a) Gain or loss on disposal of a depreciable asset – Such a gain or loss might be considered non-operating on the grounds that the asset was acquired for use and not for sale. On the other hand it might be defined as operating, on the grounds that the asset was originally acquired for, and was necessary to, the normal operation of the business. Even if the sale of a capital asset were conceded to be a non-operating transaction it might be argued that the gain or loss could easily be the result of an overgenerous or inadequate depreciation allowance charged against income in the past and should therefore form part of the ordinary income determination. But then it might be argued that gains and losses that are, in effect, adjustments of previous years' depreciation should be excluded from the current year's income figure (unless they can be said to offset continuing over or underprovision in the current year). Again, the gain or loss might be segregated from normal income, on the grounds that it is 'non-recurring'. Yet, while this would be true of that particular asset, and might even be true of a whole type of fixed assets, it certainly is unlikely that no disposals of any fixed assets will occur again.

(b) Gain or loss on disposal of an investment – Under one definition, such a gain or loss would be clearly non-operating, since investment activities are, by definition, not operation of a business. On the other hand, marketable securities are often held merely as part of the cash reserves of a business. Sometimes also, certain investments are acquired and held for business policy reasons rather than for pure investment. In addition, some companies are actively engaged in making investments, sometimes improving the operations of companies in which shares are acquired, with a view to reselling their investment at a profit. In such cases it is hard to say that the making of investments is not just part of the business operations. It may also be argued that gains or losses on sale of investments are 'non-recurring'. Under today's conditions however, it becomes less and less easy to maintain this position, at least with respect to investment in common shares. In general, shares are bought today more for the hoped for gain (or as a 'hedge against inflation' because the value of shares has tended to appreciate over the long run) than for the dividend income, which is frequently only a very small percentage of market value. Accordingly, if one is making investments the hope and expectation is that there will be 'recurring' gains.

(c) Gains or losses resulting from changes in or corrections of judgment valuations – Many valuations or estimates must be made in accounting that are based largely or wholly on judgment. For example, it would be normal in many businesses to have some small inventory write-off for obsolescence or spoilage of stock each year. The appropriate amount thereof is however very much a matter of judgment, since opinions may well differ on the potential recovery on the doubtful stock, and indeed the recovery itself may well vary depending on the energy with which disposal of the stock is pursued. It is not unusual to find that after a series of years in which a relatively optimistic view is taken of the inventory situation, opinions change and a large write-down is made. While this is clearly an operating item, it is usually arguable that some portion of the write-down is attributable to bad judgment in previous years and should be excluded from current year's income.

Consider also revisions in estimates of the economic life of fixed assets, upon which the rate of depreciation write-off is based. Such estimates must always be uncertain. It may appear today that a longer or shorter life should be assumed than was originally estimated. However, in this situation frequently it is still quite possible that the original estimate may prove to be right and the current estimate in error. In these circumstances, it may be felt that it is right to adjust the rate of write-off against current income but that present indications are not sufficiently certain to warrant the formal action of restating previous years' earnings through the medium of a charge or credit to retained earnings.

In some types of business corrections of previous estimates when the facts are finally known are commonplace. For example, consider the contractor who accrues profit on a contract in process at one year-end on the 'percentage of completion' basis, and who finds subsequently that total contract costs were underestimated, so that there was no profit on the contract. Here is a case where the earlier year's figures were clearly in error so that from one point of view, there is a strong case for making the correction by charging retained earnings account rather than income account. On the other hand, a contracting type of business is full of uncertainties and revisions of estimates occur all the time. It is hardly useful to be continually carrying such revisions to retained earnings account. Instead, the reader of statements of this type of business should understand that the income figure of any one year is highly influenced by estimates and that he should look to the results of several years to properly appraise the business.

Recent AICPA and CICA Recommendations

In view of the difficulties in finding a satisfactory definition and classification of special items, it is not surprising that reporting practice has been mixed. A number of studies over the years have shown that the treatment of extraordinary gains and losses has shown little consistency between companies, or even within one company over a period of a few years. Moreover these studies have indicated a tendency by some to put extraordinary losses through retained earnings account and extraordinary gains through income.

To improve this situation both the AICPA Accounting Principles Board and the CICA Research Committee have issued Recommendations for stricter definition of extraordinary items and standard treatment of them. The Recommendations of the two Institutes are essentially founded on the 'all-inclusive' concept of income reporting. The view is adopted that the reader of the financial statements will be best served if all items of gain and loss, suitably described, are brought together in the income statement. To implement this view, the only charges or credits that may be taken direct to retained earnings account are:

(a) Prior period adjustments – which are narrowly defined by their characteristics. They must be clearly and directly related to the business activities of particular prior periods. They arise solely from the events that took place in those periods; they are not attributable to economic events occurring after such periods. They are not influenced by current decisions or determinations by managers or owners. Since they are adjustments, it is to be presumed the final result could not be accurately estimated prior to its ultimate determination in the current period.

(b) Adjustments resulting from changes in accounting principles given retroactive effect.*

In making these rules, the Institute committees appear to have adopted the reasonable presumption that management will exercise its judgment honestly at the end of each accounting period so that any subsequent adjustments of asset or liability valuations must be deemed to be caused by developments occurring in the period reported upon or new knowledge that has come to light. For example, if in any year it is determined that a large write-down of inventory should be made because of product obsolescence, it must be presumed that such obsolescence could not have been foreseen when the inventory was taken at the previous year-end and therefore the write-down must be attributable to the year in which it takes place.

Treatment as a prior period adjustment is reserved for the relatively few cases where an estimate has been made of a specific amount payable or receivable as a result of current operations, and this estimate subsequently turns out to be in error for reasons beyond the control or determination of management. For example, provision for ultimate liability in a matter under litigation must necessarily be conjectural until final judgment or settlement. While the Canadian Institute recommendations do not deal specifically with the situation it may also, perhaps, be presumed that if prior years' statements were fraudulently prepared (say in-

---

* In Opinion No. 20 the Accounting Principles Board has recommended that the effect of most changes in accounting method should not be reflected as an adjustment of retained earnings account.

ventory was included that did not exist) or a clear mechanical error had occurred in their preparation (as distinct from a judgment estimate that subsequently proves to be faulty), a prior period adjustment would be made at the time when the error or misstatements are discovered.

Gains or losses other than 'prior period adjustments' then are treated as part of net income for the period in which they are recognized. To improve the significance of the income statement however, it was felt that a distinction needed to be made between 'extraordinary items' and the ordinary results of business operations. Such a distinction immediately involves the kinds of classification difficulties described earlier. In an attempt to shrink the area of doubt the Institute recommendations provide that gains or losses "of a character typical of customary business activities" may not be treated as extraordinary items even though they may be rare in occurrence, or abnormal in size. Thus, an unusually large bad debt loss, unusual inventory obsolescence, gains or losses on disposal of fixed assets other than an entire plant (or substantial adjustments to their carrying value not resulting from a change in accounting method), are all to be treated as part of normal income before extraordinary items.* (There is, of course, no reason why they should not be separately identified in the interests of full disclosure.)

Examples of 'extraordinary' items enumerated in the Institute recommendations are gains and losses from:

(a) sale or abandonment of a plant or a significant segment of the business (going out of business is not typical of customary business operations),

(b) sale of investments not acquired for resale (if the investments are not acquired for resale, the act of sale presumably is not typical. On the other hand, as pointed out earlier, it is hard to say in most cases that an investment is not acquired with at least the possibility of resale in mind),

(c) expropriation of properties (expropriation of an operating property is obviously an interruption to customary business activities),

(d) major devaluations of a foreign currency (in countries with relatively stable currencies such events, being unpredictable and beyond the control of management, cannot be said to be characteristic of normal activities. Where business is carried on in a country with an unstable currency however, fluctuations in it must be treated as a normal business risk and gains and losses treated as ordinary income),

(e) income tax reductions realized on the carry-forward of a loss.

In all cases, extraordinary items should be shown net of income tax, where applicable.

Principles Governing the Accounting for Special Items

The foregoing principles governing accounting for special items may be summarized as follows:

---

* Under the U.S. recommendation "the write-off of goodwill due to unusual events or developments within the period" qualifies as an extraordinary item. It is at least arguable that this also is "of a character typical of customary business activities", which only serves to illustrate how difficult it is to draw clear dividing lines. The specific case is not dealt with in the Canadian recommendation.

Extraordinary items

1. Extraordinary items (less any income tax applicable) should be separately disclosed as the last item before 'net income' in the income statement. Extraordinary items are defined as material gains and losses connected with transactions that are significantly different from those resulting from the normal or typical activities of the entity. As a result, such gains or losses would not normally have great weight in an evaluation of the business. They do not include gains or losses which would normally be regarded as a risk incidental to the business carried on, even though such gains or losses might be abnormal in amount or occurred only infrequently.

Capital transactions

1. Gains, losses or adjustments resulting from capital transactions* should in no case be credited or charged to income account.

2. A 'contributed surplus' account resulting from a capital transaction may be used to absorb charges that are the opposite to those that gave rise to the contributed surplus.

3. A charge that would otherwise have to be made against income may not be written off directly against a contributed surplus. If operations result in an accumulated deficit, such deficit should be shown as a deduction from capital and contributed surplus, and may only be written off against contributed surplus as a result of formal reorganization or quasi-reorganization proceedings. After any such write-off the accumulated earnings (or deficit) position should, for a reasonable period of years (say, five), indicate the date from which it has accumulated.

Prior period adjustments

1. Prior period adjustments are of two types:
   (a) adjustments to give retroactive effect to changed accounting methods, and
   (b) adjustments that represent corrections to previously reported figures.

2. Corrections of previous estimates are inevitable given the uncertainty underlying all economic activity. To avoid continual revision, corrections should only be treated as prior period adjustments when:
   (a) the transaction(s) whose record is being corrected clearly took place entirely in a prior period or periods, and

---

* Capital transactions may be defined as including:
  (a) transactions involving contributions of capital by, or accruing to the benefit of, the equity interest (including preferred and common shareholders in the case of a corporation),
  (b) transactions involving withdrawal or reduction of such capital,
  (c) restatement of the capital interest as a result of:
     – reorganizations (in this case, adjustments to debt interests as well as share interests may be involved),
     – quasi-reorganizations, and
     – write-up of fixed assets on appraisal.

(b) the determination of the outcome of the transaction was the result of action by forces or parties external to the entity, and not by its management alone, and either

(i) the event or transaction was unusual to the entity (e.g. a lawsuit), or

(ii) the transaction was of a kind that normally could be recorded without need for material correction (e.g. liability for income tax).

15 Measurement of assets, liabilities and equities; classification of equities

The following are some generalized definitions of the terms assets, liabilities and equity as they are used in accounting:

Assets consist of money or monetary equivalents (investments) or the expectation of future benefit arising from events and transactions prior to the accounting date, including claims on others for payment or service (receivables and pre-paids), or the earned portion of future expected claims (accrued income), the expectation of future value through sale (inventories for sale), the expectation of future value through use (fixed assets, stocks of supplies), or a generalized expectation of future benefit from past expenditure (deferred charges).

Liabilities represent the amounts that will probably have to be paid in future as a result of events and transactions prior to the accounting date, or obligations to deliver valuable goods or services in future without receipt of commensurate consideration. A contingent liability (not recorded in the accounts but merely disclosed) is distinguished from recorded liabilities by the fact that the probability of payment being required on the contingent liability is remote or, if not remote, is impossible to estimate with any reasonable degree of accuracy.

Equity is the residual of recorded assets minus recorded liabilities. In a going concern it has no other significance than this. In liquidation, it represents the amount for which the entity is accountable to its owners (after allowing for any gains or losses on liquidating the assets and liabilities).

It will be apparent from the discussion in preceding Chapters that the amounts at which assets, liabilities and equities are carried in the accounts will be determined by:

(a) the valuation placed on the transactions with parties outside the business by which assets, liabilities and equities are initially recorded in the accounts, and

(b) the subsequent processes of income accounting by which revenues are accrued and costs are allocated to (charged against) time periods.

Some authors define entries of the first type as 'external transactions' and of the second type as 'internal transactions'. Others confine the term transactions to exchanges with outside parties and use the general term 'accrual accounting' to describe the entries recording earning of revenues and matching of costs. The term 'income accounting' in place of either of these is preferred here since 'internal transaction' is an unnatural term while the term 'accrual accounting' is not always used with a consistent meaning.

It will be apparent that, in general, the values assigned to external transactions will govern the amounts assigned to accounts receivable from, or payable to, parties outside the business, and to the capital portion of shareholders' equity. Both external transactions and income accounting will influence the amount shown in the balance sheet for a much larger number of assets and liabilities such as inventories, prepaid expenses, fixed assets, deferred charges, deferred revenues, accrued assets (e.g. interest income accrued but not yet due), certain accrued charges (e.g. obligations for municipal taxes or audit fees not yet due), and other obligations to parties as yet not finally determined (e.g. provision for future pension payments). Income accounting alone will determine the credits to the retained earnings portion of shareholders' equity but dividends (a type of external transaction) will also affect the balance.

There are two situations in which balance sheet valuations may depart from those that would be established following the rules for transaction valuation and income accounting. These exist as a result of:
(a) Appraisals of fixed assets
(b) Reorganizations and quasi-reorganizations.

Appraisals of fixed assets

There are occasions when it is considered that the original cost of fixed assets is so far removed from current values that it should be abandoned as a basis of valuation in the statement of financial position. This is most often true of land values in urban areas which not infrequently multiply many times after the date the land is acquired. An additional motive for adjustment of the values of depreciable assets is to obtain a more realistic basis for computing the amount of depreciation chargeable against income. In such cases as these it is acceptable practice in Canada and the United Kingdom to write up the fixed assets on the basis of an appraisal.

The practice of recording appraisals does not, it must be admitted, fit into a cohesive theory of present generally accepted accounting principles. For most assets an upward adjustment of asset carrying values without a realization transaction is not permissible, although in many cases it may appear to be well justified. The justification for appraisal of fixed assets therefore is purely pragmatic. Fixed assets are characterized by the fact that they have a long life, that they are held for use and not for sale, and therefore their carrying values are not subject to regular adjustment through turnover. In this situation current values can diverge more widely from historic cost than with most other assets. Appraisal adjustments seek to overcome this weakness in conventional accounting procedures.

When appraisals are entered in the accounts it is important that they be made on a basis compatible with accounting objectives. Appraisals may be made for many purposes and, depending on the purpose, the basis of valuation and the resulting values will vary. Even an appraisal for insurance purposes may have more than one basis of estimation – whether 'actual cash value', reproduction cost new, replacement value and so on. It is suggested that fair market value would be the most appropriate basis of appraisal for use in accounting. Similarly, appraisal estimates of accumulated depreciation must be appropriate to accounting objectives. An engineer's 'observed depreciation' would rarely, if ever, be reasonable. The basis should be compatible with the accounting basis for depreciation write-offs, which means that it should be based on an age-life calculation using the pattern (straight-line, diminishing balance) that will be followed in the accounts thereafter.

Another factor that should be considered when recording appraisals is the fact that the amount by which assets are written up on appraisal will not be deductible in the computation of enterprise taxable income. Thus, from the standpoint of the proprietary interest, those assets are worth less than they would be if bought on the open market at arm's length. The Institute of Chartered Accountants in England and Wales has recommended (in Recommendation No. 27 in Accounting Principles) that a portion of the credit arising on revaluation of assets (equal to the tax that would be incurred if the asset were sold to realize appraisal value) should be credited to the deferred taxation account or otherwise disclosed. It is questionable whether this would fit in with tax allocation theory as it is recognized in North America, since in fact no such tax has been deferred. An alternative would be to reduce any appraisal value which is based on market value in the open market by a factor recognizing the lesser value of the appraised assets because the appraisal increment is not tax deductible. Such factor could be calculated along the lines suggested in Appendix A (Supplement to Chapter 13).

When appraisals have been recorded in the accounts, future accounting for the assets appraised is based on the appraised values in substitution for cost. That is to say, depreciation charged in arriving at income is based on the appraised values as is any gain or loss recognized on disposal of an asset.

The credit arising as a result of this appraisal is grouped as part of shareholders' equity in the balance sheet. After the initial entry such credit may be left unadjusted, until such time as a further appraisal is made. Alternatively, some entities desire to keep a record of what their accumulated retained earnings balance would have been from time to time had they continued on the basis of accounting for fixed assets based on cost. Accordingly such entities make transfers each period from the appraisal surplus credit to retained earnings account of amounts equal to the increase in depreciation charged attributable to the appraisal write-up of assets, and the portion of loss or reduction in gain recognized on disposal of an asset which is attributable to the appraisal increment in its carrying value.

Adjustments on reorganization and quasi-reorganization

This subject is dealt with in Chapter 14.

Subdivision of shareholders' equity

As noted above the total amount of shareholders' equity is a residual. It is not valued or measured directly in the accounting but rather its amount represents merely the difference between the recorded amounts of all assets less all liabilities. The total equity is, however, subdivided or classified into various categories, such as stated capital, contributed surplus and retained earnings and the basis of sub-division sometimes raises problems.

It is first necessary to consider the possible reasons for classification of share-holders' equity. At least three reasons may be adduced:

1. To show where the net resources employed by the enterprise came from – in particular to distinguish between actual contributions of capital (by equity interests and others), and retained earnings.

2. To show the amount of capital which may not legally be distributed without formal proceedings for reduction of capital.

3. To show other restrictions on dividend distributions, whether by contract (say under a trust indenture securing a bond or debenture issue) or as a matter of policy. (The latter objective may be achieved, for example, by 'appropriation' i.e. segregation of retained earnings to earmark it for a special purpose and to indicate that to that extent, at least, it is not intended to pay dividends.)

These three objectives are not entirely attainable or completely compatible one with another. For example:

1. When a stock dividend is declared any transfer from retained earnings account to capital account destroys the distinction by source between retained earnings and capital contributions unless the stock dividend is visualized as tantamount to a payment out of earnings and reinvestment of the proceeds by the share-holders. Since the shareholders receiving a stock dividend do not in fact have the opportunity to make the decision whether to reinvest, the assumption seems artificial.

2. When assets are written up on appraisal there is necessarily a credit to share-holders' equity. However such a credit does not represent a source of funds used to acquire the resources of the entity; rather it represents merely a restatement of the carrying value of some of the resources, and as such it cannot be identified in its entirety with either contributed capital or retained earnings.

3. When there are reductions of shareholders' equity other than by way of dividends (dividends are commonly considered to come out of retained earn-ings unless they are specifically indicated as distributions of capital) it may not always be obvious to what classification the reduction should be charged. The problem is particularly difficult when dealing with a company's own common shares reacquired, which will be discussed more fully later in this Chapter.

A number of writers have questioned the value to financial statement users of the information sought to be conveyed by classification of shareholders' equity. In the vast majority of cases dividends paid do not exceed current year's earnings, so that the much larger amount that can legally be distributed is information without significance. Contractual restrictions on amounts distributable more often repre-sent a potential limitation on future dividends but this information can be and usually is given by note without need to subdivide the equity. Appropriations of retained earnings can suggest specifically why the full amount of earnings have not been paid out, but this information is usually obtainable from the narrative in annual reports to shareholders or from examination of the statement of source and application of funds. Moreover if appropriations are intended to indicate *future* intended uses for assets represented by retained earnings, they do little to ensure that assets will be used as intended, in the absence of transfer of specific assets to a separate fund, which is almost never done.

It might be thought that disclosure of the total amount of retained earnings would give some worthwhile information as to whether the enterprise has been profitable. But the accumulated total of retained earnings is of little value in this regard, since it does not indicate over how long a period the retained earnings account accumulated, how much in dividends was paid out during the period of accumulation, or recent earnings and dividend history which is the most important information.

In the writer's opinion the following treatment of shareholders' equity would be sufficient:

1. Capital contributed by equity interests other than the common shareholders to be shown separately so long as the capital securities in question are outstanding.

2. The common shareholders' equity to be shown as one figure subject to any corporations act requirements to show stated or issued capital separately in the balance sheet.

3. A statement or statements showing changes in the various equity accounts for each year being reported on to be provided.

4. Restrictions on the availability of common equity for dividends to be noted where they are significant.

5. Probably, if preference equity is more clearly distinguished from common equity, an actual transfer should be made from common shareholders' equity to the preference equity where unpaid cumulative dividends exist, since the amounts of such would rank ahead of the common shareholders for distribution in liquidation.

6. Other special features of various classes of equity such as participation rights, redemption premiums, priorities in liquidation, etc. to be disclosed by note.

As has been indicated however, in present practice common equity is classified in a far more detailed fashion. Problems in present practice are discussed below under the headings:
(a) Stock splits and stock dividends
(b) Gains and losses on redemption or repurchase for cancellation of equity securities other than common shares
(c) Treatment of common shares repurchased.

Stock splits and stock dividends

From time to time a company will subdivide its stock in some ratio such as two for one, or three for one. Frequently the reason for this is that the market price for a single share has risen so high that small investors are deterred from buying shares of the company. Conversely companies sometimes reduce or consolidate the number of shares outstanding by a 'reverse split' – i.e. issuing one new share for, say, ten old ones.

It is generally accepted that stock splits or reverse splits have no accounting significance and call for no changes other than adjusting the number of shares recorded as outstanding.

The number of shares outstanding can also be affected by a stock dividend. In point of fact, a stock dividend of one common share for each share held would have exactly the same effect as a two-for-one stock split. Thus the distinction between a stock split and a stock dividend is largely formal and it is difficult to see a difference in their underlying nature. The AICPA Committee on Accounting Procedure considered this difficulty in Bulletin No. 43 Chapter 7B but felt that because many recipients look upon stock dividends as the equivalent of cash dividends they should in certain circumstances be accounted for by the issuer. The circumstances were:

(i) where the stock issuance was so small in comparison with the outstanding shares that it would have little apparent effect on the market price. (If there was a noticeable effect on the market price the dividend would be more like a stock split.)

(ii) where the issuing company was not closely held. (It was presumed that shareholders of a closely held company would not fail to realize the essential difference between a stock dividend and a cash dividend.)

It was suggested that most stock dividends of less than 20 or 25% of the shares outstanding in a widely held company should receive accounting recognition. The form of recognition to be given was a charge to retained earnings account and a credit to the contributed capital account in an amount equal to the market value of the shares distributed.

On the other hand, stock dividends which did not meet the specifications would not be accounted for other than to the extent of any transfer to stated capital required by law. Thus the anomalous result ensued that a 15% stock dividend would reduce retained earnings account, but a 25% stock dividend would not.

Stock dividends in Canada are relatively rare. One or two examples however suggest that American practice is not followed, and any amount capitalized is probably restricted to the legal minimum required to make the shares non-assessable.*

Gains or losses on repurchase for cancellation of equity securities other than common shares

American and Canadian authorities are in agreement on this question. The cost of repurchase of any security is to be applied first to reduce the par or stated capital and any paid-in surplus on shares of the same issue, on a pro rata basis. If there is a gain after this charge, it is to be credited to contributed surplus. If there is a loss after the charge it may be charged against any previously accumulated contributed surplus from gains on retirement of the same issue, and any excess is to be charged to retained earnings. (The AICPA also recognizes the possibility that a loss may be charged in its entirety to retained earnings.) It may be noted that this procedure maintains a record of equity by source on a quite narrowly

---

* It probably is not a coincidence that in the U.S. receipt of a stock dividend does not give rise to taxable income. In Canada, if the amount capitalized comes out of 'undistributed income' as calculated for tax purposes, the amount of the dividend has been taxable.

defined basis. An alternative argument might be made that the distinction between contributed capital and retained earnings would be better maintained if any loss (i.e. excess of purchase price over stated value and any contributed surplus applicable to that issue) on a capital transaction for retirement of equity shares other than common shares were chargeable in full against any contributed surplus arising from gains on previous capital transactions, regardless of what share issue those gains were related to.

Treatment of common shares repurchased

Until 1971 no company in any Canadian jurisdiction has had the right to buy in its own common shares. Ontario companies now have this right (and a similar amendment to the Canada Corporations Act has been recommended) but practice on this issue has not yet developed. We must, therefore, look to U.S. literature and practice for precedents.

There are two main issues:

(i) If a share is repurchased but not cancelled (and therefore may be reissued) should it nevertheless be accounted for as though it were retired, and if resold be accounted for as a new issue (the two transaction theory); or should the stock repurchased be accounted for at cost (as a deduction from shareholders' equity) so that when and if resold only the gain or loss would remain to be accounted for?

(ii) How should a retirement (or constructive retirement under the two transaction theory) be handled?

It may be noted that corporate law may prescribe an accounting treatment different from the preferred treatment, and if it does APB Opinion No. 6 recommended that legal requirements take precedence.

The merits of the two transaction theory vs. the one transaction theory are open to debate. The two transaction theory would often result in a fairly substantial charge to retained earnings, following which the shares might be resold (at a price close to that at which they were bought) with all the proceeds going to contributed capital accounts. This would seem to be objectionable if the shares were purchased with a definite intention to resell (perhaps just to facilitate exchanges between shareholders) and that intention was in fact fulfilled. On the other hand, if the shares were repurchased simply to use idle company funds and no definite plan for resale was in view, the purchase and any subsequent resale would definitely be two separate transactions and it would seem should be so accounted for.

APB Opinion No. 6 recommended that where shares were acquired for purposes other than retirement or when ultimate disposition has not yet been decided the cost preferably should be shown separately as a deduction from the total of shareholders' equity. (The Board, however, was prepared to accept retirement accounting as an alternative.) The writer would be inclined to reverse the emphasis and suggest that retirement accounting should be followed unless there is a fairly definite intention to resell the shares.

When shares are retired some variation in treatment is permitted. The paid-in capital accounts may be reduced pro rata to the number of shares retired, and any excess should be charged first against any other capital surplus arising from previous retirements and gains in shares of that issue and any balance against retained earnings. Alternatively (but not very logically) an excess over stated value may be charged entirely against retained earnings. Once again it is possible to wonder whether it would not be equally satisfactory to charge any excess of purchase cost over contributed capital on common shares either against any existing contributed surplus attributable to common shares, or at least pro rata against such contributed surplus. (Any contributed surplus arising from transactions in other shares retired would be considered attributable to the common shares.) In the less usual case where there is an excess of stated value over cost of shares reacquired the difference would be credited to capital surplus (contributed surplus in Canadian terminology).

In brief, it is the writer's opinion that subdivision of equity need not go beyond a basic subdivision showing separately the capital contributed by each capital source other than the common shares (plus any addition to preference share equity for cumulative unpaid dividends as might be appropriate). However if a more detailed subdivision were required, the most logical form would be as illustrated in the following example:

5% Preference shares
– par value	xxx	
– premium paid in excess of par value	xx	
Total contributed preference capital	xxx	
– unpaid cumulative dividends[1]	xx	xxx
Proceeds from issue of warrants to buy common stock		xxx
Capital contributed by way of government grant[2]		xxx

Common shares
– par value	xxx	
– premium paid in excess of par value	xx	
Total contributed common capital	xxx	
– accumulated gains on capital transactions	xx	
– accumulated retained earnings attributable to common capital[1]	xxx	xxx

[1] Retained earnings would also need to be allocated where preference shares have cumulative or unlimited participating rights, as well as in the case of unpaid cumulative dividends.

[2] This assumes a situation in which it is appropriate to treat a government grant as contributed capital rather than a reduction of asset cost (see CICA Research Recommendations, Section 3065).

On this basis if there were a retirement of, say, some preference shares, the book value as determined above would be reduced pro rata and any difference between the amount of reduction and the cost of the shares retired would be charged or credited to the common shareholder's account 'accumulated gains on capital transactions'. Any excess of charge over the balance in that account would have to be charged against retained earnings. Similarly, if common shares were retired the 'total contributed common capital' would be reduced pro rata and any difference would be credited or charged to 'accumulated gains on capital transactions' in the first instance, with any excess of charge over the balance of the account being carried against retained earnings.

Principles Governing the Measurement of Assets, Liabilities and Equities, and Classification of Equities

Based on the foregoing summarization and the income accounting rules in preceding Chapters, the following principles may be said to govern the amounts at which assets, liabilities and equities are carried in the accounts.

Assets

1. Accounts receivable arising from transactions with outside parties should be carried at their face value after allowance for discount to cover extended credit terms and for costs and losses associated with bad debts.

2. Accrued revenue should be recorded at a figure based on the contracted total revenue and proportionate to the recipient's entitlement based on his performance, the passage of time, or other factor governing the amount that may reasonably be regarded as earned.

3. Inventory should be valued at acquisition at the sum of all costs that can reasonably be attributed to it. Costs of goods remaining in inventory at any particular date are determined by the cost flow assumption adopted by the enterprise. Costs in inventory at the end of a period should be reduced to 'market' on a basis appropriate to the business. When inventory is written down to market, which is below cost, at the end of one period, the written-down value will be maintained until the inventory is sold (or further written down).

4. Fixed assets:
   (a) Land should be valued at cost except when the value of the land is dependent on some other factor that is consumed in the course of the business, in which case the land cost or an appropriate portion should be amortized as its value is exhausted.
   (b) Buildings and equipment, etc. should be valued initially at acquisition cost, which includes installation costs. The accumulated allowance for depreciation should be shown as a separate deduction from cost in the balance sheet and the net amount only shown as an asset.
   (c) An alternative acceptable basis of accounting for fixed assets is appraised value (allowing for any loss of value attributable to lack of tax-deductibility) less an allowance for accumulated depreciation appropriate to the said appraised value.

5. Prepaid expenses should be carried at the unexpired portion of their cost determined on the basis of lapse of time or other basis appropriate to the nature of the prepayment.

6. Deferred tax debits attributable to accumulated timing differences between taxable and accounting income should be carried at the actual increase in tax paid with respect to (a) revenues taxed before their recognition in the accounts as earned, or (b) expenses incurred, not deductible for tax purposes until future years. Deferred tax debits relating to loss carry-forwards (where realization of such is virtually certain) should be carried at the amount of the estimated future tax recovery.

7. Other deferred charges should be carried at cost, less amounts written off to reflect the proportion of benefits already received to total expected benefit.

8. Intangible assets (where not written off against retained earnings upon acquisition):
   (a) if of indefinite life, are carried at cost, or are systematically amortized over an arbitrary term of years;
   (b) if of limited life, are carried at cost, less amortization related to the estimated expired useful life.

Liabilities

1. Accounts payable arising from transactions with outside parties should be shown at face value (after deducting any cash discount allowed), less a discount for payment deferred beyond the normal credit terms at a discount rate established at the time the transaction was recorded.

2. Accrued costs or charges should be recorded at a figure based on contracted cost, proportionate to the creditor's entitlement based on his performance, the passage of time, or other factor governing the cost that should reasonably be recognized in the accounts.

3. Provisions for future costs or losses arising out of activities prior to the balance sheet date should be based on estimates of their amount.

4. Dividends payable should be shown at the amount declared.

5. Income tax payable should be shown at the estimated amount assessable.

6. Deferred revenue should be that proportion of revenue proceeds received which is not yet earned, determined on the basis of the degree of performance by the vendor.

7. Deferred tax credits attributable to accumulated timing differences between taxable and accounting income should be recorded at the amount of actual reduction in tax achieved (a) by postponement of taxation of revenues recognized in the accounts as earned or (b) by claiming for tax purposes costs not yet charged against income for accounting purposes.

8. Debt should be shown at the discounted present value of the amount contracted to be repaid in future, the discount rate being that established when the contract was entered into. By custom, however, debt having a nominal or face amount may be carried at that figure, and the difference between that figure and the original transaction amount be carried as a deferred charge or credit to be amortized over the period to maturity of the debt.

Equity

1. Capital contributed is carried at the amount established by the transactions through which the capital was issued. Such capital is usually subdivided between:
   (a) stated value (par value, or value assigned in the case of no par value stock), and
   (b) contributed surplus (amounts received in excess of stated capital).

2. Where share capital is redeemed for less than its stated value, the difference remains part of the equity but is transferred to contributed surplus.

3. Where share capital is redeemed for more than its stated value the difference is charged to contributed surplus to the extent that there were previous amounts paid in or gains on redemptions on the same issue, and against retained earnings if such contributed surplus is not available.

4. Any credit to equity resulting from a write-up of assets on appraisal over their former carrying value may be carried as a separate section of contributed capital indefinitely. Alternatively, to the extent that depreciation has been written on the appraisal increment, or some part of the write-up has entered into the determination of gain or loss on disposal of appraised assets, a transfer may be made from the appraisal surplus account to the retained earnings account.

5. Retained earnings represent a residual amount consisting of the accumulated sum of annual earnings since the inception of the enterprise, less dividends declared, and minus any adjustments resulting from capital transactions which could not be charged against contributed surplus.

Reorganizations or quasi-reorganizations

1. Any of the foregoing values are subject to readjustment through formal proceedings to a basis which appears to be fair and realistic. In the rare cases where this occurs, the retained earnings account for a period thereafter should be dated to indicate the 'fresh start' given to the accounting for the enterprise at the date of the reorganization.

16 Investments by trading companies other than in associated companies

To this point, attention has been focused on accounting for assets, liabilities, revenues and expenses arising from business operations. As has been noted, principles in this area have been largely shaped by the search for a fair determination of results of operations. We now come to a field of accounting not nearly so much influenced by income accounting criteria and one to which relatively little attention has been paid by accounting authority – namely that of accounting for investments.

Methods developed by commercial and manufacturing concerns for investment accounting seem to have received relatively little consideration (apart from the problems of accounting for investment in subsidiaries). Investment accounting by financial intermediaries (defined here as entities that collect funds by way of deposit, premium, etc. and hold substantial amounts invested for extended periods) is more adapted to their special situations, as might be expected from the fact that investments are of much greater importance in their financial position. It is convenient therefore to segregate the discussion of investment accounting for financial intermediaries, and this topic will be dealt with in Chapter 25.

The investments of a trading enterprise may be classified broadly as between those that are held for business policy (including investments in subsidiary companies, in 50%-owned companies, in other non-subsidiary affiliates and in unrelated companies where the investment is held for business reasons) and those that are held purely for investment purposes – i.e. for the income and/or capital gain they will bring in. The former type of investments will be discussed in the succeeding Chapter. Attention here is confined to the second type.

Questions in accounting for this restricted area revolve around the following issues:

1. The basis of classification of investments as current or non-current in the balance sheet.

2. The carrying value of the investment asset in the accounts.

3. The determination of cost or other carrying value of investments sold.

4. The basis of accounting for income from investments.

Basis of classification of investments between current and non-current

All authorities are agreed that, to qualify as a current asset, an investment must be readily marketable. Many writers, however, also draw a distinction between 'temporary' investments and 'long-term' investments on the basis of whether or not there exists an intention to sell to meet requirements for cash during the next operating cycle.[1] The intention test seems to be traceable to a confusion in working capital concepts. If current assets are, by definition, restricted to assets employed in operations during the operating cycle, it would be logical to include among them cash and temporary investments of cash that would be converted into inventory and accounts receivable at busy points during the operating cycle. Under such a definition however, cash balances themselves would have to be divided between cash required during the operating cycle and cash not required. To do so, however, would conflict with the accepted use of current assets (or working capital) as a measure of liquidity. Certainly the division of cash balances is not found in practice.

It seems arguable that so long as working capital is used as a test of liquidity ready marketability should be the only criterion for determining whether investments (not held as a matter of business policy) are current assets or not.[*] If this is accepted it also follows that the maturity date of the investment is unimportant. A mortgage portfolio could be a current asset if it were readily realizable. On the other hand, a large block of stock, even with a quoted market value, might not be readily marketable and therefore would not qualify.

However this may be, practice seems to follow the somewhat inconsistent rule that:
– all cash is included in current assets unless clearly restricted, or designated for non-current spending, but
– all investments are excluded from current assets unless it is intended to turn them into cash within the year (or operating cycle, if longer).

The latter part of the rule is probably not followed universally.

The carrying value of investments

The initial carrying value of an investment is of course cost, which includes any fees, commissions or other charges incidental to the purchase. The following deals with some of the questions that arise in connection with the carrying value:

1. Where two or more different securities are bought in one purchase – e.g. a debenture with attached warrants to buy stock – an allocation of cost must be made. If both instruments are quoted separately in the market the cost should be allocated pro rata to such market value. If only one is quoted, market value would be assigned to it and the residual to the other instrument. If no separate quotations are available it may be necessary to delay allocating cost until

---

[*] On the other hand, if the working capital test were abandoned in the balance sheet, and instead a segregation between operating assets and financial assets were recognized (as is raised for discussion in Chapter 22), the distinction between 'temporary' investments, which will be turned into operating assets at some time in the next year, and long-term investments would make eminently good sense.

quotations do become available. If one of the instruments is sold before an allocation can be made the proceeds will have to be credited against the joint cost
and the net amount shown as cost of the remaining instrument.

2. The foregoing would be one of the few cases in which proceeds on disposal
   may be credited against carrying value of an investment and no gain or loss
   recognized on the sale. Another possible case would be where a large block of
   a security is held which is not readily marketable and where the entire investment was looked upon at the time it was made as a single speculation. In the
   ordinary case however, such practice would not be acceptable.*

3. Where stock splits occur or stock dividends are received the original cost of
   the stock held is divided by the new number of shares held to arrive at a new
   unit cost. No gain or loss is recognized. If stock rights are received some writers
   advocate assigning a value to them based on their market value when originally
   traded and deducting this amount from the cost of the stock holding. In effect,
   the cost is apportioned. The more common practice, however, is to make no
   entry when rights are received. If exercised, the exercise price would be added
   to the account for investment in the stock and a new unit carrying value calculated. If sold, the proceeds from the rights would be credited to the investment
   account.

4. Where a security is voluntarily exchanged for another the exchange transaction
   should be recorded at the value of the new security acquired and a gain or loss
   recognized. In such cases, only if a value for the new security cannot be objectively assigned is it permissible to carry forward the old cost of the security
   exchanged without adjustment.

5. Where an interest bearing security is bought at a price which includes payment
   for accrued interest, the accrued interest portion should not be treated as part
   of the cost of the security but rather as a separate asset.

6. Fixed maturity date securities (such as bonds or mortgages) are usually bought
   at a discount from, or premium over, face value. If acquired for a temporary
   hold (as would more often be the case with trading companies) the discount or
   premium need not be amortized. If the security is bought for a longer term hold
   however, amortization should be written except where a discount reflects doubt
   as to eventual repayment of the principal. For purposes of description in the
   financial statements of the basis of valuation, the term 'at cost' is considered to
   include valuation at amortized cost.

After investments have been held for some time their value will usually depart
from cost. The accounting consequences of this differ somewhat depending on
whether the investment is classified as current or non-current. Current assets are
supposed, as a general rule, to be realizable at values not less than those at which

---

* Recommendation on Accounting Principles No. 28 of the Institute of Chartered Accountants in England and Wales deals with "The Accounts of Investment Trust Companies" (an investment trust company is a financial intermediary under our definition).
The Recommendation indicates that whole portfolios of investments of such companies
in some cases are carried at cost less net accumulated gains on investments realized. It is
believed this practice would not be 'generally accepted' in North America.

they are carried. If, therefore, investments are shown as current assets they should be written down below cost to reflect any material decline in market value. In other words, the basis of valuation is 'cost or market whichever is lower'. It might be thought that since only readily marketable securities may be carried as current assets, the market value must always be reasonably objectively determinable and such securities should be carried always at market rather than at cost. Market values continually fluctuate, however, and in practice to date the gain in accuracy of investment valuation in the statements has not been considered worth the nuisance of adjusting values.*

Where a write-down to market is made it may be calculated on the basis of treating each security holding separately and comparing it with its cost, or by comparing the market value of the portfolio as a whole with its aggregate cost. The former method would usually result in an overall valuation of the portfolio which is below both cost and market and would seem unduly conservative.

Since market values fluctuate the market value test can only be applied as at one date and that is the date of the balance sheet. Changes in value after the balance sheet date do not affect the accounts unless they would qualify as a 'subsequent event' of such magnitude as to require disclosure in the statements in order to make them not misleading.

If investments are not represented to be current assets in the balance sheet current market values are considered to be of less importance and a write-down to market is deemed necessary only if it is thought the decline in value will be enduring. It would be the more common practice in this case to look at each security holding individually in applying this test.

Once investments have been written down the new valuation is deemed to be cost for subsequent accounting purposes. Thus, even though the market value rises again subsequent to the write-down, the operation of the 'cost or market whichever is lower' rule does not bring about a reversal of the previous write-down.

Where investments are held for some time, their value may rise so that the cost basis may become increasingly inappropriate as a carrying value. Revaluation to a more realistic value on the same basis as appraisal revaluations of fixed assets is logically acceptable in these circumstances, although examples of this being done in North America are extremely rare.

Determination of cost of investments sold

When investments are sold the cost or other carrying value must be matched with the net disposal proceeds to determine gain or loss on disposal. Where the entire holding of a particular security is sold at one time there is no problem in this. A question can arise, however, where a sale consists of less than the complete holding, if that holding was acquired at different times and at different unit costs.

In the U.S., under the influence of tax rules, the cost to be written off is de-

---

* In recent years several accounting writers have argued that current market values would be a better basis for valuing investments in the balance sheet, particularly those held as current assets. A hearing sponsored by the AICPA Accounting Principles Board on May 25–27, 1971, however, revealed considerable opposition to this proposal from representatives of a number of companies, especially if fluctuations in market values were reflected through income account.

termined by specific identification of the security actually sold, or if this cannot be established on the first-in/first-out assumption – i.e. that the securities sold were those acquired in the earliest transaction in the security. Since all certificates of similar denomination of a security must have equal value it is hard to imagine a less rational rule than that of 'specific identification' of the security. The rule also permits manipulation of the gain or loss to be reported, merely by selection of the piece of paper to be sold.

In Canada the normal practice would be to take the average cost of the entire holding of the security as the basis of determination of cost to be written off on sale. One or two examples of the use of the LIFO assumption are also known. Where there is a large holding of a particular security, the market value of which is substantially above its carrying value, and the investor follows the practice of buying and selling small quantities of the security whenever the market appears favorable, the gain or loss on recent investment decisions may be better reflected by costing sales on the LIFO basis than on the average cost basis.

Accounting for investment income

The rules for accounting for income are relatively straightforward. If material amounts of income are received from interest-bearing securities it should be accounted for on the accrual basis rather than the cash basis. The normal practice in accounting for dividend income is to record it as cash is received, although it would be perfectly correct to record dividends as receivable on the record date.

Stock dividends paid to common shareholders are not regarded as income to the recipient since the shareholders' proportional interest in the company is not changed or increased by the stock dividend.

Gains or losses on disposal of investments would be treated either as ordinary or extraordinary income (see Chapter 14) depending on whether the investments were 'bought for resale'. Since ultimate resale is a possibility associated with virtually every purchase of investments the distinction between ordinary and extraordinary gains is hard to make. In practice, the size of the gain or loss is more likely to determine whether it is treated as 'extraordinary'.

Principles of Accounting for Investments Held by Trading Companies

The foregoing discussion may be summarized in the following principles:

1. Investments held by trading companies may be classified as:
   (a) investments in subsidiaries or in other members of an affiliated group of companies,
   (b) other investments held for continuing business advantage, which usually may be described as 'investments in associated companies', and
   (c) other investments.
   Current assets include only such of the third group as are both readily marketable and not intended to be held for an extended period of time.

2. The primary basis of valuation of investments (other than in affiliated or associated companies) is cost. Provision should be made for the diminution in value:

(a) where the market value of the investments carried as current assets is materially below cost at the balance sheet date,

(b) in other cases where the decline in value of the investment appears to be enduring.

In exceptional cases where the current value of investments held has appreciated so much that the cost figure is meaningless, investments may be reappraised at the higher value, the write-up being credited to an appraisal increment account.

3. The basis of valuation of investments should be disclosed. In addition:

(a) the market value of investments carried as current assets should be disclosed,

(b) the market value of significant holdings of marketable securities (excluding those in subsidiary and affiliated companies) which are carried as non-current assets should also be disclosed,

(c) where the current value of other investments is significantly different from carrying value, some indication of current value is desirable.

4. Where a part only of the holding of a particular security is sold, the average carrying value of the entire holding should normally be used for determining the figure to be written off against sales proceeds.

5. Receipt of a stock dividend does not constitute income to the recipient.

References

1. Finney, Miller and Byrd, *Principles of Accounting, Intermediate* (5th ed., Englewood Cliffs, N.J.: Prentice-Hall Inc. 1959) at page 296. For the opposite view see Meigs and Johnson, *Accounting, the Basis for Business Decision* (2nd ed., New York: McGraw-Hill Inc. 1962) at page 593.

17 Investments by trading companies in affiliated and associated companies

This Chapter deals with the problems associated with accounting by a trading company for investments in securities of other enterprises where such securities are held to obtain control, influence the direction of the other business, or for other reasons of business policy. It excludes consideration of investments held solely as investments – which have been dealt with in the preceding Chapter.

The distinction will not always be clear-cut. A company may invest in other companies in related lines of business because it feels it is in a better position to appraise the investment qualities of such securities as well as for reasons of business policy. However, where less than 50% ownership is held, the problems in accounting are not dissimilar, regardless of the reason for which the investment is made. Where more than 50% is held, the investor company almost inevitably takes on managerial responsibility beyond that of the pure investor.

The bases of accounting for and reporting on inter-corporate investments may be broadly classified under the following headings:
(a) Consolidation methods
(b) Investment accounting methods
    (i) cost basis
    (ii) cost plus equity in earnings ('one-line consolidation').

By consolidation methods, we mean those methods of financial reporting by which the carrying value of the investment in the accounts of the investor company is eliminated and there is substituted therefor figures representing the several assets and liabilities of the investee company. In addition, the amounts shown in the statements of income and source and application of funds of the investee company (after adjustments for the purpose of consolidation) are added to the details of income and flow of funds of the investor company to make consolidated statements.

Where the investor's equity in the investee company is less than 100%, it is possible to conceive of two methods of consolidation as a matter of mechanics. Under one, which may be called the 'partnership basis', only the investor company's pro rata share of assets of the subsidiary would be substituted for its investment account. In contrast, under the full consolidation method, all of the amounts in the accounts of the investee company would be picked up in the consolidated statements and a 'minority interest' would be recorded on the liability side of the balance sheet to allow for the equity in the investee company not attributable to the investor company. The partnership basis is applicable only in rare instances, if at all, and consideration of it is deferred until later discussion of accounting for jointly-owned companies. Full consolidation accounting, on the other hand, represents the most important single approach to accounting for inter-corporate investments.

Consolidation Accounting – Concepts and Criteria

Basic concepts underlying consolidated statements

Consolidation accounting treats a group of companies, rather than the parent company by itself, as the entity whose activities are to be reported on in the financial statements. There have been at least three separate conceptual justifications for this departure in reporting from legal form. On the one hand, the objective has been thought of as being to portray realistically the assets and operations of what is an operational unit. On this view the important test for consolidation would be whether there existed central direction and control and whether the activities consolidated contributed to a common product or service. Thus, companies might be consolidated because they were controlled through long-term lease or management contract relationships even though the parent company held no equity interest in them. A second concept of a consolidated group is that of a financial unit – i.e. one that is controlled by the parent company through the medium of share interest, direct or indirect, in the subsidiaries. A third view considers the consolidated accounts as merely a more illuminating form of presentation of the parent company's accounts, the improvement arising from the substitution of detail about subsidiary assets, liabilities, revenues and expenses for the investment and dividend income accounts in the parent company's records. On this basis it would be effective ownership of the subsidiary's assets that would be the strongest determinant of whether or not they should be consolidated.

Over the years, the first of these views has largely vanished. The idea that only companies contributing to a common product or service may be consolidated has disappeared as business has tended to become increasingly diversified (and latterly there has emerged the 'conglomerate company' engaged in a multitude of activities neither vertically nor horizontally integrated). There may be isolated instances where subsidiaries are consolidated when the residual equity is not owned by the parent, but these are likely to be cases where an examination of the facts indicates that such equity has no substance and the parent company is entitled to all or virtually all of the benefits from the subsidiaries' operations.

The other two concepts may both be identified as influencing practice. They are, of course, somewhat similar in their emphasis on inter-company share ownership as the requisite foundation for consolidation. The practical effect of the differences between them would be one of degree. Under the 'financial unit' viewpoint, control through share ownership would be the factor justifying treatment of the group as one entity. A holding of 51% of the voting shares would therefore ordinarily justify consolidation.* Under the 'parent company extended' viewpoint there would be reluctance to consolidate subsidiaries with as little as 51% ownership, especially if there were also substantial debt in such subsidiaries.

Limitations of consolidation accounting

The simple argument in favour of consolidation accounting is best illustrated by considering the case of a company which establishes a new wholly-owned subsidiary to carry on an activity or function formerly operated by the parent company itself. Unless the accounts of this new subsidiary are consolidated a substantial amount of information disappears from the financial statements. The working capital in the subsidiary, the fixed and other long-term assets and its debt, no longer appear in the parent company's balance sheet. Instead a figure for the investment in the subsidiary is shown in the non-current section of the balance sheet. The sales, costs and expenses of the subsidiary are excluded from the consolidated income statement to be replaced by one net figure representing the subsidiary's income, if the investment in the subsidiary is carried on the 'equity' basis. If the investment is accounted for on the 'cost' basis the situation is even worse. No figure at all will be included for the subsidiary's earnings unless dividends are declared by it, and the amount of such dividends is, of course, subject to the determination of the parent company. Considerable opportunity for manipulation of the parent company's income figures, thus, may exist.

For reasons such as these the long-term trend has been towards an ever increasing degree of consolidation in published financial reports. But there are some disadvantages to this as well as advantages. In the first place, consolidated financial statements may be less satisfactory as a basis for financial analysis because of the averaging effects of the consolidation on financial ratios. For example, the working capital ratio typical of a public utility is very different from that of a manufacturing operation. The gross margin on sales of a manufacturer is different from that of a wholesaler which is typically different again from that of a retailer. The combination of these figures in a consolidation produces an average which may be typical of nothing. Moreover, the consolidated ratios may change from year to year as a result solely of changes in the mix of activities carried on by the group, so that examination of trends is made more difficult. Where financial intermediaries are included in the consolidated group, the distortion is even more extreme since these companies typically have very different financing patterns, and their assets do not sensibly fit into the categories of current assets, fixed assets, etc. common to trading companies. All this of course, is true equally of companies that carry on diverse activities through divisions rather than subsidiaries. The criticism therefore is not of consolidation accounting as such, but rather of the potential inadequacy of normal financial reporting for any entity that carries on a diversified business. The general solution to the problem lies not in attempting to distinguish between cases that should be consolidated and those that should not, but rather in furnishing

---

* In a pyramid holding-subsidiary company relationship, one might well find that the investment of the so-called 'minority interest' exceeded that attributable to the shareholders of the parent company in the consolidated balance sheet.

additional information by operating 'segments' of the consolidated entity. (See further discussion in Chapter 20.)

In the second place, the consolidation of figures in the standard fashion may tend to cause the reader to overlook certain important information about legal restrictions on the free movement of assets within the group. For example, the working capital shown in the consolidated balance sheet consists essentially of the sum of the amounts of working capital shown in each company in the group (after allowing for elimination of inter-company accounts and transactions). Such consolidated working capital might consist of a combination of a very weak position in the parent company and its wholly-owned subsidiaries and a very strong position in one subsidiary with a large minority interest. In this case, it would not be apparent from the consolidated balance sheet that the working capital of the strong subsidiary would not be freely available to the group without payment of dividends, the minority share in which would substantially deplete consolidated working capital. Along the same lines it may be observed that where a substantial part of the consolidated income is earned by the subsidiaries, the availability of such earnings for dividends to parent company shareholders may be subject to such deductions as:

– restrictions imposed by covenants securing debt of a subsidiary
– foreign exchange restrictions on remittance of earnings of foreign subsidiaries
– foreign withholding taxes and domestic income taxes on dividend remittances.

Also, to the extent that consolidated retained earnings is composed of unremitted subsidiary earnings it would not legally be available for payment of dividends by the parent company. Of course, disclosure may be made in the consolidated financial statements of these matters; provision should be made for taxes likely to be payable on income remittances and may be made for potential taxes with respect to earnings retained by subsidiaries and not expected to be remitted currently. (See discussion in Appendix A.)

Another case illustrating the potentially misleading inferences which could be drawn from consolidated financial statements relates to debt outstanding or proposed to be issued by the parent company. One of the standard calculations made in appraising the quality of bonds and debentures is the number of times that interest on the obligations and on all other obligations ranking equal or prior to them is covered by income before taxes. If a consolidated income statement showed the following picture:

Income before interest, income taxes and minority interest	$7,710,000
Interest on funded debt	1,300,000
	6,410,000
Income taxes	3,290,000
Income before minority interest	3,120,000
Attributable to minority interest	528,000
Net income for the year	$2,592,000

The interest coverage would appear to be a fairly healthy 5.9 times. But these consolidated figures might be made up of the following (ignoring consolidation adjustments and eliminations):

	Parent Co.	*Subsidiary Co.*
Income before interest and income taxes	$2,280,000	$5,430,000
Interest on funded debt	1,300,000	
Income before taxes	980,000	5,430,000
Income taxes	500,000	2,790,000
Net income for year	480,000	2,640,000
Minority interest share – (20%)		528,000
Net income for parent company	$ 480,000	$2,112,000

From this it may be seen that earnings actually available to meet the interest on funded debt are only $4,392,000 ($2,280,000 plus $2,112,000) so that the interest coverage is not 5.9 times but a considerably more modest 3.4 times. To meet this point, the regulations to the securities acts of a number of Canadian provinces require that in prospectuses for the sale of debt securities there must be disclosed the consolidated earnings available for payment of interest, after deducting the amount of taxes with respect to the income or distribution of income of the subsidiaries.

Many of these limitations on the usefulness of consolidated financial statements could be ameliorated by supplementary statements and information, and to some degree such information is furnished. But there are no universally recognized standards for the additional disclosure that should be furnished in consolidated statements (although the United Kingdom Companies Act requires that parent company statements be furnished as well as consolidated statements).

As a generalization, it may be said that consolidated financial statements are virtually useless for the purpose of the short-term creditor, that they need to be treated with reserve by long-term creditors and be supplemented by a good deal of extra information, and that they have a number of weaknesses even for use by shareholders. Despite this, their use and the degree of consolidation of subsidiaries, has increased steadily in the past thirty years. It is apparent that no more effective way has been discovered to convey as much information about complex affiliated company structures as succinctly and understandably. Moreover it is also evident, as might be expected, that where there is a conflict of interest between users of annual reports the needs of the equity investor prevail. The creditor must meet his requirements for information by exacting special purpose statements as the price of lending money.

Criteria for consolidation

When should the accounts of a subsidiary be consolidated? In the light of the somewhat conflicting concepts of the objectives of consolidation and the recognized limitations of consolidated statements, it is not surprising that clearer criteria indicating just when a subsidiary should be consolidated have not developed. The following are some of the factors that influence the consolidation policies of companies:

1. *Control* through ownership of voting securities is probably the most important test. A subsidiary will rarely be consolidated if less than 50% of the voting stock

is held by the parent. Effective loss of control may also cause the exclusion of a subsidiary from consolidation. For example, a subsidiary in receivership might be excluded. A foreign subsidiary whose operations are being interfered with by the local government or which is subject to rigid foreign exchange restrictions may be excluded. Even in the absence of these conditions however, the mere existence of control is not decisive in causing consolidation of a subsidiary company.

2. Many companies use *degree of ownership* as a criterion for consolidation and require a higher percentage of ownership than merely 50% plus. At one extreme, some companies will consolidate only wholly-owned subsidiaries. Others require arbitrarily set percentages – 90%, 75%, 66⅔% and so on. This criterion seems to be losing ground in favour of effective control as the determinant of consolidation.

3. *Homogeneity of operation* in the past was considered an important criterion for consolidation. Under this test, for example, finance company subsidiaries have been excluded from consolidation with manufacturing parents, manufacturing subsidiaries from consolidation with public utility parents and so on. As indicated above, the criterion has now lost much of its influence in the face of the increasing diversification of business generally. It would still be seriously considered, however, where affiliated groups include both trading companies and financial intermediaries or regulated and non-regulated enterprises. However, APB Opinion No. 10 required that subsidiaries whose principal business activity was leasing property or facilities to parent or affiliated companies should be consolidated.

4. *Geographical location* has also been given as a reason for the non-consolidation of foreign subsidiaries. This policy developed in the United States particularly in the years just prior to the Second World War and may have been justified by the unsettled international conditions at the time. As a general policy however, it seems of doubtful merit. One would think that if a parent company places sufficient faith in the stability of a foreign country to invest in it, it should have sufficient faith to report the results of operations there in a straightforward manner. Wars and revolutions, of course, may alter the picture in any particular location, but a general ban on consolidation of foreign operations seems unnecessarily conservative. It is interesting to note that U.K. companies, in keeping with their historic world trading tradition, show no similar reluctance to report fully on foreign operations.

In summary, the criteria governing consolidation policy by companies today are not perfectly clearly established. The dominant considerations are degree of ownership and effectiveness of control, but these are not necessarily consistently evaluated by all companies. The general presumption is that consolidated statements present the financial position and results of operations of an affiliated group more realistically for the shareholders of the parent company than do unconsolidated statements, and the long-term trend is to more presentation of consolidated statements and a fuller degree of consolidation in them. It is recognized, however, that circumstances may exist which justify the exclusion of individual subsidiary companies.

There are many theoretical problems that can arise in preparing consolidated statements. These are discussed in Appendix A.

Investment Accounting Methods

The alternative to consolidation accounting for inter-corporate investments is to follow one of the recognized bases for accounting for investments, namely carrying them at cost, at cost or market whichever is lower, or on the 'equity' method. These bases of accounting are discussed further below.

As pointed out in Chapter 16, investments shown as current assets are carried on the basis of the lower of cost and market, while other investments are usually carried at cost reduced to estimated realizable value only if the decline in such value is thought to be enduring. Since investments held for reasons of business policy are not considered current assets, the cost or market rule is not applicable to them. Instead, the most common basis of accounting for inter-corporate investments is cost, subject to the proviso that a write-down below cost would be made for a substantial and apparently enduring decline in value. On the cost basis of accounting, income from the investment is recognized when, and only when, dividends are received. This is subject to a rare exception where a dividend is paid out of surplus of the investee company earned prior to the date the investment was made. In such cases the dividend is a return of capital to the investor rather than income and is credited against the cost of the investment.

An alternative basis of accounting for inter-corporate investments, and one which is increasing in popularity, is the so-called 'equity' method. On this basis the investment is initially recorded at cost but the carrying value is adjusted thereafter to show the investor company's pro rata share of the earnings of the other company.*

There is one point, however, which sometimes is overlooked in using the equity method. The amount paid by the investor company reflects a valuation of the investee company which is different from that shown on the books of the latter. Typically, the cost of the investment will exceed its book value as shown by the accounts of the investee company. If then the initial basis of accounting is cost, reflecting the investor's valuation of the investment at date of acquisition, and to it are added earnings which are based on the valuations in the investee company books, there will be an illogical mixture of valuations. To cure this it is necessary to examine the cost of the investment and relate any excess of such cost over underlying book value to specific assets of the investee company. The process is the same as that required in dealing with purchase discrepancies in consolidations (which will be discussed more fully in the next Chapter). If, on examination, some part of the excess relates to assets with a limited life (such as fixed assets or patents) the earnings reported by the investee company should be adjusted to reflect

---

* Actually, the 'equity' label is a misnomer for this accounting method. The method might more properly be described as 'cost plus equity in post-acquisition earnings'. There have been cases where companies have literally followed an equity basis of accounting for investments by writing the investment account up or down at time of acquisition to the underlying equity as shown by the accounts of the company in which the investment is made. It is clear, however, that this practice does not conform to any recognizable accounting principle.

amortization of the excess investment cost by the investor company, and only the net amount should be added to the investment account. The general rule is that the earnings reported by the investor company should be the same as they would be if the investment were consolidated.

Criteria determining the use of investment accounting methods

The chief criticism of the cost method of investment accounting is that frequently the amount of dividends received does not fairly represent the income from an investment. It has already been pointed out that companies typically plow back a substantial part of their earnings to finance growth. The result of this and other factors has been that the results of an investment policy are not fairly measured without taking into account the factor of growth in capital value of the investment. As against this, it may be argued that the increase in capital value is not realized and therefore should not be recorded. But strict adherence to a realization test is fast becoming outmoded in accounting. If companies do not pay out all earnings in dividends the requirement that gains be in a separable form is unnecessary. Recognition of income as earned, in several situations in accounting, should depend on when it can be measured reasonably accurately, not on realization.

Where an inter-corporate investment provides effective control of the investor company there is the further objection that dividends paid, and therefore income recorded by the investor company, are subject to arbitrary decision of its management. On the other hand, the equity basis, in a controlled situation, provides a measure of the achievement in an area for which the management of the investor company must take some responsibility.

We shall now consider more closely different types of inter-corporate investments.

Unconsolidated subsidiaries

There may be reasons, as previously indicated, why subsidiary companies are not consolidated. In such cases the arguments in favour of equity accounting are very strong. APB Opinion No. 18 requires this basis of accounting in consolidated statements, or in parent company statements issued to shareholders as the primary reporting medium, for investments in all unconsolidated subsidiaries except where the investment is likely to be temporary or where the majority interest has lost control (e.g. through reorganization, receivership, or bankruptcy proceedings). The cost basis of accounting continues to be used in Canada for the majority of unconsolidated subsidiaries but the use of the equity basis is increasing rapidly.

'Partnership' investments

It is quite common to find companies entering into what are essentially partnership arrangements although they are implemented through the medium of formation of a separate corporation in which the partners hold shares. There are a variety of reasons for such arrangements. The companies concerned may wish to share the costs of a common facility. They may be coming together in a joint venture because by pooling their efforts they can build a larger plant, with consequent economies of scale, than any of them could handle on their own. Or one partner may produce a by-product which is usable after further processing and the other may be looking for an assured source of supply for such processed product. By forming the joint venture they may share the processing costs and assure themselves of a secure market and a secure source of supply respectively. Frequently two companies share equally in '50%-owned companies' but partnerships of more than two companies are not uncommon.

Practice in accounting for inter-corporate investments which are essentially partnerships varies. In a majority of cases they are accounted for on the cost basis. For 50%-owned companies a trend is developing towards using the equity basis of accounting. One or two other methods are occasionally found.

On one basis, sometimes known as a 'line by line consolidation', each partner takes up in his financial statements his pro rata share of the assets, liabilities, revenues and costs of the partnership. The accounting is like a consolidation in that there is a substitution of partnership net assets for the partnership investment account, but unlike a consolidation in that only the partnership percentage is taken up, rather than all the assets and liabilities being taken up offset by a 'minority interest'.

Another basis is a mixture of the equity basis and the 'line by line' method. The investment in the venture will be shown in the balance sheet as one figure equal to that arrived at on the equity basis, but the investor's share of the revenues and costs will be added in to the income account on a line by line basis, rather than showing merely as one net figure brought into income.

In the writer's opinion, the appropriate accounting basis may vary. In a minority of cases, where the inter-corporate investment is in another company which has been set up not primarily to make profits but rather to provide a facility for joint use by the partners, a reasonable treatment would be to consolidate the proportionate interest in the jointly-owned company on the line by line method. In other cases he would think the equity basis of accounting, supplemented by condensed financial statement summaries with respect to major inter-corporate investments, would be appropriate and would reflect the financial position and results of operations of the investor company better than the cost basis of accounting.

Other substantial inter-corporate investments

Traditionally the cost basis has been used almost universally in accounting for investments where there is neither majority control nor a partnership equivalent arrangement. In recent years however, a number of writers have pointed out that where ownership of a company is widely dispersed a substantial block of shares, but considerably less than voting control, may give effective control if the one large interest can obtain proxies of the smaller shareholders. If such control exists the question arises whether the controlling investor should not be entitled to record his full share of earnings of the investee as it accrues rather than merely recording income as dividends are received.

Furthermore, the simple question may be asked whether cost can be regarded as an informative basis of accounting for investments at all, if any substantial period of time elapses after the date of investment. The plain fact is, as has already been noted, that under today's conditions the return on investments is expected to be only partly in the form of dividends and partly in the form of capital gains. Valuation at original cost ignores the second source of gain unless the investment is sold, and then attributes all of the gain to the period of sale, during which period the value of the investment may not have advanced at all. Where a company has amounts of inter-corporate investments that are significant to its financial position, it is a valid question whether the cost basis of accounting for these investments provides a fair presentation of financial position and results of operations. Disclosure of market value, while ameliorating the deficiency, does not provide a complete answer because statement readers tend not to give equal weight to supplementary disclosures.

Such considerations as these have led to extended reconsideration recently of the whole basis of accounting for investments. With respect to large holdings (but less than 50%) of the common stock of another company the following authoritative statements have recently been released: *

- "Accounting for the Results of Associated Companies" – this is the first statement of standard accounting practice prepared by the Accounting Standards Steering Committee of the Institute of Chartered Accountants in England and Wales. The statement requires that where an investor has a long-term investment in an associated company and participates in commercial and financial policy decisions of the investee, such investment should be reported (except in a parent company's unconsolidated or 'legal' statements) on the equity basis of accounting. An 'associated company' is defined as either:
  - (a) a company in which the investor's interest is essentially that of a partner in a joint venture, or
  - (b) a company in which the investor's interest is substantial (i.e. not less than 20% of the equity voting rights) and the investor is in a position to exercise a significant influence over it.
- "The Equity Method of Accounting for Investments in Common Stock" – APB Opinion No. 18. This Opinion likewise requires the use of the equity basis of accounting for investments:
  - (a) in 'corporate joint ventures',
  - (b) where the investor has the ability through his investment to exercise significant influence over the operating and financial policies of the investee (a holding of 20% or more leads to a rebuttable presumption that the investor has such ability, and vice versa).

Principles of Accounting for Inter-Corporate Investments

The foregoing discussions may be summed up in the following principles:

1. Where a holding company owns directly or indirectly over 50% of the voting shares of a subsidiary, consolidated financial statements are ordinarily necessary to a fair presentation of the financial position of the holding company. Exceptions to this general rule are:

---

* The CICA Research Committee has also issued an Exposure Draft of recommendations on long-term investments containing somewhat similar views to the statements cited here.

(a) where control is expected to be temporary or where control has been lost, e.g. because the subsidiary is in receivership or because a foreign government is creating substantial interference with its operations or its right to remit dividends;

(b) where there is an extremely sizeable minority interest;

(c) where inclusion of a subsidiary would have an extremely distorting effect on the consolidated financial statements – e.g. where the parent company controls a financial institution.

2. The aim of consolidated financial statements is to present the financial position and results of operations as though the group of companies were one company. Therefore, all interlocking accounts between companies in the group must be eliminated. Also, since one company cannot make a profit dealing with itself, provision must be made for elimination of profits made by one company on sale to another in the group where the assets sold are still included as assets in the consolidated balance sheet, so that the assets will be restated on a cost basis in accordance with normal accounting practice. Income tax paid by individual companies with respect to such profits eliminated should be deferred.

3. The consolidation policy followed by the holding company should be disclosed. If any subsidiaries are not consolidated the reasons for such exclusion and the amount of their profits for the year and since date of acquisition, to the extent that they have not been reflected in the holding company's accounts, should be disclosed. If unremitted subsidiary company profits included in the consolidation would be subject to tax on remittance this fact should be disclosed, preferably with an estimate of the amount of tax that would have been paid had all the year's earnings been remitted.

4. Investments in unconsolidated subsidiaries should normally be accounted for on the equity basis rather than the cost basis, except where control has been lost or is likely to be temporary.

5. Investments in associated companies (where ownership is 50% or less) are usually accounted for at cost. In 50% owned companies, companies which are effectively controlled with less than 50% ownership, or joint ventures, the equity basis is an acceptable alternative. (Where the joint venture is of the cost-sharing type, rather than being a profit-oriented venture, 'line-by-line' consolidation may also be appropriate.)

6. On either the cost or equity basis of investment accounting, if there appears to be a more than temporary decline in the value of the investment below the figure at which it is carried in the accounts, a write-down should be made.

18   Business combinations

The term 'business combination' refers to the bringing together under common ownership and control of businesses formerly operating independently. Such combinations may be effected in a variety of ways – through one enterprise acquiring control of the assets of another in consideration for cash, debt or the issue of shares, or through purchase of a company's shares for cash or debt, through share exchanges, through incorporation of a new company to acquire the shares of two existing companies, through statutory amalgamations or through a combination of these methods.

The decade of the 1960's and particularly the second half of the decade saw a significant surge in the number of such combinations and the value of enterprises involved. Many factors contributed to this surge – including the evolution of the so-called 'conglomerate' company – but fundamentally the buoyant economy of the decade was responsible. The growth in the business combination movement, however, threw a spotlight on a serious weakness in accounting theory – and one which in itself may have contributed to "the urge to merge".

Problems in accounting for business combinations

There are two specific accounting problems frequently associated with business combinations, namely:

1. measuring the amount of consideration paid by the acquiring party, where such consideration is wholly or partly in other than cash form.

2. assigning the measured cost (including the amount of any liabilities assumed, if any) to the various individual assets belonging to the business taken over, in the absence of bargaining with respect to individual values.

The second problem is the more prevalent, and usually the more difficult. It has already been indicated (in Chapter 6) that current accounting principles call for allocation of the cost of a 'basket purchase' in proportion to the values of the several assets acquired. It was also noted, however, that reliable valuations of individual assets of a business taken over are frequently not readily available, so that the principle is difficult to implement in practice.

Faced with this situation, there is always a temptation for the purchaser to adopt the book values of the business taken over for his own accounting with adjustments where the purchaser's accounting bases differ from those of the business acquired. As a practical matter this may not be very objectionable if the vendor's book values can be considered a reasonably close approximation of current values, and this assumption is substantiated by the fact that the total consideration paid for the business acquired is not too far different from its aggregate book values.

It may be assumed that these conditions prevailed to a much greater extent thirty or forty years ago than they do today. Moreover accounting theory then was not so highly developed. As a result it was standard accounting practice, confirmed by accounting texts, for the purchaser to carry forward the book values of assets of the business acquired (whether purchased directly, or in consolidation if the business was taken over through purchase of its shares) and to treat any purchase discrepancy between the total of these book values and the total consideration given as one figure shown separately in the balance sheet. This difference, if positive, was often called 'goodwill on consolidation' and was usually carried as one of the final assets shown in the balance sheet. If negative, the difference was shown in the balance sheet after the liabilities, or else was shown as a sort of capital surplus in the shareholders' equity section. Positive and negative discrepancies on separate acquisitions might be offset against each other. Finally it was quite common to find such purchase discrepancies written off directly to retained earnings account at the time of acquisition or later. In summary, no great significance was attributed to the accounting for purchase discrepancies, and no particular emphasis was laid on accounting for *all* the consideration involved in a business combination.

Given this approach the other problem associated with business combinations, namely that of valuation of non-cash consideration given for a business acquisition, was of minor importance. If debt was given the face value of the debt could be accepted, usually without question. If shares were given as consideration the issue price could be stated at almost any reasonable figure (not lower than par value). Indeed it was possible to set the issue price of the shares given up equal to the total book value of the assets of the business acquired, and thus prevent any 'purchase discrepancy' appearing in the transaction at all. Once again, the failure to account for the fair value of the shares issued was contrary to today's measurement principles as set out in Chapter 6.

Thus historically a weakness was built in to the standard method of accounting for business combinations. As the transaction measurement principles of accounting came to be more clearly recognized the standard method of accounting for business combinations could be seen to be in fundamental conflict with them. Nevertheless, it was difficult to come to grips with the discrepancy because:

1. When all is said and done, it is a quite difficult task to assign reasonable current values to all the assets of a business taken over. Moreover the management of one business acquiring another has usually more pressing tasks to accomplish than making such a valuation.

2. Acquisitions of another business occur only sporadically so that it is hard to build up expertise in the valuation problems involved.

The difficulty was accentuated by the tendency, as time passed, to an increase in the discrepancy between the amount of consideration given and the aggregate book values of the business acquired in the typical combination. Partly this was the result of the continuous period of inflation from 1940 onwards. (In part also, it might have reflected the ability to pay increased premiums as a result of the accounting advantages to growth by acquisition as opposed to internal growth.) In any event, allocation of the larger purchase discrepancies to individual assets such as inventory or buildings and equipment would have meant increased charges against income as such assets were sold or depreciated, thereby resulting in lower reported earnings and earnings per share. And allocation of any balance of the purchase discrepancy as the cost of true 'goodwill' (the value attaching to all the intangible advantages of a going concern) brought the accountant right up against the unresolved problem of how best to account for goodwill (see Chapter 11). Thus the managements of takeover-minded companies were given practical reasons to question the need for changes in the traditional methods of accounting for business combinations. On top of all this there developed in the United States a theory that certain business combinations represented not straight purchases of one business by another, but rather 'poolings of interests' where neither party was buying out the other. Controversy over the validity of this concept and the limits on its application bedevilled business combination accounting throughout the 1950's and 1960's.

Development of accounting applicable to business combinations

The preceding section has described the traditional method used to account for business combinations as it developed well over thirty years ago. The following are some notes on accounting developments in the last thirty years that affected, or tended to modify, the traditional method of accounting.

- AICPA Accounting Research Bulletin No. 24 on accounting for intangibles issued in December 1944 laid down the basic principle for measurement of non-cash transactions: "cost may be determined either by the fair value of the consideration given or by the fair value of the property acquired, whichever is the more clearly evident." It also stated that where practicable there should be an allocation to tangible and intangible assets of any excess of price paid for investment in a subsidiary over its net recorded assets at date of acquisition. The Bulletin, however, conceded that after establishing the cost of purchased goodwill at fair value at time of acquisition, it was permissible (though undesirable) to write off the goodwill against either paid-in capital or retained earnings.
- S.E.C. Accounting Series Release No. 50 issued in 1945 held that the write-off of purchased goodwill to paid-in capital was contrary to sound accounting principles.
- In 1946 the 'pooling of interests' accounting method was, in effect, accepted by the Securities and Exchange Commission in the merger of Celanese Corporation of America and Tubize Rayon Corporation. In this case Tubize preferred stock was converted into Celanese preferred stock share for share, and each Tubize common stock was converted into two-thirds of a share of Celanese common stock. The book values of the companies' common stocks were almost exactly in a 3 to 2 ratio, and earnings per common share were approximately in a 3 to 2 ratio.[1]
- Accounting Research Bulletin No. 40 in September 1950 was the first official

pronouncement on business combination accounting. It laid down four criteria to describe business combinations in which pooling of interests accounting was acceptable.

- Chapter 5 of Accounting Research Bulletin No. 43 issued in June 1953 reversed Bulletin 24 and stated that purchased goodwill should not be written off against paid-in capital, nor should it be written off against retained earnings immediately after acquisition. Intangibles with a limited term of existence should be amortized systematically by charges against income. Intangibles without an apparent limit to their life should be carried at cost; however if it was thought their life might eventually come to an end, they could be amortized on an arbitrary but systematic basis even without present indications that their life might be limited. Once it became evident the life of an intangible had become limited, amortization should begin.
- Accounting Research Bulletin No. 43, Chapter 7, Section C, Accounting Research Bulletin No. 48 issued in January 1957 and Accounting Principles Board Opinion No. 6 in October 1965 attempted further interpretation of the concept of 'pooling of interests', without having much apparent influence on the development of practice.
- In Bulletin No. 20 issued in July 1964 the CICA Research Committee implied that the purchase price of shares of subsidiary companies should be allocated to assets according to the value of the assets at acquisition – "The difference between (a) the cost of the shares to the parent company and (b) its equity in the net assets of subsidiaries at the dates of acquisition of the shares should be dealt with in the consolidated balance sheet according to its nature. Where such difference, or any portion thereof, is attributable to specific assets, it should be allocated to them and incorporated in their carrying value in the consolidated balance sheet. Any balance of difference not so allocated should be shown under a suitable description in the balance sheet to the extent it has not been amortized or written off." (paragraph 60)

This superseded Bulletin 14 issued in 1957 which had said "The difference between (a) the cost of the shares to the parent company, and (b) its equity in the net assets of subsidiaries at the dates of acquisition of the shares, should be shown separately on the balance sheet unless such difference has been disposed of by a procedure disclosed in the annual statements of the years in which the disposition was made." (paragraph 45)

This was an important recommendation for change in normal Canadian practice. Unfortunately its impact was obscured by the fact that it was buried in a long Bulletin dedicated to detailed recommendations on disclosure rather than to recommendations on principle.

- Accounting Principles Board Opinion No. 16 issued in August 1970 summarized arguments for and against the 'pooling of interests' concept and accepted that it was a valid concept but only under conditions that were distinguishable from those in which 'purchase accounting' was appropriate. Operational criteria were developed in place of the previous broad criteria to differentiate the situations in which each method of accounting was appropriate.
- Accounting Principles Board Opinion No. 17 was issued at the same time. The Board concluded that all intangible assets recorded should be amortized by charges against income. Where the economic life of the asset could be estimated

the period of amortization should be based on that. Where a limit to such life could not be foreseen, however, or where the life was expected to exceed forty years, a maximum amortization period of forty years should be adopted in view of the uncertainties.

The 'pooling of interests' concept

The pooling of interests accounting method has been used much less, proportionately, in Canada than in the United States. This may perhaps be explained by the fact that the advantages of the pooling method in avoiding the recording of large amounts of goodwill in the balance sheet, and the necessity to charge income with higher costs of assets acquired, have frequently been obtained in Canada without resort to pooling, merely by following the historic method of accounting for business combinations. If Canadian accounting practice for business combinations were made consistent with the rest of the body of accounting principles this result would no longer obtain and there would probably be a quickening of interest in the pooling method. The concept, therefore, is worth some discussion. The following quotation from APB Opinion No. 16 summarizes the theory of pooling:

> "Those who support the pooling of interests method believe that a business combination effected by issuing common stock is different from a purchase in that no corporate assets are disbursed to stockholders and the net assets of the issuing corporation are enlarged by the net assets of the corporation whose stockholders accept common stock of the combined corporation. There is no newly invested capital nor have owners withdrawn assets from the group since the stock of a corporation is not one of its assets. Accordingly, the net assets of the constituents remain intact but combined; the stockholder groups remain intact but combined. Aggregate income is not changed since the total resources are not changed. Consequently, the historical costs and earnings of the separate corporations are appropriately combined. In a business combination effected by exchanging stock, groups of stockholders combine their resources, talents, and risks to form a new entity to carry on in combination the previous businesses and to continue their earnings streams. The sharing of risks by the constituent stockholder groups is an important element in a business combination effected by exchanging stock. By pooling equity interests, each group continues to maintain risk elements of its former investment and they mutually exchange risks and benefits.
>
> "A pooling of interests transaction is regarded as in substance an arrangement among stockholder groups. The fractional interests in the common enterprise are reallocated – risks are rearranged among the stockholder groups outside the corporate entity. A fundamental concept of entity accounting is that a corporation is separate and distinct from its stockholders. Elected managements represent the stockholders in bargaining to effect a combination, but the groups of stockholders usually decide whether the proposed terms are acceptable by voting to approve or disapprove a combination. Stockholders sometimes disapprove a combination proposed by management, and tender offers sometimes succeed despite the opposition of management.
>
> "Each stockholder group in a pooling of interests gives up its interests in assets formerly held but receives an interest in a portion of the assets formerly held in addition to an interest in the assets of the other. The clearest example of this type

of combination is one in which both groups surrender their stock and receive in exchange stock of a new corporation. The fact that one of the corporations usually issues its stock in exchange for that of the other does not alter the substance of the transaction."

Thus the primary condition justifying pooling of interests accounting is held to be a freely arrived at exchange of shares representing the residual equity in the combining parties, independent of the business entities themselves, and not affecting the total of assets under their control. This leads to the following restrictions on the use of pooling of interests accounting as expressed in APB Opinion No. 16.

Attributes of combining companies

(a) "Each of the combining companies is autonomous and has not been a subsidiary or division of another corporation within two years before the plan of combination is initiated."

If this condition could not be met, it was felt that the exchange was more akin to one of the parties disposing of a division or part of its assets, rather than a genuine sharing of interests.

(b) "Each of the combining companies is independent of the other combining companies."

If this condition did not exist the concept of an exchange freely arrived at would be invalidated.

Manner of combining interests

(a) "The combination is effected in a single transaction or is completed in accordance with a specific plan within one year after the plan is initiated."

A merging of equity interests as a whole must obviously be arranged all at once. Successive exchanges arranged independently over a period of time suggest that groups of shareholders are disposing of their interests, not pooling them.

(b) "A corporation offers and issues only common stock with rights identical to those of the majority of its outstanding common stock in exchange for substantially all of the voting common stock interest of another company at the date the plan of combination is consummated."

The distribution of a significant amount of cash or other consideration, or the existence of a significant minority interest after the combination, would negate the concept of a free exchange of interests by the residual equity interests. Also acceptance of a security distinguishable from common equity by one or the other of the parties would be more akin to a sale of their equity interest for other consideration, than to a pooling.

(c) "None of the combining companies changes the equity interest of the voting common stock in contemplation of effecting the combination either within two years before the plan of combination is initiated or between the dates the combination is initiated and consummated; changes in contemplation of effecting the combination may include distributions to stockholders and additional issuances, exchanges, and retirements of securities."

(d) "Each of the combining companies reacquires shares of voting common stock only for purposes other than business combinations, and no company reacquires more than a normal number of shares between the dates the plan of combination is initiated and consummated."

Conditions (c) and (d) are designed to prevent arrangements to bail out shareholders or other adjustments to make it look like all the residual equity interests are joining in, when in fact they are not.

(e) "The ratio of the interest of an individual common stockholder to those of other common stockholders in a combining company remains the same as a result of the exchange of stock to effect the combination."

Again this condition supports the assumption of a pooling by all stockholders rather than a disposition of residual equity interest by some for other consideration.

(f) "The voting rights to which the common stock ownership interests in the resulting combined corporation are entitled are exercisable by the stockholders; the stockholders are neither deprived of nor restricted in exercising those rights for a period."

The combining equity interests must retain all the rights and privileges usually pertaining to such an interest.

(g) "The combination is resolved at the date the plan is consummated and no provisions of the plan relating to the issue of securities or other consideration are pending."

Provisions in the agreement for contingent issuances make it look more like a buy-sell agreement than a pooling.

Absence of planned transactions

(a) "The combined corporation does not agree directly or indirectly to retire or reacquire all or part of the common stock issued to effect the combination.

(b) "The combined corporation does not enter into other financial arrangements for the benefit of the former stockholders of a combining company, such as a guaranty of loans secured by stock issued in the combination, which in effect negates the exchange of equity securities.

(c) "The combined corporation does not intend or plan to dispose of a significant part of the assets of the combining companies within two years after the combination other than disposals in the ordinary course of business of the formerly separate companies and to eliminate duplicate facilities or excess capacity."

These are designed merely to block attempts to make a purchase look like a pooling.

The foregoing discussion indicates that, except for the primary condition that the residual equity position be pooled, the former criteria said to distinguish a pooling of interests have been largely abandoned. These included:

1. A requirement that the principal equity interests entering into a pooling combination not dispose of their interests in the combined company shortly after the combination.

2. Representation of the directors and management of both parties in the direction of the combined entity.

3. A requirement that there be not too great a disparity in size between the two parties.

4. Continuity of business carried on before the combination so that it could be presumed the combination was not in substance a scheme for liquidation of one of the parties.

Regardless of the conceptual validity of these former criteria, they were not observed in any realistic way in practice and their influence was steadily eroded throughout the period 1950–1970.

Mechanics of implementation of the pooling concept

The application of the pooling concept is simplicity itself. The book values (after any adjustment required to put them on a common accounting basis) of the assets, liabilities and equity accounts of each of the combining parties are simply added together to form the combined balance sheet of the new entity. Any new shares issued to effect the combination are assigned a stated amount equal to the stated capital of the shares acquired in exchange and therefore any contributed surplus or retained earnings of the combining parties rolls forward untouched.*

   Thus pooling accounting avoids all of the major problems associated with purchase accounting, namely the valuation of any shares issued to effect the combination, the allocation of total consideration among the assets acquired and the question of the accounting treatment to be given to purchased goodwill subsequently.

Criticism of the pooling concept

The concept of pooling is based on the proposition that in certain business combinations one entity does not acquire the resources of the other from its owners. Rather the two groups of owners have simply got together to pool their resources, which is a transaction between the owners not involving either of the entities directly and therefore should not result in adjustments to the carrying values of the resources under their administration.

   If this were all there were to the question, any share exchange transaction whereby control of one or more entities was acquired by another entity in consideration for issue of common shares of the latter would be a pooling. But this would seem to be an oversimplification. It would mean that if Co. A sold 100,000 shares to the public and used the cash to buy all the shares of Co. B, it would be a purchase. But if Co. A instead issued 100,000 shares to the shareholders of Co. B in return for their holdings of B's shares, and they then sold out by making a secondary offering of the shares of A, it would be a pooling. This would be to elevate form over substance. It would seem that at least if there are identifiable

---

* Except in a case where the par value of new shares issued exceeds the stated value of shares acquired. In such event some part of the contributed surplus or retained earnings of the combining parties must be capitalized to enable the full par value of the new shares to be recorded in the combined balance sheet. There are also some unresolved legal problems in Canada that may affect the valuation placed on shares issued. These are described in Appendix A.

major shareholders participating in the pooling their continued holding of shares of the combined entity would be needed as evidence that the transaction was a pooling, not a takeover.

Then there is the question of relative size. Can there be a real marriage between a flea and an elephant? If one party is 2% of the size of the other is there any meaningful decision by the shareholder groups to pool their interests? More often than not in such cases the question will not even be submitted to the shareholders of the larger company, and if it were they would be content to accept the recommendations of management without question. Some people object to a size test for identification of poolings on the grounds that it penalizes a large company which because of its size would be debarred from pooling with most other companies. But this would simply reflect the fact that where there is a great size disparity the larger party is inevitably predominant. It is merely a fact of life that it is difficult for a large company to enter into a true pooling.

Others have suggested that it is ridiculous to have a size test which would debar companies A and B from pooling with company C, if companies A and B could themselves pool, and thereby attain a size sufficient to enable them to pool with company C in a second transaction. The answer to this might well be that a size test should be interpreted so that a pooling of companies A, B and C in one transaction is admissible if it would be after a separate amalgamation of two of the companies, since in such a transaction the shareholders of company C would indeed be giving up a substantial part of the control over the combined enterprise.

There is also the question whether the application of pooling accounting is the most logical result in a true pooling where neither entity is taking over the other. If, for example, the book value of the common equity in both Co. A and Co. B is equal, but the common shareholders of Co. A receive two-thirds of the equity in the combined company, does this argue that book values of the combining companies form a good basis for the accounting of the combined entity? Rather it would seem the disparity in ratios is evidence of disparity in net assets contributed by the two predecessors. A few authors have suggested that a revaluation of the assets of each of the contributing parties, based on the evidence of the negotiations leading up to the combination, would provide a better basis for accounting.[2] This in itself is very likely true; in the absence of current value accounting for all companies however, it would seem to penalize the pooled entity in relation to other companies.

In summary, the idea that a pooling is a transaction between the residual equity interests in two (or more) entities and not between the entities themselves, is an elusive concept. Common shareholders do not commonly get together and hammer out bargains for exchange of their interests. Any such negotiations must be conducted for them by their representatives, the directors or management. But it is also the responsibility of these parties to make investment decisions in the ordinary course. It is hard to find bases for distinguishing the decision which a board of directors makes to buy out the shares of another company in order to take it over, from a decision on behalf of the shareholders to throw in their lot with another group of shareholders. It has to be conceded that the latter type of situation exists, and in particular cases it may not be too difficult to identify. In the abstract however, its characteristics are hard to define. Perhaps the real test is that after a true pooling combination the direction and control of the combined entity will be significantly different from that of any of the constituent entities. The only quantitative measure of this test would seem to be the relative size of the contributing entities. Perhaps, then the best practical way to distinguish poolings from purchases would be on the basis of:

(a) a fairly constrictive relative size test, and

(b) a requirement that any pooling transaction be submitted for approval to the common shareholder groups of all the combining entities.

Problems in purchase accounting

The problems in purchase accounting are more of a practical nature than conceptual. Some accountants profess to see an internal conflict in purchase accounting in that the accounting of the purchaser is based on historic cost, while the assets of the business acquired are taken on at current value. But this is no conflict. To the purchaser the current values of the assets taken over *are* his historic cost if the valuation has been done rightly. If a business buys a property from another it does not enquire as to its cost to the vendor. The purchaser has a figure for his cost, which is the price paid, and that is a current value. It is true that the purchaser will have in his accounts a mixture of values – current values for those assets recently acquired and values (costs) based on earlier price levels for assets acquired at more distant dates. But this is a feature common to all companies – not just to those which have acquired other businesses. If there is a problem, it lies with the system of accounting based on historic costs, not with the purchase method of accounting for business combinations.

The practical problems associated with the purchase method, as have been indicated, relate to valuation of non-cash consideration given, especially shares issued, and allocation of total consideration among assets acquired and liabilities assumed. The problem of subsequent disposition of goodwill, or 'negative goodwill', although not just a problem in accounting for business combinations cannot be ignored in this context.

Valuation of shares issued

The general problem of valuation of shares issued in consideration for assets has been dealt with in Chapter 6. The problem arises in a particularly acute form in some business combinations because large blocks of shares are issued relative to the total outstanding shares of the issuer. Where such shares are listed on a stock exchange or freely traded the usual practice now seems to be to value the shares issued at market price at or near the date of acquisition.

The assumption, therefore, is that the value of shares issued to make an acquisition is indicated by the market value for shares of the issuing company. This is an assumption that is open to some question. Essentially, it suggests that the issuing company could have sold the shares for cash equal to the value assigned to them, and used the cash to buy out the vendor's interest in his business. Some problems with this thinking are:

(a) The market price of a company's shares reflects the price established by buyers and sellers of relatively small quantities of shares (except for institutional block trades). Essentially it is a retail market, whereas a company issuing a large block of shares in effect is wholesaling them. It is customary to find that a new share issue by a company or a large secondary offering by individuals must be priced below the established trading price so that "the market can absorb it". The net proceeds to a company on a new issue of shares is also reduced by underwriting and other issue costs. There will almost always be some differences, therefore, between the market price of the company's shares and the net cash it could realize by issuing shares en bloc. The amount of that spread will depend on circumstances. A large company, whose shares are actively traded, issuing a small block of shares, might suffer very little discount. Smaller companies, issuing proportionately larger blocks of shares, might need to price the share issue 10% to 30% below the market. In the extreme case, a small company embarked on an active program of acquisition might find that the market would not absorb the quantity of shares which it is issuing at any price at all. In such a case vendors of businesses who accept shares rather than cash are, whether they know it or not, taking the risk of being locked in to an investment in shares of the issuing company. A valuation of shares of the issuing company at market price in these circumstances has a large element of unreality in it.

(b) The market price of the great majority of companies shows marked fluctuations over the period of a year. Even in the case of stock in large well-established companies, the high price for the year is often 50% or more above the low for the year. Such a fluctuation in the value of a business over the year would be extreme. While market prices for stock undoubtedly exercise some impact on the number of shares issued to effect an acquisition, there is no positive evidence that the vendor of a business who would sell his business for 100,000 shares (say) of the acquiring company when such shares are at their low, would be willing to accept two-thirds as many shares a few months later when they have climbed to their high. Much may depend on the marketability of the shares issued and the size of the block. In other words, spot market prices are suspect for the purpose of valuing shares issued in a business acquisition. Nor is this surprising. The typical purchaser of shares in the market is primarily interested in the dividend return and expectation of capital gain on his investment. He is not looking at the business as a potential purchaser would, and thus the underlying value of the business is not a figure with which he is primarily concerned. Investment in shares of a worthless business may be justified if someone else can be found later on to buy the shares at a higher price. While, in the long run, underlying value must be reflected in market prices, in the short run there are hundreds of other influences on the price of stock – tips, rumors, the influence of 'chartists' on the market, short-run economic effects, political events, the effect of a bull or bear mood in the market and so on. So long as investors are in for the short run, as are many of those whose trades establish a market price, the market price of shares must be a very uncertain indicator of real value to a purchaser or seller of a business.

If the problem of valuation is approached from the other direction, namely a valuation of the business acquired, there are also serious difficulties. Where the acquiring company has a well-established method of valuing businesses – say, on a discounted cash flow basis or a variant thereof – the difficulties are lessened. The use as a discount factor of the minimum acceptable rate of return to the purchasing company applied to the expected cash flow of the business acquired will produce a maximum value of the business, which would put a ceiling on the value assigned to the stock issued. But many companies have not refined their acquisition criteria to this extent and often emerge from the negotiation with only a very general idea of what total value should attach to what they have exchanged.

Nor is it possible to proceed from a valuation of individual assets of the business acquired to arrive at a total valuation. To begin with, often no attempt is made to arrive at values of individual assets other than by a look at the vendor's books and a relatively superficial tour of his plant to see the sort of condition it is in. In the second place, even if there were valuations made from the standpoint of the purchaser of the individual tangible assets and identifiable intangibles such as patents, the value of the business would differ from this by the value of intangible goodwill. In other words, the value of goodwill can only be derived from a valuation of the business as a whole. Therefore, the value of the business as a whole cannot be derived from a valuation of individual assets including goodwill.

In summary, a valuation of the purchasing company's shares determined in relation to the quoted price for them is subject to shortcomings in theory. In addition, there is need for some empirical research to guide in determining the proper or customary relationship between the value of shares issued en bloc and quoted market values for the same type of shares. Of course, if the shares of the acquiring company are not listed for trading this approach to the valuation of the purchase transaction is impossible in any event. Valuations of the business acquired made in the course of negotiations are the only alternative source of figures for valuing the transaction. In theory these should be the best indication of the value of the purchase to the purchaser. Such valuations, however, are not always made in explicit terms and where they are made, suffer from the drawback that they are usually not agreed to between the purchaser and the vendor so that they have less evidentiary value than would a price struck in a cash deal. In these circumstances the accountant must exercise his best judgment, having regard to all indicators in placing a valuation on the purchase transaction.

Allocation of total purchase consideration

The general rules for allocation of the total price paid in a 'basket purchase' have been discussed in Chapter 6. As has been already indicated the necessity for allocation of the total cost according to the values of the net assets acquired has been supported in authoritative statements by the AICPA and the CICA. Yet it appears that these principles have not been universally followed in Canada. A recent study found that in only 30 out of 93 acquisitions made by 15 sample companies in the period 1960–68 was a revaluation of assets made from the predecessor's book values.[3] One may question why this should be so.

The answer is not that the principle of allocation of cost to assets acquired is wrong – clearly it is right. In negotiations for an acquisition a purchaser is not concerned with values that may be on the books of the vendor (except to the extent that they may govern the amount of future tax deductions). He is concerned with current values. Where book values differ from current values the former are irrelevant. To take the simplest example, if marketable investments having a cost of $100,000 are carried on the books at the lower of cost and market, and current market is $200,000, the relevant value to the purchaser is $200,000 not the book value of $100,000. Similarly, in many cases real property investment is frequently carried at book values that are unrealistically low in relation to current realizable values for real estate. In addition to cases where the book values of assets based on original cost are low in relation to current value, there are frequently cases where assets are omitted completely from the balance sheet. Valuable patents developed by internal research efforts may have had no readily determinable cost and, therefore, may not be carried as assets. Other valuable assets may have been discovered, perhaps by accident, which have no cost – e.g. the mineral deposit in an area where exploration has been abandoned. In other cases, assets may have been completely written off and yet have a resurgence of value – e.g. the libraries of old films owned by film companies after television rights to films become valuable.

The existence of such 'hidden assets' in a business combination makes former book values completely inappropriate as a basis for accounting for the purchaser. If they are so used it is possible for the purchaser to sell the undervalued assets immediately after the acquisition and thus report fictitious 'instant profits', being the difference between the sale prices realized and the unrealistically low book values carried forward for the assets. Essentially the same effect occurs if the assets are not sold but rather are used to produce revenue while costs charged against revenue include only depreciation based on unrealistically low book values.

It may be objected that if book values are unrealistically low the same criticism may be levelled at the income figures reported by the acquired entity before acquisition as at the figures reported by the purchasing company after acquisition. There is this important distinction, however. The gains reported by the entity before acquisition based on low book values will merely represent delayed recognition of gains that perhaps had accrued previously (e.g. on increases in the value of investments or land) or will merely offset charges against income in previous years (e.g. when research costs resulting in valuable patents are written off). In other words the gains may be reported in the wrong time period, but they will still be part of the lifetime stream of income of the entity. On the other hand gains reported by a purchasing company which are based on unrealistically low book values of the vendor will not really be income at all. They will be return of capital, as would have been apparent if a proper value had been assigned to the assets taken over when the purchaser acquired control.

The explanation then, of the common practice of carrying forward predecessor's book values after an acquisition, must be sought on other than logical grounds. In the writer's observation two explanations may be found:

– Management of the purchasing company does not understand (or does not wish to recognize) the economics of the purchase
– The practical difficulties of allocating the total cost according to the values of the net assets acquired are substantial.

It is now generally recognized that the 'earning power' of a going concern is of much greater importance than the value of the individual assets owned by it. This is because the values of individual assets can only be realized if the business is liquidated, and the process of liquidation may destroy individual asset values since they may be valuable only as part of a going concern. Management, there-fore, rightly attaches great importance to earning power in evaluating a prospective acquisition and may well be prompted to ask "why should a purchase, which is based on the earning power of the business acquired, change the amount of earnings it reports?".

The explanation of this apparent anomaly lies in a more thorough understanding of the meaning of the term 'earning power'. The return from any enterprise comes by way of an excess of its revenues over day-to-day operating costs (i.e. by way of its 'cash flow'). However, the whole of cash flow does not represent earnings. Some part of it (usually a substantial part) merely makes good the consumption of capital invested in the enterprise. Earnings (income) only result if the cash inflow exceeds the amount necessary to make good the exhaustion of capital in the course of operations. From the standpoint of a purchaser of a business it would be more correct to say that he is buying 'cash flow generating power' rather than 'earning power'. Whether or not the cash flow generated will produce net income depends on the amount of limited life capital invested.

To take a simplified example, suppose A spends $1 million searching for a mine and bringing it into production and that it is expected the mine will produce metals worth $2 million each year for ten years while mining and other costs are estimated at $1,500,000 a year. If all goes as expected cash flow will be $500,000 a year and after an allowance of $100,000 annually for consumption of investment, earnings re-ported will be $400,000 a year. Now suppose that after three years B buys the mine from A for $1,400,000. If all other factors are the same the cash flow generating power will still be $500,000 a year but B must allow $200,000 a year for exhaustion of his investment. In other words where income to A was $400,000 annually, in-come to B is only $300,000 annually, without any change in the basic economics of the property. This perhaps would be fairly clear to anyone in the case of a wasting asset like a mine. It is not so well understood, however, in the case of the purchase of an ordinary business. And yet the principle is the same. To the extent that the purchase price is represented by assets that will be sold or used up in the course of operations (such as inventory and fixed assets), income to the purchaser from the business acquired can only be computed after allowance for replacement of his investment in those assets. And it is *his* investment (values current at the time of purchase) that is relevant, not the investment of the vendor (values as recorded on his books).

The practical problems in allocating the total consideration to assets acquired have been briefly reviewed in Chapter 6. A more extended discussion is included in Appendix A.

Subsequent accounting treatment of the remaining purchase discrepancy between amounts allocated to individual assets and liabilities taken over, and the total purchase consideration

After the most thorough evaluation of assets purchased and liabilities assumed in a business purchase there will almost always remain a 'purchase discrepancy' between the net sum of values assigned to specific assets and liabilities and the purchase price. This remainder, which may be either positive or negative, repre-sents the following:

(i) If positive,
  – Excessive payment by the purchaser because of poor bargaining
  – Payment for unidentifiable intangible assets which result in more than normal earning power or earning prospects – frequently called true 'goodwill'

(ii) If negative,
  – A 'bargain purchase' gain owing to skilled negotiation by the purchaser or the weak bargaining position of the vendor
  – Provision for costs such as employee separation payments and losses on asset disposals attendant on the proposed disposal of certain segments of the business
  – Provision for costs of plant rearrangements, etc. which are necessary to make the business efficient but which do not relate to any particular asset
  – Allowance for the fact that the business acquired is expected to operate at a loss or below normal profit for a period until management changes are made.

Since a basic assumption of accounting is that an arm's-length transaction is probably the best available evidence of value, the theory that there might be a gain due to a bargain purchase or a loss due to poor bargaining is not normally accepted in recording a purchase transaction. The remaining explanations for the existence of the purchase discrepancy are reflected in the accounting for it after the transaction.

The various ways suggested for accounting for purchased goodwill have been outlined in Chapter 11. In the United States a choice among the alternatives has been made in APB Opinion No. 17 which requires amortization for all intangible assets over a maximum period of forty years. In Canada the issue has not been resolved.

As has been indicated, in the case of the negative purchase discrepancy or 'negative goodwill' as it is sometimes called, there is more variety in the possible interpretation of its nature. To begin with, the existence of a negative purchase discrepancy should prompt reconsideration of the valuation of individual assets, especially fixed assets, to make sure they have not been overvalued. If satisfied with this, two possible explanations remain:

– The purchaser has made allowance in the purchase price for one or more specific items of cost deemed necessary to put the business acquired in good operating condition.
– A general allowance has been made to compensate the purchaser for expected below normal return on his investment for a period while its management is being straightened away.

It will depend on the facts in each case which explanation (or whether a combination of explanations) is the correct one. If specific costs are provided for, the negative discrepancy should be treated as a liability and the costs charged against it when incurred. If a general allowance has been made for losses, the negative discrepancy should be treated as a deferred credit to be taken into income in reasonable amounts and over a reasonable period of years in the future. Inasmuch as a purchaser would not normally buy a business unless he expected to be able to turn it around fairly quickly, it would seem logical that the period of amortization of the credit should not be long. Also it would be the normal expectation that operations should improve after the take-over so that the amortization of the credit should be weighted if anything towards the early years of the period.*

When a purchaser has made more than one acquisition, it is sometimes found that there is purchased goodwill in one case and negative goodwill in another. It is not uncommon in practice to find the two offset against each other in the balance sheet and carried forward as one net figure. From the discussion it will be apparent, however, that positive and negative goodwill are quite different in character and there is no more justification for offsetting them than there would be for offsetting inventory and accounts payable.

The present status of business combination accounting

The foregoing discussion has outlined the important issues in accounting for business combinations and has indicated that accounting principles in this area are in a state of flux. The following briefly summarizes recent history and the present position.

Pooling of interests

1. In Canada the pooling of interests accounting concept has been little used. The Martin Study found that only 52 combinations out of 732 where the accounting method was determinable used the pooling of interests method.[4] In the United States tabulations of acquisitions and mergers showed about half being treated as poolings in the early 1960's and a much higher proportion where stock was an important consideration in the transaction.[5]

2. It is generally acknowledged that the pooling of interests concept was widely abused and stretched far beyond any justifiable interpretation in U.S. practice in the 1960's. The issuance of APB Opinion No. 16 will no doubt greatly curb the abuses, but the full extent of its success remains to be seen. Unfortunately it has not succeeded in making the concept of pooling less fuzzy. Poolings in Canada have not been so open to criticism.[6] The weaknesses in the traditional form of purchase accounting in Canada have meant that it has not been necessary to resort to pooling in order to understate assets acquired and hence future charges against income.

Purchase accounting

1. In both Canada and the United States, for the most part shares issued to effect a combination now appear to be valued at market price at or near the date of acquisition.[7] Thus older practice has changed in this regard and present transaction measurement principles appear to be observed.** Block share issues,

---

* APB Opinion No. 16 requires that a negative purchase discrepancy be deducted from the values otherwise arrived at for non-current assets (excluding long-term investments in marketable securities). Only where these assets are reduced to zero value would the treatment of the balance of the purchase discrepancy as a deferred credit be permitted.

** The Martin Study, however, showed that out of 63 purchase transactions where assets were not revalued after the transaction 7 resulted in no goodwill. Unless purchase price was book value this suggests the possibility that shares issued were stated at amounts equal to the book value of assets acquired. (Page 27, Table IV-4) Eiteman's Study gives examples in 1956 and 1961 of the same practice in the United States. (Page 49)

however, should often be valued below current market and there is need for empirical research and authoritative guidance on this.

2. In Canada up until 1968 more often than not assets were not revalued after a combination effected through a share purchase.[8] Thus the 1964 CICA recommendations on this have been largely ignored. The requirement to disclose departures from the CICA Recommendations in audited financial statements, which was introduced in 1969, may have improved this situation but evidence is lacking on this point. In the United States the requirement to revalue assets dates back to Bulletin 24 in 1944, so that greater adherence to the principle might be expected. Moreover in taxable transactions a tax advantage is gained if the purchase cost of a subsidiary's shares can be allocated to tangible assets. Nevertheless Eiteman, writing in 1967 (before APB Opinion Nos. 16 and 17), states "accountants frequently do not write up the book values of the tangible assets acquired when using the purchase approach. Often they merely charge the excess of purchase price of the acquired assets to a catch-all account. . . ."[9]

3. In Canada the Martin Study showed the following treatment of purchase discrepancy recognized in the accounts in 61 transactions:[10]

Retained in the balance sheet		29
Written off to		
– retained earnings	19	
– capital surplus	1	20
Amortized, or written off in a		
lump sum, against income		12
		61

The Study does not distinguish between positive and negative purchase discrepancies in this table. In the United States the direct write-off to retained earnings or capital surplus was condemned in Bulletin 43 issued in 1953. Practice is divided between carrying goodwill on an unamortized basis or amortizing it against income.

Principles Governing Accounting for Business Combinations

Because business combinations accounting is in a transition period it is difficult to state the principles, except in very general terms as follows:

1. Business combinations should be classified either as purchases, where one party is clearly acquiring control of the other business or businesses, or poolings of interests where, as a result of share exchanges carried out by the residual equity interests, there is a genuine mutual exchange of proportionate interests with the result that the operations and control of the former independent entities are pooled.
   (a) Poolings of interests
      In the minority of cases that are poolings of interests the assets and liabilities of the combining entities (after adjustment to place them on a uniform accounting basis) should be added together to form the basis of the combined entity's accounts. The various equity accounts should likewise

be added together, except to the extent that surplus has to be capitalized to meet the requirements of corporate law. In historical statements of earnings the figures for the combining entities should likewise be added together.

(b) Purchases

 (i) The consideration given to effect a purchase should be valued at fair market value at the approximate date the agreement is struck. In the case of quoted share issues fair value may be taken as indicated by the market price of the stock for a reasonable period before the acquisition, but allowance should be made for limitations on marketability of the stock issued, or the pressure on market price and costs of issue that would be entailed in a direct issue of the stock to the public.

 (ii) The total consideration arrived at should be allocated to assets purchased according to their fair value. Any excess of consideration over the fair value of all the identifiable tangible and intangible assets should be carried as goodwill. Where shares of a subsidiary company are purchased, rather than assets directly, the allocation of the purchase consideration for purposes of consolidation should follow the same general principle. In this case the liabilities assumed will also have to be valued and allowance made in the valuation for any difference between the values assigned to assets and liabilities and their status for tax purposes. If the total consideration is less than the fair value of all assets conservatively valued, the difference should be treated as a provision for future identifiable costs arising from the combination or as a deferred credit, suitably described, whichever is the more appropriate. A deferred credit should be amortized against income subsequently over a period which appears reasonable according to the circumstances.

References

1. A fuller commentary may be found in S. A. Martin, S. N. Laiken and D. F. Haslam, *Business Combinations in the '60's: a Canadian Profile* (Toronto: Canadian Institute of Chartered Accountants, 1970), pp. 36–37.
2. See, for example, A. R. Wyatt, *A Critical Study of Accounting for Business Combinations* (New York: American Institute of Certified Public Accountants, 1963), pp. 81–86.
3. Martin, *Business Combinations*, p. 27.
4. *Ibid.*, p. 16.
5. See Eiteman, D. S., *Pooling and Purchase Accounting* (Ann Arbor: Bureau of Business Research, Graduate School of Business Administration, the University of Michigan, 1967), Tables 10 and 11.
6. See Martin, *Business Combinations* in Chapter V. Most of the pooling transactions reviewed met the criteria established by U.S. authoritative statements fairly well.
7. *Ibid.*, p. 26 "In cases where a relatively large amount of common stock was issued, management generally booked the value of the common stock at its market price at or near date of acquisition."
8. *Ibid.*, p. 27, Table IV-4.
9. Eiteman, *Pooling and Purchase Accounting*, p. 109.

10. Martin, *Business Combinations*, p. 28, Table IV-5. In 400 transactions for purchase of shares the average purchase premium over book value was 47%. (Table C-6) If this is typical of cases where the purchase discrepancy is written off immediately upon acquisition a substantial amount of assets disappear as a result of this accounting practice.

19 Translation of accounts in foreign currencies

The study of principles for foreign currency translation* is a study of obsolescence in ideas. The traditional approach to translation of account balances in foreign currencies was formulated many years ago in a far different environment from that of today – in a world neatly divided between countries on the gold standard and others. Moreover authoritative statements on problems of translation of foreign currency balances have been issued primarily in response to crisis – which is not a good atmosphere for sound consideration of theory. Thus, statements by committees or the research department of the American Institute were issued in 1931 (shortly after a number of countries abandoned the gold standard), in 1934 (after the U.S. dollar was devalued), in 1939 (after the beginning of World War II), and in 1949 (after the widespread devaluations of that year). The current American authoritative statement on the subject which is contained in Chapter 12 of Bulletin 43 issued in 1953 is largely based on those statements of 1939 and 1949 and reflects the exceptional conditions of the 1939 to 1949 period. Similarly, the principal English Institute statement on translation of foreign currencies was issued in February 1968 in response to the sterling devaluation of the previous November.

No statements have been made by Canadian authorities on the subject and in general Canadian companies (unless they are subsidiaries of companies incorporated outside North America) would look to U.S. pronouncements for guidance. At one time however, the practice of some Canadian companies of translating

---

* The term 'translation' is applied to the process of:
1. Expressing financial statements derived from a set of accounts maintained in the currency of one country in terms of the currency of another country – frequently to permit the inclusion of the statements of a foreign subsidiary or branch in the consolidated financial statements of a parent company, and
2. Expressing monetary assets and liabilities (cash, claims to receive cash and liability to pay cash) which are stated in terms of a foreign currency in equivalent amounts of domestic currency; an entity may acquire such foreign currency assets and liabilities without having a branch or subsidiary abroad merely as a result of foreign trading or investing or borrowing abroad.

The word 'translation' is more descriptive of what is being done than the term 'conversion' which used to be used to describe the process. The word conversion is now conventionally reserved to describe the actual act of exchanging one currency for another.

accounts of U.S. subsidiaries and branches on a dollar for dollar basis was a distinctive feature of Canadian accounting.

At the outset it should be said that the derivation of sound generalized principles for translation of foreign currency balances is a task of peculiar difficulty. Actual exchange rates are affected at any one time by a multitude of factors – the balance of trade, capital movements, government dealings in foreign exchange markets and direct government controls on foreign exchange transactions. Some of these factors are transitory, some are long run, and it is not easy to distinguish the short run from the long run influences. Accounting methods should be designed to reflect the economic environment so far as possible but in these circumstances it is hard to distinguish long-term trends which should be taken into account from meaningless fluctuations.

The soundness of particular accounting rules may be evaluated by their ability to cope with different circumstances. The traditional principles for translation probably were developed from the viewpoint of a parent company in a country with a strong currency dealing with branches or subsidiaries dependent on supplies and capital from the parent, and located in countries with less stable currencies often subject to a long-term weakening trend. Thus, a strongly conservative bias was reflected in the traditional method. This bias seems less justified when the translation is from one currency to another of relatively equal strength, or when the branch or subsidiary operates completely independently of the parent. Nor does the traditional method seem entirely suited for use in translating currencies of countries that are members of the International Monetary Fund, particularly in a year when revaluation occurs.

Thus, different procedures seem to fit different situations which makes it very difficult to frame a translation rule of general application. As a background to discussion of procedures however, it may be useful to consider some of the situations that may be encountered.

1. The currency to be translated may be rapidly and steadily weakening in relation to a standard such as the U.S. dollar. This situation has existed for a number of years in some South American countries. Such rapid weakening of the external currency value usually is associated with rapid internal inflation.

2. The currency to be translated may be stable – possibly fluctuating only within the limits set by adherence to IMF rules. Nevertheless, there may be a long-term trend toward deterioration or appreciation in the currency value, evidenced by occasional adjustments of official exchange rates. An example is the pound sterling which has declined from a value of U.S. $4.86⅔ under the gold standard (which was abandoned in 1931) to pegged rates of U.S. $4.03 at the outset of World War II, U.S. $2.80 in 1949 and U.S. $2.40 in 1967. (A small appreciation followed the suspension of convertibility of the U.S. dollar in 1971.)

3. The currency to be translated may be relatively stable with no very apparent long-term trend. For example, over a period of fifty years the exchange rate between Canadian dollars and U.S. dollars has remained very close to par taking one year with another. The period of course includes about five years when both countries were on the gold standard, a twelve-year period from 1939 to 1950 when the Canadian rate was fixed by the Foreign Exchange Control Board and the eight-year period from 1962 to 1970 when the rate was pegged

under IMF rules. In the remaining 25 years there was a period of marked instability from 1931 to 1933 when the Canadian dollar fluctuated from near par to a discount of about 25% in each year, and a period of incipient instability in the early 1960's which was checked by the pegging of the exchange rate and other government action. For most of the other years when the exchange rate was free the spread between high and low rates for the year was less than 5% and the average rate for the year was within 3% of par.

One or two comments should be made concerning this analysis. First, the word stability can only be used in relation to some standard. The standard customarily used is that of the U.S. dollar which is the currency to which other countries peg their exchange rates under IMF procedures. But the value of the U.S. dollar itself, when measured in terms of purchasing power, changes, so that to say the Canadian dollar is stable vis-à-vis the U.S. dollar does not imply that it is stable in relation to general purchasing power or to the value of other currencies or to some other standard. The term as used here is relative only. Thus, for example, the Canadian dollar could be in a stable relationship with the U.S. dollar over the long term and at the same time be in a long-run declining trend vis-à-vis, say, the West German mark.

Second, the situations described represent a continuum. There is no clear dividing line between situations which may be described as stable and those which are unstable. Moreover, a particular currency may move towards one end or the other of the scale over time. Thus, if different translation procedures are appropriate in different situations a high degree of judgment will have to be exercised in the selection of appropriate procedures.

Problems in translation may be discussed under the following headings:

1. When should a foreign subsidiary or branch be consolidated?
2. Translation procedures
   – balance sheet
   – income statement.
3. Treatment of gain or loss on translation of foreign currency statements.
4. Translation of foreign currency assets and liabilities by a company that does not have a foreign branch.
5. Sundry questions.

When should a foreign subsidiary or branch be consolidated?

Chapter 17 discussed the general question of when a subsidiary should be consolidated. The ordinary presumption is that a subsidiary should be consolidated (except for certain situations where the presentation of separate statements would be more informative) unless control of the subsidiary is likely to be temporary or does not rest with the majority owners. This ordinary rule is as valid for foreign subsidiaries as for domestic. However, a foreign subsidiary is often subject to greater risks of loss of effective control than is the domestic subsidiary. Control of a foreign subsidiary may be cut off by war or revolution. Foreign governments may expropriate without fair compensation. Foreign exchange controls may strangle a foreign business or prevent remittance of its earnings to the parent company. In these circumstances judgment has to be exercised whether (a) the accounts and liabilities of the foreign subsidiary should be consolidated and (b) if they are, whether credit should be taken in income account for earnings of the subsidiary not remitted to the parent company.

Chapter 12 of ARB No. 43 was exceedingly cautious about the desirability of consolidating foreign subsidiaries. The following quotation summarizes an extended discussion of the dangers:

> "In view of the uncertain values and availability of the assets and net income of foreign subsidiaries subject to controls and exchange restrictions and the consequent unrealistic statements of income that may result from the translation of many foreign currencies into dollars, careful consideration should be given to the fundamental question of whether it is proper to consolidate the statements of foreign subsidiaries with the statements of United States companies."

As was previously indicated, ARB No. 43 was issued in the aftermath of a world war which itself resulted in a period of great currency instability. It seems probable that the Bulletin would be less negative in tone if written today. Nevertheless the questions raised by it are still valid.

It should be noted that exactly the same considerations apply to a foreign branch as to a subsidiary. The same risks of loss of control of the business apply regardless of the legal form. In this the foreign branch is different from the domestic branch since rarely, if ever, would a company lose control of a domestic branch except of its own volition. If a subsidiary or branch is not consolidated for reasons of lack of control the net investment in it would be carried as an asset in the parent company's balance sheet, and consideration must be given to whether the amount of the investment should be written down to reflect any apparently enduring loss of value.

The need for translation of the foreign currency accounts arises primarily from the need to have statements in a common currency in order to effect a consolidation. (Equally, if the investment is carried on the 'equity' basis, translation is required to arrive at the parent company's equity in earnings on a basis equivalent to consolidation.) It is fundamental, of course, that the foreign currency statements must be prepared in accordance with accounting principles acceptable in the country of the parent company before the foreign statements can be accepted for consolidation. For example, statements prepared in some European countries where the practice is to deduct certain reserves from inventory costs as allowed by taxation law would have to be adjusted before being translated and consolidated in the statements of a North American parent company.

Translation procedures – balance sheet

There are several different theories that can be suggested leading to procedures for the translation of the balance sheet of a foreign subsidiary or branch. For purposes of discussion these theories may be characterized as follows:

(a) The current/non-current approach
(b) The monetary/non-monetary approach
(c) The single company approach

(d) The closing rate approach

(e) The par value approach for Canadian-U.S. translations.

The current/non-current approach

The current/non-current method approved by ARB No. 43 keyed its translation procedures mainly to the traditional distinction between current and non-current items in the balance sheet. The following summarizes and comments on the recommendations of ARB No. 43:

- "Cash, accounts receivable, and other current assets, unless covered by forward exchange contracts, should be translated at the rate of exchange prevailing on the date of the balance sheet.

- "Current liabilities payable in foreign currency should be translated into dollars at the rate of exchange in force on the date of the balance sheet.

- "Inventory should follow the standard rule of *cost or market, whichever is lower* in dollars. Where ... inventory is not translated at the rate of exchange prevailing on the date of the balance sheet, as is usually done with current assets, the burden of proof is on those who wish to follow some other procedure."

  There seems to be some confusion to this statement. The apparent intent is that the inventory should be valued at the lower of cost and market in the *foreign currency* at the year-end, and then this valuation should be translated at year-end rates to yield a figure that can be described as lower of cost and market in dollars. Under an alternative interpretation of this phrase however, the inventory could be valued basically at cost determined as the dollar equivalent of the foreign currency outlay at the date the inventory was acquired (prior to the year-end), subject to a market test based on year-end market values translated at year-end rates. This latter interpretation is in fact recognized as a special case in Bulletin 43 where inventory is acquired at a date when foreign currency was at a much higher exchange rate than that prevailing on the closing date of the financial period and when replacement cost in the foreign currency has correspondingly increased at the year-end. The Bulletin said "where the selling price obtainable in dollars, after deducting a reasonable percentage to cover selling and other local expenses, exceeds the cost of the article in dollars at the rate prevailing as of the date of purchase, such original dollar equivalent may be considered as the cost for purposes of inventory". A 1960 U.S. Study indicated that most companies translated locally purchased inventory by the foreign subsidiary at year-end rates of exchange, but some companies translated inventory purchased by the subsidiary for U.S. dollars at the exchange rates at the date of acquisition. The authors of the Study thought the distinction illogical and favoured the use of historic rates for all inventory, subject to the market test.[1]

- "Fixed assets°, permanent investments, and long-term receivables should be translated into dollars at the rates prevailing when such assets were acquired

---

° When fixed assets have been acquired at several dates when the exchange rates were materially different, the subsidiary's asset records must keep track of the dollar cost, or at least the total local currency cost acquired at each separate exchange rate. In this situation also accumulated depreciation in dollars cannot be computed by finding the percentage of accumulated depreciation to cost in local currency and applying this percentage to the translated dollar cost. A simple arithmetical example will indicate the error in such a procedure.

or constructed. . . . An exception to the foregoing general principle might be made where fixed assets, permanent investments, or long-term receivables were acquired shortly before a substantial and presumably permanent change in the exchange rate with funds obtained in the country concerned, in which case it may be appropriate to restate the dollar equivalents of such assets to the extent of the change in the related debt.

- "Long-term liabilities and capital stock stated in foreign currency should not be translated at the closing rate, but at the rates of exchange prevailing when they were originally incurred or issued. . . . An exception may exist in respect to long-term debt incurred or capital stock issued in connection with the acquisition of fixed assets, permanent investments, or long-term receivables a short time before a substantial and presumably permanent change in the exchange rate. In such instances it may be appropriate to state the long-term debt or the capital stock at the new rate and proper to deal with the exchange differences as an adjustment of the cost of the assets acquired."

This approach as presented by ARB No. 43 is almost identical to the 'historic rate' method which is one of two methods approved in Recommendation No. 25 of the Institute of Chartered Accountants in England and Wales. The only difference is that the English statement suggests that, in principle, inventory should be translated at historic rates rather than year-end rates. However, the statement recognizes that the use of year-end rates is often expedient.

The recommendations of ARB No. 43 have been widely criticized as not being founded in any coherent theory. Because the concept of working capital includes a non-homogeneous mixture of assets and liabilities, some carried at realizable values and some at cost (see further discussion in Chapter 22) it is claimed that translation procedures based on a current/non-current distinction cannot make sense. For example, it is pointed out that if the foreign currency declines subsequent to the acquisition of inventory but selling prices are raised to compensate, to write down the inventory by valuing it at the year-end rate will only produce a recorded loss in the period of acquisition which will be offset by a larger than normal operating profit when the inventory is subsequently sold. On the other hand, with respect to non-current accounts receivable or debt payable if a movement in the exchange rate can be assumed to be permanent the question is asked why any gain or loss should not be recognized by translating the assets and liabilities at the new, more relevant, rate.

Some of these problems are dealt with by the recommendations relating to presumed permanent revaluations. However, the logical consistency of these recommendations is also questionable. Consider for example the suggestion that debt incurred or capital stock issued to acquire fixed assets or other long-term assets shortly before a revaluation may be restated at the post-revaluation rate and the adjustment credited or charged to the asset account. Possibly this may be because it is felt that the earning capacity in dollars of such assets after the revaluation will be impaired (or enhanced) by the change. But if this is so the same will be true of similar assets bought just before the revaluation from other sources such as surplus cash resources in the subsidiary. It is inconsistent to adjust fixed asset translation values in one case and not the other. Similarly, if debt were raised just before the revaluation but the proceeds were still held in the form of cash or other liquid assets, it would be inconsistent not to adjust the amount of that debt when it would be adjusted if the funds had been spent. In short, there can be no logic to limiting the question of revaluation of either non-current assets or liabilities to the situation where an offsetting adjustment of a non-current item on the other side of the balance sheet is possible.

Grady has suggested that ARB No. 43 has become outmoded in relation to present practice particularly in the matter of translation of long-term assets and liabilities, due to the prevalence of major currency revaluations and continued substantial inflation in many countries.[2] APB Opinion No. 6 gave mild support to this view in the statement "The Board is of the opinion that translation of long-term receivables and long-term liabilities at current exchange rates is appropriate in many circumstances". Grady cited with approval NAA Research Report No. 36 "Management Accounting Problems in Foreign Operations" which espoused the 'monetary/non-monetary' approach to translation.

The monetary/non-monetary approach

This approach is founded on the distinction between a foreign subsidiary's holdings of monetary (financial) assets and liabilities (that is local currency or claims to receive or pay a fixed number of local currency units) and non-monetary items (physical assets and other debit or credit items). The value of the former category of asset and liability is clearly dependent upon the value of the currency in which it is expressed. Hence, it is argued that a movement in the exchange rate, unless it is expected to be reversed before the asset or liability is settled in cash, must cause a real loss or gain which should be recognized in the accounts. On the other hand, the value of the non-monetary asset (and the rare case of the non-monetary liability – such as the obligation to perform services or deliver goods in the future) is not directly tied to the value of the currency. An inventory asset carried at cost, for example, represents not a value certain but rather an asset with value potential from future realization. Even though its sales proceeds will be realized in the foreign currency a change in the value of that currency vis-à-vis the parent company's currency may be compensated for by adjustment of the selling price in the local currency so that the proceeds realizable in dollars may be the same before and after a currency revaluation. Thus, the approach suggests that monetary assets and liabilities should be translated at year-end rates while non-monetary items should be translated at historic rates.

The monetary/non-monetary translation procedures would differ from the current/non-current basis in the following details:
- Marketable securities which do not have a fixed income rate and maturity value would be translated at historic cost rather than a year-end rate (unless they were valued at market value, which would be a monetary basis of valuation).
- Long-term investments having a fixed income rate and maturity value would be translated at the year-end rate rather than the historic rate because of their monetary character.
- Inventories would invariably be translated at the historic rate except when the basis of accounting was realizable value or when a market value test at year-end rates indicated a lower value than the translated cost.
- Current prepaid expenses would be translated at historic rates rather than year-end rates.

– Revenues received in advance and shown as a current liability would be translated at historic rates rather than year-end rates.
– Long-term receivables and long-term debt would be translated at year-end rates rather than historic rates.

The monetary/non-monetary approach appears on the surface to have a much sounder logical foundation than the traditional approach. In a majority of cases however, there will be an excess of monetary liabilities over monetary assets. (To put it another way the total of non-monetary assets – inventory, fixed assets, etc. – will usually exceed the total of non-monetary credit balances – deferred revenue, shareholders' equity, etc.) Where this relationship holds true a devaluation of a currency in which the foreign subsidiary operates will produce an apparent gain on foreign exchange translation and vice versa. Intuitively this result does not seem reasonable; hence, further consideration is in order.

In essence, the result rests on the proposition that no adjustment to dollar carrying values of the subsidiary's inventory, fixed assets (and other net non-monetary assets) is required even though the currency in the market in which such assets are held has declined in value. In other words, it is expected prices will be raised sufficiently in the foreign currency to offset the drop in its exchange value. This proposition requires the most careful consideration. In the case of inventory a potential safeguard exists against an error in this assumption. If prices do not rise the 'market value' limitation under the lower of cost and market rule may act to force a reduction below historic dollar cost of the inventory. But this is not true for imported inventory if market is measured by replacement cost and is only partially true for inventory as a whole if market is measured by net realizable value since the latter test allows the whole profit margin to be eaten up before it becomes effective. Only a test using realizable value less normal profit margin would adequately safeguard against a failure of price rises to compensate for currency value losses.

In the case of fixed assets and other non-monetary assets an equivalent safeguard is lacking. Some accounting literature suggests that such assets should not be carried above recoverable values, but the test does not operate very effectively. With long-term assets recoverable value is very difficult to determine with any measure of certainty.

Accordingly, attention should be paid to the probability of obtaining revenue increases to compensate for currency value declines. In the situation of a continuously declining foreign currency the chances may be quite good. Business will have anticipated the currency declines in such cases and been satisfied that this risk (or probability) can be compensated for in other ways. (However, if the compensation expected lies not in the ability to increase prices but rather in the ability to hedge against losses by carrying an excess of monetary liabilities over monetary assets, it would still be inconsistent to recognize a gain on the latter position and not some loss on the non-monetary position.)

In the case of the very rapid and sudden decline in currency such as has accompanied extreme inflation in some countries in the past it seems likely also that physical assets will be found to have maintained a substantial part of their value after the foreign currency has become stabilized. However, in such chaotic conditions it would seem the course of prudence not to recognize a gain on the translation of the net monetary position, and probably the validity of consolidating the foreign subsidiary at all before conditions stabilized would be called into question.

In the case of a relatively stable currency which has been devalued (such as the 1967 sterling devaluation) the price effect is probably open to question. One of the purposes of devaluation will be to make the foreign country's products more competitive internationally. If its general price level immediately rose to offset the effect of devaluation this purpose would be frustrated. Of course prices do not move uniformly so that it may be possible to adjust some prices to offset the effect of devaluation even though the price level as a whole does not do so. Nevertheless there is reason to doubt a general assumption that prices of inventory on hand at date of devaluation of such a currency can be adjusted to compensate for loss of the value of the currency which will be received on its sale.

In the case of a currency which floats or moves in relatively small steps about a fairly stable base (such as the Canadian dollar in relation to the U.S. dollar) the general assumption of price changes compensating for currency value fluctuations seems highly unrealistic, although no doubt particular situations occur when the assumption would be valid.

One final important point should be made concerning the compensatory effect of price changes, a point which is particularly pertinent to developed nations with high income taxes. The increase in foreign currency prices necessary to recover the same return in dollars in respect of non-monetary assets will be fully subject to income tax in the absence of special provisions in a foreign country's tax system. This fact compounds the difficulty of obtaining compensatory price increases.

In summary, the revaluation of all monetary assets and liabilities at current rates under the monetary/non-monetary approach to translation has strong logical appeal upon first consideration. However, the failure to revalue non-monetary assets and liabilities rests on an assumption that changes in the revenue achievable by the foreign subsidiary will compensate for changes in the value of the foreign currency unit. This assumption is probably right in some cases and wrong in others. As a general proposition however, it seems highly questionable.

The single company approach

In theory, a company could operate in a foreign country without creating a set of accounts in the foreign currency. For example, a Canadian company might set up a sales office in London, England and translate all its expenses (and revenues if any) into dollars at the rate prevailing as the transactions were incurred (or settled). Under such a system of continuous translation the assets and liabilities of the London sales office would be carried in the books of the Canadian parent company in Canadian dollars and the problem of translation at statement dates would disappear.

For a larger foreign operation, of course, a system of continuous translation would be quite impractical and in any event, for foreign subsidiaries at least, accounts in a foreign currency are probably required to meet legal requirements. Nevertheless, the simple case makes the point that a branch or a foreign subsidiary can be regarded merely as an extension of the parent company and no new accounting principles are required if foreign currency balances are translated at the historic rates prevailing when the transaction giving rise to the balances was entered into. The only significance of fluctuations in exchange rates after transaction dates then would be their significance in calculating current market values where such are used in the accounting. In other words, the risks of fluctuation in exchange rates in foreign operations would be considered merely an added factor in the normal business risk of value fluctuations after purchase.

The single company approach to translation is based on this theory. Application of the approach results in the following differences from the traditional approach:
- Short-term marketable securities would be translated at historic rates rather than year-end rates to preserve the figure of cost in the parent company's currency. (This of course would be subject to a market test using year-end rates.)
- Short-term accounts receivable would be translated at historic rates to preserve their cost basis, subject to a write-down if year-end rates indicated a lower recoverable value in the parent company's currency.*
- Inventories would be translated at historic rates subject to the market test.
- Prepaid expenses would be translated at historic rates.
- Short-term liabilities would be translated at historic rates subject to a write-up if year-end rates indicated a higher cost in the parent company's currency necessary to liquidate the liabilities.*

The single company approach has a simple logic which is appealing. It would, however, be a considerable nuisance in practice to keep a separate record of the historical dollar equivalent of such items as trade accounts receivable or payable or prepaid expenses. It is likely that the value of the information emerging from such extra work would not be considered worth its cost and it would be found expedient to use year-end rates of exchange for translating such assets. This would bring the method close to the monetary/non-monetary basis except in its treatment of long-term monetary assets and liabilities.

Since the single company concept is a logical extension of generally accepted accounting principles for domestic enterprises, it is difficult to attack it unless one argues (1) that particular aspects of generally accepted accounting principles in general should be changed or (2) that operation in a foreign country is sufficiently different from domestic operation that modification in customary accounting principles is desirable in such circumstances. The latter argument has great force in the case of operations in countries with unstable or rapidly weakening exchange rates since the exchange rate considerations must have a pervasive effect on all operations. Where there are major currency revaluations in more stable currencies, the case for departure from normal accounting principles is also strong. Where currency fluctuations are not large, departures from normal principles have less justification. However, equally, departures for the purpose of expediency or convenience such as the use of year-end rates rather than historic rates should meet with little objection in these circumstances, because their effect would be small.

The closing rate approach

Many British companies follow the exceedingly simple procedure of translating all foreign currency balances at the closing exchange rate on the statement date. This approach is considered in Recommendation No. 25 of the English Institute as

---

* The overly conservative bias resulting from applying a cost or market test to each of these items on its own might well be avoided by netting the two (together with any open positions in currency futures) and providing for any loss indicated on the net position.

"equally acceptable" with the 'historic rate' method. The method, however, has no following in North America.

Very little discussion is available as to the theory underlining this approach. It could be argued, however, that a company with operations abroad usually has an enduring commitment of resources to foreign operations which cannot easily be withdrawn. In these circumstances the distinction between current and non-current positions is largely irrelevant. The distinction between monetary and non-monetary positions retains greater validity but, as has been argued above, the effect of exchange rate changes on non-monetary items is an important matter which is very difficult to assess. Presumably, where an enduring investment abroad has been made, its value will be dependent on expectations of the future flow of funds obtainable from the investment. If the foreign currency weakens in relation to the parent currency, other things being equal, funds remitted by the foreign operation in future will be worth less to the parent company and vice versa. Therefore, it seems reasonable to write down the net investment in the foreign country when its currency weakens and this is accomplished by translating all its assets and liabilities at the new rate of exchange.

One possible reaction to this line of argument is that the concept of a permanent investment almost suggests that foreign subsidiaries should not be consolidated at all. But this reaction would seem too extreme. It has been recognized that if controls on foreign remittances are restrictive a question is raised whether the consolidation is appropriate. But if controls are absent or not onerous the fact that the investment is committed on an enduring basis is not in itself a reason to omit consolidation. An enduring commitment is made in many domestic sub-sidiaries as well and this does not bar them from consolidation. For that matter, specific assets of the parent company may be so tied up by pledges or mortgages that they are not readily available for whatever disposition of them may be desired.

A more serious objection to the closing rate approach is that it can result in un-realistic asset write-downs in the situation of a rapidly deteriorating currency. That is to say, under certain conditions a change in foreign exchange rates is a very poor measure of changes in the ability of non-monetary assets located in the foreign country to yield an acceptable return to the parent company. Thus, in such con-ditions, if the monetary position is in balance (or favourably weighted) the invest-ment should not be written down in step with the decline in the value of the foreign currency. This was implicitly recognized in Recommendation No. 25 which said "The 'historic rate' method may, for instance, sometimes be preferred where an overseas currency has a history of instability in relation to sterling and the circumstances are such that it is judged appropriate to continue to state fixed assets on the basis of their original sterling equivalents."

The par value approach to translations between Canadian and U.S. dollars

During the period from 1951 to 1961 in which the Canadian dollar value was not pegged, the rate of exchange with U.S. dollars floated in a narrow range fairly close to par. During this period many Canadian companies and some U.S. com-panies followed the practice of translating the accounts of subsidiaries or branches in the other country on a dollar for dollar basis.

Again, this was a practical expedient. If it had a theoretical justification it was this – a dollar for dollar exchange rate was reasonably representative of the actual rate of exchange prevailing over an extended period and there was no discernible trend to change in one direction of the other. The basic investment in the other country was largely fixed and therefore to adjust its value, or that of some part of the investment such as the working capital position, according to the fluctuations in exchange rate, produced quite meaningless debits or credits which would have to be absorbed in the income account or by other means.

After the Canadian dollar was pegged at 92.5¢ U.S. in 1962 most companies abandoned the par value approach. Presumably a 7½% difference between the actual rate and the translation rate was considered too unrealistic, and in addition the formal pegging may have been considered persuasive evidence that 92.5¢ was the best rate representative of long-term value.

The experience of 1951 to 1961, however, might be generalized to suggest an approach that would be applicable for translation of the accounts of subsidiaries in countries with apparently stable currencies:

(a) whose rates are pegged under IMF rules or
(b) who have floating exchange rates but such rates historically are in a stable relationship with those of the parent company.

Under this system remittances of earnings would trigger recognition of a gain or loss. For example a dividend from a U.S. subsidiary, translated at par to a Canadian parent company when the exchange rate was $1 U.S. equal to $1.02 Canadian, would produce a 2¢ profit. In most cases this would be reasonable since the earnings of the U.S. subsidiary translated at par would have been understated if anything. On the other hand a contribution of capital from Canada to the U.S. in this situation would result in an apparent 2% loss. This result would be unreasonable and to this extent the translation method could be criticized. (Deferment of any such artificial loss or gain on contribution of capital could reduce the force of this objection.)

In summary, a variety of methods are found in practice or can be suggested in theory for translating the balance sheets of foreign subsidiaries or branches. All probably have merits in certain circumstances and all may be criticized under other circumstances. No one method seems reasonably satisfactory for every situation. The conclusion probably is that companies should use different translation methods depending on their circumstances. A Canadian company with a Brazilian subsidiary should probably use the monetary/non-monetary approach, while with a U.S. subsidiary it might well use a fixed standard translation rate considered reasonably representative of the average actual exchange rate to be expected in the foreseeable future.

It has often been observed that the problems in translating foreign currency accounts are very similar to problems in adjusting a domestic company's accounts for changes in price levels. In fact, to the extent that changes in exchange rates reflect internal inflation in a foreign country, the monetary/non-monetary approach to translation in effect achieves price-level accounting. This suggests that an even more satisfactory basis for translation of statements of foreign subsidiaries would be to first produce accounts in the local currency adjusted for changes in its price levels and then to translate the adjusted accounts entirely at current exchange rates. If price-level accounting became general, a single approach to translation – the closing rate method – could then become generally feasible.

To clarify the preceding discussion, the following table summarizes existing approaches to balance sheet translation other than those which apply just one rate to every balance sheet item.

Table I
Comparative Summary of Translation Methods

Translation rates applied $\begin{cases} \text{H} = \text{Historic rate} \\ \text{Y} = \text{Year-end rate} \end{cases}$

Balance sheet item	Current/ non-current approach	Monetary/ non-monetary approach	Single company approach
Cash	Y	Y	Y
Marketable securities – with fixed income and maturity value in foreign currency – at cost	Y	Y	H
Marketable securities without fixed currency value – at cost	Y	H	H
Marketable securities carried at market	Y	Y	Y
Short-term accounts receivable	Y	Y	H
Inventories – bought in local currency }at cost	Y	H	H
– bought in parent company currency }at cost	Y or H	H	H
Inventories carried at market	Y	Y	Y
Prepaid expenses	Y	H	H
Accounts payable and accruals	Y	Y	H
Revenue received in advance – current	Y	H	H
Long-term investments – with fixed income and maturity value in foreign currency – at cost	H	Y	H
Other long-term investments – at cost	H	H	H
Fixed assets	H	H	H
Accumulated depreciation	H	H	H
Deferred charges	H	H	H
Long-term debt	H	Y	H
Preferred stock	H	H or Y°	H
Other paid-in capital	H	H	H
Retained earnings	Amount required to balance	Amount required to balance	Amount required to balance
Minority interest	Pro rata share of equity accounts after translation	Pro rata share of equity accounts after translation	Pro rata share of equity accounts after translation

° An argument could be made that preferred stock is a monetary item since its value depends on the expectation of paying a fixed dividend in foreign currency indefinitely into the future.

Translation procedures – income statement

There are fewer problems in the translation of income statement items than in the case of the balance sheet. It is generally conceded that except where a revenue or expense arose from a balance sheet item translated at historic rates, the translation should be made at current rates insofar as possible.

There is some question whether the current rate should be that at the date the transaction is recognized in the accounts or at the date it is settled in cash. Consider a system where the accounts are continuously translated. In such a case, if a sale is made on credit should the revenue recorded be translated at the date prevailing when the sale is made, or that prevailing when the account is settled? If the former, any difference between the transaction value and the ultimate cash value would represent a gain or loss on foreign exchange; if the latter, no gain or loss separate from the results of operations would be recognized. The usual answer to this question is that the revenue should be translated at the rate prevailing when the sale is made under normal accrual principles. After that date the amount receivable could be discounted or currency futures could be sold to fix the value of the transaction. If this is not done, the risk of currency value fluctuation is a financial risk not an operating risk.

This answer seems right in the case of a stable foreign currency. However, a contrary argument might be made when operations are conducted in a steadily deteriorating currency. In such cases, if sales are made on credit management should assume that the currency will be worth less when collection is made and allow for it in the selling price. Hence, it could be argued that the revenue on such a sale should be translated at the exchange rate *expected to exist* on the collection date and such a basis of translation would properly reflect the operating responsibility in fixing prices. At the other end of the scale an argument might be made, particularly where operating in a country with a stable currency, that the rate at which operating revenues and costs should be translated should be that prevailing *when commitments are entered into* rather than when the transaction is actually recognized in the accounts. Suppose, for example, that a contractor undertook a contract with proceeds payable in sterling, payment to be made as the contract progressed. If such contract was entered into before the sterling devaluation it might be argued that all the revenues of the contract should be translated at pre-devaluation rate and if there was a loss on payments received after devaluation that was a financial loss suffered by reason of not hedging the payment receipts.

This discussion is of course somewhat theoretical since continuous translation of the operations of a foreign subsidiary is usually highly impractical. Instead an approximation to continuous translation is obtained by using an average rate for the year, a month-end rate applied to each month's transactions, or an average monthly rate. The practice selected would depend on the degree of instability in the foreign currency. Obviously the monthly average would be more accurate than a single yearly average rate. Where a major revaluation occurs it may be desirable to obtain actual figures for transactions before and after the change in rate in order to make an accurate calculation.

Recommendation No. 25 of the English Institute indicates that the continuous translation theory is not followed when the 'closing rate' translation method is adopted. Under that method profit and loss for the period is converted at the closing rate except that earnings remitted to the parent company during the period are translated at the actual rate applicable to the remittance. However, when a major currency revaluation occurs during a year, profit or loss before the change is translated at the old rate and after the change is translated at the new rate.

As indicated above, where a cost or revenue flows from a balance sheet item translated at historic rates that cost is also translated at the same historic rates. The usual example given is that of depreciation. If a fixed asset is translated at a rate of 1 local currency unit equals 1 parent company currency unit, then the depreciation thereon will be translated at that rate even though the average rate prevailing in the period of translation is, say, 2 LC units equal 1 PC unit. The principle applies to other costs besides depreciation, however, and this means that extra care must be taken if the translation is to be made accurately. For example, consider the following case:

Period 1 – closing exchange rate	1.2 LC units = 1 PC unit
– rate when closing inventory was acquired	1 LC unit = 1 PC unit
– cost of closing inventory	100,000 LC units
Period 2 – average rate for period	1.3 LC units = 1 PC unit
– closing exchange rate	1.5 LC units = 1 PC unit
– rate when closing inventory was acquired	1.4 LC units = 1 PC unit
– cost of closing inventory	160,000 LC units
– total purchases for inventory for the year	500,000 LC units

Cost of sales in local currency in period 2 would be

Opening inventory	100,000 LC
Purchases	500,000
	600,000
Less closing inventory	160,000
Cost of sales	440,000 LC

When inventory is translated at historic cost, the correct translation of cost of sales would be:

Opening inventory	$\dfrac{100,000}{1}$	100,000 PC
Purchases	$\dfrac{500,000}{1.3}$	384,615
		484,615
Less closing inventory	$\dfrac{160,000}{1.4}$	114,286
Cost of sales		370,329 PC

On the other hand, where inventory is translated at year-end rates the cost of sales translation, as it is usually done, would be at the average rate for the year:

in this illustration	$\dfrac{440,000}{1.3}$	338,462 PC units

Treatment of gain or loss on translation

In the above example, the translation rates applied to opening and closing inventory and cost of sales were consistent throughout where inventory was translated at historic cost so that no foreign exchange gain or loss would appear on inventory account. But this would not be true of other accounts. Suppose, for example, all sales and purchases during period 2 were for cash and the cash account during the year was as follows:

Cash account

Opening balance		10,000 LC
Add sales proceeds		700,000
		710,000
Deduct – purchases	500,000 LC	
– other expenses	100,000	600,000
Closing balance		110,000 LC

If there had been continuous translation or an approximation to continuous translation, the cash account in the parent company currency would appear as:

Opening balance	$\dfrac{10,000}{1.2}$	8,333 PC
Add sales	$\dfrac{700,000}{1.3}$	538,462
		546,795
Deduct purchases and other costs	$\dfrac{600,000}{1.3}$	461,538
Closing balance		85,257 PC

but the closing balance of 110,000 LC would only be worth $\dfrac{110,000}{1.5} = 73,333$ PC units so that there would be a loss of 11,924 PC units. This could be analyzed as follows:

Loss on opening balance of cash – difference between value at beginning and end of year exchange rates

Value beginning	$\dfrac{10,000}{1.2}$	8,333 PC	
Value ending	$\dfrac{10,000}{1.5}$	6,666	1,667 PC

Loss on cash generated by operations – difference between value of cash when generated, and at end of year

Value when generated	$\dfrac{100,000}{1.3}$	76,923 PC	
Value ending	$\dfrac{100,000}{1.5}$	66,666	10,257 PC

Loss on holding cash as exchange rate falls		11,924 PC

This example illustrates that when the translation rate applicable to a balance sheet item changes from one period to another or when the rate used in translating a transaction for income statement purposes and balance sheet purposes differs, the translation procedure will result in a debit or credit difference which must be accounted for in the parent company's statements. The amount of the difference in practice is usually ascertained by translating both the balance sheet and income statement by the methods previously described and finding that the net income less dividends translated into dollars, when added to the dollar balance of the opening retained earnings account, does not equal the dollar balance of the closing retained earnings shown in the translated balance sheet.

As the above example shows, the difference can be analyzed to see what gave rise to it. The reason for the difference depends upon the translation approach used. Under the monetary/non-monetary approach as illustrated, the difference in essence represents the gain or loss from holding monetary items as the exchange rate moves. Under the current/non-current approach the difference represents the adjustment to the valuation of the net current position as the exchange rate moves. Under the closing rate approach the difference would represent the result of translating the closing balance sheet of the foreign subsidiary at the previous year-end at its closing rate and retranslating that balance sheet at the following year's closing rate for the purpose of the following year's accounts.

Unless a standard translation rate is used which is unchanged from that of the previous year however, there will always be a gain or loss to be disposed of. The question then is what to do with it. The answer to this question is partly determined by the translation theory adopted. The question whether or not the gain or loss is 'realized' is also a factor. The meaning of 'realization' in relation to translation gains or losses is not clearly explained in the literature. One concept of realization relates it to remittance from the foreign subsidiary to the parent company. On this basis it could be said that no gain or loss appearing on translation is realized. Realization would only take place as funds are remitted from the foreign subsidiary to the parent company.

Advocates of the monetary/non-monetary approach usually argue that there is no such thing as an unrealized gain or loss. When the exchange rate changes the value of monetary assets and liabilities changes as well. A less extreme view might hold that such gains or losses should only be considered realized when it is considered that the change in exchange rate is unlikely to reverse itself. Still another approach might suggest a practical test for realization – losses or gains on current assets and liabilities might be considered realized and on long-term items unrealized. On the single company approach however, where assets are to be stated at the historic rate until realization, the test of realization probably would be settlement in the foreign currency. It would be unrealistic to translate foreign currency cash balances at other than current rates.

The result of the foregoing mixture of theories is as follows:

1. Under the traditional translation approach, as indicated, gains or losses are considered unrealized. The recommendation of ARB No. 43 is that gains should be deferred and not affect income unless realized losses had been written off against income in prior years. In such a case unrealized gains up to the amount of the previously expensed unrealized losses could be taken to income account. Unrealized losses should be charged against previously deferred unrealized gains and once they are exhausted should be written off against income.

2. Under the monetary/non-monetary distinction, as indicated, both gains and losses might be taken to income account when recognized. This would be especially true in dealing with countries with unstable currencies. If the method were applied in more stable situations (such as that of the Canadian/U.S. dollar) there would be considerable merit in deferring gains, and possibly losses as well, on long-term assets and liabilities.

3. As previously indicated, the single company approach would recognize gains or losses in income not later than date of realization as indicated by settlement in the foreign currency. Provision for unrealized losses on at least the net position in current monetary assets and liabilities would probably also be made.

4. Under the British closing rate approach (not followed in North America) gains or losses may be taken through income or direct to reserves.

Translation of foreign currency assets and liabilities arising from transactions not involving branches or subsidiaries

Problems in translation where no foreign branch or subsidiary is involved are somewhat simpler. In the first place the problems are confined mainly to monetary assets and liabilities. The carrying value of non-monetary assets and liabilities arising from transactions in foreign currency is normally fixed (subject to further discussion below) at the domestic currency equivalent of the transaction amount at the date of the transaction, and is not affected thereafter by fluctuations in the exchange rate. Thus the cost of, say, a machine, is fixed at the date of purchase and even though the liability to a foreign supplier is outstanding for some time and is eventually settled at an exchange rate different from that of the date of purchase, the resulting gain or loss is an item of financial income and not an adjustment to the cost of the machine.

The questions then with monetary assets and liabilities arising from trading, investment or borrowing transactions entered into by domestic entities in foreign currency are:

1. If the exchange rate changes, should the carrying value of such assets and liabilities be revised to the new rate?

2. If the carrying value is revised, should the resulting gain or loss be deferred or recognized through income?

These questions involve much the same sort of theories about realization as have been discussed earlier in connection with translation of foreign currency accounts. Advocates of the monetary/non-monetary distinction would say that all adjustments of such asset or liability values represent realized gains or losses. Others would be less extreme:

(a) It would be virtually universally conceded that the value of foreign currency cash or bank deposits owned should be adjusted as the exchange rate changes and that resulting gains or losses are realized and should be reflected in income.

(b) Most accountants would advocate that the carrying value of current accounts receivable and payable in foreign currency should be adjusted to current exchange rates. Some would regard the resulting gains or losses as realized and take them to income account. Others would regard them as unrealized and advocate provision for such unrealized losses but deferment of unrealized gains.

(c) Most accountants would consider that gains or losses on long-term amounts receivable and payable are unrealized. Many companies do not restate carrying values of such assets or liabilities. Those that do would usually defer gains as being unrealized and might defer losses as well. In part, the treatment is likely to depend on the actual situation. When the foreign currency is in a stable relationship with the domestic currency and fluctuations in exchange rates are small, such fluctuations are apt to be ignored and the carrying value of long-term items not adjusted. Where there has been a significant revaluation of the foreign currency however, there is more need to restate the carrying value. Finally, when the value of the currency is changing rapidly in what appears to be a long-term trend, there is still greater need to change the carrying values and to recognize the gain or loss as though it were realized.

(d) In the preceding discussion it is assumed that whether or not a gain or loss is recognized and deferred depends on the settlement date of the asset or liability in question. It might be argued, however, that the decision to defer a gain or loss should also be affected by the overall net position in foreign currency assets and liabilities. For example, if an entity had bank deposits in West German currency and also bonds payable in the same currency at a time when the West German mark appreciated, it would seem unsound to record a realized gain on the bank deposits and not reflect the loss on the bonds payable. This would suggest translating all foreign currency balances at current rates and deferring net gains or losses only to the extent they do not exceed amounts attributable to long-term assets and liabilities.

To return to the subject of non-monetary assets (inventory and fixed assets) purchased in a foreign currency transaction. As has been indicated, the general rule is that the cost of such assets is established at the acquisition date. The appropriate date to be considered the date of acquisition, or the appropriate exchange rate to be used in translating the foreign currency transaction, may depend upon the particular fact situation. For example, if foreign currency futures are specifically bought to liquidate the liability on the transaction, the appropriate cost for the asset would be the cost determined by the purchase of the futures. In other cases, as previously indicated, the exchange rate when the purchase commitment was entered into might be a more realistic rate at which to record the transaction than that prevailing on the day when the asset was delivered and the transaction first was recorded in the accounts. Or a more complex situation might dictate still another treatment. For example, suppose a Canadian company borrowed on long-term debt in the United States to finance a plant construction at the same time that it entered into commitments to U.S. suppliers for materials and other services required. If the proceeds of the borrowing were left on deposit in the United States until payment was due to the supplier and the exchange rate changed in the meantime, it would still be proper to charge the materials purchased to the plant cost at the exchange rate when the commitment was made, which would mean that a gain or loss on the funds held on deposit would not be recorded. However, if the funds on deposit were greater than the commitments entered into to U.S. suppliers, a gain or loss on funds on deposit should be recognized to the extent of the excess because it would have been possible to avoid any foreign exchange risks by transferring the funds to Canada before the exchange rate changed.

The principal point is that the cost of an asset bought in a foreign currency transaction is established at one particular date and subsequent fluctuations in exchange rates before the liability is settled are irrelevant to that cost. The authorities, however, make an exception to this rule in the case of major revaluation of a foreign currency. For example, the English Recommendation No. 25 states that "that part of an exceptional loss on exchange attributable to goods unsold on the balance sheet date may be treated as an increment in cost provided net realisable value in sterling is estimated to be in excess of cost so computed; this treatment is preferable if sterling selling prices of the items on hand have been increased to compensate for the change in parities". It will be recognized that this line of thinking is rather similar to some of the recommendations of ARB No. 43 in connection with translation procedures for foreign branches or subsidiaries. It may be observed, however, that such a treatment is in substance a departure from the cost basis of accounting for the assets affected. What these recommendations really accomplish is the deferment of a loss on devaluation which, in effect, has been hedged by investment in an asset that is considered to appreciate on devaluation.

Sundry matters

It is probably not possible to cover all the potential problems related to translation of foreign currencies short of a book length study. The following topics, however, may be touched on briefly:
(a) Classification of exchange gains or losses recognized in the income statement.
(b) Action required when the exchange rate changes subsequent to the year-end.
(c) The problem of multiple exchange rates.
(d) The use of a standard translation rate.
(e) Selection of a currency of account for a multi-national company.
(f) Translation of the accounts of an independent foreign company.

Classification of exchange gains or losses

As has been indicated, a company may have gains or losses on its own transactions in foreign currency. A foreign subsidiary may have gains or losses on its transactions. Finally, the parent company may have translation gains or losses on consolidating its subsidiary. Because a translation gain or loss may be reversed so long as the subsidiary remains in being, and possibly because of the variety of translation methods available, the latter type of gain or loss seems somewhat less real than the former two types. However, it is not usual to distinguish between types of gain or loss in financial statements and the average statement reader would probably not understand the significance of the distinction in any event.

U.S. and Canadian authorities, however, do call for a distinction between 'extraordinary' and other gains or losses. The extraordinary item (see Chapter 14) is defined as "a material gain or loss which is not typical of the company's normal business activities, is not expected to occur regularly over a period of years, and is not considered a recurring factor in any evaluation of the ordinary operating processes of the business".* As in any classification scheme not based on independently measurable characteristics, this definition can be difficult to interpret in relation to foreign exchange gains or losses.

First, the question what is material is often difficult. (The U.S. recommendation doubles the emphasis by referring to *material* gains and losses from a *major* devaluation.) It has been suggested earlier that whether an item is extraordinary or not is best based on the character of the event alone without much importance being given to its materiality. Second, consider how to determine whether a gain or loss is typical of normal activities or expected to recur regularly. Any entity that trades abroad or invests abroad is subject to some exchange risk unless it hedges its position completely at all times. It would seem that to qualify as extraordinary, an exchange gain or loss must be quite unexpected. Presumably, gains or losses today would be expected in trading in soft currencies or soft currency countries so that an extraordinary item can only arise in relation to dealings in hard currencies. Again, trading in currencies whose exchange rate is floating rather than pegged suggests that exchange gains or losses should be expected and cannot be treated as extraordinary when they occur. There might be an exception if a previously stable floating rate currency fell or rose to a markedly different level over a relatively short period of time. If it fell in this manner more than once however, it might be suspected that the currency had softened to a degree that losses in it should be expected and should no longer be considered extraordinary. The clearest example of a change that is extraordinary may be the case where a pegged rate has to be changed or abandoned or a previously floating rate has to be pegged to stabilize it. However, if governments changed their established practices and started making frequent small changes in pegged rates rather than infrequent large changes, even these simple cases would no longer be clear-cut. Again, it may be noted that a change in the rate of only one currency may qualify as not being expected to recur regularly but a company operating in a number of countries may find exchange rate changes occurring with some regularity. Thus, it may be questioned whether exchange gains or losses to such a company are extraordinary.

Action required when the exchange rate changes subsequent to the year-end

A movement in the exchange rate after a fiscal year-end raises the question whether the new rate should be applied in the translation of assets and liabilities in foreign currencies. This question may be considered in the general context of events subsequent to the financial statement date. Where subsequent events help to improve valuations estimated for assets and liabilities carried in the balance sheet, they should be reflected in such financial statements. Where they reflect changed conditions since the financial statement date they should not be given retroactive effect, although they may require disclosure.

In general, it would seem that changes in the exchange rate are of the second type. Such changes usually may be presumed to reflect economic conditions or political or other events arising subsequent to the year-end. However, no rule should be considered invariable on this point. For example, if a foreign currency

---

* This definition has been modified in recent revisions of the CICA Research Recommendations, and now does not contain the reference to a 'material' gain or loss.

exhibited a regular history of devaluation roughly once a year, a devaluation occurring just after a fixed year-end and, say, fourteen months after the last previous devaluation, should probably be reflected in the statements of the year just closed.

English Institute Recommendation No. 25 says "where rates of exchange have altered after the balance sheet date the alterations would normally be disregarded unless the rates of exchange on the balance sheet were not realistic and the amounts affected are material, though the implications of a change of parities which is properly excluded from the accounts may nevertheless be of such importance that it may need to be disclosed by the directors through some other medium".

The problem of multiple exchange rates

In certain countries at certain times the government has established a system of multiple exchange rates as part of a system of foreign exchange control. In such cases the general rule is that the rate applicable to dividend remittances to the parent company is the appropriate rate to select for translation purposes. For certain types of transactions however, the government may make foreign funds available at a preferential rate or perhaps only at a penalty rate. In such cases both sides of the entry recording such transactions should be translated at the appropriate rate. However, if the liability is liquidated before the inventory is sold, cash translated at the free rate is substituted for the liability translated at the preferential or penalty rate and a debit or credit or apparent loss or gain will be thrown up in the dollar account. This debit or credit should be deferred since an offsetting credit or debit will be thrown up subsequently when the inventory translated at the special rate is in turn converted into cash translated at the free rate. The same situation would be true in reverse if the inventory were sold before the liability were liquidated.[3]

The use of a standard translation rate

The practice of translating U.S. currency amounts into Canadian dollars on a dollar for dollar basis has already been referred to. In general, when currencies are in a stable relationship to each other, the use of standard rates of exchange for translation has much to commend it because it excludes the effect of meaningless, minor rate fluctuations from the income account and lessens the work of translation. Where currencies are pegged under the IMF rules the pegged rate is a natural choice for the standard bookkeeping rate.

Selection of a currency of account for a multi-national company

It has been assumed so far that a parent company will always translate its subsidiary accounts into the currency of the country in which the parent is incorporated. There are, however, a number of Canadian companies that use U.S. dollars for reporting purposes including a few that adopted this basis of reporting in 1970 as a consequence of the floating of the Canadian dollar in that year. The question arises as to what conditions warrant a company reporting in a currency other than that of its country of incorporation. In more general terms, it may be asked what criteria should a multi-national company use to select its currency of account.

This question has not been answered by any authority. Some of the major considerations are evident. Reports are primarily addressed to shareholders so that the country of residence of the majority of shareholders should be a major determinant. Secondly, it will be expedient if possible to report in a currency in which a high percentage of transactions are carried on in order to minimize the extent of translation required with its attendant artificiality. These two criteria, however, may be in conflict. For example, a company wholly owned by Canadian residents might carry on all its operations in, say, East Africa. In such a case translation into Canadian dollars is necessary for the sake of understanding by the shareholders. On the other hand, the Canadian company which carries on most or all of its operations in the United States might well report in U.S. dollars since the average Canadian is quite conversant with the exchange rate between Canadian and U.S. dollars.

In the truly multi-national company, it is conceivable that shareholders might be so widely dispersed and operations so widespread that neither of these criteria points overwhelmingly to any one currency as being the most logical choice for reporting purposes. In such a case, if the U.S. dollar is one of the possible contending currencies it would make a logical choice in view of its use as a reserve currency under present international monetary arrangements. One further point might be noted. The actual country of incorporation of such a company is of minor consequence (except for legal requirements). Foreign shareholders of a company incorporated in, say, Argentina or the Netherlands West Indies, would not find reporting in the currency of the country of incorporation very useful.

Translation of the accounts of an independent foreign company

There are occasions when a company wishes to publish its accounts in the currency of another country, perhaps in connection with financing being arranged in such other countries. In such a case it is probably impractical to attempt to translate fixed assets at historic rates of exchange prevailing when the assets were acquired. The answer therefore is to adopt something like the closing rate method of translation. Some authors question whether it is proper to translate accounts of a company operating wholly within one country into the currency of another. The information would seem to have value however, particularly if it is accompanied by a history of the exchange rates prevailing between the two countries in question.

Principles of Foreign Currency Translation

Because of the diversity in practice described in this Chapter, the principles summarized below must be thought of more as the more frequently encountered practice in North America rather than invariable rules.

Translation of accounts of foreign subsidiaries or branches

1. The usual procedure for balance sheet accounts is to translate current assets and liabilities at year-end exchange rates and long-term assets, liabilities and

paid-in capital at the exchange rates prevailing when the assets were obtained, liabilities incurred, or capital contributed. Retained earnings are translated at the rate required to balance the balance sheet when it is expressed in the parent company's currency.

Exceptions

(a) Frequently inventory is translated at historic exchange rates rather than year-end rates especially if the inventory was imported by the foreign subsidiary.

(b) Long-term monetary assets and liabilities are often translated at year-end rates rather than historic rates.

(c) After a major revaluation of the foreign currency it may be considered desirable to abandon the historic rates for translation of long-term assets and liabilities in favour of the year-end rate, possibly in conjunction with a revaluation of the assets in terms of the foreign currency.

The first two of these exceptions are more frequently encountered in connection with the translation of accounts in currencies subject to a long-term declining trend in value.

2. Income statement amounts for the most part are translated at rates designed to fairly represent the actual exchange rates prevailing during the period. This may be achieved by the use of averages, or rates changed every month or quarter, or a combination of these methods. However, income statement amounts associated with balance sheet items which are translated at historic rates (e.g. depreciation associated with fixed assets, cost of sales associated with inventory carried at historic rates, etc.) should be translated having regard to the rates used in the translation of the asset account.

3. Gains appearing in translation should be deferred until realization except to the extent they counteract losses previously written off. Losses on translation should be charged against previously deferred gains and any balance not so covered should be written off.

Exceptions

(a) After a major currency revaluation it may be considered appropriate to treat gains or losses on debt incurred just before the revaluation as an adjustment of the cost of assets acquired out of the proceeds of the debt.

(b) If a change in exchange rate may reasonably be expected not to be reversed in future (as in the case of a steadily declining currency), either gains or losses may be reflected in income account as they occur.

4. The use of standard translation rates which are changed only infrequently is acceptable when the currency to be translated is stable in relation to the parent company currency.

5. The accounts of foreign subsidiaries or branches should not be consolidated if the parent company's control is jeopardized by government action or unsettled conditions in the foreign country so that the ability of the parent company to receive the income earned from operations of the subsidiary or branch is in doubt.

Translation of foreign currency assets and liabilities arising from transactions not involving branches or subsidiaries

6. Current monetary assets and liabilities should be translated at year-end rates and any gain or loss recognized in income.

Exceptions
(a) A gain on translation at the new rate of an asset or liability other than cash may be deferred until date of settlement in cash.

(b) After a major revaluation it may be appropriate to treat *gains or losses* on liabilities incurred just before the revaluation as an adjustment of the cost of *inventory* acquired with the proceeds, if the realizable selling price of the inventory is expected to reflect the change in the cost of importing it. Similarly, it may be appropriate to treat such a *gain* as an adjustment of the cost of a *fixed asset* acquired, but ordinarily a *loss* should not be capitalized owing to the difficulty of establishing that the increase in carrying value will be recoverable.

7. Non-current monetary assets and liabilities may be treated in any of three ways:
   (a) Translation may continue at the historic rate until the asset or liability becomes current.
   (b) Translation may be made at the new rate and
       (i) gains deferred until the item becomes current or is settled, and
       (ii) losses recognized in income or deferred until the item' becomes current.
   (c) If the change in exchange rate is expected not to be reversed, translation may be made at the new rate and both gains and losses reflected immediately in income.

References

1. *Management Accounting Problems in Foreign Operations* (New York: National Association of Accountants, 1960), pp. 28–31.
2. P. Grady, *Inventory of Generally Accepted Accounting Principles for Business Enterprises* (New York: American Institute of Certified Public Accountants, Inc., 1965), p. 332.
3. See more detailed discussion in *Management Accounting Problems*, pp. 47–55.

20   Fair disclosure in financial reporting

A long standing principle in financial reporting is that there should be what has been variously called 'full', 'fair' or 'adequate' disclosure. Three questions come to mind in considering the meaning of the disclosure principle.

1. Who is the person to whom disclosure is being made?
2. What does he want or need to know?
3. What medium should be used for disclosure?

The possibility that financial statements on different bases might be prepared for different purposes has been mentioned earlier. General financial reporting, however, has grown up in the context of communication with shareholders and creditors, and it is to these two groups that disclosure rules are oriented. Originally it was thought that annual financial reporting was directed to existing shareholders only. With the development of the market in shares and especially the practice of listing on stock exchanges however, it would be generally conceded now that a corporation owes a duty to investors in general in its financial reporting, not just to those individuals who happen to be shareholders at a particular time.

Investors, of course, vary in their ability to comprehend financial reporting and it is necessary to visualize a 'typical investor' to form some idea of his needs for disclosure. The concept is rather like that of the 'reasonable man' in law – a fiction, but a necessary one. In recent years however, considerable growth and development has occurred in the profession of financial analysis. The analyst, being more highly trained, is able to comprehend more in financial reporting than the average investor. There is thus some small degree of conflict between the needs of the typical investor and those of the financial analyst, since an analyst can absorb and use detail in financial reporting that might well confuse the typical investor.

The trend of development seems clear. With increasing complexity in business financial reporting inevitably becomes more complex too. The role of the analyst takes on increasing importance and his needs must, in the long run, prevail. Some compromise, however, is possible to the extent that needs conflict. The financial statements themselves may be prepared in simple form with explanatory detail transferred to footnotes and supporting schedules. Or a few companies have gone to the length of producing a simple straightforward annual report for shareholders and a separate highly detailed report for those who are prepared to use it. The recent requirement of the Ontario Securities Commission that finance companies file a form of 'long form report' worked out jointly by the Canadian Association of Sales Finance Companies and the Investment Dealers' Association is a specific example of this type of development.

What does the investor need to know? Regulation S-X of the Securities and Exchange Commission states that financial statements should make such disclosure as would make them "not misleading". This rather vague requirement begs the question of what the investor would find misleading. One or two things are obvious. If reported income is affected significantly by an unusual or non-recurring event, this should clearly be disclosed. The classification of assets and liabilities should be accurate. Amounts which are not receivable should not be called receivable. Deferred charges should not be described as prepaid expenses, and so on. Beyond these obvious generalizations it is a matter of judgment in every case as to what the typical investor would find misleading.

In line with the developing emphasis on the needs of the financial analyst, the disclosure guidelines might be stated more positively in the form "such information should be disclosed as will assist in analysis". This is, of course, a rather open-ended statement. It would not be too far-fetched to suggest that the analyst's desire for information is like Oliver Twist's desire for food – he wants more. The drive for more disclosure, however, is limited by the objection that disclosure may be injurious to the enterprise. Two dangers are frequently seen in excessive disclosure. One is that competitors may be helped by the information disclosed to gain an advantage over the enterprise. This argument was once urged, for example, against compulsory disclosure of sales or gross operating revenue. While it probably has validity in some situations, remarkably few cases of actual injury through disclosure have been documented. A second danger is that disclosure of provisions for costs or losses may damage the interests of the entity in an adversary type of situation. For example, if a business is engaged in any litigation, or say a dispute on tax matters, a provision for cost on resolution of the matter, if known, might be taken as an admission of liability. While the provision cannot properly be omitted if the loss seems probable, it is generally accepted in these circumstances that disclosure may be minimal.[1]

The general conclusion is that the concept of disclosure is a developing and expanding one adapted to the social environment of the day. It is subject to the limitation that disclosure should not carry material risk of injuring the entity, but in other respects it has no maximum limit as long as additional information disclosed does not interfere with the readability and understandability of the basic statements. Principles of disclosure therefore can be defined only in terms of minimum recognized requirements. In view of the long-run trend also, a valid standard to apply is probably – "when in doubt, disclose".

Information may be disclosed by media outside the financial statements themselves, such as letters to shareholders, press releases and statements filed with stock exchanges or securities commissions. We are concerned here, however, only with disclosure in financial statements. In a set of financial statements disclosure may be implemented by:
– expansion in the number of categories of assets, liabilities, revenues and expenditures reported,

– expansion of descriptive material in the caption of each category,
– parenthetical information attached to each caption (e.g. quoted market value for investments),
– footnotes to statements, or notes accompanying statements,
– supplementary statements or schedules.

For easiest comprehension, it is desirable that relevant information with respect to each category in the financial statements accompany it in the statement itself or be placed as close to it as possible. On the other hand if there is very much additional information the statement soon becomes so cluttered as to be virtually unreadable. As a practical matter therefore, in all but the simplest reporting situations one is forced to attach to the financial statements one or more pages of notes and supplementary schedules. In such cases individual categories in the statements themselves should be cross-referenced on the face of the statement to the relevant note or notes and it will be helpful if the notes are set out, insofar as possible, in the order in which the reader will encounter them when reading through the statements from beginning to end. It hardly needs saying that the information given in notes should be consistent with the accounting treatment afforded the item in question. For example, if a loss is probable it is not enough to disclose the fact – provision must be made for it right in the statements.

We may now turn to a more detailed description of the various types of disclosure in financial statements required to make them not misleading and provide information for analysis.

1. A general statement of accounting policy or accounting methods followed is desirable, and special disclosure is required particularly where (a) unusual problems require the development of special accounting rules to deal with them, (b) alternative accounting methods are possible in the situation (particularly if the less common method is used), or (c) judgment is required in the actual application of the accounting method. Examples of these types of disclosure are:
   – details as to bases of valuation of assets and liabilities when such are not self-evident,
   – details as to policy re inclusion or exclusion of subsidiaries from consolidation,
   – details as to methods and rates used in translation of foreign currency assets and liabilities,
   – disclosure by contractors of basis of income recognition – whether on the completed contract method or the stage of completion method,
   – disclosure of choice of inventory costing method (LIFO, FIFO, etc.) and the method followed in writing inventory down to 'market',
   – disclosure of choice of depreciation pattern and, since this depends on judgment, disclosure of service life assumptions or rates of depreciation used,
   – similar disclosure about amortization of other capital assets.

2. Additional informative disclosure is often required or desirable for analysis. Examples are:
   – disclosure of assets and liabilities by geographical area where significant investments are held, or business activities carried on, in foreign countries,
   – disclosure of amounts of accumulated depreciation or other similar allowances deducted in arriving at the carrying value of assets,

- disclosure of any restrictions on the availability of cash for general purposes,
- disclosure if accounts receivable contain significant amounts due on extended terms,
- analysis of inventories as between raw materials, work-in-process, finished goods, etc.,
- analysis of fixed assets and accumulated depreciation by various categories (land, buildings, equipment, etc.),
- disclosure of breakdown of investments between investment in non-consolidated subsidiaries, investment in affiliates, and other investments,
- disclosure of current earnings of non-consolidated subsidiaries, and accumulated earnings since acquisition which have not been distributed to the parent company,
- disclosure indicative of the current value of other types of investments,
- disclosure of interest rates and repayment terms on debt,
- disclosure of security rights attaching to various types of debt and the assets pledged as security where this is not self-evident,
- disclosure of rights attaching to various types of shares in respect of dividend rates, premium on redemption, cumulative arrears of dividends, etc.,
- disclosure of common shares reserved for issuance upon exercise of convertibility privileges, warrants, options outstanding, etc., and the terms upon which such rights may be exercised,
- distinction between contributed capital and retained earnings in the equity section of the balance sheet and disclosure of restrictions on the right of the company to pay dividends,
- disclosure of gross revenue and cost of sales in the income statement,
- disclosure of the amount of investment income, distinguishing between income from non-consolidated subsidiaries, from affiliates, and from other investments,
- disclosure of amounts of provisions for depreciation, depletion and amortization,
- disclosure of interest expenses, segregating expense on long-term debt,
- disclosure of the amount provided for income taxes indicating the amount actually payable with respect to the current taxation year.

3. If there have been changes made from the preceding year in accounting principles followed or their basis of application, this must be disclosed indicating the effect of the change.

4. Since there may be conflicts of interest, for example between management and ownership, or minority interest and majority control of an enterprise, special disclosure should be made of such matters as:
   - remuneration, direct or indirect, of directors and senior officers,
   - amounts due from or payable to associated or affiliated companies, debts owing to a company by directors, officers or shareholders other than in the normal course of business, and loans to the company by directors, officers or shareholders,
   - the amount of loans by a company during a period to directors or officers even if such are repaid before the end of the period.

5. Contingent assets and liabilities should be disclosed unless the possibility of their realization is quite remote. Commitments which will govern the level of future costs should also be disclosed. Examples of disclosures in these categories are:
  - legal action initiated or threatened on which loss is possible but not probable (if probable, provision for loss should be made in the balance sheet),
  - possible adjustments on contract negotiation,
  - amounts of income tax loss carry-forwards where their potential value has not been recorded as an asset in the balance sheet,
  - commitments under long-term leases and details of such rental contracts,
  - obligations under pension plans for past service, not yet absorbed as cost, and disclosure of how this obligation will be absorbed against income.

6. Post-balance sheet events – financial reporting covers the income for a period and a statement of financial position at the end of the period. The report may not be completed and released until some weeks or months after the end of the period and in that time events will have occurred that have altered the financial position. What disclosure should be given to these? In the first place, some events may cast new light upon the financial position at the end of the period. For example, if a substantial debtor goes bankrupt after the end of the entity's fiscal year, the allowance for uncollectible accounts at the year-end may need to be reassessed. Any such events that permit more accurate valuation of the year-end position should be reflected in such valuation. In the second place there may be some financial or other non-operating transactions after the end of the period that significantly alter the financial position that existed at the period end. For example, a large new issue of debt or stock may be made or a significant purchase of a business may be accomplished. It is generally conceded that events of the latter type which occur between the year-end and the date the audit report is released should be disclosed in the year-end report (but not reflected in the accounts) by way of additional information to the reader. On the other hand, the course of ordinary business operations after the year-end need not be disclosed in the report. There may, for example, be a strike after the year-end which will damage the financial position. There are, however, so many factors favourable or adverse in the ordinary course of a business that it would be impractical and possibly misleading in view of all the uncertainties to single some out for comment. The current trend to more frequent financial reporting is considered the more satisfactory way to keep statement readers up to date.

One aspect of financial disclosure is currently attracting considerable attention. We refer to the disclosure of sales, profits, assets and liabilities by division of diversified entities – i.e. companies that are engaged in several unrelated lines of business. A number of years ago when full consolidation of subsidiary companies was less common than it is today, one of the arguments made against consolidation was that it obscured many important financial ratios such as profit margins on sales, debt-equity ratios, turnover of receivables and inventories, etc., when the accounts of businesses in different industries with different characteristics were consolidated. The converse of this problem occurs where a company enters into several lines of business but not through the medium of subsidiary companies.

To the extent that there was validity in the old arguments against consolidation of the accounts of diversified enterprises, there is validity in arguments that diversified companies operating through divisions should follow some form of divisional reporting. Moreover, quite apart from ratios and trends, the reporting of divisional figures would permit a much more informed assessment of a company's future prospects, by differentiating the relative importance of divisions operating in various sectors of the economy.

The problems with this proposition are practical. First the natural divisions of the reporting entity have to be determined and sometimes the accounts reorganized to produce information by division. What is a natural division will vary from one entity to another, depending not only on extrinsic factors, but also on the way the entity is organized internally. In one entity the natural division may be by type of industrial process carried on. In another, it may be by market served. In yet another, information by geographical location of plants or markets may be more important than divisional information on another basis.

After identification of divisions there may be a problem in accounting for sales of goods or services from one division to another. The basis of setting transfer prices may come into question since there may be no reliable market price for products of the type and in the quantities entering into the inter-divisional transfer. Moreover, a market price may not be the most logical transfer price where one division is a captive market for the other.

Allocation of costs that are joint or common to divisions also will present problems in logic. In many cases, allocation of all costs to divisions may be so arbitrary that it would be better to stop short of complete allocation and produce only 'contribution margin' figures in place of net divisional income figures.

Production of divisional balance sheets in many cases will be more difficult than arriving at net income by divisions, and in some cases will be a practical impossibility. Thus return on investment ratios by divisions may not be attainable.

These problems do not disprove the potential usefulness of information by divisions. They do mean, however, that information by division will rarely be comparable from one entity to another. Analysts must take care to use divisional information within its proper context and with awareness of its underlying assumptions and limitations.

Principles of Disclosure

The disclosure principle, then, may be worded as follows:

Disclosure in financial statements should be sufficient to make them not misleading to a typical investor. Assets, liabilities, revenues and expenses should be accurately described. Non-recurring factors affecting information reported should be separately disclosed. The following matters particularly should be the subject of disclosure:

(a) details of accounting policies and methods, particularly where judgment is required in the application of an accounting method, the method is peculiar to the reporting entity, or alternative accounting methods could be used;

(b) additional information to aid in investment analysis or to indicate the rights of various parties having claims upon the reporting entity;

(c) changes from the preceding year in accounting principles or methods of applying them and the effect of such changes;

(d) assets and liabilities, costs and revenues arising out of transactions with parties such as controlling interests, or directors or officers, that have a special relationship to the reporting entity;

(e) contingent assets, liabilities and commitments;

(f) financial or other non-operating transactions after the balance sheet date which have a material effect on the financial position shown by the year-end statement.

References

1. See discussion in Statement on Auditing Procedure No. 33, *Auditing Standards and Procedures* (New York: American Institute of Certified Public Accountants, 1963), p. 55.

21   Analytical data: earnings per share

We have seen that accounting is largely a process of summarizing and classifying transactions in aggregates that give some form and meaning to the raw data. We have seen also in Chapter 20 that one of the objectives of the disclosure principle is to provide information helpful in financial statement analysis and decision-making based thereon. The question then arises, how far should the financial statements go in providing information, and how much should be left to the analyst to work out for himself?

It might be argued that the role of the accountant is to furnish facts and the role of the statement reader or analyst is to draw conclusions from them. For example, the information that revenues for the year were $X and accounts receivable at the end of the year $Y is largely factual. The analyst must decide whether the information is favourable or unfavourable in forming his opinion of the enterprise. To do this he typically relies on trends, ratios and comparisons. Are the revenues increasing or decreasing from previous years? Is the indicated turnover of accounts receivable (revenues from credit transactions divided by accounts receivable) up or down? How do these trends and ratios compare with other enterprises in the same industry?

But the accountant does not narrowly confine himself to the provision of factual data. If he did, his summary of operating transactions for the year could not go far beyond a statement of cash receipts and disbursements. Revenue for the year may be factual (given a definition of revenue) but the costs to be matched against such revenues are largely a matter of opinion. Indeed the process of income accounting as a whole is largely analytical in character.

The accountant performs this analysis because he must. The statement reader is not in a position to judge which costs should be treated as expenses and which as assets, so a statement of incurred costs alone does not meet his need. The accountant must produce any analysis desired which is dependent on detailed familiarity with what is in the accounts. But after that the analyst can take the resulting product (the financial statements) and perform such further analysis based on them as he desires.

There are, however, two areas in which the accountant has assumed the prerogative of the analyst and has developed rules for arranging financial statement information for analytical purposes. In one of these, namely the production of a figure for earnings per share, the accountant's interest is relatively recent. In the other, namely the production of figures entitled current assets, current liabilities and working capital (the difference between the two preceding), his interest has been long-standing.

Earnings per Share

Any person who is making a decision is limited in the number of considerations pro or con that he is capable of taking into account. If more than a few facts or arguments are presented, he merely gets confused. Hence, there is a need in financial analysis for ratios or numbers that are both highly significant and simple. Accountants would agree that there is probably no more important information produced by the accounts than the historical record of earnings. It is probably inevitable therefore that analysts, who are interested more in values of shares than in values of companies as a whole, should have expressed this information for simplicity as 'earnings per share'. There is no more widely used statistic in the whole of financial analysis.

For many years the typical accountant's reaction to earnings per share statistics was one of caution or even disapproval. He pointed out that there could be a considerable difference in the quality of earnings. For example, earnings including substantial non-recurring gains were obviously less significant than earnings from an ongoing business. Earnings in the three-year tax-free period of a mine were obviously not as good quality as earnings of a taxable enterprise, and so on. The accountant felt, and rightly, that it was important to study the financial statements to become aware of these factors and he worried that investors, furnished with simple statistics like earnings per share, would fail to go behind them. He tended therefore to ignore earnings per share figures and the technical problems associated with them, perhaps on the theory that if he did so their use would be discouraged.

Gradually the accountant's attitude changed as two facts became evident. First, earnings per share statistics were used by, and useful to, investors and their use was not going to decrease. Second, the basis of calculation of these statistics was not consistent from one company to another or among the various financial services publishing the figures; so that there was great danger that use of the statistic would be misleading in some situations. The problems were enhanced in recent years by two factors:

1. Because of tight money conditions, companies seeking new capital were forced to issue securities having a combination of senior characteristics, preferences, etc. – and some call on the equity – through convertibility privileges, warrants to buy common shares at fixed prices, etc.

2. The common use of two-way securities in effecting acquisition of another company.

Both these factors were more noticeable in the U.S. than in Canada.

The calculation of earnings per share is only relevant with respect to shares that have a right to participate in earnings over and above those distributed as dividends – i.e. with respect to the residual equity in the company. Since the

determination of earnings was governed by accounting principles already established, the problems in calculating earnings per share for the residual equity are
limited to (a) determining the participation in earnings of senior securities and
more importantly (b) deciding the proper number of shares which represent
residual equity in order to divide their number into the reported earnings. These
problems are dealt with below:

1. What deduction should be made from reported earnings with respect to the
   rights of equity shares ranking senior to the residual equity?

   It is obvious that dividends actually declared on senior shares should be deducted in arriving at earnings for the residual equity. It is less obvious what
   should be done when dividends are not declared. If the preferential right accumulates, it seems best to deduct the cumulative unpaid dividend even though
   it was not declared, from the earnings (or add it to the loss reported) in order
   to arrive at the earnings (or loss) for the residual equity, since the cumulative
   dividend must be paid in future before common dividends can be paid. If the
   right is non-cumulative and a dividend is not declared, the preference shareholders nominally get nothing (although the security of his investment may be
   increased by the retained earnings). It may be argued then that all earnings
   should be treated as belonging to the residual equity if non-cumulative dividends are not declared. On the other hand, from the standpoint of the use of
   the figure of earnings per share, it would seem that earnings credited to common
   shareholders because no dividend is declared on the preference shares are not
   as significant as earnings where no preferential right exists at all. Special disclosure is required, therefore, where such a situation exists.

2. Where securities are outstanding which are not common shares but which have
   some characteristic of, or relationship to, the common shares, how should their
   existence be recognized in earnings per share calculations?

   Such conditions exist, for example, when:
   (a) there are two classes of common shares, or preference shares exist which
       carry rights to participate with the common in dividends declared over a
       certain amount,
   (b) common shares are issuable in future upon fulfillment of certain conditions,
   (c) there are outstanding warrants, options or other rights to acquire common
       shares at prices which may look attractive now or in the future,
   (d) debt or preference shares are convertible into common on terms which
       are or may become attractive.

   It is common ground in these cases that earnings per common share must be
   calculated after giving due credit to the participation rights of other classes of
   shares in the earnings. It is further agreed that a second calculation must be
   made on a 'fully diluted' basis – i.e. a calculation that assumes issuance of additional common shares upon exercise of option or conversion rights or fulfillment of contingencies, provided that such calculations show a lower earnings
   per share figure than the other calculation. This proviso was made because, if
   there is not such a 'dilutive' effect, in all probability the holders of convertible
   securities, warrants, etc. would not find it advantageous to exercise their rights
   to acquire the common stock and, therefore, publication of the higher earnings
   per share figure would be meaningless and possibly misleading.

Some difference of opinion exists about the calculation of the basic or primary earnings per share figure. The Accounting Principles Board takes the view that some securities are so likely to be converted to common stock that they should be regarded as 'common stock equivalents' in calculating earnings per share, and the exclusion of the dilutive effect of such common stock equivalents from primary earnings per share figures would be misleading. The CICA Research Committee on the other hand has concluded that publication of the fully diluted figure is adequate disclosure, particularly in view of the practical difficulties of defining common stock equivalents, which will be explored in the next question.

3. What criteria should be used for the identification of common stock equivalents?

   (a) Where shares are issuable in future upon fulfillment of certain conditions – e.g. maintenance of a certain level of earnings – the APB has held that they should be regarded as common stock equivalents if the conditions are being met at the close of the reporting period.

   (b) All warrants, etc. are regarded as common stock equivalents since they have no value other than that attributable to their potential for conversion into common stock. However, they would not be included in the calculation of primary earnings per share if such inclusion did not have a dilutive effect.

   (c) Convertible securities normally have an interest or dividend yield of their own and therefore their value will reflect partly this factor and partly the value placed on the conversion right. Several tests were considered by the APB to determine whether convertible securities should be considered to be common stock equivalents:

      (i) The 'investment value' (value of the security without conversion privilege) was to be compared with market value. If market value exceeded investment value by a significant percentage, the security would be considered a common stock equivalent. One objection to this test was the difficulty in getting an objective 'investment value'.

      (ii) The 'market parity' test. The market value of the security was to be compared with the market value of the number of shares into which it was convertible. If the two were more or less equal, and were in excess of the redemption price of the security, it would be presumed that the value of the security was derived mainly from its common stock characteristics, and thus it would be a common stock equivalent.

      (iii) The 'cash yield' test. The cash yield (i.e. the percentage of interest or dividend rate to market value) is to be compared with the current prime interest rate on bank loans and, if it amounts to less than two-thirds of that rate, the security is to be considered a common stock equivalent. This was the test finally endorsed by the APB.

4. Are the criteria for common stock equivalents applicable continuously?

It is evident that shares contingently issuable may be considered common stock equivalents at one year-end if the conditions for issue are being met and not at another if they are not being met. Thus, there could be a discontinuity in the number of shares used as the denominator in the earnings per share calculation. In the case of convertible securities however, the APB has recommended that their status as common stock equivalents should be determined once and for all at the time of issuance. (This is subject to one proviso where identical securities are issued at different times. In such cases, if either issue were deemed a common stock equivalent based on the conditions at the time of issue, both would be deemed to be common stock equivalents.) This limitation to the definition of common stock equivalents would seem to lessen considerably the meaning of the current figure for 'primary earnings per share' since in one company an issue could be included, and in another an identical issue excluded, because of differences in conditions existing at issuance some years back. Admittedly, the rule avoids a source of discontinuity in the figures of primary earnings per share and admittedly, discontinuity is undesirable since a trend over a number of years is useful, but the price paid in loss of relevance for the figure of primary earnings per share is very heavy.

5. What method of calculation should be used in arriving at earnings per share figures on a fully diluted basis or primary earnings per share where common stock equivalents exist?

(a) Where there are two classes of common stock or a participating preferred stock is outstanding the 'two class' method is used. Under this method, the dividend declared on each class is deducted from earnings, the balance of earnings is divided in the participation ratio, and this latter amount is added back to the dividend to arrive at the figure of earnings per share for each class.

(b) Where there are shares contingently issuable, the number is merely added to the number of outstanding shares. If the number contingently issuable depends on future conditions such as the amount of future earnings, or the future share price, the situation in this regard at the end of the most recent reporting period will be assumed to represent the situation that will exist at the issue date.

(c) Where warrants or rights are outstanding and holders will have to pay cash on exercise of such rights, the effect of receipt of cash by the entity will have to be taken into account. The Canadian recommendation is that earnings after taxes be imputed at an appropriate rate on cash receivable on the exercise of the rights. The U.S. recommendation is that the effect of cash received be reflected by the 'treasury stock' method. This method assumes, for the purpose of the computation, that the cash price is applied to purchase stock in the company at its average price over the reporting period, and that the difference between the stock issued upon exercise of the rights and the amount of stock obtainable under this treasury stock calculation be added to the number of shares outstanding in order to calculate earnings per share. Use of this method is to be limited, in that not more than 20% of the actual outstanding stock can be considered bought in under the treasury stock method, and if more cash would be available upon exercise of the rights, it is to be considered to earn an imputed return.

(d) When convertible securities exist the earnings per share will be calculated on the 'if converted' method. That is to say, dividends or interest after tax actually paid in the year on the convertible securities will be added back to the reported earnings and earnings per share worked out as if the securities had been converted to common stock at the beginning of the year.

Many additional problems can arise in calculating earnings per share, as a result of complexities in capital structures such as the existence of two class common shares with non-cumulative dividend preferences and convertible securities whose conversion rights change with time. The historical record of earnings per share may also be upset by stock dividends, stock splits or the issuance of rights to subscribe for additional stock at a figure below market.[1]

Detailed rules are contained in the AICPA and CICA statements on earnings per share, but even these may not cope with all the problems that arise in practice. The root of the difficulty lies in the attempt to reduce complicated matters to a simple statistic such as earnings per share. Any attempt to do so is bound to contain elements of unreality.

In this light the CICA refusal to follow the AICPA lead in requiring a calculation based on 'common stock equivalents', which must be artificially defined, seems wise. The other view is that a calculation based on common shares only (particularly if denoted 'basic earnings per share') may be misleading, where some securities exist which are common in all but name. The better answer to this problem, however, is not to plunge deeper into a morass of unnatural classifications requiring arbitrary dividing lines, but rather to meet complexity with full disclosure. The effect of complex capital structures cannot be adequately measured by one or two figures for earnings per share. In such cases a table should be constructed showing step by step the potential effect of the exercise of conversion and other rights attaching to securities outstanding. Such a table, as suggested by a leading accountant, would avoid the danger that a simple figure of earnings per share may conceal as much as it reveals.[2]

Principles of Accounting for Earnings per Share

The following principles summarize the rules applicable in Canada:

1. Earnings per share data should be disclosed in the financial statements so that it becomes part of the audited information.

2. Basic earnings per share should be calculated for common stock and each other class of stock which has participation in earnings such that it is similar to common. Such calculation should be on the 'two class' method.

3. Fully diluted earnings per share figures should be calculated to show the effect of the existence of other securities that may, under certain conditions, become common stock.

4. The calculation of earnings per share on the fully diluted basis should follow certain rules:
    (a) When convertible securities exist, the calculation should be on the 'if converted' basis. That is, dividends or after-tax interest on the convertible securities should be added back to earnings and the resulting total divided by the weighted average number of common shares outstanding during the period, as it would be if the securities had been converted at the beginning

of the period (or at the date of issue of the convertible securities if they were issued after the beginning of the period).

(b) When warrants or options exist, cash proceeds on their exercise should be deemed used in the business, and imputed earnings at an appropriate rate (after tax) should be added to actual earnings. The earnings so adjusted should then be divided by the weighted average number of common shares, including the shares issuable upon the exercise of the rights, assuming such rights were issued at the beginning of the period (or at the date the rights were granted if that is later than the beginning of the period).

(c) Where shares are issuable in future subject to certain conditions, the calculation of earnings per share should assume earnings and a number of shares outstanding which will be consistent with the terms and conditions applicable to the contingent issue of shares in future.

(d) Where the calculation with respect to a given security under the above rules would increase the figure of fully diluted earnings per share, such security should not be taken into account in the calculation.

References

1. The peculiar effect of stock rights issues in making the trend in historical earnings per share figures misleading is covered in N. P. Monson and J. A. Tracy, "Stock Rights and Accounting Wrongs", *The Accounting Review* (October 1964), pp. 890–893 and D. C. Shaw, "Don't Forget the Split in Stock Rights", *Canadian Chartered Accountant* (March 1969), pp. 182–184.
2. Leonard Spacek, "Umpiring the Earnings Per Share Results", *Management Accounting* (March 1969), pp. 9–27.

22 Analytical data: working capital

The rules governing the definition and disclosure of 'current assets', 'current liabilities' and their derivative 'working capital' furnish a prime example of the power of traditional practice in accounting.[1] The distinction between fixed investment and other investment seems to have been recognized in business practice two centuries ago, probably in connection with the provision of short-term credit. The business practice distinction was picked up by the earlier economists who talked of 'circulating capital' and 'fixed capital', and these terms in turn acquired legal reinforcement through their use in English cases on the legality of dividends paid by joint stock companies.

The early economists based their definition on at least two criteria which tend to shade into each other. On the one hand, circulating assets were considered those which were consumed in the production of revenue. Thus there is a continual circulation in business – money is laid out to acquire inventory; this is sold to produce cash (with accounts receivable being the way station between inventory and cash) and the cycle then begins again. Fixed assets are distinguished from circulating assets in that it is not necessary to part with them to produce revenue. They are consumed through use rather than through sale. On the other hand the distinction between fixed and circulating assets was also regarded as one based on time of realization. Circulating assets are realized quickly while the outlay on fixed assets is recovered through revenue but slowly. The two criteria are not perfectly compatible. Under the first, prepaid expenses and inventories of supplies would not be considered as circulating assets since they are consumed through use rather than sale. Under the second, they would be considered circulating assets since they normally have a short recovery period.

The first criterion is the more satisfying intellectually, since it is possible (given inventory costing methods) to make a sharp distinction between assets that will be sold and those that will not. However, for practical use it was the latter criterion that was the more important. To the short-term creditor, time is of the essence because the extension of recovery time creates uncertainty. He can assess the prospects of recovery from today's inventory, but it is another matter to look for recovery to transactions not yet in contemplation under business conditions of future years as yet unforeseeable. Moreover, a creditor's security may rest on assets other than operating assets – cash and investments, for example. Thus the rule for computation of working capital tended to become a rule of thumb based on time – assets realizable in one year and liabilities payable within one year were brought into the calculation – assets and liabilities beyond one year were excluded. This emphasis on time, as opposed to circulation of assets, was recognized by changes in terminology from the original term 'circulating capital' to 'floating assets and liabilities' and finally 'current assets and liabilities'.

But a rule based on an arbitrary cut-off point – such as one year – can never be completely satisfactory in operation. When the professional accounting societies began their program of formal consideration of accounting problems this was recognized. The most comprehensive statement on the nature of current assets, current liabilities and working capital was made by the AICPA Committee on Accounting Procedure in 1947 in Accounting Research Bulletin No. 30 (which is reproduced relatively unchanged in the codification Bulletin No. 43). In this statement the Committee emphasized anew the circulating capital criterion by recommending the substitution of the 'operating cycle' for a crude one-year period in the case of assets and liabilities arising from or related to trade transactions. In brief, the Committee said:

1. Working capital is the excess of current assets over current liabilities and identifies the relatively liquid portion of the total enterprise capital, which constitutes a margin or buffer for the meeting of obligations within the ordinary operating cycle of the business.

2. The operating cycle is the average time intervening between the acquisition of materials or services and the final cash realization from their sale.

3. Current assets are those reasonably expected to be realized in cash or sold or consumed during the normal operating cycle. Where there is no normal operating cycle, or where assets are not operating assets, the one-year test should continue to be used for distinguishing current assets from fixed.
   – Prepaid expenses are to be treated as current assets unless chargeable against several years' operations, because if they do not exist cash will have to be laid out during the operating cycle.
   – Liquid assets intended to be used to acquire non-current assets, or investments made for purposes of control, affiliation or continuing business advantage are not to be included in current assets.

4. Current liabilities are those whose liquidation is reasonably expected to require the use of existing resources classified as current assets, or the creation of other current liabilities.
   – They include collections received in advance of delivery of goods or performance of service.
   – They also include obligations not arising out of trade transactions whose liquidation is expected to occur within twelve months.

In short, working capital consists of circulating capital recoverable within an operating cycle (after deducting trade liabilities) together with cash (less cash intended for spending on long-term assets), financial assets expected to be realized in cash within a one-year period, and less debt repayable with a one-year period (except debt expected to be refunded by longer term debt).

In spite of the careful consideration given to the concept of current position, numerous writers have pointed out illogical and inconsistent aspects in it. These may be summarized as follows:

1. Confusion of objective

   Bulletin No. 43 states "*Working capital*, sometimes called *net working capital*, is represented by the excess of current assets over current liabilities and identifies the relatively liquid portion of total enterprise capital which constitutes a margin or buffer for meeting obligations within the ordinary operating cycle of the business." We may take it that the primary objective of working capital theory is to identify this 'margin' or 'buffer'. But a little consideration raises considerable doubt whether the conventional definition of working capital does in fact identify such a margin. Consider, for example, the nature of circulating assets – inventory and accounts receivable. These are by definition *circulating*. That is to say, while these assets are being turned into cash in the normal course of business, they are continually being replaced by expenditure of cash for additional inventory for further sales. In other words, seasonal factors aside, the amount of circulating assets in a going concern is rather constant so long as it remains in business, and therefore, they do *not* represent a 'buffer' or 'margin' for meeting obligations within the operating cycle of the business.* It is only in liquidation that these assets become available for meeting debts. Thus, their amount is of significance only, or primarily, to creditors who, because their loan is of a demand nature or of very short term, are able to 'pounce' to realize their security should the need arise. On the other hand, to these creditors the exclusion of assets such as investments from working capital on the grounds that it is not intended to realize upon them within one year does not make sense. If security lies in liquidation values all assets are grist to the mill. In other words, the conventional definition of working capital makes sense only in the context of short-term credit such as the typical bank loan, and for these creditors the exclusion of readily realizable assets on the grounds of intention is irrelevant.

   This limitation on the significance of working capital is often not realized, such has been the traditional emphasis on a 'sound working capital' position. Some businesses can operate perfectly satisfactorily without working capital or with negative working capital.[2] Investors who rely blindly on rules of thumb about working capital are in danger of being misled. Worse, some businesses that do not need working capital are penalized by creditors blindly working to rules of thumb about maintenance of working capital.

2. Inadequacy of concept

   If one accepts as an objective the measurement of a buffer or margin in a given time period, it is readily apparent that two important elements are missing from the normal calculation. In the first place, the cash inflow from operations within the time period is not taken into account. In the second place, commit-

---

* In point of fact, given only a break-even operation, it is the fact that fixed assets do not require continuous replacement that permits a positive cash flow, and thus there is a sense in which it could be said that depreciation on fixed assets provides the margin or buffer for meeting obligations within any given period.

ments and/or probable capital spending are not formally recorded. This latter statement is subject to the qualification that cash intended for spending on non-current purposes is to be segregated from current assets under the Bulletin No. 43 Recommendation – but this is rarely seen in practice.

These two objections simply underline the fact that a static statement of position such as a balance sheet cannot adequately portray a fluid changing position such as the margin for meeting obligations. The attempt to do so leads to the introduction of rules such as the one-year time limit but this in turn leads to such illogicalities as that a debt due in 365 days is deducted in computing working capital, while one due in 380 days is not.

3. Technical defects

Even on its own grounds the working capital concept suffers from several defects. It fails to make an adequate distinction between working assets and liabilities and financial assets and liabilities. As a result it is forced to adopt the arbitrary one-year rule for financial assets and liabilities, which is inconsistent with the operating cycle criterion used for classifying operating assets.

The figure for working capital has also been criticized on the grounds that the total is made up of assets valued on a variety of bases – cash and accounts receivable on realizable values, inventory and prepaids at acquisition costs. The difference is perhaps not too serious in practice except when inventory cost departs from current values – as is frequently the case with a LIFO inventory.

Finally, the concept overemphasizes the total of working capital which may serve to draw attention away from its composition. A marked shift from cash to inventory may be the most significant feature of a balance sheet compared with the previous year, and yet if working capital is unchanged the fact is not highlighted.[3]

Based on this discussion it is suggested that the present emphasis on definition of current assets, current liabilities and working capital and their disclosure in the balance sheet is misplaced. The balance sheet is fundamentally unsuited to analysis of liquidity over a period of time. If it is to be used however, probably greater variety in form of analysis is desirable in different situations or different industries. Appendix A contains an illustration of the form of analysis that might be made.

Principles Governing the Classification of Current Assets, Current Liabilities and Working Capital

The following rules are recognized at present as governing the classification of current assets and current liabilities:

1. Working capital is defined as the difference between current assets and current liabilities.

2. The operating cycle is the average time intervening between the acquisition of materials or services for inventory and the final cash realization from inventory sold.

3. Current assets are those assets realizable within one year from the balance sheet date or, in the case of operating assets, within the operating cycle of the business if that is longer than one year.

   (a) Certain operating assets, such as prepayments, although not held for sale and therefore not realizable in the customary sense, are includable as current assets to the extent that their existence reduces the need for cash within the next year (or operating cycle if longer than one year).

   (b) Cash not available for current spending or cash intended to be spent on the acquisition of non-current assets or liquidation of non-current liabilities should be excluded from current assets.*

   (c) Other non-operating assets (e.g. investments) are excluded from current assets if they are not intended to be realized within one year, even though they may be readily realizable.*

4. Current liabilities are those liabilities which will require the use of current assets to liquidate them:

   (a) within the longer of one year or, if the liabilities arise from operations, the operating cycle,

   (b) within one year in the case of other liabilities.

      (i) Current maturities of long-term debt are includable as current liabilities.

      (ii) Debt which is expected to be refunded on a long-term basis, however, need not be classified as a current liability.

5. Deferred tax debits or credits should be classified as current if they relate to assets or liabilities classified as current, and otherwise as non-current. If both deferred tax debits and credits occur within a category they are usually netted.

References

1. L. Goldberg, "A Note on Current Assets", *Abacus* (September 1965), pp. 31–45, presents a full discussion of the origins of the concept of working capital.
2. See comment by R. Glickman and R. W. Stahl, "The Case of the Misleading Balance Sheet", *Journal of Accountancy* (December 1968), pp. 66–72.
3. See H. I. Ross, "Some Questions about 'Working Capital' ", *Canadian Chartered Accountant* (April 1955), pp. 227–230.

---

* These principles are not always followed in practice.

23   The statement of source and application of funds

The financial statements represent the output of the accounting process – the medium through which information is communicated to the users of accounting information. The traditional statements consist of:

1. the balance sheet – a statement of assets, liabilities and equities at a point of time. In view of the primacy of the proprietorial interest in financial reporting the balance sheet is always accompanied by supplementary information (in statements or notes) detailing the reasons for changes in the amount of equity interests since the last balance sheet.

2. the income statement – a statement of earned revenues for a period, and costs allocated against that period.

In the last decade yet another statement has received increasing recognition as a valuable medium for conveying information, to the point that its inclusion in the financial statement package has been recommended as standard practice by Canadian and United States accounting authorities and is required under some of the corporate and securities legislation in the two countries. The statement in question is known by several titles, among the more common being the statement of source and application of funds and the statement of changes in financial position.

The origins of the funds statement can be traced as far back as the 1860's.[1] The statement has appeared in a variety of forms. In the period 1925–50 however, the familiar form of statement geared to produce a figure of changes in working capital during the fiscal year became predominant. Other forms are frequently found, however, such as statements of changes in cash, changes in net quick assets, or statements 'in balanced form' showing how every asset, liability and equity account is affected by the flow of funds into the business from outside sources and their expenditure.

Objectives of the funds statement

The variety of forms in which the funds statement can be found reflects a lack of consensus as to the purpose of the statement. Some accountants might say the purpose of the statement is to summarize the causes of changes in working capital.

Some would say the aim is to record the reasons for changes in liquidity. Some might say the purpose is to answer such questions as "what happened to profits (why aren't they represented by cash in the bank)?", or "how did we get the money to pay for our plant expansion or debt retirement?" And some would say the statement is merely an analytical device to focus attention on any particular aspect of the entity's operations that is desired. For example, one Canadian public utility draws up its statement to highlight the figure for expenditures on plant during the year and show where the funds came from to finance such expenditures.

It is suggested, however, that at least one theme underlies funds statements as a class. In Chapter 5 transactions carried on by an entity were classified broadly as financing, investment and operating. The income statement combined with the balance sheet summarizes the results of operating transactions that have taken place in a fiscal period. The funds statement accomplishes somewhat the same purpose with respect to financing and investment transactions. While the results of these transactions can often be deduced fairly accurately from a comparison of beginning and ending balance sheets, the funds statement portrays the flow of funds more clearly. The title given the statement by an early author – namely the 'where-got, where-gone' statement – has never been excelled as a description of the statement's fundamental objectives.

Of course, ordinary operations themselves are usually a net source of funds to a business. Since this is a recurring source, it is natural and desirable to make a distinction in the funds statement between 'funds derived from operations', or what might be described as 'internal financing' and funds derived from other sources such as borrowing or contributions of capital, which might be described as 'external financing'.

The meaning of the term 'funds'

The inclusion of operations among the sources of funds focuses attention on the precise meaning of the term 'funds'. Most (but not all) financing transactions result in receipt or repayment of cash by the entity. Similarly, most (but not all) investment transactions involve expenditure or receipt of cash by the entity. In contrast, operations carried on by an entity result in the creation of a variety of liabilities (accounts payable, accrued charges, taxes payable, etc.) and of assets (accounts receivable, inventory, prepayments, etc.). Since accounting for operations on the accrual basis reflects these assets and liabilities it is easier for an accountant to translate the results of operations as reported in the income statement into an improvement in the net current assets position rather than into an inflow of cash.

It is probably for this reason that the term 'funds' came to be used to mean net working capital. It is a somewhat unnatural usage, however, since it is hard for a layman to think of inflows and outflows of an aggregate made up of such diverse elements as inventory and demand bank loans. The average businessman is apt to think of a bank loan as a source of funds, and to become confused if told that such borrowing (if short-term) did not affect funds – in fact if the money borrowed was spent to buy fixed assets, it represented only an expenditure of funds.

Moreover, as various authors have pointed out, a statement showing only net changes in working capital can fail to disclose important shifts in the composition of working capital – such as the sale of marketable securities to finance increases in accounts receivable because of a slowing-up in collections, or the rise in accounts payable required to finance increases in inventory caused by a slow-down of sales not matched by cutbacks in production. Such considerations as these have led some accountants to search for a definition of 'funds' which corresponds more closely to the liquid position of a business and produce statements, as indicated earlier, of changes in cash, changes in cash plus marketable securities, changes in net quick assets (cash plus marketable securities, plus accounts receivable, less current liabilities) and so on.

Other accountants have taken the opposite tack and advocate dropping any liquidity connotation from the term 'funds'. To them the most useful form of funds statement is one that reports all accessions of resources to the entity (such as from borrowing or capital contributions), all distributions of resources (such as by dividends or repayment of debt) and all changes in the composition of resources (including changes resulting both from operations and investment activities). On this basis, 'funds' are defined to mean resources under the control of the entity – regardless of whether such resources are in liquid form or not. Thus acquisition of property in consideration of the issue of shares would be treated both as an inflow and outflow of funds, even though it would not be so treated in the traditional form of funds statement reporting only transactions affecting working capital. The funds statement based on this general approach naturally takes a balanced form, rather than a form whereby expenditures of funds are subtracted from sources of funds to arrive at the net change in working capital (or whatever other definition of liquidity is being used).

How the funds statement is derived

The fundamental concept of 'where-got, where-gone' is a natural adaptation of the double entry recording system. Under this system each transaction is reflected from two points of view. There are four basic types of entries, recording:

1. An inflow of funds – resulting in an increase in assets and an increase in claims upon assets arising from such causes as:
   (a) contribution of capital,
   (b) borrowing,
   (c) receipt of revenue in advance of performance,
   (d) earning of revenue (the increase in assets is associated with an increase in the claim of the equity interests upon the assets).

2. An outflow of funds – resulting in a decrease in assets and in claims upon assets, arising from such causes as:
   (a) dividends, or redemption of capital,
   (b) repayment of funds borrowed,
   (c) expense (such as administrative payroll) associated with revenue-earning activities. (The expense – i.e. decrease in asset – is associated with a diminution of the claim of the equity interests upon the assets.)

3. A change in the composition of net assets, arising from such causes as:
   (a) investment in assets held to produce income, or sale of such investments,

(b) settlement of obligations arising in previous transactions – e.g. collection of accounts receivable or payment of accounts payable.

4. An expense not involving the outflow of funds or revenue not involving an inflow of funds. For example, the amortization of the cost of assets held for use rather than for sale, or recognition of income tax expense under tax allocation accounting procedures before the tax becomes due and payable, does not represent a funds outlay. Similarly, receipts from customers in one year may not be treated as earned revenue until a later year.

It will be noted that categories 1 and 2 include all financing transactions (if funds arising from operations are regarded as internal financing). Category 3(a) embraces investment transactions. Category 4 includes internal entries made under income accounting rules that do not represent a flow of assets into or out of the business, while category 3(b) includes transactions that are merely ancillary to previous transactions. (That is to say, if we know that credit sales for a month are $100,000 we would normally expect collection of all but a very small percentage of that amount in the next month or so. Hence if we know the figure of sales for a year it does not add greatly to our information to know the amount of collections on trade accounts receivable in that same year.) Thus in drawing up a statement of funds it is necessary, or desirable, to eliminate from the summary those transactions that fall into category 4, and secondary transactions that fall into category 3(b) above.

It would be possible, but extremely laborious, to analyze each account and eliminate from the summary all such entries, leaving only the remainder to be classified as financing transactions, investment transactions or primary operating transactions involving an inflow or outflow of funds. In practice, a shortcut is achieved by using the income statement as the basis of the summary of operating transactions. This has the great advantage that it automatically eliminates from the record most secondary transactions completing primary transactions. For example, the income statement records only the revenue from sales, not the subsequent collection of cash on accounts receivable arising from the sales. In detail, the funds statement is drawn up in the following steps:

1. The income statement is adjusted to eliminate charges or credits not reflecting a flow of funds (as defined),
2. Accounts that would be affected by external financing or investment transactions (including investment in assets for the production of income) are analyzed to record the effect of such transactions as they occurred.

Modifications in this procedure are required to fit the definition of funds adopted. For example, where 'funds' are defined as working capital, financing transactions and investment transactions affecting working capital only are ignored because such transactions do not increase or decrease the net total of working capital in the business. On the other hand, where funds are defined as, say, 'cash', the figure for 'funds from operations' derived by adjustment of the income statement will usually not produce a balance, since the income statement is on an accrual basis rather than a cash basis. To correct this it is necessary to introduce into the funds statement the net change in non-cash accounts not dealt with individually in the adjustments to 'income from operations' or in the listing of financing and investment transactions.

Thus the figure for cash derived from operations might be built up as in the following example:

Net income from operations (accrual basis)		xx,xxx
Add back charges or (credits) not involving a decrease or increase in working capital:		
– provision for depreciation	x,xxx	
– deferred taxes	xxx	
– reduction in long-term deferred revenue	(xxx)	x,xxx
Net working capital from operations°		xx,xxx
Add or (deduct)		
Decrease in inventory	xxx	
Increase in trade accounts payable	xxx	
Increase in trade accounts receivable	(xxx)	
Decrease in current taxes payable	(xxx)	xxx
Net cash from operations°		xx,xxx

Illustrative forms of statement

The discussion of the various forms of funds statement may be clarified by an example. Assume the following balance sheet, income statement and supplementary information for Contract Manufacturing Ltd.:

Contract Manufacturing Ltd.
Balance Sheets December 31, 19–1 and 19–2

Assets	19–1 (000's)		19–2 (000's)	
Current assets:				
Cash	$ 480		$ 370	
Marketable securities	740		960	
Receivables	7,560		8,380	
Inventories	13,480		15,730	
Prepayments	160	$22,420	220	$25,660
Current liabilities:				
Accounts payable and accruals	3,720		4,680	
Taxes payable	1,420		1,260	
Advance payments from customers	1,500	6,640	1,240	7,180
Net working capital		15,780		18,480

° The figure for "net working capital from operations" is often referred to as 'net cash flow'. This example indicates that this description is in error. The error may not be serious in some cases, since over a period of years the average figure for 'net cash from operations' is likely to approximate 'net working capital from operations'. (Actually in a growing business 'cash from operations' will likely be somewhat less, since accounts receivable and inventory will build up as the business expands.) However in some cases, such as a business that sells on long-term credit, the use of the term 'net cash flow' may be quite misleading. Occasionally the error is compounded by a calculation of 'cash flow' which adds back depreciation, amortization and deferred taxes to net income but fails to deduct revenue earned which is in non-current form. For example, if a land developer takes back mortgages for part of the sales price of his property, his figure for revenue from property sales will not be anywhere close to being a cash inflow of the year.

	19–1 (000's)		19–2 (000's)	
Fixed assets:				
Depreciable property	13,600		14,270	
Accumulated depreciation	5,870		7,220	
	7,730		7,050	
Land	550	8,280	2,550	9,600
Deferred assets:				
Leasehold interest – less amortization	500		400	
Deferred tooling – less amortization	400	900	450	850
		24,960		28,930
Deduct – Deferred tax credit		880		930
		$24,080		$28,000
Debt and capital				
5.5% convertible debentures, due Dec. 31, 19–9	$ 3,000		$ 1,500	
Less unamortized discount	160	$ 2,840	70	$ 1,430
7.0% cumulative preference shares				2,000
Residual equity				
Common shares – no par value	4,000		7,430	
Retained earnings	17,240	21,240	17,140	24,570
		$24,080		$28,000

Statement of Income and Retained Earnings
Year ended December 31, 19–2

		(000's)
Sales		$52,640
Cost of sales		37,590
		15,050
Selling and administration costs	$10,890	
Interest and amortization of discount ($20)	200	11,090
Profit before income taxes		3,960
Provision for taxes		
Payable currently	1,940	
Deferred	50	1,990
Net income for year		1,970
Retained earnings – beginning of year		17,240
		19,210
Deduct – dividend paid – preference shares	70	
– stock dividend – common shares	2,000	2,070
Retained earnings – end of year		$17,140

ADDITIONAL INFORMATION

1. Purchases of depreciable property amounted to $820 in the year. Property having a carrying value of $150 and accumulated depreciation of $120 was sold for $80; the $50 profit on disposal was credited to income.

2. Land was acquired in consideration for the issue of $2,000 in preference shares.

3. Depreciation for the year amounted to $1,470. Amortization of the leasehold interest amounted to $100.

4. Amounts charged to deferred tooling in the year totalled $350. Amortization amounted to $300.

5. Advance payments received from customers in the year amounted to $1,860.

6. $2,000 was borrowed on demand note from the bank and repaid within the year.

7. Just at the end of the year $1,500 in bonds were converted into common stock. Unamortized discount thereon amounted to $70.

A funds statement in the common form emphasizing working capital would be as follows:

Contract Manufacturing Ltd.
Statement of Source and Application of Funds[1]
Year ended December 31, 19–2

(000's)

Source of funds:		
From operations –		
Net income for the year		$1,970
Add or (deduct) charges or (credits)		
to income not involving an outlay		
or inflow of working capital in		
the year		
Depreciation	$1,470	
Amortization of leasehold interest	100	
Amortization of deferred tooling costs[2]	300	
Amortization of debenture discount	20	
Provision for deferred taxes	50	
Profit on disposal of fixed assets	(50)	1,890
Total funds from operations		3,860
Proceeds on disposal of fixed assets		80
		3,940
Application of funds:		
Expenditures on depreciable assets	820	
Tooling expenditures deferred	350	
Dividend paid – preference shares	70	1,240
Net increase in working capital in year		$2,700

Notes:

1. In practice, this statement would probably be simplified for publication. Full details are shown here to enable the derivation of figures to be traced.

2. Although amortization of deferred tooling costs would probably be added back in practice, as shown in this illustration, there are strong arguments in favour of not doing so. See discussion on page 257.

3. Some accountants would show the acquisition of land in consideration for shares as both an expenditure and source of funds. Likewise, some would show the issuance of shares upon conversion of debentures as a source and

expenditure of funds. Neither of these transactions affects working capital. If the broader objective of showing *all* financing and investment transactions is accepted however, the land acquisition transaction (definitely), and the debenture conversion (more debatably) should be included in the statement.

4. The addition to the funds statement of a summary of the net changes in the various assets and liabilities making up working capital (as is recommended by APB Opinion No. 19) would go some distance to meeting the criticism, already referred to, of the emphasis on net working capital in this form of statement.

As indicated already, some accountants feel that if the funds statement is to focus on changes in liquidity, there are more logical measures of liquidity than working capital. The following table indicates the adjustments that would have to be made to the funds statement if it were desired to focus on changes in liquidity defined on a narrower basis than working capital.

Contract Manufacturing Ltd.
Adjustments to Funds Statement
Required by Changes in Definition of Liquidity
Year ended December 31, 19–2

		Liquidity defined as		
	Cash	*Cash plus marketable securities*	*Cash plus securities less current liabilities*	*Cash, securities, accounts receivable less current liabilities*
Net change in working capital shown by customary form of funds statement	$2,700	$2,700	$2,700	$2,700
Add resources made available from –				
a) decreases in individual current assets	Nil	Nil	Nil	Nil
b) increase in individual current liabilities:				
– accounts payable and accruals	960	960		
	3,660	3,660	2,700	2,700
Deduct resources devoted to –				
a) increase investment in:				
Marketable securities	220			
Receivables	820	820	820	
Inventories	2,250	2,250	2,250	2,250
Prepayments	60	60	60	60
b) reduce liability for:				
Taxes payable	160	160		
Advance payments from customers	260	260		
	3,770	3,550	3,130	2,310
Net change in liquid assets	($110)	$ 110	($ 430)	$ 390

Liquid assets defined as total of:

Cash	(110)	(110)	(110)	(110)
Marketable securities		220	220	220
Accounts receivable				820
Less current liabilities			(540)	(540)
	(110)	110	(430)	390

Finally, a statement showing the inflow and outflow of all resources and the changes in composition of net assets arising from investment and other activities could take somewhat the following form:

Contract Manufacturing Ltd.
Statement of Changes in Financial Position
Year ended December 31, 19–2

(000's)

The company's resources were increased by:		
Operations for the year (detailed as in the previous illustration)		$3,860
External financing		
– Short term bank borrowing[1]	$2,000	
– Issue of 7% preference shares in consideration for land acquisition	2,000	4,000
Proceeds on disposal of fixed assets		80
		7,940
Resources employed were decreased by:		
Repayment of short-term bank loans[1]	2,000	
Dividend paid – preference shares	70	2,070
Net change in resources employed		$5,870
Changes in composition of net resources employed:		
Investment in – land	$2,000	
– depreciable assets	820	
– tooling	350	
– marketable securities	220	$3,390
Net increases in – receivables	820	
– inventories	2,250	
– prepayments	60	
Net reduction in liabilities for – taxes payable	160	
– customers' advance payments	260	
Net reductions in – cash	(110)	
Net increase in liabilities for – accounts payable and accruals	(960)	2,480
		$5,870

Notes:

1. When short term borrowing fluctuates irregularly during the year, it would only be practical to show the net change therein in this statement.

2. Issued common share capital was increased during the year by two events:
   (a) conversion of $1,500 debentures (less $70 unamortized discount)
   (b) a $2,000 stock dividend.

   Some accountants favour recording these transactions in this statement as if they involved an equal and opposite flow of funds – e.g. as if the holders of convertible debentures had subscribed for common share capital and the funds received were applied to redeem the debentures. In the writer's view however, they are better omitted because:
   (a) no actual increase or decrease in resources employed by the entity occurred as a result of these events,
   (b) the changes in share capital did not result from bargained transactions in the year. The conversion of the debt was merely the completion of the earlier transaction when the debt was issued, while the stock dividend was solely at the discretion of management.

   Therefore neither event reflected management actions in the year to affect resources under the control of the entity. (Note – APB Opinion No. 19 recommends inclusion of the conversion transaction in the statement, but would exclude the stock dividend.)

Limitations on the significance of the figure for 'funds from operations'

It will be observed from these illustrations that the using up of the utility of plant and equipment and other long-lived assets is never accounted for in the funds statement. The receipt of cash on disposal of such an asset is recorded, but the loss in the value of the asset itself through use or the passage of time is not. A number of considerations flow from this fact.

1. A funds statement is not a substitute for an income statement; more particularly 'funds from operations' or 'cash flow' is not a substitute for a figure for net income. The figure for 'funds from operations' does have significance, however, since:
   (a) it indicates the funds that become available to management each year for reinvestment or other purposes;
   (b) it is an indicator of the ability of the enterprise to resist temporary periods of adversity. Most businesses if required can go for a period of time without making significant investments in new plant. In effect they can "live on capital". The figure for 'funds from operations' therefore taken together with any requirements for debt retirement indicates the margin by which operations can deteriorate before the enterprise is in danger of becoming insolvent because of lack of cash. (This, of course, is true only in the absence of further imprudent investment by management or where the funds from operations do not get tied up in illiquid assets.)

2. Accordingly, the significance of the funds statement is greatest for the short and medium term, during which period major plant replacements are postponable. Moreover the period of significance varies from one line of business

to another. For example, a trucking firm must make more or less continual replacements of its vehicle fleet in order to operate efficiently. Hence the figure of earnings plus depreciation in a trucking firm is of much less significance than the same dollar figure in a well maintained public utility, whose plant is by nature long-lived.

3. The same point is even more pertinent in connection with various types of deferred charges. In the typical funds statement amortization of deferred charges is added back to earnings so as to increase the figure for 'funds from operations' while amounts added to the deferred charges are shown separately as expenditure of funds. But many types of deferred charges are of relatively short life. For example, tooling and design for annual model changes may be regularly deferred for amortization over a twelve-month period. In such a case it is most misleading to increase the figure for 'funds from operations' by such amortization since expenditures approximately equal to the amortization will be required if next year's model is to come out. In other words management's discretion as to expenditure of that portion of the funds from operations is very small indeed.* What is needed (but does not now exist) is a rule that amortization of any asset with an initial life of, say, three or four years or less, should not be added back in arriving at the figure for 'funds from operations'.

Funds statements for companies with 'unclassified' balance sheets

Because of the predominance of the working capital form of funds statement, companies with 'unclassified' balance sheets (i.e. balance sheets in which the assets and liabilities are not classified as between current and long-term) have traditionally not presented funds statements. From the previous discussion it will be obvious that this omission is not necessitated by the nature of their balance sheets. In point of fact, the importance of the investment function in many such companies makes a statement of funds flow potentially most enlightening. To be of maximum usefulness however, the preparation of the statement might require some analysis of movement in the investment accounts which they are not ordinarily set up to provide.

Such a statement could be presented in a variety of forms. The following represents an example of a statement that might be prepared for a hypothetical deposit-accepting institution. It is not suggested as a model but merely as an illustration. Showing funds received and paid out in columns side by side is unusual, but serves to illustrate the flexibility of the statement. The form of the funds statement can readily be adapted to fit all circumstances or highlight any information desired.

---

* The reason this problem is not more generally recognized is probably traceable to the customary form of funds statement which focuses on working capital. Since deferred charges, by definition, are not part of working capital, amortization of deferred charges is not an outlay of working capital and has to be added back to arrive at a figure of 'working capital generated from operations'. If we got out of the straitjacket of the working capital concept the problems of the funds statement could be dealt with in a more rational fashion.

Statement of Funds Received and Paid Out

	Funds received	*Funds paid out*
Operations, less dividends paid	xxx	
Deposits		
– Time deposits received	xxx	
– Time deposits paid out		xxx
– Net change in demand deposits	xxx	
Borrowing:		
– Debentures issued	xxx	
Portfolio investments:		
– Maturities	xxx	
– Other proceeds from sale	xxx	
– Investments purchased		xxx
Mortgage loans:		
– Principal repayments	xxx	
– Mortgages sold	xxx	
– Mortgage advances		xxx
Other loans		
– Net change	xxx	
Purchase of property assets (net)		xxx
Net increase or decrease in other assets and liabilities:		
– Cash		xxx
– Deposits and prepayments		xxx
– Accounts payable and accruals		xxx
– Taxes payable	xxx	
Turnover of funds during year	xxx	xxx

Summary

The funds statement has a long history, but until recently was not considered an essential feature of the annual financial statements. The statement is found in a variety of forms which in part reflects some confusion as to the basic objectives of the statement. These may be listed as:

1. To show the reason for increases or decreases in total resources employed by the entity during the year.

2. To show the funds that became available in the year for investment or other disposition by management of the entity.

3. To summarize the investment decisions made by management.

4. To show the changes in composition of assets owned or liabilities owed by the entity (with particular emphasis, in the traditional form of statement, on the net change in working capital, cash, or other definition of the net liquid position).

Because the statement focuses on *flow* of funds, it does not account for the loss in utility of assets such as depreciable plant and equipment which is bought for use and not for resale. For this reason the figure for 'funds derived from operations' in the statement is not equivalent to income, and is not suitable (without adjustment) for comparison between industries.

Technical Problems in Funds Statements

A number of questions recur regularly in the preparation of funds statements and these are discussed briefly below in relation to the form of statement now common which focuses on working capital.

Presentation of results of operations

Profitable operations produce a flow of funds into a business available for rein-vestment, debt repayment, or payment of distributions on capital. The amount of such flow is not, however, identical with the amount of earnings for the period. The reason for this lies in the cost and revenue allocations which form part of income accounting. Many costs, especially purchases of depreciable assets, are incurred before the period in which they are written off as expense. Others – e.g. pension payments – may not be laid out until considerably later. Not infrequently assets from revenue transactions are received before the period in which the revenue is earned. As a result, the figure of net income for the year must always be adjusted to arrive at the actual flow of assets (or reduction of liabilities) within the period. There are two ways of showing the funds derived from operations (see below) of which the former is by far the more common:

(a) The 'add-back' method
    Funds derived from operations
        Net income for the year $xxx
        Add or (deduct) credits or charges in determining
          income not involving the flow of funds during the
          year
          Depreciation and amortization of leasehold
          improvements $xx
          Provision for deferred income taxes   xx
          Reduction in the year of revenue deferred   (xx)   xx
        Net funds derived from operations $xxx

(b) The 'adjusted income statement' method
        Revenues earned during the year less amounts received in
          advance in prior year $xxx
        Deduct costs, excluding costs such as depreciation which
          did not involve an outlay of funds in the year   xxx
        Net funds derived from operations $xxx

Several writers have pointed out that the 'add-back' presentation is a mere reconciliation, which shows accountants how the final figure of funds from operations is arrived at but which has no meaning in itself. Moreover, it encourages misconceptions such as that depreciation is a source of funds, ignoring the fact that depreciation merely reflects the apportionment of the earlier expenditures of funds on capital assets. The other method, in contrast, portrays much more meaningfully the actual flow of funds into and out of the entity in the period. On the other hand, it could perhaps be argued that if one is merely trying to show funds received and laid out in a period, the expenditures on capital assets should also be deducted. In addition, it usually is more complicated in presentation than the add-back method and some confusion could be caused by its similarity to the income statement.

In the writer's opinion, the superiority of one method over the other is not established. Under either method he would prefer presentation of just one figure for 'funds provided from operations' in the funds statement proper with a table showing how this figure is arrived at in a footnote.

Depreciation and amortization

Under many cost systems amounts written off capital assets for depreciation and amortization form part of inventoriable costs. As a result, the depreciation and amortization written in a year will not correspond exactly with the amount charged against income for the year, the difference being accounted for by the difference between the amount of depreciation and amortization cost carried forward as part of the opening and closing inventory amounts. Technically therefore, the figure for 'funds provided from operations' should be arrived at by adjusting the income statement figures for the amount of depreciation actually included therein. To do so, however, would mean that the statement would not agree with the change of working capital as shown by the balance sheet (since the depreciation included in inventory would not be counted). Customarily therefore, the adjustment to income figures for depreciation and amortization is made in the total amount provided for the year. In effect, the depreciation component in inventory is treated as though it had required an actual outlay of funds. The error in this treatment would rarely, if ever, be significant.

Presentation 'net' or 'broad'

In the funds statement there is usually a choice to be made between showing details of the changes in long-term asset or liability accounts or merely showing the net change. In connection with short life deferred tooling it was suggested earlier that the net change only should be shown. Ordinarily however, the better practice is otherwise. The *flow* of funds is usually best shown by presenting the account changes 'broad' rather than net. For example, where there has been long-term borrowing during the year and some repayment of principal, these are best shown separately as a source and application. This statement, of course, is subject to the test of materiality. Minor flows are best shown net, and frequently a number of insignificant changes may be grouped under a miscellaneous heading.

Disposals of fixed assets

Disposals of fixed assets require a complex entry in the accounts in the following form:

      Dr.   Cash or accounts receivable (for proceeds of disposal)
      Dr.   Accumulated depreciation (for depreciation accumulated on the asset)
           Cr. Fixed assets (for the carrying value of the asset)
      Dr. or Cr. Loss or profit on disposal

Only the proceeds of disposal represent a movement of funds, and only this figure should appear in the statement under the source section.

Two modifications of this treatment, however, are commonly found:

1. The proceeds of disposal are frequently netted with the outlay of funds on new capital acquisitions. Since proceeds from disposal of fixed assets are usually quite unimportant, this seems a perfectly sensible procedure. If however, a major disposal has occurred, the record would be better shown broad.

2. The profit or loss on disposal affects income for the year without representing a source or application of funds. Under the 'add-back' method therefore, it has to be shown separately and there is one more item cluttering up the reconciliation of funds provided by operations. To avoid this, it is common practice not to make the adjustment, but rather to leave the profit or loss figure in funds provided from operations and to compensate by showing the proceeds of disposal as being equal to the net carrying value of the assets sold. While technically incorrect this practice also can be condoned on practical grounds where amounts involved are not significant.

Consolidation problems

Problems in presentation arise when a parent company acquires or sells a subsidiary. To illustrate these, assume the following facts:

1. Company P acquires all the shares of Company S for $1,200,000 in cash, and $300,000 in preference shares.

2. The balance sheet of Company S at date of acquisition is:

	(000's)
Working capital	1,000
Fixed assets (net)	800
	1,800
Long-term debt	600
Common equity	1,200
	1,800

3. Accordingly, the premium over book value paid by Company P is $300,000 ($1,500 – $1,200). This is allocable $200,000 to fixed assets and $100,000 to goodwill.

The effect of this transaction on the consolidated accounts is to bring in $1,000,000 representing the working capital of Company S, offset by the payment by

Company P of $1,200,000 in current funds, for a net reduction in working capital of $200,000. This could be presented in several ways:

(a) The total investment in Company S could be shown $1,500
     Less working capital of Company S included in consolidation   1,000

     For a net application of funds   500
     Partially met by issue of preference shares   300

     Net outlay of funds as a result of transaction $ 200

Alternatively, the individual non-current assets and liabilities of Company S could be spelled out:

(b) Application of funds to acquire assets of Company S
         Fixed assets $1,000
         Goodwill   100 $1,100
     Offset by
         Debt of Company S included in consolidation   600
         Preference shares issued as partial consideration   300   900

     Net outlay of funds $ 200

On this basis the assets and debt taken over in the acquisition of Company S might be merged with the presentation of related transactions in the rest of the consolidated group. For example, if other fixed asset acquisitions were $1,500,000, total acquisitions in the consolidated statement might be shown as $2,500,000.

The writer's preference would be for the presentation shown in the first illustration, supplemented by a footnote giving the detailed breakdown of the net application of funds of $500,000 as between fixed assets acquired, goodwill acquired and debt assumed. This preference is based on the proposition that the acquisition of the subsidiary was in essence one transaction and the net effect of this on working capital should be shown. The allocation of the effect, as between various balance sheet categories, while important, can be handled by footnote.

This preference is supported by examination of the opposite situation, namely the disposal of a subsidiary. Suppose, for example, the accounts showed the same amounts for Company S as in the previous illustration and Company P sells its interest for $1,500,000 of which $300,000 is composed of a long-term receivable. This transaction would be shown in the statement of funds as follows:

     Proceeds from sale of shares of Company S $1,500
     Less long-term receivable included in proceeds   300

     Net current proceeds from sale   1,200
     Deduct working capital of Company S   1,000

     Net change in consolidated working capital as a result
         of sale of Company S $ 200

One would not expect to find the proceeds on the transactions spelled out as being so much for the fixed assets of subsidiary S, so much for its goodwill, etc., and in fact the vendor in such a situation, having sold the business as one overall going concern, will frequently not have an allocation of proceeds to the components sold.

An alternative possibility for handling the sale of a subsidiary would be to remove the subsidiary accounts from the consolidation as at the beginning of the year in which it was sold, and instead account for the investment in the subsidiary on the 'equity' basis (explained in Chapter 17). This would seem to have some justification on the grounds that the sale provides evidence that at this point of time, the subsidiary is no longer an integral part of the consolidated group. On the other hand, the treatment, as suggested in the preceding paragraph, would seem more consistent both with previous accounting and with the treatment that would be given to acquisitions of subsidiaries.

References

1. For a thorough description of the history of the funds statement see L. S. Rosen and D. T. DeCoster, "'Funds' Statements: A Historical Perspective", *The Accounting Review* (January 1969), pp. 124–136.

24 Special accounting problems of the extractive industries

This Chapter deals with certain accounting problems peculiar to the extractive industries, by which is meant those industries whose business consists of finding minerals, including petroleum or natural gas, metals and other substances found at or below the earth's surface, extracting these substances and usually performing some form of processing to put them in useable form.

These industries have a number of unique characteristics of which two have special significance for accounting:

1. They are the only industries which have to find their raw material rather than being able to buy it on the market from known suppliers;

2. Because their raw material is usually found below the surface of the earth or in remote geographical areas, the effort of finding it is usually expensive and chancy. This means that there is no close relationship between costs incurred in looking for their materials and the success achieved. The business is by nature speculative.

These two characteristics mean that the relative success of such a business may depend as much or more on its success in finding the source of its product as it does in processing and marketing it. This fact immediately raises the question whether the usual accounting rule that increases in asset value may be recognized only when realized is appropriate for the extractive industries. Moreover, the fact that costs of finding an economically developable ore deposit or an oil or gas field do not bear a close relationship to the worth of the find, means that the normal accounting process of determining income by matching costs against revenues is largely of historical significance and has limited value for the purpose of investment or other types of analysis.

That more consideration has not been given to placing a value on minerals or oil and gas reserves, when discovered, has a very practical explanation. In a typical mining operation the full extent of the ore body is not known when mining commences, and may not be fully known until many years thereafter. All that is known is that an ore body of at least commercial grade and size is thought to exist. Delineation and development of the ore body frequently proceeds just a little ahead of the mining operation. It is often, therefore, extremely difficult to place a value within reasonable limits on a mineral discovery at or near the time of discovery. In the petroleum or natural gas industry the difficulty in valuing reserves discovered may be somewhat less. Nevertheless the difficulties are severe. An accurate estimate of reserves found usually requires some years from the start of production, and adjustments of earlier estimates are very common. Valuation of reserves that may not be produced until many years in the future also involves many variables. W. B. Coutts has provided a thorough discussion of the problem.[1]

Since it has apparently not been deemed possible to value mineral reserves discovered, the extractive industries have attempted to follow the customary accounting pattern of matching costs and revenues, even though, as indicated, in exploration and development the relationship between costs incurred and eventual results may vary widely. The problem of how to account for costs incurred to find minerals is the most difficult area in accounting for the extractive industries. In discussing this topic it is convenient to deal separately with the accounting for non-producing companies, i.e. companies that have not emerged from the purely exploratory stage, and for those that have successfully reached production.

Extractive Industries Solely in the Exploratory Stage

Particularly in the mining industry, for every company that successfully comes into production, there are scores if not hundreds that collect funds, conduct an exploration program without positive results and, then, having exhausted their cash resources, become dormant or disappear.

Since such companies have virtually no revenue, the ordinary accounting rules for revenue recognition and cost matching are simply inapplicable. The important questions in these companies are:

– To what extent should cost be deferred when incurred and, if deferred, at what point must they be written off?
– How should costs incurred be classified and described in the financial statements?

A recent CICA Research Study[2] has dealt extensively with the accounting problems of non-producing mining companies. The following discussion is therefore limited.

Since all costs of a pure mine exploration company are incurred in the hope of gain, and since there is no substantial revenue against which costs may be written off, it is common practice to defer all costs initially, including general and administrative costs.* Sundry income, such as interest earned on temporary investment of cash, may be credited against the deferred charges. On this basis of accounting there is no profit or loss account, but a statement of source and application of funds or of cash is customarily provided in the financial statements, to show the flow of funds provided by the shareholders and others through to their use in the exploration program.

---

* The majority practice, however, is not invariable. A number of companies charge general and administration costs directly to deficit account. A few companies show regular income accounts to which interest and other revenue is credited and against which administration expenses are charged.

Costs deferred are classified according to the nature of the expense – assaying, diamond drilling, fees, licences and taxes, various types of administrative costs, etc. It is customary to provide a statement or exhibit showing the continuity of these costs in the financial period and a breakdown by types of cost as above, analyzing at least the direct costs by the several geographical areas in which the company is carrying on work.

Costs identifiable with mining properties or claims are capitalized in a separate asset category. Where the title is temporary it has been recommended that this asset be described as 'claim' or 'lease' rather than property.[3]

In Canada mining claims or properties and deferred exploration costs are shown as assets in the conventional balance sheet format. In the United States the SEC, under Article 5A of Regulation S-X, requires that a "statement of assets and un-recovered promotional exploratory and development costs" be presented, along with a "statement of liabilities" and a "statement of capital". In this way, the normal balance sheet is broken up into three separate pieces and unrecovered exploratory costs, etc. are distinguished from other assets.

When should costs of properties and claims and deferred exploration costs be written off? Obviously if the legal interest in claims has been allowed to lapse their cost should be written off. At such time deferred exploration costs, etc. associated with that group of claims should also be written off along with an apportionment of indirect general or administration costs which may have to be on an arbitrary basis. However, it frequently happens that although active exploration work is halted, the legal interest in claims is maintained in the hope that interest in that area may arise again in the future. In such cases it might seem that the incurred exploration costs, which have produced no results worthy of follow-up for the moment, should be written off. In some cases this is done, but more often in Canada it appears that the deferred exploration costs continue to be deferred so long as the related claims are not written off.

The foregoing comments refer directly to the accounting of non-producing mining companies. The problems of exploration companies in the petroleum industry are not greatly dissimilar; hence no separate discussion is included here.

Extractive Industries in the Producing Stage

Once a company has successfully brought sufficient oil and gas deposits or a mine into production it adopts 'profit and loss' accounting and its accounting problems and practices become more like those of a normal company. The company becomes more a going concern and less a single venture. Many companies strive to achieve greater assurance of continued existence by continuing an active exploration program.

Because of some dissimilarities in practice, mining companies and oil and gas companies will be dealt with separately below.

Mining companies

As soon as a company has determined that it has a commercial ore body it bends its efforts to development work to bring the mine into production. During the period before 'commencement of commercial production' all costs on the project will be deferred as preproduction expenses, and any revenues from initial production before commercial quantities are attained will be credited against the accumulated amount of preproduction expense.

Once commercial production begins certain changes in the accounting take place. Prior to that date all development costs – i.e. costs of outlining and gaining access to the ore body – will have been deferred. After that date costs of developing further ore will be written off as incurred unless an exceptionally large development program is undertaken, in which case some part of its costs may be deferred. Frequently the company's development work is just a little ahead of its ore requirements, and the costs of development are written off as the work is done.

Since the ore body is a wasting asset the costs accumulated and deferred before production are amortized by means of a depletion charge against income. Some part of the preproduction costs will relate to the development of ore reserves mined in the first few years of the mine's life, and the remainder will be expenditures related to the project as a whole. In theory therefore, a split rate of amortization would be appropriate. However, in view of the fact that the total amount of ore that can be obtained from the mine is not usually known very accurately, and cannot be known until further development work is done over the years, the proper rate of amortization is essentially an informed guess. The rate of amortization eventually selected is usually on the conservative side, and may consist of a dollar amount per ton of ore mined or a fixed annual percentage of total cost.

Practice is divided with respect to accounting for accumulated costs of mining properties. A survey of fifty producing mining companies showed that approximately two-thirds of the companies did not amortize the cost of properties as production proceeded. (Among the largest companies however, majority practice was to amortize such cost.) Since mining properties lose their value as ore is extracted it is hard to justify the widespread practice of non-amortization. It is true that absence of knowledge of total ore reserves often makes the appropriate rate of depletion very much a guess. But the same is true of amortization of preproduction costs and it is difficult to understand the difference in treatment.

As the mining company becomes established as a going concern, its accounting practices with respect to further exploration costs tend to become more conservative. Exploration overheads, including general and administration costs, will probably be written off when incurred rather than deferred. In addition a more conservative view is likely to be taken of direct exploration costs, and these will more often be written off in the year incurred except for very promising or very large properties.

Oil and natural gas companies

Producing oil and natural gas companies differ from mining companies in that after commencement of production and during the primary recovery stage proportionately less is involved in the way of further development cost on producing fields. Production is usually a relatively simple operation so that accounting problems continue to revolve around the treatment of costs of exploration and finding.

Under traditional accounting methods exploration costs are classified by types of cost and then deferred or written off on the basis of two tests:

(a) before results are known – whether the costs are related to a capital asset, and

(b) after results are known – whether the cost outlays have been successful in finding and developing reserves. At this time some costs previously deferred, e.g. costs of lease rights, may have to be written off.

Applying these tests results in some such practices as described below:

- Costs of exploration or drilling rights, including lease bonuses, legal costs, etc., are usually capitalized as representing a capital asset.
- Costs of land and leasing departments, carrying charges such as delay rentals, shut-in royalties, etc. are usually written off on the grounds they do not add value to the capital asset.
- Costs of exploration work may be expensed in total as giving rise to no tangible capital asset, or part may be deferred where the costs relate to, or lead to, the acquisition of land rights.
- Costs of drilling wells will be capitalized if the well is a producer, and not if it is a dry hole.

Practices of individual companies following the traditional accounting approach may vary considerably in detail – for example:

- Geological and geophysical costs may be entirely expensed, or some may be deferred if they can be identified with specific properties (particularly if the work is done by outside contractors).
- Some, but not all, companies will amortize acquisition costs capitalized with respect to underdeveloped properties on the grounds that some part of the properties will ultimately prove to be non-productive.
- Some companies will capitalize the cost of dry holes if they are drilled as development wells to outline a known producing area. Others will expense the costs of all dry holes.
- The cost centre adopted for capitalization may vary. If the individual lease is used, all costs of non-producing leases will be written off when drilling results are known and the property is abandoned. But if the cost centre is defined more broadly as a lease block, a field or a wider area of interest, a greater amount of costs will be carried forward as associated with productive properties.

The traditional accounting approach, as described, has been criticized on theoretical grounds as well as because of the undesirable range of practice.

(a) It may be argued that all costs incurred before success or failure of the program is known are laid out with the same ultimate objective in mind – namely finding and developing commercial reserves of oil or gas. It is illogical and artificial therefore to capitalize some costs on the grounds that they produce a capital asset, and write off others. So-called capital assets, such as land rights, are themselves worthless unless reserves are discovered on them.

(b) The practice of deferring only such costs as can be directly related to successful leases or fields ignores the essentially speculative character of the industry. No one can be sure that any given exploratory well will be a producer. In fact the contrary is true – one can be virtually certain that of any given number of exploratory wells drilled, some will be dry holes. Taken individually, the chances of a given well being successful are very much a toss-up. Equally however, given a program of drilling in an area selected on geological evidence as favourable, the chances are good that some will be producers.

In these circumstances it is reasonable to suggest that the costs of dry holes, as much as those of producers, are part of the necessary and inevitable costs of finding reserves, and properly may be attached to them.

Against these criticisms it is argued that conservatism is important in such a highly speculative industry. Moreover most companies carry on a more or less continuing exploration program and the results of one year's work ordinarily cannot be assessed until several years later. In these circumstances some accountants feel strongly that the practice of expensing most exploration and carrying costs as incurred is as fair a way as any of charging costs to income.

What this argument ignores, however, is the relative balance between a company's exploration work and its other activity. The income of a large integrated oil company may not be distorted by the immediate write-off of most costs of exploration. The case may well be otherwise in a smaller producing company. It seems unreasonable that a company that can defer all expenditures while it is purely in the exploratory or development stage must expense a large portion of similar expenditures once it begins to produce in commercial quantities. More generally it may be suggested that the traditional method of accounting, which reflects an immediate improvement in income as a result of a decision to suspend or curtail exploration activity (a decision which probably will have an adverse effect on future earning power), cannot be conceptually sound and must be justified on practical grounds if at all.

A diametrically opposed accounting theory, the 'full cost' theory, has received increasing acceptance in the last decade, especially in Canada. Under this theory all costs related to exploration, no matter what their nature, and all costs of developing reserves, whether individually they are successful or not, are deferred as being necessary to the finding and development of the company's reserves. The only limit to this is that if the costs deferred exceed the estimated market value of the reserves the excess must be written off.

The full cost method, however, has its anomalies, even as does the traditional method:

– in establishing a depletion rate applicable to gas and oil produced on the unit-of-production basis, all accumulated costs are included (subject to the occasional special case) even though some of the accumulated costs relate to undeveloped properties for which no reserve estimates have been made. It does not seem very logical, although it may be considered conservative, to measure the cost of current production by reference to total costs which include costs on properties not yet evaluated.

– the basis of establishing the market value ceiling on costs carried forward does not appear to be clearly established. For example, such questions as these are open to argument:

(a) Should costs of undeveloped properties be excluded when comparing market values with total costs deferred? Alternatively, if undeveloped properties have a value as such (as they often would have), should such value be added to the total value of known reserves to arrive at a total to be compared with accumulated cost?

(b) Should market values of known reserves be valued simply at net realizable value, or should estimated amounts realizable be discounted? If discounted, what interest rate would be appropriate?

– tax allocation accounting with respect to deferred allocation and development costs is not followed by most companies using the full cost method (as is true also of companies using the traditional method). It seems somewhat anomalous that tax expense should be treated on a strictly cash basis, regardless of whether deductions have been taken at the expense of amounts allowable in future, while exploration and development costs are handled on the opposite of the cash basis, all being deferred to the future.

– most important of all there is the question to what extent the costs deferred and the unit rate of depletion should be differentiated depending on the location of production area. Unit costs of finding reserves will vary on average from one area to another. In Ontario for example, exploration costs may be very similar to those in Western Canada, but because the success rate is lower and gas and oil discovered is generally in smaller pools the *cost per unit* of reserve is generally higher. In the Arctic on the other hand it is too early to say what results will be achieved, on average, in this area, but until greater experience is achieved it seems reasonable to assume that average costs per unit of reserves discovered will differ, perhaps widely. Higher costs per unit must be reflected in higher sales prices if exploration is to continue. Thus a value of 40¢ per MCF for gas at the wellhead may be necessary in Ontario as opposed to 15¢ to 20¢ in Alberta. In principle, if the company has some reserves in low cost, low sale price areas and some in higher cost, higher sale price areas, it would be misleading to use an overall average depletion rate if the actual production from the two areas is disproportionate to the total reserves. This point may not be too serious for companies whose exploration efforts have been confined mainly to Western Canada, but there appear to be some companies using the full cost method which do not define areas of interest nearly narrowly enough.[4]

These anomalies in the full cost method could be corrected by appropriate refinements of the method. The approach is also attacked, however, on more fundamental conceptual grounds. It is argued that the full cost method can conceal the relative failure of a company's exploration program for a long period of time. That is to say, if a company once establishes a quantity of reserves at a relatively low cost per unit, additional costs of exploration, even though it may be completely unsuccessful, are simply added to total deferred finding costs (up to the point where the market value of reserves exceeds the total deferred costs) and are reflected in income only very gradually as the depletion rate per unit of production rises. This, it is argued, is mere equalization of income.

Supporters of full cost accounting might reply that the averaging of successful and unsuccessful exploration results is reasonable. The expectation in conducting exploration is that there will be some successes and some failures and the one cannot be obtained without the other. Also, results of exploration cannot be known until some years after many of the costs are incurred, so that it is impossible to reflect success or failure except over a period of years. Indeed, the traditional accounting approach may be criticized on the grounds that under it a company which intensifies its exploration program will, other things being equal, show a decline in income even though the exploration may ultimately prove to have been most successful. Moreover, practices such as the amortization of costs of undeveloped properties could equally easily be attacked as attempts to equalize income, and to avoid reflecting exploration losses in the year when the results become known.

The traditional approach and the full cost approach, as here described, represent almost two different philosophies. One is conservative and pessimistic – write off all costs except those that can be associated with a narrowly defined cost centre, treatment of which will depend on the results of development. The other is optimistic in outlook – defer all costs unless it can be shown they exceed value. Modification in both approaches might tend to bring them closer together. For example, a broader definition of the cost centre and treatment of more costs as exploration overheads to be attached to direct costs would result in greater cost deferment under the traditional approach. Under the full cost approach, narrower definition of areas of interest (by geographical areas, or areas showing similar unit costs of exploration, or perhaps by management programs) would mean that lack of success in exploration would be reflected more quickly as individual areas were abandoned or costs deferred in an area hit the market value ceiling.

It would appear that some effort should be made to reduce the variety of accounting methods in oil and gas producing companies. There also appears to be some danger of a polarization of views behind something like the present traditional method on the one hand and the full cost method on the other. It would be useful to try to find some common ground before such polarization takes place.

1. In the first place it should probably be recognized that a perfect solution is not possible to the accounting problems, given the speculative nature of the business, the length of time it takes for the results of exploration activity to become known, and the frequency of revisions to reserve estimates after they are first made.

2. Secondly it should be clearly understood that the success of the exploration effort can only be successfully measured if reserves discovered are valued. That is to say, the realization criterion for revenue recognition has to be abandoned if exploration results are to be reflected in the accounts. Neither the traditional approach nor the full cost treatment of exploration costs achieves this objective.

3. Exploration is probably the most important activity of most producing companies if one excludes the integrated companies from consideration. It would seem therefore that the first question should be – "can exploration success be measured – can a reasonable valuation be made of reserves discovered?" This would involve substantial problems:
   - Costs of undeveloped properties would have to be excluded in evaluating exploration success. This would mean that some reasonable means would have to be found to allocate exploration overheads to properties.
   - Reasonable value figures would have to be assigned to reserves. To be useful, such figures would need to be standard across the industry in each (defined) area and presumably would vary from area to area.
   - It would have to be understood that value changes would result from changes in reserve estimates (and from other changes as well) which would appear as gains or losses whether through the income statement or outside it.

Obviously such an approach would contain serious practical problems – perhaps insurmountable problems. If it is deemed impractical however (as it seems to have been to date), it should be recognized that the accounts of companies with large exploration activities are inherently less useful than those of most other types of business.

4. If it is concluded that the success of exploration cannot be sufficiently reliably measured for purposes of reporting to the public, the question arises whether it is useful to continue to report in the conventional income statement format. It is often said that figures of cash flow are more important for investment analysis in oil and gas producing companies than are net income figures. Perhaps such companies should separate their reporting into two statements. One would be a statement of net contribution from production – which would show sales revenues less costs of lifting and associated overhead costs and taxes, but would exclude any figure for depletion cost. The second would be a statement of cumulative and current finding costs, classified between undeveloped and developed properties, and closely associated with figures for reserve estimates, showing the causes of change in them in the year.

5. Only if neither of the foregoing approaches is considered feasible and acceptable is it necessary to choose between the traditional and full cost methods of accounting for exploration costs, or some variant of them. If such a choice were necessary the writer leans to the full cost theory, provided some of its serious deficiencies, particularly the lack of reasonable restriction on areas of interest, were rectified. He believes the theory that all finding costs in an area of interest may reasonably be associated with reserves discovered, properly reflects the speculative character of exploration activity. The criticism that full cost accounting can, in certain circumstances, fail to give current recognition to unsuccessful exploration, is mitigated by the fact that it can only do so if previous success has likewise gone unrecognized (because total accumulated costs must be less than market value of reserves). Moreover, the possibility that the traditional accounting method can reflect heavy cost write-offs, when in fact substantial success is being achieved, is equally open to criticism. The practical effect of the conservative bias in the traditional method of accounting is that it favours the large well-established company which can afford steady write-offs that may be small relative to its other income. It is not a method that seems appropriate in a country like Canada that wishes to encourage, or at least not discourage, exploration activity.

Whatever the basis upon which costs are deferred, they must subsequently be written off against revenue from production. Apart from the costs of tangible fixed assets which may be written off by normal depreciation methods, the customary practice is to amortize costs on a unit-of-production basis. The depletion rate used is subject to recomputation annually on a cumulative basis, as new costs are incurred, reserves are added and previous reserve estimates revised. Although not without substantial problems, the estimates of gas and oil reserves are usually more reliable than those for ore reserves in the mining industry, and the depletion figure has correspondingly greater significance.

References

1. W. B. Coutts, *Accounting Problems in the Oil and Gas Industry* (Toronto: The Canadian Institute of Chartered Accountants, 1963), pp. 15–21.
2. *Financial Reporting for Non-Producing Mining Companies* (Toronto: The Canadian Institute of Chartered Accountants, 1967).
3. *Ibid.*, p. 9.
4. The case for accounting by area of interest is convincingly argued in Coutts, *Oil and Gas Industry*, pp. 26–31.

25 Accounting for financial institutions

This Chapter deals briefly with the special problems encountered in accounting for financial intermediaries. The common characteristic of financial intermediaries as here defined is that large scale investment of funds is a vital function of the enterprise. This characteristic may result from the fact that income from loans or investments is the direct objective of the enterprise (as in the case of finance companies and investment funds) or it may be a by-product of the deposit receiving function of the enterprise (as in the case of banks and trust companies) or it may result from the fact that the primary business of the enterprise entails the collection of funds from the public in advance of the time they are required (as in the case of insurance companies). Discussion of all the accounting and reporting problems of all the various types of financial intermediaries is well beyond the scope of this Chapter. An attempt will be made, however, to discuss the principal problems common to most financial institutions and brief comment will be made on the particular problems of chartered banks, trust and loan companies, general insurance companies, life insurance companies, finance companies, mutual investment funds and pension funds.

In Chapter 2 it was pointed out that the accounting methods of financial institutions exhibit significant differences from those of ordinary commercial concerns. This fact may be attributed very largely to the existence of government regulation. But it also reflects the particular nature of the accounting and other problems which face the financial institution. These problems relate to:

1. Accounting for investment portfolios;

2. Revenue recognition questions;

3. The cyclical nature of loss experience;

4. The existence of government controls.

Accounting for investment portfolios

As has been indicated previously, the usual method of accounting for investments in securities, other than investments which represent control of another entity, is to carry them at cost (or amortized cost in the case of securities with a fixed maturity date). This carrying value may be adjusted to a lower realizable value (if the security is carried as a short-term asset or if the decline in value is considered to be enduring) but a write-up to a higher market value is not permitted. Higher values are recognized only upon sale of the investment.

Even in ordinary commercial enterprises this basis of accounting has been criticized:

1. It can be argued that cost or amortized cost is a less relevant figure for balance sheet purposes than market value would be.

2. If profit is reflected only on realization, an entity with investments carried below market is in the position to choose whether or not it will increase its reported income merely by selling a security and taking a profit. On the other hand, if carrying values are above market, management may be deterred from selling securities because it means a loss must be recorded in the income account which could be avoided if the security were not sold. Thus accounting considerations may have an undesirable influence on investment decisions.

3. If the investments are freely disposable an investment decision is involved in continuing to hold them as much as it is in selling them. Thus it can be argued that the results of investment decisions are fairly represented by changes in market value during the holding period even if the changes are not realized, and therefore such changes should be reflected in income.

To some extent these same objections can be urged against the traditional investment accounting basis for financial institutions. In them however, the objections, if valid, would be much more important than they are to the average commercial enterprise because investments in securities can form such a large proportion of their total assets, and the value of investments held can be several times as large as the total shareholders' equity.

Most financial institutions (investment funds excepted) follow traditional methods in determining the carrying value of investments, sometimes modified by the provision of investment reserves (see later discussion). While these investment accounting methods can be criticized, as has been indicated above, criticism could also be directed against a straight market value basis for recording security investments of a financial institution.

1. If investments in securities such as bonds are made by the institution on a long-term basis, it can be argued that variations in market value before maturity are largely irrelevant. The significant fact in such a situation is the amount of interest being received and this is indicated by the interest credited in the income statement.

2. In any event, in the larger financial institutions investment portfolios are of such a size that their disposal could drastically affect the market. Therefore, quoted market values are not really significant to such an institution.

3. Market values for a bond portfolio are largely determined by the general level of interest rates. In the special case of the life insurance company, revaluation of bond portfolios at market would not make much sense unless the policy reserves, the calculation of which requires an interest rate assumption, were

also revalued to reflect changed interest rate levels. A similar point could be made in connection with a trust company that has a liability for monies deposited on guaranteed investment certificates or in general with any financial institution that owes a long-term liability at fixed interest rates.

4. Valuation of bond portfolios at market would be inconsistent with carrying mortgages at cost. Mortgages are like bonds in providing a fixed interest rate and value at maturity. Thus the value of mortgages also depends in part on the general level of interest rates. However, it has been traditional not to calculate or disclose a market value for mortgages since no developed market exists in which mortgages may be bought or sold. It may be noted that this argument is now losing its force as a market, for large blocks of mortgages at least, is now developing and institutions are prepared to value mortgages held in investment funds for purposes of arriving at the total market value of the fund.

5. Because of the size of investment portfolios in many financial institutions and the extent of change that can take place in market values over short periods, unrealized gains or losses, if recorded through income account, might well far exceed normal investment income and the results of other operations, which would have an adverse effect on the unsophisticated reader. In fact, for similar reasons some types of financial institutions have excluded even realized gains and losses from income account by carrying them to a reserve or direct to surplus.

On the other hand, if the market value basis is not used and if realized gains and losses are carried to income, because of the size of the investment portfolio it is even more open to management of financial institutions than to management of other enterprises to pick and choose the securities that are sold in order to produce the net income figure desired. The practice of excluding gains and losses on investment from income account entirely while solving this problem is itself open to objection, in that then an important part of operations never gets reflected in the income account.

An alternative proposal, the 'deferral and amortization' theory attacks the problem of investment accounting from the other direction. On the deferral and amortization basis gains or losses when securities are sold are spread over the period from date of sale to the maturity date of the security sold. This method thus contrasts both with the market value basis under which gains and losses are recognized as income of the period in which the value changes take place, and the traditional investment accounting basis, under which gains and losses are recognized in the period of sale.

The deferral and amortization theory has been developed specifically in the context of large investment portfolios containing fixed maturity, high grade securities which are bought primarily for income and not for trading. The theory is based on the following chain of reasoning:

1. The nature of certain types of institutions is such that they may be expected to have a steady supply of funds to invest and a net reduction in assets under administration is unlikely as far as can be foreseen.

2. The management of such an institution is likely to keep fairly fully invested at all times because of the loss of income on uninvested cash.

3. In these circumstances if an initial investment is made in a fixed interest security, the income on that portion of the investment fund is very largely determined until the maturity date of that security. For either the security will be held to maturity, or else it will be sold before maturity and the proceeds invested in a similar high grade security, perhaps even one of the same issuer with a different maturity date. When such a switch occurs, the yields on the security sold and the new security will be closely related. Such difference as exists will be largely attributable to such factors as differences in taxability of the total yield and differences in maturity dates of the securities, rather than to differences in their investment grade. In these circumstances, an apparent loss or gain on disposal of the old security will really represent an offset (during the period to maturity of the old security) to the higher or lower interest actually obtained on the new security.

An extreme example will help to illustrate the case. Suppose a $100,000 bond bearing a 3% coupon payable semi-annually (i.e. 6% per annum) was bought some years ago. Suppose it is sold today when, because of changes in interest rate levels, the yield on that bond to maturity 5 years hence is 8%. The sale price on this basis would be $91,890 and under conventional accounting a loss of $8,110 would be recorded. Then suppose the next day the $91,890 is reinvested in exactly the same bond. From then on the income on the investment would be recorded at the 8% yield rate on amortized cost rather than the previous 6%. That is to say, the income recorded in the next six months, for example, would be 4% of $91,890 = $3,676* in place of the $3,000 recorded on the previous issue. This effect would have been avoided under the deferral and amortization method by deferring the loss of $8,110 and amortizing it against income over the next 5 years.

The deferral and amortization method is as yet rarely found in practice. It has been suggested, however, on a number of occasions in connection with the permanent investment funds of non-profit organizations, pension funds and other such funds,[1] by the AICPA Committee on Bank Accounting and Auditing,[2] and by a CICA Study Group on Accounting for Trust and Loan Companies in Canada.[3]

It should be appreciated that the method is applicable in limited circumstances only and does not deal with all the problems of investment portfolios. For example, it is not applicable in accounting for equity securities or those of speculative character. If it is used under conditions where the fund invested might shrink in size from time to time, provision must be made to write off an equitable portion of the deferred balance when the fund's size is reduced. (It would be inappropriate to carry forward any deferred balance, for example, if the entire fund were liquidated.) Perhaps the greatest problem is that the theory depends on investment policy or method of operation rather than the nature of the asset. That is to say, it is only suitable for a fund operating as a long-term investor rather than a trader – seeking secure investment income primarily rather than trading gains. In practice, financial institutions may wish to play the role of both investor and trader. The bulk of their investment funds may be invested long-term but some may be held

---

* If the straight-line method of amortization of discount were used rather than the more accurate effective yield method, the income recorded would be $3,000 coupon interest plus $811 amortization.

for trading. Some institutions recognize the distinction by having separate investment accounts and trading accounts with the latter being accounted for on a market value basis. Such an arrangement would seem desirable if the deferral and amortization theory were adopted for bond investment portfolios.

Revenue recognition questions

Questions also arise in some financial institutions as to the proper basis for recognizing revenue as earned. It has been noted earlier that where revenue arises from services performed rather than the sale of goods, it is desirable if possible to accrue the revenue earned as work is performed rather than wait until it is billed or cash is collected. However, it is often difficult to accrue service revenue on a reliable basis and apart from interest and dividend income, revenue is likely to be recognized by a financial institution only as billed or as cash is collected. This can result in some income distortion – e.g. when a trust company does not have its accounts for a large estate passed until after its year-end, but in most cases the revenue not recognized would be relatively insignificant in relation to total assets and revenues.

Some difference of opinion may arise where revenues received represent partly return on investment and partly compensation for work performed. For example, in finance companies the collections from the borrower must cover interest on funds advanced to him and also costs associated with servicing his account. When the borrower is charged a percentage of the monthly unpaid balance the revenue is likely to be recorded on the same basis so that, with respect to any given loan, revenue is recognized on a diminishing pattern as though it were a pure interest return. Where the interest is 'precomputed' however (that is where the purchaser signs a note for an amount greater than the cash advanced), more variety in treatment seems to be found. A pattern of revenue recognition similar to an interest return is obtained by taking in revenue on the sum-of-the-digits basis – or the 'rule of 78' (so called because the sum of the digits for 12 months is 78). Alternatively, the total revenue is sometimes recognized on a straight-line basis on the theory that costs of servicing the loan are more or less constant. This gives no weight to the declining interest cost to the finance company as funds repaid by its customers are applied to the company's borrowing. Under either of these methods there may be immediate recognition of a given percentage of the amount of the total revenue to offset the initial heavy costs of arranging and recording the loan, with only the balance of revenue being spread over the term of the loan on the predetermined pattern.

In general insurance companies, premiums are basically spread over the life of the policy or an approximation thereto (all policies issued in a year are deemed to have been issued on July 1 so that an amount equal to one-half year's premium is deferred on all one-year policies, 5/6ths is deferred in the first year of three-year policies, etc.). Government regulations permit deferral of only 80% of this calculated amount giving an arbitrary allowance of 20% against initial costs of selling and writing the policies. Such allowance may or may not be a reasonable representation of such costs. In many cases it would be too low.

In life insurance companies revenue reported consists basically of premiums for the year together with income earned on invested assets. This revenue is unlike revenue as it is defined in a normal business, however, in that it does not represent a measure of the reward *earned* for sale of goods or rendering of service *in the year in question*. The primary service rendered by a life insurance company with respect to any policyholder in a year is to give him protection against dying in the year without adequate financial coverage. (A secondary service rendered is that of investment management of any funds accumulated to the credit of the policy.) The revenue attributable to that protection for a year to most policyholders, however, is not measured by the premium payable in any given year. Conceivably such revenue could be approximated by the premium that would be payable on a yearly renewable term (YRT) policy for the net amount at risk under the policy. The premiums payable on a whole life or endowment policy, however, will be substantially different in amount from a YRT premium and will contain payment for protection in later years and in the case of an endowment policy, a savings element as well.

As an extreme example consider a policy paid up by a single premium. After the first year no further revenue will be recorded on that policy, other than investment income on funds at the credit of the policy. Yet the policyholder will receive protection so long as the policy is outstanding.

In essence a life insurance company's accounting is not designed to yield figures comparable to revenues earned for a year and costs incurred to earn that revenue in a normal company. A life insurance policy is looked on as a long-term arrangement and until recently little consideration has been given to the desirability of relating earnings on policies to services rendered by the company year by year. The allocation of the net income from the insurance activities to years is governed by the amounts set aside each year for reserves for future policyholder benefits. Historically, these must meet certain statutory minimum tests designed to ensure solvency of the company rather than provide a fair measure of its income year by year. Later in this Chapter some current suggestions for changes in life insurance accounting are discussed.

The cyclical or irregular nature of loss experience

Some loss on loans and security investments is inevitably encountered over a period of time by any financial institution which invests in or lends money to any but the safest risks. It is frequently characteristic of such losses that they are bunched at irregular intervals. Often this is a result of fluctuations in the state of the economy as a whole. Thus losses on personal and commercial loans are likely to be heavier in a slack economy and much heavier in a major depression such as that encountered in the 1930's. Sound mortgages in the state of the real estate market for the last 30 years have been very safe, but the 1930 depression produced major losses on mortgages especially for the institution that could not afford to foreclose and hang on to the security until its value recovered. Losses on more speculative mortgages are likely to be encountered in a similar pattern to loans. Over the long term some losses on fixed charge securities are likely also to be encountered especially if their quality is less than first grade and again such losses are more likely to be realized in hard times. In the case of institutions such as chartered banks there may also be a built-in tendency to losses on securities since available resources will be invested in securities when demand for loans is low and therefore interest levels are low, and then when the demand for loan funds rises and interest rates increase securities bought at lower interest levels will have dropped in value and a loss will be realized if they are liquidated to provide funds to meet the loan demand. Trading in securities as opposed to investment for the long term will result in both losses and gains according partly to the skill of the trader. On well-managed trading however, it is to be hoped that gains will exceed losses particularly in the case of investments in common stock where the normal practice of public companies of retaining part of their earnings for reinvestment should lead to a long-run appreciation in the stock value. (This discussion is solely in terms of gains or losses in monetary terms and does not consider the possibility of loss of purchasing power through inflation.)

The insurance industry is subject to all the risks of bunching of losses on investments and as well may encounter very large claim losses on an irregular basis. Especially in the fire and casualty business large losses from the occasional hurricane, earthquake, flood or disastrous fire are predictable as an inevitable risk but are encountered only every few years. The life insurance business, although perhaps less likely to encounter the catastrophic loss experience, is nevertheless subject to a somewhat similar risk of the occasional epidemic such as the influenza epidemic of 1919. (Whether medical science has succeeded in reducing this type of risk to a negligible level in countries where widespread insurance coverage is carried is not yet proven.)

Historically financial institutions have adopted two methods to cope with the probability of irregular large scale losses. One method is to average losses over the years of a cycle by setting up reserves out of income in years of light loss and releasing the reserves to income in years of heavy loss. The other method is to exclude losses of the irregular type such as on loans or securities from income account entirely, and instead charge them direct to surplus accounts, reserves* appropriated from surplus or reserves appropriated from income before or after arriving at a figure described as net income for the year.

The existence of some such form of cyclical accounting in financial institutions has created a basic distinction between their accounting methods and those generally accepted for other business enterprises. The question may be asked why this distinction should be recognized since it is arguable that the ordinary business also has a normal expectation of some good years and some bad years – and a normal expectation that from time to time there will be some exceptional losses on, say, accounts receivable or product warranties, etc. Yet generally accepted accounting principles prohibit any such 'income equalization' devices for the ordinary business.

Several facts may provide an explanation (if not a logically satisfying answer) to this question. In the first place, it may be argued that the nature of a financial institution is such that it does not have as much ability as does a private business to avoid such cyclical or catastrophic losses so long as it is fulfilling its basic responsibility. Specifically, an insurance company cannot cease to insure during the

---

* The term 'reserve' is used here as it is used by financial institutions and is not restricted to the meaning 'amounts voluntarily appropriated from retained earnings or other surplus' as it would be in normal business enterprises.

hurricane season or a bank cease to accept deposits and invest the funds just before an expected depression. Second, the assets exposed to the risk of irregular loss in a financial institution are much greater in relation to the shareholders' equity than in the ordinary business, because in addition to shareholders' funds substantial amounts of depositors', creditors' or policyholders' funds are tied up in such assets. Third, government regulations have sanctioned the creation of loss reserves and sometimes encourage them by conservative requirements for asset valuation or by allowing charges for creation of reserves as income tax deductions. Finally, particularly in institutions which accept short-term deposits, a need has been felt to maintain depositor confidence by avoiding the showing of large unexpected losses. The old fear of a "run on the bank" straining its liquidity position or perhaps forcing it to close its doors was at one time very real. Some may think the danger remote in the more sophisticated modern world. But confidence in the financial community is a fragile attribute which is so easily upset that it is small wonder that financial institutions tend to be cautious.

The existence of government controls

Governments are interested in the operation of financial institutions because the efficient discharge of their function as financial intermediary is essential to the working of the economy, and because the public has an interest in their solvency owing to the commitment of the savings of so many individuals to these institutions. Government control takes several forms:

1. Requirements for regular and detailed reporting by the institution to government authorities and provision for periodic government inspection or audit of some aspects of their affairs.

2. Controls to ensure that the institutions remain sufficiently liquid to meet calls upon them and to see that business taken on does not overextend the company in relation to the shareholders' equity which (together with any permitted reserves) forms the margin of safety for depositors, creditors and policyholders. Such controls may consist of:
   (a) Requirements that a certain percentage of deposit liabilities be held in cash or liquid assets such as treasury bills. (Chartered banks and trust companies.)
   (b) Limitation on the ratio of liabilities (including deposits) to shareholders' equity and reserves. (Trust and loan companies and general insurance companies.)

3. Controls on valuation of assets and liabilities for accounting purposes and for measuring compliance with the tests just referred to such as:
   (a) The requirement in general insurance companies that unearned premiums be booked at not less than 80% of their unexpired portion based on the life of the policy.
   (b) The requirement to provide a liability for insurance ceded to unlicensed reinsurers.
   (c) The statutory prescription of acceptable mortality tables, interest rates and reserve calculation methods (usually producing a conservative result) for life insurance companies.

(d) The valuation of security investments at market value in general insurance companies, and a combination of values in life insurance companies not exceeding amortized cost for certain redeemable government securities and market value for other securities (subject to a complicated formula for moving towards market value over a period of years when market drops below cost).

(e) In the case of insurance companies and trust and loan companies, treatment of certain assets as 'non-admitted' for purposes of the liability coverage tests noted in the previous section, such as:

(i) investments not authorized under the governing Acts

(ii) amounts recoverable from unlicensed reinsurers

(iii) balances over a certain age due from agents

(iv) investment in equipment, furniture and fixtures and automobiles.

Summary of departures from generally accepted accounting principles

As a result of the conditions just described, the traditional accounting methods of most financial institutions have departed significantly from accounting principles generally accepted for commercial business enterprise. The following summarizes the important differences:

1. The creation of contingency or catastrophe reserves in more or less arbitrary amount by charges against income account.*

2. The creation of investment reserves by charges against income or by carrying investment gains realized direct to reserve rather than to income account, and their subsequent utilization to absorb or offset losses incurred.*

3. The practice of expensing assets which are not admitted under government regulation even though they would be perfectly valid assets under normal accounting rules.

4. The occasional failure to recognize revenue on a basis reasonably related to the time when it is earned.

5. The occasional failure to match costs with revenues on a reasonable basis – e.g. the failure to defer acquisition costs in insurance companies (except to the extent recognized in the calculation of unearned premium reserves by general insurance companies or actuarial reserves calculated under the modified preliminary term basis in some life insurance companies).

6. The frequent failure to use tax allocation accounting procedures (which may be explainable on the grounds that it is pointless to worry about such accounting refinements when other deviations from generally accepted accounting principles are so serious).

---

* If these reserves are not separately disclosed in the balance sheet either because they have been applied against assets or grouped with other liabilities, and if transfers from or to income account are not disclosed in the income statement, they are known as 'inner reserves'. Where these reserves are disclosed they would often be combined as one investment and contingency reserve.

It should be noted that not every financial institution exhibits differences from generally accepted accounting principles in its financial reporting. Also a number of institutions have made marked improvement by way of more complete and fairer disclosure in recent years. Government insurance of deposits may be an influence making depositor protection through conservative accounting less necessary than formerly and the rights of shareholders and others to obtain useful information now has higher priority. Some of this will be brought out in the following brief commentaries on various types of financial intermediaries.

Chartered banks

Until 1967 the use of inner reserves by the banks made it impossible to ascertain their earnings and financial position according to normal accounting principles and only approximate earnings and broad trends could be deduced from the published figures.

The 1967 revision of the Bank Act made significant improvements by way of:

1. Disclosure of accumulated appropriations (the amount of the former inner reserves).

2. Deduction of a provision for loss on loans from income, based on a five-year moving average of actual losses.

3. Disclosure in the Statement of Accumulated Appropriations of actual amounts of security gains, losses and write-downs, and other capital profits and losses, and of differences between actual loan losses for the year and the amount provided through income account.

The reporting methods still differ from generally accepted accounting principles in some respects, for example:

1. Security gains and losses and other capital gains and losses do not appear in the income account.

2. Arbitrary loss provisions are deducted in the Statement of Operations below a figure described as 'balance of revenue' but before the provision for income tax and a figure described as 'balance of profits'. No figure equivalent to net income for the year can be identified.

Nevertheless, the accounts in their present form provide a much better basis for analysis than formerly.

Trust and loan companies

Trust and loan companies, like the banks, have traditionally made widespread use of inner reserves. In recent years there has been a marked trend to voluntary upgrading of financial reporting policy and some companies have brought their reserves out into the open. A current CICA Study surveys the accounting methods of the industry and contains numerous recommendations concerning the best accounting and reporting policies for these companies.[4] At the present time it appears that some companies could be considered as following generally accepted accounting principles while the accounting policies of others still contain significant departures from them. In late 1970 the governing Ontario statute was amended to require the auditor of an Ontario trust or loan company to report whether his client's accounting methods were in accordance with generally accepted principles.

General insurance companies

The accounting methods of general insurance companies are more closely directed by government authorities than some of the other financial institutions. In some jurisdictions it is illegal for a company to circulate a financial statement which is different from that contained in the annual return filed with the government office.

Government prescribed accounting methods differ from generally accepted accounting principles mainly in:

1. The arbitrary limitation on the liability for unearned premiums to not less than 80% of the pro rata deferred liability (a few companies still provide a 100% reserve).
2. The requirement to show a liability for unearned premiums on risks which have been reinsured with an unlicensed reinsurer.
3. The mandatory charge-off of non-admitted assets.
4. The failure to use tax allocation accounting.

In some cases the effect of these deviations from generally accepted accounting principles might not be significant but in others they will be. Cooperation of the Superintendents of Insurance would be required to obtain changes in present accounting methods.

Life insurance companies

Differences between life industry accounting methods and generally accepted accounting principles are probably greater than for any other type of institution. These differences include:

1. The creation of inner reserves applied against invested assets.
2. The addition of contingency reserves to actuarial reserves computed on the company's regular basis, without separate disclosure of such additions.
3. The use of statutory valuation bases for actuarial reserves that are on average conservative in relation to normal expectations, with the result that income on individual policies is shifted from one year to another with an overall effect on income of any one year that is indeterminable in the absence of reserve valuation on a more realistic basis. In some cases the reserve provision required in the early years of a policy's life has been known to exceed the gross premium actually collected by the company.
4. The failure to defer substantial policy acquisition costs over the period in which the policy income will be recognized (except to the extent a partially compensatory result is obtained by setting up reserves on the modified preliminary term basis and paying some part of agents' commissions over a period of years).
5. The immediate charge-off of non-admitted assets.
6. The failure to use tax allocation accounting.

Any attempt to produce figures for a life insurance company that portray more clearly its real progress year by year encounters two substantial difficulties:

1. Matching of costs and revenues with time periods for a life insurance business is peculiarly difficult owing to the long-term nature of the policy contracts. In most commercial enterprises costs are incurred before revenue proceeds are received and the chief problem is to decide on appropriate bases for matching costs with anticipated revenues. The decision is somewhat simplified by the fact that most costs are tangible in character, such as inventory and fixed assets. Life insurance contracts, in contrast, are characterized by the fact that the bulk of revenues is received before the bulk of costs is incurred. Accordingly the primary problem, if it is desired to arrive at accounting principles that reflect a logical concept of annual income, is to find bases for deferring revenues till such time as they can reasonably be regarded as earned. (In insurance accounting terminology the problem is to find bases for providing actuarial reserves that will result in a proper determination of income.) This problem is made the more difficult by the fact that at any given time additional revenues and costs relating to policies in force remain to be received, some of which are not fixed amounts but can only be estimated.

2. Calculation of reserves on a new basis would be required which would greatly add to the work load (which has already been increased recently by the new Canadian income tax requirements).

Extensive research has been conducted recently into possible accounting methods for portraying the income and financial position of a life insurance company in a way that would be more nearly equivalent to the financial reporting of a commercial company. In December 1970 the AICPA Committee on Insurance Accounting and Auditing issued an exposure draft of a study "Audits of Life Insurance Companies" (hereafter referred to as the "Audit Guide"). In May of 1971 the joint Actuarial Committee on Financial Reporting (hereafter the Joint Actuarial Committee) of four North American actuarial societies published a commentary on the Audit Guide. These two publications have greatly illuminated the problems in financial reporting for life insurance companies.

The heart of the Audit Guide accounting proposals lies in its advocacy of the 'natural reserve' method for calculation of actuarial reserves (either implicitly or separately reflecting the deferral and amortization of initial policy acquisition costs). A brief explanation follows:

1. A natural reserve premium for a policy group is the level premium that together with expected net investment income will be just sufficient to meet the expected costs under the policy for benefits, withdrawals, and company expenses. That is to say, the natural reserve premium is a break-even premium; the difference between it and the gross premium represents the loading built-in to the gross premium for profit and margin of safety.

2. The natural reserve for a given group of policies at a given date is the amount of natural reserve premiums received since policy issue date minus the amounts of mortality, withdrawals and expenses originally estimated for the period to that date plus interest accumulated at the estimated rate in that period. Since

policy acquisition costs are typically heavy in the first year or two of a policy's life the natural reserve could be a negative (debit) figure during that period.

3. If natural reserve accounting is adopted, as recommended by the Audit Guide, and if actual experience of costs and investment earnings should be exactly equal to the estimates on which the natural reserve premium is based, the statement of operations would show a profit equal to the spread between the gross premiums received and natural reserve premiums.* On an individual policy this profit element would be a steady amount year by year. On a group of policies the profit reported would decline over the years as policies were terminated by surrender or death, but the percentage of this profit element to gross premiums received would remain constant. Gains or losses would also be reported year by year in addition to this profit loading element as actual experience of costs and interest earnings deviated from the assumptions built-in to the natural reserve premium.

4. This general description requires modification in one respect to fit the Audit Guide recommendations. The Guide states that acquisition costs used in the natural reserve calculation should be those actually incurred rather than those assumed at the time of policy issue. The mechanics of this adjustment are not clear, nor is its motive explained. It may be, however, it was felt that if actual experience on acquisition costs differed from the estimates included in the natural reserve premium calculations it would be inappropriate to reflect the difference as a gain or loss in the year the costs were incurred (at the beginning of the policy's life) rather than over some longer period.

5. For participating insurance the Guide stated that provision for anticipated dividends (as shown by published dividend projections at the date of policy issue, or as estimated in calculating the gross premium) should be incorporated in the natural reserve calculation. Alternatively, where there is a legal or other restriction on the amount of participating fund earnings that can be allocated to the shareholders, it is considered appropriate to calculate participating policy profits before dividends and treat any excess of the percentage of such profits attributable to policyholders over dividends paid to them as a deferred liability for dividends.

6. The original assumptions underlying the natural reserve calculations, under the Audit Guide proposals, would be 'locked in' for the life of the policies, except on rare occasions when unfavourable developments made it appear that a whole line of business had become or was about to become unprofitable. In such cases reserves would be adjusted to reflect current expectations and a special loss recognized.

Thus, the Audit Guide proposals accomplish two things. First, by calculating reserves using what are considered realistic assumptions, validated by the fact that they tie in with premiums actually charged, the distortion caused by the conservative bias in statutory reserves is avoided. Second, the method provides a way

---

* Except for the complicating factor that certain costs which are a percentage of premium (such as premium taxes and commissions) would increase as the gross premium charged increased.

to allocate the profit on a policy to individual years. The expected profit element in gross premiums is allocated pro rata to premiums over the period they fall due or are collected, while gains or losses resulting from deviations between expected and actual costs and revenues are assigned to the period in which they occur. While this represents one way to reflect income in the life insurance industry, it is not entirely free from question, and warrants some further comment:

1. The tie-in of profit recognition to the time of premium collection is something less than ideal. In the extreme case of the single premium policy it means that all the expected profit on the policy is recognized at the sale date. One would expect, rather, that profit would be considered 'earned' only as the insurance company rendered service – that is over the life of the policy. The suggestions made by the Joint Actuarial Committee (described later) seem better designed to achieve this objective of generally accepted accounting principles.

2. The choice of assumptions made in calculating the natural reserve premium may have a significant effect on the profit figure emerging as time progresses. For example, two companies might quote identical premiums for identical policies but one company might estimate relatively high policy service costs offset by relatively high interest earnings, while the other company estimated lower levels for both items. On the natural reserve method, the company that estimated high on service costs and high on interest would show relatively more favourable results in the early years of the policy life when interest is a negligible factor in policy experience. The situation would reverse itself in the later years of the policy as interest became a more important factor.

3. Moreover the nature of an insurance policy is such that a policy that is profitable over the whole of its life may appear to be unprofitable at particular periods. This is because the earned interest rate assumption will be held constant perhaps over the whole life of the policy while the actual expectation is that at some times the actual rate of interest earnings will be less and at other times more. Thus, even if interest rates follow a normal expected course, there will be periods when actual interest earnings are below the standard policy rate and other periods when they are above, and this will be reflected in annual reported earnings. This pattern of fluctuations in gains or losses reported from the interest factor may well be accentuated for those policies where the interest rate assumption in the natural premium is changed in steps over the life of the policy.

4. The natural reserve theory seems less convincing for participating policies than it does for non-participating policies. Gross premiums for participating insurance are not established on the basis of realistic expected assumptions as to future costs and interest earnings associated with the policy. Rather the premiums are set more or less to cover the worst situation that can arise, with the expectation that more favourable actual results will permit dividends to policyholders which in reality are closer to refunds of premiums than anything else. Thus an objective calculation of natural premium factors is not required to be made in arriving at participating policy premiums, and they will have to be made up to apply the method to this type of business.

5. The fact that in Canada the distribution to shareholders of profits from the participating business is limited to a small percentage of dividends credited to

policyholders suggests the strong desirability of segregating the results of the Par and Non-Par business in the financial statements and bringing in to the income reported for shareholders only the maximum share of reported Par profits to which they might become entitled. Also inasmuch as the amount that could legally be distributed would be controlled by profits calculated on the statutory reserve basis, it should be indicated how much of the higher profits reported on the natural reserve basis would not be available for current distribution.

For the most part the foregoing comments are not criticisms of the natural reserve proposals but rather are explanations of the inherent limitations to the significance of annual income figures for long-term contracts such as life insurance policies. Analysts will need to bear in mind the special nature of the insurance business in assessing its reported results. In view of these factors a suggestion of the Joint Actuarial Committee that companies provide an analysis of gain or loss by source is particularly appropriate.

The response of the Joint Actuarial Committee contained many useful suggestions for improvement or modification of the recommendations of the Audit Guide. Of particular significance was the suggestion that there could be other approaches than the natural reserve method to the distribution of income over the life of policy contracts. In general it was suggested that any approach should recognize that a life insurance company took a long-term risk when it issued a policy, and the income from the policy should be distributed in a way which recognized the company's 'release from risk' as time passed. (By this test, for example, recognition of total expected profit on a single premium policy at the time the premium is paid would be unacceptable.)

The Joint Committee felt that a number of methods could be devised to implement the release from risk concept and that it was not necessary to prescribe just one for general use. If just one was to be selected however, the Committee expressed a preference for use of 'percent completion of contract' reserves as producing a sounder matching (and incidentally a more conservative approach) than the natural reserve method.

The 'percent completion of contract' method calls for the actuary to increase the natural reserve premium by adjusting his most realistic estimates of future interest, mortality, etc. by a conservative factor so that the premium required is increased to equal the gross premium actually charged. The effect of calculating reserves on this basis is to eliminate recording a profit on the spread between the gross premium and the natural reserve premium when the premium is received. Instead, profit emerges only as the conservative provision made in reserves in early years is released and proved by experience not to be required.

The Joint Committee considered this method appropriate because it keeps something in reserve against the possibility of future experience that is worse than the 'most likely' assumptions allowed for in natural reserves. The method also has two advantages from the accounting point of view. First, and more important, the method spreads the profit element in the premium over the whole life of the policy rather than just over the premium paying period. Second, by relating the profit recognition to the three elements – 'investment return', 'benefit payments' and 'other expenses', the method recognizes in a rough way that it is through providing these functions, investment management, insurance protection and administration, that the insurance company becomes entitled to its profit. This latter argument cannot be pushed too far however. The Joint Committee does not suggest what weight should be assigned to each factor and it would appear this decision is to be taken arbitrarily.

Finance companies

As has already been indicated, the important question of accounting principle in finance companies is the choice of a basis for recognition of revenue on precomputed contracts. The different methods adopted in practice affect the distribution of income reported over the life of a contract with some methods resulting in a higher percentage of total revenue being recognized as earned in the early months of a contract life. In a growing business, such revenue recognition methods will result in higher net income being reported than other methods and vice versa. The difference in results is accentuated the longer the term that the average contract is outstanding.

In spite of these differences in method, which in some cases may reflect differences in the kinds of business carried on by a company, the accounting policies of finance companies are considered to be in accordance with generally accepted accounting principles.

A notable recent development has been the Cansaf long-form report which is now available to interested parties, containing much detailed financial information concerning, among other things, the breakdown of receivables outstanding by type and term, information re maturities of debt, re the company's method of taking-up income and so on.

Mutual investment funds

One dominant characteristic of mutual funds distinguishes them from other financial intermediaries – namely that the fund is required to stand ready to redeem shares or units in the fund at short notice at their net asset value per share. This fact is of overwhelming importance for the accounting. It means that:

1. The most useful basis for reporting assets of the fund is the value at which they enter into the calculation of net asset value per share.

2. The distinction between realized and unrealized gains or losses is virtually irrelevant for the fund's shareholder or prospective investor.

It follows from this that generally accepted accounting principles when applied to mutual funds require that assets be valued at fair value since this is the most useful information. Somewhat inconsistently gains or losses on investments during a fiscal year (whether realized or unrealized) are not included in the statement of income. This discrepancy is relatively unimportant since (a) what happened last year to the value of the portfolio is a very unreliable indicator of what may be expected in future years and (b) the holder of a unit obtains a very quick, clear idea of what has happened to values by examining the figure of net asset value per share which appears in the statement of net assets and shareholders' equity (balance sheet).

The requirement that assets be carried at a current value in the balance sheet creates problems in implementation to the extent that some assets are not liquid. Market quotations will be used when available but may be departed from if the market price is determined by thin trading and the block of securities to be valued is relatively large. Unquoted securities have to be valued at a fair appraisal by the directors. Where the fund has acquired stock in a private placement and has given an 'investment letter' expressing the fund's intention not to sell the stock, the value of the stock is restricted by its lack of liquidity, but the precise legal effect of the letter is not clear in Canada. Such letter stock is usually obtained by the fund at a discount from the market price (if such exists) of previously issued stock of the same company. As a normal rule, letter stock would not be valued at a figure higher than that derived by applying the same percentage discount from the current market value of the unrestricted stock of the same issue as the discount which obtained when the stock was acquired. A lower value may, of course, be appropriate in all the circumstances. SEC Accounting Series Release No. 113 (October 21, 1969) emphasizes the importance of fair valuation of restricted stock and stresses that no automatic formula can be appropriate for all situations.

Pension funds

Not many statements of Canadian pension funds are publicly available so their accounting practices do not receive much scrutiny. From a limited private survey it was found that most funds account for their investments on the traditional basis of cost less allowances for value declines where they are considered enduring. Amortization of discounts and premiums on fixed interest, fixed maturity investments is frequently ignored because of the bookkeeping work involved. Similarly, accrued income at statement dates is sometimes not picked up.

The majority of pension fund statements are confined to statements showing funds received, invested and paid out. The actuarial obligation under the pension plan is usually not included in the statement. This limits the usefulness of the statement to that of a report on the stewardship of the fund trustees over the monies entrusted to them.

Chapter 12 referred to consideration being given by actuaries in recent years to the desirability of, and best method for, reflecting long-term appreciation in the assets of pension funds. As yet, such adjustments are normally made by actuaries as part of their calculations rather than in the accounting of the fund, but it may be expected that if methods for recognizing appreciation of investments for actuarial valuation purposes become well-established, they might find their way into the financial reports of the funds themselves, especially if the actuarial obligation under the plan were also included in the statement.

References

1. R. M. Skinner, "Accounting for Profits and Losses on Investments", *Canadian Chartered Accountant* (April 1961), pp. 327–333.
2. Committee on Bank Accounting and Auditing, *Audits of Banks* (New York: American Institute of Certified Public Accountants, 1968), pp. 37–41.
3. *Accounting for Trust and Loan Companies in Canada* (Toronto: Canadian Institute of Chartered Accountants, 1971), pp. 9–15.
4. *Ibid.*

26 Accounting for non-profit organizations

This Chapter contains a survey of the special accounting practices of non-profit organizations. The term 'non-profit organization' includes those institutions that are organized for social, educational or philanthropic purposes in which there is no transferable ownership interest and from which the members or contributors do not receive any economic gain. This last test excludes those organizations such as cooperatives, which may be intended to operate on a non-profit (i.e. break-even) basis, but which are operated primarily for the benefit of members. Also excluded are utility and other business departments of government which are operated so as to yield a return on capital investment or at least to cover capital costs. Included are other governmental agencies and governments themselves, schools and universities, hospitals, charitable and welfare organizations.

Each of these various types of institution has problems peculiar to itself and it is not proposed to deal with these specialized problems here. The intention is rather to deal with problems that are typical of non-profit organizations as a class, as distinct from enterprises oriented to profit-making.

At least two characteristics of non-profit organizations have significance for their accounting practices and financial reporting:

1. The equity in a non-profit institution is not owned by, or disposable by, specific individuals. Its goal therefore is service, not profit. This means the financial objective will be to break even on average year by year, not to have a surplus of revenues over expenses. Success to a non-profit institution lies in the quality of its service and the efficiency with which it is provided. Neither of these will be ascertainable directly from its accounts. In contrast, in a profit oriented enterprise the net income figure is a rough indicator of efficiency and also whether its products or services are of acceptable quality. Because the income figure of a non-profit organization does not measure its effectiveness (other than, perhaps, in budgeting) accounting rules designed to measure profit (as many of them are) are less important if not entirely irrelevant to the non-profit institution.

2. A non-profit organization frequently receives funds for spending on special purposes under restrictions imposed by law, trust or merely by direction of the

donor.* This means that controls must be instituted to see that the funds are spent only for the special purpose intended and to enable separate account-ability for them to authorities, donors, etc. This leads to some form of 'fund accounting' as it is known, whereby the special purpose funds are accounted for as though they were entities in themselves, separate from the general funds of the institution.

Under these influences accounting for individual non-profit institutions has tended to have the following characteristics in greater or lesser degree:

1. Considerable emphasis on accountability for the liquid assets entrusted to it. The statement of operations for the year tends to resemble the statement of source and application of funds in a business enterprise rather than the income statement.

2. Because of the existence of special purpose funds, it may be necessary to look at several statements in the non-profit institution to obtain full information on funds spent.

3. Balance sheets are subdivided to show assets held for individual funds or fund groupings, and accountability for unspent fund balances. There may be con-siderable variation between institutions in the description of special purpose funds and the way they are grouped for financial statement presentation purposes.

4. Because of the emphasis on accountability for liquid assets, capital assets are frequently written off when acquired, especially if bought out of general operating funds.

5. On the other hand, frequently the acquisition of capital assets is financed by special capital donation or by long-term debt. If debt funds are used the asset balances are sometimes carried forward in order to maintain a balance between assets shown and liabilities. Even when the capital financing consists of outright grants or gifts rather than debt, it may be felt that long-term or permanent assets such as land, buildings and equipment should not disappear from the balance sheet as soon as the money to acquire them is spent. It is thus common to find a separate 'capital fund' or 'plant fund' section of the balance sheet containing asset accounts which record both liquid funds awaiting spending for capital purposes and figures representing past capital spending. In such cases, where capital assets are acquired out of general funds practice varies as to whether the amount of such spending on capital assets is added to the figures recorded in the capital fund section.

6. Under the influence of appropriation accounting which is typical of govern-mental accounting (and perhaps also because the objective of non-profit organizations is to break even over the long run), appropriations of unspent balances of funds are sometimes recorded formally in the accounts, reducing the free surplus that would otherwise be shown.

---

* The distinction here between profit and non-profit organizations is not absolute. Some enterprises organized for profit may hold trust or other special purpose funds, whereas some non-profit organizations may have little or nothing in the way of special purpose funds.

There is considerable variation in accounting practices from one institution to another. A substantial measure of uniformity in accounting practice may be obtained, however, within a particular type of non-profit institution (e.g. hospitals) through the guidance of industry associations (often assisted or stimulated by government support or regulation). In general, the accounting methods of non-profit organizations that operate on a 'fee for service' basis with fee revenue designed to recover operating costs tend to come closer to commercial practices than do those of institutions which obtain all or most of their support from governments or public subscription.

Thus, apart from the requirement to maintain the accountability for all funds received for special or restricted purposes, it is hard to identify principles which are common to all types of non-profit institutions. The practices followed by one type of institution may differ from those followed by another, and it is sometimes hard to find any justification for the difference. For example, depreciation accounting is generally followed by hospitals in Canada but not by other institutions.

If principles (rather than mere customs) are to be identified and developed for non-profit institutions it will be necessary to answer some fundamental questions. Who uses the financial reports of such institutions? What do the users want and need to know? The following are areas where diversity in practice suggests the need for clarification of accounting objectives:

1. Reporting expenditures for the year – Where expenditures are financed by special purpose funds as well as unrestricted funds, the fund basis of accounting may mean that the total expenditures on program do not appear in any one statement. If the purpose of the accounting is merely to "report on stewardship", a statement showing, fund by fund, the amounts received and paid out, and unspent balances at the year-end may be considered adequate. On the other hand, if the desire is to show a picture of the total operations of the institution there is need for a properly classified statement of all expenditures indicating the several sources from which the program is financed.

2. Distinguishing between capital and current expenditures – In a commercial enterprise, a clear distinction has to be made between capital and current expenditures in order to arrive at a correct statement of costs to be charged against income. In a non-profit organization it is often argued that the time period benefited by the capital expenditures is irrelevant and that the only important fact is the time when liquid funds are spent. Whatever the merits of this contention however, it would seem that the information value of a summary of expenditures would be improved by distinguishing between the normal recurring type of expenditure and expenditures on capital assets or major renovations and repairs.

3. Policy with respect to the carry-forward of capital costs – As indicated, many non-profit institutions have a 'capital funds' or 'plant funds' section of their balance sheet. Policy as to what costs are set up in these accounts and what are not, however, varies widely. In some cases only those costs financed out of capital grants or special capital appeals, or by capital debt, will be carried forward, while those financed out of annual revenues will be written off. In some cases land and buildings will be recorded but equipment and smaller assets will be written off. In other cases 'major' expenditures (more or less arbitrarily

defined) will be capitalized while 'minor' expenditures are written off. In still other cases all capital assets, whether acquired from special capital funds or general funds, will be set up in the capital funds section.

4. Depreciation accounting – The majority of non-profit institutions do not perform depreciation accounting. The argument for this frequently is that the capital facilities were originally donated with the intention that the user should not have to pay for their use, and that when the facilities need renewal new capital financing will be obtained in the same manner. Therefore, since capital costs will not be (and often cannot be) recovered out of current charges for services or current operating revenue, it is irrelevant or misleading to charge depreciation as an expense and thereby show a deficit on current operations. The opposite argument to this is that depreciation is a cost essential to the service performed whether we like it or not and should be shown as such. The misleading inferences that can be drawn from the resulting deficit can be overcome by proper statement presentation.

5. The basis for recording transactions – The bookkeeping basis for non-profit organizations also runs the gamut from one in which cash receipts and disbursements only are recorded, through a modified cash basis (receipts recorded on a cash basis, expenditures on an accrual basis); a modified accrual basis (major accruals of revenues are recorded but minor ones ignored); a full normal accrual basis; and finally, one in which encumbrances (commitments for expenditure) and appropriations are recorded in the accounts. Justification for the different bases varies. It is sometimes argued that receipts should be recorded on a cash basis since the organization cannot be held accountable for funds until they are actually received. An appropriation basis of accounting is based on the thinking that the institution will not build up any surplus in the long run and its financial statement should indicate its spending plans for all the resources made available to it to date. In effect it is a sort of accounting for intention. On the other hand many institutions feel that only normal accrual accounting procedures will fairly portray their actual financial position and costs and revenues.

To consider further the effect of objectives on reporting practices, let us suppose that the parties interested in the financial statements of a particular non-profit institution wanted to know the real cost of carrying out its program for a year. It would follow that:

1. Accounting should be on a full accrual basis. A cash basis would not be adequate in an institution of any size since there would be too great a risk of significant error through ignoring accruals of cost for services rendered or goods delivered to the institution. On the other hand the practice of recording encumbrances or appropriations for goods or services not yet received as though they were actual expenses would not be sanctioned. Appropriations of surplus to show future spending intentions would be permissible, but they would have to be clearly distinguished from actual costs by exclusion from the operating (income) statement.

2. Costs incurred would only be recognized as expenses of the year when the benefit of the expenditure was obtained. Thus it would be necessary to perform

inventory accounting if significant stocks of consumable supplies were held. It would be necessary to defer major prepayments. Logically, also, depreciation accounting would be followed in order to associate capital costs incurred with benefits received.

3. Costs financed by trust funds or other special purpose donations, so long as they contributed to the service objectives of the institution, would be melded with costs financed out of general revenue in order to show the whole picture of program costs in one statement. Accordingly, equal amounts of the special purpose donations would have to be treated as revenue in the statement to complete the picture. In effect revenues received for special purposes would be matched with the costs they were intended to finance, in proportion as such costs contributed to the overall program.

These suggestions would result in a financial reporting basis very similar to that of profit-oriented institutions. The similarity, however, does *not* result from a simple assumption that profit-oriented accounting is inherently superior. Rather it flows as a logical result from the objectives stated for the two types of accounting. In profit-oriented enterprises costs are matched against time periods according as they contribute to the earning of revenue, or the benefit from the expenditure is otherwise received or expires. The objective here postulated for accounting for non-profit institutions, namely to measure the cost of providing service for the year, leads to the same result. Costs are matched with time periods according to the time when the benefit of the expenditure is felt.

Many writers on the subject do not accept this objective for accounting for non-profit institutions. They argue that there is no point in worrying about an accurate measure of costs for a period if revenues are not going to be adjusted to meet the costs. In point of fact it is customary to finance the activities of non-profit institutions in two fairly distinct ways. Major capital costs are usually financed by occasional campaigns for capital funds from the public or by government capital grants. Day-to-day costs are financed by fees for service or a regular campaign for operating funds. Thus if costs financed by capital funds are not excluded from the operating statement a deficit will regularly appear which will confuse those responsible for administering the institution and have no other value.

This argument in effect implies that there is no value to knowing, for example, the real cost of providing hospital service, or university education. The only important question is whether these institutions are solvent. But the real cost of providing this service is a matter of considerable social significance. Certainly the institutions should be looked at from the financial aspect – is the money available to keep them going? But the other information is important, for example, in considering the question of the proper balance between public support and fees. What we are saying here is that non-profit institutions need both a statement of operations and a statement of source and application of funds. The latter is not a substitute for the former. It should not be beyond the wit of accountants to devise a form of operating statement that discloses the cost of service on an annual basis without confusing those who read the statements. But first a consensus must be reached as to the objectives of the reporting.

27 An evaluation of generally accepted accounting principles

Part I of this Study has been devoted to tracing the historical development of accounting principles, suggesting the logic underlying their development and their interrelationships and describing solved and unsolved problems in present accounting practice. It remains to attempt some overall assessment of currently recognized accounting principles.

What are the characteristics of the system as a whole? It has the following strengths. It is substantially based on exchange transactions between parties. Thus, initial recording in the accounts is based on facts and these facts are easily verifiable. Moreover, where the transactions reflect arm's-length bargaining, transaction values are as good evidence of fair value as one is likely to find. Certainly they are much more convincing evidence of value *at the date of the transaction* than would be furnished by appraisal or any other basis of valuation. Also, since most economic activity is carried on through the medium of repetitive transactions, the system is able to reflect fairly the substantial majority of activities that are carried on in this way. These factors give enormous strength to the whole fabric of the system, a fact which tends to be overlooked amid the widespread criticism of individual weaknesses or shortcomings of the system.

The weaknesses of the system in large part reflect the limitations of transaction-based accounting:

1. Complex transactions require separation into their component parts or other forms of estimation in order to account fairly for the costs and revenues involved. This estimation reduces the automatic objectivity inherent in accounting for simple transactions. Since 1940 there has been a large increase in the number of complex business transactions and also the number of transactions extending over many years in which the commitment aspect becomes relatively more important. One form of complex transaction that has vastly increased in comparatively recent years is the purchase of a business, either directly or through acquisition of a controlling share interest. Other examples of complex transactions include long-term leasing which may include payments for services or percentage of sales clauses, and pension undertakings which may be based on final average earnings or profit sharing and thus are dependent on future events.

The commitment aspect of transactions becomes important in long-term 'take or pay' contracts, or contracts involving guarantees of debt of the vendor by the purchaser.

2. Transactions not at arm's length do not provide good evidence of fair value, yet many such transactions do occur and their legal effect (transfer of title to property, etc.) requires that some recognition be given to the transaction in the accounts.

3. The emphasis on transactions in accounting means that increases in the value of assets which are not confirmed through a sale are not ordinarily reflected in the accounts. Such increases may occur by chance or may be a result of planned policy.

   (a) In the case of businesses whose activity is growing things, income is understated in the growth period – e.g. timber lands will increase in value over a long period without accounting recognition.

   (b) A failure to recognize 'holding gains' is more serious for capital assets such as investments or fixed assets than for assets held for sale such as inventory, since the latter will be turned over sooner or later and the value increase recognized (except under the LIFO method of valuation). In the case of capital assets, holding gains and current values are all the more significant if the assets are separable from the enterprise without disrupting its activity.

4. The system tends to flounder when it cannot rely on transactions as a guide. For example, LIFO and FIFO inventory valuation methods give quite different results in the accounting and yet in certain circumstances the choice of methods is an open question. Similarly, clear criteria are lacking to guide the selection of depreciation patterns. As for deferred charges and intangible assets, the problem is both one of finding a reasonable pattern for amortization and also determining a reasonable time period or other basis for write-off.

5. In a period of inflation (or deflation for that matter) costs recorded as a result of earlier transactions tend to lose their significance over a period of time, and therefore do not form a good basis for determining income currently through the matching process.

Apart from the effect of inflation, on balance the system is clearly conservative in its effect on the recorded financial position. Revenues and hence income are not reflected until sale – late on in the cycle of economic activity. Some costs are written off as period costs when incurred, even though all costs if incurred on a rational basis must bring some future benefit no matter how transitory. Where there is doubt about the proper period for depreciation or amortization of a cost the common (although not invariable) practice is to amortize over too short a period. Frequently costs that might legitimately be treated as deferred charges (e.g. research and development costs) are written off as incurred to avoid coming to grips with the problem of a reasonable amortization policy. Recognition of losses in value while holding assets is permitted, but not of holding gains (except when appraisals are recorded).

Accountants, however, are not always conservative. For example, there was at one time considerable resistance to depreciation accounting. Much more recently many accountants have opposed accruals for pension cost, or allowance for deferred taxes, or deferment of the investment tax credit (in the U.S.). Also, when it comes to recognition of losses on capital assets, the accountant is prone to avoid the issue because of the practical difficulty in valuing this type of asset and thus being sure of the loss or its amount. Although not by any means the whole explanation, these inconsistencies in part arise because the accountant is influenced by the desire to avoid estimation and uncertainty in his work, and such avoidance can sometimes result in unconservative accounting.

From the standpoint of the reader of financial statements, the conservative bias in generally accepted accounting principles may be an acceptable price to pay for a system that has a high degree of objectivity and verifiability. What is most harmful to the analytical investor is the inconsistent or uneven application of the conservative bias. Moreover, inconsistencies in the degree of conservatism between companies, particularly in the same industry, must detract from the significance of financial reporting. Yet these problems are inescapable. If we are to have truthful reporting we cannot avoid estimates, valuation and the exercise of professional judgment. If we leave open the use of judgment we accept the likelihood of occasional inconsistent judgment. On the other hand, if we do not permit some judgment, such is the complexity of business activity that we will not be able to reflect it accurately. We shall return to these problems in Part II.

Part II

Change and development

28 The development of accounting principles: introduction

Part I consisted of an explanation of accounting principles as they exist today together with a brief commentary on their historical development. The central concern of Part II is with the process of change and development in accounting principles. For, as has been seen, accounting principles do change over time. Should this change be directed or not? What is the role of accounting research and of accounting authority in the development of accounting principles? Granted that accounting principles do change, how are the purveyors and users of accounting information to be informed about and participate in the change? Finally, in what directions should changes in current accounting principles be made?

There are basically two approaches to the development of accounting principles. The first may be labelled as the inductive approach, under which principles represent generalizations of accounting methods found in practice. The justification for this pragmatic approach may be set out as follows. Accounting principles are justified by the usefulness of the results of accounting to decision-making by the users. Since accounting methods found to be commonly used are in all probability useful, 'general acceptance' of an accounting method justifies such a method being regarded as a principle. Thus, accounting principles can be derived by observation of usage.

This pragmatic, inductive approach appears to have dominated the development of accounting in the past. Accounting theory correspondingly has consisted largely of an attempt to rationalize and reconcile observed practices into one harmonious structure. Essentially this is what has been attempted in the first part of this Study. Implicit in this approach is a belief that truth – or at least usefulness – will out. It implies that users of accounting information know what they want, that all important groups of users want the same information, and that those who furnish the information know what the users want and want to give it to them.

Under the alternative deductive approach it is necessary to agree upon some fundamental premises upon which a logical theory can be built. First the objectives of accounting must be stated. Then consideration must be given to how they can be satisfied. When the objective is simple the principles of accounting may flow directly from the statement of objective. For example, the objective of recording the stewardship of the executor of an estate is satisfied readily by the traditional statement of 'charge and discharge' whereby the executor records the assets that have come under his control and his disposition of them. On the other hand, if the objective is to convey information that will be useful for decision-making, further assumptions are required before principles can be derived. It will be necessary to consider, for example, what decisions are influenced by accounting reports, what information the users need and how the information is to be conveyed to them. Accounting principles then would be those rules that would link the objectives sought with possible means for their accomplishment.

Under the utilitarian, pragmatic view, little positive action is necessary – or even desirable – to develop accounting principles, since direct action would tend to inhibit the natural development of useful principles in response to changing circumstances. All that is necessary to reduce conflicting accounting practices is to set up a sort of nose-counting authority, publish those principles receiving the necessary majority acceptance and proscribe those that do not.

In practice however, it is often very difficult to do even this. There is first of all the problem of defining the field in which particular principles have application. For example, if we are considering the applicability of depreciation accounting, on what basis can we differentiate between profit-making enterprises and not-for-profit organizations, or on what basis can we differentiate between, say, hospitals which do follow depreciation accounting and universities which do not? How do we know also what is the majority practice when there is no way of ascertaining how often the question comes up for decision, nor what differences in circumstances may have existed to justify different conclusions? Also, what is the answer when it is evident that opinions are relatively evenly divided and two mutually inconsistent accounting practices exist?

In essence the pragmatic approach to development of accounting principles has been followed by accounting authority in the past, and attempts to reduce conflicting practices have until recently been extremely cautious and tentative. It is apparent on the basis of experience that this approach will never, by itself, come close to solving the problem of conflicts in accepted accounting principles.

On the other hand the deductive approach to the development of accounting principles is also beset with difficulty. In the first place there is the intellectual problem of selecting sound premises upon which to build a structure of theory. The attempts made so far to develop statements of 'the postulates of accounting' have not been notably persuasive. The unfortunate truth is that we all have different preconceptions about the economic environment and the way it operates. As Lord Keynes said, "Practical men, who believe themselves to be quite exempt from any intellectual influences, are usually the slaves of some defunct economist." Accountants are no less subject to the force of unconscious intellectual tradition than are self-made businessmen. If assumptions are to be made therefore, they need to be supported by thorough research. Moreover, although his experience gives the perceptive accountant some unique qualifications for making observations about the economic and social environment, such observations are likely to be immeasurably improved by drawing upon the knowledge and background of other disciplines.

In the second place the internal consistency of principles developed on the deductive approach requires some recognized centralized authority controlling the selection of postulates and development of principles from them. Otherwise there could be a considerable variety of theories developed by reasoning from different assumptions. Such a situation is of course the common experience in social sciences such as economics. The difference with accounting however, as was explained in Chapter 2, is that the requirement to communicate through such a compact condensed medium as a set of financial statements makes recognized rules a clear necessity. In this respect accounting theory is subject to more rigorous demands than any other branch of the social sciences. The theories of economists have great influence on the conduct of national and international affairs but no one demands that economists get together and produce one, and one only, consistent coherent economic theory to guide action.

Inevitably many accountants are disturbed by proposals for centralization of accounting authority. They know the variety of circumstance that can be encountered in the affairs of an enterprise and rightly doubt the ability of any authority to foresee the whole range of circumstances that may be encountered in particular cases and frame rules capable of accounting fairly for all of them. There is a real danger if an attempt is made to develop accounting principles to a high degree of detail. This danger can be ameliorated however if the chain of reasoning leading from the postulates to the principles is clearly set out, so that actual situations encountered may be readily differentiated as between those to which the principle does and does not apply.

In real life choices such as that implied in this description of the inductive and deductive approaches are never simple or clear-cut. Probably, as in most human affairs, a middle course is best – steering a passage between the unchecked proliferation of accounting practices no matter how conflicting they may be, and a rigid authoritarianism which suppresses experiment and forces all practice into a confined structure not readily adaptable to special circumstances or changes in the environment.

In the opinion of the writer however, accounting theory at the present time would profit from a heavy dose of deductive logic and a vigorous effort to suppress alternative accounting practices which do not reflect differences in underlying circumstances. The other danger – that there might be suppression of legitimate experimentation and adaptation of accounting practice to fit varying circumstances and changing need – seems sufficiently remote at present that it can be ignored for the time being. It is of course necessary, in establishing an authority over accounting principles, that there be opportunity for opposing views to be heard and that there be opportunity for presentation of accounts in forms differing from the standard.

In the next Chapter the requirements of a deductive approach to the development of accounting principles will be discussed along with amplification of the very real difficulties inherent in the approach.

29   The deductive approach to the development of accounting principles

In Part I it was stated, "Accounting seeks to hold a mirror up to economic activity and reflect it, with minimum distortion, in a condensed form that all may read." This means first of all that accounting should be based on fact since it can only reflect that which exists. But it means more than this. A mere listing of, say, all the purchases made by a business in a year, showing the supplier's name, a description of the purchase and the price, would be a true reflection of facts about the business, but it would not be accounting. Accounting must convey information, and to do this the raw data or facts must be given some meaning or pattern by the processes of classifying assets, liabilities, revenues, and expenses. Finally, the information conveyed should be advantageous to the user in making judgments and decisions – i.e. it must be useful. We can therefore sum up the ultimate objective of accounting as:

"To convey information that is relevant to the needs of the user."

This statement of ultimate objective does not of itself lead directly to the formulation of accounting principles. Four questions at least must first be answered:

1. Who are the users for whose benefit accounting information is prepared?
2. What information is useful for these users?
3. What generalizations or assumptions about the economic environment form a logical foundation for principles for measuring and communicating data required by the users?
4. What practical standards should be observed in formulating rules for providing information to the users?

Who are the users?

The first problem, and a fundamental one, is the identification of the users of accounting information.* There are a number of serious difficulties with this. More

---

* It may be worth repeating here that this Study is not concerned with management accounting needs because management is able to specify the information it wants and does not need principles of accounting to ensure that it gets it. (Information which is useful for management, of course, is very likely to be useful to other parties.)

than one group of users can be identified and such groups may have various needs. Some of these groups, such as the taxation authorities, have the power to require special statements (returns) so that the problem so far as they are concerned is solved by the provision of special purpose reports.* Other users include creditors, investors, members of non-profit organizations, special interest groups such as labour unions, and society generally, as represented by government agencies responsible for the collection of statistics, the administration of anti-combines legislation and so on. These groups often have to make do with general purpose statements which may be less than perfectly adapted to their needs. For example, for purposes of economic statistics the 'separate enterprise' theory of the accounting entity is probably more useful than the 'proprietary' theory, but the latter generally prevails under the influence of investor-oriented accounting.**

An obvious answer to the problem of different groups of users would be to present information in several forms, i.e. prepare financial statements on several bases. Although this possibility has been recognized for many years there has been, historically, a reluctance to adopt this course. There are probably several reasons for such reluctance:
- The additional work caused by preparing information on several different bases, and the difficulty in adequately explaining them.
- The danger that the differences between various bases may not be properly understood, and erroneous conclusions may be drawn.
- Possibly the danger that presentation of statements on several bases may undermine the confidence of readers in *all* statements. There is an instinctive supposition in the minds of those unfamiliar with the problems that there can only be one 'true' figure for 'income' or 'cost'. Presentation of several figures, even if carefully described and differentiated, could be upsetting to those who have this feeling.

As a practical matter therefore, there are distinct limitations on the desirability of multi-value financial reporting. Probably, however, accounting could go farther in this direction than it has yet gone.

What information is useful?

In spite of the fact that accounting information is produced primarily to be useful to a particular group of users, there is very little communication of their needs by the users to those who furnish accounting information. Some writers have suggested the need for much more research into what users want to guide the develop-

---

* Its solution creates another problem however, since there is often a reluctance on the part of management to produce accounting information in more than one form – "to keep two sets of books". Probably the best example of this tendency is given by the observed fact that many businesses adopted diminishing balance depreciation patterns after the change in the Canadian Income Tax Act in 1949, and have continued with these patterns in spite of the fact that frequently they are inappropriate for fair measurement of income.

** On the other hand, as indicated in Chapter 25, the whole body of accounting rules for certain regulated financial institutions, such as life insurance companies, has been so adapted for the purposes of policy holder or depositor protection that the usefulness of their financial statements for investor purposes is seriously diminished.

ment of accounting principles. But this raises questions also. For example, most experts would agree that the cost of acquisition of an investment held (or any other asset for that matter) has no relevance to a decision whether or not the investment should be held or sold today. Yet accountants regularly find that those responsible for making decisions *want* to know the cost (or book value) figures before making decisions. To some extent, of course, this reflects the reluctance on the part of managers to "show a loss" that may put their management in a bad light. But more than this, there seems to be an intuitive feeling that cost is relevant. In such situations should accounting be geared to give the users the information they want, even though it is not logically relevant to their decision-making, or should there be some independent assessment by accountants of the worth of the information made available?

In the absence of any direct communication of users' needs, accounting has proceeded on certain implicit assumptions as to the information desired. In the early period of modern accounting, as has been indicated, the aim was to produce a statement of worth. In the last 30 years the emphasis shifted to a statement of income, with the balance sheet being relegated to a position of second place. More recently a statement of funds flow, or changes in financial position, has received strong support. Accounting principles and practice have developed under the guidance of these unwritten and unspoken assumptions as to needs.

The influence of assumptions as to information needed can be illustrated by brief consideration of possible alternatives. Suppose for example that the information desired was considered to be a statement of return on investment. If this were so, the practice of writing off goodwill against retained earnings – now permissible in Canada – would obviously be unacceptable because it would understate investment. The LIFO inventory convention, now used as an aid to a better calculation of income, would probably not be acceptable because of the unrealistic figure it yields for investment in inventory after price levels have changed – and in general, the question of current values for assets owned would become even more important than it is now. Or consider the somewhat belated recognition now being given in accounting to the users' need for reliable figures of earnings per share. A whole new series of accounting principles is required for the proper calculation of such figures, giving guidance how to deal with such problems as share issues part way through a year, two class common shares, potential dilution from conversion and option rights, etc.

If, however, we accept for purposes of further discussion that the users' primary need from accounting is a reliable statement of income, and secondly a statement giving some detail of assets held and liabilities owed, we still have to specify much more precisely what is meant by income, assets and liabilities for the purpose at hand. In other words we have a problem of defining, describing and specifying what is required to meet the felt needs of the users. It is here that many accounting writers are led astray. They start with a proposition that users want a statement of income. They then search for a definition of income, and select, for example, the economist's definition "income is the amount an entity can spend and still be as well off at the end of the period as at the beginning" as being the 'true' definition. They then readily demonstrate that the accounting process does not yield a figure of income anything like the definition selected. They then proceed to suggest changes in accounting principles aimed at coming much closer to their definition of income, with little consideration as to whether in the process of changing principles the resulting accounting might become less, rather than more, relevant to the users' needs.

If we consider the needs of investors as predominant, for example, we must ask ourselves what the investors want by way of information. It is not enough to say they want a statement of income, we must ask *why* they want a statement of income. Two major reasons, among others, are:

1. As a guide to the value of their investment.

2. As an aid in assessing management performance.

Income is only a guide to value, of course, if it can be assumed that the income earned in the past will be repeated in the future. Therefore the investor does not just want to know how much better off the business was in the period, he wants to know whether the gain was the result of regular recurring business operations or was a once-in-a-lifetime gain on assets held. Likewise, to evaluate management, he wants to know to what extent profit or loss was attributable to management direction and to what extent it was fortuitous.

This is not to say it is wrong to have an ideal in mind as to concepts embodied in accounting statements. On the contrary an ideal goal, even if unattainable by reason of practical difficulties, is necessary to give coherence and direction to accounting rules. What is meant is that these ideals have to be carefully considered in the light of users' needs and spelled out. A brief all-purpose definition of income may not be very satisfactory as a guide to principles in action.

What useful generalizations or assumptions can be made about the economic environment?

In Chapter 3 on concepts underlying accounting principles three observations about the economic environment were listed, namely (1) economic activity is carried on by identifiable entities, (2) most enterprises are operated on a continuing basis, and (3) the existence of an exchange economy permits a system of accounting in monetary terms. Appendix A (supplement to Chapter 3) contains an amplification of the significance of these concepts to currently recognized accounting principles. It is probably fair to say, however, that the relationship between these 'postulates'* and accounting principles is not very direct.

One would think that postulates with greater operational content could be derived from consideration of the information desired by users. If users want statements of wealth and measurement of changes in wealth one of their primary concerns must be with values and changes in values. The following list suggests

---

* The term 'postulate' has been used with a variety of meanings. An AICPA Committee described postulates as ". . . the basic assumptions on which principles rest. They necessarily are derived from the economic and political environment and from the modes of thought and customs of all segments of the business community". This definition broadly describes the sense in which the term is used here. Some accountants, however, argue that the only postulate of accounting is 'fairness'. Such use of the term is closer to a description of the objective of accounting rather than to axioms which can be derived by empirical observations of the economic and political environment.

a number of possible observations concerning the economic environment that might lead to accounting principles which are valid in the light of these concerns.

Observation or 'postulate'	Significance for accounting principles
1. Most goods and services are distributed through transactions bargained at arm's length.	Costs resulting from arm's-length transactions are the best evidence of value at the time of the transaction.
2. Cash to be received in future is not worth as much as cash in hand, both because creditors demand a reward for waiting for payment and because of risk of non-collectibility.	Values assigned to assets and liabilities should be discounted to recognize both risk and payment delay factors.
3. An asset acquired for business purposes as opposed to personal consumption has value only insofar as it is likely to result in net cash receipts in future.	Where cash flows are predictable a possible basis of asset valuation is discounted cash flow.
4. The purchasing power of a currency changes over time.	Gains and losses of purchasing power result from holding monetary assets and liabilities and should be measured to give complete information.
5. Profit (value added) from a business is attributable to the whole activity carried on.	In theory value increases (profits) should be recognized as work is done. Consequently postponement of profit recognition, until some critical event (such as sale), is only satisfactory if the scale of operations is fairly constant and the critical event occurs on a regular recurring basis.
6. Gain or loss may result from business activity or from mere holding of assets.	While the critical event basis for revenue recognition may be satisfactory for repetitive business activity, postponement of recognition of gain or loss on assets held for investment or for speculation until realization is undesirable.
7. Investment in a project or in individual capital assets, if rational, is predicated on a calculation that net returns from the investment will recover cost plus an acceptable rate of return on the investment. Any benefit associated with capital investment will be treated as a reduction of capital cost (or an increase	In the normal case government capital assistance should be treated as an offset to capital costs, rather than a gain of the year in which the assistance is received.

in project returns) in a project feasibility study. Therefore, government assistance, whether by way of direct grant, or indirectly by way of income tax reductions, will encourage investment. If such assistance is available to one entity only, it may serve to make an uneconomic, or marginal, project economic. If such assistance is generally available the forces of competition should tend to reduce project output prices to the point where the rate of return is reduced to the former acceptable rate.

This list is intended to be illustrative only, not exhaustive. An adequate survey of possible postulates would require much more extended consideration.

Practical standards for the formulation of accounting principles

After definition of the users' information needs and identification of observations about the environment which relate to such needs, the next step is to consider how such needs can be met in practice. Only at this stage is it possible to formulate accounting principles. It is a truism to say that ideals are rarely attainable. Anyone familiar with business must be aware of the difficulty – in large measure the impossibility – of precise measurement of certain intangible factors which are an essential ingredient of economic income. What is the goodwill of a business and how much has it increased over the most recent accounting period? What will be the useful life of fixed assets and accordingly what is a fair proportion of their cost that should be charged off in the determination of income? Accounting is full of approximations and unverifiable presumptions. The best that can be hoped for is that it will point generally in the right direction, and that users will be cognizant of its limitations.

To say this is not, as some seem to think, a counsel of despair. Rules which are practical and which are pointed in the right direction produce a better answer than no answer, especially if the reader knows of any bias inherent in them. A compass does not point to the true north but to magnetic north. However, if we want to get to the true north, it is still useful to have a compass even though it will not in itself lead us to the exact spot.

There must then be a decision as to what rules are most useful having regard to all the circumstances. Essentially such determination is a matter of judgment which must be arbitrary. Certain standards for the exercise of judgment may be suggested, however.

To be relevant to users, it is submitted that accounting information should have the following characteristics:

1. It must be reliable.
2. It must be effectively communicated to the users.
3. It should be worth its cost.

If given accounting principles produce information that fails to meet any of these tests, the principles are unacceptable. The meaning of these criteria is enlarged upon below:

(a) Reliability – If users are going to take action on information, they will want to be able to depend on it. Essentially this means that the information must be measurable and thus verifiable to some degree. The Committee to prepare a statement of basic accounting theory of the American Accounting Association stated that "verifiability requires that essentially similar measures or conclusions would be reached if two or more qualified persons examined the same data. It is important because accounting information is commonly used by persons who have limited access to the data. The less the proximity to the data, the greater the desirable degree of verifiability becomes."[1] The scope of information acceptable from the standpoint of reliability could probably be expanded if the practice developed of indicating the range of possible error in the measurement (plus or minus) and/or the degree of probability that the measurement is correct within the limits stated.

(b) Communicability – Accounting statements are necessarily compressed representations of reality, which poses a difficult problem in communication. Given this constraint, the following will contribute to understanding by users:

(i) Freedom from bias – Since users normally have no access to the basic data of the accounting statements, they are entirely dependent on a fair presentation. The AAA Committee defines freedom from bias as follows: "Freedom from bias means that facts have been impartially determined and reported. It also means that techniques used in developing data should be free of built-in bias."[1]

(ii) Quantifiability – As has been pointed out earlier, expression in monetary terms, or more broadly in statistical terms, is the only way to convey a great deal of economic information in a brief statement. Some information of course cannot be expressed in quantitative terms and such additional means of communication as explanatory notes to statements must be resorted to.

(iii) Disclosure – The information required over and above quantitative data includes definitions of terms where such are not necessarily clear in their context, explanations of accounting methods followed unless these are clearly evident, indications which of possible alternative accounting methods have been followed if more than one method could have been selected in the circumstances, indication of any inconsistency with accounting methods followed in previous periods and a clear statement of its effect, and an indication of the result of judgment where the accounting method followed required judgment decisions (e.g. the judgment decision as to the useful lives of assets required in depreciation accounting).

(iv) Simplicity – Broadly speaking, the difficulty in seeing the forest increases proportionately with the number of trees. Too much information can be almost as inimical to human understanding as too little. Accounting information should be presented simply, without gobbledygook. Here the criterion of materiality is applicable. If information separately presented is of insignificant importance, by and large it is better merged with the aggregate of the most closely related material data.

(v) Timely periodic reporting – To be useful information must be available promptly. In addition it should be furnished often enough to indicate trends, without coming out so often that real trends are obscured by the minor fluctuations characteristic of all economic activity. This criterion would indicate the need for establishing a regular reporting cycle, with provision for special reports upon the occurrence of non-recurring events of special importance.

(c) Practicality – Finally, there is the common sense criterion that information should be worth the cost required to prepare it. This may seem so obvious that it needs no elaboration. But it opens up a considerable field for speculation. The value of information supplied, for example, may depend on whether the user is sufficiently intelligent to use it so as to obtain the potential payoff. If it is not so used efforts to educate the user may be the right response rather than ceasing to supply the information.

To sum up – To develop a structure for logical deduction of accounting principles we need:

1. A statement of the overall objective of accounting – to convey information about the accounting entity that is relevant to the needs of the users.

2. Identification of the users whose needs are to be considered – it is the proposition of this Study that, whether or not we think it desirable, existing accounting principles are primarily aimed to meet the needs of investors. (On the other hand, in certain areas where the investor interest is absent or not predominant, as in non-profit organizations or financial institutions, the users of information are not well-defined and this contributes to the fuzziness of accounting principles in these areas.)

3. Identification of the concepts that are considered to be relevant to the needs of the users, and definition of such concepts in terms that would be ideal (if attainable) for the users. We refer here to such concepts as income, asset, liability, working capital, net worth, etc.

4. Identification of assumptions or 'postulates' about the economic environment and its working that may form the premises upon which accounting rules ideally should be built.

5. Identification of criteria to be applied in the development of operational accounting rules to give practical expression to the ideal concepts selected under 3 above.

In diagrammatic form the above process can be set forth as follows:

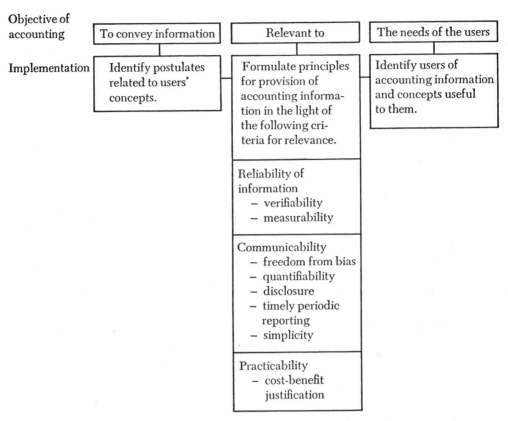

Objective of accounting	To convey information	Relevant to	The needs of the users
Implementation	Identify postulates related to users' concepts.	Formulate principles for provision of accounting information in the light of the following criteria for relevance.	Identify users of accounting information and concepts useful to them.

		Reliability of information
		  – verifiability
		  – measurability	

		Communicability
		  – freedom from bias
		  – quantifiability
		  – disclosure
		  – timely periodic reporting
		  – simplicity	

		Practicability – cost-benefit justification	

What must strike one immediately from examination of this diagram is that at every turn decisions are required whose rightness depends on judgment, experience, and lack of bias. What is also obvious is the need for much more research than has been accomplished to date into questions such as:

– Who are the users of accounting statements?
– What information do they need to aid in decision-making?
– What is the potential value of such information?
– What costs are involved in provision of information beyond that now generally furnished?
– What observations can be made about the economic and social environment that are valid foundations for accounting principles? What is the evidence to substantiate such observations?
– How much information can be conveyed in general purpose statements without overwhelming the user's powers of comprehension?
– What alternative media are available for supplying information of value for special purposes?

It would seem probable that disciplines other than accounting may have solved questions similar to these in other contexts and could make valuable contributions to such research.

References

1. *A Statement of Basic Accounting Theory* (Evanston, Ill.: American Accounting Association, 1966), p. 7.

30 The formulation of accounting principles: a quasi-legislative function

Advocacy of greater emphasis on a deductive approach to development of accounting principles raises the question of who is to assume responsibility for such development. In practice, three parties have an interest in the formulation of accounting principles:

1. Managements of enterprises who have the primary responsibility for a fair reporting of their position from time to time. They have the facts or are in the best position to get them. They are most thoroughly acquainted with all aspects of the particular problems encountered in their organization.

2. The users of financial reports who need fair and accurate reporting on a comparable basis to help in their decision-making.

3. The public accountants who undertake the responsibility on behalf of the users to report on the fairness of the accounting. They derive their status in this context solely from the fact that they have no personal interest in the results shown by the accounts, and thus are in a position to arrive at an independent view of what is fair.

Traditionally, management has been the innovative force in the development of accounting principles. It has the immediate contact with the problems, and it is in a position to develop and propose solutions with a fair chance of acceptance. Users of financial reports have virtually no opportunity to influence the development of accounting principles. Certain bodies which may be taken in a sense to represent the users' interests, such as the stock exchanges and securities commissions, have exercised some influence, but mainly in the direction of pressure for greater uniformity in accounting and greater disclosure in financial reports. The accounting profession, which stands between management and the users of financial reports, has from time to time pioneered in the development of accounting principles (it can probably claim most responsibility for the adoption for depreciation accounting, the abandonment of the practice of using secret reserves and the adoption of tax allocation accounting), but until recently its efforts have mainly been directed to confirm the best of existing practice rather than to lead in the development of practice.

The consequences of this dependence on management initiative have been as follows:

1. A case by case development of accounting principles and a proliferation of accounting methods with relatively little regard for the requirements of a coordinated overall theory.

2. Strong interest in accounting methods which would serve to reduce income taxes and conversely little interest in accounting innovation that was unlikely to have that result. The pressure for widespread adoption of the LIFO inventory method in the U.S., for example, reflects at least as much its long-run tendency to reduce taxable income as it does the merits of the theoretical argument for the method. On the other hand, the lack of practical interest in the development of accounting methods to compensate for the distortion caused by inflation probably stems from doubt that such methods would be accepted for taxation purposes.

3. An interest in accounting methods that have a favourable effect on reported earnings without in themselves affecting income taxes. The widespread use of the pooling of interests accounting method in business combinations probably owes much to this factor.

4. A reluctance to tackle problems that are complex and take a long time maturing. For example, a proper accounting for the costs accruing under a trusteed pension plan is a matter of some complexity. When the adoption of such plans became widespread in the years after the last war, many managements gave little thought to the question whether payments actually made into the pension fund represented in every case a fair measure of the cost of the plan to the entity.

5. Most notably of all, the adoption of several different, sometimes conflicting, solutions to the same problems by managements of different companies using their independent judgment.

So marked has been the last named characteristic that Grady has suggested "diversity in accounting among independent entities"[1] as a basic concept of accounting.

While enterprise management has traditionally been the innovative force in the development of accounting methods, the accounting profession through its professional associations has taken responsibility for codifying methods and, through official recognition, giving them status as principles.* The profession may also take credit in large part for elimination of undesirable accounting methods to the extent that has occurred. (In some cases securities commissions have refused to accept certain accounting methods but such occasions have been relatively few.)

As was noted in Chapter 4, the professional societies became active in shaping accounting principles in the 1930's and 1940's with the commencement in the

---

* One should also acknowledge that the writings of accountants in the universities over a period of time inevitably influence the thinking of accountants both in public practice and in industry. Thus the profession, through its academic wing, may be said to play an innovative role indirectly, as well as a regulatory role.

United States, England and Canada of series of bulletins or recommendations on accounting methods. Over the years since then these bulletins have covered a wide variety of questions and exercised great influence. The citations scattered through this Study and the extracts from authoritative statements included in Appendix B provide ample evidence of this. Three substantial criticisms however have been levelled at these statements:

1. They did not deal with problems in an organized way based on a recognized theory of accounting. In other words, they did not use the 'deductive approach' as described in the previous Chapter. Instead they tended to operate as firemen putting out fires, meeting problems on which 'generally accepted' practice had not developed satisfactorily, after the problems arose and often not until they became pressing.

2. The authority of the statements was not clear-cut. The Institute committees were trapped by the logic of their own beliefs. If "the accounts of a company are primarily the responsibility of management" and "the authority of opinions reached by the committee rests upon their general acceptability" the recommendations could only be regarded as advisory.[2] Moreover, it was believed that "no rule of general application can be phrased to suit all circumstances or combination of circumstances that may arise, nor is there any substitute for the exercise of professional judgment in the determination of what constitutes truthful presentation in a particular case".[3] On the other hand, the committees evidently believed their recommendation should have some authority. "The burden of justifying departure from accepted procedures, to the extent that they are evidenced in committee opinions, must be assumed by those who adopt another treatment."[2]

3. Possibly because of their unclear authority, the statements frequently sanctioned alternative treatments and thus did not contribute as much as they might have done to the reduction of diversity in practice.

These criticisms and the preceding discussion of the division between the innovative role of management and the codifying and regulating role of the accounting profession are probably less valid now than once they were. In recent years the following trends may be noted:

1. The professional societies have evinced a greater interest in development of a coherent accounting theory. The American Institute published Accounting Research Studies No. 1 and 3 on "The Basic Postulates of Accounting" and "A Tentative Set of Broad Accounting Principles for Business Enterprises" in 1961 and 1962. These unfortunately did not command a favourable reception partly because they were "too radically different from present generally accepted accounting principles...." In Accounting Research Study No. 7 published in 1965, Paul Grady drew up an "Inventory of Generally Accepted Accounting Principles for Business Enterprises" to assist in consideration of the subject as a whole. This was followed in 1970 by APB Statement No. 4 on "Basic Concepts and Accounting Principles Underlying Financial Statements of Business Enterprises" which contains an integrated summary of presently accepted accounting principles. Currently studies have been commissioned on "The Objectives of Financial Accounting" and "The Operations of the Accounting Principles Board". The Canadian Institute, for its part, commissioned the present Study

some years ago, with objectives which straddled those of the several American Studies referred to.

2. The authority of statements issued has been strengthened in the United States, Canada and England by recommendations or requirements that departures from principles recommended in the statements be disclosed in financial statements or, failing that, in the auditors' report. Such disclosure does not preclude an enterprise from following accounting methods other than those recommended if its management thinks it proper to do so, nor from receiving an unqualified audit report if the auditors agree, but it does put the reader on notice if such departures exist.

3. Recommendations made have been more innovative, and on the whole less apt to sanction alternative practices. Examples which may be cited are the recommendations on accounting for pension costs, income tax allocation, and the calculation of earnings per share.

These trends suggest that the profession has been moving away from the inductive approach to development of principles towards the deductive approach. This implies that the criterion of 'general acceptance' has reached the end of its usefulness. In the opinion of the writer the following chain of reasoning is valid:

1. Recognized clear accounting principles are necessary for effective financial reporting. Furthermore such principles must deal with specific subject areas. It is not enough to have a broad principle such as 'match costs with revenues' if it permits such divergent practices as providing or not providing for deferred income taxes or accruing or not accruing for past service pension costs, to name only two examples.

2. It is unrealistic to expect the development of a 'generally accepted' consensus for the proper solution of each accounting problem, given the absence of a consensus on basic assumptions of accounting and the fact that managements, which are primarily responsible for accounting presentations, are inevitably greatly influenced by circumstances and pressures peculiar to their own situation.

3. It is equally unrealistic, given the same absence of consensus on basic assumptions, to expect that individual public accountants in the exercise of their professional judgment will arrive at similar conclusions on all, or even a majority of, difficult accounting questions.

4. Accordingly it must follow that 'general acceptance' cannot be relied upon as a criterion for the development and selection of accounting principles. At most, acceptance is a limiting factor to the logical development of principles, not a guide.

We come then to the position that if we expect to formulate a set of accounting principles that will be consistently applied they must be formulated by some authority. In effect, someone must exercise a legislative function.* This conclusion raises the following immediate questions:

---

* We are here drawing an analogy between principles in the conduct of accounting and laws in a society. No suggestion is intended that the legislation of accounting principles would be performed by governmental action – quite the contrary, in fact.

1. What persons or institutions are qualified to undertake such a legislative function?

2. What opportunity is to be left for accounting presentations that do not conform to authoritative recommendations?

3. What role is left for professional judgment under a legislative approach to the formulation of accounting principles?

The legislation of accounting principles

Financial reporting is for the benefit of the users. But as a group they are unorganized and not in a position to specify what they want in the way of accounting. Only two organizations are possible of consideration for the role of legislating accounting principles – the professional societies of accountants and the securities commissions.

Both of these institutions may be considered to be active on behalf of the users. Both are independent. Either could do the job. The ambit of the securities commissions' influence is narrower than that of the profession since they are concerned only with companies raising money from the public or listed on stock exchanges, but effective regulation of these companies' accounting would control that of all profit-oriented enterprises.

As a practical matter, in Canada the choice is obvious. Modern securities legislation is relatively recent and the commissions are sufficiently hard pressed to perform their regulatory and control function without taking on the additional function of legislating accounting principles. Moreover, the divided jurisdiction under the Canadian federal system is a further factor militating against effective action by government bodies in this area.

In the United States the Securities and Exchange Commission has much greater resources than any Canadian securities commission and has been a potent regulatory force for thirty-five years. The Commission has the power to prescribe accounting principles acceptable to it. Yet it has used this power sparingly, preferring to concentrate on obtaining full disclosure and to rely on the profession for development of both generally accepted and acceptable principles. There have been occasions when the SEC has felt called upon to make rules where a situation was unsatisfactory. With the increasing activity and effectiveness of the APB, it seems less likely that this will be required in the future. Thus the pattern of legislative authority residing with the profession, with reserve power in the Commission, seems securely and satisfactorily established in the U.S.

In Canada matters have not progressed so far. While the profession is the logical vehicle to undertake a legislative function, it has not yet fully faced up to the implications and necessity of the role. The Accounting and Auditing Research Committee was originally set up as an advisory and educational body. It has acquired a degree of authority over the years but that authority has never been defined. If the Institute is to recognize openly its responsibility to take the lead in the legislation of accounting principles, the status of the Committee must be strengthened, co-operation of interested parties outside the Institute secured, and financial problems resolved. The achievement of these objectives presents difficult problems. Discussion of them however would go beyond the scope of this Study.

A further problem unique to Canada should be dealt with. That is the problem of the relationship between accounting principles as recognized in the U.S. and in Canada. The Canadian and United States economies are intertwined and their capital markets are interconnected to a greater degree probably than exists anywhere else in the world. Naturally therefore, accounting principles in the two countries have developed along similar lines. Canadian accountants have looked to U.S. practice for a lead, and it has in the past been true that any accounting principles recognized in the U.S. would be acceptable in Canada. In making recommendations to date, the CICA Research Committee has always studied the AICPA position most carefully and has been very reluctant to proceed along different lines although it has sometimes felt it necessary to do so.

The development of the legislative function separately in both countries however raises problems. When two distinct bodies are conducting studies and making recommendations, particularly when such recommendations are detailed in form, it is inevitable that there will be differences in what is recommended. A good example is furnished by the difference in the U.S. and Canadian positions on earnings per share. Other examples occur in the pension cost recommendations and the tax allocation recommendations. As the professional bodies in the two countries issue further recommendations these differences will proliferate and considerable confusion will occur. There are two possible answers to this:

1. The professions in the two countries could agree to merge their legislative authority so that only one set of recommendations would emerge.

2. Provision could be made for a distinction in financial statements and auditors' reports to show whether the statements were drawn up on the basis of accounting principles recognized in Canada or in the U.S.

An argument can be made that the former solution, if co-operation between the two Institutes were feasible, would be clear-cut and in the public interest. (Provision would of course be necessary for differences in principles where differences in law or custom altered the basic situation accounted for.) On the other hand, Canadian thinking would unquestionably have more influence in a separate body, and it may be that separate Canadian consideration of accounting problems would, in the long run, contribute more to sound accounting principles than would be contributed by our joining in (and being submerged by) the U.S. effort. This is a most serious question which members of the Canadian profession need to think about.

The opportunity for dissent

When the suggestion is made that the authority of Institute pronouncements be strengthened, many people are concerned with the possibility that worthwhile innovation will be suppressed and the flow of ideas stifled by the dead hand of authority. They prefer to depend on competition in the "market place for ideas" to produce generally accepted and satisfactory accounting and financial reporting methods.

This is not a question that can properly be discussed in black and white (although it often is). The risks of dependence on authority are well-known and have had practical illustrations in many fields. It is however a question of alternatives.

Can we hope to attain accounting *principles* as opposed to a mixed bag of diverse practices without some medium for researching and thinking through the problems in an organized fashion? It is the thesis of this Part II that we cannot. This is not to say that authority cannot make mistakes. It obviously can. The question is, will the achievement of more comparable financial reports, based on accounting principles arrived at by a more consistent reasoning process, compensate for the occasional faulty recommendation?

Knowing the dangers associated with authority we can also arrange some checks and balances. Here are some points:

1. A responsible authority will provide opportunity for all points of view to be expressed and will give the widest exposure to its draft proposals. Thus there should be no stifling of ideas, at least before a recommendation is settled upon. Moreover, independent research should be fostered and more will be said about this in the next Chapter.

2. In the nature of things, accounting innovation will continue to rest very largely with management. The role of the legislative authority will, in large part, consist of selecting between alternatives, both of which have support in practice.

3. Management will continue to have primary responsibility for preparation of financial reports. If it cannot accept the recommendations of the Institute, it is free to prepare its report on some other basis. (A few companies have done this already when they find they cannot agree with generally accepted accounting principles.) If the legislative authority found that a substantial number of companies were ignoring its recommendations on a given point it would have notice that they should be reconsidered.

The role of professional judgment

In addition to the concern that innovative ideas will be stifled, many worry that strengthening the authority of Institute pronouncements will produce a rigid uniformity and deny to the individual accountant the use of his professional judgment. There is a danger here, but in the writer's opinion it can be avoided if practitioners show themselves as in fact willing to use their judgment.

There are two kinds of questions that a legislative authority may attempt to deal with. The first type of question involves merely a difference of opinion as to the proper accounting treatment. There is no question of one treatment being appropriate in one set of circumstances and the other in other circumstances. The two treatments are just mutually inconsistent. An example is the tax allocation controversy. Apart from a few special cases such as the regulated public utilities, there were no special circumstances that justified accountants adopting one practice in one case and a different position in another. And yet accountants using their professional judgment did come to different conclusions. In such situations as these it seems best that there be some medium for expressing a collective judgment. Individual practitioners, even though they may disagree with the opinion of the designated authority, should be willing to accept it rather than have the chaos of conflicting practice.

The second type of question involves matters of form and substance. Suppose for example that it is agreed that when two businesses are combined under one management it represents a purchase if one constituent dominates the other and a pooling of interests if neither constituent is clearly dominant, and the accounting is different depending on the substance of the transaction. In such a case it would be desirable that accounting authority define the accounting methods appropriate for each type of transaction, offer examples and guidelines to help distinguish between the two types, but leave the decision in actual cases to professional judgment acting in accordance with guidelines. Such decisions are not black and white and properly represent an area where professional judgment should be exercised. Questions of this type are very common in accounting, so common that we can be confident that the need for the exercise of professional judgment will never disappear.

And yet the room allowed to professional judgment could be greatly narrowed. For the fact is that in many instances such judgment has not been exercised and the result has been unsatisfactory accounting. If judgment had been really exercised pooling of interests accounting would never have been used in cases where the size of one constituent of a business combination was less than 5% of the size of the other constituent. If judgment had been used, practitioners would have insisted on a capitalization of leases with 'dummy leasing companies'* regardless of their opinion as to the merits of lease capitalization generally. Practitioners faced with difficult judgment decisions are tempted to seek definitive, even if arbitrary, rules set out by authority. In the absence of such rules they have to look to 'generally accepted' practice, and in hard cases the most elastic interpretation tends to find its follower until the principle is entirely eroded. In such circumstances the need for some authority to step in becomes apparent and rules are indeed drawn up that dispense with the need for the exercise of judgment, to the relief of all concerned but at the risk that the rules may have to be rigidly applied in situations where they are not appropriate.

What would be helpful is a distinction somewhat like that understood in law between a 'question of law' and a 'question of fact'. The legislature makes laws to govern certain situations or relationships and questions how such laws are to be interpreted are 'questions of law'. But questions how a given situation should be treated in accordance with the law are 'questions of fact'. To draw the analogy in accounting terms, it is a law (or accounting principle) that obsolete stock in inventory should be written down to realizable value. It will be a question of fact (requiring professional judgment) in any case as to what stock is obsolete and what is its realizable value. If the legislative authority in accounting seeks to confine itself to statements of principle as illustrated, there will be ample room

---

* A 'dummy leasing company' is one specifically set up to own a large facility and lease it to one (or occasionally a few) parties. Only a nominal amount of equity is put into the company and the facility is financed virtually 100% by a debt obligation. The facility is leased entirely to the company or companies that set up the dummy leasing company and the debt is secured by payments under the lease and usually a further guarantee of the lessee(s). In the circumstances, it is clear that the parties financing the dummy leasing company are looking to the credit worthiness of the lessees as their primary security. Yet the debt does not show on the balance sheet of the lessee unless the lease is capitalized.

and need for professional judgment. It would only be if, in our example, the authority went on to set down rigid rules for the ascertainment of what is obsolete stock and estimation of its realizable value that judgment would be eliminated. It may be true that it will not always be clear where an accounting legislative authority should stop, but there is no reason to suppose that it will in general go too far if in fact accountants do stand ready to exercise their judgment. There should however be some place where accountants may go to reinforce their judgment and this is dealt with in the next Chapter.

References

1. P. Grady, *Inventory of Generally Accepted Accounting Principles for Business Enterprises* (New York: American Institute of Certified Public Accountants, Inc., 1965), pp. 32–35.
2. Committee on Accounting Procedure, *Bulletin 43 – Restatement and Revision of Accounting Research Bulletins* (New York: American Institute of Certified Public Accountants, 1953), pp. 9–10.
3. The Committee on Accounting and Auditing Research, *Preface to Bulletins (Revised)* (Toronto: The Canadian Institute of Chartered Accountants, 1948), p. 2.

31 Support for the legislative function: interpretation, research and education

The preceding Chapter has suggested the need for a legislative authority over accounting principles; it argued that the Institutes of professional accountants should play a primary role in the establishment of any such authority and discussed the possible dangers to independent thought and action and to the use of professional judgment that could result from unwise exercise of authority.

Such dangers are inherent in the existence of authority. The answer to this, it is suggested, lies in a system of checks and balances rather than in a refusal to recognize authority. Some constraints on authority have been described. We suggest below certain other proposals that would contribute towards the effective functioning of an accounting authority.

The interpretative function

Legislation of accounting principles in an excessively detailed form would be most undesirable for the following reasons:

1. Because of the variety of business operations and of the financial and legal frameworks in which they are carried on, no accounting legislation to deal with the details of every situation is possible.

2. Complexities in legislated accounting principles would encourage legalistic interpretations of the rules in individual cases, to produce accounting treatments that might be in accordance with the words of the principles but not with their real intent. Experience with income tax legislation must surely prove to accountants how difficult it is to prevent abuses when complex rules are drafted.

3. As has been pointed out, the exercise of professional judgment could be inhibited by overly detailed rules.

An accounting authority therefore should attempt to confine itself to a general expression of the principle under discussion, reserving specific recommendations to those cases where a clear choice has to be made between conflicting accounting methods found in practice. In making rules an authority ought to state as simply as possible the objective of its recommendation, the premises upon which its recommendations are founded and the chain of reasoning by which they are arrived at. It would be helpful also if the authority provided examples showing how its recommendation should be interpreted in specific situations. Beyond this it should not go.

If this is done, professional judgment will guide the application of principles to specific cases. Inevitably however, there will be cases where opinion is legitimately divided as to the proper application of the principles to the particular case. For these reasons it would be helpful if some medium could be established to give interpretations of the rules in stated cases. Such an agency would be particularly helpful in cases of disputes between an auditor and his client. On the one hand, managements of business organizations occasionally consider their auditor to be unreasonably rigid over genuinely debatable points and are frustrated by the lack of effective means of appeal if the auditor remains adamant. On the other hand, an auditor is often under great pressure to accept an accounting treatment which he considers of doubtful merit but finds it difficult to resist such pressure if examples of the (to him) undesirable practice can be found apparently being used by other companies. In either case the ability to refer the question to a disinterested outside party for adjudication would help to defuse the issue and reduce the tension between auditor and client.

Such an agency likewise might in appropriate circumstances deal with stated cases put to it by bodies such as securities commissions, stock exchanges or societies of financial analysts. It would have to be careful, however, to restrict itself to the interpretative function. If the issue raised were not covered by authoritative pronouncements, the question should properly be referred to the legislative authority for study.

Proposals have been made elsewhere for an 'accounting court'. Some of these however are more in the nature of a proposal for a legislative authority than for a true court. The suggestion herein for the creation of an interpretative agency is intended to be rather a natural complement to the accounting legislative function suggested previously, not a substitute for it.

The mechanics of setting up and operating an interpretative agency would present obvious problems. Constitution of the membership of the agency would be one. The most logical source of members for the agency would be accountants drawn from public practice having a broad background of experience in financial accounting problems, perhaps former members of the legislative authority. However, unless such an agency were staffed by full-time members, which seems unlikely at least at first, there would be the problem of potential or apparent lack of impartiality. A member could obviously not consider cases involving clients of his own firm. He might even have difficulty dealing with cases involving companies in the same industry as clients of his firm. Another obvious difficulty would be that of providing opinions on stated cases fast enough to meet the need. Accounting problems frequently are not recognized as such until shortly before the established date for financial reporting. These difficulties however do not invalidate the general idea of some impartial adjudicative body; they merely indicate that it should not be expected to be a panacea for all problems.

An alternative approach or perhaps a complementary approach would be to set up a technical question-answering service within the Institute. Such a service has been provided for many years by the American Institute of Certified Public Accountants. Latterly this service has been supplemented by the publication of "Interpretations" of APB Opinions. Answers given by Institute staff members without reference to a formal adjudicative body would inevitably carry less weight than would the opinion of such a body but nevertheless a valuable service would be performed in some cases.

In either case it would be valuable to publish (without identification of parties concerned) a description of the situations submitted and the opinions given. In this way there would be built up in the field of accounting principles something similar to a body of case law. The precedents so established would have a valuable influence in reducing diversity of accounting practice.

The research function

The increased emphasis on a deductive approach to the formulation of accounting principles, as advocated herein, suggests a need for better knowledge of and research into the functioning of our economic and social environment to form a foundation for the deduction of accounting principles. In the past, as problems have been tackled on an ad hoc, case-by-case basis, relatively little research in depth has been done as support for opinions expressed. The chief reliance in arriving at accounting recommendations has been upon the pooled knowledge and experience of members of the committee studying the problems. The membership of such committees has largely been drawn from accountants in public practice, and this has probably meant that recommendations have been influenced more by concern that they be applied easily in practice and be generally acceptable and less by a concern for rigor in the logical process underlying the recommendation. This is not intended to suggest that a concern for practical functioning of accounting recommendations is a bad thing – on the contrary, it is essential.

It is suggested however that certain desiderata may not be satisfied in the process just described. If a primary consideration is the immediate acceptability of a recommendation, the best answer to a problem may not be adopted because a lengthy process of education of managements, financial statement users and accountants themselves would be required to persuade them of the merits of the recommendation. Moreover if a problem involves considerations outside the scope of accountants' regular experience – as many problems do – recommendations will be hampered by the lack of basic knowledge on the part of those responsible for making the recommendation. This has been true in the case of a number of important problems in the last twenty years. For example, the problems of pension cost accounting cannot properly be evaluated without some familiarity with actuarial concepts. The problem of accounting for long-term leases cannot reasonably be dealt with in the absence of an extremely detailed familiarity with the variety of financial arrangements available and a thorough grasp of the economic effect of alternative arrangements.

In the face of these actual or potential weaknesses, committees on accounting principles have taken two steps:

1. They have broadened their membership to include members teaching at universities and members whose primary background of experience has been in industry or government rather than in public practice.

2. They have commissioned independent research studies to investigate some of the more fundamental or complicated accounting issues and the backgrounds to them. The present work is one such study. These studies have been carried out in general by members of the Institute staff, by university professors, or by members of large public accounting firms.

These research studies have a potentially far-reaching effect. First they provide a more thoroughgoing and fundamental investigation and analysis of difficult problems than is attained by a mere pooling of experience of accounting committee members no matter how widely the membership is drawn. Secondly, given wide circulation and readership, the studies may in themselves have an educative effect which may help to overcome resistence to new and untried ideas.

Has this potential been completely fulfilled? There has been enough experience to date to suggest two difficulties with a research study program, in Canada at least. In the first place there is a problem in getting research done of the desired quality. The problem is partly financial – obtaining support for researchers – but goes beyond the financial aspect. It goes to the difficulty of finding people with the ability, experience and time available to conduct proper research studies. It goes also, in some cases, to the failure to enlist the support of disciplines other than accounting or of people with experience backgrounds other than that of the researcher. In the second place, probably because of their technical nature, the distribution of research studies to date has been limited and consequently their educative effect is limited. Readership of research studies has been confined largely to the public accounting firms and to accounting classes in universities. A wider audience would obviously be desirable.

The question then is – can the program of fundamental research be strengthened? From time to time, suggestions have been made for the development of an accounting research foundation. The idea of a foundation has several points of advantage. It may broaden the financial base for research. A foundation would be to some degree removed from the pressure for immediate results and should be able to conduct broad studies of a long-term character. A foundation can more readily engage in education of the public at large.

There is a question however whether these potential advantages could not be more readily attained by a foundation in some degree divorced from the professional accounting association. If wide-spread membership in the foundation is a goal, it would seem that more might be obtained by joint sponsorship of the foundation by the CICA and other bodies such as the Financial Executives Institute, the Society of Industrial Accountants and the Societies of Financial Analysts.

Such a joint sponsorship would also strengthen an accounting foundation by affording a wider background for research. In addition if a university connection could be established, valuable strength would be contributed through the access it would provide to interdisciplinary research, merging the insights of economics and other social sciences with the specialized knowledge of the accountant.

Finally, it is possible that an independent research foundation would provide a valuable counterpoise to research done within the Institute. If the results of independent research did not agree with the Institute's own research, the accounting legislative authority would be on notice to proceed very carefully in any recommendations it proposed to make. On the other hand, if a fully independent study concurred with the research results obtained by the Institute, any recommendation of the accounting legislative authority would carry additional weight and should be the more readily accepted by the business community generally.

The educational function

It has become the practice in the United States and more recently in the United Kingdom and Canada for the professional Institutes to issue 'Exposure Drafts' of recommendations proposed by their committees dealing with questions of accounting principle. The practice has much to recommend it. Because of it many impractical recommendations are eliminated from official pronouncements, unforeseen difficulties in the recommendations are raised and dealt with, and fuller explanations may be given of the reasons for certain recommendations which do not initially meet with acceptance. But this in essence is a program of communication, not education. It does not meet the difficulty where more fundamental disagreements exist about the nature of accounting principles and the need for improvements in them.

Part of the problem at this level lies in the seeming simplicity of accounting presentations. When we stop to think about it, it is well-nigh incredible that we should expect to convey any useful information at all about a multi-million dollar corporation, which is party to thousands of business transactions in a year, all within the compass of the four or five pages devoted to the financial statements in the typical annual report. And yet financial statements do manage to convey substantial information to any reasonably intelligent reader who has a minimal understanding of accounting concepts.

This very success of financial communication creates problems. On the one hand analysts complain that they don't get enough information to really appraise a company's performance. On the other hand, other people complain that statements are too complicated for the average reader to understand. Some people complain about the rigid artificial accounting conventions (such as adherence to historical cost in financial statements) while others complain about the variety of accounting methods possible under the umbrella of 'generally accepted accounting principles'. Very few people, even very few accountants, are conversant with the fundamental reasons underlying accounting rules as we know them.

In these circumstances, the professional Institutes could usefully perform an educational function in financial accounting directed to three constituencies – its own members who are some years away from their courses in accounting education – non-accounting members of management who have some responsibility for the communication of financial results, including top management – and financial analysts who have responsibility for interpreting financial statements even though they may have only an elementary grounding in accounting. Some such educational effort would be extremely valuable in improving the effectiveness of accounting communication and may be essential to gain support for voluntary improvement in accounting and financial reporting methods.

32 Recommendations for development in accounting principles

The preceding two Chapters have argued the need for a legislative authority in accounting and suggested how it should reason out the development that should take place in presently accepted accounting principles. The purpose of the next three Chapters is to present briefly the writer's opinions as to the desirable direction of change.

Before commencing this, a few practical comments are worth making:

1. In accounting we attempt to portray economic realities primarily, not legal relationships. Thus, in accounting any condition which is expected to have a favourable effect on future cash flows is an asset, regardless of whether any legal title can be asserted to some thing. Any obligation likely to have an unfavourable effect on future cash flows is a liability regardless of whether a legally enforceable obligation exists. This point is worth making since accounting, especially for limited companies, has grown up in an environment greatly influenced by laws – corporation laws, securities laws, income tax laws, etc. Many businessmen are apt to think that the main purpose of accounting is to compute (and sometimes to minimize) total taxable income. They have difficulty grasping the fact that a statement arriving at taxable income may accurately do that job and yet not fairly present business income.

2. Essentially what we are reiterating is that in accounting, substance must have precedence over form. For example, income should not be recognized at time of passage of legal title if some other cut-off point more fairly represents the conjunction of completion of income-earning activity and reasonable certainty as to the amount of revenue earned. Leases should be treated as instalment purchases if that in substance is what they are. To say this is not to deny that legal relationships may have an economic effect on an entity. They can and do, and when they do legal relationships should be given such disclosure or other recognition in the accounts as is justified by the circumstances.

3. If we depart from legal form, of course, we lose a great deal of certainty. It must be clear that fair presentation requires judgment as to the probability of future events. Accountants are accustomed to certain types of estimates involving the future – e.g. the estimate of useful lives required for depreciation account-

ing – but many are instinctively reluctant to face new situations which require judgment estimates. Nevertheless, estimates are essential to fair accounting. An important purpose of research in accounting should be to examine areas where judgment estimation is required and to produce guidelines helpful to the exercise of judgment. An accounting legislative authority that makes recommendations for accounting practices that will involve the exercise of judgment should feel obligated at the same time to consider the practical problems and develop guidelines and illustrative material bearing on the subject.

4. Along the same lines we need not be concerned with the ultimate in precision in our judgments. We should resist the tendency to choose an answer that is clearly wrong just because it is easily measurable. For example, if a transaction is entered into today with a price payable in instalments some time into the future, clearly there should be a discount factor applied to the future payments to arrive at the present valuation of the transaction. Yet, because the appropriate rate of discount might vary within a range of plus or minus 2%, depending upon the judgment of the person selecting the rate, there is a strong temptation to use the face amount of the contract without discount, as a figure that requires no judgment. Auditors are particularly prone to want rules that prize certainty above fairness, in order to avoid extension of the number of situations in which their judgment may differ from their clients'. This temptation should be resisted.

5. In legislating accounting principles the profession must be concerned with the pace of change. For a long time the profession was too timid in coping with accounting and reporting problems. In very recent years the production of pronouncements has vastly speeded up. At the same time the aim has become more ambitious – from an objective of confirming and standardizing the best of current practice to one of leading practice. In coping with pension cost accounting, tax allocation and earnings per share, the profession has introduced complicated rulings based on closely reasoned and complex theory. These rulings are not easily understood or appreciated by ordinary businessmen or the public generally and they sometimes face the opposition of important vested interests. Also many people, accountants among them, instinctively question the need for change in established practices. In these circumstances, there is a practical problem involved in gaining and maintaining acceptance of the profession's authority. It may be that a more deliberate approach to major accounting changes and a considerably expanded effort to explain the need for them, and thinking underlying them, would be desirable.

6. On the other hand, there have been several examples of particular accounting problems, perhaps affecting only a narrow segment, that have arisen in a very short period of time, and about which the profession has done very little. These problems often relate to practical difficulties in the application of recognized accounting principles in a particular industry. They may not have a broad theoretical content but they may be of considerable practical import to the financial reporting of the industry. For example, there have been, and perhaps still are, acute revenue recognition problems in the finance companies, real estate development, and franchise-type industries. The accounting profession often receives very bad publicity because it does not deal quickly with these issues

which, although narrow, are important in their own field. More attention needs to be paid to particular industry problems.

Change and Development in Accounting Principles for Business Enterprises

To reason out the desirable direction of changes in accounting principles we must first make some assumptions as to who uses accounting information and what they want to know. It has already been indicated that many parties have an interest in the financial reporting of business enterprises. Historically however, financial reporting was devised to meet the needs of investors and creditors and these interests still predominate. As between investors and creditors, the point of view of the latter carries relatively less weight. The trade creditor does not normally have access to the statements of his debtor and usually relies on secondary sources of information such as credit rating agencies. Lenders of funds often find they want more detailed information than is suitable for investors and potential investors in shares. For them special purpose statements may be provided – for example, bond and debenture lenders may arrange to get consolidating balance sheet figures and other data as a condition of their loan. Bankers usually arrange to receive interim statements from their customers and may also ask for 'long-form' audit reports. Bankers sometimes complain that customary accounting statements do not fully meet their requirements. If so, the answer seems to be to make special arrangements to get additional information. The accounting bodies and bankers' associations could usefully work together to produce standardized statement forms reporting detailed information desired by bankers – but this would be specialized reporting outside the scope of accounting principles as such.

Assumptions as to information desired

What then do investors want to know about a business? They want to know its current worth. They want to know how its wealth has increased in the past, particularly the recent past. Information as to increase in wealth is desired not so much for its own value as for:

1. The basis that it affords for prediction of the future.
2. The light it sheds on the performance of management.

To facilitate this we need to know not only the net change in wealth but also we need to:

1. Distinguish that portion of the change which arises from additions or withdrawals of capital (including payments of a return on capital) from changes resulting from the operation of the business.
2. Classify the results of operations of the business so far as possible to distinguish between the results of the normal repetitive activity carried on and those results that are of a fortuitous or non-recurring nature.
3. Provide further analysis that will assist in understanding the essential elements of the business carried on.

With all this, investors want the information simply presented so that it can be comprehended without excessive difficulty and they want the information to have a high degree of reliability. Uncertainty quickly erodes the usefulness of information for decision-making purposes.

The distinction between 'worth' and 'wealth'

In the preceding paragraph we have referred to the 'worth' of a business and its 'wealth'. These two terms are not synonymous. Consider for example a normal operating business. Each of its assets will have a value, or rather a set of values, which may be measured in several ways. For example, the value of each asset may be taken as the figure for which it could be disposed of in the normal course of business, or the amount obtainable upon liquidation, or the amount it would take to replace the asset's productive capacity and so on. But however measured there will be a difference between the sum of the values of the individual assets and the worth of the business as a whole, that is to say the amount for which the business as a whole can be disposed of. The difference between the total worth of the business and the sum of the amounts for which its assets' productive capacity can be replaced, if positive, may be denoted as goodwill.[*]

In the normal business goodwill is an amount of some magnitude and importance. And yet its value cannot be measured objectively since goodwill cannot be produced to order and no market exists for definable units of goodwill. A frequent approach to the valuation of goodwill is to calculate a normal expected return on the replacement value of the assets bound up in the business and capitalize the excess of future predicted profits over this normal return at a discount rate appropriate to the risk involved. Alternatively the form of the calculation may be to determine a capitalized value of the whole predicted future earnings stream and subtract from this the replacement value of other business assets to arrive at a net valuation for goodwill.

The point of all this is that only when a business is sold as a going concern (or a controlling interest is sold) can there be any objective indication of the 'worth' of the business as a whole, including the goodwill associated with it. Therefore, as a practical matter normal accounting rules can aim to arrive at a valuation of the

---

[*] Elsewhere it has been suggested that the amount of goodwill in a publicly-held company is represented by the difference between the total value of its individual assets (less debt) and the value of its share capital at current market quotations. In this view, the goodwill of a company fluctuates daily and it is therefore ridiculous to bring it into account in financial reporting. We do not here accept such a definition of goodwill. On any given day the number of shares traded which establishes quoted market value is only a small fraction of the total number of shares outstanding. The considerations which influence an individual trading a small number of shares of a company, although not entirely unrelated, are markedly different from those that govern the behaviour of an owner of a controlling interest in a business who is disposing of that interest. The other view may be based on the observable fact that many transactions involving sale of a controlling interest do take place at a figure close to market valuations then current. A partial explanation of this may be that would-be purchasers (and vendors) are to some extent influenced by stock market prices, but also it may be that transactions only are consummated when the vendor's basic valuation of the business happens to approximate its current quoted market value.

wealth tied up in an entity, but not the *worth* of the entity. There is considerable confusion on this score and the point is worthy of emphasis because much of the pressure for a valuation approach to accounting rests on an assumption that in this way the worth, or value, of a business as a whole can be determined. The fact is that it cannot.

Approaches to the measurement of wealth

As explained earlier in this work there are basically two theoretical approaches to the measurement of the wealth and income of a business. One may be called the 'direct valuation approach'. It involves four steps:

1. Value the net assets of the business at the end of the period to ascertain its total wealth.

2. Subtract the valuation at the beginning of the period to find out the net change.

3. Ascertain how much of the change resulted from capital transactions (contributions or withdrawals of capital or payment of a return on capital).

4. Analyze the balance (income for the year) to distinguish the various elements contributing to it to show whether it arose from trading in assets, or holding assets, and so on.

This approach explicitly abandons the realization test for recognition of income. Its usefulness obviously depends on the reliability of the valuations and this is the chief difficulty with it. Here we should distinguish two cases:

1. Most businesses will have certain assets that are separable from it without disrupting the operations. The only problem with these assets is to ascertain representative market values which could be obtained if they were put up for sale. This problem may range from a very simple one, as in the case of small quantities of securities traded on a stock exchange, to a very difficult one.

2. In the overwhelming majority of businesses however, the bulk of assets will not be transferable without causing suspension of, or great disruption of, the business. In such a case, there is no point in valuing the individual assets even if objective market values were obtainable. Replacement values, for example, are meaningless if no one in his right senses would replace the assets. In other words, such assets can only sensibly be valued as part of an operating whole. But as we have seen there is no objective basis for valuation of a business as a whole. It has value (in excess of break-up value) only insofar as it has power to generate future net cash inflows. But a valuation based on a subjective capitalization of expected future cash flow cannot be used to measure past income, or else the reasoning is close to being completely circular.

The alternative approach to measurement of financial position and results of operations has been called a 'transaction analysis' approach (and is also known in the literature under the description 'income accounting' or 'accrual accounting'). This approach takes the following form:

1. All outlays of funds are classified among various types of assets acquired, or as period costs. (In some accounting literature this process has been described under the title 'costs attach'.)

2. Rules are devised for recognition of revenue as earned, usually at the time of some 'critical event' (frequently the time of realization).

3. Asset costs are matched either against revenues recognized, or against time periods, to determine periodic income.

4. Remaining asset costs are kept under continual review and any that appear to have lost their utility, or power to generate future revenue, are written off as losses.

The chief difficulty with this approach is that it gives no recognition to gains that arise other than through sale, and these in particular cases may be substantial, such as:
– gains from discovery – e.g. the mineral exploration company
– gains from growth – e.g. the company growing timber
– gains from holding assets – e.g. the company whose business is investing, or the company which has been fortunate enough to hold real estate that has greatly appreciated in value.

In addition, the recognition of losses on valuation is subject to the same sort of difficulties as were mentioned above under the valuation approach. These difficulties are so substantial that write-downs of non-current operating assets tend to be ignored in practice, even though prescribed in theory.

The time now seems ripe for a reappraisal of the two approaches to financial reporting. In the writer's opinion a combination of the two should be attempted. Where assets are separable from a business their current realizable value is the most important information desired by the reader of financial statements. Fluctuations in such value do fairly measure the decisions taken (perhaps taken by default, if the possibility of sale is not kept under regular review) and therefore are fairly included in income. The principle should be that current value should be shown, and only substantial practical difficulty in measuring current value reliably should be justification for not recording current values in the financial statements.

On the other hand, where assets are not separable from the business there seems much less point in adjusting their values individually to current realizable value since it is the value of the business as an operating unit that counts, not the value of the individual assets per se. The collective value of such a business will be a reflection of its expected future income stream. Direct valuation of operating assets is therefore unnecessary. This does not mean that some adjustment of the carrying value of the assets in the accounts may not be made in the interests of a better matching of costs and revenues, but such adjustment will not be made as part of a simple valuation approach. The subject of adjustment for changes in price levels over time is deferred here until a later point in the discussion.

Valuation of separable assets

Investments

Investments often represent the simplest valuation problem. Small blocks of marketable securities are freely disposable. Valuation at market price clearly reflects the results of a policy of holding such securities in the period in which they are held.

A more difficult valuation problem is presented when large blocks of a particular security are held, perhaps for reasons of business affiliation with another company, perhaps not. Such a holding may be less liquid and the business may have longer term objectives in investing in it. Yet the valuation approach is still valid since the asset will normally be separable from the business and since the dividend income (if any) from the holding will not normally provide a good indicator to its value. There are, however, some grounds for departing from current quoted market values in such a case:

1. The quoted market price may not be indicative of the price obtainable for a large block of securities.
2. If the current market value is depressed but may reasonably be expected to recover, it may well be that the entity would not sell at such a price.

As noted in Chapter 17, both the English and American Institutes have recommended that such large blocks of securities be valued on the 'equity method'. This method presupposes that the investor is in a position to value the assets of the investee company at date of acquisition of the investment, to adjust its reported results if necessary in order to put them on a consistent basis with that of the investor, and to obtain information from the investee on a timely basis. Such a presumption may well not be valid when the investor holds less than control. However, even an approximation on an estimated basis is likely to provide fairer results than adherence to the cost basis of valuation. This is a good example of a case where a valuation that is less than perfectly precise is better than one that is absolutely certain but irrelevant.

Conclusion – In the writer's view, it is difficult not to conclude that small holdings of marketable securities should be valued at market. Also in the interest of a more realistic valuation of business investments and the income from holding them, some method should be adopted for valuation of sizeable blocks (below control) of securities held. A method such as the equity basis of accounting, even though to some degree artificial, would more closely reflect the value of the investments over the long term.

Real property

Real estate is the other type of asset most commonly grossly undervalued in the accounts. Two situations can be distinguished here. On the one hand there is the case where the land use by the entity is the 'highest and best use' for the land. In such a case the land may become undervalued relative to other fixed assets because property costs have appreciated more than other costs. Nevertheless the higher value of the land will presumably be reflected in the pricing of the business product, and hence its income, so that the undervaluation is relatively unimportant. On the other hand, there are frequently cases where the land becomes more valuable for another purpose than that to which it is put, or becomes valuable enough to support a more intensive development. In such a case the increased value of the land is not reflected in the income derived from its existing use. Some disclosure of this situation should be made if it exists. In theory the best practice would be to write up the value of the land to the extent that it exceeds the total of:

1. the net carrying value of the land and buildings on the books,
2. the cost of demolition of the building, and

3. the cost of moving the operation to equivalent premises elsewhere, all adjusted for the tax effects of such a hypothetical move.

Given sufficient reliability to the measurement, the credit could be shown as a holding gain in the income statement.

Conclusion – Financial statements would be more useful if material excess values of real property, on the basis described above, were reflected in the accounts. Since investment in real property is usually a long-term proposition, and the real estate market does fluctuate, it may be that the valuation in the accounts should be based on a moving average of property valuations over a short period in the past – say two or three years. There may be some hesitation about reflecting such a revaluation in income, based on doubts as to the reliability of estimates of property values. If such were the case it would be reasonable for a trial period to carry the credit on revaluation to an appraisal surplus account. Finally, if it should be considered that even this gives too much weight to an estimate of this sort, the minimum requirement should be that the directors of a company give their estimate of any such excess value by way of additional disclosure to the financial statements.

Other problem areas requiring the valuation approach

Natural growth assets

Yet another cause of asset understatement is the situation that exists when assets increase by natural growth rather than by purchase and manufacture. This occurs for example in farming, cattle raising and forestry. It must be obvious in such cases that if the growing period extends over any considerable length of time the realization principle cannot lead to a fair statement of results of operations and financial position. The extreme case would be the forestry industry where decades must elapse before seedling trees grow to maturity.

Conclusion – Only a valuation approach would appear capable of giving satisfactory results in these situations. The writer does not have the familiarity with the forest industries to enable him to assess the reliability of estimates of value in growing timber and timber rights. At the very worst, it would seem that a careful calculation of the full actual cost of growing timber should be capitalized. Theoretically however, this would be much less satisfactory than evaluation if such could be accomplished.

Discovered assets

Assets can also come into being by discovery. This typically occurs in the extractive industries. The mineral exploration company, for example, may at one moment have total valuable resources of, say, $100,000 and may almost overnight become worth many millions. Similar results occur in exploration for oil and gas. Under transactional accounting these mineral resources receive no recognition in the balance sheet. Neither will the value of the asset be revealed even remotely accurately by its income stream. The income for a year of a mine with one year's ore reserves left may be the same as that for a mine with ten years – yet their values will be enormously different.

Conclusion – If at all possible an estimate of the value of mineral reserves ought to be recorded in the balance sheet. It is conceded that a valuation would necessarily be very approximate and would vary widely depending on the sale price of the mineral concerned over the life of the mine. For these reasons and because the discovery of value occurs as a result of a single event rather than a repetitive activity, it would seem better that the credit not be carried to income but rather be made to a sort of appraisal surplus account which could be adjusted from time to time with fluctuations in the apparent long-term demand for and price of the material. If it should be decided that such a valuation would be too unreliable to be incorporated in the balance sheet, an alternative would be to give a directors' valuation by way of additional note disclosure. In either event it should be a rule of accounting disclosure that the dollar figure should be supplemented by figures for physical reserves to the extent they are known. Further consideration of accounting for the extractive industries is given in Chapter 24.

A non-extractive industry may upon rare occasions encounter something similar to an asset discovery. For example, the motion picture companies discovered with the advent of television that their libraries of old films previously written off became again very valuable. The value of such a discovered asset is not always reflected fully and immediately in income. A treatment similar to that described above for the extractive industries would be valuable in such circumstances.

33 Recommendations for development in accounting principles (continued)

Under the transaction analysis approach, problems may be classed as:
– transaction recognition and measurement problems
– revenue recognition problems
– cost matching problems.

Transaction recognition and measurement problems

Commitments generally

As pointed out in Part I, the current rule is that a transaction receives no recognition in the formal accounts until one or other of the parties performs some or all of his responsibility. Beyond this it is recognized that disclosure should be given to commitments for capital expenditure, to material long-term leases (which are in effect substitutes for capital expenditures) or to additional financing which has been arranged. Disclosure is also given of contingent commitments such as guarantees of debt of third parties, etc. Disclosure is not, however, required for commitments in the normal course of business or of unfilled orders – i.e. transactions that have not yet reached the performance stage.

    Conclusion – The performance criterion for transaction recognition seems a logical one. However, an entity's position can also be materially affected by the existence of contracts governing future performance in the normal course of business. A long-term purchase or resale contract, for example, particularly if it involves a 'take or pay' clause, may be very material to a business. Disclosure of such commitments would seem desirable. Disclosure of the unfilled order position would also be useful information in contractor types of business and in most other businesses outside the retail field.

Lease transactions

In the case of leases of property the question is whether by turning over his property the lessor has completed performance so that the whole lease transaction should be recognized in the accounts, or whether the lessor's performance in effect is continuous through permitting the lessee quiet enjoyment of the property over the term of the lease. The argument that performance has occurred when the property is initially turned over is a strong one, particularly under a 'net lease' whereby the lessee is responsible for running expenses and taxes. The argument is strengthened if the facility is designed to the order of, or especially for, the lessee, and becomes well-nigh irrefutable if the lessee guarantees any debt of the lessor incurred in connection with the property. Arguments for capitalization of lease transactions thus rest on two observations:

1. Leasing is a substitute for ownership of property.

2. To a going concern a lease rental obligation is similar in effect to debt – i.e. it involves regular payments of known fixed amounts over a fixed term.

Such property rights and rental obligations would seem to be information of significance to the investor. The picture, however, is often muddied by other factors in the lease contract – possibly the existence of services to be provided by the lessor – possibly provisions for a type of profit sharing built into the lease rental, such as a percentage of sales clause. Technical problems in determining amounts to be capitalized also exist. Finally, where taxes are based on capital they would or could be increased by capitalization of leases.

Conclusion – Greater comparability of financial position between entities would be achieved if leases were generally capitalized. The principle should be that the portion of lease rentals not attributable to service or profit sharing should be capitalized if it can be done. Because of the complexity of the problem, however, rule making should proceed with great caution and be supported by thorough research into the practical problems involved.

Non-arm's-length transactions

The chief justification and support for the transaction analysis approach to accounting lies in the fact that the basis for entries – i.e. completed transactions – represents bargained values at the date of the transaction. The presumption that a transaction figure is fair value, however, loses most of its persuasiveness if the transaction is between parties that do not deal at arm's length. In fact transactions are often consummated at figures other than fair value for perfectly valid reasons – frequently reasons connected with an entity's arrangements of its taxation affairs. There is a rule that has some status in accounting – that an entity cannot make a profit by dealing with itself – and this is recognized, for example, in the consolidation of accounts. But this rule has not been phrased broadly enough to reach all the problems.

Consider first transactions between a holding company and a wholly-owned subsidiary. (Much the same comments would apply to transactions between an individual and a company or business owned by him outright.) For purposes of consolidated statements, the effect of such transactions on valuation of assets and reporting of operations is eliminated in the consolidation process. But what of the statements of the individual entities? The transactions cannot be eliminated there because the legal status of the entity has been affected – it has incurred liabilities or paid cash or obtained title to assets and so on. Can we say that the financial position and operations of each of the entities is fairly presented according to generally accepted accounting principles? For example, if there is a large management fee paid by one entity to another, is the income of each fairly presented after including the cost or revenue from the management fee? Some would say that since these transactions actually took place, the income account reporting them must be correct. On the other hand, it may well be that the payment of a fee from one to another was in substance a gift, or partly a gift, rather than a factor in earning income. As another example, if a property asset is transferred from one entity to the other at a value different from its previous carrying value, can that revised value be reflected fairly in the financial position of the transferee at the new figure? What is the evidence that the new value is a fair one if the transaction is not at arm's length?

Consider again the case of the self-constructed capital assets. Under the rule that an entity should not record a profit on work done internally such an asset will be recorded at the sum of actual cost outlays. These may include interest capitalized if interest was actually incurred to finance construction of the asset. (In practice many companies, perhaps a majority, do not capitalize interest in such circumstances.) But no cost with respect to capital funds tied up in construction is recognized to the extent that equity capital is used in the financing (except in the case of public utilities). In contrast, if the asset were bought from outside parties the price would normally include a profit for the vendor.

Finally, consider the joint venture to which each party contributes assets. If party A embarking on a 50-50 joint venture with party B contributes (say) a capital asset at a valuation higher than his carrying value, is party A entitled to record 100% of the apparent profit on the sale of his asset to the joint venture, 50% of the profit, or none? Does it make a difference if B's contribution for his 50% interest is in the form of cash rather than other assets? If so, does it make a difference if A and B are entering into other joint ventures at about the same time, to which sometimes A contributes cash for his share and sometimes B contributes cash?

Conclusions – The situation where a minority interest is in existence means that non-arm's-length transactions cannot just be ignored by in effect valuing them at the transferor's book value. The transaction will need to be reflected at a fair value and the auditor will have to satisfy himself so far as possible as to its propriety. It must be recognized however that the auditor, as a practical matter, can only judge the fairness of certain amounts within limits. For example, it would be a matter of opinion what is the fair amount of a management fee, within a margin of plus or minus 50%. Similarly, the transfer price for inventory products in a semi-finished form would be very difficult to audit effectively. In these circumstances there is a strong case for very full disclosure of the amounts involved in non-arm's-length transactions, including the value of sales to affiliated companies, the value of product purchases and, separately, the value of service purchases (including management fees) from them. In addition to transactions in the normal course of business, there should be a description of major transactions in the year involving transfer of fixed assets, intangible capital assets and investments, and description of the terms of any intercompany debt assumed, etc. As with many disclosure rules, it would be desirable in order to obtain conformity that such provisions be incorporated into corporation and securities legislation.

In the case of transactions involving wholly-owned subsidiaries, a treatment similar to that available to subsidiaries with minority interests would logically have to be allowable. However, rather than incur the extra expense of having an auditor satisfy himself as to valuation (insofar as possible), an alternative might be to produce a special limited purpose statement. In such a statement intercompany operating transactions (such as sale of product) would obviously have to be allowed to stand, but the auditor would disclaim any attempt to verify that these had taken place at a fair value. On the other hand, transactions involving capital assets would be accounted for at the vendor's carrying value. If the contracted transaction price was a different figure, the vendor's carrying value would be restored in the accounts of the purchaser and the difference (after allowing for allocation of any tax effects of the transaction) would be treated according to its nature – e.g. as a credit to contributed surplus if a write-up was made from the transaction value, or a debit to retained earnings if a write-down was made.

Where capital assets are constructed by an entity existing practice should be revised. It ought to be possible to record a reasonable profit on self construction in order to make the carrying values consistent with what they would have been if bought from an outsider. In the case of structures this could be accomplished by capitalizing interest (really a charge in lieu of a return on capital) during construction, regardless of how the project was financed. If the project was financed by equity however, rather than treat the credit as income earned (or an offset to interest expense), it might be better to carry it to contributed surplus account. The theory would be that the amount of return capitalized represented a contribution made by the equity interest to the enterprise in the form of return foregone, which the equity interest might have earned had the funds been otherwise invested.

When assets are contributed to a joint venture the fact that other parties have put up matching contributions may be evidence that the value at which the property was contributed was fair. If the assets are separable from the business and earlier recommendations are accepted there should be little problem since the contribution value and the value on the books of the predecessor would vary by very little. However, if the asset was a capital asset whose value was dependent on income from the business carried on and whose carrying value was therefore not regularly revised, there could be a problem. Consistent with the theory of not revaluing such assets, it might be best to recognize a gain on contribution to the joint venture only to the extent of the outsider's interest in it. That is to say, if it was a 50-50 joint venture, 50% of the gain would be recognized and 50% deferred (offset against the carrying value of the joint venture) to be brought into income when picking up the entity's share of the income from the joint venture. On the other hand, where inventory assets are sold to the joint venture, it would seem more appropriate to defer 100% of the profit and recognize it only as the inventory is resold.

Delayed payment and other non-cash transactions

Most transactions are made on terms which require payment outright or within 10, 30 or 60 days. These are customarily recorded at the contracted transaction amount. Frequently however, terms of payment are longer – perhaps extending over several years. If a commercial rate of interest is allowed for in the contract term, there is no problem. However if no interest is allowed for, or only a nominal amount, it is clear that the present value of the transaction is worth less, possibly much less, than the stated contract amount. In practice however, sometimes such transactions are booked at the face amount. Not infrequently this is done to add support to the intention by the vendor to treat the whole proceeds received as a capital receipt for tax purposes.

Other transactions do not involve cash payment, now or in the future. The rule for dealing with barter transactions is that they should be valued at the value of the asset given up or the thing taken in exchange, whichever is the more clearly evident. In practice, however, in face of uncertainty as to current values there sometimes is a desire to value the asset received at the book value of the asset exchanged. The exchange of shares for assets forms a particular case of the barter exchange problem. Here two situations can be distinguished. One is where the market value of the class of shares being issued is well established, or at least the company is well established so that some idea can be formed of the worth of its shares. The other is where a company is in a promotional or development stage and it is an open question to what extent its shares or the assets being acquired through the issue of shares have value. In mineral exploration companies the practice seems to have become established that shares issued for property cannot be assigned a higher value than shares being sold about the same time for cash. The question is, however, could shares be issued at a lower valuation? Or what is the situation if shares are issued for property when there is no concurrent public issue?

Conclusions – Although the theory is clearly established that a delayed payment transaction must be discounted to arrive at a proper value to be recorded, practice frequently does not conform to theory. The principle should be reiterated by authority and some guidance given concerning discount rates to be used. These would vary with the situation. If payment of the sale price is secured only upon the property sold, the appropriate discount rate would be one thing, if general security is given it would be another, and if the price is totally unsecured it would be still another. Judgment must be involved, within limits, in arriving at the appropriate rate, but there is no justification for avoiding the use of judgment by not discounting the transaction at all.

There are two provisos to this. Some delayed payment transactions which are sales in form may be little more than options, whereby the purchaser will only pay if he is successful in reselling the property. If the terms of the transaction are such that there is no effective way to recover from the purchaser if he does not fulfill the transaction, there would be grounds for not recording any profit on the sale, except to the extent it was measured by cash received or secured.

The operative rule in barter transactions likewise needs reiteration. It is highly unlikely that a barter transaction would take place at all if one of the parties had no feel for the real value either of what he was getting or what he was giving up.

In the valuation of transactions involving the issue of shares for property, frequently the share value is easier to establish. There are some questions however about valuation of a relatively large block of shares. Frequently the value of such shares should be discounted below current traded market value. If the block were issued in an underwriting, for example, there would be expenses of the issue and underwriting commission involved, and the block might have to be priced below the retail market to sell. In a particular transaction also the block of shares may not, in fact, be immediately marketable because of escrow provisions, etc. A further discount would be appropriate for this. A study needs to be made of this question of valuation of shares issued and guidelines published.

The question of valuation of shares issued for property that is entirely speculative in character is debatable. As noted above, Canadian practice, at least in the mineral exploration field, is to record shares issued for property at a figure consistent with the cash price of shares concurrently being offered. But can this be reconciled with the position in this or other fields where shares are issued to promoters at a valuation of perhaps a few cents a share, and some time later, frequently while a company is still in the development stage, the company is publicly underwritten at perhaps several dollars a share? This question can be argued two ways. On the one hand it may be thought that it is misleading to prospective investors if they see a large value in the balance sheet for properties and rights and do not appreciate its speculative character. On the other hand the inclusion of this figure, to a reasonably informed reader, shows him graphically how much has been paid to insiders and promotors for their contribution, valued on the same scale as the investment which the reader is invited to put up. Both points of view have some appeal, but both cannot be acceptable for general practice. On balance it would seem that where shares are issued for property or services that are speculative in character, and where there is no independent measure of the share value at the time of issue (such as concurrent issues for cash), the present practice of placing a nominal value only on the shares issued is preferable. When shares are subsequently sold to the public before the company has established an earnings record, disclosure should be made in the prospectus either of the value of the shares previously issued for property, etc. at the same price as they are being offered for sale, or (as is now done) of the dilution that new shareholders suffer in the tangible asset backing behind their shares.

Basket purchase and sale transactions

Included under this heading are all transactions where the total bargained exchange value must be assigned to more than one asset or must be divided between more than one form of consideration or both. In such cases the bargained transaction price is evidence of overall value but not of the value of the individual pieces of the transaction. However, the individual parts of the transaction must be valued if they are to be properly accounted for thereafter.

Chapter 6 contains a discussion of the problems with these transactions. A particular form of basket purchase is the purchase of a business discussed in Chapter 18. Accounting for business combinations has probably been the most unsatisfactory area of accounting in the past decade. The problems are discussed in Chapter 18 and conclusions suggested.

The problems associated with basket sale transactions have received relatively less attention. Consider for example the case where securities are sold by a company in units consisting of shares plus a debt security. In such cases there has to be a division of proceeds between the types of security issued. If the debt security carries a reasonable interest rate, the valuation of the shares can be derived by subtracting the face value of the debt from the total issue price of the unit. However, if the interest rate on the debt security is not reasonable, both the debt security and the shares need to be valued to form a basis for proration of value between them.

Securities are often issued with warrants entitling the holder to buy shares (or some other security) at a stated price for a stated time. These warrants usually have a value, even though the exercise price of the warrant would not make it attractive to subscribe for the shares immediately. In Canada it is general practice to ignore the warrant value in allocating the consideration. In the U.S.A. a proper allocation of value to a detachable warrant must be made which will then be carried in the shareholders' equity section of the balance sheet. Obviously, the U.S. practice is the more defensible in logic.

Securities which are convertible into shares are also frequently issued. The existence of the conversion privilege usually permits a lower interest cost than if the security were issued without such privilege. Thus the privilege has a value just as a warrant has a value. It differs from the warrant, however, in that the conversion privilege cannot be exercised without giving up the basic security. This lack of separable characteristics ostensibly led the Accounting Principles Board to the opinion that a valuation of the conversion privilege need not be made and separated out on the balance sheet. As a result of this decision the interest cost recognized in the accounts on a convertible security is not increased (by way of amortization of extra discount) as it would have been if some part of the consideration received were allocated to the conversion privilege. In the writer's opinion the APB decision is not well-founded in theory. Admittedly there would be some practical difficulty in valuing the conversion right and the debt payment obligation separately. But an approximate answer would have been more correct than no answer.

Revenue recognition problems

1. Fundamentally, income is the result of all the activity that ends up with an excess of revenue over costs. If we were certain that revenue would be realized, and certain as to its amount, there is little question but that we would take up income as work progresses, by the expedient of valuing inventory in progress in relation to its ultimate selling price. This, in fact, is what is done in measuring a contractor's income on the stage of completion method. Thus it is clear that *realization* cannot, and should not, be the ultimate guiding principle for recognition of revenue.

   On the other hand the majority of businesses does not produce to order on contract, so that realization at a particular price cannot be said to be certain. Nevertheless in many businesses it can be said that it is highly probable that inventory will be sold according to the price lists established from time to time. It is open to question in these circumstances whether an inventory valuation method based on selling price, and reflecting profit in proportion to work done, might not be at least as acceptable as inventory methods based on cost. The following table suggests one way in which inventory valuations based on selling price might be calculated.

	Direct labour	*Over-head*	*Current standard cost*	*Profit distribution proportionate to activity**	*Cumula-tive standard cost*	*Inven-tory value*
Raw material			$ 20.00		$20.00	$20.00
Manufacturing cost:						
Process A	$ 8.00	$12.00	20.00	$ 2.00	40.00	42.00
Process B	16.00	14.00	30.00	4.00	70.00	76.00
Process C	6.00	4.00	10.00	1.50	80.00	87.50
	30.00	30.00				
Non-inventoriable cost:						
Administration			5.00	1.25		
Selling			5.00	1.25		
Profit margin			10.00			
Selling price			$100.00	$10.00		

* The measure of 'activity' is taken as direct labour plus administration and selling costs.

Conclusions – Such a method of valuation would be impractical in many cases – e.g. where selling prices are unpredictable, or are changed with great frequency. Where it is possible however, it would have certain advantages:

1. Being based on market, it would eliminate the double valuation test implicit in 'lower of cost and market'.

2. Slow-moving stock, or an overstocked position, could be explicitly recognized by applying a discount factor to the inventory price to allow for delay in realization.

Also, where practical, it would be at least as capable of reliable and objective determination as methods purportedly based on cost.

2. In cases where revenue recognition is associated with a 'critical event' (commonly point of sale) such problems as exist appear to be peculiar to particular industries or special situations. There are the cases where a sale may be in substance little more than an option, or 'best efforts' agreement. For example, in property companies a sale to a land speculator may be made on terms which provide little real certainty of realization of cash. In companies selling franchises the sale to the franchisee may constitute little more than a promise by the franchisee to pay certain sums if successful. There are also cases of instalment sales which raise several problems. In the first place, the question may be whether the purchaser is sufficiently committed to the deal to warrant recognition of revenue at the time of sale at all. In the second place, there is the question of the division of revenue as between the manufacturing or trading proceeds at point of sale, and the financing revenue to be recognized over the term of the instalment sale contract. Finally, there is the problem of the proper pattern in which to recognize revenue on the financing portion of the contract. Conversely,

there are cases where a manufacturer may lease out his products on lease-option contracts, on terms which make it highly probable that the lessor will sooner or later exercise his option to buy. In such cases the lease contract is in substance a sale, and it would seem justifiable to record the manufacturing profit at the date of the lease.

Conclusion– In such cases as these, principles must necessarily be generalizations. Much can be gained by studying the business practices of particular industries and suggesting guidelines to practice. In the last analysis, however, fair presentation must rest on proper judgment as to the substance of the transaction. To proclaim as an immutable principle that revenue is only to be recognized on sale is to run the risk that undue weight will be given to the legal form of sale, and not enough to the degree of probability of performance according to the contract terms.

Cost matching problems

Inventory accounting

A few paragraphs earlier, it was suggested that inventory valuation might be based on selling prices, if conditions were such that revenue recognition before point of sale were deemed reasonable. If however revenue recognition is postponed until point of sale, we are left with the problems of deciding what costs are proper to carry forward in inventory. These problems were discussed in Chapter 9.

First as to the question of overheads in inventory. We seem now to have arrived at the point where it is generally accepted that some recognition must be given to manufacturing overheads in inventory. There remains, however, the question whether a proportionate share of all such overheads must be included (absorption costing) or whether only overheads that vary with volume should be carried forward (direct costing).

Conclusions – As was suggested in Chapter 9 the writer is of the opinion that the absorption costing method has the stronger theoretical justification, but the direct costing method avoids certain practical difficulties – notably the danger that exists under absorption costing that income of a period will be improperly bonused if goods are overproduced and an overlarge inventory is carried forward at the end of the period. It is suggested that an authoritative statement should be made as to the acceptability of direct costing, and that the danger of carrying forward excessive amounts of overhead under absorption costing should be emphasized.

Then there is the problem of the order in which product costs are matched against revenues. The average cost and FIFO methods are reasonably similar in effect but these differ substantially from the LIFO or base stock methods. Apart from arguments for price level adjusted accounting (which will be treated as a separate issue later) the arguments for the LIFO type of inventory method run along the following lines:
– Where product costs increase, a business must aim to recover a current level of cost in its selling price, or else it will be unable to stay in business without injection of additional capital to finance carrying inventories at higher cost levels.
– Because of this some businesses which deal in commodities subject to wide price

fluctuations follow a policy of adjusting their selling prices to reflect directly and immediately fluctuations in their material costs.

- A rise in a material cost to such a business does not necessarily mean the business is better off. Indeed the consequent increase in its selling price may make the business less competitive. In other words, a rise in the current replacement cost of the assets owned by a business and required by it for carrying on its business does not necessarily mean that the worth of the business has increased. Such a change in cost structure may well make the business less of a viable going concern. (We come back, therefore, to our earlier point – an increase in the wealth of an entity (wealth meaning the value of resources at its disposal) does not mean an increase in its worth.)

These are strong arguments. But several points may be noted:

1. These arguments do not just apply to a narrow range of industries which deal in commodities subject to wide price fluctuations and which base their selling prices on current cost conditions. Virtually every business must follow the same pricing policy if it is to stay in business. The problem of fluctuating product cost may be particularly serious in some industries, but no business is exempt from changes in its costs, and every business in the long run must seek to cover its costs. These arguments really suggest that (with the rare exception of businesses that are speculators in products rather than producers) all businesses should value inventory at current replacement cost when matching inventory cost against revenues. (It may be noted in passing that the LIFO and base stock methods are only approximate ways to reflect current cost in the cost of goods sold, and a deliberate pricing at current replacement cost would better implement the basic concept underlying these methods.)

2. If replacement cost is the most appropriate figure for matching against sales revenues then replacement cost would also be the more appropriate figure for valuation in the balance sheet.

3. To the extent that actual costs incurred are adjusted to replacement costs, there will be 'holding gains or losses'. These adjustments, related to the holding of operating assets over the period of time elapsing between purchase and sale, differ markedly from gains or losses on holding assets separable from the business. In the latter case the real worth of the business is changed and the holding gains and losses are therefore part of income. In the former case the individual resources tied up in the business may be valued at higher or lower figures, but this is independent of the question whether the worth of the business as a whole has changed. Accordingly, it is arguable that holding adjustments in this case should not be treated as part of income.

Conclusions – The foregoing comments suggest that a policy of valuing inventory at current replacement cost, and treating changes in value from original cost as capital adjustments, is logically defensible and may well be the preferable method of inventory accounting. The objections to the method lie more upon the grounds of practicality. Not many businesses are able to keep a continuous record of replacement cost of all products at date of sale. Those businesses that now use LIFO accounting probably do have this capability, but many others would not. It hardly seems practical to look for general adoption of this accounting method except by a process of proving its merit over an extended period of time. In the circumstances, the best policy might be merely to encourage its use, particularly by those companies now using LIFO or base stock. Valuation at current replacement cost would improve the usefulness of the balance sheet figures of such companies. (It might also be argued that by including holding gains and losses in a separate section of the income statement the final income figure would be more comparable with that of companies reporting on other inventory methods. This might, however, be considered inconsistent with the underlying theory and hence undesirable.)

The questions associated with inventory valuation when 'market' is below cost are also discussed in Chapter 9. There will always be practical problems in valuing obsolete stock at estimated recoverable amounts. Other problems associated with valuation at market would be largely overcome if some of the earlier suggestions were adopted – i.e. if inventory valuation were derived from selling price, or if inventory were valued at direct cost. Where problems remain, the nature of their solution may be suggested by the discussion at pages 82 to 84 of Chapter 9.

Depreciation accounting

The basic problems underlying depreciation accounting – namely determination of asset life and pattern of write-off – are discussed in Appendix A, in the supplement to Chapter 10. There is nothing particularly new about these problems. Accountants have been aware of them for years. The question is, are they dealt with satisfactorily in practice? In the writer's observation the common practice in depreciation accounting is overly conservative. Even in spite of the increasing importance of obsolescence as a factor in determining useful asset lives, the tendency is to assume too short a useful life for the purpose of making depreciation calculations. The error is compounded by the overly frequent use of a diminishing balance pattern of write-off. Such a pattern should be assumed only when the net revenues from use of an asset (after deducting repairs and maintenance costs, etc.) fall off very rapidly over time. If the revenues do tend to decline, but do so only slowly, the straight-line pattern is more appropriate, since the declining reported return on the asset will be in step with its declining net book value in the accounts. On the other hand, although most depreciation accounting is overly conservative, there certainly are cases which err the other way. We cannot, therefore, conclude that depreciation provisions between accounting entities are comparable overall.

Conclusions – The use of judgment in the selection of asset lives is inescapable in depreciation accounting. Problems in depreciation accounting, therefore, are not the kind that can be solved by laying down hard and fast rules. The role of accounting authority in this field should be directed towards improvement of the necessary judgment decisions. The following suggestions are directed to this end:

1. Studies of actual experience in asset lives should be conducted to serve as a guide in the adoption of depreciation rates. While past experience will not necessarily be repeated in the future, knowledge of the past at least forms a useful background to judgment. If studies can be fostered within identifiable industries, so much the better.

2. Companies should be required or encouraged to review their depreciation assumptions regularly – say, once every five years. Too many companies adopt

a depreciation rate and pattern and never bother to consider whether it gives the most appropriate result.

3. Because diminishing balance patterns are used so widely where their use is inappropriate (under the influence of taxation regulations) some special effort should be made to discourage them. A straight-line pattern is appropriate over the widest range of situations.

4. There may be a few situations of long-lived assets where an increasing charge depreciation pattern would be justified in theory. In recent years, for example, a number of real estate companies have adopted sinking fund depreciation for rental property. The practical difficulty with sinking fund depreciation is that because of the use of an interest factor, a very high percentage of the asset balance is left to be depreciated until towards the end of the assumed life. For example, if a sixty-year life is chosen with a 5% interest factor, approximately 41% of the asset cost is left to be written off in the last ten years. As a practical matter, there could easily be an error of ten years in the life of an asset estimated to last sixty years, and if such error overstates the life, the consequence for the accuracy of the accounts could be serious. Moreover, it may well be unrealistic not to assume that there will be increasing costs associated with maintenance of the asset in the second half of its life. In these circumstances, consideration might be given to developing a write-off pattern which would:

(a) provide for early retirement of any components of the asset likely to need renewal before the end of its useful life (e.g. elevators, wiring, plumbing and roofs in a building)

(b) be on an increasing charge basis for (say) the first third of the asset's estimated life and switch to a straight-line pattern subsequently.

Because depreciation methods and judgments as to useful lives can never be completely standardized, and because judgments may differ, companies should be *required* to disclose methods and rates used in the depreciation calculation. Such disclosure is now given only by a minority of companies. The disclosure also should be more comprehensive than is now customary. It is of little value to read that equipment is depreciated at rates varying from 4% to 20%. A table or schedule should indicate how much of the total carrying value of depreciable assets is depreciated at each rate, or group of rates (with rate groupings being permitted only within a fairly narrow range), and should disclose the consequent depreciation written for each rate grouping.

Deferred charges and period costs

The problems associated with accounting for costs which do not attach to tangible fixed assets or inventory are discussed in Chapter 11. In general, the problem is to judge to what extent costs will benefit future periods and hence may be deferred, and on what basis they should be written off once they are deferred.

Conclusions – It does not seem feasible to attempt general rules in this area. Individual situations will vary widely. The danger is, however, that because of the lack of effective rules inconsistent accounting may become possible. That is to say, a certain type of cost might be deferred one year and not the next, and possibly might not be incurred at all in the following year. It would seem desirable, therefore, to strengthen disclosure vis-à-vis such 'discretionary' costs – i.e. costs which may or may not be deferred. Among the costs in this category are research and development costs, repairs and maintenance costs, promotion costs in a consumer product company and so on. Required disclosure for each such category of costs might be:

– The amount of cost absorbed against income for the year, distinguishing between costs written off directly in the year and amortization of costs deferred.
– Description of the basis of deferment where costs are deferred, and a general description of the projects to which the deferred costs relate.

The practice of capitalization of initial losses goes one step beyond the mere deferment of costs. As suggested in Chapter 11, the *theory* is not necessarily unsound. There *are* business establishment costs, and a period of operation before reaching a break-even point is frequently a necessary accompaniment to beginning a business. However, most businesses are continually phasing out old operations and commencing new, and as a practical matter it would be very difficult and potentially open to abuse, to attempt to identify and defer losses associated with new business.

Conclusions – The practice of capitalization of initial losses should be narrowly circumscribed. Losses should be deferrable only in relation to clearly identifiable projects which are clearly separate from the business being carried on. A business that intends to defer losses should be required to 'call its shots'. If losses are deferred on opening new branches, a policy should be laid down to determine the number of months for which operating results may be deferred and the subsequent basis of amortization. If establishment losses are to be deferred in a large new undertaking, the company should state at the outset its estimate of costs and losses to be deferred and the period required to arrive at a break-even position. In the absence of a change to the planning of the undertaking, this forecast should set a limit to the costs to be capitalized and the period in which losses are to be capitalized, since if there is a cost overrun it cannot be assumed that the amount of the overrun is recoverable.

Goodwill

The problem of treatment of goodwill that does not have a predictable limit to its life has been discussed in Chapter 11. Essentially the same question arises with respect to amortization of business establishment losses (if they have been deferred) and purchase costs of such intangibles as trademarks, brand names, etc. There does not seem to be any demonstrably right answer to this dilemma. Strong arguments can be made in favour of any of the three possible treatments discussed in Chapter 11.

Conclusions – The writer's opinion – arrived at only after much hesitation – is influenced primarily by considerations that go beyond the measurement problem. It is a fact that there is usually a cost, in terms of loss of profits as well as actual expenditures, to the establishment of a business. If an entity goes into a new line of business on its own these losses are reflected as a deduction from its income until the new business becomes successful. On the other hand if an entity buys another business as a going concern it will not have to suffer such costs and losses. This is one reason why it will be willing to pay something more than the replacement cost of the tangible assets of the other business. Accordingly, failure to require amortization of purchased intangibles gives the management of the acquiring company virtually a free pass to increased profits without having worked for them. Such accounting favours the management that buys a business over the one that builds its business. The writer therefore believes that amortization of purchased intangibles should be required, as a general accounting principle, over a period and at a rate that must be determined in each case from the facts but which, in the nature of things, should rarely be longer than twenty years. Because the rate of amortization must be so greatly influenced by judgment there should be full disclosure in the financial statements of the write-off pattern being followed.

34 Recommendations for development in accounting principles (concluded)

This Chapter continues with commentary on a miscellany of questions, chiefly related to accounting for normal business entities, followed by a brief comment on accounting for non-profit organizations.

Extraordinary items

Chapter 14 reviewed the history of the development of accounting for extraordinary gains and losses, culminating with the recent adoption in the U.S. and Canada of the 'all-inclusive' concept of income reporting, together with rules for the classification of items as 'extraordinary' in the income statement. Some comments based on experience with the new rules follow:

1. The emphasis on materiality of an item in determining whether or not it should be classified as extraordinary is inappropriate. It means that management and the auditors must continually be making decisions as to whether an extraordinary item is material or not. It means also that the trend of the figure for income before extraordinary items (a figure given some importance in financial analysis) may be quite distorted by showing an item as extraordinary one year, because its size is barely considered material and showing a slightly smaller item as ordinary income in the following year, because its size is below the materiality limits. If historical summaries of earnings are to have significance, size must be downgraded as a classification test in this area and chief reliance placed upon the nature of the item.

2. It is, however, open to question whether the nature of extraordinary items can be described sufficiently clearly to avoid difficulties. Extraordinary items are defined as being "of a character significantly different from the typical or customary business activities of the entity ... events and transactions which would not be expected to recur frequently and which would not be considered as recurring factors in any evaluation of the ordinary operating processes of the business". What will be considered as extraordinary under this definition may well be a matter of opinion. Part of the difficulty may lie with the use of the

word 'extraordinary' to denote the items in question, since many events that the man in the street might consider extraordinary are 'ordinary' under the intent of the rules. The following discussion illustrates the difficulty of distinguishing extraordinary items:

(a) Gains or losses on sale of investments not bought for resale are considered 'extraordinary'. Who is to say what the intention was on acquiring an investment? Realistically speaking the possibility of resale is always present in an investment decision, even though it may not be the primary motivation of the decision to purchase.

(b) Revaluations of a foreign currency are cited as an extraordinary event. To a company with operations in only one foreign country this might be true. To a multi-national company however, currency revaluations are a normal risk of business. To still other companies speculation in currencies may be an integral part of their operations.

(c) The loss or provision for loss on sale or abandonment of a plant or significant segment of a business seems at first sight to be clearly extraordinary. But consider the large company with a large number of plants. Plant closings and relocations may occur fairly regularly in such a company. Even in a smaller company is it easy to distinguish between the closing of a plant, the shutting down of a production line in the plant, or the disposal of a particularly large piece of equipment?

(d) Income tax reductions realized as a result of a loss carry-forward are stated unequivocally to be extraordinary. This item is at least clear-cut, but does it make sense? This treatment means that the losses show up in ordinary income, but the carry-forward recoveries (which are not an uncommon feature of financial reports) always appear as extraordinary. Contrast this with the treatment of large bad debt losses. It is argued (correctly) that such losses must be treated as part of ordinary items because they are a normal risk of business. Neither are they prior period adjustments, even if the account was outstanding at the previous year-end, because the loss (if not prevously provided for) must have been caused by or made evident by events of the current period. Can we not argue similarly that tax reductions realized from loss carry-forwards are items associated with normal business operations which are not considered prior period adjustments because profits must arise in the current period before such credits can be recognized?

In historical perspective the concept of 'extraordinary items' was a useful and probably necessary step in resolving the longstanding controversy between the 'all-inclusive' and 'current operating performance' views of the income statement. Now that the former concept has become accepted however, it may be time to abandon the attempt to draw artificial distinctions between ordinary and extraordinary events. Instead it should be made an explicit rule of disclosure that all large exceptional items affecting income of the year be disclosed (preferably by using separate lines in the income statement). An item would be regarded as exceptional either by reason of its irregular infrequent occurrence, or by the fact that even though the event itself was of a normal character (e.g. the bad debt loss) the amount involved was unusual in relation to normal operations.

There may be some concern, if this were done, that where items were debatable some managements would be tempted to disclose the debits (the exceptional losses) and bury the credits (the exceptional gains). It would be a shortsighted management that did so however, since this would mean that next year they would be faced with a comparison of current income with figures for the previous year inflated by the undisclosed exceptional gain.

The question of manner of presentation of earnings per share always is associated with the problem of dealing with extraordinary items. Once again, provided the final figure for results reported for the year was given on a per share basis, it could be left to management as to what was the most informative presentation. Probably most managements would want to identify a figure before unusual items separately disclosed, in order to bring out underlying trends.

Changes in accounting methods

The action required when a change is made in accounting method requires some consideration. There are three conceivable ways of handling such a change. The first way is to make the change with retroactive effect. When this is done, balance sheet figures at the beginning of the year of change are adjusted as though the new method had been in use previously, and historical figures of earnings, etc. are recomputed accordingly. (Occasionally it may be impractical to recalculate the effect which the new method would have had on earnings of previous years, and in such cases disclosure can only be given of the discontinuity in the historical record of earnings.) Under the second method the balances carried forward from previous years are left undisturbed, and the new accounting method is applied only to transactions occurring after the date of change. Under the third method no adjustment to historical figures is made but closing balances in the year of change are calculated on the new method and disclosure given of the effect of the change on earnings in the year of change. The last method would only be used where the change in method is more by way of a refinement of the previous basis of calculation, rather than a basic change in approach.

Instinctively, one would think that if a new accounting method is adopted, it is presumably considered superior to the old and therefore it should be made retroactive. Moreover, if this is not done the results for the years after the change may be distorted because of the inconsistency in method. Consider for example the case of an oil company that changes from the traditional method of accounting for oil exploration costs to the 'full cost' method. Under the traditional method substantial exploration and development costs will be written off when incurred which would be deferred under the full cost method. If such costs are not reinstated in the balance sheet when the new method of accounting is adopted amortization of deferred exploration costs will be lower than normal for several years, while at the same time all current costs of exploration will be deferred. Thus reported profits will tend to increase above a level that would be sustained if either method of accounting had been used consistently throughout.

Two arguments are made against retroactive accounting adjustments. One is a practical argument against the abuse that can occur when a change results in the write-off of an asset cost previously deferred, or the setting up of a liability previously ignored. For example, suppose a company has followed the practice of deferring product development costs and changes to a method requiring the immediate write-off of such costs. Profits in previous years will not have borne a full charge for development costs. If the deferred amounts are now written off, profits of future years will not have to bear the charge either. Even if a retroactive recalculation of the previous year's figures is made, little attention may be paid to it, with the result that the company gets the best of both worlds, over the whole period, in reporting its results. The other argument against restatement rests upon the feeling that a change in previously reported figures is inequitable. Securities have been bought and sold in relation to figures previously reported and it may be felt that these should not be changed. Retroactive adjustment of figures may also affect the application of tests under bond indentures and trust deeds in a manner not contemplated when the tests were written.

As beween making a change retroactively or only prospectively, in the writer's opinion the former is clearly superior in logic. A change should only be made if the new method is considered preferable and if so the best portrayal of results and the trend in them over the years is provided by giving the new method retroactive effect. There should be curbs against abuse to the extent possible. The effect of the change on previous years' figures should be emphasized by requiring disclosure of restated income figures for five years back, not just for the preceeding year as is the usual custom. Some thought might be given to prohibiting a retroactive write-off of deferred costs where the deferments were clearly justified in previous years and the policy of deferment had the effect of raising the general level of reported profits in the most recent two or three years. Similarly, a retroactive change in method which has the effect of writing off a type of deferred costs not now incurred (e.g. business establishment costs) should be prohibited.*

That changes in accounting methods can affect the covenants under trust deeds in unintended ways is not uncommon experience. To permit this to impede desirable changes, however, would be to place the cart before the horse. Writers of trust documents and indentures need to spell out the accounting methods underlying proposed tests in detail, and not merely refer in general terms to accounting principles. Alternatively, trust deeds should provide that tests are to be measured in accordance with the accounting methods followed by the entity at the date of the document.

One or two other minor points may be made in relation to changes in accounting methods. A change in method should be distinguished from the adoption of a new method because of changed circumstances. For example, if a company for years followed the practice of expensing small amounts of development costs as incurred and then embarked on an ambitious major development program quite unlike its

---

* APB Opinion No. 20 (published after this was written) attacks the problem of potential abuse in accounting changes by providing that:

(1) No change may be made except to a method considered superior in the circumstances, and

(2) For the most part the adjustments required to balance sheet assets and liabilities to put them on the new accounting basis shall be reported as a separate item in income of the year of change rather than being treated as a prior period adjustment. Pro forma figures for prior years reflecting the changed accounting methods should however be provided.

previous programs, it would not be a change in method or inconsistency to defer the new program costs, while continuing to expense the former type of costs.

The consequences of a change in estimate should also be distinguished from a change in accounting method. For example, if the estimated useful lives of fixed assets are adjusted the consequent change in rate of write-off is not a change in accounting method. In contrast, a change in the pattern of accounting, say, from diminishing balance to straight-line depreciation, would be a change in method. Usually a change in estimate should be applied prospectively not retroactively. For example, if the useful life of fixed assets is thought to be longer than originally estimated, the depreciation rate can be adjusted to stretch out the write-off of remaining book value over remaining useful life. If depreciation has been kept under regular review, this would be the only sensible method. On the other hand, cases do occur when the depreciation rate has been much too slow or too rapid for a number of years, and the company does not wake up to the fact until the bulk of the assets are near retirement or the bulk of the asset value has been written off. In such cases a practical argument can be made for retroactively adjusting the accounts to recognize the error. CICA Handbook Recommendations however appear to rule that any such adjustment must be made as one amount through the income account in the year when the change in life is recognized.

Consolidation accounting

Questions related to consolidation accounting are dealt with in Chapter 17. The most important open questions concern the criteria which should govern whether a subsidiary company should or should not be consolidated. In the writer's opinion, the most important criterion should be effective control, as evidenced by holding more than 50% of the voting stock. The governing rule should be that all subsidiaries will be consolidated where this condition prevails, unless:

1. control is likely to be temporary because of options given on stock or because of an intention to sell

2. control has been lost because the company is in receivership, or because of the action of a foreign government or for other reasons

3. control is likely to be lost because of warrants, options or other rights held by outsiders to buy stock in subsidiaries.

The fact that the parent company does not use its voting control to supervise the management of the subsidiary should not be accepted as a reason for non-consolidation. If the power to control is in existence it must be assumed it would be used should the parent company have any reason to be dissatisfied with the results of the subsidiary.

Exceptions to the basic control tests should be allowed in limited circumstances:

1. Where the subsidiary is a financial intermediary it need not be consolidated in the interest of not distorting the financial ratios in the consolidated statements.

2. Where inclusion of the working capital of the subsidiary would materially improve the consolidated working capital position *and* where the free use of the subsidiary working capital is effectively restricted by the existence of

conditions in debt agreements of the subsidiary or the existence of a major minority interest in the subsidiary it need not be consolidated.

The mere existence of a substantial debt interest or minority interest in the subsidiary should not in itself justify non-consolidation in the absence of the other conditions referred to in (2) above. A 'pyramided' holding company structure is more clearly displayed by a consolidated balance sheet than is otherwise possible.

If a subsidiary company is not consolidated it should be required to be carried on the equity basis of accounting. This is subject to the proviso that where the value of the investment in the subsidiary is less than the figure that would be derived from the equity basis of accounting, and the loss in value appears to be more than temporary, the carrying figure should be reduced to a realistic figure. In addition, where the carrying value of non-consolidated subsidiaries equals more than (say) 15% of the shareholders' equity of the parent company, it should be required to publish the statements of the larger subsidiaries separately or at least condensations thereof, along with its own statements.

Translation of accounts in foreign currencies

The discussion in Chapter 19 has indicated that the question of proper methods for translation of accounts in foreign currency is highly confused. That this should be so is not surprising in view of the complexity of the topic. While it is clear that the same translation rules are not appropriate in every situation, the economic causes underlying movements in the exchange rates are so varied and so intertwined that it is virtually impossible to define clearly those situations where one set of rules should apply, and those where a different set should apply.

Faced with conditions like these it would be unrealistic to hope to attain translation principles perfectly adapted to every situation. What should be sought is not an impossible 'ideal' answer, but rather one that is sufficient to go along with. Moreover if we cannot have a perfect answer there is much to be said for looking for a simple answer, so that readers of financial statements can understand for themselves the results of the translation procedures applied. Given this background the following represents a few observations on the subject.

Translations of foreign currency assets and liabilities arising from transactions not involving branches or subsidiaries

We start with the problem of translating individual assets and liabilities that are expressed in foreign currencies (as opposed to the problem of translation of financial statements of foreign branches or subsidiaries). This problem is simplified by the fact that only monetary assets and liabilities are involved. A reasonable set of rules for such translations would be:

1. All such balances should be translated at rates of exchange prevailing at the statement date. (The parity rate would be reasonable where the exchange rates between two countries are pegged and move only within a narrow band. Where the exchange rate concerned is floating rather than fixed, an arbitrary bookkeeping rate would be acceptable if it approximates the actual year-end rate.)

2. Gains or losses resulting from changes in the translation rate applied on such assets and liabilities:

(a) should be recognized in income if the asset or liability is close to maturity (such as would be the case with cash balances or trade accounts receivable or payable)

(b) should be deferred and amortized over the term to maturity of longer term receivables and payables in recognition of the fact that there is a financing element in such items, and exchange gains or losses can be considered an adjustment of the implicit interest revenue or cost in such arrangements.

3. The foregoing rules should be modified where there are both short-term and long-term balances in foreign currency. In such cases the gains and losses on translation of all items should be offset and the net result deferred only to the extent that it does not exceed the amount that would be deferred on the net long-term position.

A gain or loss recognized on restatement of a foreign currency liability should not be treated as an adjustment of the cost of non-monetary assets whose acquisition was financed by such liability. In spite of some authoritative support this idea is totally unsound. The cost of an asset is not different depending on whether or not the liability for it has been settled. If the purchaser did not hedge his position vis-à-vis the liability, the adjustment when the exchange rates move is an adjustment relating to the financial management of the business not to the cost of its assets.

When an asset is bought or sold for a foreign currency amount however, usually the relevant exchange rate is that existing when the purchase commitment was made, not that when the asset was received. Once an order is placed or a sale is made to be settled in a foreign currency the person entering into the transaction in effect has taken a position in that currency which he should hedge if he wishes to avoid the exchange risk. In general, then, it may be stated that transactions in foreign currencies should be recorded in the accounts (even if only in memorandum form) at the commitment date rather than the performance (delivery) date, if an accurate record of real foreign exchange gains and losses is to be maintained.

Translation of the accounts of foreign branches or subsidiaries

When we think about the translation of accounts of foreign branches or subsidiaries we should remember that setting up a business normally involves a commitment of funds that is largely fixed. It takes inventory to operate a business as well as fixed assets. Thus the distinction between current and non-current assets is relatively unimportant in assessing the risk of exchange rate changes in foreign operations. Even the monetary/non-monetary distinction may be unimportant since business operations customarily require carrying accounts receivable and working cash balances. It is the whole investment that is at risk of changes in currency values and that risk does not vary materially depending on the character of the assets. Except for surplus cash held abroad the risk that there will be a change in the balance of value between the two currencies is a long-term risk related to the period over which the investment will be held. Some part of that long-term risk can be avoided by borrowing in the foreign currency. If this is done it is only the equity in the foreign operation that is at risk. If the foreign currency deteriorates or appreciates it will mean that earnings in the foreign currency are worth less or more to the parent company. In considering how changes in exchange rates should affect translation procedures, therefore, we should be thinking mainly of the long term. A long-term investment should not be written down, for example, unless the loss appears to be of an enduring nature.

Some other considerations that should affect translation procedures for the accounts of a foreign branch or subsidiary are listed below:

– Is the foreign operation in a country with a stable currency or an unstable currency? (While no precise dividing line between 'stable' and 'unstable' currencies can be stated it is suggested that by and large developed countries which are members of the International Monetary Fund may be considered to have stable currencies. Some other currencies may be considered stable on the basis of past history and an assessment of their current economic position. Other currencies are fairly obviously unstable.)

– Is the exchange rate between the currencies in question pegged or floating?

– Is the foreign operation independent of the business of the parent company? That is to say, is the reason for ownership of the foreign business merely that it appears to be a good investment, or is the foreign operation set up as ancillary to the business of the parent company? If the latter, does the foreign operation function as a sales outlet for the parent company or a supplier of materials or both?

– Is the purpose of the foreign operation to conduct a business adding value to goods or providing services, or is it merely to make profits by trading or speculation in commodities, currencies, etc? (The latter would be a special situation which would call for special rules. The best accounting basis for a trader or speculator would be market value for the assets or contracts in which it trades. This would suggest that current exchange rates should be used for all its translations. This example is mentioned merely to illustrate that there will always be exceptions to a general rule, and is not discussed further here.)

Unless accounting generally adopted current values as the basis for recording assets and liabilities there seems to be no general rule that would be appropriate in all situations. (On a current value basis of accounting the current exchange rate at the statement date would obviously be the most logical translation basis.)

While a valuation approach to accounting is not now generally accepted, consideration of the possibility does suggest the most desirable translation basis for accounts maintained in countries with unstable currencies. In such countries one of the most pervasive causes of currency instability is rapid internal inflation. If such a situation existed in the parent country it is doubtful that the historical cost basis of accounting would persist; rather some form of current value or price-level adjusted accounts would in all probability become generally accepted. Accordingly it can be argued that when an operation is conducted in a highly inflationary foreign environment, generally accepted accounting principles may, or should, be interpreted to permit or require a valuation adjustment to assets and liabilities in the foreign currency accounts. Then translation of all items at current exchange rates would naturally follow.

The following discussion of possible translation rules is based on the assumption that no price-level or current value adjustment of the foreign currency accounts has been made.

1. Translation of accounts in stable foreign currencies.
   (a) Currencies with fixed parities.

Where a fixed parity has been declared by government action it is suggested that translation should be made at that rate. Actual exchange rates will fluctuate within a permitted range but this may reasonably be ignored in view of the long-term nature of investment in a foreign business.

Where parities are changed by official action there would be a presumption that the new parity rate is the best translation rate that can be used in the circumstances. Whether that rate should be applied to all assets and liabilities however and whether gain or loss should be recognized in the situation is open to question, and the considerations involved may differ.

   (i) The autonomous foreign business. Where the foreign business is not tied in with the business of the parent company (and is conducted wholly within the foreign country), the change in exchange parities has no meaning from the standpoint of local management. There seems no reason therefore to apply different translation rates to different components of the foreign accounts such as fixed assets or inventory. All items in the financial statements should be translated at the new parity rate after the change. If the foreign currency has appreciated in terms of the parent company currency this will produce a credit adjustment (assuming assets in the foreign operation exceed liabilities), and conversely a debit adjustment if the foreign currency has depreciated. If the foreign currency appreciated future earnings would be worth more, and vice versa. This would suggest that the credits or debits might be recognized as gains or losses in income immediately (or credits only might be deferred if conservatism were deemed important). On the other hand, if it were considered quite possible that the exchange rate would reverse itself at some future date either credits or debits might be deferred. A general rule might be suggested to defer recognition of gains or losses unless it is considered that the movement in exchange parities is probably irreversible in the foreseeable future (say, ten years or so).

   (ii) The foreign sales outlet. Where the foreign division acts as a sales outlet for the parent company the investment abroad is likely to be less permanent in character. Also a change in parities does affect the business carried on. An appreciation of the foreign currency makes the foreign business supplied from the parent company more competitive, and vice versa. In these circumstances when there has been an appreciation it would seem appropriate to adjust all assets and liabilities to the new rates (with the exception of inventory purchased from the parent company if it is desired to adhere to a strict realization test) and reflect the gain in income immediately. Where there has been a devaluation in the foreign currency, inventory purchased from the parent company would be reflected on the lower of cost and market rule in the foreign currency, assets and liabilities then translated at the new rates, and the loss reflected in income immediately.

(iii) The foreign supplier. When the foreign division acts as a supplier to the parent company, the permanency of the foreign investment may vary from one case to another. An appreciation of the foreign currency will have an adverse effect on the costs of the parent company to the extent materials are bought abroad and vice versa. In these circumstances any credit or debit arising on translating the net foreign assets should definitely be deferred initially. It might be appropriate, however, to amortize such items as an adjustment to costs of purchases from the foreign subsidiary over an arbitrary period.

(b) Currencies on floating rates.

When basically stable currencies are floating, the situation is not so different from that of fixed parities. It will be convenient to maintain a standard translation rate so long as it is considered reasonably representative of the actual rate prevailing from time to time. It may be that a policy should be adopted of adjusting to a new standard rate whenever current exchange rates on average depart from the standard rate by an arbitrary percentage – say, more than 3% – for a period of six months or a year. Changes in the standard rate could then be handled much as changes in fixed parities discussed above.

2. Translation of accounts in unstable foreign currencies.

In the absence of price-level or current value accounting in the foreign currency, translation of accounts in unstable currencies should probably follow the monetary/non-monetary approach which might be considered as giving somewhat the same result as price-level accounting. (It will eliminate the effect of inflation to the extent that the foreign currency is losing purchasing power faster than the parent company currency.) In the usual situation there will be an excess of monetary liabilities over monetary assets, so that when the foreign currency weakens the translation of the net monetary position at the new rate will produce a net credit. Unless there is a high degree of certainty that the foreign currency prices can be raised sufficiently to provide a profitable recovery of the investment in inventory and fixed assets which is still translated at the historic rate, the credit adjustment should be deferred and amortized into income over a reasonable period to offset the 'heavy' charge against income on account of such assets in future when the foreign currency income statement is translated into the parent country's currency using historic rates for cost of sales and depreciation. If there is a debit adjustment when the foreign currency weakens (representing an excess of monetary assets over liabilities) this should be recognized as a loss immediately. If the foreign currency should appreciate, normally it could be presumed that this was temporary, and debit or credit adjustments might both reasonably be deferred.

Disclosure

Chapter 20 discusses the problem of defining adequate disclosure in financial statements. Although a matter of degree, the principles underlying fair disclosure are reasonably apparent. It would however be helpful if accounting authority made a comprehensive general statement of the principles of disclosure.

One principle that needs particular emphasis relates to the selection of accounting methods and the exercise of judgment in applying them. Whenever alternative methods are available with respect to accounting for a particular type of asset or transaction, the entity ought to disclose which method it has adopted. Moreover, where the application of a method requires judgment – for example in determining useful lives of fixed assets for the purpose of setting depreciation rates – the judgment estimates ought to be made known. To implement this principle it might be desirable, at least for public companies, to require that companies compile a descriptive list of their accounting principles and methods (following a model format), have it approved by their Board of Directors, and file it with stock exchanges and/or securities commissions. Such a list might be too long to include in the annual report on a regular basis, but it could be required to be published periodically – say, once every five years – with changes published at the time of adoption.

If this step were taken some present methods of disclosure could be dropped. For example, a reader of financial statements gains little information by reading that inventory is carried at 'lower of cost and market' if he knows neither how cost or market is arrived at nor whether, in fact, any write-downs from cost were made. Descriptions of the basis of valuation of assets became a requirement some years past, largely to smoke out undesirable practices such as the deduction of undisclosed reserves from inventory valuations. Financial reporting practice has now improved to the point where such checks are no longer necessary. If the reader can be assured that an entity's accounting practices are not contrary to accepted accounting principles, he does not need brief descriptions of bases of valuation. He must have a good deal more detail about accounting methods used for it to have any value.

Another suggestion for additional disclosure that has been raised in recent years is the idea that a business should provide a forecast of expected financial results for a period of, say, one year ahead, along with the historical figures in the annual report. The initial reaction to this by many accountants is a fear that the forecast might be given more weight than it deserves and be misleading to investors and the public. Management also is likely to resist the idea because of the confidentiality of the information and the effect its disclosure might have on such matters as labour and other contract negotiations.

On the other hand some advantages to the idea appear on further reflection. In the first place the necessity to make a public forecast might well stimulate managements to make better forecasts. This in turn would increase the awareness of the factors that make their business tick, and potentially would improve their management ability. (To one who has had some experience of business it is often a surprise to note how frequently budgetary procedures are very casual and inaccurate, based on hunch or guess, or even are non-existent in spite of the voluminous literature in existence on the value and uses of proper budgets.) In the second place, as the year proceeded and variances from the forecast figures arose, management might be stimulated to take corrective action more rapidly than if their forecast had not been published. In the third place, the explanations that would be made in annual reports of the reasons for deviations of actual results from the forecast would be enlightening to the readers as to the factors and risks which affect the business, and thus over a period of time their investment judgment would be improved.

Naturally, some practical difficulties can be seen with the idea. In certain types of business (e.g. a contracting business) at certain times it is very hard to see beyond the immediate order position. Perhaps such businesses would need to be given an exemption from the requirement, or be given the option of forecasting more frequently for shorter periods. The auditors' responsibility with respect to the forecast would have to be defined. Other difficulties, no doubt, would occur. Basically, the idea presents many problems and seems too radical to win acceptance at this time. But with the gradual evolution of higher standards of reporting, particularly for companies in which there is a public interest, the idea seems likely, ultimately, to become accepted.

Analytical data – working capital, source and application of funds, earnings per share

In general, accounting authority should be reluctant to institute rules related to artificial concepts. The following discussion illustrates what is meant by 'artificial' – the distinction between 'inventory' and 'fixed assets' corresponds to a real difference between the things described. A classification of costs in these categories therefore is natural rather than artificial. However, a classification of certain items as being 'working capital' depends not on the natural characteristics of the items described, but rather on the prior definition of working capital. While it may well be useful in certain cases to make up definitions such as working capital to help in the comparison of one business with another, no such simple artificial concept can allow for all the differences in situations that occur in real life.

Consider the situation of a company owning a rental property which is financed largely by mortgage or other form of debt. The repayment of debt principal is usually scheduled so that it can be taken care of by cash flow from the rentals from time to time. If a balance sheet of such a company is drawn up shortly after a debt instalment payment date, it may show very little by way of liquid assets on hand. If the debt instalments for the next year are shown as current liabilities, the company will display a serious working capital deficiency. Yet this picture is entirely misleading since the probability is that the cash necessary will become available before the debt falls due.

To a greater or lesser degree, all working capital calculations are shot through with such anomalies. And yet a considerable number of accounting rules are concerned with decisions as to whether a given item should or should not enter into the working capital position. In the writer's opinion accounting authority should abandon the attempt to impose rules for the calculation of working capital since these will inevitably be misleading in particular situations. An authority should confine itself to balance sheet presentation guidelines that will assist interested readers to make such comparisons as may be desired. The type of presentation that might be appropriate is indicated by Appendix A in the supplement to Chapter 22.

Chapter 23 follows the discussion of working capital with the related topic of the statement of source and application of funds. The chief conclusions of the discussions in Chapter 23 are:

1. The objective of the funds statement at present is not clear to everyone. Is it to show the sources or causes of the net change in assets under the control of a business? Is it to focus on the liquidity of a business? Is it to show how much of the increase (or decrease) in assets (or liquid assets) came about as a result of the ongoing operations of the business (as opposed to financial transactions)? Or is it a combination of these?

2. In the writer's opinion the statement will have most general usefulness if it is in two parts – one part showing the causes of the net change in total assets under administration – the other part analyzing in what manner the balances in individual asset categories have changed, focussing on the liquidity position if desired.

3. Funds statements for companies with unclassified balance sheets would require some information not now routinely provided by most accounting systems, such as an analysis of the movement in investment accounts, but are potentially very informative.

4. There are a number of problems of detail to be looked at in the traditional funds statement. The most important of these relates to the manner in which 'funds arising from operations' is calculated, and concerns the add-back of short-term depreciation or amortization in arriving at the figure of funds from operations. To take an extreme example, consider a company that defers the cost of product tooling and development when incurred, to be amortized over the succeeding twelve months. A figure of funds inflow arrived at by adding back such amortization to net income would have very little significance, and will certainly be non-comparable with the figures for another company that follows a policy of expensing such costs when incurred. Similar comments could be made about tools and dies capitalized in the accounts and depreciated over a very short period. To cure this it is suggested that a practical rule should be adopted to the effect that, where a company incurs a given type of capital or deferred cost on a regular recurring basis and such cost is depreciated or amortized over a short period of years, say, three or four years or less, such depreciation or amortization should be excluded from the figure of funds from operations.

Earnings per share is another artificial analytical concept concerning which accounting rules have recently been instituted. The writer agrees that rules were necessary in this area because of the abuse or potential abuse of the calculation. However, again it is difficult to make rules for production of a single figure (or two figures) that makes sense in every situation. The artificiality of the APB definition of 'common stock equivalents' well exemplifies the sort of difficulties encountered. The Canadian approach of illustrating the whole possible range of calculation by providing a figure both for earnings per share issued and outstanding, and for fully diluted earnings, seems superior. However, in view of the possible complexity in situations that may be encountered, and the effect of assumptions that necessarily have to be made, there is a strong case for giving still more detailed information consisting of a schedule of the earnings per share calculations, showing and explaining the dilutive effect of each assumed right to acquire common shares, on a step-by-step basis.

Interim financial reports

Amidst all the literature on financial reporting problems, remarkably little consideration seems to have been given to the special problem of financial reports for periods of less than a year. In recent years, largely owing to legislative and stock exchange requirements, there has been a considerable expansion in the number of companies reporting financial results more often than annually. Most of the problems peculiar to such interim reports arise because the revenues and costs may fall irregularly through the year, and the consequent fluctuations in reported earnings may be misleading. Answers need to be given to the following questions:

1. If a certain type of revenue is received only at intervals, should it be accrued in interim reports even if it is recognized only on a cash received basis for annual reporting? For example, if dividend income on investments is received only once or twice a year, should it be accrued or deferred so as to be spread evenly over the year rather than being reflected only in the quarter in which it is received?

2. If certain types of costs are incurred irregularly through the year, should they be deferred or accrued and written off over the year in proportion to expected sales rather than be expensed as incurred as is the case with annual reporting? For example, advertising and promotion costs, development costs and many other types of costs may be incurred in bunches and will distort the results for short periods if they are entirely written off in the period in which they are incurred.

3. If certain costs are only established on an annual basis, how should they be calculated in interim periods? Examples are income taxes and profit sharing provisions. If a particular quarter usually shows losses, should these losses be reduced by expected tax recoveries if the year as a whole is expected to be profitable? Should a profit sharing arrangement be treated similarly to income tax in this respect?

4. If manufacturing activity is seasonal, should unabsorbed overhead in slack seasons and overabsorbed overhead in busy seasons be carried forward to be absorbed over the remainder of the fiscal year? If so, how should the proper amount to be carried forward be established?

5. If the sales pattern is seasonal so that certain quarters customarily show losses on conventional accounting methods, should fixed costs be deferred and absorbed proportionately to sales so that the quarter shows a profit margin on sales consistent with that which it is expected will be realized for the year as a whole? If so, how could such 'predictive' reporting be assured of reasonable accuracy?

It is likely that there is some variation in practice in the answers to all the above questions. Consideration of the problems and an attempt to furnish standard acceptable answers would seem desirable.

Accounting adjustment for price-level and/or value changes

One of the most discussed subject areas in accounting literature of the past twenty-five years has been that of the effect of price-level changes on the validity of financial reports. The interest stems from the continuous and well-nigh universal erosion in the purchasing power of money over this period. On the other hand, the interest has been largely academic. There has been virtually no demand from financial analysts for accounts adjusted for price-level effects. Nor have managements evinced any great desire for such reports. In view of this lack of interest on the part of those most concerned with accounts in practice, and the fact that adjustment of accounts for the effect of changing price levels contains practical difficulties and makes for a good deal of additional work, it is not surprising that price-level accounting has not made more headway.

Nevertheless it is doubtful that it is safe to let this state of affairs continue. Recent years have seen an acceleration of the pace of inflation in the English speaking countries. When the loss of money value appeared to be at the rate of 2% a year or less, it could well be ignored for practical purposes, partly because the indices measuring the change in price level probably overstate the real loss of value (since price indices may not take adequate account of improvement in quality) and partly because the margin of error was well within that inevitable in accounting measurements generally. In the last few years however, we have seen inflation grow to a stated rate of 4% to 6%. It is becoming apparent also that forces tending towards inflation are generally stronger than the countervailing forces. Inflationary policies by and large are more popular politically than deflationary policies. The desirable policy goal of maintaining relatively full employment of national resources often involves monetary and fiscal policies with inflationary effect. The long-term tendency to expansion in the role of government action and the concomitant regular increase in government spending tends also to be inflationary. Moreover a government has a natural vested interest in a little bit of inflation since the combination of rising monetary incomes and progressive income tax rates means that inflation provides greater government revenues automatically without the politically unpopular necessity to raise tax rates. At present rates of inflation and with the long-term prospect of more to come, it is becoming apparent that financial reporting must be adjusted to allow for the deterioration of currency values if it is to reflect the real economic situation fairly.

Accounts that are not adjusted for rising price levels or changes in current values of assets or liabilities contain the following errors. (Opposite results would be true if prices fell.) First, they do not show the loss to an entity that occurs as a result of holding money or claims to money (receivables, investment in bonds, mortgages, etc.) or the gain that results from owing money when the purchasing power of money declines. Second, they do not show the gain to an entity that results from holding other assets whose current value has increased by more than the general price level or the loss from the opposite situation. Third, they do not measure the income from operations properly if cost figures incurred in earlier years are set off against revenues received in current years.

It is not the purpose of this work to describe the methods of making adjustments for changes in the general purchasing power of the currency of account or adjustments to current values of specific assets held and the practical difficulties in implementation of such adjustments. Suffice it to say that two types of adjustment may be involved in compensating for the above three shortcomings of conventional accounts. A restatement of account balances in accordance with a general price-level index can deal with the first shortcoming. The practical problems connected with methods of adjustment are discussed in a number of works. The second and third shortcomings described above require valuation of specific assets at current values (replacement costs or other values). This in practice may be much more difficult to do. It has been suggested earlier that separable assets can and should be valued at current realizable value. Later on it was suggested that, for best measurement of operating income, inventory and cost of sales should be regularly restated at current replacement cost. This may be easy to do in some cases and difficult in others. By similar reasoning, fixed assets and depreciation thereon should be stated at current replacement cost. This will usually be difficult. It may be possible in some cases to use specific price indices, but many businesses have not in practice kept their fixed asset records in such a way that index adjustments can be easily applied to them, even if reliable indices were available.

Perhaps more work is required to explore the practical difficulties of calculating price-level adjusted accounts. It is however time that some decisions were taken. We may hope that current efforts to contain and reduce the rate of inflation will be successful. We would be foolish to count on it. We need to decide at what point price-level adjusted accounts, even if done imperfectly on the basis of a general price index, should be required, and whether they should be presented as the primary accounts or as supplementary information. It will be recognized that the profession cannot decide these matters on its own. But it can seek co-operation of management and other parties more vigorously than in the past, and it should do so. The day may not be too far distant when the force of economic events will have robbed conventional financial statements of much of their meaning.

Accounting for non-profit organizations

Chapter 26 contains a brief commentary on the accounting practices of non-profit organizations and points out the very wide diversity in practice in these organizations. In the writer's opinion, the fundamental reason for the confusion that exists as to the best methods of accounting in non-profit organizations is that the readers of the financial statements of such organizations have not made known what they want to know. Consequently, the accounting practices have grown like Topsy under a number of influences, without any particular rhyme or reason to them.

It is submitted that:

1. The primary purpose of the financial report of a non-profit organization should be to display the cost of its program for the fiscal year. This objective goes a good deal beyond giving a mere description of the receipt and spending of funds in the year.

2. In order to portray cost properly, ordinary rules for recording capital assets, inventories and prepayments should be followed except to the extent that amounts involved are unimportant in the financial picture.

3. Cost classification is important and in all but the smallest organizations costs should be reported according to the purpose of the expenditure – e.g. case work, educational costs, campaign expenses, administration, etc. – rather than by nature of expenditure – e.g. wages, salaries, supplies, etc.

4. Different types of non-profit organizations should promote cooperative effort to arrive at standard formats for reporting costs best suited to their particular type of operation.

5. The picture of costs incurred should not be confused by arbitrary appropriations of funds for various special purposes.

6. Revenues should be matched with costs rather than costs with revenues as in the case of commercial business. That is to say if donations, grants and other support are received for special purposes, they should be reported as revenues in the period in which the money is spent for that purpose rather than the period in which the money is received by the organization.

7. Revenues for a year should be classified by source to provide the most useful information.

8. While the accounts should make clear any restrictions applicable to the spending of funds on hand, fund accounting should not be permitted to fragment a comprehensive picture of the costs of a year's program and the various sources from which support has been received. In some cases both purposes could be achieved by preparing a statement showing costs and revenues both by individual funds and combined.

9. The balance sheet should display all the assets of the organization. As in the case of businesses, separable assets should be revalued if their disposable value changes in a fiscal period.

35   Conclusion

The theme of this Work, and particularly of Part II, has been as follows:

1. Financial accounting (a poor nomenclature) is a medium of communication of pertinent economic information by those responsible for managing an entity to other parties (owners, investors, creditors and the public generally) having some interest in it but who do not have access to its internal information systems. Financial accounting is also distinguished by the fact that it aims to give a rounded comprehensive view of the activity of an entity for the period and its resources at the end of the period, not just a view of one aspect. A set of financial statements represents a kind of economic model of the functioning of the entity, showing how the capital has been contributed by way of equity or debt, how the funds so received have been disposed of, the revenues generated by the operations, whether the result has been a gain or loss, and the disposition of any gain or loss generated.

2. Since people can only absorb a limited amount of information about a subject at one time financial statements must necessarily be condensed in form. The act of classifying and arranging data to achieve such condensation, if well done, adds to the sum total of information conveyed by bringing out the essential pattern of economic activity from the myriads of transactions. The art of accounting is therefore both descriptive and analytical.

3. The choice of method for classifying and presenting data ought to depend first on what users need to know, and second on what information really has some meaning in an economic sense. Thirdly, there is the practical consideration that information should be worth the cost of developing it.

4. If communication through the medium of the accounts is to be successful, users of accounting data must be able to grasp the significance of what they are being told. This simple statement underlies the whole idea of accounting principles, including the concept of adequate disclosure. It underlies the proscription of completely arbitrary practices such as the creation of 'inner reserves'. It supports the practice of disclosing the basis of the accounting methods used. It is the driving force behind the struggle to reduce the number of cases where the

same economic events can be accounted for by different methods, yielding widely different results.

At one time great reliance was placed on disclosure, such as of the basis of valuation of assets, as a means of compensating for the use of diverse accounting methods. As a practical matter however, such reliance is ill founded. A high percentage of statement users are interested in comparisons between entities and for them the work of adjusting statements to achieve comparability (even if possible, which is frequently not the case) limits the usefulness of financial statements severely. Many other users are not sufficiently skilled to realize the significance of disclosure as to accounting methods. As a practical matter, it may be conceded that the manner in which business is carried on and the legal, social and economic environments are so complex that complete standardization of accounting methods will never be achieved. But this is a far cry from the belief by one writer that "diversity in accounting among independent entities" is a basic concept of accounting. Such a belief is in essence an admission of failure.

5. It is argued then that the goal, however difficult of attainment, must always be to provide useful economic information by methods which in identical situations will be identical, and which will vary only with variations in the situation to be described. The question is, by what means can we best move towards that goal? For thirty-odd years the accounting profession has adopted generally accepted practice as its standard and has directed its efforts to improve the quality of practice through education and persuasion of those whose responsibility it is to issue financial reports. The results have been good – but have they been good enough? The efforts made have been limited by these weaknesses in the whole process:
   - A failure to agree upon any coherent articulated view of the nature, goals and objectives of financial reporting.
   - A failure to enquire deeply into the needs of the users of financial information.
   - A failure to agree upon 'postulates' or truths about the economic environment and to use them as aids in choosing which, among conflicting accepted accounting methods, have the greater validity.
   - A tendency to leave the initiation of accounting methods almost solely to those responsible for the results portrayed by the accounting, without provision for a referee where the methods so developed have been contradictory and without adequate provision for the situation where practice has not developed at all.

6. On this view 'general acceptance' should be abandoned as a standard for derivation of accounting methods. Taken literally, it is nonsense – no new method in relation to an existing problem could be adopted, no matter how superior, if it differed from the method used in the past. On the other hand, in the case of an entirely new problem virtually no guidance is given beyond certain broad generalizations that have little guidance value.

7. In the place of general acceptance as a means of deciding on accounting methods, it is urged we should substitute the authority of an accounting legislative body. Indeed this process has begun already and has come some distance, particularly in the U.S.A. with reference to the Accounting Principles Board.

The financial press not infrequently makes such references as "the CICA which determines what are generally accepted accounting methods". This association in the public mind, if it exists and develops, is potentially dangerous to the accounting profession since criticisms of weaknesses in accounting methods would then, inevitably, be turned into criticism of the profession. There is no real alternative for the profession to a clear assumption of responsibility and authority, and action to fulfill its responsibilities.

8. Once this is accepted, the question becomes one of how best to fulfill that responsibility. The following points have been made:

(a) The legislative body should observe three guidelines in its statements:

(i) So far as possible the enunciation of principles should be set forth in the broadest possible terms. This will avoid the situation where a detailed recommendation appears on the face of it to apply to a situation which was never contemplated when the recommendation was made. It will also avoid the possibility of people trying to avoid the impact of a recommendation that should apply, simply because the wording of the recommendation is slightly ambiguous when applied to their fact situation. The application of the broadly enunciated principles would then be left to the professional judgment of the accountants participating in the particular case. Only if this procedure were obviously failing to produce satisfactory results should more detailed recommendations be considered.

(ii) Each recommendation should be supported by the chain of reasoning by which the legislative body arrived at its conclusion. Traditionally accounting committees have stated recommendations without much supporting reasoning. Even the APB Opinions, while presenting arguments for and against certain practices, have not really stated step by step how the majority arrived at their conclusion. Presentation of such a chain of reasoning would be valuable assistance to practitioners considering whether particular situations fell within the scope of the recommendation.

(iii) Although the enunciation of a principle may be in broad terms, wherever the situation is complex it should be accompanied by examples showing how it is expected the principle would be applied.

(b) Particularly if the legislative body confines itself to broad statements of principle, it would be useful to set up some agency to give opinions on the application of the recommendations to specific cases.

(c) A further check upon the opinions of the legislative body and a stimulus to improvement in them would lie in a strong research capability. While there will always be need for research within the Institute supporting the legislative body, there are strong arguments in favour of an independent research foundation with wider sponsorship and independent membership, probably directing its research efforts to other fields as well as that of financial reporting.

(d) The accounting institutes might well direct more attention to wider education in the problems of financial reporting. For maximum effectiveness the Institute must be interested in the education of management and users of financial information as well as its own members. Greater exposure to the points of view of these participants would have a return value to professional accountants.

9. Finally, Canadian accountants have a particular problem of some urgency to resolve with respect to differences in accounting principles recognized in the United States and Canada. In the longer term, the answer to this may lie in some form of international co-ordination but that effectively appears to be years away. In the meantime it seems probable that some rules will have to be adopted by Canadian accountants to determine when Canadian rules must be followed and when U.S. rules may be followed in accounting for Canadian companies, and to make clear in financial reporting which set of rules has been followed. This requires thought now.

Appendix A
Specialized topics

This Appendix contains investigations in greater depth of some of the specialized problem areas in accounting theory and practice. The problems reviewed are arranged in the order in which they are mentioned in the general development of theory in Part I, so that this material can be considered as supplementing, Chapter by Chapter, the ideas expressed in that Part. A good many of the recommendations in Part II also touch on the matters discussed in this Appendix. Hence, the Appendix, in a sense, provides a bridge between the two Parts.

Supplement to Chapter 3 – Accounting Concepts

Accounting entity

The decision as to the entity whose activities are to be reflected is primarily a matter of definition, which to some extent at least is subject to the wishes of interested parties. For example, Smith, who owns several drug stores, might set up a separate system of accounts for each store, or might have one set of accounts for all his stores. In the former case, the accounting entity would be the store unit; in the latter case it would be the chain.

As another example, consider the accounting for pension fund assets held by trustees. If the purpose of the accounting is to show how the trustees have fulfilled their responsibility for custody of the fund assets, the accounts need show only the source and disposition of assets entrusted to them. If, however, the purpose is to show the financial position of the pension *plan* (as distinct from the pension *fund*), the accounts must necessarily incorporate an actuarial valuation of the liabilities of the plan, and a calculation of the surplus or deficit of assets in the fund.

In other words, the choice of the accounting entity blocks out an area of interest and, so to speak, conceives of an artificial person in this area, holding assets, owing debts, and receiving revenues and paying expenses. This conception is similar to the legal concept of a corporation as an artificial person but is not coterminous with, or dependent on, it. An accounting entity must represent a recognizable unit or body carrying on some economic activities. Such entity may be a corporation. But it may equally be a group of corporations connected by ties of ownership or control. Or, as indicated, it may be an unincorporated enterprise, distinguished by the activity it carries on.

An accounting entity therefore can be set up to provide information about almost any activity. Businesses can, and frequently do, set up separate systems of accounts to reflect the activities of separate plants, branches, or departments. It has already been observed however that accounting principles have been developed primarily in relation to communication between the management of an organization and outside interested parties. The whole basis of such communication is that management is to account fairly for the resources entrusted to it, showing what has been bought with such resources, and what resources have been used up in the course of carrying on the enterprise. In the normal situation, where purchase and sale transactions are consummated at arm's length with third parties, the record of such transactions is an adequate basis for reporting in the financial statements. Where such transactions have not been made at arm's length, however, serious doubt exists that the transactions constitute sufficient evidence of value to justify a representation to outside parties that the accounts are fairly presented.* In such cases, additional evidence of the value of the consideration is required before the accounts can be accepted as fairly presented. As a practical matter, satisfactory evidence of this nature is usually rather difficult to obtain. It would be rare therefore that the accounts of a branch of a business could be said to be fairly presented according to generally accepted accounting principles.

Even in the absence of non-arm's-length relationships, identification of a particular entity as the focus for accounting does not solve all the problems associated with the concept of entity. A number of writers have developed various theories about the relationship between an accounting entity and the parties interested in it. Discussion in this area tends to be highly theoretical, and somewhat reminiscent of a 13th century Thomist contemplating a fine point in theology. The following review is not exhaustive, and may not do justice to all the arguments bearing on the subject.

There are two main theories as to the relationship between an accounting entity and the parties interested in it. Under the 'entity' theory the entity is viewed as a separate person, owning the resources of the enterprise and liable to the claims of the proprietors in much the same fashion as it is liable to the claims of creditors. The fundamental balance sheet equation, thus, is viewed as:

$$\text{Assets} = \text{Claims on assets (equities)}.$$

---

* In the Thomascolor case the United States Securities and Exchange Commission held that where negotiations for purchase of patents and patent application rights were substantially not at arm's length it was improper to value these intangible assets at an amount equal to the par value of the stock issued to acquire them, when (i) there were no real indicators of the value of the patents, and (ii) the company stock had not been traded in the market and there was no other standard by which the value of the stock would be judged. (United States Securities and Exchange Commission, Accounting Series Release No. 73, U.S. Government Printing Office, 1952.) This case, however, would not necessarily be a good precedent in a Canadian jurisdiction where the corporations act requires that the directors determine in good faith that the consideration received is the fair equivalent of the par value of the shares, or the value assigned to no par value shares.

On the other hand, under the 'proprietary' theory the entity is viewed simply as the agent of the proprietor group. Thus in substance the proprietors own the assets and owe the liabilities, and the balance sheet equation should be viewed as:

$$\text{Assets} - \text{liabilities} = \text{Proprietors' equity.}$$

Goldberg holds that both theories are mistaken in focussing on ownership. Under his 'Commander' theory, the management of an enterprise (its commander) is responsible for producing reports about entity activities that meet the needs of the different parties at interest. Such reports may be different if the needs are different. In other words the financial statements are statements *about* the entity, but not the statements *of* the entity, and thus a unique theory about the nature of the entity is not required.[1] This however is a prescription for the production of a variety of special-purpose statements, rather than one general purpose statement for each entity, which may be impractical. Vatter has argued that it is a mistake to personalize accounting. He would choose the 'fund' as the basic reporting unit, the fund being a unit which records both sources of funds for a particular purpose, and the resources acquired with them. The concept has not won acceptance in practice.[2]

Each of the main theories has more than one form. Under the 'entity' theory Gilman conceived of the proprietor's equity as being similar to a creditor's interest, and profits earned immediately became a debt due to the proprietor.[3] Husband suggested that since a corporation's income does not become income to a shareholder until a dividend is declared, retained income cannot be considered part of the shareholders' equity.[4] Li went further and argued even capital supplied by a shareholder is not part of a shareholder's equity since he has no claim upon the corporation for return of capital (except in liquidation).[5] These ideas all seem somewhat forced.

Under the 'proprietary' concept the focus is on proprietors as a group. This is just as artificial as the entity concept in the case of most corporations, since the individuals making up the shareholder group are continually changing. Most writers include preference shareholders among the proprietary interest, presumably because of their legal status as owners. Some, however, have argued that the point of view adopted should be that of the residual equity only.

What is the significance of these theories? It is this – the concept adopted may suggest or dictate the correct accounting treatment of certain transactions. For example, consider the incorporation fee and organization expenses of a company. From the viewpoint of the economic entity as such, this cost adds nothing to its resources available for carrying on business. It should therefore be written off rather than carried as an asset. From the viewpoint of the proprietors however, it is advantageous to carry on business in corporate form. The cost therefore is properly carried as an asset from their point of view. While this is an insignificant example there are more important differences (discussed below) and the danger is that accountants may unconsciously espouse one theory in answering one question and a different theory in connection with a different question.

Before discussion of individual problems, a preference will be expressed as to the best form of each concept. These can conveniently be illustrated by classification of a typical balance sheet. The writer's version of the entity theory (which will be called hereafter the 'separate enterprise' concept to avoid talking about the 'entity theory of the accounting entity') would call for a balance sheet divided as follows:

> *Net assets of the entity*
> Cash
> Receivables
> Inventory
>   etc.,
> Less trade payables, taxes payable, etc.,
>
>   in balance with
>
> *Net capital employed in the entity*
> Bank loans
> Long-term debt
> Preference shares
> Common shares
> Retained earnings

The focus of attention is upon the resources actually used by the entity to carry on operations and which give rise to its income. These are balanced by a summation of the interests of the several parties that have provided resources to the entity. The dividing line between liabilities deducted from resources and liabilities grouped as capital employed is, generally, that the former arise in the ordinary course as a result of day-to-day operation of the business and usually are short-term, and non interest-bearing, whereas the latter are borrowed specifically as financing, and usually bear interest. Consistent with the division in the balance sheet one might expect to find the income statement divided in two sections, the first containing revenues and costs resulting from business operations, culminating in a figure of net operating income before tax, and the second section showing the distribution of income to the various suppliers of capital in the form of interest and dividends. Corporation income tax would necessarily be included in this section since it is only imposed on income after deduction of interest. (It may be noted that tax law appears to be following the proprietary theory in allowing a deduction for interest but then is inconsistent with it in taxing proprietors' income again when dividends are distributed, without allowing a compensating deduction for income taxes paid by the corporation.)

Under the proprietary concept the focus of attention is essentially on the lower right hand corner of the normal balance sheet – the shareholders' equity section – and the amount of income to be credited to the shareholders. The present customary form of financial statements fits the proprietary concept, except that, in the writer's opinion, there is a strong argument for focussing attention not just on the legal proprietorship, but rather on the owners of the *residual equity*. Consistent with this view, the income statement would be extended to deduct preference share dividends and arrive at earnings available for the residual equity (which then would fit in with the customary calculation of earnings per common share).

In presenting these views of the logical form of financial statements under the 'separate enterprise' theory on the one hand, and the 'proprietary' theory on the other, the writer does not intend to suggest that these forms are commonly found in practice, or that these particular variations of entity theory are widely held.

We return now to the significance of the two theories in terms of accounting principles. For the most part principles and practices would be unaffected by the choice of theory. But in the following cases different principles might logically flow from the different points of view:

1. Costs of raising capital – as these do not contribute to the resources employed by the entity, they should be written off, or deducted from contributed capital under the separate enterprise theory. Under the proprietary concept they may properly be considered assets and deferred in the balance sheet, to be amortized over the duration of the capital subscription if it is for a limited term.

2. Government grants or subsidies relating to acquisition of capital assets – under the separate enterprise theory these would automatically be credited to contributed surplus upon receipt. Under the proprietary concept a decision would need to be made about the economic value of the asset eligible for subsidy. To the extent that the subsidy was required to induce acquisition of this asset, the proprietary interest has received no benefit and the grant should be applied to reduce the effective cost of the asset to an economic value. Grants not so required would be credited to contributed surplus.

3. Investments in other companies not considered part of the entity (i.e. not eligible for consolidation) – under the separate enterprise concept it is arguable such investments should be carried at cost. Under the proprietary concept one might lean to writing up the carrying value to reflect earnings retained by the other company.

4. Employee stock options – these require no outlay of funds by the entity and therefore would require no accounting under the separate enterprise concept. From the point of view of the proprietorship however, something of value is given up and, to the extent it can be measured, employee compensation expense should be recognized and charged against income.

5. Goodwill – it might be argued that goodwill earned should be recorded as an asset (if it could be measured) under the proprietary concept, but that it should not be set up under the separate enterprise theory since it does not represent an increase in the resources devoted to the business of the entity. Purchased goodwill is a more debatable case, but it might still be argued under the separate enterprise theory that its cost should be written off immediately when incurred.

A decision as to the relative merits of these two theories (or other theories) depends essentially on what the information is wanted for. One would imagine for example that the separate enterprise concept would be more attractive as a basis for compilation of national statistics of economic activity. It might also be fairly useful for creditors of an entity. On the other hand shareholders and potential shareholders who are interested in the return to them on their investment would presumably be better served by the proprietary concept.

For general purpose financial reporting the question is which view is to prevail. In our present society the legal background of financial reporting is oriented to the presentation of information to the shareholders. Their interests must be presumed to weigh more heavily therefore, which would seem to justify the selection of the proprietary concept under present conditions.

References

1. Louis Goldberg, *An Inquiry into the Nature of Accounting* (Evanston, Illinois: American Accounting Association, 1965).

2. W. J. Vatter, *The Fund Theory of Accounting and its Implication for Financial Reports* (Chicago: The University of Chicago Press, 1947).

3. Stephen Gilman, *Accounting Concepts of Profit* (New York: The Ronald Press Company, 1939).

4. G. R. Husband, "The Entity Concept in Accounting", *The Accounting Review* (October 1954), pp. 552–563.

5. D. H. Li, "The Nature of Corporate Residual Equity under the Entity Concept", *The Accounting Review* (April 1960), pp. 258–263.

The going concern

It is an observable fact today that most businesses, and indeed most organized activity, are carried on within the framework of institutions that have a continuing existence. The fact has been recognized in law through the institution of the corporation – an artificial person having an indefinite life. Accounting recognition is embodied in the concept of the 'going concern'.

The going concern concept has a profound effect upon the direction of accounting:

1. To a going concern, the values that could be obtained on liquidation for assets that are tied up in the business and not separate from it are largely irrelevant, and usually may be ignored.*

2. Some idea of the future stream of revenues from continuing operations is more important to the assessment of a business than knowledge about its assets and liabilities at any particular point of time. It follows that the income statement has come to be regarded as having greater significance than the balance sheet. Also, within the income statement, it is important to distinguish between the regular recurring type of income and the fortuitous or non-recurring gain or loss.

3. If income is to be determined fairly, the accounting cannot be based merely on a counting up of legal rights or possessions and legal debts or obligations. A balance sheet may fairly carry forward as an asset any measurable cost that demonstrably gives rise to future benefits, even though no saleable asset or right exists. Similarly, it should count as a liability any obligation likely to give rise to future costs, even though no legal liability to specific persons exists.

---

* This is not always true. If values obtainable through liquidation exceed the present value of future income from continuing in business, they are significant. This could only occur when some of the assets are being put to a use in the business that is not their most advantageous use. Since most business assets are special purpose in nature, this occurs relatively infrequently.

4. As a result of this emphasis on fair determination of income for a going concern, accounting income can less and less be considered as disposable income. The most important consideration is whether the business is better off as a result of its operations, not whether it is in a position to pay out its income in cash. Many businessmen have been perplexed by the paradox that their apparently profitable business is always short of cash. They fail to realize that earnings often are plowed back almost automatically if a business is growing, and that it is possible for a business to get into financial difficulty even though its earnings are perfectly satisfactory, if too much of its resources become invested in illiquid assets – e.g. new product development costs. The increasing emphasis on the statement of source and application of funds reflects in part the fact that the health of a business depends on keeping an eye on its financial resources as well as its earnings.

While accounting development has been much influenced by the fact that most enterprises can fairly be regarded as going concerns, it does not follow that accounting rules which are dependent on an assumption of continuing operation should be used if it is clear that an entity will only have a limited life. In such cases special purpose accounting and reporting are called for.

Monetary expression in the accounts

Wealth takes many forms. It may consist of cash in the bank, rights to payments of money in the future, share interests in companies, real estate, machinery, equipment, vehicles, materials and supplies, goods in various stages of completion, and so on. The job of accounting is to provide measures of wealth, show how it increases or decreases over an accounting period and report to interested parties. The task of classifying the quantities of data involved and expressing them in meaningful aggregates demands the use of a common medium of expression. Money, the medium involved in most exchanges of wealth, provides the natural medium for expression.

Consider for example the representation that a business holds inventory of $1,467,932. Such an inventory may consist of thousands of items at varying stages of production. If no monetary valuation were attached to the inventory, how else could some idea about it be conveyed to the average reader of a financial report?

The fact that some monetary expression must be attached to assets, liabilities, revenues and expenses in the accounts does not imply a bias in favour of any particular basis of valuation. Original cost in dollars is perhaps the easiest basis of valuation for assets acquired by purchase; but other bases are possible – current replacement cost, original cost adjusted by a general price index or a special price index, and so on. Any one basis would fulfill the requirement that the accounts be expressed in monetary terms.

Periodic and timely reporting

As has been stated, the purpose of financial accounting is to convey relevant information about the operations of a business or institution to outside interested parties. If such information is to be useful for decision-making however, it must be provided regularly and it needs to be up-to-date. Late accounting is bad accounting.°

The proper length of the accounting period could be the subject of argument. On the one hand it should not be so short that the results reported may be drastically affected by the transient currents of business. For most businesses a month would be too short. On the other hand it should not be so long that unfavourable trends are given opportunity to grow undisclosed and unchecked.

The traditional accounting period is the year, and this has considerable merit when it is considered that so much of business is still affected by the seasons and religious holidays. The retailer and manufacturer of consumer goods depends on the Christmas trade. The processor of farm and fishing products depends on the seasons. The automobile manufacturer and dealer, and makers of many other consumer durables have seasons considerably tied to the climate.

On the other hand some businesses are relatively unaffected by seasons and are more influenced by factors such as the business cycle. The construction and heavy engineering industries and supporting primary producers may feel that a two or three year period would be a more reliable indicator of average profitability than a one year period. Moreover, in any business, a one year period is often too short to show the effect of long-range planning or research and product development that has gone on in the period. Nevertheless, most people would agree that a reporting period longer than one year would be unacceptable. The reader should temper the conclusions he draws from financial statements with the knowledge that business activity by its nature fluctuates from season to season and year to year. If not, he may be misled – but to avoid the risk of misleading the reader by providing him with no information at all would seem an unsatisfactory solution.

Instead, the trend is all the other way, towards reporting, at least in brief, on semi-annual or quarterly figures. There are special problems bound up with such reporting and there is room for further development of accounting principles in this area, as well as that of annual reporting.

Conservatism

Accountants are traditionally 'conservative' – that is to say, they prefer performance to promise, they are skeptical about asset values, and they are alert to the possibility of understated liabilities. This conservative frame of mind is justified as a practical matter. For the natural tendency in business is that assets dissipate themselves, but liabilities adhere. Inventory not watched becomes shop-soiled or obsolete. Plant and equipment not maintained deteriorates. Receivables not followed up become harder to collect, while creditors can be relied upon to press their claims.

° The converse however is not necessarily true – i.e. that early accounting is good accounting. It is not unknown for companies to give a spurious appearance of accounting efficiency by rushing to publish their annual reports when in reality the speed has involved a considerable risk of inaccuracies and bad judgment. Also the expedient used by some financial institutions of closing off their records for the calendar year before the fiscal year-end in order to get their reports out early in the following month is merely laughable.

On the other hand the doctrine of conservatism has sometimes been used to justify deliberate understatement of financial position. In the nineteenth century, when investors committed their funds for the long pull, the practice was less harmful. Then, conservatism frequently found expression in the creation of 'secret reserves' through deliberate understatement or omission of asset values from the balance sheet or the recording of fictitious liabilities. The possibility of abuse inherent in such accounting, however, and at the very least the damage done to the usefulness of the accounts, is generally recognized today.

There is therefore little justification for a conservative bias in accounting where no doubt exists as to asset or liability measurement in accordance with the principles of accounting consistently followed by the business. The legitimate use of conservatism is confined to situations where genuine doubt exists about the item in question.

The problem, even with this limited use of the concept, however, is that there is virtually no authoritative guidance existing as to the permissible degree of conservatism. In the writer's opinion such guidance could be expressed in terms of probability. A priori, the amount at which an amount receivable or payable is carried in a balance sheet should be the best estimate of the amount that will ultimately be realized or paid (discounted to present value where appropriate). If that amount is uncertain, so that it is desired to depart from the most probable estimate to a conservative estimate, the degree of conservatism can be stated in probability terms. For example, it would seem intuitively reasonable that if a company were in the midst of a contract dispute, with the probability being that damages assessed or settled would be within a range of $100,000 to $300,000, the liability might be recorded at a figure of $240,000 – which has a 70% probability of not being exceeded. Conversely, the injured party might record in his accounts an estimated recovery of $160,000 on the grounds that he had a 70% expectation of getting at least that much.

Materiality

"De minimis non curat lex." The law does not concern itself with trifles – and so it is with accounting. The standard of 'materiality' simply implies that it is impractical to be overly meticulous about trivial amounts. Some matters may not be handled in accordance with accounting principles, simply because it is too much trouble to do so. For example, small stores of factory and office supplies are frequently written off when purchased rather than being dealt with through normal inventory accounting. Similarly, small items of furniture and equipment may be written off on acquisition rather than be capitalized and amortized by depreciation accounting.

The idea of materiality may have some similarity to mathematical concepts of significant figures. It is well known that if a number having five significant figures is multiplied by one having only two significant figures, the product cannot have more than two significant figures. Similarly, certain figures in accounting are necessarily approximations or estimates, the accuracy of which cannot be known until perhaps years have passed – e.g. the provision for depreciation. If depreciation can only be estimated in approximate terms, say within X dollars, there may be no reason to worry about a misstatement of fixed asset costs of the same general order. This argument should not be carried too far, however. A misstatement of marketable securities by $100,000 would ordinarily be a good deal more serious than a misstatement of the net carrying value of fixed assets by the same amount.

The amount which it is permissible to treat as immaterial will vary from item to item and also from business to business. The degree of distortion in the financial statements caused by ignoring immaterial items will obviously be a function largely of the size of the business. A multi-million dollar corporation may well be able to expense all capital purchases under $1,000 without distortion. The corresponding figure for the small owner-operated business might well be $25. General guidance as to what is material is contained in the Preface to the Research Recommendations of the CICA Research Committee:

> "While materiality is a matter of professional judgment in the particular circumstances, the Committee believes that, as a general rule, materiality may be judged in relation to the reasonable prospect of its significance in the making of decisions by the readers of the financial statements. If the item might reasonably be expected to affect the decision, it should be deemed to be material."

Supplement to Chapter 8 – The Distinction Between Revenue Offsets and Costs

Questions sometimes arise as to whether certain charges should be regarded as revenue offsets or revenue reductions on the one hand, or as costs incurred to earn revenue on the other. The definition adopted will control the reporting of these items in the financial statements. These questions are discussed below:

1. Trade discounts – These amounts represent reductions granted customers from a theoretical list price. The amount of reduction varies with the class of customer reflecting differences in the degree of service given or cost of service given to each class. The discount is almost invariably deducted in the billing and thus the amount of discount is never received. Accordingly trade discounts are normally treated as revenue offsets.

2. Volume rebates – These represent amounts refunded to customers who purchase more than certain basic quantities of goods over specified periods. Unlike trade discounts, they represent refunds to customers of amounts collected from them, rather than amounts deducted at the time of the original billing. They are, however, broadly similar in purpose to trade discounts since they should reflect savings in unit costs in dealing with larger volume purchasers. Accordingly they are usually treated as deductions in arriving at revenue.

3. Allowances – These represent price adjustments made to customers after sale for such reasons as damage to goods in shipment, poor quality, errors in delivery, etc. Once again they represent amounts never received and are usually treated as revenue offsets.

4. Returns – Charge-backs arising from cancellation of sales and return of goods obviously represent amounts to be deducted from gross revenue.

5. Federal sales and excise taxes required to be collected at point of sale by the manufacturer or licensed wholesaler – These are taxes imposed on the vendor at point of sale and calculated by reference to the selling price. In principle, such taxes do not represent recompense for any service performed by the

vendor and therefore do not represent costs on which the vendor is entitled, or will normally attempt to earn a return.

The latter statement however is subject to some qualification. The vendor bears the credit risk on such taxes included with his billings. If the purchaser defaults on payment, the vendor is still liable for the tax. Also taxes may be imposed sufficiently early that an allowance for interest on them becomes a factor in the vendor's prices.

Certain manufacturers pay sales tax under the 'unlicensed wholesale branch method'. In some cases tax may be paid when goods are shipped from the factory to the branch based on a price equivalent to the price the manufacturer would charge to an independent wholesaler. In such cases the vendor is in effect carrying on two businesses, that of a manufacturer and, through his branch, that of a wholesaler. His ultimate sale price for goods sold out of the branch will represent recompense for both the manufacturing and wholesaling functions. When he is viewed as a manufacturer, the tax is not part of his revenue. When he is viewed as a wholesaler, however, the tax is part of his costs and hence must be covered by revenue.

In some of these borderline situations described above, it may be a matter of opinion whether or not the tax should be deducted in reporting revenue. In the normal case however, sales and excise taxes would be treated as revenue offsets.

6. Provincial sales taxes – These taxes are imposed on the consumer but are collected by the vendor. Since the vendor receives the tax as agent for the government it should not be included in gross revenue.

7. Freight out – Prices for goods sold may be quoted delivery included or F.O.B. factory. If a delivered price is quoted, delivery may be made by the vendor's own equipment, or by hiring outside freight or cartage firms. A theoretical argument can be made that the charge by outside freight or cartage agents should be deducted from revenue, since some of the sales price must be considered to be on account of services not rendered by the vendor. As a practical matter however, the inconsistency in treatment of delivery charges would probably detract from the usefulness of the accounts. If the vendor performs any deliveries, it would probably be better to charge all costs of deliveries whether internal or external as costs. Only if the vendor has no facilities for making deliveries, would it seem better to treat delivery charges by outsiders as revenue offsets.

8. Cash discounts – These discounts are offered by the vendor to encourage payment within a specified short period of time. Usually the discount is sufficiently generous that the purchaser should take advantage of it even if he has to borrow to do so. The expectation, therefore, is that customers will take advantage of discounts and it follows logically that the revenue figure should originally record only the amount billed less the cash discount offered. This practice of originally recording revenue on a net basis, however, is pretty well confined to the utility companies. Some businesses record as revenue the gross amount billed but deduct from it actual cash discounts allowed, which comes to much the same sort of thing. The more frequent practice, however, is to record as revenue the gross amount billed and to charge off cash discounts allowed as a financial expense.

9. Bad debts – Whenever sales are made on credit there exists a possibility, in some cases a virtual certainty, that some accounts will never be paid because of default by the debtors. It could be argued then that some allowance for this loss should be deducted from the revenue account on the grounds that this estimated amount will never be received. The more customary practice, however, is to leave the revenue figure at the total of amounts billed (less returns, adjustments, etc.) and treat any allowance required for doubtful accounts as a cost or loss.

Apart from the first four items mentioned above, variations are found in practice whether the items are treated as revenue deductions or costs. Some of these variations are justified by differences in circumstances, while others reflect merely differences in opinion. In most cases, however, the amounts at issue are not sufficiently large that differences in treatment will materially distort the revenue figures shown.

Supplement to Chapter 10 – Criteria for Selection of a Depreciation Pattern

The choice of a depreciation pattern determines how the cost of a fixed asset is allocated to time periods over its economic life. The pattern chosen is supposed to be 'rational' – but how may rationality be demonstrated? Many accountants give a very simple answer to this. If an asset is expected to show level net proceeds from its use a straight-line pattern is considered appropriate. If net proceeds are expected to tail off over its life (because of increasing operating and maintenance costs or decreasing revenues) a diminishing charge pattern is preferred. If the asset's life will be terminated only when it is worn out through use, a unit-of-production method may be used.

This simple approach suggests two questions:

1. How do we know what net proceeds are to be expected from the use of an asset?

2. What account should be taken of the time value of money in the calculation? That is to say, net proceeds from the use of an asset ten years from now are not worth as much as the net proceeds we are earning today. Is a straight-line depreciation pattern really appropriate if these values are unequal? In other words should the depreciation pattern take into account a factor for interest or cost of capital?

Proceeds from utilization of a fixed asset

A moment's reflection should serve to convince us that in many situations we do not know what net proceeds are to be expected from the purchase of a capital asset. For example, what proceeds can we attribute to the carpet on the floor of an executive's office? This may seem an extreme illustration, but in fact it is not. The same point applies to all capital assets bought for administrative purposes (office equipment, head office building, etc.) and if it applies to them it also applies (at least to a degree) to fixed assets used in manufacturing, since you cannot carry on manufacturing without some administration. Moreover, even if we ignore the dependence of the manufacturing process on administration, we have to recognize that much of the time the final product will have been worked on by more than one piece of capital equipment, so that allocation of the net proceeds among machines must be arbitrary. The basic point is that most of the time the net proceeds of a business as a whole represent the joint product of all its capital investment and cannot be allocated on a factual basis to parts of it.

In a few cases, a reasonably accurate estimate of revenues and costs associated with an asset can be made – e.g. for investment in cars by a taxi company or airplanes by an airline. In other cases where purchase of an asset has been justified by estimates of cost savings, these can be considered as the proceeds attributable to the asset. In still other cases where a whole new project has been undertaken, projections made in connection with evaluation of the investment may give guidance to the depreciation pattern. (It is somewhat ironic that it is easier to deduce an appropriate depreciation provision for the project as a whole from such evaluations than for individual assets.) But many cases remain where judgment as to the benefits derived from investment in a capital asset, and hence the appropriate pattern for depreciation, must be largely intuitive.*

The significance of the time value of money

Suppose the management of a business is considering the purchase of a machine which it is estimated should make a net contribution to income of $1,000 a year for the next ten years, or a grand total of $10,000. What will the management be willing to pay for the machine? There are a number of ways by which, in practice, the management of a business would approach this question. One thing is sure however, and that is that they would not pay as much as $10,000 since the present worth of sums of money to be received in the future is not equal to face value. It must be discounted. If the management adopted a 'discounted cash flow' approach, and aimed for a 10% return in investment it would make the following calculation:**

---

* In a stimulating work, W. T. Baxter suggests that it is not necessary to assume a particular level of revenue from the use of an asset if it can be assumed the asset will be replaced at the end of its life. In such a case a 'deprival value' can be assigned the asset which equals the difference between the present value of all future outlays (for replacement, etc.) that would be required if the firm did not now own the asset, and the present value of future outlays assuming it does own the asset. Future outlays associated with the use of the asset include costs of exceptional repairs, etc. attributed to its ageing and also include any estimated *reductions* in normal revenues due to age. The decline in 'deprival value' over the years provides a measure of the appropriate depreciation charge year by year. (Presumably, if special outlays for repairs, etc. were charged directly to income in a year, the depreciation charge for that year would be reduced. The Study is not explicit on this point.) See W. T. Baxter, *Depreciation* (London: Sweet & Maxwell, 1971).

** This and subsequent illustrations are oversimplified and not strictly accurate in detail because of the assumption that earnings accrue at the end of the year, rather than gradually throughout it. They are however adequate for the purpose of illustration.

	Estimated earnings	*Discount factor*	*Present worth*
Year 1	$1,000	.909	$ 909
2	1,000	.827	827
3	1,000	.751	751
4	1,000	.683	683
5	1,000	.621	621
6	1,000	.564	564
7	1,000	.513	513
8	1,000	.467	467
Subtotal			5,335
9	1,000	.424	424
Subtotal			5,759
10	1,000	.385	385
Total			$6,144

On this basis, it would appear that the business could afford to pay $6,144 for the machine and attain its objective of a 10% return.

If after purchase, a straight-line depreciation pattern were applied to this machine, the accounts would show a steady annual amount of earnings ($1,000–$614.40) over the years from the use of the machine. To some this would seem natural and logical when the net cash earnings of the machine (before depreciation) are a steady annual amount. However, it does mean that the accounts would show a steadily increasing percentage return on the investment over the years, as follows:

Year	*Investment at beginning of year*	*Net income per accounts*	*% return on investment*
1	$6,144	$386	6.3%
2	5,530	386	7.0
3	4,915	386	7.9
4	4,301	386	8.9
5	3,686	386	10.5
.	.	.	.
.	.	.	.
10	614	386	62.9

In no year would the accounts show the actual rate of return aimed for by the management of the business: – viz. 10%.

An alternate depreciation pattern then might aim at maintaining the net carrying value of the machine at an amount equal to the present worth of its remaining service values, just as the initial investment represented the present worth of service values over its whole life. Reference back to the original illustration will indicate that with nine years' remaining life the present worth would be $5,759, with eight years $5,335, and so on. The depreciation provision required in the first year, therefore, would be $385 ($6,144–$5,759), in the second year $424, in the third year $467 and so on. The accounts would then show a constant 10% return on investment, as follows:

Year	Investment at beginning of year	Net income per accounts	% return on investment
1	$6,144	$615	10%
2	5,759	576	10
3	5,335	533	10
.	.	.	.
.	.	.	.
.	.	.	.
10	909	91	10

Here we have developed the 'annuity' pattern of depreciation, familiar to most accountants in theory, but rarely seen in practice. The name derives from a comparison of the initial investment in machinery with the purchase of an annuity yielding cash payments of a fixed amount for a period of years. It is well known that the annual payments on an annuity consist of two elements – interest and a return of capital – and that the interest portion steadily decreases as the investment is reduced over the years by the return of capital. Similarly, the net cash return from a machine is visualized as being in part a return of capital (to which the depreciation charge should be equated) and the remainder is true income. And, just as with an annuity, it is felt that in the early years the income element in the net cash return is large, and the return of capital element is small.

Some accountants would argue that this is the most logical way to approach an evaluation of depreciation patterns, because it is consistent with the approach that sophisticated management takes towards its investment decisions. A little further analysis therefore may be in order. It will be noted that an assumption that service values will be *level* over the life of the asset produces a depreciation charge that *increases* over that life. Conversely, one can assume that if the appropriate depreciation charge is *level* over the life of the asset, there is a presumption that the service values are *declining*. To generalize, if one accepts the theory underlying the annuity method of depreciation, one can deduce (given the implicit discount rate) what service values are assumed in any given depreciation pattern, whether it be the annuity pattern itself, the straight-line pattern, the diminishing balance pattern, or any other pattern.

The following graph shows the course of service values over the life of a 10-year asset (with 10.74% salvage value at the end of the period) that are implicit in the annuity pattern of depreciation, the straight-line pattern, and the diminishing balance pattern, given a 10% per annum discount factor. It will be noted that the annuity pattern assumes steady service values over the life of the asset. The straight-line pattern assumes declining service values over the life of the asset, from 18.93% of cost in the first year to 10.90% in the tenth year. The diminishing balance method assumes a precipitous decline in service values from 30.0% of cost in the first year to 4.02% in the tenth year.

If we wish to evaluate a depreciation pattern against this background therefore, we must look to the patterns of service values of the assets being depreciated. A clue to the pattern of service values may be found in an examination of the causes of asset retirements. If retirement is caused by wear and tear, it is likely that it will be foreshadowed some years before the actual retirement by increasing repair and maintenance costs, greater downtime, greater scrap costs because of the increasing inaccuracy of the machine, and possibly a declining rate of output.

Accordingly there is some reason to expect a decline in service values towards the end of a machine's life. Again if we consider the effect of obsolescence upon an item of capital equipment, it will be observed that it will have its greatest effect towards the end of the asset's life. Accordingly it is fair to expect that in many if not the majority of cases, service values will tail off over the life, or at least in the second half of the life of a capital asset.

DEPRECIATION PATTERNS INCORPORATING A 10% INTEREST FACTOR

SERVICE VALUES IMPLIED BY VARIOUS DEPRECIATION PATTERNS – FOR ASSET WITH 10 YEAR LIFE AND 10.74% RESIDUAL VALUE

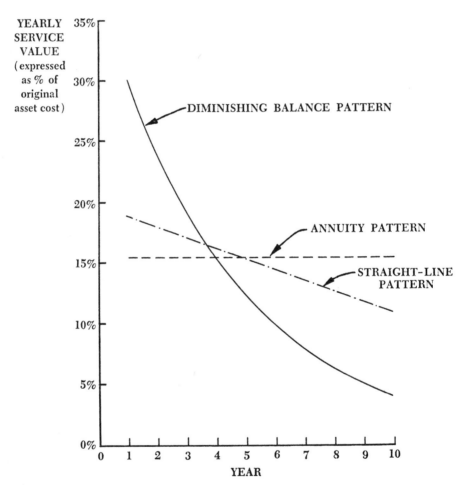

Unfortunately, very little has been published as to actual business experience with the course of service values over an asset's life, and the typical business does not have records from which it can report its own experience with any degree of certainty. Any conclusions as to the appropriateness of the various depreciation patterns must therefore be tentative.

It would seem however that the annuity method (or the sinking fund method, which is much the same in result) would appear to be appropriate only where there is very little probability of obsolescence through changes in technology or shifts in the pattern of consumer demand. Also the decline in efficiency of the asset with age and use should be negligible. These conditions are rare. They are likely to be found only with relatively long-lived assets. They may be found in some public utilities where the risk of obsolescence is relatively small. In the equipment category of asset, the conditions might be applicable to office furniture, but probably to no other. The straight-line method of depreciation is appropriate where some decline of service values with time is expected but the decline is not rapid. It is likely to be more appropriate for longer-lived assets than for shorter-lived assets. Its best application is probably with buildings and structures. The diminishing balance method of depreciation is most appropriate where the decline in service values is likely to be rapid. This would hold where there is a high risk of obsolescence of the asset, or a considerable decline in its physical efficiency over life. Automobiles appear to be an ideal application for diminishing balance depreciation. Short-lived machinery and equipment could probably also appropriately use this method. Longer-lived machinery might be better adapted to the straight-line method, and in general it would appear that the diminishing balance method will often give too rapid a write-off in the early years of asset lives.

There is of course no reason why a business should not construct a depreciation schedule which would fit its own conditions and still meet the tests of being orderly and rational. For example, it may well be that for some assets a straight-line write-off would be appropriate for the first half or three-quarters of the asset life and a diminishing balance method thereafter. Alternatively, it might be appropriate for some machinery to write it off on the diminishing balance method during its intensive use period in, say, the first half of its life, and on a straight-line basis thereafter. In practice, very little consideration has been given to these matters in ordinary business accounting.

Supplement to Chapter 13 – Evaluation of Tax Allocation Theory

The main controversy in income tax accounting has concerned whether, and to what extent, tax allocation procedures are necessary to arrive at a fair portrayal of income for a year. As noted in Chapter 13, this issue has now largely been settled with general acceptance of comprehensive tax allocation procedures. The statements of the Canadian and American Institutes, however, differ from the English Institute in the application of the procedures. The North American Institutes advocate the 'deferral' concept;* the English Institute recommends the 'accrual' concept; none of them favour the once-popular 'net-of-tax' concept.

---

* This 'deferral' theory of tax allocation contains one rather unusual feature. In no other case can the allocation of a cost to accounting periods give rise to a deferred *credit* in the balance sheet. Deferred credits normally can arise only in connection with the allocation of *revenues*. In the case of income tax allocation however, the net tax cost is visualized as being composed of positive and negative elements, a tax cost (positive) associated with revenues taxed and a tax reduction (negative) associated with costs allowed for tax purposes. Where costs are allowed for tax purposes before they are written off in the accounts, it is the *tax reduction* element that is deferred under tax allocation procedures and this is represented by a deferred credit in the balance sheet.

The theory espoused has some significance to the determination of the net income figure and to the presentation of the statements. The explanation for such possible differences is as follows:

1. Under the 'deferral' theory, the amounts of deferred tax debits or credits are not regarded as valuations of assets or liabilities, but merely the amounts resulting from transferring the actual or estimated tax effects of revenues or costs from the period when the tax is imposed to the period when the revenues and costs are recognized in determining accounting income. As a consequence no problem of valuation of the deferred debits or credits arises.

2. Under the accrual theory, the deferred debits or credits are regarded as estimates of amounts of tax reductions that will be realized in future, or liabilities for tax that will become payable in future. Two consequences flow from this view:
   (a) if tax rates are expected to be different in the future when the tax becomes recoverable or payable the valuation of the deferred tax debits and credits should be adjusted;
   (b) a discount factor could be justified if recovery or payment were long delayed.*

3. The 'net-of-tax' theory, strictly speaking, is not a *tax* allocation theory, but rather calls for consideration of the tax status of assets and liabilities in their measurement and allocation to income account. Thus, if a liability for warranty cost is not allowable for tax when set up, but warranty payments when made will be, the provision for future warranty payments may be reduced to allow for the future tax benefit. Or if fixed asset costs are claimed for tax purposes before depreciation is written, the loss of tax deductibility should itself be recognized as depreciation of the original carrying value of the asset. In practice, where the net-of-tax method was used the amount of adjustment to the asset or liability valuation was made exactly equal to the tax effect of the timing difference, but this was not necessary under the theory. Rather the logical conclusion to the theory would have been an examination of the real value of tax deductibility of costs, which (as will be shown later) requires recognition of a discount factor if such deductibility is delayed for some time after the cost is incurred.

In view of these differences, a closer analysis is attempted here. Four situations give rise to timing differences between taxable and accounting income:

1. where revenues are included in accounting income in one period but are not taxable until some later period, e.g. profit on instalment sales;

2. where revenues are deferred in the accounts to a later period but are taxable in the current period, e.g. unearned profits on certain types of construction contracts, and intercompany profits in inventories which are eliminated on consolidation;

3. where expenses are charged against income for accounting purposes in one period but are not deducted for tax purposes until some later period, e.g. pro-

---

* In Opinion No. 10 issued in 1966 the Accounting Principles Board recommended that deferred taxes should not be determined on a discounted basis pending further consideration. No further discussion of this subject has yet been made public.

visions for warranties, provisions for deferred compensation payments, and depreciation of fixed assets or write-downs of inventories in excess of amounts allowed for tax purposes;

4. where expenses are claimed for tax purposes in one period but are not charged against income for accounting purposes until some later period, e.g. capital cost allowances in excess of depreciation charged, and certain other costs which are sometimes deferred in the accounts but claimed immediately for taxes, such as exploration and development costs, start-up costs, past service pension contributions, and accounting and legal expenses in connection with bond or debenture financing.

In the first case above, revenues have been recorded as earned in the accounts, but have simply not yet come into taxable income. In the normal course however, within a short period of years they will become taxable. It would seem here that the 'accrual' concept best explains the charging-off of a tax cost currently that becomes payable (in all probability) in future.

In the second case taxes have actually been paid with respect to revenue not yet recognized in the accounts. This being so, taxes will not again be paid with respect to that revenue when it is recognized in the future. The deferment of the tax charge currently, to be matched with the future year when revenues are recognized but not taxable, fits the deferral theory.

In the third case costs have been absorbed against accounting income without being allowed against current taxable income. In all probability however, a benefit will be derived from tax deduction in the future and it seems reasonable to accrue for the estimated benefit then receivable. Here again the accrual concept seems more appropriate.

In the fourth case taxes have been reduced by allowances for costs not yet written off in the accounts. As a result, no tax benefit will be received in future when such costs are absorbed against accounting income. If one accepts the idea of deferment of tax *reductions* (the negative element in income tax cost) the deferral theory may be accepted. In the alternative however, a strong argument may be made for the net-of-tax theory in this situation. It is clear that no rational business man would pay as much for an asset not claimable for taxes as he would for an identical asset that is claimable for taxes. In other words, the tax-deductible status of an asset has a value and, to the extent it is used up, that value should be written off. If in the case of fixed assets, an asset is being depreciated over its service life, but its tax-deductible status is being absorbed over a shorter period, depreciation should be adjusted to compensate.

The conclusion from this analysis then is that no one theory about the basis of tax allocation procedures is necessarily valid for every situation involving timing differences between accounting and taxable income, and a choice of one and one only theory is unnecessary in this connection. The traditional accounting techniques of accruals, deferments, and depreciation and amortization in step with benefits received, are sufficient, if properly applied, to deal with the income reporting problems involved in tax/accounting timing differences.

It has been noted earlier (in Chapter 6) that transactions giving rise to amounts payable or receivable should, in theory, always be stated at discounted values. Application of this proposition to accruals of income tax liabilities or recoveries in the applicable situations described above, leads to the conclusion that these accruals too should, in theory, be discounted. Usually in such cases however (i.e. where revenues or expenses are recognized for accounting purposes before they affect taxable income), the postponement of tax, or tax relief, is relatively short-term, and discounting the accruals would not be significant.

Depreciation adjusted to compensate for exhaustion of tax-deductible status

The situation where the effect of tax/accounting timing differences is of longest duration, ordinarily, is where costs are claimed for tax purposes before being written off in the accounts, and specifically where depreciation is claimed more rapidly for tax purposes than it is booked. It was suggested above that the deferment concept might be (and is) applied in this situation, in which case no argument can be made for the discounted approach. The same is not true however where provision is made for tax/accounting timing differences on the 'net-of-tax' basis, by way of additional depreciation.

When the suggestion is made that additional depreciation should be written to reflect the using up of an asset's tax-deductible status, the first question that arises is as to the determination of the initial value of the tax deductible status. A quick answer would be that, with a 50% tax rate, each dollar of plant investment produces a 50¢ tax benefit, so one-half the value of an asset lies in its tax-deductible status. This however ignores the fact that the tax benefit is received only over a period of years. Hence the value today of future tax deductibility is something less than 50¢ on the dollar. On a discounted basis, the actual present value of tax reductions which are allowed on the diminishing balance method is given by the formula:

$$PV = AT \frac{(r)}{(i + r)}$$

Where A = undepreciated capital cost of the asset
T = the tax rate
r = the diminishing balance rate
i = the interest rate used in discounting

For example, if the tax rate is 50% and the interest rate is 10% the value of future tax deductions on a class 8 asset claimable for tax purposes on a 20% diminishing balance basis, is (assuming continued profitable operations):

$$50\% \frac{(.20)}{(.10 + .20)} = 33\frac{1}{3}\% \text{ of undepreciated capital cost.}$$

When the above formula is used, the tax rate and diminishing balance rate are known, but the appropriate interest rate must be chosen. There might be some theoretical argument about this in the normal company – arguments could be made in favour of its internal earnings rate, its average overall cost of capital or its cost of debt. Since we are concerned with the value to the shareholders of the tax allowance, such rate has to be expressed in 'after-tax' terms. For general use a rate in the range of 8% to 12%, which would be equivalent to the average after-tax cost of capital for a wide range of business would seem appropriate.

Using a 10% discount rate and a 50% tax cost, the present value of the tax-deductible status of various classes of assets (as described in the tax regulations) would be:[*]

	Capital cost allowance rate	Value of tax-deductible status
Class 3	5%	16⅔%
Class 8	20%	33⅓%
Class 10	30%	37½%
Class 12 and costs of other assets claimable 100% in the year incurred, such as costs of exploration and development in the extractive industries		45.45%

The effect of accelerated allowances is illustrated by the following figures:[**]

	Capital cost allowance rate	Value of tax-deductible status
Class 19	50%	43.68%
Class 20	20%	38.40%

In general, as is to be expected, the lower the capital cost allowance rate (i.e. the longer it takes to obtain tax deductions) the lower is the discounted value of future tax reductions. Consequently, the lower the capital cost allowance rate, the greater the difference between the deferred tax that would be provided on the normal tax allocation basis and the depreciation to be provided on the basis described above. On average for most businesses it may be guessed that the extra book depreciation required to recognize the exhaustion of tax deductible status as a result of capital cost allowances in excess of depreciation would be about two-thirds of the deferred tax provided on the recognized tax allocation basis.

Application of the 'additional depreciation' concept

An example may clarify the 'additional depreciation' concept. Suppose a company invests $3,000,000 in a year in Class 8 assets. Suppose further that these assets are expected to have a 10-year life, and consequently would normally be depreciated at a 10% straight-line rate.

Under the proposal, the cost of these assets would be assigned to two categories – a 'tax-deductible value' category equal to 33⅓% of the total cost (if using a 10% interest factor) and the remainder to a 'service value' category. The 'tax-deductible value' category would be depreciated on the diminishing balance basis at the rate

---

[*] This calculation assumes that the cash effects of these allowances on taxes payable are received at the end of each fiscal year after the capital asset is acquired. This would be a reasonable practical approximation to the actual cash effect in most situations.

[**] Calculated on a different formula, because these allowances are granted on the straight-line rather than the diminishing balance basis.

allowed for tax purposes, since this would appropriately match the tax reductions obtained through claiming capital cost allowances. The 'service value' category would continue to be amortized at the 10% straight-line rate, assuming that basis properly reflects the expected capability of the assets to produce revenue over a 10-year period. Total depreciation on the new basis, compared with depreciation as it normally would be calculated, may be scheduled as follows:

	Depreciation base	*Depreciation provision*			
		Year 1	*Year 2*	*Year 3*	*Etc.*
New basis					
Service value	$2,000,000	$200,000	$200,000	$200,000	–
Tax-deductible value	1,000,000	200,000	160,000	128,000	–
	3,000,000	400,000	360,000	328,000	–
Normal depreciation provision	3,000,000	300,000	300,000	300,000	–
Extra depreciation – new basis		$100,000	$ 60,000	$ 28,000	–

This extra depreciation may be compared with the amount of deferred tax which would be recorded on the normal tax allocation basis as follows:

	Depreciation base	*Depreciation provision*			
		Year 1	*Year 2*	*Year 3*	*Etc.*
Normal depreciation	$3,000,000	$300,000	$300,000	$300,000	–
Capital cost allowance	3,000,000	600,000	480,000	384,000	–
Excess capital cost allowance		300,000	180,000	84,000	–
Deferred tax – 50%		150,000	90,000	42,000	–

It will be observed that for a Class 8 asset, the 'additional depreciation', on the assumptions given, is exactly two-thirds the amount of deferred tax as provided on the normal tax allocation basis.

Conclusion on tax allocation accounting

It has been argued here that in strict logic several different methods should be used to recognize the effect of differences in the timing of revenues and costs for accounting and taxation purposes. The comprehensive tax allocation method on the deferral theory follows one basis only for dealing with these differences. In so doing it lays itself open to criticism on particular points. Yet it is necessary to remember the environment in which comprehensive tax allocation was adopted. Until the Institute statements of 1967, the nature of timing differences and the problems in accounting for them had been matters of debate for close to fifteen years. In the course of this period practice had hardened to the point that the opposing sides, as a practical matter, could probably not have been reconciled. The professional accounting societies had to do something to eliminate the gap between the diametrically opposed positions that had developed. The method they chose had some elements of artificiality in it. But it was a great deal better than the near chaos that preceded it, and may well have represented the most constructive practical action that could have been taken in the situation.

Supplement to Chapter 17 – Problems in Consolidation Accounting Procedures

Many problems arise in the mechanics of consolidation. These problems and the procedures developed to cope with them are dealt with below under the following headings:

1. Problems at date of acquisition of a subsidiary
   (a) determination of the date of acquisition
   (b) step-by-step acquisitions
   (c) uniformity of accounting practice
   (d) consistency in fiscal years
   (e) inter-company transactions before acquisition.

2. Allocation of purchase discrepancies at date of acquisition.

3. Changes in parent company interest after acquisition of control.

4. Elimination of inter-company accounts and transactions.

5. Minority interest problems
   (a) valuation of minority interest at date of first consolidation
   (b) minority interest share in inter-company profits eliminated
   (c) minority interest in gain or loss on inter-company bond holdings
   (d) minority interest calculation where there are interlocking shareholdings
   (e) minority interest share in deficit of subsidiary
   (f) presentation of minority interest in the consolidated statements.

6. Problems in consolidation of foreign subsidiaries.

7. Stock dividends issued by subsidiary companies.

Problems at date of acquisition of a subsidiary

Determination of the date of acquisition

The first problem is to establish the effective date of acquisition of the subsidiary, that is the date from which the operating results of the subsidiary are included in the consolidated income. From a legalistic viewpoint the proper date would be the closing date when title to the subsidiary company shares is vested in the parent company. From the standpoint of reflecting the decision-making involved however, a better date is probably that on which the contract to purchase is signed. In some cases, a still earlier date may be justified. The negotiations may have been carried on using the most recent financial statements of the acquired company as a basis, and it may be reasonable to assume the date of those statements as the one from which operations enure to the benefit of the new parent. In some cases, for example, the purchase price will be specifically related to the financial position at a date, and the agreement will ensure that operations subsequently are for the benefit of the purchaser by prohibiting payment of dividends or any special distribution by the subsidiary after that date until title of transfer is effected.

A point to watch in the determination of the effective acquisition date is that it should not predate the payment date by too long a period. For example, suppose a purchase were made in mid-year based on the previous year-end's audited financial statements (with provision for investigation by the purchaser and the usual vendor's warranties concerning subsequent material adverse changes). It would be misleading to include the profits of the subsidiary in the consolidation from the first of the year because this would mean a full year's subsidiary profits would be taken in, whereas only half a year's interest on money borrowed, or half a year's loss of interest on funds used to finance the purchase, would be taken into account. If the acquisition is made through the medium of a share issue, there would be no interest effect, but the acquisition date similarly should not predate the time at which the shares are assumed to be outstanding for the purpose of calculating earnings per share. In general the acquisition date and payment date should coincide or be separated by a period not longer than trade credit terms would allow. If for some reason a longer time gap seems justified, it would be logical, when recording the transaction, to discount the liability for payment.

A practical problem may be to obtain reliable financial statements of the subsidiary at the date selected as the logical acquisition date. Typically, it will be necessary to go to the nearest month end. If the monthly statements are unreliable or non-existent it may be necessary to go back to audited statements and prorate earnings of the subsidiary for the period before and after the acquisition date selected. In many cases however, special audited statements will be obtained at the date of acquisition to substantiate the position at that date and, incidentally, to provide verification of matters covered in the agreement for sale and to ascertain whether the accounting methods of the new subsidiary conform with those of the parent.

Step-by-step acquisitions

Where control of a subsidiary is acquired in a series of two or more transactions, the question arises whether the date of acquisition of the subsidiary is to be taken as the date of the acquisition which finally gave the parent control, or whether more than one acquisition date will be assumed. The practical significance of the question relates to the inclusion of the parent's share of the subsidiary's earnings in consolidated income. For example, suppose control was acquired in two separate purchases of 30% of the subsidiary shares each. On the step-by-step basis, 30% of the subsidiary's earnings would be included in consolidated income from the date of the first purchase and 60% after the second purchase. On the single-step basis, no subsidiary earnings would be taken up until after the second purchase unless the subsidiary had happened to pay dividends in the interim.

If the purchases are part of a more or less deliberate program of acquisition by the parent company, the step-by-step basis would seem theoretically superior. On the other hand, if some years elapse between the initial purchase and the date of acquisition of control, there would be a presumption that there was no organized program for acquisition. Even where there is a relatively brief series of transactions, a difficulty arises on the step-by-step basis when the parent company's year-end intervenes between the date of the first transaction and the date of acquisition of control. In these circumstances, it is doubtful that consolidation of what is still a minority interest would be justified at the year-end and therefore the parent's share of the subsidiary's earnings will not be taken up unless the investment is carried on the equity basis. Accordingly, in the year when control is finally acquired, a step-by-step accounting basis would require correction of earnings previously reported, which is usually done only with reluctance. As a result of these various considerations, both treatments of step-by-step transactions are found in practice.

Uniformity of accounting practice

A single company must follow uniform accounting practices. In principle, one would expect the same requirement in a consolidated group. This does not mean that the same accounting method must be followed, even though the underlying factual circumstances differ. For example, in one subsidiary or division, it may be felt that LIFO inventory accounting is appropriate because of the nature of its business while other divisions use FIFO. But when underlying conditions are the same, one would expect to find similar accounting methods.

This general rule encounters some difficulties in practice. For example, when a company acquires a foreign subsidiary, it might be found that the foreign company follows a different depreciation pattern than that of its new parent, perhaps under the influence of taxation practice in the foreign country. Provided such depreciation pattern is recognized as acceptable in the country of origin of the parent company, there seems to be no absolute necessity for requiring a change in a subsidiary's depreciation accounting methods. This would be particularly true where a minority interest remains in the subsidiary. On the other hand, if the subsidiary's accounting method is not acceptable in the parent company's country, adjustment must be made to the subsidiary's figures for purposes of consolidation. For example, certain European countries permit substantial write-downs of inventory below cost for tax purposes and require that these be recorded in the accounts if claimed for tax. Such inventory reserves would obviously have to be eliminated in the consolidated accounts (with allowance for associated tax effects). The practical general rule in a consolidated group (and the same would logically also be appropriate for a divisionalized company) is that where alternative accounting practices are considered acceptable, different divisions or subsidiaries may follow different alternatives provided the operations of the several divisions or subsidiaries involved are not integrated. This last proviso suggests for example, that it would be wrong, if inventory were transferred from one affiliate to another for further processing, to have different costing methods – one of which included certain overheads and one of which did not.

Consistency in fiscal years

Not infrequently a subsidiary may have a different fiscal year-end from that of its parent. Reasons for this may vary. The natural business year of the subsidiary, for example, may differ from that of the parent. Foreign subsidiaries may have to close off earlier than does the parent company in order to get their financial statements completed in time for consolidation.

If the accounts of the subsidiary are consolidated, the discrepancy in year-ends is a source of inaccuracy in the consolidated financial statements. The question is, how much inaccuracy may be tolerated? At one extreme, the difference in fiscal year-end may be given as a reason for non-consolidation. But if the subsidiary on all other grounds qualifies for consolidation, to omit it because of the difference in fiscal year-end merely substitutes one inaccuracy for another. The U.S. Securities and Exchange Commission, as an administrative rule, permits consolidation of subsidiaries where the difference in year-end is not more than 93 days, and this is probably reasonably representative of what is done in general practice in published reports. If the subsidiary's financial statements are older than this, the company may be included in the consolidation on the basis of later interim statements, even though such are unaudited (the auditor reporting on the consolidated financial statements must then decide whether the lack of an audit report on the subsidiary is material to his opinion).

Where stale-dated subsidiary financial statements are included in the consolidated statements, the inter-company accounts between that subsidiary and other members of the affiliated group will not be in agreement (unless there have been no transactions between them in the period intervening between the fiscal year-ends). In such cases the transactions accounting for the differences should be analyzed so as to make the most reasonable disposition of the difference in the consolidated statements.

The general conclusion is that differences in fiscal year-ends are not normally a sufficient reason for omitting a subsidiary from the consolidation. When the difference in year-end is not too great (normally not over three months) the accounts of the subsidiary may be consolidated as though they were up-to-date with provision for reasonable disposition of differences arising in consolidation of inter-company accounts in the affiliated group. When the time difference is greater, consolidation may be done on the basis of interim financial statements of the subsidiary unless these are considered likely to be unreliable by an amount material to the consolidation. In this, as is generally true, efficient accounting is basic to accurate financial reporting.

Inter-company transactions before acquisition

Some authorities have suggested that where assets have been sold between companies that later become affiliated, and such assets remain in the accounts of one of them after the affiliation is established, the inter-company profit on the transaction should be eliminated. The theory behind this proposition is that, from the standpoint of the affiliated group, the proper basis of asset valuation is cost when the asset was first acquired by the group.

In the writer's opinion this is an unnecessarily purist view. Cost as a basis of asset carrying value in the accounts is essentially justified because, as the product of an arm's-length transaction, it is objective evidence of value. If the sale between the companies before they became affiliates was truly at arm's length, the sales value forms an equally objective and proper basis for carrying the asset in the consolidated accounts.

Allocation of purchase discrepancies at date of acquisition

The process of consolidation, as has been indicated, is essentially one of substituting the assets and liabilities of the subsidiary for the amount of the investment in it in the balance sheet of the parent company. Where a subsidiary has operated independently before acquisition, the value of its identifiable net assets (less minority interest if any) will rarely be exactly equal to the amount paid for its shares by the parent company. There will be, therefore, a 'purchase discrepancy' arising in the consolidation at the date of acquisition which must be dealt with in the accounts in some fashion. The manner in which such purchase discrepancies are handled is discussed in Chapter 18 which deals with the problems peculiar to business combinations – i.e. amalgamations, mergers or acquisitions.

Changes in parent company interest after acquisition of control

Some rather subtle intellectual problems are presented when a change occurs in the parent company's percentage interest in the subsidiary after the date when control is acquired and consolidated statements are first prepared. The solution to these problems may depend partly on one's concept of the essential nature of the consolidated statements – whether they represent merely a more illuminating form of the parent company statements or whether they represent an attempt to account for an economic entity unified through the legal control exercised by the parent, but whose capital is financed by other sources as well. This same question is relevant to the manner of presentation of the minority interest in the consolidated balance sheet (see below).

Consider first the case where the parent company sells some of its shareholdings in a subsidiary at a price above their carrying value on the equity basis of accounting. Probably the majority of accountants would view this as a realization by the parent of part of its investment so that the gain would be credited to income and flow through to consolidated retained earnings. In effect they would be espousing the 'parent company' view of the consolidated accounts. From the 'economic entity' point of view on the other hand, no assets have been parted with by the consolidated group so there can be no business gain to be credited to income. Instead the transaction would be treated as a capital transaction involving a readjustment of ownership interest between majority and minority shareholders in the subsidiary, the net result of which is an overall increase in the assets of the entity. From the viewpoint of the entity, this would have to be regarded as an additional capital contribution.

Then take the case where the subsidiary itself issues shares so that the interest of the parent company has been diluted. Here the 'parent company' viewpoint does not seem nearly so persuasive. The parent company by itself has participated in no transaction. One has to postulate a notional issue of shares from the subsidiary to the parent company at a figure equal to average book value and a subsequent resale of the shares by the parent to justify accounting for a gain to the parent company. The simpler view on the other hand, and one more clearly in accord with the facts, is that capital has been contributed to the subsidiary and hence to the consolidated entity, and the whole is a capital transaction. The problem that arises however is that the new minority interest will in all probability have paid more than the amount at which its proportional interest in the subsidiary is shown on the books of the latter. What this really means is that there can be 'purchase discrepancies' with respect to minority interest as well as majority interest in consolidated statements. For example, if the minority interest pays $100,000 for a one-sixth share interest in a subsidiary company and the accounts of the subsidiary show the following position before and after the transaction:

Shareholders' equity:	*Before sale of shares*		*After sale of shares*
Capital – 100,000 shares	$100,000	120,000 shares	$200,000
Retained earnings	160,000		160,000
	$260,000		$360,000

the minority interest will only be credited with $60,000 under normal consolidation procedures and there will be a 'purchase discrepancy' of $40,000. In the writer's view the most logical treatment of this would be to include it with the minority equity account in the consolidated balance sheet. He is unaware of any case however in which this has been done in practice. An alternative, which would seem to be less logical, would be to show the $40,000 as contributed surplus. A third alternative, which seems still less logical, is to credit the $40,000 to consolidated retained earnings. A limited survey indicates that practice is divided between these latter two alternatives.

Finally, consider the case where the parent company buys out a minority interest some time after acquiring control. The universal practice in such a case is to treat any excess cost over underlying book value as an addition to the original purchase discrepancy (if any). This is only consistent with the treatment of the transactions by which the parent company acquired control. In other words, it is clear that in the original transactions giving rise to control and therefore consolidation, and in recording any transaction whereby such a control is increased, the viewpoint is clearly that of the parent company.

In summary, assets in the consolidated financial statements are to be carried at cost to the parent company including the purchase discrepancy. If subsequently an interest in such assets is sold through the medium of a sale of a part interest in a subsidiary, a gain or loss by the parent company proprietary interest may be recognized. On the other hand this does not prejudge the case where a minority interest invests directly in a subsidiary rather than buying shares from the parent company. It is much more straightforward to view this as a capital contribution to the affiliated group by the new minority interest than it is to consider it as a sort of sale of the parent company interest to the minority.

Elimination of inter-company accounts and transactions

Consolidated accounts basically try to portray the activities of an affiliated group of companies as though they were one company. Accordingly, assets and liabilities which merely represent amounts due from or owing to other companies in the group must be eliminated by offsetting them against each other as part of the consolidation process. Similarly, inter-company transactions are eliminated and only sales to or purchases from outsiders are reflected in a consolidated income statement. If inter-company transactions are made at a markup over cost and the assets sold remain in the books of the purchasing company at the end of the reporting year, the profit on such assets must also be eliminated from consolidated income in order to restate the asset at cost to the consolidating group. This reflects the rule that an entity cannot make a profit by dealing with itself.

The elimination of inter-company profits in inventory or fixed assets is usually a straightforward procedure (unless a minority interest exists – this will be discussed in the next section). The amount of inter-company profit to be eliminated from inventory will ordinarily be the gross margin recorded by the vendor company, but this is not invariably true. Some of the costs of the vendor might be properly added to inventory if the purchaser and vendor were operating as one unit. For example, freight costs absorbed by the vendor on sales to the purchasing company might well add to the utility of the inventory. Similarly, in the case of inter-company sales of fixed assets, some of the costs absorbed by the vendor company could represent installation costs which could properly be capitalized by the purchaser to reflect the total cost of putting the asset into service.

The eliminating entries dealing with inter-company profit in fixed assets are a little more complicated than for inventory. In the year of the inter-company sale, the profit must be charged back against consolidated income to reduce the asset to cost. In subsequent years that portion of the depreciation written by the purchasing company which relates to the inter-company profit must be reversed on consolidation to relate the consolidated depreciation provision to cost as carried for consolidation purposes.

While inter-company profits may be eliminated for consolidation purposes, they are of course realized from the standpoint of the individual companies, and usually this means that they will be taxed. Since this tax relates to income which will not be reported by the consolidated entity until subsequent periods, it should be deferred under normal tax allocation principles and, as such, will appear as a tax prepayment asset.

The elimination of inter-company receivables and payables is simply achieved by offsetting them as part of the consolidation mechanics. A difference may occur, however, where one company in the group has issued bonds or debentures in the open market and, subsequently, an affiliate has purchased some or all of the bonds outstanding. The stated amount of the bonds in the accounts of the issuer (par value plus or minus unamortized premium or discount on issue) will normally not correspond exactly with the carrying value of the investment asset in the accounts of the purchasing company. On consolidation, therefore, a difference is thrown up which from the group point of view is a realized gain or loss, although from the standpoint of the individual companies it is not. This gain or loss would be reflected through consolidated income account.

Subsidiary companies may also hold shares in the parent company or in other affiliated companies. The former situation is rare in Canada because of prohibition of such acquisitions by several corporations acts. Where the situation does exist, the parent company shares held by the subsidiary would logically be treated in the consolidated financial statements according to the rules for accounting for stock reacquired. (See Chapter 15.) Where subsidiary companies hold shares in each other, there is no problem unless a minority interest exists in one or both companies. Such cases are referred to in the next section.

Minority interest problems

Valuation of minority interest at the date of first consolidation

The mechanics of consolidation involve in part the elimination by the parent company of its account for investment in the subsidiary and the substitution for it of the net amount of assets, liabilities and minority interest (if any) in the subsidiary. At the date of acquisition of the subsidiary, as pointed out previously, there is usually a purchase discrepancy between the amount of the parent company's investment and the net book value of the subsidiary. This in effect represents the difference between the value which the parent company puts on the net assets of the subsidiary and the amounts at which these are shown on the books of the latter. The difference may in part represent a different valuation by the parent of the assets shown in the subsidiary's accounts, in part it may represent payments for identifiable tangible and intangible assets not valued in the subsidiary's accounts, and in part it may represent payment for unidentifiable intangibles – commonly known by the omnibus term 'goodwill'.

Where a minority interest exists, the purchase discrepancy will of course only apply to the parent company's interest in the subsidiary. From this it has been suggested that the calculation of minority interest should reflect its share of the asset revaluation represented by the purchase discrepancy. The effect of this suggestion is shown by the following illustration. Suppose a company acquires 80% of the shares of another company for $360,000 when the balance sheet of the latter shows net assets of $300,000. On the basis of the subsidiary company balance sheet, the minority interest would be calculated as 20% of $300,000 = $60,000. The purchase discrepancy on consolidation then would be $360,000 – ($300,000 – $60,000) or $120,000.

Alternatively, it might have been calculated that if an 80% interest was worth $360,000, 100% of the subsidiary should be worth $\frac{100}{80} \times \$360,000 = \$450,000$. Accordingly on consolidation the amount shown for minority interest would be $90,000 and for the purchase discrepancy would be $150,000.

In practice the former consolidation procedure is usually followed. The latter method is occasionally encountered but is not widespread. It might be argued however that the latter is the more logical approach. It has been stated that consolidated statements are prepared primarily for the enlightenment of parent company shareholders (the minority interest can tell very little about its particular share of the group from a consolidated statement). To the parent company shareholders the relevant figure for assets (when initially acquired) is their cost to the consolidated group. In the case of assets acquired through purchase of a subsidiary, the proper measure of this cost, as has been indicated, is value current at the time of acquisition and this forms the basis of future accounting for the group. It follows logically that a minority interest share in such assets must, for purposes of the same consolidated statements, be based on the same values.

Purchased goodwill may represent an exception to this general rule. In the case of all other assets it may be assumed that the purchaser could not acquire the assets in the form he did (i.e. through purchase of shares in the subsidiary) without the minority interest attaching to them. In the case of purchased goodwill however, it can be argued that some or all of its value attaches to the controlling interest alone and no recognition of it should be given in valuing the minority interest. This would seem to be an open question to be determined in each case on its own facts.

Minority interest share in inter-company profits eliminated

In an earlier section, the standard practice of eliminating inter-company profits in the inventories and fixed assets of the affiliated group was discussed. Where minority interests exist in either the vendor or the vendee, questions arise as to whether a part of the inter-company profit, as it relates to the minority interest, may be deemed to be realized.

Consider first the situation where the vendor company has a minority interest. In this case at least three techniques for elimination of inter-company profit have been proposed. Under one technique, only the majority percentage interest of the inter-company profit would be eliminated. This is on the theory that the minority interest is entitled to the profit on sale by the company in which it is interested, and the markup attributable to the minority can properly be regarded as cost to the parent company. This thinking rests on a concept of the consolidated statements as solely an extension of the parent company statements and it makes a sharp distinction between the parent company and minority interest in the consolidated group – the latter being regarded almost as dealing at arm's length with the group. The technique is rarely found in practice and has little to commend it.

Under another technique 100% of the profit is eliminated by a charge to consolidated income account. No part of the elimination is allocated against the minority interest, however, with the result that the amount of the minority interest in the consolidated balance sheet reflects the minority's percentage interest in the vendor company calculated on the basis of its own balance sheet (which is obviously unaffected by the elimination of inter-company profit). It is claimed that this reflects the legal realities of the situation – namely that the rights of the minority interest with respect to a completed transaction are not affected by the fact that the other party to the transaction may have been the majority shareholder or a company controlled by it. The practice has the anomalous result, however, that consolidated earnings are depressed by inter-company sales from subsidiaries in which a minority interest exists if the goods sold are still in inventory of the purchasing company at the year-end. From a group point of view reported profits are affected by what is a transaction internal to the group – not with outsiders. In the writer's opinion this technique is conceptually faulty. The main argument, that it fairly reflects the legal position of the minority interest, overlooks the fact that consolidated statements are prepared primarily for the benefit of the shareholders of the parent company and are effective largely because they do ignore legal restrictions in favour of portraying the economic situation of the controlled group. The method however is simple and in many situations would not be materially in error.

The technique preferred by the writer would eliminate the entire inter-company profit from inventory also, but would charge the minority interest share therein against earnings attributable to the minority interest in the consolidated income statement, leaving the majority to bear only its pro rata share.

In the opposite situation, that is where the minority interest is in the purchasing company rather than the vendor company, the profit on the inter-company sale has occasionally been deemed realized to the extent of the percentage of minority interest (i.e. only the parent company's share of the inter-company profit has been eliminated in the consolidation). However this ignores the basic objection to recording profits in inter-company sales, namely that arm's-length bargaining in the transactions is absent; accordingly the usual and proper practice is to eliminate 100% of the profit on this type of transaction.

Minority interest in gain or loss on inter-company bond holdings

Where debt securities have been issued by one company in a group and subsequently some have been bought in by another company, as was pointed out earlier the consolidated group has realized a gain or loss to the extent of the differences in carrying values in the accounts of the issuing and purchasing companies. If minority interests are present in either or both of those companies, the question arises whether some of the consolidated gain or loss should be attributed to them. Again there are different opinions on this. One school of thought holds that no part of the gain or loss should be assigned to the minority interest since, from the point of view of the individual company in which the minority interest rests, no gain or loss is realized (until the bonds are repaid). A second view is that the gain or loss must be split between the minority and majority interests since ultimately the differences between the par value redemption price and the carrying value of the securities in the books of *both* the issuing and purchasing companies will have been taken to income account in the individual companies and thus will be shared by the minority interests therein. On this basis the portion of gain or loss assigned to the minority interest will be (1) in the issuing company the minority percentage of the difference between par value and carrying value of the securities at date of purchase, and (2) in the purchasing company the minority interest percentage of the difference between par value and purchase cost. A third theory would allocate the total gain or loss on consolidation between the majority and minority interest according to the percentage of minority interest in the company *issuing* the securities. The thinking here is that the issuing company could have bought in its own securities just as well as an affiliate, so that all the gain or loss should be attributed to the issuer.

In the writer's opinion the third theory mentioned is unrealistic. It ignores the fact that the resources of the issuing company were probably not available to acquire its own securities and that the minority interest in that company is only entitled to share in results produced by employment of that company's resources. The technique would also require recalculation of minority interests to the end position achieved by the second method when the securities were ultimately redeemed.

From the standpoint of technical accuracy the second method would seem to be superior to the first. It is however more complicated in operation and the differences in result between it and the first method would rarely be significant.

Minority interest calculation where there are interlocking shareholdings

In unusual situations two or more subsidiary companies in an affiliated group may hold shares in each other. In such a case each company has an interest in the income and retained earnings of every other company in which shares are held. If a minority interest exists in any of the companies with interlocking shareholdings it is necessary to solve a set of simultaneous equations to ascertain the amount of income and retained earnings attributable to such minority interest. The technique is illustrated in standard text books.

When a subsidiary company with a minority interest holds shares in the parent company simultaneous equations may similarly be used to determine the amount of the minority interest including its share of income and retained earnings of the parent company. Alternatively, however, the investment of the subsidiary in shares of the parent company may be treated on consolidation in a manner similar to shares repurchased by the parent company (see Chapter 15) and in such case the minority interest in the subsidiary company would be calculated without reference to the retained earnings of the parent company.

Minority interest share in deficit of subsidiary

When a subsidiary in which there is minority interest loses money, the minority interest share of the loss is charged against it in the consolidation process thereby reducing the amount standing to the credit of the minority interest in the consolidated balance sheet. If, however, a time comes when the minority interest in the subsidiary deficit equals its share of the capital of the subsidiary no further share of losses should be charged against the minority interest. In other words, the minority interest in a subsidiary cannot be shown as a net debit balance since it cannot be forced to contribute further capital to the subsidiary. If the subsidiary is continuing to operate in these circumstances it is usually being financed by advances from the parent company or other affiliates and in these circumstances the full risk of loss is attributable to the parent.

Presentation of minority interest in the consolidated statements

The presentation of minority interest in consolidated financial statements tends to suggest the underlying concept held as to the nature of the minority interest. In a substantial number of cases minority interest is classified as a liability in the consolidated balance sheet. In probably the majority of cases however, it is shown as a separate item, more or less in limbo, between liabilities and the shareholders' equity section. Cases where it is included in the shareholders' equity section are rare.

The minority interest in earnings is almost universally shown in the consolidated income statement as a deduction before arriving at the figure of net income for the year. Most often it is shown as a separate and final deduction before the net income figure. It is not uncommon however to find it grouped with other expenses.

In summary, the minority interest seems to be regarded as similar to a liability and its share of the subsidiary profits as akin to interest expense. This view has probably evolved from thinking of the consolidated statements as an extension of the parent company statements.

In the writer's opinion however, the character of the minority interest is essentially an equity interest, albeit one restricted in scope. It is not altogether unlike a participating preference share. If this view were accepted the minority interest would be grouped in the shareholders' equity section of the balance sheet. It would also follow that the minority interest shown in profits would not be deducted in the consolidated income statement. Instead it might be presented as follows:

Consolidated income for the year	$3,120,000
Attributable to	
Minority interest in Subsidiary Co. Ltd.	$ 528,000
Preference dividend requirements	260,000
Common shareholders of Parent Co. Ltd.	2,332,000

Alternatively, under the 'residual equity' version of the proprietary concept of the entity (see Supplement to Chapter 3, page 374, herein) *both* the minority interest and the preference dividend requirements would be deducted in the income statement to arrive at the income attributable to the residual equity.

Problems in consolidation of foreign subsidiaries

The existence of foreign subsidiaries raises questions as to the proper bases for translation of statements expressed in foreign currency into the currency of the parent company, the treatment of potential tax on unremitted earnings and the disclosure of these matters in the financial statements.

Consideration of possible bases for translation of foreign currency amounts is included in Chapter 19 which deals comprehensively with the accounting problems associated with transactions in foreign currency. We need mention here only that it is customary to disclose as part of a general note on consolidation policy the basis on which the accounts of foreign subsidiaries are included in the consolidation. Some companies, as well, provide supplementary information showing the distribution of assets and liabilities included in the consolidated balance sheet and of revenues and profit shown in the consolidated income statement, as between the geographical areas in which business is carried on.

Usually not all profits earned by foreign subsidiaries are remitted to the parent company. To the extent that earnings are remitted they will frequently be subject to withholding taxes by the foreign country and possibly income taxes in the parent company's country. The question then arises whether provision should be made for such taxes with respect to earnings not remitted. In other words, is it proper to record as profits in the consolidated income statement amounts which could not actually be distributed to the parent company shareholders without payment of further tax?

In practice, some companies make provision for taxes with respect to unremitted earnings but the majority do not. The argument for the latter practice is somewhat as follows. It is standard practice today that companies do not pay out all their earnings in the form of dividends. Such retained earnings are reinvested and serve to finance a company's growth. In this capacity they should increase future earnings and thus are valuable to the shareholders. At one time studies of the stock market indicated that shareholders placed a higher value on a dollar of earnings paid out in dividends than they did on earnings retained by a company. However, favourable tax treatment of capital gains vis-à-vis dividend income and other factors have made investors value retained earnings more highly and now no distinction between the investor's valuation of paid-out and retained earnings is apparently provable. Therefore, so long as investment opportunities exist in a foreign country, and the investment climate is favourable, there is reason to expect that part of a subsidiary's earnings will be retained for reinvestment and will never be remitted to the parent company. In these circumstances, provision for taxes with respect to unremitted earnings is unnecessary.

In the writer's opinion, this argument is reasonable even though it does mean that the provision for tax on unremitted earnings must depend on a judgment assessment of the probability of future remittances of such earnings. It would seem however that the accounting policy followed and the estimated amount of taxes that would have been paid, had all the earnings for the year been remitted should be disclosed. Only a minority of companies now give the latter disclosure.

Stock dividends issued by subsidiary companies

When a subsidiary issues a stock dividend (out of post-acquisition earnings) in common shares, so that some part of its retained earnings becomes unavailable for dividend payment to the parent, the question arises whether the parent should show a transfer of equivalent amount from consolidated retained earnings to contributed surplus to earmark the amount not available for dividends.

In the writer's opinion, the answer is *no*. In Chapter 15 it was noted that there should be no presumption under today's conditions that the entire balance of retained earnings is necessarily available for dividends. In fact, because of the practice of reinvestment of earnings, it would usually be impossible economically, even if not legally, to distribute the amount at credit of retained earnings account. Accordingly legal restrictions on the amounts available for dividends are a matter for disclosure if considered significant information, not for reflection in the accounts. The situation of a stock dividend by a subsidiary is somewhat analogous to the requirement under Section 61 of the Canada Corporations Act to capitalize surplus when preferred shares are redeemed. On this question, the CICA Research Committee said:

> "Compliance with statutory requirements as to special designations of certain items of realized surplus should not distort the basic classification as to source, e.g., the statutory item 'Capital surplus' under the Canada Corporations Act should be classified as appropriated retained earnings."
> (Research Recommendations, paragraph 3250.08)

Supplements to Chapter 18

Possible Legal Impediments to the Use of Pooling of Interests Accounting

The adoption of the pooling of interests basis of accounting means that the asset, liability and equity accounts of the entities entering into the pooling should be added together at the pooling date without change (except for such changes as are necessary to put the accounting methods of all the combining entities on the same basis). Suppose, for example, a business combination were effected by means of issuance of 250,000 no par common shares of Co. A for all the shares of Co. B at a time when the balance sheets of the two companies were as follows:

	Co. A		Co. B	
Net assets	$50,000,000			$20,000,000
Capital stock –				
1,000,000 shares	10,000,000	100,000 shares		1,000,000
Retained earnings	40,000,000			19,000,000
	50,000,000			20,000,000

Where a pooling combination is accomplished by one company issuing its shares in exchange for those of another it is necessary to assign a value to the shares issued equal to the amount of contributed capital in the balance sheet of the company whose shares are acquired, in order that the equity accounts of both companies may carry forward unchanged in amount in consolidation. In the preceding example therefore a value of $1,000,000 or $4 a share would have to be assigned to the 250,000 no par shares of company A issued to effect the combination.° After the issue then the balance sheet of company A would appear as follows:

	Company A	
	Unconsolidated	*Consolidated*
Net operating assets	$50,000,000	$70,000,000
Investment in Co. B	1,000,000	
	51,000,000	70,000,000
Capital stock – 1,250,000 shares	11,000,000	11,000,000
Retained earnings	40,000,000	59,000,000
	51,000,000	70,000,000

This basis of accounting, however, might be precluded by the operation of the corporations acts in certain circumstances, although conflicting legal opinions have been expressed on the issues involved. The potential legal problems are discussed below.

If par value shares are issued to effect a combination, a problem exists whenever the aggregate par value of the shares issued exceeds the contributed capital of the company acquired. In the foregoing illustration, for example, if Co. A's common shares had a $10 par value, they could not be issued as fully paid for a consideration less than $2,500,000. Accordingly, Co. A's balance sheet after the combination would be:

	Company A	
	Unconsolidated	*Consolidated*
Net operating assets	$50,000,000	$70,000,000
Investment in Co. B	2,500,000	
	52,500,000	70,000,000
Capital stock – 1,250,000 shares	12,500,000	12,500,000
Retained earnings	40,000,000	57,500,000
	52,500,000	70,000,000

The effect of this is that $1,500,000 of the combined retained earnings has been capitalized as a result of the combination. Any historical summary of retained

---

° In the U.S. under varying state laws no par value shares may have a 'stated value' ascribed to them. In such cases the stated value determines the minimum amount which must be assigned to shares issued just as par value establishes a minimum amount to be attributed to capital for par value shares. If such minimum exceeds the amount of contributed capital shown in the balance sheet of the company whose shares are being acquired, the difference, on consolidation of the two companies, is deducted first from any other contributed capital accounts in excess of par or stated value in the combined companies, and to the extent such amounts are insufficient is charged to retained earnings. The problems in such cases are similar to those discussed in this section from a Canadian viewpoint with respect to the issue of par value shares.

earnings account would show this capitalization almost as though it were an issue of a stock dividend at the date of pooling.

In some situations there may not be a sufficient balance of retained earnings to cover the amount required to be capitalized. Suppose, for example, that Co. X were issuing 100,000 shares with a par value of $50 each for all the shares of Co. Y in the following situations:

	Co. X	*Co. Y*
Net assets	$15,600,000	$1,350,000
Capital – 300,000 shares	15,000,000	100,000
Retained earnings	600,000	1,250,000
	15,600,000	1,350,000

To solve such a problem it would probably be necessary to take proceedings to have the capital of Co. X reclassified as shares without par value, or as shares of having a low par value (say $1 per share).

The foregoing problems may be regarded as more or less mechanical. Problems of legal interpretation are also involved, however. The Canada Corporations Act states:

> 13(15) Shares having a nominal or par value shall not be issued as fully paid except for
>
> (a) a consideration payable in cash at least equal to the product of the number of shares allotted and issued multiplied by the nominal or par value thereof; or
>
> (b) a consideration payable directly or indirectly in property . . . that the directors in good faith determine . . . to be in all the circumstances of the transaction the fair equivalent of the cash consideration mentioned in paragraph (a).

The wording of this section does not clearly indicate its intent. However, it might be read to the effect that once the directors have determined a figure of consideration to be assigned to the shares (which must be at least equal to their par value) they must, if the shares are issued for property, resolve that the property is "the fair equivalent" of the consideration stated "in all the circumstances of the transaction".

If the section should be read in this way the question is what is the meaning of the words "the fair equivalent" bearing in mind that usually the market value of the shares of a company being acquired in a pooling transaction is well above the net book value of that company's assets, and well above the amount of its issued capital. Some lawyers interpret this section to the effect that the consideration assigned to the shares issued cannot be less than the fair market value of the shares of the company being acquired. Others give weight to the words "in all the circumstances of the transaction" and are of the opinion that if the circumstances are such that pooling accounting is appropriate then a corresponding valuation of the consideration is appropriate for the purpose of this section of the Act. Others take a position in between, to the effect that the consideration assigned to the shares issued may be less than market value of the shares acquired but cannot be less than the book value of these shares.

The Act's provision dealing with the issue of no par value shares is somewhat similar:

> 13(13) Shares without nominal or par value shall not be allotted as fully paid except for
>   (a) the consideration fixed by the directors ... payable in cash to the total amount of the consideration; or
>   (b) a consideration payable directly or indirectly in property ... that the directors in good faith determine ... to be in all the circumstances of the transaction the fair equivalent of the cash consideration mentioned in paragraph (a).

Again the meaning of "the fair equivalent" is in question.

The wording of The Business Corporations Act, 1970 of Ontario is somewhat different, but seems to pose a similar problem.

> 44(4) No share shall be issued until it is fully paid and a share is not fully paid until all the consideration therefor in cash, property or services ... has been received by the corporation.
>   (5) For the purposes of subsection 4 ... the value of property or services shall be the value the directors determine ... to be in all the circumstances of the transaction the fair equivalent of the cash value.

It has been suggested that even if the acquiring company is required to record shares issued on its books at fair value, there are no legal rules governing the preparation of consolidated statements so that the pooling concept may be given effect to in these statements. For example, if in our first illustration the fair value of all the shares of Co. B were considered to be $40,000,000 the financial statements of Company A could be presented as follows:

| | *Company A* | |
	Unconsolidated	*Consolidated*
Net operating assets	$50,000,000	$70,000,000
Investment in Co. B.	40,000,000	
	90,000,000	70,000,000
Capital stock – 1,250,000 shares	50,000,000	11,000,000
Retained earnings	40,000,000	59,000,000
	90,000,000	70,000,000

Even if this possible solution were adopted a company would face the corporations acts requirements that the balance sheet disclose "the issued capital and the amount received therefor that is attributable to capital" (section 121(1)(w) of the Canada Corporations Act and section 177(1)(23) of the Ontario Act).

Problems in Allocation of Purchase Price in a Business Combination

The following comments outline some of the difficulties in allocating the total consideration in a business combination accounted for by the 'purchase' method among the various assets and liabilities taken over.

Valuation of liabilities assumed

1. If the purchaser assumes the liabilities of the business (as he does in effect when he buys shares) he must make allowance for estimated and contingent liabilities assumed. Some of these may by the terms of the agreement be left the responsibility of the vendor. However, some – e.g. liabilities for ordinary product warranty – are customarily assumed by the purchaser. Not uncommonly, there is no warranty provision in the books of the vendor and warranty costs are dealt with on a pay-as-you-go basis. If the purchaser has allowed for them in his valuation however (as he should), he should make some provision for them in allocating his purchase price.

2. Usually the purchaser takes on the pension obligations of the vendor. Frequently, there is a sizeable obligation for unfunded past service cost which the vendor has been amortizing over a period of years since the date of last revision in his pension plan, on the theory that he will receive benefits from the improvement in his plan over such periods. The purchaser should consider whether he too will receive future benefits justifying the charging of past service amortization to future years' income or whether he should provide for the past service liability along with his allocation of the purchase obligation. Furthermore, if a consequence of the purchase will be an improvement in the pension arrangements for the vendor's employees, provision for the extra cost of this should probably be made along with the allocation of the purchase price.

3. If the liabilities assumed (or the liabilities of a company that is taken over as a subsidiary) include interest-bearing debt, it is highly probable that the true weight of the debt to the purchaser will be different from the figure at which it is shown on the books of the vendor. For example, suppose the vendor has funded debt outstanding which was originally borrowed on a 5% cost basis. If it would cost the purchaser 9% to borrow on similar security and maturity terms, the payments schedule on the debt (interest, plus principal retirement at maturity) should be discounted at 9% less a factor to allow for the difference in tax treatment of the extra interest cost assumed, to arrive at the real weight of the debt to the purchaser. While this treatment is not yet in general use in Canada it is recommended in APB Opinion No. 16.

4. It could be argued on similar grounds that preferred stock outstanding in a subsidiary company taken over, if carrying favourable dividend terms, should be included in the minority interest figure at a valuation below par, unless it is likely to be redeemed.

5. Arrears of cumulative preference dividends, while not on the books of the company taken over, should probably be provided for by a purchaser in the allocation of his purchase price since they will have to be paid before the purchaser can draw earnings up from the new subsidiary.

Revaluation of assets which are recorded on the books of the purchaser

1. Readily marketable securities held by the vendor should be revalued to current market value at the date of the purchase.

2. The same principle holds good for all other assets of the vendor which are sale-

able without disrupting the operations of the business. Vacant land owned, for example, should be valued at disposable value.

3. Assets which are held to further business operations present a more complicated problem. For example, frequently land held by a company becomes very valuable over a period of years, but it is not possible to realize on the land without wrecking the building on it and moving or discontinuing operations. The proper apportionment of the purchase price in such circumstances may depend on economic studies of the alternatives open. If the business is worth continuing in another location, the proper value of the assets that can be moved is their depreciated replacement cost. The proper value of the land is its market value reduced by, or with separate provision for, prospective costs of moving the business and demolition of structures on it. The value of assets that could not be moved would obviously be limited to scrap value.

4. Inventories may, under accepted accounting principles, be carried at costs which are well below the figure that a vendor would accept for them. The best example of this would be inventories of materials costed by the LIFO basis of accounting. In such a case, the inventory should be revalued by the purchaser at current cost even though he will then continue the LIFO method of inventory accounting from this higher base. A more difficult and probably more common situation would be that found when inventories are carried by the vendor on a costing method that omits certain overheads from the valuation – say, a 'direct costing' method. Although not the subject of negotiation directly, it seems reasonable to assume that the vendor would value his inventories more highly for purposes of sale – even in a bulk sale – than their valuation on the direct cost basis. Theoretically, then, the purchaser should also value these inventories at this higher price in allocating the purchase price. However, it may be that he will wish to continue the vendor's inventory costing methods or adopt some other method which does not produce the purchase valuation of the inventory. If so, he will be faced with the problem of having different bases of valuation for his initial inventory and the inventory at the end of the first fiscal year which of course would distort income reported for that period. The practical answer seems to be to value the inventory taken over by the methods that will be used in future accounting, but to keep in mind that some portion of the unallocated 'purchase discrepancy' (dealt with below) relates to inventory valuation.

Valuation of unrecorded assets

1. In a typical business there may be a fair quantity of tangible assets such as supplies, spare parts, tools, dies, patterns, etc. that have accumulated over a number of years but which were written off when purchased rather than incur the work necessary to keep track of them. These are elements of value in any purchase and theoretically should be recorded as assets. Again however, the purchaser is faced with a problem. He may not wish to carry such items as assets in his accounts because of the work of accounting for them. The answer may be similar to that suggested above for overheads not booked in inventory – namely to consider that some portion of the purchase discrepancy applies to those assets not specifically valued.

2. Very similar to these unrecorded tangible assets are certain unrecorded intangibles. Any business where engineering is important will have built up files of blueprints and designs that will have value but which will not be carried as assets because of the difficulty of costing and keeping track of them. Development work-in-process is another intangible asset which may or may not be valued in the accounts. Research and development may have resulted in patents that have immense value. Marketing efforts may have developed valuable trade marks and trade names. In all these cases the purchaser must consider whether to account for these as specific assets or to leave them unaccounted for as part of the purchase discrepancy. Here there is room for practical considerations. There is less reason to account meticulously for normal design and development work that goes on year after year and that has relatively short value-life because, in the usual course, this asset replaces itself out of current expenditure. In the case of patents however, or any abnormal research and development project, there is greater need for specific accounting because one cannot assume that as these assets lose their value with time they will be replaced with similar assets of equal value out of current operations.

3. Another unrecorded asset frequently found in companies taken over is the right to a loss carry-forward deduction for income tax purposes. This right, under normal accounting rules, is not recorded as an asset unless its recovery is 'virtually certain'. Usually however, a purchaser has more ways than the vendor to assure recovery and the right is undoubtedly a valuable asset acquired as a result of the purchase. If not recorded separately as an asset by the purchaser, it would seem best that some portion of the purchase discrepancy be considered as representing the loss carry-forward, and to this extent a future recovery should be credited against it, rather than taken as a gain through the income account.

Differences between allocated purchase values and values recognized for tax purposes

1. When a purchaser has bought shares of a company, and occasionally when he has bought assets, the valuations placed by him on the assets and liabilities taken over will differ from those used in the determination of taxable income thereafter. This in itself is a factor to take into account in the assignment of purchase cost to individual assets and liabilities. No businessman in his right senses would pay as much for an asset not fully claimable for tax purposes as he would for an identical asset that does carry a full tax deduction. If, therefore, the assignment of values is based on values in a going market such valuation should be discounted somewhat for lack of tax deductibility. If, for example, fixed assets are to be valued at depreciated replacement cost determined by an appraisal, and if the replacement cost is derived from current market prices (as it normally would be), the appraisal figure should be discounted to allow for the lack of tax deductibility. The method of doing so would be the same as that suggested in Appendix A supplement to Chapter 13. An alternative suggestion might be that instead of discounting the asset value for lack of tax deductibility, the asset should be shown at full value and a deferred tax credit set up equal to the amount of asset value not deductible, multiplied by the current tax rate. This has a rather strong pragmatic appeal, since by this means all differences

between tax and book values in the purchaser's balance sheet would in effect be embodied in the deferred tax accounts. In the writer's opinion however, it can be criticized as being an artificial procedure since:
- no tax has actually been deferred with respect to these assets, and
- the valuation would be theoretically incorrect since deferred tax accounting would require that the implicit discount factor that must be present in a properly bargained purchase price be ignored.

Contingent payments

1. Not infrequently, contracts for the sale of a business include provision for additional payments to the vendor if specified profit levels from the business acquired are attained or maintained for a number of years in the future. The proper interpretation of such a clause may be a question of fact. The contingent payment might be inserted merely because the vendor thought the business would earn more and therefore was worth more than the purchaser thought possible, and this was the only way to bring them together to make a deal. In such a case the contingent payment would be clearly an intrinsic part of the purchase contract and the vendor would have done everything to fulfill his part in the bargain by turning over control of the business on the closing day. The accounting consequences would follow from this. To the extent that liability under the contingent payment clause was considered likely, provision for it should be made by the purchaser. If the likelihood of payment were small, a note to the financial statements disclosing the contingency would be adequate. If and when the liability was set up, the proper charge would almost always be to the account 'purchased goodwill', since the payment would be caused by higher than normal profits and goodwill may be defined as the expectation of above normal profits. Purchased goodwill may properly be amortized against income over the period of expected super profits, but it is unlikely that such period would be as short as the year in which the contingent payment was made. In other words, it is unlikely a direct write-off of the payments made under the contingency clause would be justified on this interpretation.

2. On the other hand, if the vendor were retained to manage the business taken over, it might be that a contingent payment clause would be inserted to give him incentive. In such a case, the vendor would not have fulfilled all his part in the contract and the contingent payment should not be recorded as a liability by the purchaser until earned by the vendor. In these circumstances, there would be more justification for regarding the payment as a form of bonus or profit sharing to be absorbed as a charge in the year of payment.

3. APB Opinion No. 16 makes a distinction between a contingent payment based on earnings, and one based on the market price of a specific security issued to effect the combination. The former type of arrangement indicates that the contingent payment is an adjustment of the cost of the acquisition to be accounted for as indicated in paragraph 1 above. The latter type of arrangement suggests merely that the value of the consideration given was to be guaranteed. The contingent payment therefore should not be treated as an adjustment of the cost of the acquisition, but rather as an adjustment of the valuation placed on the securities previously issued.

Supplement to Chapter 22 – Possible Substitutes for the Working Capital Concept

Chapter 22 has indicated that the working capital classification of a balance sheet is a rigid and unsatisfactory tool for analysis. If balance sheet figures are to be used for this purpose much greater variety in form of analysis is desirable in different situations or different industries. Merely as an example of one form of analysis Exhibit A (page 414) has the following features:

1. A basic division of the balance sheet between one side showing the net resources (assets employed) in the business, and the debt and capital which has financed the acquisition of these resources. Trade accounts payable and other non-interest bearing liabilities incurred in the course of the business are treated as deductions from committed resources rather than as invested capital.

2. A division of resources between the assets required for and consequent upon carrying on the business (operating assets) and other resources (financial assets). Investments in affiliated and associated companies which are carried to further business policy are classified as operating assets rather than as financial assets.

3. Classification of the operating assets primarily according to their nature. A division is also made between short-term and long-term assets, mainly based on the operating cycle theory, but this could be considered unnecessary.

4. Arrangement of the financial assets in order of liquidity.

5. Listing of debt in order of maturity.

6. Note disclosure of the portion of debt maturity that may be said to have 'accrued'. For example, if a debt were incurred due five years hence, one-fifth would be deemed to have accrued at the end of the first year and so on. This would be a substitute for the arbitrary one-year rule in working capital wherein none of the debt is shown as a current liability for four years and all of it for the fifth year. If the 'accrued' debt maturity figure were increasing relative to the financial assets available for liquidation of the debt, it would become apparent that refunding of the debt would be necessary.

Any balance sheet must have its limitations, however, as has been indicated, and if a better indicator of buffer or margin of liquidity is required, a special statement is needed consisting essentially of a forecast source and application of funds statement, one form for which is illustrated by Exhibit B (page 415).

EXHIBIT A

Elho Appliances Limited
Consolidated Balance Sheet
December 31, 1971

RESOURCES EMPLOYED		1971 *(000's)*	1970 *(000's)*
Net operating assets			
Short-term assets –			
Working funds and cash in transit	$ 300		$ 240
Accounts receivable – trade	5,660		5,100
Inventory	11,460		9,190
Prepayments	70		50
		$17,490	14,580
Short-term liabilities –			
Cheques outstanding	180		
Accounts payable and accrued charges	3,240		
Provision for warranties	1,090		
Taxes payable	630		
	5,140		4,800
Short-term working position	12,350		9,780
Investment in associated company	300		300
Fixed assets	10,470		4,740
Less accumulated depreciation	4,110		
	6,360		
Long-term prepayments	120		150
Deferred tooling less amortization	440		290
Trademarks and goodwill	70		70
Net investment in operating assets		19,640	15,330
Net financial assets			
Cash not required for operations	50		220
Marketable securities – at market	680		1,550
Other investments – at cost (estimated value $300)	240		240
	970		2,010
Less liabilities for capital spending (note 1)	480		
Net financial resources		490	2,010
Total resources employed		$20,130	$17,340

DEBT AND CAPITAL		1971 *(000's)*	1970 *(000's)*
Debt			
Due to bankers – demand loan		$ 3,000	$ 2,900
Due to bankers – term loan (note 2)		3,000	3,300
Debentures payable – 8¾% due June 30, 1990		2,000	
Total debt		8,000	6,200
Shareholders' equity			
Minority interest in subsidiary company		380	360
Preference shares – series A – 5.5% $50 par value, redeemable at par: Authorized 40,000 shares Outstanding 25,600 shares		1,280	1,280
Residual equity –			
Common shares without par value Authorized 2,500,000 shares Outstanding 1,700,000 shares	2,300		
Consolidated retained earnings	8,170		
		10,470	2,300
			7,200
Total shareholders' equity		12,130	11,140
Total debt and capital		$20,130	$17,340

Notes:

1. Commitments for additional capital spending outstanding at December 31, 1971 amounted to $1,600,000 ($2,500,000 in 1970).

2. The term loan is secured by demand notes, but scheduled for repayment by instalments on December 1 each year of $300,000 for two years, $360,000 for the next four years, and $500,000 for the last two years.

3. Based on spreading the original principal amount of debt outstanding evenly over time period elapsing to final scheduled maturity date, the accrued maturity of the debt outstanding, after deducting repayments, is –

	1971	1970
Demand bank loan	$3,000	$2,900
Term bank loan	150	90
Debentures payable	50	

EXHIBIT B

Elho Appliances Limited
Forecast Flow of Financing
1972–76

	Financial position Dec. 31/71	1972	1973	Forecast 1974	1975	1976
Net financial assets						
Cash	50					
Marketable securities – at market	680					
Other investments – estimated value	300					
	1,030					
Less liabilities for capital spending	480					
	550					
Forecast funds provided from operations with currently planned expansion (after dividends)		1,600	1,800	2,000	2,000	2,000
Requirement for						
Capital spending on current expansion program, replacements of existing plant and major maintenance		1,950	350	400	1,000	400
Debt retirement		300	300	360	360	360
		2,250	650	760	1,360	760
Forecast funds available						
For business expansion, increased dividends, additional debt retirement, or investment (reduction in available financial assets, or requirement for new borrowing)	550	(650)	1,150	1,240	640	1,240

Appendix B
Authoritative
statements

This Appendix contains excerpts from authoritative statements of three accounting bodies on the subject matter of various Chapters in Part I. The following abbreviations will be used to identify the sources of quotations:

Canada
CRR — Recommendations of the Accounting and Auditing Research Committee of The Canadian Institute of Chartered Accountants.[1]

Great Britain
BR — Recommendations on Accounting Principles issued by The Institute of Chartered Accountants in England and Wales[2]
BSSAP — Statements of Standard Accounting Practice of the Institute.[2]

United States
APBO — Opinions of the Accounting Principles Board of the American Institute of Certified Public Accountants[3]
ARB — Accounting Research Bulletins of the Committee on Accounting Procedure of the American Institute of Certified Public Accountants. (Note — this committee's responsibilities were assumed by the Accounting Principles Board, Sept. 1, 1959.)[3]

This Appendix does not contain references to Statement No. 4 of the Accounting Principles Board issued in October 1970 and entitled "Basic Concepts and Accounting Principles Underlying Financial Statements of Business Enterprises". Statement No. 4 provides a comprehensive generalized discussion of accounting principles and therefore surveys most of the territory covered in Part I of this book. Pertinent quotations from Statement No. 4 would be too numerous to reproduce here, but it should be referred to by anyone researching authoritative statements on the subject of generally accepted accounting principles. Recommendations or statements for guidance of members of other professional institutes such as those of the Institutes of Chartered Accountants of Scotland and in Australia are also omitted for reasons of space.

[1] Copyright 1972 by The Canadian Institute of Chartered Accountants.
[2] Copyright 1972 by The Institute of Chartered Accountants in England and Wales.
[3] Copyright 1972 by the American Institute of Certified Public Accountants, Inc.

Chapter 6 – Transaction Measurement

Problems in transaction measurement have been dealt with in the following statements:

1. Delayed payment transactions.

> "*Note exchanged for property, goods, or service.* When a note is exchanged for property, goods or service in a bargained transaction entered into at arm's length, there should be a general presumption that the rate of interest stipulated by the parties to the transaction represents fair and adequate compensation to the supplier for the use of the related funds. That presumption, however, must not permit the form of the transaction to prevail over its economic substance and thus would not apply if (1) interest is not stated, or (2) the stated interest rate is unreasonable (paragraphs 13 and 14) or (3) the stated face amount of the note is materially different from the current cash sales price for the same or similar items or from the market value of the note at the date of the transaction. In these circumstances, the note, the sales price, and the cost of the property, goods, or service exchanged for the note should be recorded at the fair value of the property, goods or service or at an amount that reasonably approximates the market value of the note, whichever is the more clearly determinable. That amount may or may not be the same as its face amount, and any resulting discount or premium should be accounted for as an element of interest over the life of the note (paragraph 15). In the absence of established exchange prices for the related property, goods, or service or evidence of the market value of the note, the present value of a note that stipulates either no interest or a rate of interest that is clearly unreasonable should be determined by discounting all future payments on the notes using an imputed rate of interest as described in paragraphs 13 and 14. This determination should be made at the time the note is issued, assumed, or acquired; any subsequent changes in prevailing interest rates should be ignored.

> "*Determining an appropriate interest rate.* The variety of transactions encountered precludes any specific interest rate from being applicable in all circumstances. However, some general guides may be stated. The choice of a rate may be affected by the credit standing of the issuer, restrictive convenants, the collateral, payment and other terms pertaining to the debt, and, if appropriate, the tax consequences to the buyer and seller. The prevailing rates for similar instruments of issuers with similar credit ratings will normally help determine the appropriate interest rate for determining the present value of a specific note at its date of issuance. In any event, the rate used for valuation purposes will normally be at least equal to the rate at which the debtor can obtain financing of a similar nature from other sources at the date of the transaction. The objective is to approximate the rate which would have resulted if an independent borrower and an independent lender had negotiated a similar transaction under comparable terms and conditions with the option to pay the cash price upon purchase or to give a note for the amount of the purchase which bears the prevailing rate of interest to maturity.

> "The selection of a rate may be affected by many considerations. For instance, where applicable, the choice of a rate may be influenced by (a) an approximation of the prevailing market rates for the source of credit that would provide a market for sale or assignment of the note; (b) the prime or higher rate for notes which are discounted with banks, giving due weight to the credit standing of the maker; (c) published market rates for similar quality bonds; (d) current rates

for debentures with substantially identical terms and risks that are traded in open markets; and (e) the current rate charged by investors for first or second mortgage loans on similar property."

(APBO 21 – pars. 12–14)

2. Barter transactions.

"*Aquiring assets*. The general principles to apply the historical-cost basis of accounting to an acquisition of an asset depend on the nature of the transaction:

a. An asset acquired by exchanging cash or other assets is recorded at cost – that is, at the amount of cash disbursed or the fair value of other assets distributed.

b. An asset acquired by incurring liabilities is recorded at cost – that is, at the present value of the amounts to be paid.

c. An asset acquired by issuing shares of stock of the acquiring corporation is recorded at the fair value of the asset – that is, shares of stock issued are recorded at the fair value of the consideration received for the stock.

The general principles must be supplemented to apply them in certain transactions. For example, the fair value of an asset received for stock issued may not be reliably determinable, or the fair value of an asset acquired in an exchange may be more reliably determinable than the fair value of a noncash asset given up. Restraints on measurement have led to the practical rule that assets acquired for other than cash, including shares of stock issued, should be stated at 'cost' when they are acquired and 'cost may be determined either by the fair value of the consideration given or by the fair value of the property acquired, whichever is the more clearly evident'. 'Cost' in accounting often means the amount at which an entity records an asset at the date it is acquired whatever its manner of acquisition, and that 'cost' forms the basis for historical-cost accounting."

(APBO 16 – par. 67)

3. Basket purchases – allocation of cost to assets.

"*Allocating cost*. Acquiring assets in groups requires not only ascertaining the cost of the assets as a group but also allocating the cost to the individual assets which comprise the group. The cost of a group is determined by the principles described in paragraph 67. A portion of the total cost is then assigned to each individual asset acquired on the basis of its fair value. A difference between the sum of the assigned costs of the tangible and identifiable intangible assets acquired less liabilities assumed and the cost of the group is evidence of unspecified intangible values."

(APBO 16 – par. 68)

4. Basket sales of securities.

"Differences of opinion exist as to whether convertible debt securities should be treated by the issuer solely as debt or whether the conversion option should receive separate accounting recognition at time of issuance. The views in favor of each of these two concepts are contained in the following paragraphs.

"The most important reason given for accounting for convertible debt solely as debt is the inseparability of the debt and the conversion option. . . .

"Another reason advanced in favor of accounting for convertible debt solely as debt is that the valuation of the conversion option or the debt security without the conversion option presents various practical problems. . . .

"The contrary view is that convertible debt possesses characteristics of both debt and equity and that separate accounting recognition should be given to the debt characteristics and to the conversion option at time of issuance. This view is based on the premise that there is an economic value inherent in the conversion feature or call on the stock and that the nature and value of this feature should be recognized for accounting purposes by the issuer. The conversion feature is not significantly different in nature from the call represented by an option or warrant, and sale of the call is a type of capital transaction. . . .

"The Board is of the opinion that no portion of the proceeds from the issuance of the types of convertible debt securities described in paragraph 3 should be accounted for as attributable to the conversion feature. In reaching this conclusion, the Board places greater weight on the inseparability of the debt and the conversion option (as described in paragraph 7) and less weight on practical difficulties.

"There is general agreement among accountants that the proceeds from the sale of debt with stock purchase warrants should be allocated to the two elements for accounting purposes. This agreement results from the separability of the debt and the warrants. The availability of objective values in many instances is also a factor. There is agreement that the allocation should be based on the relative fair values of the debt security without the warrants and of the warrants themselves at time of issuance. The portion of the proceeds so allocated to the warrants should be accounted for as paid-in capital. The remainder of the proceeds should be allocated to the debt security portion of the transaction. This usually results in issuing the debt security at a discount (or, occasionally, a reduced premium)."

(APBO 14 – pars. 6–9, 12, 15)

Chapter 7 – Allocation of Revenue to Accounting Periods

Authoritative statements lay heavy emphasis upon sale as the point of time at which it is proper to regard revenue as earned. For example, among the six rules adopted by the membership of the American Institute in 1934, the following statement is found:

. . ."Profit is deemed to be realized when a sale in the ordinary course of business is effected, unless the circumstances are such that the collection of the sale price is not reasonably assured. An exception to the general rule may be made in respect of inventories in industries . . . in which owing to the impossibility of determining costs it is trade custom to take inventories at net selling prices, which may exceed cost."

(ARB 43 – Ch. 1, par. 1)

This statement was reinforced in 1966 in the following words:

". . . The Board reaffirms this statement; it believes that revenues should ordinarily be accounted for at the time a transaction is completed, with appropriate provision for uncollectible accounts. Accordingly, it concludes that, in the absence of the circumstances° referred to above, the installment method of recognizing revenue is not acceptable.

°"The Board recognizes that there are exceptional cases where receivables are collectible over an extended period of time and, because of the terms of the transactions or other conditions, there is no reasonable basis for estimating the degree of collectibility. When such circumstances exist, and as long as they exist, either the installment method or the cost recovery method of accounting may be used. (Under the cost recovery method, equal amounts of revenue and expense are recognized as collections are made until all costs have been recovered, postponing any recognition of profit until that time.)"

(APBO 10 – par. 12)

The attitude is set out more fully in a discussion of accounting for government contracts as follows:

"It is recognized that income should be recorded and stated in accordance with certain accounting principles as to time and amount; that profit is deemed to be realized when a sale in the ordinary course of business is effected unless the circumstances are such that collection of the sales price is not reasonably assured; and that delivery of goods sold under contract is normally regarded as the test of realization of profit or loss.

"In the case of manufacturing, construction, or service contracts, profits are not ordinarily recognized until the right to full payment has become unconditional, i.e., when the product has been delivered and accepted, when the facilities are completed and accepted, or when the services have been fully and satisfactorily rendered. This accounting procedure has stood the test of experience and should not be departed from except for cogent reasons.

"It is, however, a generally accepted accounting procedure to accrue revenues under certain types of contracts and thereby recognize profits, on the basis of partial performance, where the circumstances are such that total profit can be estimated with reasonable accuracy and ultimate realization is reasonably assured. Particularly where the performance of a contract requires a substantial period of time from inception to completion, there is ample precedent for pro rata recognition of profit as the work progresses, if the total profit and the ratio of the performance to date to the complete performance can be computed reasonably and collection is reasonably assured. Depending upon the circumstances, such partial performance may be established by deliveries, expenditures, or percentage of completion otherwise determined. This rule is frequently applied to long-term construction and other similar contracts; it is also applied in the case of contracts involving deliveries in instalments or the performance of services. However, the rule should be dealt with cautiously and not applied in the case of partial deliveries and uncompleted contracts where the information available does not clearly indicate that a partial profit has been realized after making provision for possible losses and contingencies."

(ARB 43 – Ch. 11A, pars. 11–13)

On construction-type contracts in general the committee said:

"The committee believes that in general when estimates of costs to complete and extent of progress toward completion of long-term contracts are reasonably dependable, the percentage-of-completion method is preferable. When lack of dependable estimates or inherent hazards cause forecasts to be doubtful, the completed-contract method is preferable. Disclosure of the method followed should be made."

(ARB 45 – par. 15)

Similar views are expressed in recommendations of the English Institute:

"In some types of businesses, such as tea and rubber producing companies and some mining companies, it is a recognised practice to bring stocks of products into account at the prices realised subsequent to the balance sheet date, less only selling costs. By this means the whole of the profit is shown in the period in which the crop is reaped or the minerals won. This basis has come to be accepted as customary in the industries concerned.

"In manufacturing businesses which carry stocks of by-products the separate cost of which is not ascertainable these stocks are normally included at current selling price (or contract sale price where applicable) less any expenses to be incurred before disposal; the cost of the main product is reduced accordingly.

"In businesses which involve the acceptance and completion of long-term contracts it is often appropriate to spread over the period of the contracts, on a properly determined basis, the profits which are expected to be earned when the contracts are completed. This procedure takes up in each period during the performance of the contract a reasonable amount as representing the contribution of that period towards the eventual profit; it thus recognises to a prudent extent the value of the work done in each period and restricts the distortion which would result from bringing in the whole of the profit in the period of completion. The principles which determine whether an element of profit is to be included are:

(a) profit should not be included until it is reasonably clear from the state of the work that a profit will ultimately be earned; it is therefore inappropriate to include any profit element where at the balance sheet date the contract has been in progress for a comparatively short time or to include an amount in excess of the profit element properly attributable to the work actually done

(b) provision should be made for foreseeable losses and allowance should be made as far as practicable for penalties, guarantees and other contingencies

(c) a clear basis for including a profit element should be established and adhered to consistently."

(BR 22 – pars. 20–22)

Chapter 8 – Cost Allocation: The Matching Principle

The following general statements of the matching principle were made in connection with discussions of accounting for income taxes:

"A basic concept in the accounting measurement of income is that costs incurred in the process of earning income should be charged in the period in which the related revenues are reflected in the accounts. In the case of income taxes, the problem is one of selecting the basis for computing the tax charge which can be appropriately related to the income reflected in the accounts."

(CRR 3470.04)

"d. Matching is one of the basic processes of income determination; essentially it is a process of determining relationships between costs (including reductions of costs) and (1) specific revenues or (2) specific accounting periods. Expenses of the current period consist of those costs which are identified with the revenues of the current period and those costs which are identified with the current period on some basis other than revenue. Costs identifiable with future revenues or otherwise identifiable with future periods should be deferred to those future periods. When a cost cannot be related to future revenues or to future periods on some basis other than revenues, or it cannot reasonably be expected to be recovered from future revenues, it becomes, by necessity, an expense of the current period (or of a prior period)."

(APBO 11 – par. 14)

Chapter 9 – Inventory and Cost of Sales

Citations from the authorities on the subject matter of this Chapter are as follows:

1. On determination of inventory cost:

> ". . . In the case of merchandise purchased for resale, or of raw materials which are to enter into production, cost may be said to be 'laid-down' cost, for example, invoice cost (in terms of Canadian dollars) plus customs and excise duties and freight and cartage. In the case of inventories of work in process and finished goods, cost will include the laid-down cost of material plus the cost of direct labour applied to the product and ordinarily the applicable share of overhead expense properly chargeable to production. Where the storage of goods for a significant period of time is an integral part of the manufacturing process, cost may also include the applicable share of warehousing expense and, in a few cases, carrying charges.

> "Sometimes certain costs are excluded in determining inventory values. Usually expenditures arising out of abnormal circumstances, such as rehandling of goods and idle facilities, are not included. Similarly, in some cases, a portion of fixed overhead is excluded where its inclusion would distort the net income for the period by reason of fluctuating volume of production."
>
> (CRR 3030.02–.03)

> "The primary basis of accounting for inventories is cost, which has been defined generally as the price paid or consideration given to acquire an asset. As applied to inventories, cost means in principle the sum of the applicable expenditures and charges directly or indirectly incurred in bringing an article to its existing condition and location.

> ". . . Although principles for the determination of inventory costs may be easily stated, their application, particularly to such inventory items as work in process and finished goods, is difficult because of the variety of problems encountered in the allocation of costs and charges. For example, under some circumstances, items such as idle facility expense, excessive spoilage, double freight, and rehandling costs may be so abnormal as to require treatment as current period charges rather than as a portion of the inventory cost. Also, general and administrative expenses should be included as period charges, except for the portion of such expenses that may be clearly related to production and thus constitute a part of inventory costs (product charges). Selling expenses constitute no part of inventory costs. It should also be recognized that the exclusion of all overheads from inventory costs does not constitute an accepted accounting procedure. . . ."
>
> (ARB 43 – Ch. 4, par. 5)

> "The elements making up the cost of stock are:
> (a) direct expenditure on the purchase of goods bought for resale, and of materials and components used in the manufacture of finished goods
> (b) other direct expenditure which can be identified specifically as having been incurred in acquiring the stock or bringing it to its existing condition and location; examples are direct labour, transport, processing and packaging
> (c) such part, if any, of the overhead expenditure as is properly carried forward in the circumstances of the business instead of being charged against the revenue of the period in which it was incurred

> "Opinions differ on the extent to which overhead expenditure should be included in computing the cost of stock, though it is generally agreed that it

cannot properly include selling and finance and other expenses which do not relate to the bringing of stock to its existing condition and location. . . .

"If overhead expenditure is included in the amount attributed to stock an adjustment will be necessary in the event of disruption in production by events such as a strike, a fire, an abnormal falling off in orders, or temporary difficulties in obtaining materials, with the result that the volume of production is abnormally or unexpectedly low. In such circumstances the amount included in respect of overhead expenditure ought not to exceed an appropriate proportion on the basis of normal activity . . ."

(BR 22 – pars. 4, 7, 9(c))

2. On determination of cost of sales:

"The method selected for determining cost should be one which results in the fairest matching of costs against revenues regardless of whether or not the method corresponds to the physical flow of goods.

(CRR 3030.09)

"Cost for inventory purposes may be determined under any one of several assumptions as to the flow of cost factors (such as first-in first-out, average, and last-in first-out); the major objective in selecting a method should be to choose the one which, under the circumstances, most clearly reflects periodic income.

". . . ordinarily the identity of goods is lost between the time of acquisition and the time of sale. In any event, if the materials purchased in various lots are identical and interchangeable, the use of identified cost of the various lots may not produce the most useful financial statements. This fact has resulted in the development of general acceptance of several assumptions with respect to the flow of cost factors (such as *first-in first-out, average,* and *last-in first-out*) to provide practical bases for the measurement of periodic income . . ."

(ARB 43 – Ch. 4, par. 6)

"Apart from the variations which occur in calculating the amount to be attributed to each of the elements of cost there are various methods of computing cost. In a small business one method only will normally be used but in a large composite business carrying on a variety of activities different methods may be used for different activities; once selected however the methods should be applied consistently to those activities from period to period. The following are the principal methods:
(a) 'Unit' cost. . . .
(b) 'First in, first out'. . . .
(c) 'Average' cost. . . .
(d) 'Standard' cost. . . .
(e) 'Adjusted selling price'. . . ."

(BR 22 – par. 11)

3. On determination of 'market':

"A departure from the cost basis of pricing the inventory is required when the utility of the goods is no longer as great as its cost. Where there is evidence that the utility of goods, in their disposal in the ordinary course of business, will be less than cost, whether due to physical deterioration, obsolescence, changes in price levels, or other causes, the difference should be recognized as a loss of the current period. This is generally accomplished by stating such goods at a lower level commonly designated as *market.*

. . . .

"As used in the phrase *lower of cost or market* the term *market* means current replacement cost (by purchase or by reproduction, as the case may be) except that:

(1) Market should not exceed the net realizable value (i.e., estimated selling price in the ordinary course of business less reasonably predictable costs of completion and disposal); and

(2) Market should not be less than net realizable value reduced by an allowance for an approximately normal profit margin.

. . . .

"Because of the many variations of circumstances encountered in inventory pricing, . . . [this statement] . . . is intended as a guide rather than a literal rule. It should be applied realistically in the light of the objectives expressed in this chapter and with due regard to the form, content, and composition of the inventory. . . .

"Depending on the character and composition of the inventory, the rule of *cost or market, whichever is lower* may properly be applied either directly to each item or to the total of the inventory (or, in some cases, to the total of the components of each major category). . . .

"When no loss of income is expected to take place as a result of a reduction of cost prices of certain goods because others forming components of the same general categories of finished products have a market equally in excess of cost, such components need not be adjusted to market to the extent that they are in balanced quantities. . . ."

(ARB 43 – Ch. 4, pars. 8–12)

"When the cost of the stock has been determined it is then necessary to establish whether any portion of the outlay on stock is irrecoverable; to that extent a provision for the loss needs to be made. This calculation may be made either (i) by considering each article separately or (ii) by grouping articles in categories having regard to their similarity or inter-changeability or (iii) by considering the aggregate cost of the total stock in relation to its aggregate net realisable value. The third method involves setting foreseeable losses against expected but unrealised profits and would not normally be used in businesses which carry stocks which are large in relation to turnover.

"The irrecoverable portion of the cost of the stock is the excess of its cost, as computed by the method of cost ascertainment which is deemed appropriate for the business, over the net realisable value of the stock. 'Net realisable value' means the amount which it is estimated, as on the balance sheet date, will be realised from disposal of the stock in the ordinary course of business, either in its existing condition or as incorporated in the product normally sold, after allowing for all expenditure to be incurred on or before disposal.

"In many businesses it is important to have regard to the price at which stock can be replaced if such price is less than cost. The considerations which lead to the use of replacement price include the following:

(a) *Uncertainty as to net realisable value.* . . .

(b) *Selling prices based on current replacement prices.* . . .

(c) *Recognition of uneconomic buying or production.* . . .

Where the replacement price basis is adopted the stock is stated at the lowest of (a) cost, (b) net realisable value, (c) replacement price, with the effect that the profit and loss account is charged with any reductions necessitated by an excess of (a) over (b) or (c) as the case may be."

(BR 22 – pars. 12–13, 16–17)

Chapter 10 – Fixed Assets and Depreciation

The following excerpts indicate a large measure of agreement in authoritative statements on depreciation.

1. On the requirement that depreciation be based on the carrying value of fixed assets in the books:

> "Fixed assets are normally accounted for on the basis of their historical cost. . . . It is recognized, however, that there may be instances where it is appropriate to reflect an appraisal in the accounts, e.g., where it is confirmed by an arm's length purchase (as in the acquisition of a subsidiary) or in a reorganization.
>
> "If an appraisal of fixed assets has been recorded, subsequent charges against income for depreciation should be based on the new values."

(CRR 3060.01, .06)

> "The Board is of the opinion that property, plant and equipment should not be written up by an entity to reflect appraisal, market or current values which are above cost to the entity. . . . Whenever appreciation has been recorded on the books, income should be charged with depreciation computed on the written up amounts."

(APBO 6 – par. 17)

2. On depreciation patterns:

> "The different natures of asset involve consideration in deciding on the method of depreciation appropriate in each case. Unless the methods adopted are applied consistently the usefulness of periodic accounts for the purpose of comparison of one period with another may be vitiated."

(BR 9 – par. 9)

> "Subject to any periodic adjustment which may be necessary, the straight-line method (computed by providing each year a fixed proportion of the cost of the asset) spreads the provision equally over the period of anticipated use. . . . Though other methods may be appropriate in the case in some classes of assets, the balance of informed opinion now favours the straight-line method as being the most suitable for general application."

(BR 9 – par. 5)

3. On round amount depreciation:

> "A fourth method, . . . [of depreciation] . . . is the renewals reserve method, under which round sums, not necessarily computed by reference to the useful lives of the assets, and sometimes determined largely by the results of the year's trading, are provided and set aside as general provisions towards meeting the cost of future renewals. This method does not accord with a strict view of depreciation and may distort the annual charges to revenue."

(BR 9 – par. 8)

4. On the difference between depreciation and tax allowances:

> "It cannot be too strongly emphasized that capital cost allowances are a tax measure which permit a taxpayer to deduct from income, over a period of years,

amounts expended on the acquisition of depreciable fixed assets. In many cases the capital cost allowances for any year may be equal to, or at least not materially different from, the provision for depreciation reflected in the taxpayer's books. Nevertheless, the two are distinct and the amount of capital cost allowance may, in some cases, be more, and in other cases less, than a proper provision for depreciation."

> (CICA Bulletin No. 8 on 'Deferred Depreciation', issued March 1952. This Bulletin was not included in the consolidation of Research Recommendations issued in 1968.)

". . . However, the committee believes that when the amount allowed as amortization for income-tax purposes is materially different from the amount of the estimated depreciation, the latter should be used for financial accounting purposes."

> (ARB 43 – Ch. 9C, par. 9)

5. On periodic revision of depreciation:

"Treatment as prior period adjustments should not be applied to the normal, recurring corrections and adjustments which are the natural result of the use of estimates inherent in the accounting process. For example, changes in the estimated remaining lives of fixed assets affect the computed amounts of depreciation, but these changes should be considered prospective in nature and not prior period adjustments . . ."

> (APBO 9 – par. 24)

". . . Provisions for depreciation are therefore in most cases matters of estimation, based upon the available experience and knowledge, rather than of accurate determination. They require adjustment from time to time in the light of changes in experience and knowledge, including prolongation of useful life due to exceptional maintenance expenditure, curtailment due to excessive use, or obsolescence not allowed for in the original estimate of the commercially useful life of the asset."

> (BR 9 – par. 3)

Chapter 11 – Intangible Capital Assets, Prepaid Expenses, Deferred Charges and Period Costs

References in authoritative literature to some of the foregoing topics are as follows:

1. On intangible capital assets and their amortization:

"The Board concludes that a company should record as assets the costs of intangible assets acquired from other enterprises or individuals. Costs of developing, maintaining, or restoring intangible assets which are not specifically identifiable, have indeterminate lives, or are inherent in a continuing business and related to an enterprise as a whole – such as goodwill – should be deducted from income when incurred.

"The Board believes that the value of intangible assets at any one date eventually disappears and that the recorded costs of intangible assets should be amortized by systematic charges to income over the periods estimated to be benefited. . . .

"The cost of each type of intangible asset should be amortized on the basis of the estimated life of that specific asset and should not be written off in the period of acquisition. Analysis of all factors should result in a reasonable estimate of the useful life of most intangible assets. A reasonable estimate of the useful life may often be based on upper and lower limits even though a fixed existence is not determinable.

"The period of amortization should not, however, exceed forty years. Analysis at the time of acquisition may indicate that the indeterminate lives of some intangible assets are likely to exceed forty years and the cost of these assets should be amortized over the maximum period of forty years, not an arbitrary shorter period.

". . . The Board concludes that the straight-line method of amortization – equal annual amounts – should be applied unless a company demonstrates that another systematic method is more appropriate. The financial statements should disclose the method and period of amortization. Amortization of acquired goodwill and of other acquired intangible assets not deductible in computing income taxes payable does not create a timing difference, and allocation of income taxes is inappropriate.

". . . A company should evaluate the periods of amortization continually to determine whether later events and circumstances warrant revised estimates of useful lives. If estimates are changed, the unamortized cost should be allocated to the increased or reduced number of remaining periods in the revised useful life but not to exceed forty years after acquisition. Estimation of value and future benefits of an intangible asset may indicate that the unamortized cost should be reduced significantly by a deduction in determining net income (APB Opinion No. 9, paragraph 21). However, a single loss year or even a few loss years together do not necessarily justify an extraordinary charge to income for all or a large part of the unamortized cost of intangible assets. The reason for an extraordinary deduction should be disclosed."

(APBO 17 – pars. 24, 27, 28–31)

2. On bond discount:

"In the committee's opinion it is a sound accounting procedure to treat such discount as a part of the cost of borrowed money to be distributed systematically over the term of the issue and charged in successive annual income accounts of the company. The anticipation of this income charge by a debit to income of a previous year or to surplus has in principle no more justification than would a corresponding treatment of coupons due in future years."

(ARB 43 – Ch. 15, par. 3)

"Questions have been raised as to the appropriateness of the 'interest' method of periodic amortization of discount and expense or premium on debt (i.e., the difference between the net proceeds, after expense, received upon issuance of debt and the amount repayable at its maturity) over its term. The objective of the interest method is to arrive at a periodic interest cost (including amortization) which will represent a level effective rate on the sum of the face amount of the debt and (plus or minus) the unamortized premium or discount and expense at the beginning of each period. The difference between the periodic interest cost so calculated and the nominal interest on the outstanding amount of the debt is the amount of periodic amortization.

"In the Board's opinion, the interest method of amortization is theoretically sound and an acceptable method."

(APBO 12 – pars. 16–17)

Chapter 12 – Complex Transactions

1. Lease transactions.

   (a) accounting by lessees:

   "It seems clear that leases covering merely the right to use property in exchange for future rental payments do not create an equity in the property and are thus nothing more than executory contracts requiring continuing performance on the part of both the lessor and the lessee for the full period covered by the leases. The question of whether assets and liabilities should be recorded in connection with leases of this type is, therefore, part of the larger issue of whether the rights and obligations that exist under executory contracts in general (e.g., purchase commitments and employment contracts) give rise to assets and liabilities which should be recorded.

   "The rights and obligations related to unperformed portions of executory contracts are not recognized as assets and liabilities in financial statements under generally accepted accounting principles as presently understood. Generally accepted accounting principles require the disclosure of the rights and obligations under executory contracts in separate schedules or notes to the financial statements if the omission of this information would tend to make the financial statements misleading. The rights and obligations under leases which convey merely the right to use property, without an equity in the property accruing to the lessee, fall into the category of pertinent information which should be disclosed in schedules or notes rather than by recording assets and liabilities in the financial statements.

   "On the other hand, some lease agreements are essentially equivalent to installment purchases of property. In such cases, the substance of the arrangement, rather than its legal form, should determine the accounting treatment. The property and the related obligation should be included in the balance sheet as an asset and a liability, respectively, at the discounted amount of the future lease rental payments, exclusive of payments to cover taxes and operating expenses other than depreciation. Further, in such cases, it is appropriate to depreciate the capitalized amount for property over its estimated useful life rather than over the initial period of the lease.

   "The property and the related obligation should be included as an asset and a liability in the balance sheet if the terms of the lease result in the creation of a material equity in the property. It is unlikely that such an equity can be created under a lease which either party may cancel unilaterally for reasons other than the occurrence of some remote contingency. The presence, in a noncancelable lease or in a lease cancelable only upon the occurrence of some remote contingency, of either of the two following conditions will usually establish that a lease should be considered to be in substance a purchase:

   a. The initial term is materially less than the useful life of the property, and the lessee has the option to renew the lease for the remaining useful life of the property at substantially less than the fair rental value; or

   b. The lessee has the right, during or at the expiration of the lease, to acquire the property at a price which at the inception of the lease appears to be substantially less than the probable fair value of the property at the time or times of permitted acquisition by the lessee. . . .

   ". . . the existence, in connection with a noncancelable lease or a lease cancelable only upon the occurrence of some remote contingency, of one or more circumstances such as those shown below tend to indicate that the lease arrangement is in substance a purchase and should be accounted for as such.

a. The property was acquired by the lessor to meet the special needs of the lessee and will probably be usable only for that purpose and only by the lessee.

b. The term of the lease corresponds substantially to the estimated useful life of the property, and the lessee is obligated to pay costs such as taxes, insurance, and maintenance, which are usually considered incidental to ownership.

c. The lessee has guaranteed the obligations of the lessor with respect to the property leased.

d. The lessee has treated the lease as a purchase for tax purposes.

"In cases in which the lessee and the lessor are related, leases should often be treated as purchases even though they do not meet the criteria set forth in paragraphs 10 and 11, i.e., even though no direct equity is being built up by the lessee. In these cases, a lease should be recorded as a purchase if a primary purpose of ownership of the property by the lessor is to lease it to the lessee and (1) the lease payments are pledged to secure the debts of the lessor or (2) the lessee is able, directly or indirectly, to control or influence significantly the actions of the lessor with respect to the lease. . . .

(APBO 5 – pars. 7–12)

(b) accounting by lessors:

"There are two predominant methods in general use for allocating rental revenue and expenses over the accounting periods covered by a lease. These may be termed the 'financing' and the 'operating' methods.

"*Financing method* – Under the financing method, the excess of aggregate rentals over the cost (reduced by estimated residual value at the termination of the lease) of the leased property is generally designed to compensate the lessor for the use of the funds invested. Since this excess is in the nature of interest, it is recognized as revenue during the term of the lease in decreasing amounts related to the declining balance of the unrecovered investment or, in other words, as an approximately level rate of return on funds not yet recovered. When rentals are level, this results in a decreasing percentage of each succeeding rental being accounted for as revenue and an increasing percentage as recovery of investment. This is comparable to the method followed by most lending institutions in accounting for level repayment plans.

"*Operating method* – Under the operating method, aggregate rentals are reported as revenue over the life of the lease. The amount of revenue to be recognized in each accounting period will ordinarily be equivalent to the amount of rent receivable according to the provisions of the lease unless distortion of periodic revenue would result, e.g., when the rentals depart radically from a straight-line basis without relation to the economic usefulness of the leased property. The income statement reflects, as expenses, depreciation of the leased property, maintenance and other related costs, as well as the cost of any other services rendered under the provisions of the lease. The amount of these expenses to be recognized in each accounting period should be determined by methods which are appropriate in the circumstances and which are conventionally used for such expenses when incurred in activities other than leasing.

"*Basis for selection* – The objective of fairly stating the lessor's net income during each of the periods covered by the leasing activities is the most important consideration in differentiating between the use of the financing or operating method. . . . Pertinent factors in making the choice, among others, are the following: the nature of the lessor's business activities; the specific objectives of its leasing activities, including the relationship to other business activities of the lessor, if any; the term of the lease in relation to the estimated useful life of the property; the existence of renewal or purchase options and the likelihood that the lessee will exercise them; provisions of the lease which indicate the extent to which the usual risks of ownership (e.g., obsolescence, unprofitable operation, unsatisfactory performance, idle capacity, dubious residual value) or rewards of ownership (e.g., profitable operation, gain from appreciation in value at end of lease) rest with the lessor or the lessee.

"The financing method is generally appropriate for measuring periodic net income from leasing activities of entities engaged in, perhaps among other things, lending money at interest – e.g., lease-finance companies, banks, insurance companies or pension funds. Lease agreements of institutions of this kind typically are designed to pass all or most of the usual ownership risks or rewards to the lessee, and to assure the lessor of, and generally limit him to, a full recovery of his investment plus a reasonable return on the use of the funds invested, subject only to the credit risks generally associated with secured loans. Usually, the financing method is similar to the method of accounting for revenue already in use for other lending activities of the institutions. The financing method is also appropriate for a leasing activity of an entity which is not identified as a financial institution, such as a manufacturer, if the lease agreements have the characteristics described earlier in this paragraph.

"On the other hand, there are companies (e.g., the owner-operator of an office building, the lessor of automotive equipment on short-term leases – daily, weekly or monthly) which retain the usual risks or rewards of ownership in connection with their leasing activity. They may also assume responsibilities for maintaining the leased property or furnishing certain related services which will give rise to costs to be incurred in the future. Rental revenues are designed to cover the costs of these services, depreciation and obsolescence, and to provide an adequate profit for assuming the risks involved. In these cases the operating method is appropriate for measuring periodic net income from leasing activities. The operating method is also appropriate if the leasing activity is an integral part of manufacturing, marketing or other operations of a business which generate revenues and costs which must be considered along with revenues and costs from the leasing activities in arriving at appropriate methods for measuring the overall periodic net income (examples are leases of retail outlets with lease provisions deliberately made favorable to induce lessee to handle lessor's product and leases which generate significant servicing revenues and costs). The operating method likewise is appropriate for leasing activities for an otherwise strictly financing institution if such activities are characterized as set forth in this paragraph.
"When manufacturers use leases to assist in marketing products or services, the Board believes that the guidelines described in Paragraphs 7, 8 and 9 indicate whether the financing or operating method is appropriate. Manufacturing revenues (amounts which would have been obtained in a regular sale or the discounted amount of future rentals whichever is lower), costs and profit should be determined at the time of entering into the lease and reported in the income statement of the lessor on the same basis as outright sales of similar manufactured

property, provided all of these conditions are met: (a) credit risks are reasonably predictable, (b) the lessor does not retain sizable risks of ownership of the nature described in Paragraph 7 and (c) there are no important uncertainties surrounding the amount of costs yet to be incurred or revenues yet to be earned under the lease. If any of these conditions is not met, manufacturing profit should be recognized, using the operating method, only as realized in the form of rental revenue over the term of the lease. If manufacturing revenue is determined at the time of entering into the lease, the conditions described above having been met, the financing method should be used and the amount of the manufacturing revenue becomes the 'cost of the leased property' as that term is used in Paragraph 5. When it is feasible to determine normal selling prices, then revenues, costs and trading profits of dealers and other middlemen should be recognized in the same manner and under the same conditions described above for manufacturers."

(APBO 7 – pars. 4–9, 12)

2. Pension cost accounting.

    (a) accrual of cost:

"Pension entitlements of employees covered by a pension plan should be viewed as an integral part of their compensation accruing over their working lives from the inception of the plan even though the plan may contain a cancellation clause and may provide that there is no liability for any unvested benefits in the event of cancellation. Therefore, to produce a proper allocation of pension costs to accounting periods, the full cost of accruing pension entitlements should be absorbed in the period in which the service that gave rise to the entitlement was rendered.

"In the case of cost based plans, the employer's cost for each period is a definite and readily determinable amount. With benefit based plans, the annual costs are estimated by the actuary with reference to the benefits which accrue to the employees as a result of services during the current period."

(CRR 3460.12–.13)

"In the preparation of the accounts of an employer who is under contractual obligation to provide or contribute towards retirement benefits for employees, due consideration should be given to all aspects of that obligation in addition to the normal charge against revenue in respect of insurance premiums or contributions to a scheme. In particular:

    (a) where the employer has given a guarantee (for example, to maintain the solvency of the scheme or to ensure a minimum rate of interest on or rate of accumulation of the funds) there should be an appropriate note on the accounts if the amount is or may become material in relation to the accounts of the employer; in view of the effects of inflation special consideration of this matter is necessary where benefits are based on salaries at or near to retirement date

    (b) where there is an obligation to provide retirement benefits which are not covered by contributions to a retirement benefits scheme (for example benefits to which employees will be entitled under individual service agreements or their general terms of employment or by way of supplement to insured benefits) provision should be made therefor if the amount is material; if provision is not so made the position should be stated by note.

"Where it is the policy of an employer to pay retirement benefits to employees or their dependants although under no contractual obligation to do so, this expense can be dealt with either by charging against current revenue the retirement benefits payable or by setting aside amounts against which to charge retirement benefits as they become payable in the future. Whichever method is adopted should be used consistently. If the method used is to set amounts aside it is desirable that these should be computed on a consistent basis by making each year an estimate of the benefits which are likely to become payable in the future as a result of service during that year. (The recommendation in paragraph 32 (b) would however apply where a retiring allowance, though made voluntarily, has been granted in such a way that its continuance constitutes a contractual obligation.)"

(BR 21 – pars. 32, 34)

"The Board recognizes that a company may limit its legal obligation by specifying that pensions shall be payable only to the extent of the assets in the pension fund. Experience shows, however, that with rare exceptions pension plans continue indefinitely and that termination and other limitations of the liability of the company are not invoked while the company continues in business. Consequently, the Board believes that, in the absence of convincing evidence that the company will reduce or discontinue the benefits called for in a pension plan, the cost of the plan should be accounted for on the assumption that the company will continue to provide such benefits. This assumption implies a long-term undertaking, the cost of which should be recognized annually whether or not funded. Therefore, accounting for pension cost should not be discretionary."

(APBO 8 – par. 16)

(b) actuarial gains and losses:

"Where complete calculations of the actuarial liability for the accrued pension benefits are made, a change in the liability since the previous calculation may result from changes in or variations from the actuarial assumptions. In view of the substantial degree of uncertainty involved in pension calculations, and because an actuarial revaluation is usually carried out at regular intervals, an adjustment brought about by an actuarial revaluation (as distinct from an adjustment arising from a modification of the benefits under a plan) normally may be included in the pension costs of the current period or allocated to operations over the period which is expected to elapse before the next revaluation.

"An adjustment in pension calculations brought about by an actuarial revaluation should be included in the pension costs of the current period or allocated to operations over the period which is expected to elapse before the next revaluation."

(CRR 3460.21–.22)

"Actuarial assumptions necessarily are based on estimates of future events. Actual events seldom coincide with events estimated; also, as conditions change, the assumptions concerning the future may become invalid. Adjustments may be needed annually therefore to reflect actual experience, and from time to time to revise the actuarial assumptions to be used in the future. These adjustments constitute actuarial gains and losses. They may be regularly recurring (for example, minor deviations between experience and actuarial assumptions) or they may be unusual or recurring at irregular intervals (for example, substantial investment gains or losses, changes in the actuarial assumptions, plant closings, etc.)

"In dealing with actuarial gains and losses, the primary question concerns the timing of their recognition in providing for pension cost. In practice, three methods are in use; immediate-recognition, spreading and averaging. Under the immediate-recognition method (not ordinarily used at present for net losses), net gains are applied to reduce pension cost in the year of occurrence or the following year. Under the spreading method, net gains or losses are applied to current and future cost, either through the normal cost or through the past service cost (or prior service cost on amendment). Under the averaging method, an average of annual net gains and losses, developed from those that occurred in the past with consideration of those expected to occur in the future, is applied to the normal cost.

"Unrealized appreciation and depreciation in the value of investments in a pension fund are forms of actuarial gains and losses. Despite short-term market fluctuations, the overall rise in the value of equity investments in recent years has resulted in the investments of pension funds generally showing net appreciation . . .

"The amount of any unrealized appreciation to be recognized should also be considered. Some actuarial valuations recognize the full market value. Others recognize only a portion (such as 75 per cent) of the market value or use a moving average (such as a five-year average) to minimize the effects of short-term market fluctuations. Another method used to minimize such fluctuations is to recognize appreciation annually based on an expected long-range growth rate (such as 3 per cent) applied to the cost (adjusted for appreciation previously so recognized) of common stocks; when this method is used, the total of cost and recognized appreciation usually is not permitted to exceed a specified percentage (such as 75 per cent) of the market value. Unrealized depreciation is recognized in full or on a basis similar to that used for unrealized appreciation.

"The Board believes that actuarial gains and losses, including realized investment gains and losses, should be given effect in the provision for pension cost in a consistent manner that reflects the long-range nature of pension cost. Accordingly, except as otherwise indicated in Paragraphs 31 and 33, actuarial gains and losses should be spread over the current year and future years or recognized on the basis of an average as described in Paragraph 26. If this is not accomplished through the routine application of the method . . . the spreading or averaging should be accomplished by separate adjustments of the normal cost resulting from the routine application of the method. Where spreading is accomplished by separate adjustments, the Board considers a period of from 10 to 20 years to be reasonable. Alternatively, an effect similar to spreading or averaging may be obtained by applying net actuarial gains as a reduction of prior service cost in a manner that reduces the annual amount equivalent to interest on, or the annual amount of amortization of, such prior service cost, and does not reduce the period of amortization.

"Actuarial gains and losses should be recognized immediately if they arise from a single occurrence not directly related to the operation of the pension plan and not in the ordinary course of the employer's business. An example of such occurrences is a plant closing, in which case the actuarial gain or loss should be treated as an adjustment of the net gain or loss from that occurrence and not as an adjustment of pension cost for the year. Another example of such occurrences is a merger or acquisition accounted for as a purchase, in which case the actuarial gain or loss should be treated as an adjustment of the purchase price . . .

"The Board believes unrealized appreciation and depreciation should be recognized in the determination of the provision for pension cost on a rational and systematic basis that avoids giving undue weight to short-term market fluctuations (as by using a method similar to those referred to in Paragraph 29). Such recognition should be given either in the actuarial assumptions or as described in Paragraph 30 for other actuarial gains and losses. Ordinarily appreciation and depreciation need not be recognized for debt securities expected to be held to maturity and redeemed at face value."

(APBO 8 – pars. 25–26, 28–32)

(c)   past service costs:

"Although past service benefits are calculated by reference to service in prior periods, they are granted as additional remuneration for continuing service and the costs therefore relate, not to the past, but to the current and future periods. In contemplation of these present and future services, it is considered appropriate to spread these costs as charges to operations over a reasonable period of years, which may or may not coincide with the period over which funding payments are made. It is at this point that, in the interests of simplicity, accounting for the costs of past service benefits may depart from the general proposition that accounting for costs is related to the build-up of pension obligations during employees' working lives.

"When a pension plan is amended to change the retirement benefits, the change may apply to the benefits accrued to employees prior to the date of the amendment as well as those subsequent to that date. An increase in prior service costs resulting from an amendment of a pension plan is similar to the past service costs arising when a pension plan is created. Accordingly, the considerations and accounting treatment relating to past service costs apply equally to such increases.

"Past service costs arising from the introduction of a pension plan or from a modification of the benefits payable under an existing plan should not be treated as a prior period adjustment. Since costs of pension commitments should be considered as relating to the years following the introduction or the modification of a plan, the practice of charging past service pension costs to retained earnings would have the effect of relieving those subsequent years of charges that should properly be borne by them.

"Past service costs, arising from the introduction of a pension plan or from the modification of the benefits payable under an existing plan, should be charged to operations over a reasonable period of years which may or may not coincide with the period over which any related funding payments are made. Such costs should not be treated as prior period adjustments."

(CRR 3460.15–.18)

"There is broad agreement that pension cost, including related administrative expense, should be accounted for on the accrual basis. There is not general agreement, however, about the nature of pension cost. Some view pensions solely as a form of supplemental benefit to employees in service at a particular time. Others see a broader purpose in pensions; they consider pensions to be in large part (a) a means of promoting efficiency by providing for the systematic retirement of older employees or (b) the fulfillment of a social obligation expected of business enterprises, the cost of which, as a practical matter, constitutes a business expense that must be incurred. Those who hold this second viewpoint associate pension cost, to a large extent, with the plan itself rather than with specific employees. In addition, the long-range nature of pensions causes significant uncertainties about the total amount of pension benefits ultimately to be paid and the amount of cost to be recognized. These differences in viewpoint concerning the nature of pension cost, the uncertainties regarding the amount of the estimates, and the use of many actuarial approaches, compound the difficulty in reaching agreement on the total amount of pension cost over a long period of years and on the time to recognize any particular portion applicable to an employee or group of employees. . . .

"One view is that periodic pension cost should be provided on an actuarial basis that takes into account all estimated prospective benefit payments under a plan with respect to the existing employee group, whether such payments relate to employee service rendered before or after the plan's adoption or amendment, and that no portion of the provision for such payments should be indefinitely deferred or treated as though, in fact, it did not exist. . . . Among those holding this view there is general agreement that cost relating to service following the adoption or amendment of a plan should be recognized ratably over the remaining service lives of employees. There is some difference of opinion, however, concerning the period of time to use in allocating that portion of the cost which the computations under some actuarial methods assign to employee service rendered before a plan's adoption or amendment. As to this cost, (a) those viewing pensions as relating solely to the existing employee group believe that it should be accounted for over the remaining service lives of those in the employ of the company at the time of the plan's adoption or amendment, whereas (b) some of those holding the broader view of pensions, referred to in Paragraph 11, believe that this cost is associated to a large extent with the plan itself and hence that the period of providing for it need not be limited to the remaining service lives of a particular group of employees but may be extended somewhat beyond that period. . . .

"An opposing view stresses that pension cost is related to the pension benefits to be paid to the continuing employee group as a whole. Those holding this view . . . point out that, in the great majority of cases, provision for normal cost plus an amount equivalent to interest on unfunded prior service cost will be adequate to meet, on a continuing basis, all benefit payments under a plan. . . . They see no reason therefore to urge employers to provide more than normal cost plus an amount equivalent to interest on unfunded prior service cost in these circumstances, because additional amounts never expected to be paid by a going concern are not corporate costs, and thus are not appropriate charges against income. They acknowledge, however, that corporations can and do make payments to pension funds for past and prior service cost, with the result that reductions will be effected in future charges for the equivalent of interest on unfunded amounts, but they consider this to be solely a matter of financial management rather than a practice dictated by accounting considerations.

"In many pension plans, cost recorded on the basis described in Paragraph 13 will accumulate an amount (whether funded or not) at least equal to the actuarially computed value of vested benefits. . . . However, this result might not be achieved in some cases. . . . Some hold the view that when periodic provisions are based on normal cost plus an amount equivalent to interest such periodic provisions should be increased if they will not, within a reasonable period of time, accumulate an amount (whether funded or not) at least equal to the actuarially computed value of vested benefits. Others would require the increases in provisions only if the company has a legal obligation for the payment of such benefits.

"Another view is that, if the company has no responsibility for paying benefits beyond the amounts in the pension fund, pension cost is discretionary and should be provided for a particular accounting period only when the company has made or has indicated its intent to make a contribution to the pension fund for the period. Others believe that pension cost is discretionary even if the company has a direct responsibility for the payment of benefits described in the plan.

"All members of the Board believe that the entire cost of benefit payments ultimately to be made should be charged against income subsequent to the adoption or amendment of a plan and that no portion of such cost should be charged directly against retained earnings. Differences of opinion exist concerning the measure of the cost of such ultimate payments. . . . The Board has concluded, in the light of such differences in views and of the fact that accounting for pension cost is in a transitional stage, that the range of practices would be significantly narrowed if pension cost were accounted for at the present time within limits based on Paragraphs 12, 13 and 14. Accordingly, the Board believes that the annual provision for pension cost should be based on an accounting method that uses an acceptable actuarial cost method . . . and results in a provision between the minimum and maximum stated below. The accounting method and the actuarial cost method should be consistently applied from year to year.

a. *Minimum.* The annual provision for pension cost should not be less than the total of (1) normal cost, (2) an amount equivalent to interest on any unfunded prior service cost and (3) if indicated in the following sentence, a provision for vested benefits. . . .

b. *Maximum.* The annual provision for pension cost should not be greater than the total of (1) normal cost, (2) 10 per cent of the past service cost (until fully amortized), (3) 10 per cent of the amounts of any increases or decreases in prior service cost arising on amendments of the plan (until fully amortized) and (4) interest equivalents under Paragraph 42 or 43 on the difference between provisions and amounts funded. The 10 per cent limitation is considered necessary to prevent unreasonably large charges against income during a short period of years."

(APBO 8 – pars. 11–15, 17)

3. Stock options:

"The practice of granting to officers and other employees options to purchase or rights to subscribe for shares of a corporation's capital stock has been followed by a considerable number of corporations over a period of many years. To the extent that such options and rights involve a measurable amount of compensation, this cost of services received should be accounted for as such. The amount of compensation involved may be substantial and omission of such costs from the corporation's accounting may result in overstatement of net income to a significant degree . . .

". . . Where the inducements [granted to employees to take up stock under a stock option plan] are not larger per share than would reasonably be required in an offer of shares to all shareholders for the purpose of raising an equivalent amount of capital, no compensation need be presumed to be involved.

". . . When compensation is paid in a form other than cash the *amount* of compensation is ordinarily determined by the fair value of the property which was agreed to be given in exchange for the services to be rendered. The time at which such fair value is to be determined may be subject to some difference of opinion but it appears that the date on which an option is granted to a specific individual would be the appropriate point at which to evaluate the cost to the employer, since it was the value at that date which the employer may be presumed to have had in mind. In most of the cases under discussion, moreover, the only important contingency involved is the continuance of the grantee in the employment of the corporation, a matter very largely within the control of the grantee and usually the main objective of the grantor. Under such circumstances it may be assumed that if the stock option were granted as a part of an employment contract, both parties had in mind a valuation of the option at the date of the contract; and accordingly, value at that date should be used as the amount to be accounted for as compensation . . .

"The date of grant also represents the date on which the corporation foregoes the principal alternative use of the shares which it places subject to option, i.e., the sale of such shares at the then prevailing market price. Viewed in this light, the *cost* of utilizing the shares for purposes of the option plan can best be measured in relation to what could then have been obtained through sale of such shares in the open market . . .

"Freely exercisable option rights, even at prices above the current market price of the shares, have been traded in the public markets for many years, but there is no such objective means for measuring the value of an option which is not transferable and is subject to such other restrictions as are usually present in options of the nature here under discussion. Although there is, from the standpoint of the grantee, a value inherent in a restricted future right to purchase shares at a price at or even above the fair value of shares at the grant date, the committee believes it is impracticable to measure any such value. . . . On the other hand, it follows in the opinion of the committee that the value to the grantee and the related cost to the corporation of a restricted right to purchase shares at a price *below* the fair value of the shares at the grant date may for the purposes here under discussion be taken as the excess of the then fair value of the shares over the option price.

"While market quotations of shares are an important and often a principal factor in determining the fair value of shares, market quotations at a given date are not necessarily conclusive evidence. Where significant market quotations cannot be obtained, other recognized methods of valuations have to be used. Furthermore, in determining the fair value of shares for the purpose of measuring the cost incurred by a corporation in the issuance of an option, it is appropriate to take into consideration such modifying factors as the range of quotations over a reasonable period and the fact that the corporation by selling shares pursuant to an option may avoid some or all of the expenses otherwise incurred in a sale of shares . . .

"If the period for which payment for services is being made by the issuance of the stock option is not specifically indicated in the offer or agreement, the value of the option should be apportioned over the period of service for which the payment of the compensation seems appropriate in the existing circumstances . . ."

(ARB 43 – Ch. 13B, pars. 1, 4, 10–14)

Chapter 13 – Income Taxes and Income Tax Allocation

1. On intra-period tax allocation:

"The related tax effect for extraordinary items should be shown separately in the income statement with the extraordinary items and not as part of the provision for income taxes included in 'income before extraordinary items'.

"To provide a proper matching of costs and revenues, reductions or increases in income taxes attributable to items included in retained earnings should also be included and disclosed in retained earnings."

(CRR – 3470.33–.34)

"The need for tax allocation within a period arises because items included in the determination of taxable income may be presented for accounting purposes as (a) extraordinary items, (b) adjustments of prior periods (or of the opening balance of retained earnings) or (c) as direct entries to other stockholders' equity accounts.

"The Board has concluded that tax allocation within a period should be applied to obtain an appropriate relationship between income tax expense and (a) income before extraordinary items, (b) extraordinary items, (c) adjustments of prior periods (or of the opening balance of retained earnings) and (d) direct entries to other stockholders' equity accounts. The income tax expense attributable to income before extraordinary items is computed by determining the income tax expense related to revenue and expense transactions entering into the determination of such income, without giving effect to the tax consequences of the items excluded from the determination of income before extraordinary items. The income tax expense attributable to other items is determined by the tax consequences of transactions involving these items. If an operating loss exists before extraordinary items, the tax consequences of such loss should be associated with the loss."

(APBO 11 – pars. 51–52)

2. On the concept of tax allocation:

"In financial statements drawn up for submission to shareholders, corporate income taxes are, for practical purposes, considered to be a cost incurred in the process of earning the income attributable to their shareholdings.

"A basic concept in the accounting measurement of income is that costs incurred in the process of earning income should be charged in the period in which the related revenues are reflected in the accounts. In the case of income taxes, the problem is one of selecting the basis for computing the tax charge which can be appropriately related to the income reflected in the accounts.

"Present tax laws stipulate that certain expenses and losses as well as certain revenues and gains will never be included in the computation of taxable income. In addition, some deductions may be allowable for tax purposes even though they have no counterpart in the determination of accounting income. Such items create no special problem in accounting for income taxes although, if the amounts are significant, they may need to be disclosed in the financial statements.

"Other differences between accounting and taxable income arise when the time of including items of revenue and expense in the computation of accounting income and the time of their inclusion in the computation of taxable income do not coincide. There are four situations which lead to such timing differences: ...

"The Research Committee ... has concluded that the tax allocation basis provides the most satisfactory method of achieving the prime objective of a proper matching of costs and revenues in the case of tax timing differences."

(CRR – 3470.03–.06, .12)

"The charge for corporation tax should be based on the profits shown by the accounts. The charge would usually be expected to be in appropriate relationship to the profit (excluding franked investment income and group income). This relationship will, however, be distorted if, in computing the income assessable to tax, the profits shown by the accounts have to be adjusted by:

(a) adding back expenses not allowable for tax in this or any subsequent period, such as depreciation of non-industrial buildings or excess remuneration of the directors of a close company; or

(b) excluding income not taxable such as interest on tax reserve certificates; or

(c) the difference between depreciation charged in the accounts and capital allowances computed for tax purposes; or

(d) the difference arising as a result of allocating items to different periods for accounting and taxation purposes as, for example, provisions and accrued charges on income which do not rank for taxation relief until the expenditure provided for is actually incurred or the charge actually paid.

"The allocation of items to different periods for accounting and taxation purposes referred to in paragraphs 7 (c) and (d) will usually result in the taxation charge based on the taxable profit of the year not being in appropriate relation to the profit shown by the accounts. The extent of the distortion may vary from year to year and may not always be material. Nevertheless, such distortions should be avoided by providing for taxation on the accounting profit without regard to items allocated to other periods for taxation purposes. The difference between the corporation tax on the accounting profit and the corporation tax on the taxable profit should be dealt with through the deferred taxation account. . . . There is normally no need to disclose separately in the profit and loss account the amount transferred to or from the deferred taxation account.

"Recommendations

(a) The corporation tax charge should be based on the accounting profit without regard to the fact that some items are allocated to other periods for taxation purposes.

(b) If material items are altogether disallowed or excluded for taxation purposes, any consequent distortion of the corporation tax charged should be explained by note. . . ."

(BR 27 – pars. 7, 9, 11)

"The Board has considered the various concepts of accounting for income taxes and has concluded that comprehensive interperiod tax allocation is an integral part of the determination of income tax expense. Therefore, income tax expense should include the tax effects of revenue and expense transactions included in the determination of pretax accounting income. The tax effects of those transactions which enter into the determination of pretax accounting income either earlier or later than they become determinants of taxable income should be recognized in the periods in which the differences between pretax accounting income and taxable income arise and in the periods in which the differences reverse. Since permanent differences do not affect other periods, interperiod tax allocation is not appropriate to account for such differences."

(APBO 11 – par. 34)

3. On the nature of deferred taxes:

"There are two methods of applying the tax allocation basis. Under the accrual method, the accumulated tax allocation balances are adjusted to reflect changes in tax rates; under the deferral method, the balances are not adjusted.

"Accrual method (Adjustments made for changes in tax rates). The amount by which the current tax provision differs from the amount of taxes currently payable is considered to reflect the recognition in the current period of taxes expected to be recoverable or payable in a future period. The current computation is considered to be tentative, and subject to adjustment in future periods as more certain knowledge of the probable amount of future recoveries or payments becomes available. Therefore, the current tax provision is computed at current tax rates, but the accumulated tax allocation balance is adjusted in future periods to reflect changes in tax rates, such adjustment being reflected in the accounts as an extraordinary item.

"Deferral method (No adjustments made for changes in tax rates). The amount by which the current tax provision differs from the amount of taxes currently payable is considered to represent the deferring to future periods of a benefit obtained or expenditure incurred currently, and is accordingly computed at current tax rates without subsequent adjustment of the accumulated tax allocation debit or credit balance to reflect changes in tax rates.

"There are differences of opinion as to which of these two methods of tax allocation is preferable. There are some who feel that the accrual method is preferable because in most cases tax allocation consists of allocating a future tax liability to the current year and that a more precise determination of this future liability would require adjustment for significant changes in tax rates. The Research Committee, however, is of the opinion that the deferral method is the preferable method of applying the tax allocation basis.*"

* "A variation of accounting for income taxes is the so called net-of-tax method. It is based on the proposition that the effects of taxes enter into the valuation of individual assets and liabilities. Under this method, the tax effects of timing differences are treated as adjustments of the related revenue and expense items in the income statement rather than as an adjustment of the provision for income taxes, and the accumulated tax effect is shown in the balance sheet as an adjustment of the related asset or liability accounts. The net-of-tax method distorts results by mixing the tax effect with other items in the income statement and in the balance sheet. In the view of the Research Committee, it should not be used.
(CRR – 3470.14–.15, .17, .19)

"As mentioned ... the corporation tax charge in the profit and loss account should be based on the accounting profit without regard to items allocated to other periods for taxation purposes. In the balance sheet, the liability for corporation tax will represent the amount actually assessable in respect of the accounting period. The difference between the charge and the liability, if material, should be passed through the deferred taxation account, although in order to avoid undue complexity, its use is normally restricted to those items which cause major differences between accounting profit and assessable profit. The purpose for which the account will most frequently be used is to adjust for the differences between capital allowances given for tax purposes and depreciation charged against profit in respect of the same assets, and this will usually ensure that a credit balance is maintained on the account. Other credits to the account will result from following the recommendations set out in section VI below regarding capital surpluses not immediately taxed. The presumption is that amounts included in the balance at the credit of the deferred taxation account will be required at some future date or dates to meet taxation liabilities relating to profits or surpluses already brought into account, or resulting from the acceleration of tax relief in relation to the corresponding charges against profit. The balance should therefore be regarded not as a reserve but as a deferred liability. The fact that as elements of this liability mature they are replaced by the new deferments does not alter the character of the balance.

"Recommendation

(a) A deferred taxation account should be established and maintained at current rates of taxation whenever there exist material taxation liabilities which may crystallize at some future date on profits and surpluses already brought into account.

(b) As regards assets on which capital allowances cumulatively exceed the charges for depreciation in the accounts, the deferred taxation account should provide for tax on the excess of:

(i) the net amount at which the relevant assets are stated in the balance sheet over

(ii) the written down value of those assets for taxation purposes. . . .

(c) A credit balance on the deferred taxation account should not be treated in the balance sheet as a reserve or grouped with reserves. It should be separately stated, but may be grouped with any liabilities or provisions which fall outside the heading of 'current liabilities'.

"The deferred taxation account is intended to provide for a future liability at future rates of tax, but as those rates are unknown this object can never be achieved with certainty or precision. Nevertheless, as changes in the rate of corporation tax take place, it should be recognized that the basis on which past provision has been made has become out of date, and the balance of the account should be adjusted accordingly.

"Recommendation

When a change in the rate of corporation tax has taken place, the entire balance of the deferred taxation account (and any amount of future tax or tax relief shown by way of note) should be correspondingly adjusted. To the extent that the adjustment relates to entries made in previous years, the amount, if material, should be disclosed."

(BR 27 – pars. 32–33, 37–38)

"Interpretations of the nature of timing differences are diverse, with the result that three basic methods of interperiod allocation of income taxes have developed and been adopted in practice. . . .

"Interperiod tax allocation under the *deferred method* is a procedure whereby the tax effects of current timing differences are deferred currently and allocated to income tax expense of future periods when the timing differences reverse. The deferred method emphasizes the tax effects of timing differences on income of the period in which the differences originate. The deferred taxes are determined on the basis of the tax rates in effect at the time the timing differences originate and are not adjusted for subsequent changes in tax rates or to reflect the imposition of new taxes. The tax effects of transactions which reduce taxes currently payable are treated as deferred credits; the tax effects of transactions which increase taxes currently payable are treated as deferred charges. Amortization of these deferred taxes to income tax expense in future periods is based upon the nature of the transactions producing the tax effects and upon the manner in which these transactions enter into the determination of pretax accounting income in relation to taxable income.

"Interperiod tax allocation under the *liability method* is a procedure whereby the income taxes expected to be paid on pretax accounting income are accrued currently. The taxes on components of pretax accounting income may be computed at different rates, depending upon the period in which the components were, or are expected to be, included in taxable income. The difference between income tax expense and income taxes payable in the periods in which the timing differences originate are either liabilities for taxes payable in the future or assets for prepaid taxes. The estimated amounts of future tax liabilities and prepaid taxes are computed at the tax rates expected to be in effect in the periods in which the timing differences reverse. Under the liability method the initial computations are considered to be tentative and are subject to future adjustment if tax rates change or new taxes are imposed.

"Interperiod tax allocation under the *net of tax method* is a procedure whereby the tax effects (determined by either the deferred or liability methods) of timing differences are recognized in the valuation of assets and liabilities and the related revenues and expenses. The tax effects are applied to reduce specific assets or liabilities on the basis that tax deductibility or taxability are factors in their valuation.

"The Board has concluded that the deferred method of tax allocation should be followed since it provides the most useful and practical approach to interperiod tax allocation and the presentation of income taxes in financial statements."

(APBO 11 – pars. 18–21, 35)

4. On tax loss carry-forwards:

"For loss carry-forwards, the potential tax recovery should not be recognized in the accounts in the period of loss unless it appears virtually certain that the carry-forward benefit will be realized within the carry-forward period allowed by the tax authorities. There may be circumstances, however, where in a period of loss all or part of an existing tax allocation credit may be brought into account in determining the reported results for the period.

"Where a tax reduction associated with the tax loss carry-forward is not recognized in the accounts, the existence of the loss carry-forward should be disclosed in a note to the financial statements. If the carry-forward benefit is realized in a later period, the resulting tax reduction should be reflected in the income statement of the period of realization as an extraordinary item."

(CRR 3470.31–.32)

"Recommendations
(a) If a loss is set against other income of the same accounting period, corporation tax should be provided on the net income.
(b) If a loss is set against the profits of the preceding accounting period, the corporation tax recoverable should, if material, be disclosed separately.
(c) If a loss is available to be set off against the profits of succeeding accounting periods, the existence of the loss, if material, should be indicated by way of a note. It should be made clear that any tax relief is dependent on there being future profits of sufficient amount.
(d) If the corporation tax charged for a particular accounting period has been eliminated or materially reduced by losses brought forward, the amount of the relief should be indicated.

"Recommendations
(a) When a trading loss has been incurred, and is to be carried forward, a transfer should be made from the deferred taxation account to the credit of the profit and loss account of an amount equal to the notional tax relief

attributable to the loss, but not exceeding that part of the balance of the deferred taxation account which represents tax on income from the same trade. If account is taken in this manner of the whole of a loss, the need for the note recommended in paragraph 15 (c) above will be obviated. If only part of the loss is so treated, any amount given in the note should be appropriately reduced.

(b) When a transfer has been made under (a) above, then as and when a trading profit is subsequently earned against which the loss can be set for assessment purposes, a transfer should be made from the profit and loss account to the credit of the deferred taxation account of an amount equal to the actual tax relief resulting from the loss, but not exceeding the amount previously transferred in accordance with (a). In indicating the relief obtained, as recommended in paragraph 15 (d) above, it should be borne in mind that a part or the whole of the loss relief will have been credited to the profit and loss account under (a) above in an earlier year."

(BR 27 – pars. 15, 40)

"The tax effects of any realizable loss carry*backs* should be recognized in the determination of net income (loss) of the loss periods. The tax loss gives rise to a refund (or claim for refund) of past taxes, which is both measurable and currently realizable; therefore the tax effect of the loss is properly recognizable in the determination of net income (loss) for the loss period. Appropriate adjustments of existing net deferred tax credits may also be necessary in the loss period.

"The tax effects of loss carry*forwards* also relate to the determination of net income (loss) of the loss periods. However, a significant question generally exists as to realization of the tax effects of the carry*forwards*, since realization is dependent upon future taxable income. Accordingly, the Board has concluded that the tax benefits of loss carry*forwards* should not be recognized until they are actually realized, except in unusual circumstances when realization is *assured beyond any reasonable doubt* at the time the loss carry*forwards* arise. When the tax benefits of loss carry*forwards* are not recognized until realized in full or in part in subsequent periods, the tax benefits should be reported in the results of operations of those periods as extraordinary items.

"Net deferred tax credits arising from timing differences may exist at the time loss carry*forwards* arise. In the usual case when the tax effect of a loss carry*forward* is not recognized in the loss period, adjustments of the existing net deferred tax credits may be necessary in that period or in subsequent periods. In this situation net deferred tax credits should be eliminated to the extent of the lower of (a) the tax effect of the loss carry*forward*, or (b) the amortization of the net deferred tax credits that would otherwise have occurred during the carry*forward* period. . . ."

(APBO 11 – pars. 44–45, 48)

Chapter 14 – Special Items

1. Extraordinary items:

"Extraordinary items may be defined as gains, losses and provisions for losses which result from occurrences the underlying nature of which is not typical of the normal business activities of the enterprise, are not expected to occur regularly over a period of years, and are not considered as recurring factors in any evaluation of the ordinary operations of the enterprise. Examples of occurrences giving rise to extraordinary items, provided they meet the criteria above, would be:

(a) the discontinuance of, or substantial change in, a business programme or policy such as sale or abandonment of a plant or significant segment of the enterprise or sale of investments not acquired for resale;

(b) intervention by government or other regulatory bodies such as expropriation of properties or revaluation of a foreign currency;

(c) acts of God such as earthquakes or floods;

(d) realization of income tax reductions on the carry-forward of a loss.

"Each extraordinary item should be shown separately and its nature described. Items resulting from events and transactions of a similar nature may be shown in the aggregate and dissimilar items should be shown individually. The amount of any income taxes attributable thereto should be disclosed.

"Gains, losses and provisions for losses resulting from normal business activities which are both abnormal in size and caused by rare or unusual circumstances, have sometimes been considered to be extraordinary items. However, because such items result from occurrences the underlying nature of which is typical of the customary business activities of the enterprise, even though caused by unusual circumstances, they are not extraordinary items. Such items would include:

(a) losses and provisions for losses (regardless of size) with respect to bad debts or inventories;

(b) gains, losses and provisions for losses from normal fluctuations of foreign exchange rates;

(c) adjustments with respect to contract prices;

(d) adjustments arising from changes in the estimated useful life of fixed assets."

(CRR 3480.04, .10–.11)

The Canadian recommendations very largely follow those of the Accounting Principles Board in Opinion No. 9 so the latter are omitted here. The English recommendations are similar to the practice prevailing in North America before the recent recommendations on extraordinary items.

"All profits and losses of a revenue nature should normally be reflected in the profit and loss account. Additions to or utilisations of revenue reserves and the application of capital reserves to the relief of charges on revenue should therefore normally be passed through that account. They should be dealt with either as items entering into the ascertainment of the result shown for the year or as adjustments of the unappropriated balance from the accounts of the current and prior years as may be appropriate. This does not however prevent wholly exceptional items of material amount which do not relate to the accounting period from being taken direct to reserves if a true and fair view will be better presented in that way.

"Items of an exceptional or non-recurrent nature should be dealt with in such a way as to show in the particular circumstances a true and fair view of the result of the year. Such items, other than tax adjustments of earlier years, may be dealt with as follows:

(a) where the items arise from the trading operations of the company, they may be dealt with in arriving at the trading surplus or deficit and disclosed separately by one of the methods recommended in paragraph 41

(b) they may be shown separately in the section of the account which includes other income and non-trading expenditure of the year

(c) they may be shown separately after the 'profit after taxation'

(d) they may in appropriate circumstances be omitted from the profit and loss account and taken direct to reserve (see paragraph 11).

"Where exceptional or non-recurrent items have been taken into account before arriving at 'profit before taxation', any tax charges or reliefs arising because of the items should be included with the tax charge on such profit.

"Where exceptional or non-recurrent items are not taken into account before arriving at 'profit before taxation', the effect of these items on the amount shown in respect of tax should be considered; where appropriate the relevant tax charges or reliefs should be shown as separate adjustments to the respective items."

(BR 18 – pars. 11, 43–45)

2. Prior period adjustments:

"Situations occasionally arise where the financial statements for a period include gains or losses which should be related to the income of prior periods. Such gains or losses are distinguishable from extraordinary items and are referred to below as 'prior period adjustments'. They are limited to those adjustments which have all four of the following characteristics:

(a) are specifically identified with and directly related to the business activities of particular prior periods;

(b) are not attributable to economic events, including obsolescence, occurring subsequent to the date of the financial statements for such prior periods;

(c) depend primarily on decisions or determinations by persons other than management or owners; and

(d) could not be reasonably estimated prior to such decisions or determinations.

"Examples of prior period adjustments (provided they have all four characteristics) might be:

(a) non-recurring adjustments or settlements of income taxes;

(b) settlements of claims resulting from litigation.

"Gains or losses which qualify as prior period adjustments are rare. They would not include normal corrections or adjustments arising from modification of estimates commonly used in accounting, such as adjustments arising from changes in the estimated useful life of fixed assets. They also would not include, regardless of size, bad debt losses, inventory losses, amounts written off deferred development costs or income tax reductions realized from the carry-forward of a loss."

(CRR 3600.01–.03)

Once again the Canadian recommendations are in substance the same as the American.

3. Capital transactions:

"Capital transactions should be excluded from the determination of net income and shown separately in the statement to which they relate (at least for the year in which the transactions occur).

"Capital transactions include items such as:

(a) changes in capital, including premiums, discounts and expenses relating to the issue, redemption or cancellation of share capital;

(b) gains or losses

(i) on purchase and resale by a company of its own issued common shares;

(ii) on purchase and cancellation by a company of its own issued common shares;

(c) contributions by owners or others, such as government grants in certain circumstances;

(d) transfers to and from reserves;

(e) appraisal increase credits;

(f) dividend distributions (including stock dividends)."

(CRR 3610.01–.02)

Chapter 15 – Classification of Equities

1. Stock splits and stock dividends:

"As has been previously stated, a stock dividend does not, in fact, give rise to any change whatsoever in either the corporation's assets or its respective share-holders' proportionate interests therein. However, it cannot fail to be recognized that, merely as a consequence of the expressed purpose of the transaction and its characterization as a *dividend* in related notices to shareholders and the public at large, many recipients of stock dividends look upon them as distributions of corporate earnings and usually in an amount equivalent to the fair value of the additional shares received. Furthermore, it is to be presumed that such views of recipients are materially strengthened in those instances, which are by far the most numerous, where the issuances are so small in comparison with the shares previously outstanding that they do not have any apparent effect upon the share market price and, consequently, the market value of the shares previously held remains substantially unchanged. The committee therefore believes that where these circumstances exist the corporation should in the public interest account for the transaction by transferring from earned surplus to the category of per-manent capitalization (represented by the capital stock and capital surplus accounts) an amount equal to the fair value of the additional shares issued. Unless this is done, the amount of earnings which the shareholder may believe to have been distributed to him will be left, except to the extent otherwise dictated by legal requirements, in earned surplus subject to possible further similar stock issuances or cash distributions.

"Where the number of additional shares issued as a stock dividend is so great that it has, or may reasonably be expected to have, the effect of materially reducing the share market value, the committee believes that the implications and possible constructions discussed in the preceding paragraph are not likely to exist and that the transaction clearly partakes of the nature of a stock split-up as defined in paragraph 2. Consequently, the committee considers that under such circumstances there is no need to capitalize earned surplus, other than to the extent occasioned by legal requirements. . . .

"In cases of closely-held companies, it is to be presumed that the intimate knowledge of the corporations' affairs possessed by their shareholders would preclude any such implications and possible constructions as are referred to in paragraph 10. In such cases, the committee believes that considerations of public policy do not arise and that there is no need to capitalize earned surplus other than to meet legal requirements.

"Earlier in this chapter a stock split-up was defined as being confined to trans-actions involving the issuance of shares, without consideration moving to the corporation, for the purpose of effecting a reduction in the unit market price of shares of the class issued and, thus, of obtaining wider distribution and improved marketability of the shares. Where this is clearly the intent, no transfer from earned surplus to capital surplus or capital stock account is called for, other than to the extent occasioned by legal requirements. It is believed, however, that few cases will arise where the aforementioned purpose can be accomplished through an issuance of shares which is less than, say, 20% or 25% of the previously outstanding shares."

(ARB 43 – Ch. 7B, pars. 10–12, 15)

2. Treatment of common shares repurchased:

"The Board considers that the following accounting practices . . . are acceptable . . .

a. When a corporation's stock is retired, or purchased for constructive retirement (with or without an intention to retire the stock formally in accordance with applicable laws):

i. *an excess of purchase price over par or stated value* may be allocated between capital surplus and retained earnings. The portion of the excess allocated to capital surplus should be limited to the sum of (a) all capital surplus arising from previous retirements and net 'gains' on sales of treasury stock of the same issue and (b) the prorata portion of capital surplus paid in, voluntary transfers of retained earnings, capitalization of stock dividends, etc., on the same issue. For this purpose, any remaining capital surplus applicable to issues fully retired (formal or constructive) is deemed to be applicable prorata to shares of common stock. Alternatively, the excess may be charged entirely to retained earnings in recognition of the fact that a corporation can always capitalize or allocate retained earnings for such purposes.

ii. *an excess of par or stated value over purchase price* should be credited to capital surplus.

b. When a corporation's stock is acquired for purposes other than retirement (formal or constructive), or when ultimate disposition has not yet been decided, the cost of acquired stock may be shown separately as a deduction from the total of capital stock, capital surplus, and retained earnings, or may be accorded the accounting treatment appropriate for retired stock, or in some circumstances may be shown as an asset in accordance with paragraph 4 of Chapter 1A of ARB 43. 'Gains' on sales of treasury stock not previously accounted for as constructively retired should be credited to capital surplus; 'losses' may be charged to capital surplus to the extent that previous net 'gains' from sales or retirements of the same class of stock are included therein, otherwise to retained earnings."

(APBO 6 – par. 12 as amended by APBO 16)

Chapter 16 – Investments – Other Than in Associated Companies

1. Classification as current; carrying value:

"Investments should be classified as current assets only if capable of reasonably prompt liquidation. Such investments would include not only temporary holdings of marketable securities but also funds placed in other investment mediums, such as treasury bills, investment certificates, and call loans."

(CRR 3010.01)

"It is recommended that the following principles should normally be applied in connection with the treatment of investments in the balance sheets of trading companies whose normal business does not involve either dealing in investments or the holding of investments other than in subsidiaries.

"Investments which it is intended to hold continuously, for example trade investments and interests in subsidiaries, should be classified as fixed assets.

"Where interests in associated companies are material they should be stated separately under the general heading of 'Trade investments' or under a heading of their own.

"Quoted and other readily realisable investments (other than trade investments, investments in subsidiaries and fellow subsidiaries, and other investments intended to be held continuously, even though they may happen to be quoted or are otherwise readily realisable) should be classified as current assets; to do otherwise would distort the view of the current asset position.

"Provision should be made for the diminution in the value of investments:
(a) where the market value at the date of the balance sheet of investments which are current assets is lower than cost
(b) where the value to the business of investments which are fixed assets appears to have decreased permanently below cost.

"Provision for diminution in value ... should not exceed the amount required to reduce cost to market value at the date of the balance sheet in the case of investments which are current assets or to long-term value in the case of investments which are fixed assets."

(BR 20 – pars. 37–38, 41–42, 45–46)

2. Stock dividends received not income:

"In applying the principles of income determination to the accounts of a shareholder of a corporation, it is generally agreed that the problem of determining his income is distinct from the problem of income determination by the corporation itself. The income of the corporation is determined as that of a separate entity without regard to the equity of the respective shareholders in such income. Under conventional accounting concepts, the shareholder has no income solely as a result of the fact that the corporation has income; the increase in his equity through undistributed earnings is no more than potential income to him. It is true that income earned by the corporation may result in an enhancement in the market value of the shares, but until there is a distribution, division, or severance of corporate assets, the shareholder has no income. If there is an increase in the market value of his holdings, such unrealized appreciation is not income. In the case of a stock dividend or split-up, there is no distribution, division, or severance of corporate assets. Moreover, there is nothing resulting therefrom that the shareholder can realize without parting with some of his proportionate interest in the corporation."

(ARB 43 – Ch. 7B, par. 6)

Chapter 17 – Investments in Associated Companies

1. Criteria for consolidation:

"The purpose of consolidated statements is to present, primarily for the benefit of the shareholders and creditors of the parent company, the results of operations and the financial position of a parent company and its subsidiaries essentially as if the group were a single company with one or more branches or divisions. There is a presumption that consolidated statements are more meaningful than separate statements and that they are usually necessary for a fair presentation when one of the companies in the group directly or indirectly has a controlling financial interest in the other companies.

"The usual condition for a controlling financial interest is ownership of a majority voting interest, and, therefore, as a general rule ownership by one company, directly or indirectly, of over fifty per cent of the outstanding voting shares of another company is a condition pointing toward consolidation. However, there are exceptions to this general rule. For example, a subsidiary should not be consolidated where control is likely to be temporary, or where it does not rest with the majority owners (as, for instance, where the subsidiary is in legal reorganization or in bankruptcy). There may also be situations where the minority interest in the subsidiary is so large, in relation to the equity of the shareholders of the parent in the consolidated net assets, that the presentation of separate financial statements for the two companies would be more meaningful and useful. However, the fact that the subsidiary has a relatively large indebtedness to bondholders or others is not in itself a valid argument for exclusion of the subsidiary from consolidation.

"In deciding upon consolidation policy, the aim should be to make the financial presentation which is most meaningful in the circumstances. The reader should be given information which is suitable to his needs, but he should not be burdened with unnecessary detail. Thus, even though a group of companies is heterogeneous in character, it may be better to make a full consolidation than to present a large number of separate statements. On the other hand, separate statements or combined statements would be preferable for a subsidiary or group of subsidiaries if the presentation of financial information concerning the particular activities of such subsidiaries would be more informative to shareholders and creditors of the parent company than would the inclusion of such subsidiaries in the consolidation. For example, separate statements may be required for a subsidiary which is a bank or an insurance company and may be preferable for a finance company where the parent and the other subsidiaries are engaged in manufacturing operations."

(ARB 51 – pars. 1–3)

2. Use of the equity basis for unconsolidated subsidiaries:

"The Board reaffirms the conclusion that investors should account for investments in common stock of unconsolidated domestic subsidiaries by the equity method in consolidated financial statements, and the Board now extends this conclusion to investments in common stock of all unconsolidated subsidiaries (foreign as well as domestic) in consolidated financial statements. The equity method is not, however, a valid substitute for consolidation and should not be used to justify exclusion of a subsidiary when consolidation is otherwise appropriate. The Board also concludes that parent companies should account for investments in the common stock of subsidiaries by the equity method in parent-company financial statements prepared for issuance to stockholders as the financial statements of the primary reporting entity."

(APBO 18 – par. 14)

3. Use of the equity basis for associated companies:

"... where a company conducts an important part of its business through the medium of other companies, whether more or less than 50 per cent owned, the mere disclosure of dividend income (or mere inclusion of dividend income alone) is unlikely to be sufficient to give shareholders adequate information regarding the sources of their income and of the manner in which their funds are being employed.

". . . In recent years there have been two important developments. One has been the growing practice of companies to conduct parts of their business through other companies (frequently consortium or joint venture companies) in which they have a substantial but not a controlling interest. The other is the importance which investors have come to attach to earnings (as distinct from dividends), the price/earnings ratio (P/E ratio) and, increasingly, earnings per share. Thus, in order that the investing company's accounts as a whole may give adequate information, and provide a total of earnings from which the most meaningful ratios can be calculated, it is considered necessary that the coverage of consolidated accounts be extended so that they shall include (within the framework of the existing law) the share of earnings or losses of companies which are described in this Statement as associated companies (see paragraph 6).

"This approach recognises a difference in principle between the nature of investments in associated companies (as defined in this Statement) and other forms of trade investment. The essence of the distinction is that the investing company actively participates in the commercial and policy decisions of its associated companies; it thus has a measure of direct responsibility for the return on its investment, and should account for its stewardship accordingly, whereas it will not normally seek to exert direct management influence over the operating policy of other companies in which it invests, and should continue to deal with them in accordance with traditional accounting methods.

"The broad concept underlying the accounting treatment of the results of associated companies here stated is the adoption in modified form of the consolidation procedures used for subsidiary companies. It follows from this that the investing group's share of associated companies' profits and losses will be reflected in its consolidated profit and loss account, and its share of their post-acquisition retained profits or surplus will be reflected in its consolidated balance sheet, though not in its own balance sheet as a legal entity.

"A company (not being a subsidiary of the investing group or company) is an associated company of the investing group or company if:
(a) the investing group or company's interest in the associated company is effectively that of a partner in a joint venture or consortium
   or
(b) the investing group or company's interest in the associated company is for the long term and is substantial (i.e., not less than 20 per cent of the equity voting rights), and, having regard to the disposition of the other shareholdings, the investing group or company is in a position to exercise a significant influence over the associated company.

In both cases it is essential that the investing group or company participates (usually through representation on the board) in commercial and financial policy decisions of the associated company, including the distribution of profits.

"Income from investments by a company or its subsidiaries in associated companies (as defined in paragraph 6 above) should be brought into account on the following bases:
(a) *In the investing company's own accounts*
   (i) Dividends received up to the accounting date of the investing company; and

(ii) dividends receivable in respect of accounting periods ending on or before that date and declared before the accounts of the investing company are approved by the directors.

(b) *In the investing group's consolidated accounts (see paragraph 8)*
The investing group's share of profits less losses of associated companies (see paragraph 12 for exceptions).

"An associated company's results should be omitted from the consolidated accounts only on the same grounds as those which would permit group accounts not to deal with a subsidiary, notably if the inclusion of such results:

(a) would involve expense or delay out of proportion to the value to the members of the investing company
or

(b) would be misleading.

The reason for omission should be stated.

"Unless shown at a valuation, the amount at which the investing group's interests in associated companies should be shown in the consolidated balance sheet is:

(a) the cost of the investments less any amounts written off
and

(b) the investing company or group's share of the post-acquisition retained profits and reserves of the associated companies.

The investing company which has no subsidiaries, or which does not otherwise prepare consolidated accounts, should show its share of its associated companies' post-acquisition retained profits and reserves by way of note to its balance sheet. Information regarding associated companies' tangible and intangible assets and liabilities should be given, if materially relevant for the appreciation by the members of the investing company of the nature of their investment."

(BSSAP 1 – pars. 2–7, 12, 19)

"The Board concludes that the equity method best enables investors in corporate joint ventures to reflect the underlying nature of their investment in those ventures. Therefore, investors should account for investments in common stock of corporate joint ventures by the equity method, both in consolidated financial statements and in parent-company financial statements prepared for issuance to stockholders as the financial statements of the primary reporting entity.

"The Board concludes that the equity method of accounting for an investment in common stock should also be followed by an investor whose investment in voting stock gives it the ability to exercise significant influence over operating and financial policies of an investee even though the investor holds 50% or less of the voting stock. Ability to exercise that influence may be indicated in several ways, such as representation on the board of directors, participation in policy making processes, material intercompany transactions, interchange of managerial personnel, or technological dependency. Another important consideration is the extent of ownership by an investor in relation to the concentration of other shareholdings, but substantial or majority ownership of the voting stock of an investee by another investor does not necessarily preclude the ability to exercise significant influence by the investor. The Board recognizes that determining the ability of an investor to exercise such influence is not always clear and applying judgment is necessary to assess the status of each investment. In order to achieve a reasonable degree of uniformity in application, the Board concludes that an investment (direct or indirect) of 20% or more of the voting stock of an investee should lead to a presumption that in the absence of evidence to the contrary an investor has the ability to exercise significant influence over an investee. Conversely, an investment of less than 20% of the voting stock of an investee should lead to a presumption that an investor does not have the ability to exercise significant influence unless such ability can be demonstrated. When the equity method is appropriate, it should be applied in consolidated financial statements and in parent-company financial statements prepared for issuance to stockholders as the financial statements of the primary reporting entity."

(APBO 18 – pars. 16–17)

Chapter 18 – Business Combinations

1. The choice between the purchase and pooling methods of accounting:

"The Board finds merit in both the purchase and pooling of interests methods of accounting for business combinations and accepts neither method to the exclusion of the other. The arguments in favor of the purchase method of accounting are more persuasive if cash or other assets are distributed or liabilities are incurred to effect a combination, but arguments in favor of the pooling of interests method of accounting are more persuasive if voting common stock is issued to effect a combination of common stock interests. Therefore, the Board concludes that some business combinations should be accounted for by the purchase method and other combinations should be accounted for by the pooling of interests method.

"The Board also concludes that the two methods are not alternatives in accounting for the same business combination. A single method should be applied to an entire combination; the practice now known as part-purchase, part-pooling is not acceptable. The acquisition after the effective date of this Opinion of some or all of the stock held by minority stockholders of a subsidiary – whether acquired by the parent, the subsidiary itself, or another affiliate – should be accounted for by the purchase method rather than by the pooling of interests method."

(APBO 16 – pars. 42–43)

2. Application of the pooling of interests method:

"The recorded assets and liabilities of the separate companies generally become the recorded assets and liabilities of the combined corporation. The combined corporation therefore recognizes those assets and liabilities recorded in conformity with generally accepted accounting principles by the separate companies at the date the combination is consummated.

"The combined corporation records the historical-cost based amounts of the assets and liabilities of the separate companies because the existing basis of accounting continues. However, the separate companies may have recorded assets and liabilities under differing methods of accounting and the amounts may be adjusted to the same basis of accounting if the change would otherwise have been appropriate for the separate company. A change in accounting method to conform the individual methods should be applied retroactively, and financial statements presented for prior periods should be restated.

"The stockholders' equities of the separate companies are also combined as a part of the pooling of interests method of accounting. The combined corporation records as capital the capital stock and capital in excess of par or stated value of outstanding stock of the separate companies. Similarly, retained earnings or deficits of the separate companies are combined and recognized as retained earnings of the combined corporation. . . . The amount of outstanding shares of stock of the combined corporation at par or stated value may exceed the total amount of capital stock of the separate combining companies; the excess should be deducted first from the combined other contributed capital and then from the combined retained earnings. The combined retained earnings could be misleading if shortly before or as a part of the combination transaction one or more of the combining companies adjusted the elements of stockholders' equity to eliminate a deficit; therefore, the elements of equity before the adjustment should be combined."

(APBO 16 – pars. 51–53)

3. Problems in application of the purchase method:

"The same accounting principles apply to determining the cost of assets acquired individually, those acquired in a group, and those acquired in a business combination. A cash payment by a corporation measures the cost of acquired assets less liabilities assumed. Similarly, the fair values of other assets distributed, such as marketable securities or properties, and the fair value of liabilities incurred by an acquiring corporation measure the cost of an acquired company. The present value of a debt security represents the fair value of the liability, and a premium or discount should be recorded for a debt security issued with an interest rate fixed materially above or below the effective rate or current yield for an otherwise comparable security.

"The distinctive attributes of preferred stocks make some issues similar to a debt security while others possess common stock characteristics, with many gradations between the extremes. Determining cost of an acquired company may be affected by those characteristics. . . .

"The fair value of securities traded in the market is normally more clearly evident than the fair value of an acquired company (paragraph 67). Thus, the quoted market price of an equity security issued to effect a business combination may usually be used to approximate the fair value of an acquired company after recognizing possible effects of price fluctuations, quantities traded, issue costs, and the like (paragraph 23). The market price for a reasonable period before and after the date the terms of the acquisition are agreed to and announced should be considered in determining the fair value of securities issued.

"If the quoted market price is not the fair value of stock, either preferred or common, the consideration received should be estimated even though measuring directly the fair values of assets received is difficult. Both the consideration received, including goodwill, and the extent of the adjustment of the quoted market price of the stock issued should be weighed to determine the amount to be recorded. All aspects of the acquisition, including the negotiations, should be studied, and independent appraisals may be used as an aid in determining the fair value of securities issued. Consideration other than stock distributed to effect an acquisition may provide evidence of the total fair value received."

(APBO 16 – pars. 72–75)

"An acquiring corporation should allocate the cost of an acquired company to the assets acquired and liabilities assumed. Allocation should follow the principles described in paragraph 68.

First, all identifiable assets acquired, either individually or by type, and liabilities assumed in a business combination, whether or not shown in the financial statements of the acquired company, should be assigned a portion of the cost of the acquired company, normally equal to their fair values at date of acquisition. Second, the excess of the cost of the acquired company over the sum of the amounts assigned to identifiable assets acquired less liabilities assumed should be recorded as goodwill. The sum of the market or appraisal values of identifiable assets acquired less liabilities assumed may sometimes exceed the cost of the acquired company. If so, the values otherwise assignable to noncurrent assets acquired (except long-term investments in marketable securities) should be reduced by a proportionate part of the excess to determine the assigned values. A deferred credit for an excess of assigned value of identifiable assets over cost of an acquired company (sometimes called 'negative goodwill') should not be recorded unless those assets are reduced to zero value.

Independent appraisals may be used as an aid in determining the fair values of some assets and liabilities. Subsequent sales of assets may also provide evidence of values. The effect of taxes may be a factor in assigning amounts to identifiable assets and liabilities (paragraph 89).

"The market or appraisal values of specific assets and liabilities determined in paragraph 88 may differ from the income tax bases of those items. Estimated future tax effects of differences between the tax bases and amounts otherwise appropriate to assign to an asset or a liability are one of the variables in estimating fair value. Amounts assigned to identifiable assets and liabilities should, for example, recognize that the fair value of an asset to an acquirer is less than its market or appraisal value if all or a portion of the market or appraisal value is not deductible for income taxes. The impact of tax effects on amounts assigned to individual assets and liabilities depends on numerous factors, including imminence or delay of realization of the asset value and the possible timing of tax consequences. Since differences between amounts assigned and tax bases are not timing differences . . . the acquiring corporation should not record deferred tax accounts at the date of acquisition."

(APBO 16 – pars. 87, 89)

Chapter 19 – Translation of Accounts in Foreign Currencies

1. Translation procedures:

"The fundamental uncertainties involved in exchange operations make it impossible to lay down hard and fast rules for conversion into sterling of the accounts of overseas branches and subsidiaries, and emphasise the need for each case to be judged on its merits in the light of particular circumstances.

"Where there have not been exceptional changes in exchange parities two main methods are however normally accepted for converting overseas branch and subsidiary accounts into sterling for the purposes of the financial accounts of United Kingdom companies. For convenience they are termed here the 'closing rate' (sometimes also called the 'balance sheet date') and the 'historic rate' methods. Both methods are described in broad outline below though no attempt is made to discuss the variations in detail often found in practice.

" 'Closing rate' method

"Under the 'closing rate' method, all items in the overseas branch or subsidiary accounts are converted at the rate ruling on the balance sheet date, subject to special considerations relating to the following items.

"*Stocks* acquired locally are stated at closing rate, but stocks bought out of sterling funds, or shipped from other foreign branches or subsidiaries in the group are stated at actual sterling cost or sterling equivalent of the currency with which it was purchased, after elimination of profits attributable to transfers within the group. The normal rules for reducing stocks to net realisable value if this is less than cost apply.

"*Profit or loss for the year* is converted at the closing rate of exchange except for remittances during the year, which are converted at the actual rate.

" 'Historic rate' method

"The 'historic rate' method of converting accounts regards overseas branches or subsidiaries from an accounting point of view as adjuncts of the parent, and their activities are measured in terms of sterling, which in normal circumstances is regarded as remaining constant while foreign currencies fluctuate.

"*Fixed and other non-current assets* are converted into sterling at the rates of exchange ruling when they were acquired or constructed, or at actual sterling cost.

"*Depreciation of fixed assets* is converted at the rate or rates used when the relevant assets were acquired.

"*Cash, debtors and other current assets* (excluding stocks) are converted at the rate of exchange ruling on the balance sheet date ('closing rate').

"*Stocks* are converted at the rates ruling at the time when they were acquired or produced, or at actual sterling cost if purchased out of sterling funds. This procedure is consistent with 'historic rate' principles, but in practice, even where the 'historic rate' method is used, it is often found expedient to convert stocks at the closing rate used for other current assets. The normal procedures for determining whether any part of the cost of stock is irrecoverable are applied (see Recommendation 22).

"*Current liabilities* are converted at the closing rate.

"*Long-term liabilities and share capital stated in overseas currency* are converted at the rates ruling when they were incurred or issued, or at actual sterling cost.

"*Profit and loss account.* Depreciation, as noted, is converted at the exchange rates ruling when the relevant fixed assets were acquired. Consequently, depreciation is added back to the profit or loss for the period under review before conversion into currency. Conversion is then effected at the average rate for the period: a weighted average is applied where profits (or losses) do not accrue evenly throughout the period.

" 'Closing rate' and 'historic rate' methods compared

"In normal circumstances both the 'historic rate' and 'closing rate' methods are widely used and equally acceptable in practice. The 'historic rate' method is the more traditional. It measures overseas operations from the standpoint of a stable and unchanging home currency, and was evolved in the context of overseas branches and subsidiaries largely financed and stocked from the United Kingdom. The 'closing rate' method, which has been increasingly adopted in recent years, recognises overseas branches and subsidiaries as viable units existing apart from their parent, and by no means necessarily relying on their parent for finance or stocks. It expresses overseas operations in current and realistic sterling amounts, and has the practical advantage over the 'historic rate' method of simplicity of operation. The method of conversion to be selected is however a matter for judgement in the light of the facts of individual cases. The 'historic rate' method, may, for instance, sometimes be preferred where an overseas currency has a history of instability in relation to sterling and the circumstances are such that it is judged appropriate to continue to state fixed assets on the basis of their original sterling equivalents."

(BR 25 – Appendix)

"Fixed assets and permanent investments should be translated into dollars at the rates prevailing when such assets were acquired or constructed. Long-term receivables may be similarly translated, although translation of such receivables at current exchange rates is appropriate in many circumstances. When large items are purchased for United States dollars (or from the proceeds of sale of such dollars), the United States dollar cost will, of course, be used. If, however, the purchase is made in some foreign currency (obtained from earnings or borrowings), then the cost of the assets should be the equivalent of the amount of foreign currency in the United States dollars, at the rate of exchange prevailing at the time payment is made. An exception to the foregoing general principles might be made where fixed assets, permanent investments, or long-term receivables were acquired shortly before a substantial and presumably permanent change in the exchange rate with funds obtained in the country concerned, in which case it may be appropriate to restate the dollar equivalent of such assets to the extent of the change in the related debt.

"In consolidating or combining the accounts, depreciation should be computed on the amount of fixed assets as expressed in United States dollars, even though for purposes of local taxation it may be impossible to show the foreign currency equivalent of the full amount of depreciation on the foreign statements.

"Cash, accounts receivable, and other current assets, unless covered by forward exchange contracts, should be translated at the rate of exchange prevailing on the date of the balance sheet.

"Inventory should follow the standard rule of *cost or market, whichever is lower* in dollars. Where accounts are to be stated in which the question of foreign exchange enters and the inventory is not translated at the rate of exchange prevailing on the date of the balance sheet, as is usually done with current assets, the burden of proof is on those who wish to follow some other procedure.

"There are, however, undoubtedly many cases where the cost or a portion of the cost of an article was incurred when the foreign currency was at a substantially higher rate of exchange than existed on the closing day of the financial period. In many cases such an asset could not be replaced for the amount in foreign currency at which it appears in the records of the branch or subsidiary company. In some cases the replacement price in foreign currency would undoubtedly have increased since the fall in exchange, and it would be inequitable to treat *the lower of cost or market* as a mere translation at the closing rate of the foreign currency cost price, where the article could now be replaced only at a much higher amount in foreign currency. Where the selling price obtainable in dollars, after deducting a reasonable percentage to cover selling and other local expenses, exceeds the cost of the article in dollars at the rate prevailing as of the date of purchase, such original dollar equivalent may be considered as the cost for purposes of inventory.

"Current liabilities payable in foreign currency should be translated into dollars at the rate of exchange in force on the date of the balance sheet.

"Capital stock stated in foreign currency should not be translated at the closing rate, but at the rates of exchange prevailing when originally issued. Long-term liabilities payable in foreign currency may be similarly translated, although translation of such liabilities at current exchange rates is appropriate in many circumstances. These are general rules, but an exception may exist in respect to long-term debt incurred or capital stock issued in connection with the acquisition of fixed assets, permanent investments, or long-term receivables a short time before a substantial and presumably permanent change in the exchange rate. In such instances, it may be appropriate to state the long-term debt or the capital stock at the new rate and proper to deal with the exchange differences as an adjustment of the cost of the assets acquired.

"The operating statements of foreign branches or subsidiaries, or of domestic corporations conducting their business in foreign currencies (buying, selling, and manufacturing), should preferably, where there have been wide fluctuations in exchange, be translated at the average rate of exchange applicable to each month or, if this procedure would involve too much labor, on the basis of a carefully weighted average.

"Where a major change in an exchange rate takes place during a fiscal year, there may be situations in which more realistic results will be obtained if income computed in foreign currencies is translated for the entire fiscal year at the new rates in effect after such major fluctuation. This procedure would have the practical advantage of making unnecessary a cutoff at the date of the change in the exchange rate. Where dividends have been paid prior to a major change in the exchange rate, out of earnings of the current fiscal year, that portion of the income for the year should be considered as having been earned at the rate at which such dividend was paid irrespective of the rates used in translating the remainder of the earnings."

(ARB 43 – Ch. 12, pars. 12–20,
as amended by APBO 6)

2. Effect of extraordinary revaluations:

"For United Kingdom companies engaged in substantial overseas trade, or owning substantial overseas trading branches or subsidiaries, the normal fluctuations of exchange rates, whether the rates are pegged or floating, may give rise to differences on exchange whenever one currency has to be converted for accounting purposes into another. Such gains and losses on exchange are a normal feature of overseas operations and do not in themselves usually present any special problems. In general, where there has been no substantial shift in parities, exchange differences on direct trading with foreign customers or suppliers are dealt with in the profit and loss account in arriving at the profit or loss for the period. Where the accounts of overseas branches or subsidiaries have to be converted into sterling for inclusion in the parent's or group accounts the normal accounting conventions for conversion are straightforward and are used consistently from year to year. (The Appendix to this Recommendation contains a note on the conversion conventions usually adopted.)

"Where, however, exchange rates are subjected to a sudden, significant and evidently permanent adjustment outside the run of normal exchange fluctuations, such as happened when on 18th November 1967 sterling was devalued in terms of the United States dollar from $2.80 to $2.40, United Kingdom companies may encounter special accounting problems. In these circumstances exceptional exchange gains or losses attributable to the abnormal change in parities may arise as regards both direct trading transactions and the accounts of overseas branches and subsidiaries. It then becomes necessary to determine the amount of exceptional loss or gain involved, and how it should be dealt with in the accounts.

"For companies with overseas assets and liabilities other than those attributable to overseas branches and subsidiaries, a major change in currency parities will give rise to a sterling gain or loss on exchange in respect of those of their overseas assets or liabilities affected at the date currency rates change.

"In these circumstances the general rule is that overseas assets and liabilities, both current and long term, at the date the parities change should be converted into sterling at the new rate of exchange and the resultant exceptional losses or gains on exchange, if material, presented in the accounts so as to show a fair view of the effects of the alteration in exchange parities.

"Exceptional gains or losses on exchange attributable to changes in parities and relating to overseas assets and liabilities of a normal trading nature are normally dealt with in the profit and loss account, and separately disclosed as an exceptional item if material. Due account is taken of any consequential effect on liability to tax.

"There may be exceptions to the general rule to the extent that any part of the gain or loss may properly be taken into account in arriving at the amount at which items to which it relates are to be stated in the balance sheet. For instance, that part of an exceptional loss on exchange attributable to goods unsold on the balance sheet date may be treated as an increment in cost provided net realisable value in sterling is estimated to be in excess of cost so computed; this treatment is preferable if sterling selling prices of the items on hand have been increased to compensate for the change in parities.

"Similarly, exceptional losses or gains attributable to liabilities outstanding at the relevant date for purchase of fixed assets from overseas are normally dealt with by adjustment of the cost in sterling of the relevant asset account.

"Exceptional gains or losses which may be regarded as not of a revenue nature, such as those relating to long-term loans granted or received may be shown in the profit and loss account or dealt with by direct transfer to or from reserve according to which method will better present a true and fair view, as suggested in paragraph 3 above. Where there are both gains and losses of other than a revenue nature, they are set-off in the first instance.

"The object of converting the accounts of United Kingdom companies' overseas branches or subsidiaries into sterling is to enable them to be incorporated into the home company's or group accounts at a sterling equivalent which fairly expresses their state of affairs and results. Normally the two main methods of converting other currencies for this purpose, as outlined in the Appendix to this Statement, are the 'closing rate' and 'historic rate' methods.

"Where a major revision of exchange parities has taken place during the financial period it is necessary to determine whether the effect on the sterling equivalent of overseas branches' or subsidiaries' accounts gives rise to an exceptional difference on exchange. In theory, as noted above, the gain or loss attributable to a change in parities could be directly arrived at by converting the accounts of overseas branches or subsidiaries at the dates the rates changed into sterling at the old and new rates and measuring the difference.

"In practice the exceptional gain or loss attributable to the change in parities is normally calculated by adjustment of net assets in the opening or closing balance sheets; for instance, by taking net assets at the last accounting date before the change and adjusting them by reference to the profit earned or loss incurred in the period up to the date of change: the difference between the resultant amount converted at the old and new rates of exchange is the exceptional gain or loss. This achieves the same result as converting net assets at the date the rates changed. . . .

"Under the 'closing rate' method assets and liabilities at the balance sheet date are converted at the rate of exchange then ruling, so that the effect on them of any major change of parities is automatically recognised. Under the 'historic rate' method, however, fixed assets and long-term loans and liabilities are normally stated at their original sterling equivalents. A major change in parities calls in question these amounts. Bearing in mind that proper provision must be made for depreciation of fixed assets and repayment of long-term liabilities it would be unrealistic not to recognise that a change in parities implies an adjustment in the sterling equivalents of fixed assets and long-term loans. In these circumstances it may be desirable either to adjust their sterling amounts by reference to the balance sheet rate of exchange, or to carry out a valuation of fixed assets; if the 'historic rate' method of conversion is to be followed, the latter amounts would continue to be used for future conversion purposes in place of original sterling equivalents. . . ."

(BR 25 – pars. 1–2, 5–9, 11–15)

Chapter 20 – Fair Disclosure

Disclosure recommendations in the authorities are too numerous to reproduce in detail.

Chapter 21 – Earnings Per Share

Recommendations on earnings per share are detailed in form and hence unsuitable for reproduction here. The problems involved are discussed in:

CICA Research Recommendations – Section 3500,
APB Opinion No. 15.

Chapter 22 – Working Capital

Statements on the nature of current assets, current liabilities and working capital are as follows:

"As a balance sheet classification, current assets should include those assets ordinarily realizable within one year from the date of the balance sheet or within the normal operating cycle, where that is longer than a year. The current asset classification should also include current accumulated tax allocation debits.

"As a balance sheet classification, current liabilities should include amounts payable within one year from the date of the balance sheet or within the normal operating cycle, where this is longer than a year (the normal operating cycle should correspond with that used for current assets). The current liability classification should also include current accumulated tax allocation credits.

"The current liability classification should include only that portion of long-term debt obligation, including sinking-fund requirements, payable within one year from the date of the balance sheet.

"The current liability classification should also include amounts received or due from customers or clients with respect to goods to be delivered or services to be performed within one year from the date of the balance sheet, if not offset against a related asset.

"Obligations, otherwise classified as current liabilities, should be excluded from the current liability classification to the extent that contractual arrangements have been made for settlement from other than current assets. Examples would be a maturing bond issue where contractual arrangements have been made for long-term refinancing and trade accounts where contractual arrangements have been made for settlement by the issue of share capital."

(CRR – 1510.01, .03–.06)

". . . in the past, definitions of current assets have tended to be overly concerned with whether the assets may be immediately realizable. The discussion which follows takes cognizance of the tendency for creditors to rely more upon the ability of debtors to pay their obligations out of the proceeds of current operations and less upon the debtor's ability to pay in case of liquidation. It should be emphasized that financial statements of a going concern are prepared on the assumption that the company will continue in business. Accordingly, the views expressed in this section represent a departure from any narrow definition or strict *one year* interpretation of either current assets or current liabilities; the objective is to relate the criteria developed to the operating cycle of a business.

"Financial position, as it is reflected by the records and accounts from which the statement is prepared is revealed in a presentation of the assets and liabilities of the enterprise. In the statements of manufacturing, trading, and service enterprises, these assets and liabilities are generally classified and segregated; if they are classified logically, summations or totals of the *current* or *circulating* or *working* assets, hereinafter referred to as *current assets*, and of obligations currently payable, designated as *current liabilities*, will permit the ready determination of working capital. *Working capital*, sometimes called *net working capital*, is represented by the excess of current assets over current liabilities and identifies the relatively liquid portion of total enterprise capital which constitutes a margin or buffer for meeting obligations within the ordinary operating cycle of the business. If the conventions of accounting relative to the identification and presentation of current assets and current liabilities are made logical and consistent, the amounts, bases of valuation and composition of such assets and liabilities and their relation to the total assets or capital employed will provide valuable data for credit and management purposes and afford a sound basis for comparisons from year to year. It is recognized that there may be exceptions, in special cases, to certain of the inclusions and exclusions as set forth in this section. . . .

"For accounting purposes, the term *current assets* is used to designate cash and other assets or resources commonly identified as those which are reasonably expected to be realized in cash or sold or consumed during the normal operating cycle of the business. Thus the term comprehends in general such resources as (a) cash available for current operations and items which are the equivalent of cash; (b) inventories of merchandise, raw materials, goods in process, finished goods, operating supplies, and ordinary maintenance material and parts; (c) trade accounts, notes, and acceptances receivable; (d) receivables from officers, employees, affiliates, and others, if collectible in the ordinary course of business within a year; (e) instalment or deferred accounts and notes receivable if they conform generally to normal trade practices and terms within the business; (f) marketable securities representing the investment of cash available for current operations; and (g) prepaid expenses such as insurance, interest, rents, taxes, unused royalties, current paid advertising service not yet received, and operating supplies. Prepaid expenses are not current assets in the sense that they will be converted into cash, but in the sense that, if not paid in advance, they would require the use of current assets during the operating cycle.

"The ordinary operations of a business involve a circulation of capital within the current asset group. Cash is expended for materials, finished parts, operating supplies, labor, and other factory services, and such expenditures are accumulated as inventory cost. Inventory costs, upon sale of the products to which such costs attach, are converted into trade receivables and ultimately into cash again. The average time intervening between the acquisition of material or services entering this process and the final cash realization constitutes an *operating cycle*. A one-year time period is to be used as a basis for the segregation of current assets in cases where there are several operating cycles occurring within a year. However, where the period of the operating cycle is more than twelve months, as in, for instance, the tobacco, distillery, and lumber businesses, the longer period should be used. Where a particular business has no clearly defined operating cycle, the one-year rule should govern.

"This concept of the nature of current assets contemplates the exclusion from that classification of such resources as: (a) cash and claims to cash which are restricted as to withdrawal or use for other than current operations, are designated for expenditure in the acquisition or construction of noncurrent assets, or are segregated for the liquidation of long-term debts; (b) investments in securities (whether marketable or not) or advances which have been made for the purposes of control, affiliation, or other continuing business advantage; (c) receivables arising from unusual transactions (such as the sale of capital assets, or loans or advances to affiliates, officers, or employees) which are not expected to be collected within twelve months; (d) cash surrender value of life insurance policies; (e) land and other natural resources; (f) depreciable assets; and (g) long-term prepayments which are fairly chargeable to the operations of several years, or deferred charges such as unamortized debt issue costs, bonus payments under a long-term lease, costs of rearrangement of factory layout or removal to a new location, and certain types of research and development costs.

"The term *current liabilities* is used principally to designate obligations whose liquidation is reasonably expected to require the use of existing resources properly classifiable as current assets, or the creation of other current liabilities. As a balance-sheet category, the classification is intended to include obligations for items which have entered into the operating cycle, such as payables incurred in the acquisition of materials and supplies to be used in the production of goods or in providing services to be offered for sale; collections received in advance of the delivery of goods or performance of services; and debts which arise from operations directly related to the operating cycle, such as accruals for wages, salaries, commissions, rentals, royalties, and income and other taxes. Other liabilities whose regular and ordinary liquidation is expected to occur within a relatively short period of time, usually twelve months, are also intended for inclusion, such as short-term debts arising from the acquisition of capital assets, serial maturities of long-term obligations, amounts required to be expended within one year under sinking fund provisions, and agency obligations arising from the collection or acceptance of cash or other assets for the account of third persons.

"This concept of current liabilities would include estimated or accrued amounts which are expected to be required to cover expenditures within the year for known obligations (a) the amount of which can be determined only approximately (as in the case of provisions for accruing bonus payments) or (b) where the specific person or persons to whom payment will be made cannot as yet be designated (as in the case of estimated costs to be incurred in connection with guaranteed servicing or repair of products already sold). The current liability classification, however, is not intended to include a contractual obligation falling due at an early date which is expected to be refunded, or debts to be liquidated by funds which have been accumulated in accounts of a type not properly classified as current assets, or long-term obligations incurred to provide increased amounts of working capital for long periods. . . ."

(ARB 43 – Ch. 3A, pars. 2–8, as amended by APBO 21)

Chapter 23 – The Statement of Source and Application of Funds

1. Objectives of the funds statement:

"The objectives of a funds statement are (1) to summarize the financing and investing activities of the entity, including the extent to which the enterprise has generated funds from operations during the period, and (2) to complete the disclosure of changes in financial position during the period. The information shown in a funds statement is useful to a variety of users of financial statements in making economic decisions regarding the enterprise.

"The funds statement is related to both the income statement and the balance sheet and provides information that can be obtained only partially, or at most in piecemeal form, by interpreting them. An income statement together with a statement of retained earnings reports results of operations but does not show other changes in financial position. Comparative balance sheets can significantly augment that information, but the objectives of the funds statement require that all such information be selected, classified, and summarized in meaningful form. The funds statement cannot supplant either the income statement or the balance sheet but is intended to provide information that the other statements either do not provide or provide only indirectly about the flow of funds and changes in financial position during the period."

(APBO 19 – pars. 4–5)

2. Meaning of the term 'funds':

"The concept of *funds* in funds statements has varied somewhat in practice, with resulting variations in the nature of the statements. For example, *funds* is sometimes interpreted to mean *cash* or its equivalent, and the resulting funds statement is a summary of cash provided and used. Another interpretation of *funds* is that of *working capital*, i.e., current assets less current liabilities, and the resulting funds statement is a summary of working capital provided and used. However, a funds statement based on either the cash or the working capital concept of funds sometimes excludes certain financing and investing activities because they do not directly affect cash or working capital during the period.

For example, issuing equity securities to acquire a building is both a financing and investing transaction but does not affect either cash or working capital. To meet all of its objectives, a funds statement should disclose separately the financing and investing aspects of all significant transactions that affect financial position during a period. These transactions include acquisition or disposal of property in exchange for debt or equity securities and conversion of long-term debt or preferred stock to common stock."

(APBO 19 – par. 6)

3. Presentation of results of operations:

"The ability of an enterprise to provide working capital or cash from operations is an important factor in considering its financing and investing activities. Accordingly, the Statement should prominently disclose working capital or cash provided from or used in operations for the period, and the Board believes that the disclosure is most informative if the effects of extraordinary items ... are reported separately from the effects of normal items. The Statement for the period should begin with income or loss before extraordinary items, if any, and add back (or deduct) items recognized in determining that income or loss which did not use (or provide) working capital or cash during the period. Items added and deducted in accordance with this procedure are not sources or uses of working capital or cash, and the related captions should make this clear, e.g., 'Add – Expenses not requiring outlay of working capital in the current period.' An acceptable alternative procedure, which gives the same result, is to begin with total revenue that provided working capital or cash during the period and deduct operating costs and expenses that required the outlay of working capital or cash during the period. In either case the resulting amount of working capital or cash should be appropriately described, e.g., 'Working capital provided from (used in) operations for the period, exclusive of extraordinary items.' This total should be immediately followed by working capital or cash provided or used by income or loss from extraordinary items, if any; extraordinary income or loss should be similarly adjusted for items recognized that did not provide or use working capital or cash during the period."

(APBO 19 – par. 10)

Selected bibliography

General

Accounting Principles Board Statement No. 4. *Basic Concepts and Accounting Principles Underlying Financial Statements of Business Enterprises.* New York: American Institute of Certified Public Accountants, 1970.

Arthur Andersen & Co. *Accounting and Reporting Problems of the Accounting Profession.* 3rd ed. Chicago: Arthur Andersen & Co., 1969.

Baxter, W. T. and S. Davidson (eds.). *Studies in Accounting Theory.* 2nd ed. Homewood: Richard D. Irwin, 1962.

Davidson, S., D. Green, Jr., C. T. Horngren, and G. H. Sorter (eds.). *An Income Approach to Accounting Theory.* Englewood Cliffs: Prentice-Hall, 1964.

Gilman, S. *Accounting Concepts of Profit.* New York: Ronald Press, 1939.

Grady, P. *Inventory of Generally Accepted Accounting Principles for Business Enterprises.* New York: American Institute of Certified Public Accountants, 1965.

Study Group on Business Income. *Five Monographs on Business Income.* New York: American Institute of Accountants, 1950.

Study Group on Business Income. *Changing Concepts of Business Income.* New York: Macmillan, 1952.

Chapter 3

Moonitz, M. *The Basic Postulates of Accounting.* New York: American Institute of Certified Public Accountants, 1961.

Paton, W. A. and A. C. Littleton. *An Introduction to Corporate Accounting Standards.* Evanston: American Accounting Association, 1940.

Gibbs, G. "Accounting Principles: 'Generally Accepted' by whom?", *Accounting and Business Research* (Winter 1970), pp. 39–43.

Lorig, A. N. "Some Basic Concepts of Accounting and Their Implications", *The Accounting Review* (July 1964), pp. 563–573.

Chapter 4

Edey, H. C. and Prot Panitpakdi. "British Company Accounting and the Law, 1844–1900", in *Studies in the History of Accounting* by Littleton, A. C. and B. S. Yamey (eds.). London: Sweet & Maxwell, 1956, pp. 356–379.

Chapter 5

Burns, J. S., R. K. Jaedicke and J. M. Sangster. "Financial Reporting of Purchase Contracts used to Guarantee Large Investments", *The Accounting Review* (January 1963), pp. 1–13.

Wojdak, J. F. "A Theoretical Foundation for Leases and other Executory Contracts", *The Accounting Review* (July 1969), pp. 562–570.

Chapter 7

Audits of Construction Contractors. New York: American Institute of Certified Public Accountants, 1965.

Thomas, A. L. *Revenue Recognition.* Ann Arbor: Bureau of Business Research, University of Michigan, 1966.

Windal, F. W. *The Accounting Concept of Realization.* East Lansing: Bureau of Business and Economic Research, Michigan State University, 1961.

1964 Concepts and Standards Research Study Committee – The Realization Concept. "The Realization Concept", *The Accounting Review* (April 1965), pp. 312–322.

Arnett, H. E. "Recognition as a Function of Measurement in the Realization Concept", *The Accounting Review* (October 1963), pp. 733–741.

Bowers, R. "Tests of Income Realization", *The Accounting Review* (June 1941), pp. 139–155.

Horngren, C. T. "How Should We Interpret the Realization Concept?", *The Accounting Review* (April 1965), pp. 323–333.

Myers, J. H. "The Critical Event and Recognition of Net Profit", *The Accounting Review* (October 1959), pp. 528–532.

Sprouse, R. T. "Observations Concerning the Realization Concept", *The Accounting Review* (July 1965), pp. 522–526.

Storey, R. K. "Cash Movements and Periodic Income Determination", *The Accounting Review* (July 1960), pp. 449–454.

Chapter 9

Mulcahy, G. *Use and Meaning of "Market" in Inventory Valuation.* Toronto: Canadian Institute of Chartered Accountants, 1963.

Walker, J. K. and G. Mulcahy. *Overhead as an Element of Inventory Costs.* Toronto: Canadian Institute of Chartered Accountants, 1965.

Green, D. Jr. "A Moral to the Direct Costing Controversy?", *The Journal of Business* (July 1960), pp. 218–226.

Johnson, C. E. "Inventory Valuation – The Accountant's Achilles Heel", *The Accounting Review* (January 1954), pp. 15–26.

Miller, R. A. "Inventory Measurement at the Lower of Cost or Market", *The New York Certified Public Accountant* (September 1965), pp. 648–660.

Mitchell, C. L. "Direct Costing – An Opinion Survey", *Canadian Chartered Accountant* (August 1966), pp. 106–107.

Most, K. S. "The Value of Inventories", *Journal of Accounting Research* (Spring 1967), pp. 39–50.

Parker, R. H. "Lower of Cost and Market in Britain and the United States: An Historical Survey", *Abacus* (December 1965), pp. 156–172.

Sorter, G. H. and C. T. Horngren. "Asset Recognition and Economic Attributes – The Relevant Costing Approach", *The Accounting Review* (July 1962), pp. 391–399.

Staubus, G. J. "Direct, Relevant or Absorption Costing?", *The Accounting Review* (Jan. 1963), pp. 64–74.

Chapter 10

Baxter, W. T. *Depreciation.* London: Sweet & Maxwell, 1971.

Coughlan, J. D. and W. K. Strand. *Depreciation – Accounting, Taxes, and Business Decisions.* New York: Ronald Press, 1969.

Grant, E. L. and P. T. Norton Jr. *Depreciation.* Revised Printing. New York: Ronald Press, 1955.

Harvard Business School Round Table. *The Measurement of Property, Plant and Equipment in Financial Statements.* Boston: Graduate School of Business Administration, Harvard University, 1964.

Bierman, H. Jr. "Depreciable Assets – Timing of Expense Recognition", *The Accounting Review* (Oct. 1961), pp. 613–618.

Brief, R. P. "A Late Nineteenth Century Contribution to the Theory of Depreciation", *Journal of Accounting Research* (Spring 1967), pp. 27–38.

Brief, R. P. and J. Owen. "Depreciation and Capital Gains: A 'New' Approach", *The Accounting Review* (April 1968), pp. 367–372.

Johnson, O. "Two General Concepts of Depreciation", *Journal of Accounting Research* (Spring 1968), pp. 29–37.

Reynolds, I. N. "Selecting the Proper Depreciation Method", *The Accounting Review* (April 1961), pp. 239–248.

Scott, D R. "Defining and Accounting for Depreciation", *The Accounting Review* (July 1945), pp. 308–315.

Chapter 11

Catlett, G. R. and N. O. Olson. *Accounting for Goodwill.* New York: American Institute of Certified Public Accountants, 1968.

Moffet, H. S. *Accounting for Costs of Financing.* Toronto: Canadian Institute of Chartered Accountants, 1964.

Sands, J. E. *Wealth, Income, and Intangibles.* Toronto: University of Toronto Press, 1963.

Gynther, R. S. "Some 'Conceptualizing' on Goodwill", *The Accounting Review* (April 1969), pp. 247–255.

Nelson, R. H. "The Momentum Theory of Goodwill", *The Accounting Review* (Oct. 1953), pp. 491–499.

Spacek, L. "The Treatment of Goodwill in the Corporate Balance Sheet", *The Journal of Accountancy* (Feb. 1964), pp. 35–40.

Walker, G. T. "Why Purchased Goodwill should be Amortized on a Systematic Basis", *The Journal of Accountancy* (Feb. 1953), pp. 210–216.

Chapter 12

Coutts, W. B. and R. B. Dale-Harris. *Accounting for Costs of Pension Plans.* Toronto: Canadian Institute of Chartered Accountants, 1963.

Five Articles on Accounting for the Cost of Pension Plans. New York: American Institute of Certified Public Accountants, 1968.

Hicks, E. L. *Accounting for the Cost of Pension Plans.* New York: American Institute of Certified Public Accountants, 1965.

Myers, J. H. *Reporting of Leases in Financial Statements.* New York: American Institute of Certified Public Accountants, 1962.

Nelson, A. T. *The Impact of Leases on Financial Analysis.* East Lansing: Bureau of Business and Economic Research, Michigan State University, 1963.

Axelson, K. S. "Needed: A Generally Accepted Method for Measuring Lease Commitments", *The Financial Executive* (July 1971), pp. 40–52.

Dewhirst, J. F. "A Conceptual Approach to Pension Accounting", *The Accounting Review* (April 1971), pp. 365–373.

Graham, W. J. and H. Q. Langenderfer. "Reporting of Leases: Comment on APB Opinion No. 5", *The Journal of Accountancy* (March 1965), pp. 57–62.

Hall, W. D. "Current Problems in Accounting for Leases", *The Journal of Accountancy* (Nov. 1967), pp. 35–42.

Halliwell, P. D. "Basic Principles of Pension Funding and APB Opinion No. 8", *Management Accounting* (July 1969), pp. 15–19, 23.

Hennessy, J. L. "Recording of Lease Obligations and Related Property Rights", *The Journal of Accountancy* (March 1961), pp. 40–46.

Jenkins, D. O. "Accounting for Funded Industrial Pension Plans", *The Accounting Review* (July 1964), pp. 648–653.

Osborne, O. D. "Accounting for Finance-Type Leasing Operations", *NAA Bulletin* (June 1963), pp. 47–53.

Philips, G. E. "Pension Liabilities and Assets", *The Accounting Review* (Jan. 1968), pp. 10–17.

Seago, W. E. "Accounting for Pension Costs – An Illustrative Case", *The New York Certified Public Accountant* (June 1971), pp. 425–432.

Shillinglaw, G. "Leasing and Financial Statements", *The Accounting Review* (Oct. 1958), pp. 581–592.

Simmons, M. O. "New Light on Actuarial Cost Methods", *The Financial Executive* (July 1968), pp. 69–75.

Sloat, F. P. "Accounting Recognition of Appreciation and Depreciation of Equities Held in Retirement Plan Funds", *The New York Certified Public Accountant* (Jan. 1966), pp. 35–38.

Trowbridge, C. L. "Fundamentals of Pension Funding", *Transactions of the Society of Actuaries* (Vol. 4. 1952), pp. 17–43.

Zises, A. "Disclosure of Long Term Leases", *The Journal of Accountancy* (Feb. 1961), pp. 37–47.

Chapter 13

Black, H. A. *Interperiod Allocation of Corporate Income Taxes.* New York: American Institute of Certified Public Accountants, 1966.

Bierman, H. Jr. "A Problem in Expense Recognition", *The Accounting Review* (Jan. 1963), pp. 61–63.

Carr, G. K. "Accounting for Income Taxes", *Canadian Chartered Accountant* (Oct. 1963), pp. 238–244.

Chapter 14

Bernstein, L. A. *Accounting for Extraordinary Gains and Losses.* New York: Ronald Press, 1967.

Arnett, H. E. "Application of the Capital Gains and Losses Concept in Practice", *The Accounting Review* (Jan. 1965), pp. 54–64.

Arnett, H. E. "The Distinction Between Ordinary and Non-Ordinary Gains and Losses", *The New York Certified Public Accountant* (April 1967), pp. 267–278.

Bernstein, L. A. "Netting of Extraordinary Items – Effect on the Determination of Materiality", *The Journal of Accountancy* (June 1971), pp. 74–75.

Block, M. "Distinction Between Prepaid Expenses and Deferred Charges", *The New York Certified Public Accountant* (April 1967), pp. 298–299.

Powell, W. "Extraordinary Items", *The Journal of Accountancy* (Jan. 1966), pp. 31–37.

Wright, A. W. "Periodic Net Income and Extraordinary Items", *Management Accounting* (May 1966), pp. 35–42.

Chapter 15

Birnberg, J. G. "An Information Oriented Approach to the Presentation of Common Shareholders' Equity", *The Accounting Review* (Oct. 1964), pp. 963–971.

Eiteman, D. S. "Are There Two Kinds of Stock Dividends?", *NAA Bulletin* (Oct. 1963), pp. 53–58.

Frielich, R. and R. Lauver. "Accounting for Subsidiary's Stock Dividend", *The New York Certified Public Accountant* (Oct. 1967), pp. 782–784.

Lowe, H. D. "The Classification of Corporate Stock Equities", *The Accounting Review* (July 1961), pp. 425–433.

Paton, W. A. "Postcript on 'Treasury' Shares", *The Accounting Review* (April 1969), pp. 276–283.

Ray, J. C. "Amount to be Capitalized for a Stock Dividend", *The New York Certified Public Accountant* (Aug. 1962), pp. 511–517.

Ray, J. C. "Accounting for Treasury Stock", *The Accounting Review* (Oct. 1962), pp. 753–757.

Chapter 17

Childs, W. H. *Consolidated Financial Statements.* Ithaca: Cornell University Press, 1949.

Galvin, B. J. B. *Survey of Consolidation Practices in Canada.* Kingston: Queen's University, 1958.

Kocan, Peter. "Reporting the Operations of Jointly Owned Companies", *The Journal of Accountancy* (Feb. 1962), pp. 54–59.

Maclean, F. D. "The Unacknowledged Subsidiary in Consolidated Financial Statements", *The New York Certified Public Accountant* (Nov. 1964), pp. 838–841.

Perry, K. W. "Intercompany Profits and ARB 51", *The Accounting Review* (July 1963), pp. 626–628.

Russell, J. D. "Group Accounts", *Accountancy* (Jan. 1966), pp. 19–25. (Feb. 1966), pp. 85–90.

Chapter 18

Eiteman, D. S. *Pooling and Purchase Accounting.* Ann Arbor: Bureau of Business Research, University of Michigan, 1967.

Martin, S. A., S. N. Laiken and D. F. Haslam. *Business Combinations in the '60s: a Canadian Profile.* Toronto: Canadian Institute of Chartered Accountants, 1970.

Wyatt, A. R. *A Critical Study of Accounting for Business Combinations.* New York: American Institute of Certified Public Accountants, 1963.

Report of the Committee of the Ontario Securities Commission on the Problems of Disclosure Raised for Investors by Business Combinations and Private Placements. Toronto: Province of Ontario, Department of Financial and Commercial Affairs, 1970.

Beyer, R. "Goodwill and Pooling of Interests: A Re-assessment", *Management Accounting* (Feb. 1969), pp. 9–15.

Briloff, A. J. "Dirty Pooling", *The Accounting Review* (July 1967), pp. 489–496.

Gunther, S. P. "Contingent Pay-Outs in Mergers and Acquisitions", *The Journal of Accountancy* (June 1968), pp. 33–40.

Hinton, P. R. "Accounting for Mergers: Is the ASSC Mistaken?", *The Accountant* (April 1, 1971), pp. 411–415.

Lay, D. W. "Accounting for Business Combinations", *Canadian Chartered Accountant* (Nov. 1967), pp. 329–334.

Salmonson, R. F. "Reporting Earnings After an Acquisition", *The Journal of Accountancy* (March 1964), pp. 51–54.

Sciarrino, J. A. "FEI Surveys Accounting for Business Combinations", *The Financial Executive* (Aug. 1969), pp. 30–34.

Chapter 19

Hepworth, S. R. *Reporting Foreign Operations.* Ann Arbor: Bureau of Business Research, University of Michigan, 1956.

Management Accounting Problems in Foreign Operations. New York: National Association of Accountants, 1960.

Elliott, C. W. "The Lower of Cost or Market Test for Foreign Inventories", *NAA Bulletin* (Feb. 1965), pp. 12–17.

Elliott, C. W. "Choosing Appropriate Exchange Rates for Translating Foreign Income Statement Accounts", *The New York Certified Public Accountant* (Sept. 1966), pp. 683–689.

Frederikson, E. B. "On the Measurement of Foreign Income", *Journal of Accounting Research* (Autumn 1968), pp. 208–221.

Parker, R. H. "Principles and Practice in Translating Foreign Currencies", *Abacus* (Dec. 1970), pp. 144–153.

Seidler, L. J. and J. Dowling. "Unsettled Currency Devaluation Problems in International Accounting", *The New York Certified Public Accountant* (Sept. 1968), pp. 623–627.

Thompson, A. E. J. "Foreign Exchange – Accounting and Tax Features", *Canadian Chartered Accountant* (Sept. 1964), pp. 166–170.

Watt, G. C. "Unrealized Foreign Exchange Gains Arising from Funds Borrowed in Local Currency", *NAA Bulletin* (Feb. 1965), pp. 3–11.

Chapter 20

Backer M. and W. B. McFarland. *External Reporting for Segments of a Business.* New York: National Association of Accountants, 1968.

Mautz, R. K. *Financial Reporting by Diversified Companies.* New York: Financial Executives Research Foundation, 1968.

Rappaport, A., P. A. Firmin and S. A. Zeff (eds.). *Public Reporting by Conglomerates: The Issues, the Problems, and Some Possible Solutions.* Englewood Cliffs: Prentice-Hall, 1968.

Chapter 21

Monson, N. P. and J. A. Tracy. "Stock Rights and Accounting Wrongs", *The Accounting Review* (Oct. 1964), pp. 890–893.

Shaw, D. C. "Don't Forget the Split in Stock Rights", *Canadian Chartered Accountant* (March 1969), pp. 182–184.

Spacek, L. "Umpiring the Earnings Per Share Results", *Management Accounting* (March 1969), pp. 9–14.

Chapter 22

Fess, P. E. "Improving Working Capital Analysis", *The New York Certified Public Accountant* (July 1967), pp. 506–512.

Glickman, R. and R. W. Stahl. "The Case of the Misleading Balance Sheet", *The Journal of Accountancy* (Dec. 1968), pp. 66–72.

Goldberg, L. "A Note on Current Assets", *Abacus* (Sept. 1965), pp. 31–45.

Hirschman, R. W. "A Look at 'Current' Classifications", *The Journal of Accountancy* (Nov. 1967), pp. 54–58.

Leach, C. W. "A New Look at Working Capital", *Canadian Chartered Accountant* (March 1962), pp. 237–243.

Sorter, G. H. and G. Benston. "Appraising the Defensive Position of a Firm: The Interval Measure", *The Accounting Review* (Oct. 1960), pp. 633–640.

Chapter 23

Mason, P. *'Cash Flow' Analysis and the Funds Statement.* New York: American Institute of Certified Public Accountants, 1961.

Brace, W. M. "Statements of Source and Application of Funds", *Canadian Chartered Accountant* (Aug. 1968), pp. 93–97.

Corbin, D. A. "Proposals for Improving Funds Statements", *The Accounting Review* (July 1961), pp. 398–405.

Dunn, G. R. "A Proposed Funds Statement for Financial Institutions", *Management Accounting* (Nov. 1968), pp. 9–12.

Rosen, L. S. "Funds Statement Concepts", *Canadian Chartered Accountant,*
  I History and Cash Reports (Oct. 1968), pp. 275–277.
  II The Liquidity Perspective (Nov. 1968), pp. 369–372.
  III The Perspective of Inter-Entity Transactions (Dec. 1968), pp. 445–449.

Rosen, L. S. and D. T. DeCoster. " 'Funds' Statements: A Historical Perspective", *The Accounting Review* (Jan. 1969), pp. 124–136.

Staubus, G. J. "Alternative Asset Flow Concepts", *The Accounting Review* (July 1966), pp. 397–412.

Chapter 24

Coutts, W. B. *Accounting Problems in the Oil and Gas Industry.* Toronto: Canadian Institute of Chartered Accountants, 1963.

Financial Reporting for Non-Producing Mining Companies. Toronto: Canadian Institute of Chartered Accountants, 1967.

Field, R. E. *Financial Reporting in the Extractive Industries.* New York: American Institute of Certified Public Accountants, 1969.

Chapter 25

Accounting for Trust and Loan Companies in Canada. Toronto: Canadian Institute of Chartered Accountants, 1971.

Committee on Bank Accounting and Auditing. *Audits of Banks.* New York: American Institute of Certified Public Accountants, 1968.

Committee on Insurance Accounting and Auditing. *Audits of Fire and Casualty Insurance Companies.* New York: American Institute of Certified Public Accountants, 1966.

Committee on Insurance Accounting and Auditing. *Audits of Life Insurance Companies (Exposure Draft).* New York: American Institute of Certified Public Accountants, 1970.

Cramer, J. J. *Accounting and Reporting Requirements of the Private Pension Trust.* Bloomington: Bureau of Business Research, Indiana University, 1965.

Report of the Canadian Committee on Mutual Funds and Investment Contracts. Ottawa: The Queen's Printer, 1969.

Joint Actuarial Committee on Financial Reporting. *Response to the December 1970 Exposure Draft of "Audits of Life Insurance Companies".* Society of Actuaries (et al.), 1971.

Larkin, E. L. *Accounting for the Realities of Bank Portfolio Management.* New York: Haskins and Sells, 1970.

Baker, R. E. "Income of Life Insurance Companies", *The Accounting Review* (Jan. 1966), pp. 98–105.

Comiskey, E. E. and C. S. Colantoni. "Accounting Alternatives and Finance Company Earnings", *Financial Analysts Journal* (March-April 1969), pp. 55–59.

Kidd, R. N. A. "Fire and Casualty Insurance Company Accounts", *Canadian Chartered Accountant* (Sept. 1967), pp. 171–175.

Mitchell, B. N. "Financial Statements of Life Insurance Companies", *The New York Certified Public Accountant* (July 1966), pp. 519–527.

Raymond, R. H. "Life Insurance Company vs. Traditional Financial Statements", *The Journal of Accountancy* (Dec. 1965), pp. 39–45.

Stewart, R. D. "Disclosure Deficiencies in Life Insurance Company Reports", *Canadian Chartered Accountant* (April 1964), pp. 266–271.

Chapter 26

Audits of Voluntary Health and Welfare Organizations. New York: American Institute of Certified Public Accountants, 1967.

Canadian Hospital Accounting Manual. Toronto: Canadian Hospital Association, 1968.

Canadian Standards of Accounting and Financial Reporting for Voluntary Organizations. Toronto: Canadian Institute of Chartered Accountants (et al.), 1967.

Chart of Accounts for Hospitals. Chicago: American Hospital Association, 1966.

College and University Business Administration. Washington, D.C.: American Council on Education, 1968.

Henke, E. O. *Accounting for Nonprofit Organizations: An Exploratory Study.* Bloomington: Bureau of Business Research, Indiana University, 1965.

Henke, E. O. *Accounting for Nonprofit Organizations.* Belmont: Wadsworth Publishing, 1966.

National Committee on Governmental Accounting. *Governmental Accounting, Auditing and Financial Reporting.* Chicago: Municipal Finance Officers Association, 1968.

Skinner, R. M. *Canadian University Accounting.* Toronto: Canadian Institute of Chartered Accountants, 1969.

Standards of Accounting and Financial Reporting for Voluntary Health and Welfare Organizations. New York: National Health Council and National Social Welfare Assembly, 1964.

Bordner, H. W. "Fund Concepts as Accounting Postulates", *The Journal of Accountancy* (July 1961), pp. 52–60.

Bruegman, D. C. and G. D. Brighton. "Institutional Accounting – How it Differs from Commercial Accounting", *The Accounting Review* (Oct. 1963), pp. 764–770.

Ellenberger, J. O. "A Look at Depreciation Accounting in Nonprofit Organizations", *NAA Bulletin* (Jan. 1961), pp. 55–62.

Fluckiger, W. L. "A Philosophy of Fund Accounting", *The Journal of Accountancy* (Aug. 1963), pp. 66–71.

Steinwurtzel, S. L. "Statement on Accounting Postulates and Principles for Nonprofit Organizations", *The New York Certified Public Accountant* (Sept. 1962), pp. 577–580.

Williams, R. W. and R. L. Leonard. "Financial Reporting by Nonprofit Organizations", *The Journal of Accountancy* (April 1962), pp. 46–50.

Wojdak, J. F. "A Comparison of Governmental and Commercial Accounting Concepts", *The New York Certified Public Accountant* (Jan. 1969), pp. 29–38.

"Report of the Committee on Accounting Practices for Not-for-Profit Organizations". *The Accounting Review* (Supplement to Vol. XLVI, 1971), pp. 81–163.

Chapter 29

A Statement of Basic Accounting Theory. Evanston: American Accounting Association, 1966.

Pattillo, J. W. *The Foundation of Financial Accounting*. Baton Rouge: Louisiana State University Press, 1965.

Arnett, H. E. "The Concept of Fairness", *The Accounting Review* (April 1967), pp. 291–297.

Bedford, N. M. "The Nature of Future Accounting Theory", *The Accounting Review* (Jan. 1967), pp. 82–85.

Catlett, G. R. "Sound Accounting Requires a Solid Foundation", *Canadian Chartered Accountant* (Jan. 1963), pp. 29–33.

Mepham, M. J. "Towards A Definition of Accounting", *The Accountant* (Oct. 28, 1967), pp. 548–552.

Snavely, H. J. "Accounting Information Criteria", *The Accounting Review* (April 1967), pp. 223–232.

Sterling, R. R. "A Statement of Basic Accounting Theory: A Review Article", *Journal of Accounting Research* (Spring 1967), pp. 95–112.

Chapter 30

Powell, W. "The Development of Accounting Principles", *The Journal of Accountancy* (Sept. 1964), pp. 37–43.

Spacek, L. "The Need for an Accounting Court", *The Accounting Review* (July 1958), pp. 368–379.

Spacek, L. "A Suggested Solution to the Principles Dilemma", *The Accounting Review* (April 1964), pp. 275–283.

Vance, L. L. "The Road to Reform of Accounting Principles", *The Accounting Review* (Oct. 1969), pp. 692–703.

"Report of the Committee on Establishment of an Accounting Commission", *The Accounting Review* (July 1971), pp. 609–616.

Chapters 32–34

Edwards, E. O. and P. W. Bell. *The Theory and Measurement of Business Income*. Berkeley: University of California Press, 1961.

Corbin, D. A. "Comments on 'The Accretion Concept of Income'", *The Accounting Review* (Oct. 1963), pp. 742–744.

Lemke, K. W. "Asset Valuation and Income Theory", *The Accounting Review* (Jan. 1966), pp. 32–41.

Philips, G. E. "The Accretion Concept of Income", *The Accounting Review* (Jan. 1963), pp. 14–25.

Snavely, H. J. "Current Cost for Long-Lived Assets: A Critical View", *The Accounting Review* (April 1969), pp. 344–353.

Index